# Early Books
## and Manuscripts

# Early Books
# and Manuscripts

*Forty Years of Research*

*by Curt F. Bühler*

THE GROLIER CLUB

THE PIERPONT MORGAN LIBRARY

MCMLXXIII

# FOREWORD

THE making of books, their content, and their history, are subjects of perennial fascination and mystery. To these Dr. Curt F. Bühler has devoted his working life, whether in the Pierpont Morgan Library or in other fertile sources of knowledge in this country and abroad, for his extensive travels have been always in search of information. From his days of graduate study in Dublin and Munich (both, be it noted, centers rich in library resources), he has never ceased to pursue the elusive and to clarify the obscure, as determined as any detective in the discovery of clues, and as rational as the best judge in weighing facts and probabilities.

A scholar who is also a librarian risks being neither one nor the other. In his forty years at the Morgan Library, Dr. Bühler has always performed his staff duties in generous measure, and helped others to perform theirs, with a sense of dedication and a sense of humor that have lightened many an hour of tribulation and made him an ideal colleague. At the same time, he has followed with steady energy the trails and mazes of research in his principal area of investigation, the intellectual activity of the fifteenth and sixteenth centuries. The resulting textual editions, monographs, and catalogues would alone have made him a respected member of the international sodality of scholars, but to these he has continuously added a rich harvest of briefer contributions to knowledge. These are fugitive pieces, not in the sense of being minor or insignificant, but because, having been published in learned journals or out-of-the-way periodicals and collections, they have escaped more general notice and acclaim.

With the present publication of Dr. Bühler's opuscula (reviews excepted), we now have ready to hand some forty bibliographical studies, chiefly concerned with incunabula, and an equal number of textual investigations. They are the products, and occasionally the by-products, of research undertaken in the period 1927-1965, the terminal date being purely a matter of choice, since the author's output happily still continues.

Nothing is included here of Dr. Bühler's work on the *Missale Speciale*, printed in an early state of a type designed by Johann Gutenberg, and used in a refined version in the Psalter issued by his successors, Fust and Schöffer, in 1457. Scholars have differed throughout this century as to whether the *Missale* was printed about 1450 or as late as the 1470's. The fruits of Dr. Bühler's intensive study of its text, type, paper, and the development of the printing art are appearing in learned journals and his findings will ultimately be assembled in a publication entirely devoted to the *Missale*.

The topics dealt with in the present volume cover aspects of bibliography, codicology, literature, and history, representing research in architecture, astrology, biography, law, medicine, politics, and science, among other fields. The papers concern material written or printed in Greek, Latin, English, French, German, Italian, Catalan, and Spanish. Though primarily connected with the period when the Renaissance spirit spread through the countries of Europe, the subject matter of the studies ranges chronologically from the writings of the classic Greek philosophers to reprinting in the nineteenth century, and penetrates our own time with an appreciation of Miss Belle da Costa Greene.

One way to honor a distinguished scholar is to publish a *Festschrift*, a collection of essays written by his peers on subjects more or less germane to the interests of the person honored. This rarely succeeds in adding to the glory of either the recipient or the contributors. A more homogeneous and far more useful volume results when the approbation takes the form of an edition of the scholar's own scattered articles and papers, and we can be grateful to the wisdom of the Grolier Club and the Pierpont Morgan Library that their tribute to a long-time associate has taken this enduring form.

FREDERICK B. ADAMS

# CONTENTS

## TEXTUAL STUDIES

## LIBRI IMPRESSI

## A REVIEW

# ILLUSTRATIONS

*following page 312*

# Subscribers

Jere Abbott

Mrs. Werner Abegg

Frederick B. Adams, Jr.

Reginald Allen

Frank Altschul

Elmer L. Andersen

Duncan Andrews

Anonymous Subscriber

H. Richard Archer

Gabriel Austin

Frank L. Babbott, *In Memoriam*

C. Waller Barrett

Francis W. Bartlett

Dr. Howard T. Behrman

Dr. Elmer Belt

Pierre Berès

Abel E. Berland

Beatrice Bishop Berle

Walter D. Binger

Eugene R. Black

Lyman G. Bloomingdale

Joseph Blumenthal

Bodleian Library

William H. Bond

Boston Athenaeum

Boston Public Library

B. H. Breslauer

British Museum

T. Kimball Brooker

Bryn Mawr College Library

Commander C. Alexander Buhler, USN

C. Walter Buhler

Mrs. Ludlow Bull

Herbert T. F. Cahoon

Bancroft Library, University of California

David G. Carter

Carlo Alberto Chiesa

Herman Cohen

Morris L. Cohen

H. Dunscombe Colt

Columbia University Libraries

Cornell University Libraries

John M. Crawford, Jr.

William J. Dane

William P. Davisson

Everett L. DeGolyer, Jr.

Beeckman J. Delatour

Robert O. Dougan

John Dreyfus

Mrs. Philip C. Duschnes

J. M. Edelstein

Dean S. Edmonds

Mrs. Milton B. Eulau

E. A. Evans, Jr.

Douglas C. Ewing

Mrs. DeCoursey Fales

Haliburton Fales, 2nd

Burrel C. P. Farnsley

Mrs. W. R. Fay

Charles E. Feinberg

P. William Filby

John F. Fleming

Folger Shakespeare Library

Mrs. William Logan Fox

Mrs. H. Clifford Gayley

Henry E. Gerstley

John Goelet

Frederick R. Goff

Mrs. John D. Gordan

Paul and Marianne Gourary

Robert D. Graff

The Grolier Club

Morris Hadley

Sinclair Hamilton

William A. Hanway

George L. Harding

Dr. Ernst Hauswedell

James H. Heineman

Kenneth E. Hill

Philip Hofer

Arthur C. Holden

Dwight A. Horne

Arthur A. Houghton, Jr.

The Houghton Library, Harvard University

Alfred H. Howell

Warren R. Howell

E. Harold Hugo

Mrs. Donald F. Hyde

Howard W. Johnson

Walter J. Johnson

Kungliga Biblioteket, Stockholm

Dr. Gordon W. Jones

Herman William Kapp

Bayard L. Kilgour, Jr.

King's College, Cambridge

Alfred A. Knopf

H. P. Kraus

Valerian Lada-Mocarski, *In Memoriam*

Mrs. William F. Lamb

Lawrence Lande

Wheaton J. Lane

Langsdale Library, University of Baltimore

George H. M. Lawrence

Edward J. Lazare

Rensselaer W. Lee

Herman W. Liebert

Charles J. Liebman

Linda Hall Library

Albert E. Lownes

Milton McGreevy

James G. McManaway

David Jackson McWilliams

Daniel Maggin

H. Clifford Maggs

Otto Manley

Thomas E. Marston

Louis L. Martz

Professor Millard Meiss

Paul Mellon

Walter S. Merwin

Charles F. Morgan

Henry S. Morgan

John P. Morgan II

Henry Morris

Peter M. Mortimer

Wing Foundation, Newberry Library

The New-York Historical Society

The New York Public Library

Mrs. George Nichols

Dr. H. F. Norman

University of Oregon Library

Mrs. Walter H. Page

Michael Papantonio

Albert J. Parreño

John F. Peckham

Mrs. Paul G. Pennoyer

Robert M. Pennoyer

University of Pennsylvania Library

Boies Penrose

Carl H. Pforzheimer Library

The Pierpont Morgan Library

Edward S. Pinney

Lawrence Clark Powell
Richard E. Priest
Princeton University Library
Dr. Russell W. Ramsey
Otto H. Ranschburg
Gordon N. Ray
S. Wyman Rolph
Mrs. James J. Rorimer
The Philip H. & A.S.W. Rosenbach Foundation
A. M. Rosenbloom
Charles J. Rosenbloom
Bernard M. Rosenthal
Samuel R. Rosenthal
Lessing J. Rosenwald
Charles Ryskamp
Dr. Morris H. Saffron
John A. Saks
William Salloch
Mrs. Robin Satinsky
Henry L. Savage
Otto Schäfer
William H. Scheide
George McKay Schieffelin
Stuart B. Schimmel
Leonard B. Schlosser
Edgar Scott
Eric H. L. Sexton
John J. Slocum
L. M. C. Smith

Dr. George E. Staehle
Nathaniel E. Stein
Mrs. Carl Stern
Henry Root Stern, Jr.
E. Clark Stillman
Roderick D. Stinehour
Prof. Dr. Hans Strahm
Norman H. Strouse
G. Thomas Tanselle
Robert L. B. Tobin
Benjamin H. Trask
Trinity College, Hartford
Miss Alice Tully
Decherd Turner
Abraham Uchitelle
Giorgio Uzielli
Jacques L. Vellekoop
Arthur E. Vershbow
James E. Walsh
Dr. Jerome P. Webster
Joseph Francis Weiler
Monroe Wheeler
Miss Julia Wightman
Laurence Witten
Edwin Wolf, 2nd
Richard S. Wormser
William P. Wreden
Jacob Israel Zeitlin
Ben D. Zevin

# ACKNOWLEDGMENTS

THE author of the articles here reprinted is deeply indebted for the generous help of numerous friends and scholars, many of whom are named at the appropriate places in the several chapters. For the present publication, he is under the very greatest obligation, extending in some cases over many years, for the moral and material support of Dr. Frederick B. Adams, Mr. Gabriel Austin, Mr. Robert D. Graff, and Dr. Charles A. Ryskamp. Special thanks are due to the trustees of the Pierpont Morgan Library and the Council of the Grolier Club, whose financial assistance alone made this publication possible. Mr. P. J. Conkwright and the Princeton University Press have earned the author's gratitude, the former for his splendid design of the book and the latter for the remarkable accuracy of its compositors and proofreaders. Their co-operation has made the heavy task of seeing this volume through the press much lighter.

Lastly, but by no means least, it is a pleasant duty to acknowledge the fact that this book would never have appeared without the enduring patience and continuous encouragement of Lucy Jane Ford Bühler.

CURT F. BÜHLER

## PUBLISHERS' ACKNOWLEDGMENT

THE publishers desire to express their sincere thanks to the editors and copyright owners of the following periodicals for the kind permissions to reprint articles which first appeared in their journals: *Anglia, La Bibliofilia, Bulletin of the History of Medicine, Chymia, English Language Notes, Gutenberg-Jahrbuch, Isis, Journal of English and Germanic Philology, Journal of the Walters Art Gallery, The Library, The Library Quarterly, Medievalia et Humanistica, Modern Language Notes, More Books, New Colophon, Osiris, Papers of the Bibliographical Society of America (PBSA), Philological Quarterly, Proceedings of the Hampshire Field Club and Archaeological Society, Publications of the Modern Language Association of America (PMLA), Renaissance News* (now *Renaissance Quarterly), Review of English Studies, Scriptorium, Speculum, Studies in Bibliography, Studies in Philology, Studies in the Renaissance,* and *Traditio.* Similar thanks are due to the owners, administrators, and trustees of: Erasmus Antiquariaat en Boekhandel (Amsterdam), Folger Shakespeare Library (Trustees of Amherst College), New York Public Library, The Philip H. and A.S.W. Rosenbach Foundation, University of Pennsylvania, Walters Art Gallery, and Mr. Frederick R. Goff.

# Early Books
## and Manuscripts

# CHAPTER B1

## *THE DICTES AND SAYINGS OF THE PHILOSOPHERS*

THE importance of the *Dictes* lies chiefly in the fact that Caxton's first edition of it is the first book printed in England not only giving the place of printing but also the year of issue.

Here endeth the book named the dictes or sayengis of the philosophhres enprynted by me William Caxton at Westmestre the yere of our lord MCC-CCLXXVII etc. (fol. 74.)

The books that appeared from Caxton's press are so well known and have been so minutely examined that, from a typographical point of view, it would appear that the last word had been said.[1] Caxton printed three editions of the *Dictes*; the first (I) appeared in 1477 (Duff 123, with the unique variant in the John Rylands Library, Duff 123a); the second (II) in 1479 or 1480 (Duff 124); and the third (III) in 1489 (Duff 125). The variant of the first edition (Ia) has the added colophon:

Thus endeth this book of the dyctes and notable wyse sayenges of the phylosophers late translated and drawen out of frenshe into our englisshe tonge by my forsaide lord Therle of Ryuers and lord Skales and by hys comandement sette in forme and emprynted in this manere as ye maye here in this booke see Whiche was fynisshed the xviij day of the moneth of Nouembre & the seuententh yere of the regne of kyng Edward the fourth.

and this is preserved in the subsequent editions together with the date of the original colophon. In addition, there are two contemporary manuscripts: British Museum Additional 22718 (Ad) on paper and the famous MS. 265 of the Lambeth Palace Library (L) on vellum. Strangely enough, although the typographical studies of the prints have been so thoroughly and painstakingly done, the manuscripts and the texts of these prints have, to say the least, been

[1] See William Blades, *The Life and Typography of William Caxton*, London, 1861-3; Gordon Duff, *Fifteenth Century English Books*, Bibliographical Society, 1917; Seymour de Ricci, *A Census of Caxtons*, Bibliographical Society, 1909; W.J.B. Crotch, *The Prologues and Epilogues of William Caxton*, E.E.T.S. 1928 (with bibliography); Hain's *Repertorium Bibliographicum; Short Title Catalogue*, &c.

only cursorily examined. The present article does not intend to discuss in full the problems that will confront the reader (a task which must, of necessity, be left to a larger and more detailed examination), but it will at least serve to point out some of the questions which the learned bibliographers of Caxton either overlooked or considered irrelevant.

W.J.B. Crotch, in his edition of *The Prologues and Epilogues of William Caxton* (p. cvii), summarizes, in effect, the findings of the bibliographers;

The second edition was printed from the re-issue of the first and repeats the colophon. Throughout the Epilogue the wording compares page for page but not line for line. The third edition was probably not set up from the second but from the first.

and, speaking of the second edition, Blades says, 'Lastly, the orthography varies throughout the whole volume.'

As Crotch pointed out the third edition was reprinted not from the second but from the first edition. That the differences between I and II are numerous and more important than mere orthographical changes will be made clear later. In every single case we shall find that III perpetuates the readings of I, whether II represents a perfectly obvious improvement or not. In short, III was reset from I and not, as might normally be expected, from II. Why?

The manuscript in the British Museum was presented by Sir W. C. Trevelyan in 1859. From various autograph notes in the volume, the former owner and Blades surmised that the manuscript had been in the possession of the Trevelyan family since 1479. Blades (vol. ii, p. 37) describes it as 'apparently a copy from the first printed edition' and 'The other English manuscript, Addit. 22718, is on paper, and a verbatim copy from Caxton's printed edition, bearing date 28th November, 1477'. The 'colophon' of this manuscript, however, reads:

Thus endith this book of the dytees & notable wise seyengges of the philisophers late translated and drawen owt of ffrenshe in to our englysshe tong by my forsaid Lord Skales and bi his commandment set in forme in this maner as ye may here in this book see whiche was ffynysshid the xxviii day of þe moneth of Novembir And þe seventh yere of þe reygne of Kyng Edward the ffourþe.
　　Si tho ponatur et mas sibi associatur
　　Et Cokke addatur qui scripsit sic uocitatur.

It is probable that 'Thomas Cokke' wrote November 28th by mistake; he apparently transposed an 'x' from the date of the year to the day of the month. The year could not possibly be the seventh of the reign of Edward IV (1467). As it will be shown later that this manuscript is a transcript not of the first but of the second edition, the book was possibly not even 'ffynysshid' the 28 November 1477. Now it is perfectly self-evident that, if Ad was continuously in the hands of the Trevelyan family[2] since 1479, it cannot be a copy of a book printed in 1480, or, alternatively, the book from which this manuscript was copied must be dated before 1479. Of course, it is quite possible that the autograph notes in Addit. 22718 are not *of* any year but were written in *for* that year, possibly some years later. In any case, it is obvious that either the dating of Ad or that of the print is wrong. Unless II was printed early in 1479, such evidence as we now have is mutually exclusive.

With the Lambeth manuscript we encounter a further difficulty. Blades describes the manuscript thus (vol. II, p. 38),

> The writing is the usual secretary hand of the 15th Century, and the date of the transcription, as given in the colophon, is December 29th, 1477, or about six weeks after the publication of Caxton's printed edition, of which it is a verbatim copy, etc.

but in his preface to the facsimile edition of the *Dictes* (London, 1877, p. xi), he says, 'There is in the Library of Lambeth Palace, a manuscript copy of Caxton's third edition'. Dr. M. R. James's description of the Lambeth Manuscripts (Cambridge University Press, 1930–2, p. 412) states that 'it is a verbatim copy of Caxton's printed edition of the *Dictes* published in Nov. 1477, and is dated about six

---

[2] Entries in the manuscript record the births of several members of the family of 'Hyll' or 'Hill'. The earliest is 'Agatha Hille' on 30 May 1479. These entries may be of a slightly later date. On folio 86v is this rather amusing poem;

> God wote grete cause these wyffys haue a-mong ⎫
> But dowte ye not there hertis be strong   ⎬ In besenysse
> ffor they may suffur no maner wrong    ⎭
> ffor yf they dyde there hertis wold brest ⎫
> Wherfor ffor-sothe I holde it best    ⎬ In be[senysse]
> Let h[e]m a-lone with evylle rest    ⎭
> Ye husbondis alle by on asent ⎫
> Let your wyffys haue there intent   ⎬ In be[senysse]
> Or els by my trowthe ye wylle repent ⎭
> Hit ys harde a-yenst the streme to stryve ⎫
> ffor he þat casteth hym for to thryve   ⎬ In be[senysse]
> He most aske leve of hys wyffe ⎭
> Or els be God & by the rode ⎫
> Be he neuer so wylde or wode   ⎬ In be[senysse]
> Sche wille make hys here grow thorow hys hode ⎭

weeks later'; the manuscript, we are told, is of the fifteenth century 'very carefully written with interesting ornaments', and (p. 414)

The decorative initials throughout the book are remarkable. They are modelled not very skilfully on the contemporary Italian work: the letter in fine burnished gold, the ground divided into fields of blue, pink, and green, dotted with white and filled with white branch-work. See Blades, *Caxton*, 1861, i. 81, ii. 38. He speaks of the miniature as being defaced and of the engraving as 'beautified'. I do not agree: the miniature is in good condition and the engraving quite faithful.

Now the colophon of the manuscript reads,

Thus endeth the boke of the dictes and notable wise sayenges of Philosophres late translated out of ffrensshe into Englisshe by my forsaide lord Therle of (*erasure*) and by his comaundment sette in fourme & enprinted in right substanciale maner / And this boke was ffinisshed the xxiiij day of Decembre, the xvijth yere of our liege lord King Edward þe iiijth. (106ʳ).

The seventeenth year of the reign of Edward IV extended from 4 March 1477 to 3 March 1478, so that the date on which the manuscript was finished must be 24 December 1477. If the date given in the colophon were 18 November, one would be inclined to say that the scribe had merely copied the date of the Caxton print. As the date is not the same, one cannot escape from the conclusion that the work of transcription was actually completed on 24 December 1477. Scarcely six weeks elapsed between the date of Caxton's print and the completion of L, during which, apart from the mere transcription of the text, the 'copyist' had to obtain Caxton's book; collect, arrange, and rule the vellum; complete one rather ambitious miniature and occasional decorative initials; and, possibly, bind the volume (though it is more probable that the book was bound after the date given in the colophon). The scribe must have worked under exceptional pressure if he had merely contented himself with an accurate transcription of I, but the manuscript is *not* a verbatim copy of the first edition. In most of the important variations, as we shall see later, L *agrees with the second edition*. As L and II are so nearly alike, one must, if one agrees with the accepted order of the three editions, conclude that L is the prototype of II; in that case Edward IV either gave or lent to Caxton this 'presentation' manuscript. In no other way can one account for the text of II (if the date of that edition is 1479 or 1480); surely it cannot be a coincidence that the 'corrections' in L are identical with those in II. Though II has some additional changes (in common with Ad), this does not in any way weaken the argument; the variants the two have in common are, in general, desirable, but one cannot suppose that two correctors working independently chose practically identical emendations. The only possible alternative is that the Lambeth manuscript of 1477 was derived from II, but that print is generally dated 1479. Ad, incidentally, cannot be a copy of L, as Ad and II agree in certain readings which do not occur in L. Neither L nor II was, in turn, derived from Ad, as this manuscript has many faults entirely its own.

The list of the textual variants given below does not, in any way, pretend to be complete nor are all the major variations noted. On the other hand, it will, I believe, amply illustrate the textual changes that I have spoken of.

Among the more important variants are:

Fol. 7ᵛ, l. 17   'a grete prouffitable wynnyng'  I, III.
                 'a grete & a profitable w.'  Ad, II; *so in* L *by* MS. *correction.*
Fol. 12ᵛ, l. 11  'wherfore suche thinges wol be gretely kept'  I, III, L.
                 'wherfore suche wol be kept'  II, Ad.
Fol. 35ʳ, l. 3   'semblably he bad and thanked god'  I, Ia, III.
                 'semblably he badde thanke god'  II, Ad, L.
Fol. 37ʳ, l. 6   'And said be wele ware that in bataille thou truste not all onely in thy strength dispreysing thyn naturall witte† causeth victorie withoute might/but vn[n]ethe may men haue victorie by strength withoute vse of natural wit.'  I and III.

            † Clearly something has been omitted by I and III. The French text reads (Morgan MS. 10) 'Et dist garde toy en bataille que tu ne te fies seullement en ta force en desprisant ton sens raisonnable car aucune fois le sens suffit pour vaintre sans force/mes, etc.' In II, Ad, and L, the omission has been corrected: 'witte for often engin causeth victorie, etc.'

Fol. 40ᵛ, l. 12  'he taught the science and lerned it and after the deth of plato' I, Ia, and III.
                 'he taught the sciences and learned than (thaim L) after the deth of plato'  II, Ad, and L.
                 *but* 'il aprenoit la science. ¶ Et apres ce que le dit platon fut mort' (Morgan MS. 10; similarly Morgan MS. 771).
Fol. 54ᵛ, l. 27  'impossible thing that the man may kepe him'  I and III.
                 'impossible thing a man to kepe him'  II, Ad, and L.
                 *but* 'il est impossible que celui se puisse garder'  (MS. 10).
Fol. 66ʳ, l. 8   'take hede whedre they charge hym wyth gold or grauell'  I, Ia, and III.
                 'take hede whedre they be charged with gold or grauel'  L, Ad, and II.

The French text is somewhat different but in the essential part it reads 'qui sont chargees' (Morgan MSS. 771 and 10).

Fol. 69ʳ, l. 23   'And he ansuerd that one is not sure to kepe long in one degre & is most difficile to be founde' I, Ia, and III.

'And he aunswerd helth whiche is not sure to be kepte long in one degree and is mooste difficile to be founde' L.

'And he ansuerd helthe whiche is not sure to be kept long in one degree & is moste diffycile' II and Ad.

*but* 'et il respondit celle qui ne peult longuement demourer en vn estat et donc on peult le mains finer' (MS. 10; similarly MS. 771).

Fol. 70ʳ, l. 29   'a gouge doth the iron' I and III.

'a gonge doth euery swetnesse' II, Ad, and L.

*but* 'La lime fait le fer' (MSS. 10 and 771).

## Those of less importance include:

Fol. 2ʳ, l. 7   'haue had my parte' I and III; 'haue' *omitted in* L and II.

Fol. 6ʳ, l. 28   'Hermes departeth thens' I and III; 'departed' *in* Ad, L, and II.

Fol. 10ʳ, l. 12   Ad inserts 'And saide sapience is lyke a thynge that shal not profite'. Apparently a scribal error caused by misreading the lines.

Fol. 12ᵛ, l. 17   'royaume or prouynce' I, III, and L.
'royaumes or prouinces' II and Ad.

Fol. 15ʳ, l. 18   'whiche was a cyte' I and III; 'whiche athenes' Ad, II, and so, *by correction,* in L.

Fol. 19ʳ, l. 27   'god is not worshipped' I and III; 'not onely worshipped' II, Ad, and so, *by correction,* in L.

Fol. 40ʳ, l. 26   'that more vseth of reason' I, III, and L.
'that mooste vseth reason' II and Ad.

Fol. 41ʳ, l. 1   'And yaue grete almesdedis' I, Ia, and III; for 'yaue', *read* 'ded' in Ad, L, and II.

Fol. 46ᵛ, l. 25   'What he doth' I and III.
'his doyng' Ad, L, and II.

Fol. 51ᵛ, l. 6   'And he sayde to him ayen Syr if I am not worthy to haue so moche' *omitted only in* Ad.

Fol. 55ᵛ, ll. 11–13   'And he sayth Kinges . . . enduryng' *omitted only in* Ad.

Fol. 60ᵛ, ll. 7–8   'surmounteth alle other wordes and thoughtes as he him self' *omitted only in* Ad.

Fol. 61ᵛ, l. 9   'For King' I and III; 'For þaire Kyng' Ad, L, and II.

Fol. 65ʳ, l. 22   'whom that I truste' I and III; 'that' *omitted in* II, Ad, and L.

Fol. 65ʳ, l. 29   'cōme' I and III; 'cometh' in II, Ad, and L.

(The text in Addit. 22718 is occasionally quite corrupt. I have recorded here only four of Ad's special faults, but these are enough to prove that neither II nor L is a copy of Ad.)

The prints and the manuscripts, on the basis of the evidence considered above, would be related thus,

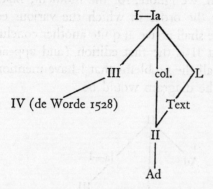

Why was III reprinted from the variant of I? One might conjecture that Caxton delegated the task of issuing the third edition of the *Dictes* to an apprentice, who was possibly ignorant of the existence of II. As Crotch says (p. cxxii)

'Be that as it may, the year next saw a revival of energy, for no less than eleven extant books appear to have been printed in 1489, although much of the work involved mere revision, such as might readily have been done by Caxton's assistants.'

The connexion between the manuscripts, and the prints may be taken to be more or less established, but the explanation of the manner in which these texts of the *Dictes* are related, is far from satisfactory. It necessitates the exceedingly unlikely supposition that the King permitted Caxton to make use of, or copy, the manuscript presented to him by Earl Rivers; secondly, this explanation demands that Caxton, for his second edition, made use not only of this manuscript but also of the variant of I (for the colophon); thirdly, we must suppose that the date of MS. Addit. 22718 is incorrect in two respects, viz. in the day of the month and in the year of the reign of Edward IV; and lastly, after we have corrected the date of Ad to read 18 November 1477, we must presume that this manuscript was *not actually written* in that year but in 1479/80. It may incidentally be mentioned that the variant of I has not been adequately accounted for by any bibliographer, nor does the reconstruction given above help materially. From the fact that the colophon of the variant (with the exception of the date) is reproduced in L, it must be assumed that L was copied from the variant and not from I; II, in turn, has the text of L, but the colophon (including the date) of Ia, so that Caxton must have made use of both in printing II.

If, on the other hand, we ignore, for the moment, Blades's typographical evidence for the order in which the various editions of the *Dictes* appeared, we shall arrive at quite another conclusion. One need only suppose that II is the first edition (and appeared on 18 November 1477), and all the problems that I have mentioned above are logically solved. The diagram would be

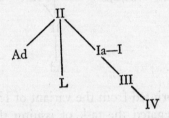

The question concerning the date of Ad is answered; the manuscript may have been finished on the 'xxviij day of þe moneth of Novembir And þe seven(teen)th yere of þe reygne of King Edward þe ffourþe'; or, if one prefers to see in the date of Ad merely a contortion of Caxton's colophon, at any time after 18 November 1477, and before 30 May 1479. L was copied from II [the only evidence against this supposition rests on the date of the manuscript (1477) and the date (1479) that Blades assigns to II] and this manuscript was duly presented to Edward IV. The vexing problem, whether the King lent the manuscript to Caxton and why, is eliminated. If II is really the first edition, it offers this ready solution to the variant of I. When Caxton decided to reprint the *Dictes*, he altered the text of II, possibly making the emendations with the French text before him (see my list of variants). After a few copies (perhaps only one) of the work had come off the press, Caxton, realizing that he had reprinted the original colophon of II without changing the date, decided to rectify this error by the simple expedient of cutting out the colophon entirely. Possibly Caxton did not consider the task of resetting the type on folio 74ʳ (in order to correct that date too) worth the trouble. This, at least, would offer a reasonable explanation for Ia. The problem of III is also disposed of without undue speculation. Caxton probably retained all copies of the variant and when III came to be printed, it was reprinted from this issue.

The only possible argument against this theory, rests upon the typographical evidence. II is printed in type 2*, and the evidence for dating II *post* 1479 is derived from Blades's analysis of Caxton's type (vol. ii, p. xxxii)

> Never finding that the two founts (2 and 2*) are mixed; and seeing that all the books dated *ante* 1479 occur in Type No. 2; and all those dated *post* 1479 in No. 2*; the two types appear to indicate two periods: and, taking into consideration the peculiarities just noticed, it would seem that, upon the types becoming worn, some of the best were selected, trimmed up with a graver, and used for making matrices for a new casting. If this were not the case how are we to account for the new fount being so nearly like the old? for, the two not being used together, there was no reason for such care to make them match.

It is not impossible, in my opinion, that Caxton cut this type specially for the first edition of the *Dictes* in order to please his powerful patron, Earl Rivers; the next time the type 2* was used it was to print Rivers's translation of the *Cordyale* (completed 24 March 1479). Between 1476 and 1483, Caxton made use of four types (2, 2*, 3, and 4); of these, 2 and 3 were used in 1476–8; 2* and 3 (separately and together) from 1479 to 1483; and 4 from 1479 on. Does this absolutely preclude the possibility that 2* was first employed in 1477 but reserved for publications of special importance (i.e. the *Cordyale*)? I can, in that case, be dated after 24 December 1477, and probably before 24 March 1479 (after this date 2 was no longer used). This is doubtlessly a bold conjecture, but it is apparently the only logical solution to the vexing problems we have been considering. A critical edition of Caxton's *Dictes* is most desirable and will, no doubt, show conclusively whether or not my conjecture concerning the order in which the various editions and the manuscripts appeared is tenable.[3]

### POSTSCRIPT TO DR. CURT BÜHLER'S ARTICLE
#### BY R. B. MCKERROW

SOME eight or ten years ago, having occasion to look at the three early editions of the *Dictes and Sayings*, I noticed a small typographical point which suggested to me a doubt whether the generally accepted order of the first two of these was correct. Any further investigation of the matter seemed, however, to involve a study of

---

[3] Since writing this article, I have heard that Professor Hittmair of Tübingen is contemplating such an edition. It will be most useful, indeed, to all interested in the typography of Caxton. [No modern edition of the work has yet appeared. CFB]

Caxton's types, for which I had no time, and I therefore put my note aside with the intention of returning to it later should an opportunity arise. This never did: but now that Dr. Bühler has on quite different grounds arrived at a conclusion which tallies with my vague suspicion, I have obtained his permission to add to his paper a brief postscript as to the bibliographical point which I had noticed and which—so far as it goes—seems to give some slight support to his view.

Using the same notation for the three editions as Dr. Bühler does, we may note that I and II correspond page for page and generally line for line, while III does not follow its predecessors in these respects; and further that whereas the line-endings of both I and II are uneven, in accordance with Caxton's practice in his early period, the endings of I are much more uneven than those of II. It may also be remarked that on the whole the setting of I appears to have been less careful than that of II, the use of hyphens in words divided at the end of a line being particularly erratic in the former.

Now, although it is undoubtedly true that, in the work of a particular printer, books printed with irregular line-endings generally precede those in which the lines end evenly, it by no means follows that, of two books both of which have uneven line-endings, the more uneven one will be the earlier; and especially does this not follow when one is a line-for-line reprint of the other. Indeed, the contrary seems more likely to be true. A compositor setting up a book from a manuscript will naturally make his lines end with some approach to evenness. He will insert into each line as many words as it will conveniently admit, and if by using an abbreviation or by slightly reducing the spacing of the last two or three words of a line he can find room for an extra word instead of leaving the line noticeably short, he may be expected to do this. The result will be, as a general rule, that though the lines do not end evenly as in modern printing, the unevenness will seldom exceed the width of a letter or two. On the other hand, a compositor who is following printed copy line for line will, unless he takes extraordinary care with his spaces, find that his lines will vary considerably in their relative length from those of his copy.[4]

---

[4] It is generally recognized that the quickest way of determining whether two prints of anything having uneven line-endings, such as verse, belong to the same setting of type, is to notice whether the relative positions of the line-endings in the two do, or do not, correspond with one another.

If, for instance, he uses by chance somewhat thin spaces he may find that there is plenty of room at the end of his line for the first word of the next. Had he been printing a first edition from the manuscript he would naturally have inserted this additional word, but if he is following a printed book line for line he will, as naturally, not do this, for if he does, he will upset the length of the next line and perhaps to an even greater extent. There is thus at least a probability that a reprint of an irregular-lined book will be more irregular than the original.

Of course this is only a probability, and it is indeed only probable on the assumption that the compositor would take no very great care with his work, or no more than would ordinarily be taken with a reprint. It would doubtless be possible, by taking trouble, to render the line-endings of a reprint even *more* regular than those of the original, but it may, I think, fairly be argued that this would only be done at a time when even line-endings had become customary, and neither of the editions of the *Dictes* under discussion shows signs of a conscious attempt at such regularity.

In II, as I have said, the irregularity is seldom great; it amounts as a rule to the space of a letter or two; and there seem to be very few cases in which an additional word could have been got into the line without considerable alteration in the spacing. In I, however, there are many such cases. Occasionally, indeed, a line is so short that it seems that the compositor could have added the first word of the next line without any readjustment at all, and quite frequently a slight change in spacing or the use of a contraction would have allowed this. One is constantly puzzled by the failure to take up a word or syllable and by the unnecessarily awkward division of words when the compositor apparently had ample space at his disposal, until one notices that the mechanical following of the lines of II would produce just this result.

Thus, therefore, though we cannot arrive at proof by considerations of this kind, I venture to think that the greater relative regularity of the line-endings in II may not unreasonably be regarded as supporting the view that this is the earlier edition and that I, the supposed first edition, is actually the reprint.

There are two other small typographical points which seem to tell in the same direction, namely, that the type of II (Caxton's so-called type 2*) contains, as well as the looped k of I, a k of the same form as the Recuyell type (Caxton 1), whereas I seems to use the looped k alone.[5] Also that II does not appear to use the ligatured ll, whereas I has both ligatured and nonligatured forms. It seems perhaps unlikely that if Caxton possessed the ligatured form he would cease to use it, but I must leave such questions to those more expert in early type forms.

[5] See Duff, *Fifteenth Century Books*, plate 1, line 7 from foot, 'knowe', and plate 3, line 13, 'make', where the k's seem to me identical. It should be noted that there is in type 2*, besides the occasional looped k, another k of the same general form as that of type 1, but with a shorter curl over the top, see plate 3, line 17, 'knewe', and line 4 from foot, 'take'.

(From *The Library* (1934), pp. 316-329).

# CHAPTER B2

## MORE ABOUT *THE DICTES AND SAYINGS*
## *OF THE PHILOSOPHERS*

SOME years ago, the present writer contributed an article to *The Library* (December 1934) in which he questioned the traditional order in which the first two editions of *The Dictes and Sayings of the Philosophers* were believed to have appeared. By the discovery of a variant setting for one of the sheets in this book, it is possible to shed still more light on this problem.[1]

The sheet in question is the second sheet in the fourth (unsigned) quire and comprises the conjugate folios 26 and 31 [d2–d7]. The variant settings may be readily identified by the reading of the last line on each page; for the sake of convenience, the variants are respectively marked Ib and Ic:

Folio 26 recto:
    men shulde be guyded aftre .iij. ordres that is to saie in (Ib)
    men shulde be guyded after thre ordres. that is to saye in  (Ic)

Folio 26 verso:
    to do harme And said the goode saule graffeth goodnesse & (Ib)
    to do harme And saide the good saule graffeth goodnes &  (Ic)

Folio 31 recto:
    the ende of the werke / ther was awoman that called him old (Ib)
    thend of the werke. ther was awoman that called him old  (Ic)

Folio 31 verso:
    diseases of this world / ther was neuer ioye withoute sorowe (Ib)
    diseases of this worlde. there was neù ioye without sorow (Ic)

Of the nine copies whose readings are known to me only two represent the variant Ic, these being one of the copies in the Pierpont Morgan Library (PML 673) and the copy in the library of Trinity

---

[1] The designations of the manuscripts and printed editions here used are the same as those used in the previous paper; the explanations need not, therefore, be reprinted. Another manuscript has, however, come to light since 1934; this is MS. Ry. 20 of the Newberry Library, Chicago, and it is referred to as N in the present paper. Although it differs widely from all the Caxton editions of the *Dictes*, it has Earl Rivers's Prologue stating that the translation was made by him. For further details the reader is referred to my edition of the *Dicts and Sayings of the Philosophers* (Early English Text Society, Original Series No. 211, 1941; reprinted 1961).

College, Cambridge. The remaining copies all have the reading given in Blades's facsimile (Ib); they comprise the second copy in the Morgan Library (PML 773), both copies in the John Rylands Library, two copies in the British Museum (IB 55004 and IB 55005), and those in the Henry E. Huntington Library and the University Library, Cambridge.

In a number of cases there are important differences between the two variant issues. In the order of their appearance, they are the following:

Folio 26 verso, line 1:
Clergie / in knyghthode & in cōmones / and ordeigned the || clergie aboue the knyghthode / . . . (Ib)
Clergye / in knighthode & in cōmones / and ordeigned that || clergye aboue the kmghthode. . . . (Ic)

Folio 26 verso, line 4:
peple the knyghthode sholde defende the clergie & the peple / the (Ib)
peple / & þe knighthode sholde defende the clergye & the peple / the (Ic)

Folio 26 verso, lines 18–21:
And || sayd / right as a man is heled of his sekenesse / by vertue || of a medycine / right so is an euyl man heled of his malice || by vertue of the lawe (Ib)
And || sayde Right as a man is heled of his sekenesse. by vertue || of a medicine / right so is an euil man heleth of his malice || by vertue of his lawe (Ic)

Folio 31 recto, lines 24–8:
One axed him what was a goode purchasse. he || ansuerd that / that groweth in the spēding therof / And saide || drōkenship vndoth amā. & said one ought not to axe ɔseile || of him that hath his herte al sette to the world for his aduis || shalbe but after his pleasāce. (Ib)
One axid him what was a good purchassh / he || ansuerd that groweth in the spēding therof / And said dron||kenship vndoth aman / & saide one ought to axe  ceyle of || him that hath his hert al sett to the world for his aduys || shalbe but after his plesance / (Ic)

Now it is self-evident from the text that, in at least the third and fourth examples,[2] Ib is correct and Ic is not. If we are to believe that Ib was printed in order to correct the misreadings of Ic, then Ic most certainly represents the first issue. In short, the order of appearance of the issues would be: first issue—Ic, second issue with corrected text—Ib, third issue with corrected text and added colophon

[2] In the first two examples either reading might be correct, though in each case the reading of Ib seems better if the whole passage is taken into consideration.

—Ia. Although this appears to be, at first glance, a most reasonable sequence, it does not fit the facts which must now be presented.

If we follow William Blades and Dr. James in the belief that the Lambeth manuscript (L) is a copy of what Blades believed to be the first edition (I), we encounter a seemingly inexplicable problem. L, as is well known, is a carefully written and decorated manuscript, completed (on the evidence of the colophon) on 24 December 1477, or (according to Blades) some six weeks after Ia had come off the press;[3] Ia is also considered by Blades to have been the prototype of the British Museum manuscript (Ad)[4] and of Caxton's second edition (II). Again (if we follow Blades) the question must be raised: why were these three texts all taken from the *third* issue and not from the earlier ones? Furthermore, with the exception of the variant sheet here noted and the addition of the colophon in Ia, all the remainder of the book was printed at one and the same time, so that there cannot have been a very great lapse of time between the issues of Ic, Ib, and Ia. Why did Caxton go to so much trouble as to print three separate issues for the corrections and additions here made, which, after all, cover very insignificant points?

Turning now to Blades's second edition, we note that in each case II has the readings of Ib–Ia and not of Ic. Furthermore II has one[5] special fault on folio 31 recto, lines 18–20; here II reads:

> And sayd || whan a man speketh he ought to considere what he wil seye || for better it is he cōsidere. than another shold.

In all the issues of I, this reads (orthographical variants disregarded):

> And said || whan a man speketh he ought to ɔsidere afore what he wil seie || for better it is he ɔsidere. than another shold.

In this instance Ad also omits 'afore' while L writes 'bifore'.[6] If we follow the order designated by Blades, we find that, for no very good reason, L (though copying I) altered the 'afore' to 'bifore'; furthermore it must then be noted that II, although drawn from

---

[3] It was copied from Ia as the manuscript has a colophon which closely resembles that in Ia; neither Ib nor Ic have this colophon. As it has not got the variant readings of Ic, L could not have been copied from this issue.

[4] Ad has a colophon similar to Ia and does not have the readings of Ic.

[5] There are two minor slips on folio 31 verso. In line 7, II has 'desireth' where I has 'desired'; in line 28, II prints 'they' for 'thy', a misprint found nowhere else.

[6] Similarly N, where the passage reads: 'he awth to consydyr be fore what he wyl sey for bettyr yt ys þat he consyder þan a odyr shold.'

both L and Ia,[7] ignored *both* these readings and entirely omitted the word. Next Ad, being also derived from I and not from II according to Blades, by a well-nigh incredible coincidence also omitted 'afore'. Finally, the third edition (III) ignored the readings of all its immediate predecessors (L, N, Ad, and II) and returned to the text of I. Although such a circumstance may not be completely inconceivable, the weight of the evidence seems to lie in a somewhat different and more plausible direction.

Assuming for an instant that II is the first edition, we find a much more reasonable explanation for this problem. Ad, as a copy of II, followed his original in omitting the word; the scribe of L, realizing that II had an omission here, supplied 'bifore'; I, who also noted the omission but whose readings were not taken from L, chose 'afore'; and finally III followed his immediate predecessor in this reading. In such a reconstruction all theoretical coincidence is eliminated.[8]

If II is again taken to be the earlier edition, it follows that Ia must be the first issue of the second edition and Ib the second. As I pointed out in the previous paper, this readily explains the presence of the colophon in one issue of this edition and its omission in the others. Caxton merely set up his type for Ia from II and, after printing one or more copies before he realized that he had included a colophon with a wrong date, simply deleted it. On the other hand, if I, as is usually supposed, is really the first edition, it seems strange that Caxton should have gone to the trouble to add a colophon for only the one copy known to us as against the thirteen others that have not got it. As I know of no apparent reason why Caxton should have done this, the explanation based on the theory given above seems much more credible.

If we believe the order in which the editions appeared to be II–Ia–Ib, we must still account for Ic. The present writer has previously pointed out[9] that Caxton occasionally reprinted certain leaves either in order to correct obvious errors or because he had insufficient sheets for some quires to complete the number of desired copies. In such cases, when he needed additional sheets, he simply reprinted the necessary folios and bound them up with the other sheets. This

[7] Compare my note and the stemma *supra*, p. 9 ff.

[8] Compare the stemma and note in my first paper, p. 10 ff.

[9] Compare my notes in *The Library*: 'Caxton Variants' (June 1936); 'Three Notes on Caxton' (September 1936); 'Two Caxton Problems' (December 1939).

must have been the origin of Ic and the mistakes in these reprinted leaves are merely the faults of a hurried and slipshod compositor. The order of the appearance of the issues would then be: Ia (with the colophon of II), Ib (with the text of Ia but with the colophon deleted), and Ic (Ib with the reprinted leaves inserted).

Turning now to the third edition, we must note that III has not the mistakes either of II or Ic already spoken of but derives directly from the text of Ib and Ia.[10] Here I should like to correct an accidental misstatement in my first paper dealing with the *Dictes*. I stated there that III was printed from the variant Ia. As the texts of Ia and Ib (save for the colophon) are identical, it cannot be definitely established whether III was printed from the variant Ia or Ib, but since III has not the colophon of Ia, the inference is that it was, very probably, not set up from Ia but from Ib. This belief is strengthened by the fact that, as we have seen, Ib is the most accurate of the three issues of III's predecessor, as it has not the wrong colophon of Ia (copied from II) nor the incorrectly reprinted sheet of Ic. It is probable, therefore, that when Caxton wanted to print his third edition of this text he set up his type from the most correct issue of his second edition, viz. Ib.

This paper seems to add some further proof for the theory that II was the earliest edition of the *Dictes*. The present writer, at least, is convinced that, on the basis of the evidence here produced together with that in the first paper, Blades's second edition (II) must actually be the first and that it is thus the earliest book printed in England giving not only the place of printing but also the actual date as well.[11]

(From *The Library* (1941), pp. 284-290).

[10] On folio 26 recto, line 11, Ic prints 'seyng' while Ia and Ib have 'seynig'. Significantly enough III also has the misprint of Ia–Ib and this may be further proof that III was not set up from Ic.

[11] The only objection to this theory is on the basis of the types. I is printed with Caxton's type 2, while II has type 2*. Blades contended that only type 2 was in use in 1477 and that type 2* was not used till 1479. Here the present writer does not agree with Blades; for a full discussion of this problem, see my paper 'Three Notes on Caxton'. It must also be remarked that the order in which, according to Blades, the types appeared was upset by the discovery of portions of type 3 in the 'new' *Indulgence* of 1476; on this point, see Prof. A. W. Pollard's article in *The Library*, vol. ix, pp. 86–9.

# CHAPTER B3

## SOME OBSERVATIONS ON *THE DICTES AND*
## *SAYINGS OF THE PHILOSOPHERS*

SOME years ago I set forth the theory that the traditional order of the first two editions of the *Dictes* might have to be reversed and that what was generally believed to be the second edition (II) was actually the *editio princeps*. Since this theory has recently been questioned (*The Library* (1948), 155–85), I should like to explain what my position in the matter is at present.

My interest in the Caxton printings of this translation was the result of preparatory work for an edition of the two other English versions. In the course of this study I stumbled upon the fact that the Lambeth manuscript (L) was not an exact copy of the presumed first edition (I) as had been affirmed by other scholars, and on the basis of the dates in the manuscript and in the printed editions[1] and from the fact that in all the most important instances L agreed with II (not with I), I came to the conclusion that L must have been copied from II and that II (on the basis of the dates) might be judged the first edition. At that time I had had no bibliographical training; after an interval of fifteen years, I can only say that I would write the article quite differently were I to do so now. I am not quite so sure of anything nowadays as I was in the early 1930s and I would certainly be less dogmatic about the conclusions to which the evidence seemed to point.

In any event, I soon had doubts that my papers were the final word on this problem (the second paper was written in 1938 but its appearance was somewhat delayed by the outbreak of war) and I expressed this point of view quite freely, both in private conversations and in print.[2] I have since undertaken a thorough study of the

---

[1] Lambeth MS. No. 265 is dated 24 December [1477] and the Rylands copy of I, with the extra colophon, has the date: 18 November [1477]. This latter date also appears in II, which Blades believed was printed *c.* 1479. Additional MS. 22718 of the British Museum is a copy of II but appears to have been in the hands of the Trevelyan family since 1479, a date which conflicts with the supposed dating of II.

[2] Compare my *The Dicts and Sayings of the Philosophers*, E.E.T.S., o.s., ccxi (1941), p. lvii, and also my two short notes: 'A Survival from the Middle Ages: William Baldwin's Use of the *Dictes and Sayings*', *Speculum*, xxiii (1948), p. 79,

French and English manuscripts and a careful comparison of every copy of the first two editions. This work I have in hand, as my copy of Blades's facsimile edition bears witness. At this stage of my investigations I can only say that there is a wealth of evidence both to support my theory and to contradict it.

The evidence advanced in the article 'A Word on Caxton's *Dictes*' is (unfortunately) not viewed impartially but from the firm conviction that I is the first edition. This has led the writer into a series[3] of contradictions, inconsistencies, and errors of fact, one of which is perfectly unnecessary and extraneous to the argument. Furthermore, two of the most significant pieces of evidence for the order in which the editions may have been printed are not even mentioned in this paper (see pp. 29-32 and note 29).

The article is vitiated, as I have said, by a number of contradictory statements and of these the following may be cited. On p. 172 we find a remark as to the 'superior correctness of II'—only to be told, two pages later, that half of the sample readings just cited 'are erroneous in II in a way too inconsiderable to lend itself to tracing'. Again, on p. 177 it is stated that 'I is noticeably inferior' to II, following hard upon a demonstration which purports to establish the inferiority of II in a most significant reading. On p. 174 we are informed that in 'four of the six cases, the reading of I *is* more in conformity with the French than the reading of L and II'. But surely, in a translation that one which is nearer the original must necessarily be the better text, and thus II must be viewed as certainly inferior.

One error of fact may be mentioned here; others will be noted in their proper places. The implication is made (on p. 178) that Rivers had known and used the Scrope translation.[4] If Rivers had used such

---

n. 25, and 'New Manuscripts of *The Dicts and Sayings of the Philosophers*', *Modern Language Notes,* lxiii (1948), p. 28, n. 15.

[3] See the statement on p. 156: 'fol. 16ʳ was the last page in its forme.' Surely the last page must always be a verso. My belief that Caxton did not immediately bind the copies as soon as they came off the press but that he stored the quires in unbound lots is also disputed (p. 179, n. 3, and p. 180). By a curious coincidence, it can be proved beyond the shadow of a doubt that Caxton's contemporary, Le Petit Laurens, did *not* bind the copies of his edition of the French *Dits moraux* (Pellechet 4362) as soon as the sheets were printed but that he stored the quires separately. See my discussion, *Gutenberg-Jahrbuch,* 1950, pp. 182-185.

[4] It was William Blades (a printer) who first suggested that Rivers might have used the Scrope translation, and this theory was echoed by Hermann Knust and Ezio Franceschini, distinguished scholars in the field of romance literature. None of

a manuscript,[5] how can one account for the ludicrous blunders in translation, the omissions of text (in Plato), the disarranged sentences (in Socrates), and the other slips to which attention is called repeatedly in my notes to the Early English Text Society edition. Two scholars well known in the field of Middle English literature (one of whom has written extensively about Caxton and who is the announced editor of a new edition of Rivers's translation) have stated categorically that Rivers had not made use of Scrope's version. In view of my somewhat extensive analysis and the concurring opinions of Professors Alois Brandl[6] and Rudolf Hittmair,[7] I do not believe that there will be many scholars who will agree that Rivers knew and used the earlier versions.[8]

The theory of the order in which the printed editions were produced rests (in essence) on four basic points—text and time, type and typography. Turning first of all to the text,[9] we come immediately to what seems to me the crux of the whole problem—and here I should like to reserve judgement for the present. The evidence —at the moment—seems to point both ways. In any case, what must first be determined is which is the superior text, I or II; and by

---

these ever claimed to be a student, or to have any specialized knowledge, of English literary history.

[5] Where Rivers speaks of 'other of the same bookes whiche difference and be of other inportaunce', he does not, in my opinion, refer to other translations of the *same* book but more probably to the *De Vita et moribus philosophorum* by Walter Burley, the *Vitae et sententiae philosophorum*, the *Auctoritates de vita et moribus philosophorum*, or Alart of Cambrai's *Moralités des philosophes*.

[6] 'On the Dictes and Sayings of the Philosophers', *An English Miscellany Presented to Dr. Furnivall*, Oxford, 1901.

[7] 'Earl Rivers' Einleitung zu seiner Übertragung der *Weisheitssprüche der Philosophen*', *Anglia*, xlvii, p. 340.

[8] For an additional bit of mistranslation by Rivers, see my *Speculum* paper cited above.

[9] Some of the arguments based on grammar and tautology are not clear to me. For example, on p. 173, 'come' is not an incorrect or ungrammatical form at all, but a perfectly proper third person singular preterite. Since the sentence on that page contained four verbs, three of which are certainly in the past tense, it could easily be argued that the compositor altered the 'cometh' of his copy to 'come' for the sake of consistency. Naturally the present tense is correct as the verso of the leaf proves but the compositor in reprints would normally just set to the end of the page. And as for thinking that Caxton would be averse to 'tautology'—why it was his favourite stylistic device! See Leon Kellner (*E.E.T.S.*, E.S., lviii, p. cxi): 'What makes Caxton's style appear so awkward in the eyes of the modern reader, is his repetitions, tautologies and anacolutha. But these irregularities are, for the most part, conscious sins, committed not only by him, but also by all the writers of his time.' For Caxton's use of 'who that', see ibid., p. xl.

'superior' text is meant that one which is closer to the French manu-script used by Rivers. As in the case of Scrope's translation not only of the *Dicts* but also of the *Epistle of Othea*,[10] it is incorrect to say that a certain reading is wrong because it does not agree with the reading of the *standard* version of the original. In both of Scrope's translations I have been able to show that many of his 'mistransla-tions' are actually quite correct renderings of corrupt originals. One must not confuse modern translations made from a standard and authorized text with medieval ones which were made from whatever manuscript (good, bad, or indifferent)[11] came to the hand of the translator. How far this condition may apply to Rivers remains to be determined—but on the basis of the variations in the English edi-tions and in the French manuscripts it ought to be possible to estab-lish the nature of the manuscript which Rivers used. Again it must be borne in mind that as far as the Caxton text is concerned, the best text is not necessarily that which is closest to the ideal French text but that which is closest to the French manuscript from which Rivers made his translation. Once this has been determined it will materially simplify the problem of establishing the order in which the editions appeared.

As for the time element, it was precisely the fact that L was not a copy of I but an emended version closer to II and dated thirty-six days later which first aroused my interest in the matter. I felt then (as I do now) that it was most doubtful that the scribe could have produced the manuscript in so short a time. Indeed, though we are given the date when the manuscript was finished, no one knows for certain when it was begun—so that (under the hypothesis as set forth) a period of thirty working days is the maximum which one may allow for the scribe to perform all the tasks which I outlined in the first of my papers.[12] Yet we are now asked to assume that

[10] See my article 'Sir John Fastolf's Manuscripts of the *Épître d'Othéa* and Stephen Scrope's Translation of this Text', *Scriptorium*, iii (1949), 123–8, as well as my edition of the *Dicts*.

[11] The phrase 'filth of a gonge doth every swetnesse' (see p. 175) presents a diffi-cult problem. Could it possibly be that Rivers's manuscript read 'feir(e)' or that he misread 'fer' as such. [OF Feire (= MF Foire) → ME Feire = ME Faire (*O.E.D.* Fair sb²)]. It is possible, of course, that Rivers originally translated OF 'lyme' by some pleonasm like 'file or a gauge'. Anyone familiar with Middle English hand-writing could easily understand how this might be read as 'filþ of a gonge'.

[12] Compare the estimate given by Fritz Milkau, *Handbuch der Bibliothekswissen-schaft*, Leipzig, 1931–40, I, 734, to the effect that Vespasiano da Bisticci employed 45

there was a further, intermediate step of a time-consuming nature. The contention is that a copy of Ia was corrected and that this model was furnished to Haywarde and then further emended by him.[13] The only result of this hypothesis that I can see is to make the time schedule even more difficult to accept. Surely, one can hardly give credence to a theory that the quires were sent to the corrector as fast as they came off the press, that they were revised by him and immediately sent to Haywarde, that the scribe thereupon made his copy and ultimately returned the corrected sheets in good order to Caxton. This practically implies proof-reading of a sort which normally leads to stop-press corrections. Caxton had already used this practice in this work[14] and in other volumes as well, so that if he carefully proof-read his text immediately after printing, one would expect to find variant states of the sort commonly found in *S.T.C.* books. One would, under such circumstances, certainly not anticipate any need for an *extensively revised* second edition. Furthermore, if one accepts the outline given above, one must then believe that the corrected copy of Ia was carefully preserved for a year or more in anticipation of a second edition—but that when the third edition (III) was planned, all memory of this corrected copy and the existence of the officially revised second edition had slipped the printer's mind. What the validity of a comparison may be between the work of a medieval scribe writing carefully and presumably emending an unfamiliar text and that of a contemporary, professional writer mechanically repeating a familiar one, I shall leave to others to decide. The expert eye of Montague Rhodes James, in any case, saw in the Lambeth manuscript one that was 'very carefully written, with interesting ornaments'; one may also cite his observation that 'the decorative initials throughout the book are remarkable'. This

---

scribes for 22 months to prepare 200 volumes for Cosimo de' Medici. This indicates that each scribe would require at least four months in the production of one manuscript.

[13] Emendation by Haywarde must be assumed since L does not correspond exactly with either I or II; for further details, see note 29, below, where it is suggested that the date of the Lambeth MS. may be immaterial anyway for the purposes of this discussion.

[14] As an example of stop-press corrections in I, note that the last word on signature [a4] of I appears as both 'lepeop' (B.M. IB. 55004–5) and 'people' (Morgan and Huntington copies). So also in II, the Huntington copy has 'leasepd' in the last line of signature [e5] verso, where the British Museum example correctly has 'pleased'.

is not the sort of comment one usually finds associated with the work of a scribe working at top speed.

I have always felt most uncertain about my discussions of Caxton's types and I have said so quite freely. I do not pretend to have any special competence in type-analyses or experience in the *minutiae* of type-cutting. But one must note, in observing the many, completely divergent, opinions which competent scholars have expressed as to the nature and order of the earliest Mainz and 'Coster' types, that few discussions based on these points seem to have led to any permanent, generally accepted, conclusions. One must also point, in passing, to the sentence on p. 181 of the recent study which affirms that 'the combined use of types 2 and 3 in *Boecius de consolacione philosophie* appears to show that *Boecius* was the transitional volume, and definitely shows that Caxton was working on new types about 1479, where there is not a scrap of evidence that he was doing anything of the sort in 1477'. This statement is *most* unfortunate since both types 2 and 3 appear in the 'new' *Indulgence* of 1476 (so far as we know, the earliest piece of printing on English soil). Caxton, then, was certainly working with new types almost a year before the first *Dictes* (whichever one that may have been) was printed—and *not* in 1479.[15] And was type 3 not used by Caxton between December 1476 and the printing of the *Boecius* some two years later?

The bibliographical and typographical discussion[16] has been left for the last since it includes what I have known for many years to be the most damaging piece of evidence against the theory that II is the *editio princeps*, though this evidence has not hitherto been presented in full. It is certainly not the argument set forth under the heading 'copy-fitting by crowding [spacing]'. That argument depends, it seems to me, entirely on one's *point de départ*. Certain it is, as Dr. McKerrow and I also believed, that the one edition was set up from the other—but which from which? Assuming that I is

[15] Doubt is expressed (pp. 166 and 181–2) that Caxton could have cut type 2* in 1477 and 'then did not use it again for over a year'. But according to Blades's account one must now assume that type 3 was cut in 1476 and not used again for *two* years!

[16] In regard to the uneven right-hand margins in I, we are informed (p. 158) that 'there is little reason to believe that Caxton had caught the knack [of making the lines end evenly] by November 1477, only to lapse back to uneven margins after a year or more'. But one should note that if Duff 39 (the Cologne Bartholomaeus) was actually produced by him or that he had a hand in its production, then Caxton knew how to make lines end evenly as early as 1472—and yet 'lapsed back' to uneven ones anyway.

the earlier, then II would appear to be 'copy-fitted' by spacing on some pages and crowding on others—but viewing II as the earlier, one observes just the opposite phenomenon. Much is made in the recent essay of 'gaping' spaces, and the illustrations are selected to emphasize that point. But let the reader consider this! The third edition is neither a line-for-line nor a page-for-page reprint of I, yet one observes similar spaces to those found in II in the last few lines of signatures A2 recto, E1 verso, F8 recto, and G7 recto.[17] If II was set from Rivers's manuscript one would also expect to find evidences of 'copy-fitting' of a different sort, that is, spacings and crowdings to accommodate the amount of text assigned to a certain page or section. The 'blank spaces' and 'improper blanks' are certainly present in II[18]—but they are also present, in a much aggravated form, in such books as the only Caxton edition of the *Book called Caton*. The lines in this volume measure about 117 mm. in length—yet one finds blank spaces (in the middle of the lines and interrupting the text) of 40 mm. on a2 verso, of 43 mm. on b4, of 47 mm. on d2 verso, and of no less than 50 mm. (almost half the total width) on e2. What purpose they were expected to serve (aesthetic or practical) I do not know; in any event, so far as we *do* know, in the *Book called Caton* they have nothing to do with copy-fitting to another edition.[19]

[17] On E1 verso, there is a space of 45 mm. in the middle of a line of text with an overall length of 117 mm.—and the space occurs in the middle of a sentence.

[18] On p. 159 one finds the comment: 'The rubricator then disguised the unsightly and meaningless gaps by putting large paragraph marks in them, whether paragraphs began there or not.' The work of the rubricator was, of course, not part of the printing process at all and one finds both rubricated and unrubricated copies (so, for example, the Huntington copy). As a general observation, this remark is quite valueless.

[19] Spacing out and leaving 'gaping' blanks at the bottom of the page are particularly noticeable when Caxton was setting from manuscript copy. In reprints he was always able to avail himself of orthographical variants, contractions or expanded abbreviations, punctuation, &c., to even out the spaces encountered in his type copy. In the *Pilgrimage of the Soul* (Duff 267), for example, the line generally measures 122 mm. yet the last line on g3 verso has a 33 mm. blank and the last one on k1 has a gaping space of 39 mm. The verso of the same leaf has a last line which measures only 46 mm. though k2 does *not* begin a new paragraph. Again, line 3 from the bottom of m4 has a 60 mm. space internally! The same practice may be observed in the books printed by Wynkyn de Worde. In his *Treatise of Love* (Duff 399) column 2 of A4 recto is short a line and a half though the sentence *continues* on the verso; similarly B4 recto has a second column short four lines, though again the sentence continues on the verso. Under these circumstances, I do not see how loose spacing and large blanks at the bottom of pages can be considered as valid evidence for copy-fitting against an earlier edition.

It is also claimed that one of the 'weakest' points in my original contention for the priority of II was the explanation of the variant colophon in Ia. Now it is argued that if I was set from II and the pressman, noting that the colophon was wrong, deleted it for that reason, he would also have altered the date on folio 74$^r$. I think one need only reflect on the fact that this is presumably what happened in the case of the third edition; certainly it has not got the extra colophon and it certainly is dated 1477 where the other editions have this date. In short, the third edition may well illustrate that something *did* take place which, it is claimed, could not have occurred.

We have now arrived at what I am entirely willing to admit may be viewed as the most damaging piece of evidence against my tentative theory that II was the first edition. This evidence is damaging— but not fatal, since it represents a curious phenomenon noted in several other cases. The reference is naturally to the repeated text, the last line on folio 37 in I being repeated (plus an extra word from the line above) on the verso of the same leaf.[20] Normally in a line-for-line reprint such a condition would seem to be an impossibility, since the error would certainly be caught in the course of composition (if it existed in the original). It happened with reasonable frequency when a printer was setting from manuscript—but how can one account for either omissions or repetitions of lines in close reprints, when such errors do not occur in the original? Yet there are other cases of this sort and we can now examine just a few of them.

In the case of a typical page-for-page reprint, we find, for example, in the Marchesinus, *Mammotrectus super Bibliam* (Venice: Jenson, 23 September 1479), that, though it is a reprint of the edition by Renner and Bartua of the previous year, it omits a line and a half of text on signature y8. This text is supplied by means of stamping below the text-page, at any rate in the copy belonging to the writer. Again, in the case of the two editions of Ludolphus de Suchen, *Weg zu dem heiligen Grab*, the later edition by Hohenwang follows (page-for-page) the earlier one by Günther Zainer (1477)[21]

---

[20] In Blades's facsimile edition (London, 1877) the text reads: '. . . And sayd. Whan thou shalt se Aman of | good disposicion. and full of parfectyon. thou ought to | do after hym. for couetise is bothe weke and seke in hym || to do after him / for couetise is bothe weke and seke in him'.

[21] Zainer's edition is often set loosely in the last few lines when compared with Hohenwang's, yet the latter is the reprint. One must also note that in both editions the last line on folio 6 verso is repeated at the top of folio 7 recto! It is not certain whether Zainer's edition was set from manuscript or from an earlier edition. A most

but it omits the last line on folio 19 verso which is also supplied by stamping. As for the two editions of Laurentius Valla's *Compendium octo partium orationis*, the one produced by Johann Otmar at Reutlingen is a page-for-page reprint of the Basle edition by Johann Amerbach, yet (as Mlle Pellechet 3893 pointed out) the reprint omits text in its proper place and supplies it elsewhere in the volume. Thus page-for-page reprints can differ widely from their models.

The omission of lines is not peculiar to page-for-page reprints but occurs even in line-for-line reprints, though this is still more incredible. Thus the *Pforzheimer Catalogue* (iii, 968, no. 941) notes such an occurrence in *S.T.C.* 22,600 (Skelton's *Certayne bokes*, London: John Day [1563]). With this one arrives at an example very significant for the *Dictes*. The two editions of Juvenal printed by Vindelinus de Spira normally agree page-for-page (and, of course, line-for-line) —yet a line is repeated at the top of folio 60 verso in the reprint. And an even worse example of needless repetition may be cited for the Gregorius Britannicus, *Sermones funebres et nuptiales*, printed at Venice, 4 April 1498. As the *BMC* (V: 588) points out:

> A close reprint, in the same number of leaves, of A. and I. Britannicus's Brescia edition, 1495 (IA. 31148). The correspondence is thrown out by the repetition in the first column of quire b of the matter already printed in the last column of quire a, but restored by the omission of the equivalent of one column of text at the end of quire c.

Probably the most astonishing example of all is the one cited by Victor Scholderer (*Gutenberg–Jahrbuch* (1931), 107–9) where there are described two printings of the *Achilleis* from the *same setting of type*—yet the reprint dropped out one line completely and subsequently repeated a line. With these facts in mind, it seems that one may believe that almost anything might happen to reprints.

When one compares folio 37 verso in editions I and II of the *Dictes*, a series of curious facts emerges. Especially noteworthy is the fact that lines 1 to 21 of II correspond exactly to lines 2 to 22 of I and that the same text found in lines 23 to 29 of I is contained in lines 22 to 29 of II. Now, if one assumes that II was set from I, one would

---

curious and instructive case of a repeated line in a line-for-line reprint is cited from two undated editions of Valla's *De donatione Constantini* by A. C. Clark, *The Descent of Manuscripts*, Oxford, 1918, pp. 448–9. The edition of Petrarch's *Canzoniere*, Hain 12750, is set up from the Venice 1473 edition (H 12757), yet the first lines on f4 verso and f9 verso are the same as the last lines on the corresponding rectos.

normally expect to find that the compositor, having just omitted one line,[22] would proceed immediately to make good this omission. But not in this case, for (under this premiss) the compositor must here have set twenty-two lines almost exactly like his model—and only then have started to space out his text to make up the line he had gained.

Another peculiarity must be noticed. In lines 1 to 22 of I there are found two contractions and three ampersands, these numbers comparing favourably with an average of four ampersands and three contractions found in ten characteristic pages selected at random. But in lines 23 to 29 of I (seven lines corresponding to the last eight in II) there are no fewer than four contractions and four ampersands. A count based on letters and punctuation is equally striking. Leaving aside the ('repeated') first line of I, we obtain the following results. Lines 2 to 8 of I contain 308 characters, an average of 44 to the line.[23] Now while lines 23 to 29 of II include 301 characters (average: 43 to the line), lines 23 to 29 of I contain 331 characters. Here the average is more than 47 characters to the line, and the excess of 23 or 30 in these seven lines corresponds to at least half a line elsewhere. Combining these findings with the fact that the last few lines in I contain an exceptional number of contractions and ampersands, it should be self-evident that I shows crowding and not that II is spaced out. One *might* infer from all this that a line had been added to I rather than that a line had been deleted in the setting of II. However this may be, it is certainly worthy of note that earlier in the same decade when Vindelinus de Spira and Stephanus Corallus required an extra line, they obtained it by the simple expedient of reprinting the last line on the previous page.

No, it is not the repeated text found in some copies of I which is so significant—but rather the previously unrecorded fact that this repetition does not appear in *all* copies. The text in the Huntington copy, for example, reads:

... And sayd. Whan thou shalt se Aman of | good disposicion. and full of parfectyon. thou ought ‖ to do after him / for couetise is bothe weke and seke in him

[22] Because of the presence of a number of 'run-overs'—no matter which edition is the first—it is certain that the compositor of the reprint habitually set from the top of the page, not from the bottom.

[23] II agrees line-for-line with I except for a slight divergence in the first two lines common to both.

This piece of evidence appears to contradict flatly the argument recently advanced (p. 160): 'Furthermore, folio 37ʳ is the last page of the inner forme (of the sheet containing fols. 36ʳ, 36ᵛ, 37ʳ, 37ᵛ), and the compositor could then pause, as 37ᵛ would not be needed until the sheet was ready to back up.' Since *O.E.D.* defines 'to back' as 'to print on the back', one is obliged to conclude from this statement that the inner forme was printed first. However, if Caxton did not compose the verso until the recto was printed, how could he have foreseen that there was going to be repetition which would necessitate deletion at the foot of the page? Again, if the verso was being composed while the recto was printing and the repetition then came to Caxton's notice, it seems more likely that he would have corrected the text on the verso rather than omitting text on the recto.

But there are more probable lines of reasoning. On the basis of the omission of the repeated text, it *might* casually be assumed that Caxton, having noted the error while the recto was printing and when (for one reason or another) it was impossible to make the correction in the verso, deliberately cut out the offending words at the foot of 37ʳ probably by the simple expedient of not inking these characters.[24] But this theory leads us into unexpected difficulties.

A point of no little consequence is the fact that, compared with the 'standard' state, the Huntington copy shows text omitted at the foot of the recto—not the omission of an entire line on the verso. It would obviously have been almost as easy and much more effective for Caxton to have got rid of the duplicating text by resetting part of the verso page rather than by the simple (though clumsy) method of not inking a line—plus an extra word from the line above—on the recto. The reason for Caxton's not pursuing the former course can only be explained, it seems to me, on the theory that he was

[24] It seems impossible to conclude that Caxton eliminated the duplicating words by unlocking the forme, by removing the last line plus the 'to' of the penultimate line and replacing these words by quads, and then by locking up the type again. In that event—and with but little more trouble—Caxton might have removed three or four lines, reset the whole text, and by spacing out and leaving 'improper blanks' have made good the omitted text without leaving the page a line short.

That printers often prevented whole lines as well as separate characters from printing by the simple process of not inking them is common knowledge. It habitually occurred when type-bearers were used (see footnote 28, below). This method was also employed when both black and red printing appeared on the same page; on this point, see my 'Notes on Two Incunabula Printed by Aldus Manutius', *Papers of the Bibliographical Society of America*, xxxvi (1942), 18-26.

unable to do so, probably because the verso had already been printed off.

One must also recall the truism that, among Tudor books anyway, the number of printed copies of the first state of a sheet would *normally* have been fewer than of the second (altered) state.[25] It seems reasonable to expect that time would not reverse this proportion. Consequently, since the Huntington copy represents the numerically rarer form, it would (according to this line of argument) be in the first state.

Now if I was set from manuscript and the Huntington copy is the first state, there seems to be no logical way to account for the variant. Obviously the type as composed could be machined, for we have the Huntington example and it is textually correct. True, the page was one line short but it is difficult to believe that this would have caused Caxton any special anxiety.[26]

If it be argued that the 'standard version' of I was the first state of the first edition, one must then assume that Caxton became aware of the misprint only after the entire outer forme had been printed and after a majority of these sheets had been perfected. This line of argument, however, runs directly counter to two accepted bibliographical principles which hold (1) that the first state is the scarcer and (2) that the inner forme was ordinarily printed first.[27] If the inner forme of 'standard' I *was* actually printed first and the repetition was discovered during the course of printing, I am at a loss to explain the variant states, for the necessary corrections could then have been made in *all* copies of the outer forme.

[25] See, for example, footnote 14. The copies with the misprints are the more uncommon. Of the twelve copies of *Dictes* I whose readings are known to me, only the copy belonging to Mr. William H. Scheide and that in the library of Trinity College, Cambridge (VI. 18. 2), have folio 37$^r$ in the same state as the Huntington Library copy.

[26] Examples of pages short one line of text will be found in the earlier *History of Jason* and in the later *Canterbury Tales* (prose section).

[27] From what one must infer from the quotation cited above, this is also the view held by my critic. While it is 'normal' for books to have the inner forme printed first (especially when—as here—it is the inner forme of the innermost sheet of a quire, since this is of necessity the first part of the gathering that can be printed), instances are known where the printing of the outer forme preceded that of the inner. Again, while it is 'normal' for a printer to discover an error and correct it early in the course of printing rather than very late, the opposite condition is not entirely unknown and cannot be disregarded. However, to follow the line of reasoning set forth above, one must here assume two simultaneous abnormalities in order to explain the variant states if I is the first edition. It is perhaps safer to prefer

Assuming, however, that II is the first edition and that I was set up from an emended copy, one would arrive at a totally different explanation for the variant states. The printer set the recto of folio 37 to agree with his copy. Before printing the inner forme and while composing folio 37$^v$, he contracted too much at the bottom of the verso page; finding himself a line short, he simply repeated text from the previous page as his Continental colleagues had done before him. Conscious of the repetition, Caxton determined to treat the duplicate text of the recto as a bearer rather than that at the top of the verso. This is logical enough since readers of printed books as well as manuscripts were accustomed to have the tops of the pages evenly aligned no matter how raggedly uneven the bottoms of these pages might be. It would therefore be inevitable that the printer would prefer to be short a line at the foot of the recto than short one at the top of the verso. In order to print an accurate text, it may be supposed that he did not ink the words at the bottom of the page, giving us the state of the Huntington copy. Subsequently the pressman either forgot about—or was simply indifferent to—the repetition and, inking the whole page, printed it off and thus produced copies of the 'standard' state.[28] This hypothesis, in any case, accords with the two bibliographical principles which deal with the relative scarcity of first states and the priority of printing of inner formes.

What, then, may one say as to the order of the first two editions of the *Dictes*? I hold the very strong conviction that overwhelming evidence is required in order to upset accepted bibliographical beliefs and I am frank to confess that the evidence in favour of the priority of II is far from overwhelming. I do not, at the moment, know for a fact which is the earlier edition. Under these circumstances and until all the evidence is in, especially that which may result from the textual and literary studies now in progress,[29] I think one should

---

arguments based on normality rather than those based on abnormality when explaining bibliographical phenomena.

[28] For examples of the accidental inking and consequent printing of 'type-bearers', see my paper 'A Note on a Fifteenth-Century Printing Technique', *The Library Chronicle of the Friends of the Library, University of Pennsylvania*, xv (1949), 52–55.

[29] Although it is perhaps premature to express an opinion at this point of my investigations, present circumstances compel me to mention a new conviction which offers a partial and plausible solution for at least one phase of the problem. It seems not improbable that the differences between the Lambeth MS. and the Caxton edition (whichever one may have been the first) may be accounted for by the hypothesis that both derive from different manuscripts, each made (directly or indirectly) from Rivers's original text. Since we know of some eight early manuscripts of Scrope's *Dicts* and four of his *Othea*, multiple manuscripts with startling differences

(provisionally in any case) regard I as the 'accepted' first edition with the note that it has not been certainly established whether I or II was actually the earlier.[30] This is the view I held at the time that the checklist of the Morgan incunabula was printed[31] and that is why the Morgan copies of *Dictes* Ib and Ic hold their traditional place and have not been assigned new Proctor numbers.

(From *The Library* (1953), pp. 77-88).

of text need occasion no surprise. The argument, if it proves to be a valid one, would run something like this:

In 181 instances (individual words or phrases), I differs from II. In 98 cases (usually the most significant), L agrees with II and 59 times with I; on 14 occasions L is made to read like II by manuscript correction, while the readings for 10 divergencies still need to be checked. In at least 29 further cases, however, L differs from *both* I and II.

Again, at the very end of Rivers's text, Haywarde has written the meaningful note: 'And one William Caxton atte desire of my lorde emprinted many bokes after the tenour and forme of this boke whiche William saide as foloweth after.' This is the only original passage in the text; it is followed immediately by Caxton's section and the colophon, in the slightly revised form described in my first paper.

Now it seems possible that Haywarde was supplied with one manuscript of the text for his copy while Caxton was supplied with another. Haywarde, having completed the copy of Rivers's text, discovered the additional material printed by Caxton and transcribed this section from the printed edition, making slight modifications in the colophon. Hence the special note by Haywarde just mentioned.

This will certainly account for the difficulties surrounding the element of time, since Haywarde may have started writing at any time (not necessarily after 18 November) and conveniently completed his work on 24 December. The effect of this hypothesis, if proved, on the priority of I or II still needs to be established.

With the date of the Lambeth MS. in mind, one would expect that the corrections made in that manuscript would have been made from the first edition and not from the later reprint. Since, however, they are made from II, this would seem to be another argument for the priority of II. It seems so unlikely that a manuscript written for the king in 1477 could be corrected against a book not printed till 1479.

[30] Although the above theory accounts for the problem of timing, it does not explain why III was set from I and not from the (presumed) second edition, nor does it settle the question as to the origin of the extra colophon in the Rylands copy. Curiously enough, in the case of the repeated text found on folio 37 of I, the third edition repeats the first four words of the text found on the verso of I (about a third of the line), to the confusion of the sense. What sort of a copy of I was used for this reprint?

The arguments regarding the availability of copies, discussed on pp. 167-8 of the recent article, seem to me highly inconclusive. Why would II, if it was the second edition, not have been more available to Caxton than I? Modern figures seem to prove nothing. Of the five manuscripts based on Caxton's printings which have come down to us, four are certainly (I believe) copies of II and *none* can be proved to be a copy of uncorrected I. These 'statistics' would indicate that in the early days II was much the most common of the Caxton editions—but no one would seriously accept such figures as proof that this condition actually prevailed.

[31] *Check List of Fifteenth Century Printing in The Pierpont Morgan Library*, New York, 1939.

# CHAPTER B4

## ON THE HORACE PRINTED IN ROME
## BY WENDELINUS DE WILA
## OR BARTHOLOMAEUS GULDINBECK

A RECENT study of the undated Horace printed with the de Wila-Guldinbeck type 1: 108R (Proctor †3559) brought to light certain points of some importance, not only for the printing of this work, but also for the history of early printing in Rome, as the period covers those critical years for the Italian book-trade, the early 1470's. The Horace is printed in the pure state of the de Wila-Guldinbeck type (without the admixture of the gothic characters for d, v,[1] etc. or the *rum* abbreviation ℞) and with two forms of *et*, i.e. & and z. The unsigned quires of the copy preserved in The Pierpont Morgan Library occur in the following order: [*⁴ a-b¹⁰ c-k⁸&¹⁰ l-n⁸ o⁶ p-q¹⁰ r-s⁸ t¹⁰ v-z⁸ A⁸ B-C⁶].

The most important point which the examination produced (and one which Proctor failed to note) is that a Greek type is used in the commentaries. Careful scrutiny of Plate 1 will show that the type is Ulrich Han's earlier Greek type (103 mm.) in a late state, as the $\theta$ punch has been damaged. Proctor (*The Printing of Greek in the Fifteenth Century*, The Bibliographical Society, Illustrated Monograph VIII, p. 30) noted that Han's later Greek type was the 103 mm. type recast on a larger body with certain modifications, among which he pointed out 'the punch of the $\theta$ has suffered damage, and has been broken in on the right-hand side'. This state may be noted in the first line of the Greek passage reproduced; on the other hand, in line 3 as elsewhere in the text, the $\theta$ shows a break on the left-hand side, doubtless due to inverted type. The *eta* is still the H of the earlier state, whereas Han made use of a new character (N) in 1474.

If the separate quires are examined for Greek type, it will be seen that it appears wherever necessary in every quire of the book except in signatures [A] and [B]. In these quires, spaces are left for the insertion of Greek words by hand. As it is most unlikely that the printer should have used Greek type both before and after these

---

[1] The *ver*-contraction is used by de Wila.

signatures and, for some reason or other, not have had the type at the time the other two quires were printed, we may deduce from this the manner in which the book was printed. From the beginning of the text with the *Vita Horatii Secundum Acronem* on folio 6ª (a²; a¹ being a blank), the text is printed without a break through folio 196ª [y⁸]; the verso of this leaf is blank. On folio 197ª [z¹] the *De arte poetica* begins and continues (with the added commentaries) through the end of the book. In quire [z] there was no need for Greek type; [A] and [B] have spaces in place of Greek printing, while [C] again has Greek passages wherever necessary. As a result we may infer that the printing of the Horace began with the *Poetica* and that after the first three quires of this work had been struck off, the printer obtained the necessary Greek type from Ulrich Han and used it subsequently wherever necessary.

It is possible that a chain of circumstances can help us to identify the year in which this book was printed. Han adopted the use of Greek type in 1471; in 1474 Han's new Greek type was employed. In 1474 Han ended his association with Simon Nicolai Chardella. In this same year, de Wila and Johannes Reinhardi also parted company, and when the latter issued his Festus on 1 October 1475, he left spaces for the Greek words. The earliest known book signed and dated by Guldinbeck appears to be the Tuberinus, *De Simone puero* of 19 June 1475 and there is no evidence to show that he used Greek type in any book ascribed to him. Indeed the Aesop, *Vita et fabulae* (Hain 270), attributed to Guldinbeck by the Gesamtkatalog (No. 336, *um* 1475), has spaces for Greek and the Festus of 31 December 1477 (Proctor 3563) printed in Guldinbeck's type 2: 97G, also leaves the Greek words unprinted.

From these facts, we may deduce the following:

1. In 1474 Han no longer used his earlier Greek type, as the Lactantius of 12 February already has the later type.

2. In 1474, Chardella (apparently Han's financial backer during the difficult years of the early '70's) and Han ended their partnership.

3. If one supposes that Han disposed of his stock of the earlier type, the most likely year would be 1474, when the business was reorganized and a new type was already in use. There is no ground to suppose that he gave or sold the type to Chardella, as the other types seem to have remained in Han's hands.

4. It is evident that the type passed to the de Wila-Guldinbeck press but it appears to have been obtained by this press after de Wila

had parted from Reinhardi, as the latter apparently knew nothing of Greek printing.

5. The printer of the Horace did not have Greek type when he began to print the book but acquired it while the book was at press.

6. The earliest book definitely identifiable with Guldinbeck was not printed until 17 June 1475 and two books attributed to him have no Greek type but only spaces for the insertion of the letters by hand. This would indicate that Guldinbeck either did not know how to print in Greek or had no Greek type.

7. As Han had new matrices for Greek type in 1474, it seems unlikely that the material of the earlier type would have lain about his shop unused for any long period, particularly as in that year Han's printing establishment was probably reorganized. Therefore if the type was sold, the most likely year in which it was sold would be 1474; if, on the other hand, the printer of the Horace rented or borrowed the type from Han at a later date, one would expect to find the later, and not the earlier, Greek type in the Horace.

In short it does not seem unreasonable to assume that the Horace was printed in the winter of 1474-5, and as the roman type is in the same state as in the books signed by de Wila and as it cannot be clearly shown that Guldinbeck was actively engaged in printing before the spring of 1475 or that he ever used Greek type, the book may perhaps best be ascribed to de Wila.

The Greek passage in the reproduction reads:

νιρευς αν συμηθεν αγεν τρεις νηας ειγας
νιρευς αγλαιης υιος χεροποιο ταν αρτος
νιρευς ος καλλισος ανηρ υπ ιλιον ηλθε
των αλλων δαναων μεταμυμονα πιλιωνα

Porphyrio extracted this quotation from the second book of the Iliad, which reads correctly:

Νιρεὺς αὖ Σύμηθεν ἄγε τρεῖς νῆας ἐίσας
Νιρεὺς Ἀγλαίης υἱὸς Χαρόποιό τ᾽ ἄνακτος
Νιρεύς ὃς κάλλιστος ἀνὴρ ὑπὸ Ἴλιον ἦλθε
τῶν ἄλλων Δαναῶν μετ᾽ ἀμύμονα Πηλείωνα

Apart from the mistakes in the Greek, the printer shows great unfamiliarity with the handling of this type. Proctor pointed out (p. 30):

The ε in 1471 rises above the line of type, the lower half being level with the short letters; in 1474, it goes below the line, and the upper curve is on the general level.

The ε in the reproduction seems to show an intermediate stage in which it extends just above and just below the level of the short letters. The lines at best are very uneven, possibly caused by the type slipping in the chase, the body of the Greek type being smaller than that of the Latin; elsewhere (particularly in quire C), it appears that the Latin text was set up first with spaces for the insertion of the Greek type, as in at least one instance insufficient space was left and the Greek word barely squeezed in.

Two distinct differences between Han's Greek type[2] and that of the Horace may be seen. Apparently the printer did not obtain (in any case did not use) Han's *upsilon* or *iota*; for the former he used his Latin v and for the latter the i. The most notable feature of the i is that in a large majority of the cases (about 75 per cent) it is inverted when used as the *iota*. In the Latin text also, the i is frequently found upside down; a rough estimate would be one inverted i to every fifteen correctly printed. (The proportion varies from 1 in 60 on folio 13[a] to 1 in 5 on folio 190[a]). This may, of course, simply be due to inverted type, but the extraordinary frequency with which these misprints occur appears to argue in favour of faulty type. This may be explained as follows: after a certain matrix had been made, it was incorrectly fitted into the type-mould (that is, inverted); whatever type was cast from such a mould would have the face reversed. If, therefore, the type was correctly placed in the form (that is, with the nick corresponding to those of the other pieces of type), the i's cast from that particular matrix would print upside down. Other letters occasionally occur inverted, such as the u and n, but not more than once in three hundred times and are thus only misprints. The Cicero *Rhetorica ad Herennium* of 1474, signed by de Wila, shows the same high percentage of inverted i's (my count shows a ratio of 1 in 12). On the other hand, in the books printed in the later state of the same type and signed by Guldinbeck, the Turrecremata *De efficacia aquae benedictae* and the Bartolus de Saxoferrato *Tractatus procuratoris*, the proportion of inverted i's to those correctly printed is hardly greater than one would expect from ordinary misprints (1 in 150 or more). Does this distinguish Guldinbeck's work

[2] Incidentally the character v̈ stated by Proctor to have been added in 1474 occurs in the Tortellius of 1471 (for example in the chapter: De Y littera).

from de Wila's? Unfortunately The Pierpont Morgan Library has
no copy of the Tuberinus *De puero Simone* or of the *Stilus Romanae
Curiae* which would show if any book signed by Guldinbeck has as
high a percentage of inverted i's.

(From *La Bibliofilia*, 37 (1935), pp. 376-380).

# CHAPTER B5

## GEORGE MAYNYAL: A PARISIAN PRINTER
## OF THE FIFTEENTH CENTURY?

FOR almost a century and a half the name of George Maynyal has appeared from time to time in the lists of early Parisian printers. Although such eminent authorities as Panzer, Pellechet, Maignien, Proctor, Burger, Claudin, Duff, Pollard, Voulliéme, Schramm, Haebler, and Polain[1] have noted him, there is no evidence to the effect that a *George* Maynyal was ever engaged in printing in the fifteenth century, as no book seems to be known to which he set his name. Despite the fact that this 'ghost' was laid some thirty-five years ago in a footnote to Claudin's *Histoire de l'im-primerie en France au XV⁰ et au XVI⁰ siècle* (vol. ii, p. 552, n. 3),[2] the name George Maynyal reappears with astonishing regularity in the discussion of early Parisian printing. It is hoped that this paper

---

[1] The name George Maynyal may be found as follows: Panzer, ii. 282. 68; Pellechet-Dijon, p. 125, and Pellechet-Versailles, p. 134; Edmond Maignien, *Catalogue des incunables de la Bibliothèque Municipale de Grenoble*, Mâcon, 1899, p. 399; Proctor, *Index*, ii. 564; Burger, *Index*, p. 98; Claudin, ii. 1; Duff, *A Century of the English Book Trade*, London, 1905, p. 103; Pollard, *Catalogue of Books mostly from the Presses of the First Printers . . . collected by Rush C. Hawkins*, Oxford, 1910, p. 243; Voulliéme-Berlin, p. 252, and Voulliéme-Trier, p. 145; Albert Schramm, *Katalage des deutschen Buchmuseums zu Leipzig. Die Inkunabeln*, Leipzig, 1925, p. 65; Haebler, *Frühdrucke aus der Bücherei Victor von Klemperer*, Dresden, 1927, pp. 339 and 346, and *Typenrepertorium*, ii. 275; Polain, iii. 785, no. 3633. Titles have only been supplied where the reference is not perfectly self-evident.

[2] 'Tous les bibliographes donnent à Maynial le prénom de Georges, que rien 'ne justifie. Nous avons examiné les livres signés de Maynial pendant son associa-'tion avec Gering, et nous n'y avons trouvé que l'initiale G de son prénom. Dans 'aucun d'eux on ne lit *Georgius* en toutes lettres, comme l'indique Panzer, dont 'on a admis l'autorité sans la contrôler. D'éminents bibliographes, tels que 'MM. Robert Proctor et Gordon Duff, se sont laissé tromper et ont reproduit 'cette assertion sans avoir remarqué l'erreur. Après avoir rédigé, longtemps 'après, le passage concernant l'association de Maynial avec Gering (voir t. 1ᵉʳ, 'p. 86), nous avons cru nous être trompé en donnant à Maynial le prénom de 'Guillaume, imprimé en toutes lettres sur des volumes d'une date postérieure, et 'nous avons fait de Georges et de Guillaume deux imprimeurs différents, sans 'doute parents, mais qu'il ne fallait pas confondre. (Voir pp. 1 et 4.) Nous avons 'procédé à une contre-vérification qui peut permettre de les identifier. Le prénom 'de Georges doit être remplacé par celui de Guillaume, sous lequel sont signées 'les autres productions de sa seconde presse.'

may serve to eliminate George Maynyal definitely from the list of
Paris printers and to call attention to a work frequently overlooked
when the Maynyals are noted.

The fact that a G. Maynyal was an associate of Ulrich Gering in
the early 1480's has been common knowledge at least since Maittaire's
day;[3] it is also well known that a Guillaume Maynyal was engaged
in printing religious books in the later years of this same decade.
That these two Maynyals have not been recognized as being one and
the same person is very probably the result of a gratuitous assumption on the part of Georg Panzer.[4] In the *Annales Typographici*
(Nuremberg, 1794, vol. ii, p. 282, no. 68), a copy of the *Speculum Aureum* (Hain 14905) is attributed to 'Udalricum Gering et Georgium
Maynyal', although the colophon (contractions expanded) reads
merely: 'Impres||sumque Parisius per magistrum Vdalricum co||-
'gnomento Gering / et G. Maynyal. Anno sa-||lutis millesimo. cccc.
'lxxx. xxix. Aprilis.' Panzer (or his source) apparently took for
granted that the G stood for Georgius, and most bibliographers seem
to have adopted this statement without troubling too much to verify
Panzer's notation.

The most curious notices concerning George Maynyal may be
found in Claudin's work. Claudin says (vol. i, p. 86): 'En 1479, nous
' trouvons Gering travaillant avec un nouvel associé, Guillaume May-
' nyal. Il imprime avec lui les *Postilla Guillermi* dans le format in-
' quarto.' In the notice on the press of Guillaume Maynial (ii. 1)
there is the following statement: 'Il existait un Georges Maynial,
' associé d'Ulrich Gering en 1480, au *Soleil d'Or* de la rue Saint-
' Jacques, après le départ des compagnons de ce dernier, Friburger
' et Crantz. Guillaume Maynial était probablement un proche parent,
' le fils ou le neveu de ce Georges Maynial, comme on peut le con-
' jecturer.'[5] In the footnote referred to above, Claudin definitely admitted that there was no evidence to the effect that the G stood for
Georgius and substituted Guillaume instead. We shall see that there

---

[3] See Michel Maittaire, *Annales Typographici*, Amsterdam, 1733, i. 405.

[4] I have not bothered to examine Panzer's sources to see if any of them have
this same error. In any case, Maittaire does not make this mistake, merely noting
G. Maynal. In the list of printers Maittaire significantly includes G. Maynal
under the heading 'Gulielmus'.

[5] There is no notice under Ulrich Gering that he was ever partnered by a
*Georges* Maynial, only the Guillaume already noted. Claudin also says (ii. 4):
' Nous avons tout lieu de croire que Guillaume Maynial était originaire du même
' pays que Caxton pour lequel il a travaillé à Paris.'

is very good evidence indeed for the fact that the G was intended to stand for Guillaume (or Guillermus).

The books in which the name Maynyal occurs fall into two classes: the first group includes those printed in collaboration with Ulrich Gering, the second those signed by Guillaume Maynyal alone. The following books belong to the first press:

1. *Manipulus Curatorum.* 22 April 1480. (Cop. II, 2838) signed G. Maynial
2. *Speculum Aureum.* 29 April 1480. (Claudin I, 86)   "   G. Maynyal
3. *Summa in Virtutes* 16 August 1480. (Polain 3633)   "   G. Maynial
   *Cardinales.*

Three books are likewise known which bear, in each case, the name Guillermus Maynyal as printer. They are:

1. *Missale Sarum* (for Caxton). 4 December 1487.     (Duff 322)
2. *Psalterium Latinum.* 18 May and 19 July 1489. (Polain 3272)
3. *Manuale Ecclesiae Carno-* 29 July 1490.     (Claudin II. 3)
   *tensis.*

One book has been consistently overlooked, although it is noted in the *Histoire de l'imprimerie en France*, the *Postilla Guillermi*.[6] Apparently Claudin had not actually seen the volume, as he gave no further details than those already quoted. This *Postilla Guillermi* is sufficiently accurately described in a work not frequently referred to, the *Catálogo de Incunables y Libros Raros de la Santa Iglesia Catedral de Segovia*, by D. Cristino Valverde del Barrio (Segovia, 1930, pp. 145–6, no. 245), so that no further description is necessary, but the colophon is shown (Plate 2) in order to settle once and for all the question of George Maynyal. The *Postilla Guillermi* is important for two reasons: first of all it definitely proves that the Christian name of Gering's partner was not Georgius, and secondly it gives a slightly earlier date for this partnership than that recorded by Proctor. The date in the colophon is '29 March 1479', but the year is probably not that of our reckoning. The book is almost certainly dated 'more Gallicano', as in France the year habitually began with Easter. In 1479 Easter fell on April 11 and in 1480 on April 2, so that the date of the *Postilla Guillermi* must be set down as 29 March 1479/80. There is further evidence for believing that the book was

[6] The copy in The Pierpont Morgan Library bears the accession number 20994. It is not described in the usual bibliographies and the only mention in Peddie (*Conspectus Incunabulorum*, ii. 307) refers to the St. John's College, Cambridge, magazine *The Eagle* (December 1910, pp. 75–105), where the incunabula of the college library are listed. See illustration, Plate 2.

printed in March 1480 (according to our reckoning), for we know
that, as late as 19 August 1479, Gering produced a *Manuale Con-
fessorum* (Proctor 7861) in which the name of G. Maynal as a
partner is not found. Presumably, then, the partnership began some
time between August 1479 and March 1480. Since Gering is found
working with a Guillaume Maynyal in March 1480, it is reasonably
certain that the G. Maynyal who collaborated with Gering in the
production of three more signed books in that year must be this same
Guillaume Maynyal and not an otherwise unheard-of George
Maynyal.

(From *The Library* (1937), pp. 84-88).

# CHAPTER B6

## CAXTON STUDIES

IN the course of re-cataloguing the sixty-odd Caxtons in The Pierpont Morgan Library, New York, the present writer came across two small points which seemed to him of more than passing interest. The problems that were brought up in attempting to account for these details concern in the main only Caxton's printing technique and type. Although perhaps not recognizably so at first reading, the three sections of this paper are roughly interrelated. The first deals with a piece of accidental printing and the last with an equally accidental impression of a piece of Caxton's type; both these, in turn, lead to the conclusions drawn in the second section, which differ somewhat from the accepted tradition as to the method of early printing.

### I

In his *Census of Caxtons* (Bibliographical Society, Illustrated Monograph No. xv, p. 33), Seymour de Ricci added this note to his description of the Pierpont Morgan copy of Christine de Pisan's *The Fayttes of Armes and of Chyualrye*: 'On the blank verso of folio 3 is a curious set-off, not yet identified.' This rather interesting point seems to have attracted no particular attention and the matter was summarily dismissed in the Early English Text Society's edition of this work (1932, and reprinted 1937, page xxxv), where the editor, Dr. A.T.P. Byles, noted that 'this is a misprint for folio 2, the verso of which is blank and in most copies shows a strong set-off from folio 1 recto, owing to the first gathering (unsigned) being piled together while the ink was still wet'. That neither of these statements is entirely correct will be shown hereafter.

The first gathering of this volume consists of two leaves of table, and the verso of the second one, as Dr. Byles correctly pointed out, bears the off-set of the recto of the first in all the copies that I have seen; there are seven of these and they are the copies found in the following libraries: The Pierpont Morgan Library, Henry E. Huntington Library, British Museum, Columbia University Library and Yale University Library, the last-named being de Ricci's untraced copy no. 40. It was not to this off-set, though, that de Ricci appears to refer but to a rather singular fragment of printing plainly legible in the Morgan copy and, to a slightly lesser degree, in the copy now in the Huntington Library. As a set-off must necessarily appear in reverse and as the present piece cannot, from its very appearance, be judged to be a double set-off (that is, a set-off of a set-off), it is clear that it must be an actual piece of printing and the sharpness of the impression obviously confirms this. The fragment extends the length of the inner margin of the type-page for a total of 31 lines, the length of the normal type-page in this volume; it varies in width from the portion of a single character to a maximum width of four complete characters.

We may first of all turn to the physical appearance of the fragment itself; an explanation for its presence in the volume will be given later. Twenty lines of it measure approximately 120 millimetres and the type represented is Caxton's no. 6, the identical type used throughout the *Fayttes of Armes*; unless it is merely printer's 'pi' which its appearance belies, the page does not correspond to any page printed in the volume itself. The identity of the fragment has not been revealed by a reasonably careful search in such similarly printed Caxtons as I have seen, which comprise the *Statutes of King Henry VII*, *The Boke of Eneydos*, *The Dictes or Sayengis of the Philosophers* (third edition), and *The Myrrour of the World* (second edition). It would appear, though, that the most interesting part of the fragment lies not so much in establishing the identity of it with any known page of Caxton printing as in the appearance of the fragment itself. When enlarged four times as in the illustration, Plate 3, it will be noted that the face of the type is actually seen in outline. Apparently what happened at the time of printing was that the type for this fragment had been inked and that subsequently the ink had been wiped off so that the protruding face of the type was reasonably clean but that some vestiges of ink still clung to the edges and along the sides of the letters. When the paper and the type were brought into contact with a certain amount of pressure in the course of the printing, the ink from the edges of the type was transferred to the paper whereas the actual face of the type in some instances remained quite clean and elsewhere shows only a light touch of ink. In the normal process of printing in the fifteenth century, the face of the type was inked, the paper and the type brought into contact, and when the necessary pressure was applied the ink was thus transferred from the face of the type to the paper. As the ink tended to spread, particularly if it was a trifle thin, and consequently to run over the edges, the frequent result was a slightly blurred and irregular impression, and the actual face of the type was scarcely ever exactly reproduced.[1]

In the instance of this fragment, the usual result has been exactly reversed. In this particular case, the ink was unable to run into the face of the type, when the type and the paper had once come into contact, but was forced to spread further outward and away from the edges of the type. When examined in the enlargement, the face of the type is thus revealed in outline, exactly as the metal type itself would have appeared to the printer, and without that distortion which characterizes the printed impressions made from the type. The examination of the actual 'face' of Caxton's type is thus made possible and is worthy of study. As our knowledge of the exact appearance of the face of fifteenth-century type is limited to a mere handful of examples, the present specimen is of considerable importance. Although it is impossible to make any sweeping statements on the basis of the limited number of characters here represented, it is nevertheless possible to point to a few significant details. The care with which the type was originally cut is particularly note-

---

[1] William Blades, *The Life and Typography of William Caxton*, London, 1861-63, vol. II, p. xlvi, makes particular note of this. 'His [Caxton's] ink was of the weakest description, and the amount of power required for a "pull" of the press proportionally weak, the one necessitating the other. His presses, in the earlier part of his printing career, did not take more than a post folio page; and, with a very sloppy ink, the pull, if strong, would have made a confused mass of black instead of a legible impression. As it is, the ink has been almost invariably squeezed over the side of the letters, and has contorted their shape. Few indeed, although practical men, would imagine the deceptive nature of an impression taken from new types, with a weak ink and light pressure. In such case the type appears now much thicker than it is, from the "spuing" of the ink—and now battered, with some portion of it broken—and now, to use a technical term, as if it were all "off its feet". To prove this, as well as to illustrate how little we can judge from first appearance, the two specimens in Plate IX B have been printed under my own inspection. The upper portion is printed with weak ink and a low pressure: the type looks worn— no two copies are exactly the same in appearance; indeed scarcely any two of the same letter look as if cast in the same matrix, and most people would come to the conclusion that it was too bad ever to be used again. Now look below:—it is the same identical form re-printed; not a letter has been changed, and yet the whole edition of the upper half was worked off before one copy of the lower half was pulled. Good ink and a strong impression have caused all the difference, and had these been at Caxton's command we should never have seen the rudeness so visible in most of his books.' As Blades's work is probably available to the reader, the plate is not reproduced here.

worthy; the bound th, the graceful sweep of the curve in the r and ampersand, the carefully executed decorative flourishes and serifs in the l, a and s, and the sharply angled comparatively heavy design of the o and the d may be specially singled out. The resulting conclusion that may be drawn from a study of this fragment is that the occasionally blurred face and typographically not very pleasing appearance of a page of Caxton printing is due rather to the use of an inferior quality of ink than to a poorly designed and badly cut type.

## II

The question as to how this fragment came to be printed at all brings up a most interesting point as far as the technique of printing in the fifteenth century is concerned. In his valuable *An Introduction to Bibliography for Literary Students* (Oxford, 1927, p. 58), Dr. Ronald B. McKerrow describes the method of printing with two pulls to the forme: 'By this method the whole forme is placed on the bed of the press at one time and the paper being placed on the tympan in the ordinary way, the carriage is first run under the platen to the distance of half its length; the platen is then brought down and raised again; the carriage is then run further in and the lever pulled a second time. Thus each page (in a folio) is actually printed separately, but as the pages of type are on the bed together and rigidly fixed with respect to one another, and as the paper does not (or should not) move between the two pulls, we ought to find no difference in register or in parallelism of the pages from what we should have if the whole forme had been printed by one pull of the lever.'[2] From his observations, Dr. McKerrow deduced that the platen in the typical early press was considerably smaller than the tympan, in point of fact somewhat less than half its size. It is clear, of course, that the platen, if it was at all smaller than the tympan, could have been no greater than half its size, for it is obvious that the printing could only have been accomplished by either one or by two pulls of the lever. If it had been that the platen was to any considerable extent larger than one half the size of the tympan, it follows that at the first pull not only the whole of one half of the forme would be printed but a portion of the other half as well. Under such circumstances, this would cause a portion of the second half of

---

[2] Elsewhere (p. 61) Dr. McKerrow says: 'And here I think that I may perhaps surprise some bibliographers by saying that always until about 1800 a normal full-sized forme was printed by two pulls of the lever.'

the forme to come under the platen twice and the remainder but once, with the possibility that a consequent heavier impression would result on one part of the page than on the other, or at the very worst, a double impression. Also it is, I think, inconceivable that (let us say) two-thirds of a forme would be printed with one pull and the remaining third by another.

As we have seen, the fragment here under discussion appears on the verso of the second leaf, the remaining three pages being fully printed; this sheet furthermore constitutes the whole of the first (un-signed) gathering. That the fragment represents the portion of a page used as a type-high support seems to be self-evident, but the questions as to why such a 'bearer' was necessary or, assuming that it was necessary, how it came to be printed still need to be answered. Presuming that these folio sheets were printed with two pulls to the forme, the platen would descend on half the tympan and print the text now found on folio 1 recto; as no pressure would thereby be brought on the other half of the sheet and the paper was firmly held on the tympan, a support, at least a bearer equal to the height of the type-page, seems quite unnecessary. Again presuming that a page of such supports was necessary to fill out the forme or for some similar reason and that a portion of it had indeed been inked, it is difficult to see how so sharp an impression as the one here found could have been obtained when no pressure was directly applied to it, for, as we have seen, the platen could not have covered more than half of the forme and would not have touched the other at all. If each folio page was printed with one pull, the only reasonable ex-planation for the presence of the fragment is that a bearer was essen-tial (though it need not have been so high as an actual page of type and might have been any other manner of 'furniture'), that by some accident the inner margin of this page of type had been inked and improperly wiped clean, and that the printer as a matter of habit had completed the usual practice and had pulled the lever twice, possibly not being aware that only half the sheet was to be printed. From this, it also follows that a frisket was not used by Caxton to cover up the blank half of the sheet, for a properly cut frisket would have pre-vented the blank page from receiving any impression whatsoever, or, if by accident it had slipped a trifle out of place, the resulting impression would have been even at the edges and not irregular as it actually is.

A few words of further explanation may, I think, be added to

Dr. McKerrow's comment. As we have seen, Dr. McKerrow stated that 'thus each page (in a folio) is actually printed separately' but this is not necessarily true in every instance. The number of pages printed with one pull of the lever is obviously not dependent on whether a book is printed 'in folio' or 'in quarto'; on the contrary the number of pages printed at one time depends solely on the size of the pages and the size of the platen. Although there is no direct evidence as to the size of Caxton's press, the approximate dimensions can be inferred from an examination of the books themselves. The largest sheet known to have been printed by Caxton is found in the *Golden Legend* and, according to Blades, measures about 22 x 16 inches. The tympan of Caxton's press could not, accordingly, have been any smaller but might very well have been considerably larger. If, for the sake of argument, we assume this same measurement for the tympan and that the sheet was printed with two pulls, the size of the platen could not have been greater than 11 x 16 inches or smaller than 7 x 11½, the size of the type-page in the *Golden Legend*. That this was a 'standard' size of printing press from the earliest days seems likely; Moxon, in his *Mechanick Exercises* (1683), gives the size of the tympan as about 22 x 15 inches and that of the platen as 9 x 14. It will be noted that this measurement for the platen is just half way between the smallest possible size of Caxton's platen and the greatest, as determined by the size of the largest sheet and its type-page. If, then, we assume the size of his platen to be that of Moxon's, Caxton could easily have printed two pages of his smaller folios with one pull. The diagram on page opposite, drawn to scale, will show this clearly.

The outer dimensions are those of the sheet in the *Golden Legend*; next the size of the type-page with its approximate position has been drawn in. The dotted lines show how the pages of Caxton's smaller folios might have fitted into the press. If, in the case of the smaller folios, Caxton placed his text on the bed of the press in the same manner as for his larger folios (B), he would, as a matter of course, have had to print with two pulls of the lever. Unless he used a smaller press than he did for the *Golden Legend* or the same press with a smaller tympan, a considerable loss of paper would have resulted. However, as the diagram shows, he could easily have fitted two pages into the coffin of half the press if he laid them side by side (A). This means of course that he used a different size of paper, which, though exactly half the size of the *Golden Legend* sheet, was not

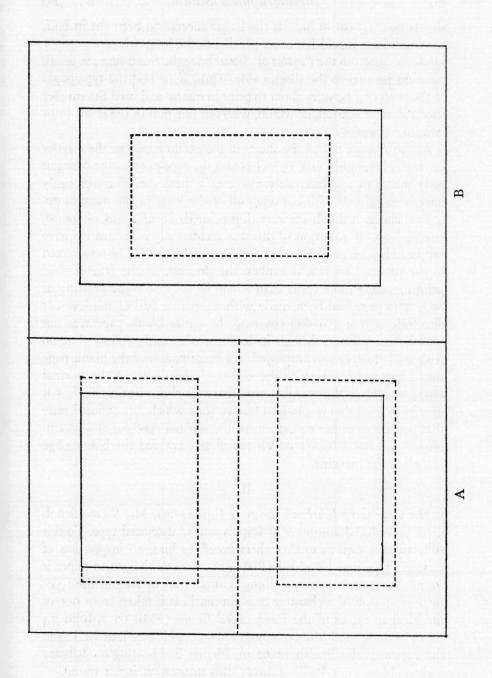

this same sheet cut in half. If the larger sheets had been cut in half, the chain-lines would have run parallel to the long side of the paper while the sheets in the *Fayttes of Armes* have the chain-lines, as usual, running parallel to the shorter side. Thus, if he laid the type-pages in the press as if he were about to print in quarto and used the smaller sheets above discussed, he would, with but one pull of the lever, print two folio pages at a time.

As the average size of the sheets in the extant copies of the *Fayttes of Armes* is roughly 11 x 15 inches and the type-page in the Morgan copy measures approximately 7½ x 4½, these sheets[3] could easily have been printed with but one pull of the lever in the manner described above. If the sheets were thus printed, a bearer was, of course, essential, and if a portion of this was accidentally inked, as we have supposed before, an impression of this would naturally be transferred to the paper. This would explain the presence of the fragment of printing rather more easily than would be the case if the printing of each folio page had been made with a separate pull of the lever. It also follows that a frisket covering the entire blank page was not used by the printer, though it does not necessarily follow that no frisket whatsoever was employed. An examination of the blank page shows signs of printing to the extent of the width of the normal type-page, while the margins are otherwise clean. From this fact it may be argued that a standard frisket (one which left exposed only that portion of paper equivalent to the normal type-page) was employed and not a frisket which completely covered the blank page as well as the margins.

## III

In the *Gutenberg-Jahrbuch* for 1927 (pp. 24–25), Mr. Victor Scholderer reproduced a number of impressions of displaced type. To this collection, as well as to the others noted by him, an impression of Caxton's type may be added (Plate 4a). Here the height to paper is 20 mm, but unfortunately nothing unusual may be seen in the type; there is no sign of a chamfer or a pin-mark. It is taken from one of the Morgan copies of the *Book called Caton* (PML 691), folio g 4 recto. In the second Morgan copy (PML 690, Plate 4a), as well as in the copies in the British Museum, Henry E. Huntington Library and the New York Public Library, this impression is not found.

---

[3] Blades (p. xvii) notes that one size of Caxton's paper measured 16 x 11 inches, which is probably the size he employed for printing the smaller folios.

It is generally supposed that such pieces of type as the present one were accidentally pulled out of the forme in the process of inking it. Dr. McKerrow says of it (p. 204): 'it need only be said that the method of inking by dabbing the type with ink-balls was especially likely to draw out loose type.' The presence of an impression of a piece of type seems generally to be accompanied by a disturbance of the type somewhere else, but in the present instance there is no such disturbance and not one character in the whole sheet (g 4 recto – g 5 verso) is wanting. The fact that this piece of type is lying on a corner of the signature and is consequently higher than the rest of the type-page is clearly seen in the depth of the impression, which has very nearly torn through the paper and is, except for the lack of ink, as distinctly visible on the verso as on the recto.

Now it is, of course, quite possible that a piece of type lying by chance near the press accidentally fell on the forme and thus came to be printed. If such be the case, it must have been a very unusual occurrence to have loose type lying on or near the press for, if it were common to have pieces of type lying about loose, one might expect to find many more such impressions than we now have. There is another explanation, but it is purely a conjectural one and, though reasonable, one that will require further confirmation from other sources.

As we have seen in the second section of this paper, Caxton could have printed two pages of a small-sized folio at one time if he employed but half the press. It is equally possible that, using the entire available space in the bed of the press and two sheets of paper on the tympan, the printer would have been able to print four pages with two pulls of the lever; in short, he would be printing 'in quarto' but with two sheets of folio paper. That this is possible is, of course, quite obvious; and if we assume for the moment that he did make use of this practice, the origin of the piece of type, which appears in the *Book called Caton*, becomes apparent. As will be seen in Plate 4b, PML 691, a violent disturbance in the type has taken place in the last line of folio g 8 recto. That this disturbance is found only in that copy which also has the impression of the piece of type (PML 691) seems to me significant; the other copies listed above correspond to the second Morgan copy (Plate 4b, PML 690). Now if the sheet (g 4 recto – g 5 verso) occupied one half of the coffin and the sheet (g 1 verso – g 8 recto) the other half, it is possible that, in the inking, one piece of type from g 8 recto was accidentally jerked by the ink-ball on to the forme of g 4 recto and thus gave the impression here reproduced.

One objection to this theory might very well be raised and that is why, if Caxton had his type-pages arranged as if he were printing in quarto, did he not actually do so. That he did not do so seems to be proved by the paper itself, for each sheet has one watermark approximately in the centre of half of the sheet, and the chain-lines on each page run parallel to the long side of the paper. Unless the paper which Caxton used was made entirely different from any other paper known to us, it is impossible to conclude that the *Book called Caton* was actually printed in quarto. The only explanation that occurs to me is that the paper of the size used in the *Golden Legend* was unsuitable for this. This paper is unusually thick and heavy;[4] possibly the size of this sheet made it necessarily so. In any case, it might have proved difficult to fold such a sheet twice, or when it was so folded, it might have given a bulky appearance to the book. It is possible that a thinner paper with a weight comparable to that used in the *Caton* was not available in a larger size, so that printing in quarto with a large sheet was not possible.[5]

(From *Gutenberg-Jahrbuch* (1940), pp. 169-176).

[4] Blades (p. xvii) notes that Caxton made only sparing use of the largest size of paper because it 'was probably found too unwieldy'.

[5] Blades has two curious notes on Caxton's method of printing. He says (vol. 1, p. 53): 'Caxton, even when using the quarto size, cut up his paper into half sheets, and then, as with folios, printed in single pages'. Again (vol. 11, p. xlviii) he states: 'It has been already observed that the quarto sizes were treated, both in printing and binding, as folio, the paper being cut in half before going to the press'. This seems indeed to have been a laborious process. The present writer plans at some future time to discuss the Caxton quartos.

# CHAPTER B7

## A NOTE ON ZEDLER'S
## COSTER THEORY

IN the past four centuries so much has been written about Lourens Coster and the question of his contribution to the invention or development of printing that the present writer would be extremely reluctant to add his opinion to this vexed question were it not for the fact that the beliefs of the most recent and most learned supporter of Coster's claims do not seem to have been analyzed in the light of his own discoveries. There is a rather important point which can (and should) be raised in connection with Gottfried Zedler's *Von Coster zu Gutenberg*, Leipzig, 1921, and his *Der älteste Buchdruck und das frühholländische Doktrinale des Alexander de Villa Dei*, Leiden, 1936, the two most important analytical works in which Coster is set forth as the inventor of printing. The question as to whether it was Gutenberg or Coster who discovered printing has been raised over and over again. The present writer has no wish to re-open the question or to take a position either one way or the other, but the contradictions that may be found in Zedler's own works make it seem worth while to examine this reconstruction.

Zedler's earlier book is divided into two parts: in the first he deals exhaustively with the earliest books and fragments obviously produced in the Netherlands and sets forth his theory as to how and when they were printed; in the second part, he endeavors to show that the account given by Hadrianus Junius in his *Batavia*, Leiden, 1588, is substantially correct and that from this one must conclude that Coster was the printer of these works. In short, Zedler's book is based squarely on (1) his theoretical deductions concerning these early prints and (2) Junius's account of Coster. Now it is a matter of no small consequence that if Zedler's typographical arguments are valid, Junius's account is demonstrably impossible and (vice versa) if Junius correctly relates the events that took place, Zedler's theories as to the dates of these imprints are clearly incorrect. If then Zedler's work is based squarely on two accounts which in turn contradict each other, what value can we set on Zedler's book?

The story as related by Junius is so well known that it need not here be repeated at length. Suffice it to say that, in this account, it is stated that Coster invented printing apparently in the late 1430's, that by this method he printed a *Speculum humanae salvationis*, and that, on Christmas eve 1440/41, a certain apprentice named Johannes Faustus stole Coster's type and equipment which he took to Mainz and commenced printing there, producing a *Doctrinale* with these same types. It is, of course, clear that Zedler relies entirely on Junius's story since the slightly earlier accounts of the invention of printing in Haarlem told by Jan van Zuren, Dirck Volkertszoon Coornhert, and Ludovico Guicciardini[1] do not name the inventor. Obviously there were other citizens of Haarlem equally capable of inventing the art of printing so that in order to identify Coster with this invention only Junius's story is of value. The account given by Junius of the historical details has been rather generally rejected as false by most historians and bibliographers, but since Zedler accepts it in modified form, it may be of interest to review the narrative in the light of Zedler's own discoveries.

Turning now to Zedler's typographical deductions, we learn the following. Apparently some time before the year 1440, the early printer (Coster) had fashioned two founts of type. The earlier of these, the Pontanus or Donatus type, was in use, we are told, from about 1435 to 1472 or later; the second type was the Saliceto or Doctrinale type, which the early printer is supposed to have used from about 1440 to 1472, or again somewhat later.

Here the discrepancy between the two accounts becomes perfectly self-evident to the reader and no satisfactory explanation for it has been offered by Zedler. If the theft of *all* of Coster's printing type and equipment (Junius leaves us in no doubt on this score as he specifically states that the thief "choragium omne typorum involat,

[1] The full texts of these accounts, together with a German translation, are printed in Zedler-Coster, p. 126 ff. Alfred W. Pollard (*Fine Books*, New York & London, 1912, p. 36, n. 1) says: "The first trace of the legend is in a reference to Coster as having 'brought the first print into the world in 1446' in a manuscript pedigree of the Coster family compiled about 1559." Father Bonaventura Kruitwagen (*Die Ansprüche Hollands auf die Erfindung der Buchdruckerkunst* in *Gutenberg Festschrift*, Mainz, 1925, pp. 353-370) points out that these are not separate accounts but all of them have a common origin. For complete bibliography of the Gutenberg-Coster controversy, the reader is referred to Douglas C. McMurtrie's recent and excellent *The Invention of Printing: A Bibliography*, Chicago, 1942, especially pp. 111-156, 201-202, 209-211, etc.

instrumentorum herilium ei artificio comparatorum supellectilem convasat") took place in 1440/41, it is difficult to see how Coster could have continued to make use of this material till 1472. On the other hand, if the entire equipment was stolen when Junius says it was, it follows that all the books printed by Coster with this equipment must be dated prior to 1440/41, a fact that is in direct contradiction with Zedler's typographical deductions. Manifestly both these accounts cannot be true and yet Zedler's hypothesis is based equally firmly on both of them.

According to the story as told by Junius, Coster must have printed his *Speculum* before 1440/41, yet Zedler gives excellent reasons for believing that this book could not have been printed before 1470. Again, if Junius is correct, the *Singularia juris* by Ludovicus Pontanus must have been printed before 1440, if printed by Coster, since after that date the type was no longer in Coster's possession. But this is most doubtful since the Roman lawyer, Ludovicus Pontanus, died (at the youthful age of thirty) only in 1439. It seems rather unlikely that a serious legal book, such as this one is, could have been completed much before his death, even less likely that a manuscript of the book could have reached Haarlem in somewhat less than two years, and entirely unlikely that Coster would have undertaken to print in 1440 a legal work by an obscure Italian when more suitable texts were at hand. It may be pointed out that printing had been practised for more than six years in Italy before the *Singularia juris* found itself put into type by an Italian press, where, it is reasonable to suppose, Pontanus's reputation would be the greatest. There is another book, however, which leaves no room for doubt, the edition of the *De salute corporis* by Guilelmus de Saliceto. This was printed, according to Zedler, by Coster and since it is printed in the same type as the *Doctrinale* must have been completed before the theft of that type in 1440/41, if one is to believe Junius's story. In this volume there are included several works by Aeneas Sylvius who is called "Pius Secundus Pontifex Maximus"; since Aeneas only became Pope on the death of Calixtus III on August 6th, 1458, it is certain that the book was not printed before that date. We must therefore either believe that Junius's account of the theft is entirely inaccurate or that the book was printed at Mainz by "Johann Faust." The latter theory is equally untenable since printing of so inferior a quality could scarcely have been sold at Mainz in competition with the remarkable products then issuing regularly from the press of Fust and Schoeffer and thus goes to prove that it is impossible to identify Johann Faust with either Fust or Gutenberg.

With the veracity of Junius's account (to which of course full credence must be given if Coster is to be identified with the inventor of the art) thus endangered, Zedler[2] endeavors to bolster the story as told by the old bookbinder Cornelis (from whom Junius obtained the facts) by saying that, though the theft took place, it was by a different man at a different time. Zedler believes that Cornelis's report is somehow connected with an entirely different event. Sometime early in the 1470's a new printer, the printer of the Abcdarium, makes his appearance. This printer, according to Zedler's surmise, must have learned his trade at Coster's printing office before setting up his own shop and this is the event that lies behind the theft reported by Cornelis. In that case what has happened to the theft which is one of the two main points in Junius's narrative? If we believe the printer of the Abcdarium stole all Coster's equipment in 1470 or earlier, how could the latter have continued for several years to print with it? If he did not steal the type, what did he steal? And if he did not steal anything at all, why was the old bookbinder so enraged with him? The small output attributable to this press would hardly have made it an active competitor of Coster's firm and so become the object of Cornelis's ire.

On the basis of Zedler's own reconstruction of the development of the earliest printing in the Netherlands and on the evidence supplied by the books themselves, it is evident that most of Junius's account is untrue. Other writers, notably Father Kruitwagen,[3] have shown that Junius has elsewhere misrepresented and distorted historical facts, that the evidence of the old bookbinder Cornelis is untrustworthy, and that the story of the theft of type, a common enough literary motif, is paralleled by similar accounts in other countries. The only item left in Junius's story which has not been clearly set aside as untrue is that the printer of the early Dutch incunabula was named Lourens Coster and that he resided in Haarlem in the 1440's. In the light of the other untruths, can one really accept Junius's account without outside corroborative evidence which has never been

[2] Zedler-Coster, p. 157 ff.

[3] Kruitwagen, *op. cit.*, p. 361. Compare also the evidence as weighed by Pollard, *op. cit.*, pp. 38-43 and by A. van der Linde, *The Haarlem Legend of the Invention of Printing by Lourens Janszoon Coster*, London, 1871.

produced? Perhaps one should echo Guicciardini's cautious note: "quel che ne sia alla verità, non posso ne voglio giudicare."

That printing was practised at a reasonably early date in the Netherlands cannot be disputed since we have the books to prove it. At what date these were produced is, however, not clear. The chief testimony on this score seems to be Ulrich Zell's famous comment about the "prefigurations" which took place in Holland before the invention of printing in Mainz in 1440,[4] as well as the fact that in January 1445/6 the Abbot Jean le Robert of Cambrai[5] purchased in Bruges a *Doctrinale* "jetté en molle" (whatever that may mean). As for Zell, it is rather more than likely that his evidence is only hearsay; furthermore, he says nothing of Gutenberg's trial efforts in Strassburg.[6] One must infer from Zell's statement that the Dutch "prefigurations" appeared before 1440, but it is somewhat unlikely that Zell could have had any first-hand acquaintance with such books before 1440.[7] If he did not actually see the "prefigurations" before 1440, but saw them in 1450 or 1460 he may have misjudged their antiquity from the crudeness of the impression. This would leave the question of date very uncertain, since, though the "Coster" imprints might have been coeval with or even later than the early Mainz products, their crude appearance would have led an early enquirer to believe they were much older than was actually the case. The purchase of a copy of the *Doctrinale* by the worthy Abbot offers no further evidence, since no one seems to know what is meant by "jetté en molle" and there is no way of identifying this book with

[4] The famous passage occurs in the *Cronica van der hilliger Stat Coellen* printed at Cologne by Johann Koelhoff in 1499. A good translation may be found in Pollard, *op. cit.*, pp. 34-35.

[5] Zedler-Doktrinale, pp. 1 and 30 ff.

[6] For the latest discussion of Gutenberg's work in Strassburg as well as for the other claims to the invention of printing, see Otto W. Fuhrmann, *Gutenberg and the Strasbourg Documents of 1439*, New York, 1940.

[7] Although we do not know the year of Zell's birth, he died in 1507 or later. Assuming that he saw the "prefigurations" in 1437 at the age of 15, he must have been born not after 1422. This would mean that he was 55 at the time he married, 44 when he commenced printing and continued at this trade till he was 72, and that he died at the age of 85. While not impossible, this seems somewhat unlikely. If Zell is the same Ulricus de Hanau who matriculated at the University of Erfurt (which is generally considered to be the case) in 1453, he must have been 31 at that time, a most unusual age to enter a university in the fifteenth century. On the other hand, if Zell is the Ulricus of the Erfurt University register and he had entered the university at the prevalent age of 16, he *could not* have had any personal knowledge of the existence of Dutch "prefigurations" before 1440. See E. Voulliéme, *Die deutschen Drucker des fünfzehnten Jahrhunderts*, Berlin, 1922, pp. 40-41.

one of Coster's editions. Even if one sees in this a reference to one of the early Dutch *Doctrinales,* which may or may not have been the case, this merely proves that the Dutch printer was a contemporary of Gutenberg's, since the earliest Gutenberg *Donatus* is considered to have been printed in 1444 and the *Weltgedicht* in 1445.

What is left of Zedler's book with which one can safely agree is a careful analysis of the earliest Dutch founts. As to the date which may be assigned to them, we are as much in the dark as ever. The weakest point in Zedler's chronological discussion is that he supposes that the early printer used the same fount of type for fully half a century even after he had cut newer and better founts. This seems somewhat counter, as far as we know, to the usual practice of the early printing-houses, and Zedler's reply to such criticism is hardly convincing.[8]

As we have seen, Zedler's effort to identify the early Dutch printer with Lourens Coster rests on evidence too scanty and questionable to be admissible and his dating of the products of this press, based in large part on the evidence submitted by Cornelis and Zell together with the reported purchase of a *Doctrinale* in 1445/6, seems inconclusive. The present writer is not aware of any other evidence, conclusive or otherwise, which would lead one to believe that the earliest printing in the Netherlands took place in the 1430's and that the printer was Lourens Coster. On the other hand, the *Gesamtkatalog's* dating of the earliest *Doctrinales* as "vor 1470?" is equally unjustifiable, in view of Zell's statement and the record of an earlier purchase of such a book. The present writer is inclined to believe that the anonymous printer undertook his experiments at or about the same time that Gutenberg did and that the two must be regarded as contemporary and independent ventures. The belief that two men, working independently, could make the same invention at about the same time is not beyond the bounds of credulity; indeed it is amply attested by numerous other cases in the history of invention and discovery.

(From *PBSA* 37 (1943), pp. 61-68).

[8] Zedler-Doktrinale, p. 49, explains that Coster's types suffered less damage in the course of time because they were cast in sand with the use of wooden punches. The present writer is not impressed by this argument.

# CHAPTER B8

## JUNIUS AND THE THIEF
## OF HAARLEM

To the Editor of MORE BOOKS
Dear Sir:

With a thoughtfulness and courtesy not often accorded to one holding a different belief in bibliographical matters, Mr. Haraszti has offered me space in which to reply to his remarks (appearing in the January issue of MORE BOOKS, pp. 23–26) concerning my paper "A Note on Zedler's Coster Theory." Since it is entirely self-evident that I failed to make my point sufficiently clear to Mr. Haraszti (and to many others, I have no doubt), I welcome this opportunity.

The entire point of my paper, as I thought the title would suggest, was to analyze Zedler's theory in the light of his own explanations—not (primarily) to add further complications to the existing confusions relating to the "Coster" legend (or fact). Such facts and arguments as I have used may all, I believe, be found in Zedler's works, with but little recourse to other sources. Thus it was not so much with the Coster theory itself that I was concerned as with Zedler's account of it. I accepted Zedler's typographical deductions and I accepted Zedler's version of what his historical account (Junius) relates—and then showed (or sought to show) that these two contradicted each other.

Bearing this in mind, we may turn to Mr. Haraszti's objections. He refers to *my* interpretation and translation—but these are not mine at all, they are Zedler's. As Mr. Haraszti points out, the Latin text may be subject to various interpretations. My concern was not with this but with what Zedler said it meant. There may be doubt as to the Latin—there is none with regard to the German translation which Zedler supplies. It reads:

Nämlich gerade in der Nacht, in der die Geburt Christi gefeiert wird, und alle ohne Unterschied der heiligen Weihe beizuwohnen pflegen, nimmt er den ganzen Typenvorrat an sich, packt die Werkzeuge und das Geräte seines Herrn, die für die auszuübende Kunst geschaffen waren, zusammen und macht sich mit den gestohlenen Sachen aus dem Hause.

Zedler clearly believes the Latin to say that the thief took everything appertaining to the press—lock, stock, and barrel—a statement in direct conflict with Zedler's belief that the Haarlem printer continued to use this equipment for thirty-odd years. It was *most* unfortunate that I quoted the Latin text and not Zedler's rendition of it; I should have said something like "Junius, according to Zedler's own translation, leaves us in no doubt etc." Incidentally Mr. Haraszti is wrong when he states in note 51 that I omitted the word *supellectilem*. It is there exactly as it appears in Zedler, though Mr. Haraszti overlooked it in his transcript (p. 23).

If I were to give my own translation of these words *choragium omne typorum involat*, it would be: "he seizes the entire equipment of types." Granting that *involare* can mean "to fly into" and *choragium* may designate "a place," I do not believe they hold these meanings in this instance. This may be argued both from the point of view of grammar and of context. When the verb *involare* means "to fly into," it normally—though not invariably—requires a preposition; when it occurs with a simple accusative object, I should think the preferable reading is "to seize." Again, for *choragium* I should prefer the meaning in which it is used by Vitruvius and others, i.e. "mechanical equipment." Most significant for this interpretation, I think, is the presence of the adjective "omne." Using Mr. Haraszti's meanings, one would have to translate these words as: "he flies into the whole (every) place of types." Since it seems likely that, for practical purposes, Coster would have kept all his type in one place and because one does not normally fly into a *whole* room, the wording of the Latin, as in the English translation, seems awkward. In order to render this passage as "he flies into the room (place) of the types," Mr. Haraszti must assume that Junius forgot an important (though not vital) preposition and added an entirely superfluous "omne."

Mr. Haraszti further feels that to translate *involare* as "to steal" (I should prefer "to seize") and *convasare* as "to pack up" creates a contradiction and that one of these verbs is superfluous. Such a contradiction is not apparent to me nor could it have been to Pollard whose summary (it is not a translation) states that the thief had the occasion "to pack up and steal all the tools and appliances." Thus Pollard also believes Junius to say that *all* the equipment was stolen —and surely types are not the least important of the printer's tools. Finally, as for the wine flagons, one must note that Junius speaks of these not in relation to the story of the theft but earlier in regard to the new types of tin which, he states, superseded those of wood and lead. One is supposed to infer, I expect, that the remnants of his experiments with lead and tin were used to make pewter jugs.

As for the *Doctrinale* "jette en molle," this is a thorny question and perhaps I was a bit too arbitrary in what I said. For the contradictions in Zedler's book produced by Zedler's own statements, this *Doctrinale* is of very minor importance; it is of value chiefly as corroborating the date of Zell's "prefigurations." However, I suggested in my paper that this book gives good grounds for believing that printing in Mainz (or Strassburg) and in the Low Countries began about the same time.

I regret that I failed to make all these points as clear as I should have done in the first instance. I trust this will rectify my oversight —albeit somewhat late. I should like to congratulate Mr. Haraszti on his clear exposition of this "perdifficilis et perobscura quaestio" and the Boston Public Library on its acquisition of these valuable Donatus fragments.

Faithfully yours,

Curt F. Bühler

(From *More Books* (1945), pp. 122-123).

# CHAPTER B9

## VARIANTS IN ENGLISH INCUNABULA

THE fact that, particularly among early printed books, copies of the same edition frequently exhibit variant settings of type or changes of text is a matter of common knowledge to all bibliographers. So common is this in the case of English incunabula that one is tempted to observe that it would be a matter of the utmost difficulty to find two identical Caxtons. The present writer has, from time to time, called attention to the variant settings in the works of William Caxton; a similar situation exists in the case of some of his English colleagues. Before turning to the examples to be cited here, it seems fitting to make a few general remarks on how and why variant settings of type came into being, since this is not, I believe, a subject that has been as fully treated as its importance demands.[1] These will be found in Part One.

The second part will be devoted to an examination of three previously unknown variants, while the third will discuss the reasons for a variant issue that has long been known but never fully explained.[2]

## PART I

The variant-settings in incunabula, sometimes referred to as "issues," may range from the alteration of a single character on a single page of text to completely reprinted pages extending through several successive quires; they involve alterations in text, type, illustrations or other embellishments. I do not think it is necessary to enter here into a discussion of the variants brought about by physical causes

---

[1] Discussions along similar lines will be found in R. B. McKerrow, *An Introduction to Bibliography for Literary Students*, Oxford, 1927, p. 204 ff.; Konrad Haebler, *Handbuch der Inkunabelkunde*, Leipzig, 1925, p. 132–136; W. W. Greg, *The Variants in the First Quarto of 'King Lear,'* London, 1940, *passim*; and in numerous short papers. The best of these discussions is that by Dr. McKerrow, but he points out but two kinds of variation against the six I have listed. The other writers have treated fully only the questions raised by errors of composition.

[2] I wish to express my thanks for help received from Dr. John D. Gordan of New York, Dr. A. S. W. Rosenbach of Philadelphia, Miss Margaret B. Stillwell of the Annmary Brown Memorial, Mr. Robert B. Anderson of the Harvard Law Library, Dr. James G. McManaway of the Folger Shakespeare Library, and my colleagues at The Pierpont Morgan Library, Miss Helen Franc and Miss Ann Mosher.

(fire, damage to the press, accidental or wanton destruction of type, etc.)[3] since these would appear to be quite self-explanatory. Apart from such variants, it is safe to assume, I believe, that the reason for the existence of variant settings lies either in technical causes or in accidental ones. Issues having their origin in technical causes generally contain variants clearly involving an improvement of text, while those that are the result of accidental errors have variants displaying no noteworthy textual improvement and may even exhibit a deterioration of text. The frequent and hastily assumed theory that the variant issue displaying the more correct text must inevitably be the later issue (since it is assumed, on quite gratuitous grounds, that it is a corrected re-issue of its corrupt predecessor) is not necessarily a correct deduction. The possibility is always present that an ignorant compositor, setting up copy for a second issue, may have misread his original and thus introduced corrupt readings in the later variant which did not exist in the earlier. Of this we shall have more to say in Part Three.

Errors of imposition are probably the commonest and certainly the most easily recognized of the technical causes leading to variant issues. An adequate example is given by Blades in his description of the copy of the *Recuyell of the Histories of Troy*, then in the possession of the Duke of Devonshire and now in the Huntington Library. Blades[4] writes: "The inmost sheet of the 3rd quinternion has an error in the printing, which no folding can rectify, as the fourth page of the sheet is printed so as to back the first, and the second takes the place of the fourth." Since other copies have the correct imposition, it is self-evident that the printer discovered the error in time to make the necessary corrections before all the copies had been struck off.

The second technical cause leading to variant issues is brought about by errors of composition. This may again be divided into two

[3] This type is defined by Dr. McKerrow as "accidental variation owing to displacement of type during the actual machining." He adds: "it need only be said that the method of inking by dabbing the type with ink-balls was especially likely to draw out loose type." I have altered Dr. McKerrow's definitions as I did not find them sufficiently flexible to cover all the variations. There are, as we shall see, "accidental variations" due to other causes than machining. I have therefore determined to call this type "physical," since it has its origin in physical causes, reserving "accidental" for those variants brought about by "accidents" of whatever sort.

[4] William Blades, *The Life and Typography of William Caxton*, London, 1861–63, vol. II, p. 6.

parts: either that the compositor's errors necessitated the correction of misprints (or improvements in typography) or that similar errors required the addition of further information or deletion of existing portions of text. As I have previously pointed out,[5] Caxton's *Boke of Eneydos* shows variant issues brought about by the correction of a single misprint, while the variants of the *Book callid Caton* are the result of the printer's desire to improve the typographical appearance of the volume.[6] For the addition or deletion of further information, we may note the variants of Caxton's first *Chess Book*, noted in the same paper, or the question of the extra colophon in the Rylands copy of the *Dictes and Sayings of the Philosophers* which I have dealt with elsewhere.[7]

The easiest of the accidental errors to be identified is that of "imperfection," for which Blades[8] found a perfect example in a Bodleian copy of the *Recuyell*: "There is in this volume a curious accident: the verso of the 29th leaf has not been printed by the pressmen, although the corresponding page on the same side of the sheet shows a good impression." A variation of this constitutes the second group of accidental errors; that is when it was discovered, after the type had been distributed, that certain sheets had been left unperfected. This necessitated resetting the type in order to perfect the leaves and thus caused the appearance of variant issues. I believe the variants of Caxton's *Jason*[9] are a satisfactory example of such an occurrence.

[5] "Caxton variants," *The Library*, vol. xvii, June, 1936, p. 62–69.

[6] In the *Caton*, the opening line of one issue shows a paragraph mark (¶) which does not appear in the other. I argued, at the time, that this new piece of type arrived at Caxton's shop while he was in the process of printing this sheet and that he reset the first line in order to use the new character. With this explanation, I am still satisfied, though it should be amplified. The ¶ is also found on the inner forme of the fourth sheet of the last quire as well as on both inner and outer formes of the innermost sheet of this same quire. Apparently the new ¶ arrived while both the last and the first quires were being printed, indicating that Caxton had more than one press. The first quire was usually the last printed by the early printers if it contained (as this one does) a table of contents with page or leaf references.

[7] See articles reprinted *supra*.

[8] William Blades, op. cit., vol. ii, p. 5. "To perfect" is a technical expression meaning "to complete the printing of a sheet of a book, etc. by printing the second side." (OED)

[9] "Caxton's 'History of Jason,'" *Papers of the Bibliographical Society of America*, vol. xxxiv, 1940, p. 254–261. We may note in passing that two minor misprints

The last mistake in this group is perhaps the most difficult to speak of with certainty and I must digress on it at somewhat greater length. It has been pointed out that several pages in Caxton's *Morte d'Arthur* are found in variant states[10] which show only minor variations and no improvement of text. My belief is that these variants were the result of the following mishap: while the volume was being printed, the pressmen did not keep an accurate account of the number of sheets they printed for each quire, so that in some instances they had too many sheets for certain signatures and in other cases too few. The extra sheets were easily disposed of by using them for the bindings of the volumes.[11] If there were too few, however, the printer in most cases felt obliged, as a practical measure, to make good the deficiency by reprinting these sheets. Since the scantness of his supply of type forced the early printer to distribute the formes as soon as he was through with them,[12] no type remained standing when the books were made up. He was thus obliged to reset the pages if he wished to reprint the necessary sheets and by these means the variant pages such as those in the Malory came into being.

It has been suggested to me by some of my colleagues that this explanation is based rather too heavily on the above assumption, since it would have been a relatively simple matter for the pressmen to have kept an accurate tally on the number of sheets they printed. The letters of the Koberger family,[13] however, prove beyond doubt that such a tally was not kept. On August 13, 1501, Anton Koberger complained to Hans Amerbach: "Ich hab Collationiren lassen Tertia vnd Quarta partes So jr mir gesant hand vnd jn tertia parte mangelt mir jn 28 buchern jn jedem 1 qtn .q. jm ersten alphabett hab 28

---

were corrected while the *Jason* was being printed. On leaf 6 recto, line 4, the Morgan copy has "aud" while "and" appears in that belonging to The New York Public Library; again on leaf 55 recto, last line, the Morgan copy reads "thsi" whereas the Public Library example has "this." These, therefore, represent variants caused by errors in composition.

[10] See my paper "Two Caxton problems," *The Library*, vol. xx, December, 1939, p. 266–268.

[11] For an account of how such sheets were used, see Blades, op. cit., vol. ii, p. 70, and my paper "Three Notes on Caxton," *The Library*, vol. xvii, September, 1936, p. 155–162.

[12] Lawrence C. Wroth, *The Colonial Printer*, New York, 1931, p. 142–143, points out that the early American printer was faced with the same difficulty.

[13] Printed by Oscar Hase, *Die Koberger*, Leipzig 1885, p. v ff.

Defect bucher gemacht wollet mir Die Selben qtn schicken So jr am nachsten bucher schickt. Ich hab ettlich qtn r übrig Die an des .q. stat gewest sind." Again on the ninth of January, 1506, Koberger writes to the same printer: "Also sind Die abgeczelt vnd von blat zw blat Collationirt vnd ettlicher bletter zw wenig vnd ettlicher zw vill funden." That Amerbach was not alone guilty of this fault is demonstrated in Koberger's letter to Johann Froben (12 January 1509): "Jr habt Das werck woll Collationirt Aber wir vinden alle tag ettwas zw vill oder zw wenig Als ich euch woll anczeigen will." It was not, then, uncommon that an incorrect number of sheets were printed. If, on occasion, this mistake was discovered only after the type had been distributed, the printer would have no alternative other than to reset the type in order to supply the lacking leaves. This would give an adequate explanation for the variant sheets which show no improvement of text. Indeed, if the resetting of the leaves was given to an ignorant or incompetent compositor, it is easy to see how the text of these reprinted leaves might show a deterioration from the original.

In order to sum up, the reasons for the existence of variant issues in English incunabula may be set down as follows:

### Physical Causes

### Technical Causes

Errors of imposition
Errors of composition

### Accidental Causes

Imperfection left uncorrected
Imperfection corrected by reset type
Incorrect number of leaves or quires printed

We may further note that in the case of variants created by technical errors, there was a deliberate attempt to improve upon the text of the work, while those caused by accidental errors were motivated by no such purpose.

## PART II

The three variants to be noted here have not, to the best of my knowledge, been cited before. In addition, an explanation for their origin, along the lines discussed above, will be attempted.

*A*

In Richard Pynson's edition[14] of the *Canterbury Tales* [London, circa 1491], the text printed on signature H2 verso is found in two different states, both issues being represented in The Pierpont Morgan Library. In Morgan No. 751, the text is set up thus (beginning at the foot of H2 recto, column 2, line 37):

". . . And || this is in many thynges as in speche || in contenaunce in out-rageousnes. || [verso] of aray of clothing Cryst wolde not || so sone haue noted & spoken of the || clotyng of that riche man in the gos || pel but yf it had be synne . . ."

In Morgan No. 750, the same text reads:

". . . And || this is in many thynges as in speche || in contenaunce in out-rageousnes. || [verso] clotyng of that riche man in the gos || pel but yf it had be synne . . ."

Turning to the bottom of the second column, line 37, H2 verso, we find that Morgan No. 751 reads:

". . . I saye yot [*sic*] þat || honeste in clotyng of man and wo- || man is vncouenable || [H3] But certes the superfluyte or dysordi || nat skarcete of cloting is reprouable ||"

In Morgan No. 750, the same text appears as:

". . . I saye yot [*sic*] þat || honeste in clotyng of man and wo- || man is vn-couenable || But certes the superfluyte or dysordi || nat skarcete of cloting is reprouable || [H3] But certes the superfluyte or dysordi || nat skarcete of cloting is reprouable ||"

When the two issues are laid side by side, it is quite apparent how the misprint came about. In setting up the type originally, the compositor accidentally omitted two lines; apparently his eye had skipped from one phrase to a similar one further down, a common enough omission in manuscripts where this type of error has received the formidable title "omissio ex homoeoteleuto." When this was noted, the press was stopped,[15] the two lines inserted at the top of column 1 of H2 verso and two lines moved from the bottom of column 2 to the top of the next page [H3 recto]. Except for the necessary reshifting in the lines, no other changes were made and the misprints

[14] E. Gordon Duff, *Fifteenth-century English Books*, Bibliographical Society, 1917, no. 89.

[15] For a thorough discussion of what took place in the printer's office, see Greg, op. cit., p. 51 ff.

"wasteo" for "wasted," "Adn" for "And," "calour" for "colour," and "yot" for "not" remain uncorrected in the second issue. The remaining leaves were then run off. This made the text of the later issue correct, but in those copies containing the leaves of the first setting there is a lacuna of two lines at the top of column 1 and a repetition of two lines at the end of column 2. The variants are therefore the result of a technical error in composition. Similar to Morgan 751 are the Gordan-Goodhart, Berg Collection (Young-Royal Society), and Rosenbach copies, while the copy in the Reserve Room of The New York Public Library belongs to the other issue.

## B

The second variant is found in Lathbury, *Liber moralium super threnis Jeremiae*, [Oxford] 1482. Here the outer forme of the fourth sheet of quire o [o4 recto – o5 verso] occurs in two entirely different settings. The two issues may be identified as follows:

|  |  |  | Morgan 706 | Morgan 707 |
|---|---|---|---|---|
| o4 recto, col. | 1, l. | 4 : | propteria | propterea |
|  | l. | 5 : | ni | in |
| col. | 2, l. | 4 : | olī gra- | olim gra |
|  | l. 22/3: |  | lo- ‖ quētis | lo- ‖ quentis |
| o5 verso, col. | 1, l. | 1 : | ethnici | ethinci |
|  | l. | 2 : | salamon | salomon |
| col. | 2, l. | 2 : | fabrifacta | fabrefacta |
|  | last line: |  | mnlachrum | mulachrum |

The Folger copy is like Morgan 707, while the Annmary Brown Memorial example belongs to the other issue. It is probable, as we shall see, that these variants were caused by the accidental failure to perfect the sheet, making it necessary to reset the type in order to complete the text. The fact that the variants occur in the outer forme rather than in the inner need cause no surprise since, as the late Dr. Ronald B. McKerrow has shown,[16] the printing of the inner forme would normally precede that of the outer.

Turning to the text itself, the issue represented by Morgan 707 is slightly the better. The major differences are three: on o4 recto, col. 1, line 34, Morgan 707 has "attritio responsionem" while Morgan 706 lacks the word "attritio"; in col. 2, line 26, Morgan 707 reads "culpe

---

[16] op. cit., p. 31–32.

iudeorum" whereas Morgan 706 has "cuple rudeorum"; and on o5 verso, col. 1, line 3, Morgan 707 correctly has "alienigenas," the other issue reading "aligenigenas." Since, in the first example, the compositor need only have reset two lines of type in order to make room for the added word, and the other two cases involve the resetting of but one line each, it seems unlikely that the entire forme was reset in order to present a better text. That the printer was perfectly capable of resetting certain words and lines without disturbing the rest of the page is amply shown elsewhere in the text;[17] as the Morgan catalogue notes:[18]

There are two issues of this book, some, like the present copy, with, and some without the woodcut border. On leaf k7 verso (*should read* kk7) some copies read "super capitulum s'm trenorū," others (of which this is one), "sup capitulū secūdu trenorū." As noted by Mr. Madan (*The Early Oxford Press*, p. 255), "clearly the type was altered because s'm is a fair contraction when meaning 'according to,' but not properly used when meaning 'second.'"

Since there was no need for the printer to reset an entire forme in order to make three changes, it does not seem reasonable to conclude that the variant arose primarily out of a desire to improve the text. This could have been accomplished just as well by resetting only four lines and, as we have seen, the printer was fully able to do this. Furthermore, Morgan 707 contains minor misprints which, if the printer had been striving for accuracy, one would not expect to find. The most likely explanation for the presence of these variant settings that occurs to me is that some sheets accidentally escaped "perfection" and that, when the printer came to reset the type for this forme, he introduced the three improvements of which we have spoken.

[17] There are numerous corrections, made while the book was at press, scattered throughout the text. The following examples may be noted; for convenience, I shall use the sigla 6 for Morgan 706, 7 for Morgan 707, A for Annmary Brown and F for the Folger copies: t3 recto, col. 2, l. 3 from bottom, "nichilum" (6) and "nullam" (7AF); v5 recto, col. 2, l. 2 from bottom, "peccatum" (6AF) and "pectatum" (7); D1 verso, col. 2, l. 2, "deficiunt" (6AF) and "difficiunt" (7); H6 recto, col. 1, l. 5, "Docet ypocras de secretis nature et" (6F) and "sic docet ypocras de secretis nature &" (7A); kk3 verso, col. 1, last line, "retributionis" (6AF) and "retribntionis" (7).

[18] *Catalogue of . . . Early Printed Books . . . now Forming Portion of the Library of J. Pierpont Morgan*, London, 1907, vol. III, p. 185. Also noted by Duff, no. 238. It is curious that the printer made the correction here, since on the very same page, at the bottom of the second column, he prints "primū s'm & quartū capitulū." That the printer regularly uses "s'm" for "second" is shown elsewhere in the book; for example, in the last line of col. 2 of z8 verso, he prints "s'm" where he had sufficient room to print "secundum" in full.

## C

The last variant issue occurs in the Lyndewode, *Constitutiones Provinciales*, Westminster, Wynkyn de Worde, 31 May 1496. Although Duff (No. 279) notes that the first four quires are found in two different states, he did not seem to notice that the printer made extensive corrections in quire K while the volume was at press. In all, there are thirty-seven alterations in text and these occur on twelve of the sixteen pages in the quire. Both issues are represented in The Pierpont Morgan Library and a comparison of the texts reveals that Morgan 727 has the correct version in all but one instance. The following characteristic examples may be singled out:

|  | Morgan 727 | Morgan 733 |
|---|---|---|
| K1 recto, l. 17: | ppter vacca 24 | ppter vaca 24 |
| verso, l. 1: | aut | ant |
| K2 recto, l. 12: | moneat | moueat |
| verso, l. 3: | sēinū. fructuū | seminū. fructū |
| K3 recto, l. 3: | compellant | compelant |
| K4 verso, l. 1: | maiores | maioris |
| K5 recto, l. 20: | canonico | cononico |
| K6 recto, l. 6: | veīre | venire |
| verso, l. 4: | e- ‖ piscopi | e- ‖ piscoi |
| K7 recto, l. 15: | collegis | collegiis |
| K8 recto, l. 5: | vl' monia ‖ lis | vel moni ‖ lis |
| verso, l. 14: | moniales | maniales |

The Gordan-Goodhart and Rosenbach copies listed in the *Census*[19] belong to the less correct issue, while Morgan 727 is similar to the Harvard and Annmary Brown examples. These last two copies show that still further corrections were made while the work of printing was proceeding. In line 17 of K1 verso, Morgan 733 prints "sacra eloquio iubuente" which was slightly improved to "sacro eloquio iuuente" in Morgan 727. However, the printer saw that the text was still not correct and made still another alteration;[20] the Harvard and Annmary Brown copies read "sacro eloquio iubente."

A close study of the two Morgan copies shows that we are here dealing with variant settings that are the result of the printer's de-

[19] Margaret B. Stillwell, *Incunabula in American Libraries*, New York, 1940, no. L 65.

[20] For a similar instance, see Greg, op. cit., p. 41.

sire to improve the text. When the printer saw the misprints in his text, he interrupted the printing to make the necessary corrections. This did not involve the resetting of entire pages as a careful investigation reveals. The same broken characters and the same errors in alignment occur in both Morgan copies at the same places. Furthermore, both copies have the same misprints left uncorrected: K3 verso, l. 3, "nnllaten"" for "nullatenus;" K5 recto, l. 9, "dilgenter" for "diligenter;" K5 verso, l. 12, "pepulum" for "peplum;" K7 verso, l. 2, "versauicce" for "versavice;" and K8 verso, ll. 6/7, "furint" for "fuerint." It is safe to assume, therefore, that the reason for these variant issues is a technical one, the printer's errors in composition having made necessary the corrections we have noted.

## PART III

As we have had occasion to remark, Duff pointed out that the first four quires (A-D) of the *Constitutiones Provinciales* were known in two different settings. Duff made no particular comment as to which was the earlier or how the two issues came into being; a close scrutiny of the text in both copies will provide an answer for both queries.

A comparison of the text of the issue described by Duff (A) with that of his variant (B) shows an astonishing number of variant readings. It is almost certain that two different compositors set up the text, though the issues agree page for page, and often line for line. The compositor of A nearly always prefers, when he has such a choice, to use "t" instead of "c," "x" rather than "xs," "y" in place of "i," and "s" for "ss;" thus A prints *etiam, gratiam, executione, synodo, suspensionis* where B has *eciam, graciam, exsecutione, sinodo* and *susspensionis*. Most astonishing of all, however, is that in the thirty-two leaves there are no fewer than 159 misprints in B while A has no more than nine such errors. In addition, the compositor of B shows that he was either extremely careless or possessed of an insufficient knowledge of Latin for this sort of work. The following misprints in B seem to indicate that the latter is true: *sacramento* for *sacramentum* [A8 verso]; *alienauit* for *alleuiabit* [B1 recto]; *liberos* for *libros* and *subplicio* for *suppellicio* [B6 recto]; *pusilaminitas* for *pusillanimitas* [C2 verso]; *talia* for *taliter* [D3 verso]; *grauimus* for *grauius* [D6 verso]; etc. In these circumstances, one would, on first thought, be inclined to assume that the variant issue B was the earlier and A the later, a corrected version of its unusually corrupt predecessor. In this case, however, I believe it can be definitely shown that A is actually the earlier. The proof for this rests on a curious misprint. In the variant issue B, the text of the last and first lines on D6 verso — D7 recto, respectively, reads as shown in Plate 5. The last word on D6 is "capitu" and the first on D7 is "ah*uius*modi." This makes no sense; indeed there are no such Latin words. In Morgan 727, the same text reads as in Plate 6.[21] Morgan 733, though it belongs to the same issue, shows that a disturbance in the type has taken place on D7 recto, where the text now reads as shown in Plate 7.

What took place, apparently, is this:[22] in Morgan 733, the "l" had dropped out of the forme, the "s" in the line below was shoved out of place and the line "loosened up." When the compositor of the variant issue B came to set up his text, he had before him some copy with the readings as in Morgan 733. In his ignorance of Latin, he did not realize what had happened and merely set up what he saw; thus, instead of printing *capitula huiusmodi*, the compositor set up the type with the impossible reading *capitu ahuiusmodi*. This appears to be the obvious, indeed the only plausible, explanation for this misprint, and thus the variant issue B must be the later one.[23]

If then A is the earlier, how can we explain the existence of B? The answer for this, it seems to me, is that de Worde originally did not print enough sheets for the first four quires; possibly he planned to increase the size of the edition while the book was at press, which amounts to much the same thing. In any case, he was forced to reprint these quires and handed over the copy to one of his lesser helpers with the result which we have seen. The reason for these variants is thus an accidental one, since the printer originally failed to produce the necessary number of sheets to complete all the copies in this edition.

It is hoped that the present paper has adequately covered the problems with which it has sought to deal. It is, of course, common knowledge that the fifteenth-century printers did not keep the sheets

[21] This is also the reading of the Harvard and Gordan-Goodhart copies.

[22] An exactly similar case is noted by Greg, op. cit., p. 37, example VI. See also my paper "Caxton studies," *supra*. These are adequate examples of variants brought about by physical causes, in this case accidental destruction of type.

[23] There is, also, another instance which shows that A is the earlier. On D5 verso, line 2, B has "nisiq*uam*" (an impossible form) while A correctly has "nu*m*quam." Apparently the compositor of B misread the "ū" of A as "ſi" which, when the stroke marking the contraction is slightly bent, it closely resembles.

for the various "issues" together but mixed them up indiscriminately.[24] While this complicates matters for the bibliographer, it presents no fresh problems which cannot be solved by proper application.

[24] On this point, see McKerrow, op. cit., p. 209 ff. and Greg, op. cit., p. 42 ff.

(From *Bookmen's Holiday, Notes and Studies
Written in Tribute to Harry Miller Lydenberg.*
The New York Public Library
(1943), pp. 459-474).

# CHAPTER B10

## THE BINDING OF BOOKS PRINTED BY
## WILLIAM CAXTON

WITH the possible exception of Ludwig Hain's *Repertorium Bibliographicum*, Stuttgart & Paris, 1826-1838, no bibliographical reference work has stood the test of time more successfully than William Blades's *The Life and Typography of William Caxton*, London, 1861-1863. Though I have from time to time found occasion to disagree with some of the observations made by Blades and noted a few minor inaccuracies, no one is more aware of the enormous labor and great learning which the eminent bibliographer of Caxton has bestowed upon his work than I am. It is not, then, for the sake of offering further criticism of minor points in this book but rather in the hope of supplementing it that I should like to call the reader's attention to a deduction made by Blades which the evidence afforded by the books themselves seems to contradict.

Blades was clearly of the opinion that, as soon as the printed sheets had dried sufficiently, they were placed in the hands of the binders. He states (II, p. xlviii): "[They] went, without further process, from the press side to the hands of the Binder." As proof for this he adds: "The edition of 'Eneydos,' 1490, was hurried through the Binder's hands so soon after the first section (which, containing the prologue and table, necessarily went to press last) was printed, that all the leaves of that section, in every copy I have seen, show a very bad 'set off' from the type on the opposite pages." Two types of bindings, according to Blades,[1] were employed by Caxton's binder; for the smaller books and those requiring less durable bindings, the binder was supposed to have used vellum wrappers while the larger—or more important—volumes were encased in stamped leather over wooden boards. While E. Gordon Duff[2] denied that Caxton ever

[1] Op. cit., II, p. lii.

[2] *William Caxton*, Chicago, 1905, pp. 84-85. Blades had suggested (II, p. 221) that the Bodleian copy of the second edition of the *Directorium Sacerdotum* was "still in the original parchment wrapper, as issued from Caxton's workshop." As to this, Duff remarks (p. 75): "All evidence goes to prove that Caxton never made use of parchment or vellum as a binding material, and in the case of the present book it is quite clear, on close examination, that it has been made up from two imperfect copies, and that the binding is not earlier than the seventeenth century."

made use of vellum for binding purposes, he also suggested that Caxton "numbered bookbinders amongst his workmen and issued his books ready bound." All genuine Caxton bindings, he maintained, were of stamped brown calf over wooden boards. These suggestions have been generally accepted by students of the earliest English printing.[3] However, Duff did not indicate how soon after the completion of the printing the books were bound, and it is with this small point that we are at present concerned.

It must be recognized at the outset, of course, that Caxton's printing practice was probably quite different from that employed on the Continent, at least as it was practised there in the latter part of the fifteenth century. Caxton was far removed from the centers of the new art; his books tell us that his technique remained primitive and show that only reluctantly and slowly did he utilize the improvements which took place on the Continent after his departure from Bruges.[4] Furthermore, Caxton was concerned only with printing books for local demand; their very contents made them non-exportable. Not a single item in the entire list of books printed at Westminster could have been designed for sale abroad; indeed very few would have been acceptable in the northern counties, let alone Scotland. While we cannot, therefore, base our beliefs as to how and when Caxton bound his books on principles known to have been employed on the other side of the Channel, it may nevertheless be useful to see what, it is generally considered, was the method followed there. As for such methods, we find a wonderful difference of opinion among modern bibliographers; these range from Gruel's assertion[5] that printers always bound their own books, through Haebler's belief[6] that some firms probably sold all their books bound, to

---

[3] Compare, for example, R. B. McKerrow. *An Introduction to Bibliography for Literary Students,* Oxford, 1927, pp. 121-122.

[4] According to Blades (II, p. xlii), it was not until 1480 that Caxton was able to print with lines of an even length although this was common practice abroad long before this. Caxton did not make use of printed signatures till the following year (Blades, II, p. 80) though they appear in books printed in Cologne during the time of his stay there (1471-1472). Title-pages were not used by Caxton, though they do occur in the works of his successor, Wynkyn de Worde.

[5] Léon Gruel. *Manuel historique et bibliographique de l'amateur de reliures,* Paris, 1887, I, p. 17: "tous les livres, *sans exception,* aussitôt qu'ils venaient d'être imprimés, étaient reliés par les libraires qui les éditaient."

[6] Konrad Haebler. *Handbuch der Inkunabelkunde,* Leipzig, 1925, p. 179: "Man hat ja annehmen zu müssen geglaubt, dass sogar manche Firmen der Wiegendruckzeit ihre Erzeugnisse in gebundener Form auf den Markt gebracht haben."

Goldschmidt's contention[7] that all printers bound a few of their
books for immediate sale or for display purposes but that the greatest number were sold unbound. It seems likely that Goldschmidt's
conclusions are correct in regard to the big publishing houses which
appeared towards the close of the century; certainly the business
records of the Kobergers[8] bear him out in some detail. That this was
universally true and that the smaller firms generally sold their books
unbound (or in sheets), I would hesitate to assert in view of the fact
that Goldschmidt's theory is not conceded by many of his colleagues,
not even for the Kobergers or Aldus Manutius,[9] the greatest printers
of their day. While it is nevertheless probable that the bigger houses
often sold their books in sheets, it is equally certain that some form
of "edition" binding was known in the fifteenth century; it is only
reasonable to suppose that the smaller printers—having few or no
representatives to retail their publications—probably sold their copies
bound at the printing office.

If, then, we agree with Duff and others that Caxton habitually sold
his books already bound, must we follow Blades in the belief that
Caxton had these books bound as soon as the sheets came off the
press? With this belief I hardly concur. The proof which Blades
brings forward in the case of the *Eneydos* appears very unconvinc-
ing. Indeed it seems impossible to conclude that the set-off to which
Blades refers could possibly have come about in the manner he suggests. Assuming that the edition consisted of but one hundred copies
(the smallest number for which Haebler[10] could discover any evi-

[7] E. Ph. Goldschmidt. *Gothic & Renaissance Bookbindings*, London, 1928, p.
36 ff. He maintains that "in the fifteenth and sixteenth centuries books were always
sold all over Europe in rough, unfolded sheets, and never otherwise." For the booksellers' practice at a somewhat later date, see the recent interesting paper by William A. Jackson, *Notes on English "Publishers' Bindings" of the Sixteenth and
Seventeenth Centuries,* in: *Bookmen's Holiday, Notes and Studies Written in Tribute
to Harry Miller Lydenberg,* New York, 1943, pp. 483-488.

[8] The Koberger business correspondence is printed on pp. v-cliv of Oscar Hase's
*Die Koberger,* Leipzig, 1885.

[9] Compare Friedrich Bräuninger. *Verlegereinbände bei Aldus,* in *Jahrbuch der
Einbandkunst,* III, pp. 54-60, and Adolph Schmidt. *Verlegereinbände Anton Koberg-
ers zu Nürnberg in der Landesbibliothek zu Darmstadt,* in: *Archiv für Schreib-und
Buchwesen,* II, pp. 113-129.

[10] Haebler, op. cit., pp. 142-145. He adds: "So kleine Auflagen wurden aber wohl
nur da hergestellt, wo mit dem Druck erst schüchterne Anfänge gemacht wurden,
den Unternehmern geschäftliche Erfahrung fehlte oder ein kaufmännisches Interesse
überhaupt nicht in Frage kam." None of these reasons is suitable here. Haebler suggests that the usual size of an edition at this time was between 400 and 500 copies.

dence) and that the binders immediately proceeded to bind the sheets without waiting for the ink to dry thoroughly, it may be true that the first few copies would show such set-offs but that all of them would do so, as Blades suggests, seems unlikely. By the time the binders (if indeed Caxton had more than one) had finished their preparatory work on the first dozen or so copies, the ink on the remainder would very probably have been quite dry.[11] What the set-off does indicate with any certainty—and it indicates nothing more than this—is that the sheets were folded soon after printing, a simple enough operation and not necessarily a part of the binder's tasks at all. The sheets may have merely been folded in this manner preparatory to storing them.

If we turn to the extant Caxtons themselves, there seems to be ample evidence to prove that the printer did *not* bind all the books of an edition directly it was off the press. A glance either through Blades or Seymour de Ricci's *A Census of Caxtons*, [English] Bibliographical Society, 1909, reveals many important hints; among these, one may note numerous instances where several Caxtons are recorded as having been (or still are) bound together in an "original binding." For example, at the Whitley Beaumont sale (Hodgson's, November 23, 1906, Cat. no. 188) Quaritch obtained for the British Museum a volume that originally contained three Caxtons (the *Royal Book* of c. 1488, the *Doctrinal of Sapience* of May 7, 1489, and the *Book of Good Manners* of May 11, 1487) in the "original leather binding." At a sale at Sotheby's (May 20-21, 1909) there was sold a volume in the original Caxton binding containing books printed by him between March 24, 1479 and August 12, 1481. De Ricci notes (under 74.2) that the Huntington copy of Lydgate's *Stans Puer ad Mensam* "was in original vellum wrapper after 'Paruus Catho II'" (de Ricci 14.1). In addition one may note that all three of the known copies of *Cato* III (de Ricci 15) were at one time or another bound with other Caxtons while the five Caxtons owned by R. Johnson in 1510 (de Ricci, p. 168) appear to have been purchased in sheets and bound together at that time.[12] There are other examples. This seems

[11] It would have taken a binder at least a day to bind a copy in stamped leather over wooden boards, though he might have bound several in vellum wrappers in the same length of time. It is hardly likely, then, that the set-off came about as the result of binding (except possibly in the first few copies bound) but rather as the result of folding the sheets. This, obviously, may or may not have been done by the binder but in itself it does not prove that the copies were bound immediately after printing.

[12] Apparently the purchaser could, if he chose, buy several different works and

to give adequate proof that Caxton did not bind all copies as soon as they were off the press but rather that he stored the sheets, binding them only as requested by the purchaser. The fortunate discovery of a previously unknown Caxton in 1931 gives added weight to this reasoning. In the October issue of *Apollo* of that year, W. Loftus Hare described the newly-found copy of Lydgate's *Pilgrimage of the Soul*, then in the possession of Messrs. William H. Robinson, Ltd. The peculiar interest which this copy holds for us is that signature e belongs not to the *Pilgrimage* (printed June 1483) but to Lydgate's *Life of our Lady* (printed about 1484). It is difficult to believe that this error is due to the eighteenth-century re-binder; it is much more likely that the mistake originally took place in Caxton's workshop where the binder by accident picked up the wrong signature e from the shelves. The books are, of course, very similar, representing two works (in verse) by the same author, printed in types displaying only the minutest differences (Blades 4 and 4*), and produced about the same time. Since these sheets have such a great superficial resemblance, it is not at all surprising to find the binder mistaking the sheets of the one book for the other.[13]

---

have Caxton bind them up together. This, of course, reduced the cost of binding considerably. This practice was not confined to Caxton; see my paper, *Notes on a Pynson Volume*, in: *The Library*, December, 1937, pp. 261-267.

[13] A very similar instance occurs in a volume belonging to the present writer. This is a copy of the Italian translation of the *Vitae et Sententiae Philosophorum* of Diogenes Laertius, printed in Florence by Francesco Bonaccorsi and Antonio di Francesco, July 5, 1488; although bound in a modern vellum binding, my copy is quite large, measuring 217 x 142 mm. compared with the British Museum copy which measures but 201 x 132 mm. In the upper right hand corner (recto) of the first leaf of each quire (except for the first such gathering which of course has its printed indication), a fifteenth-century hand has written "filoxofi." This was obviously intended to identify the unbound quires as belonging to the *Vitae*; when the sheets reached the binder's hands, it was apparently expected that this word would be cut off in the trimming. However, this copy was not cut down sufficiently to eliminate the "filoxofi" entirely, though in one or two instances it has been partially cut into. Although signature f is so marked in my copy, it does *not* belong to the *Vitae* but to the Phalaris *Epistolae* (also in Italian) produced by the same printers on May 17, 1488. Thus despite this precaution the same mistake has occurred as in the Robinson copy of the *Pilgrimage*. It also proves that all copies of the *Vitae* and of the *Epistolae* were not bound directly after printing. [It may seem strange to find the Venetian form (with the characteristic "x") for "philosopho" in a Florentine book, but this does not necessarily indicate that the book was first bound in Venice. Bonaccorsi's partner was a Venetian—here he signs his name as Antonius Venetus—and by 1499 he had returned to that city and had set up another press. The British Museum's incunabula catalogue (VI, p. xvii) suggests that Antonio was doubtless the foreman of Bonaccorsi and this may account for the form "filoxofi" in my copy.]

If further proof be needed that Caxton did not bind the copies at once but kept the sheets unbound until they were required, this is conclusively furnished by other facts which may be gleaned from Caxton's own bindings. In a paper published in *The Library* (*Three Notes on Caxton*, September, 1936, pp. 155-162), the present writer discussed at length the copy of the Boethius found by Blades at the King Edward VI Grammar School at St. Albans. From the covers of the original binding, Blades recovered "56 half-sheets of printed paper" which comprise fragments of books printed by Caxton (according to Blades) between 1477 and 1484. If Blades is correct, the Boethius (printed before 1479) could not have been bound before 1484. If my theory is accepted, namely that the Boethius may have been printed somewhat later (say 1481) and the *Life of our Lady* somewhat earlier (or about 1482), it still follows that the Boethius was not bound immediately upon completion of the printing.[14]

If, then, Caxton did not bind his books at once, one may enquire as to whether they were stored as assembled copies or by separate signatures. The *Pilgrimage of the Soul* certainly indicates that the unbound sheets were not stored as copies, for if they were it would be difficult to explain the presence of the quire from the *Life of our Lady* in the Robinson copy of the *Pilgrimage*. If the sheets for each signature were kept together, were they stored flat or folded? Here the evidence is not quite clear. Blades's discussion of the *Eneydos* tends to show, as we have seen, that the sheets were folded as soon as possible, indeed in this particular case too soon. Caxton's *Fayttes of Armes and of Chyualrye* seems to confirm this.[15] In this case the blank verso of folio 2 in most copies shows a set-off from folio 1 recto, which could only have resulted from the *folded* sheets having been stacked together when the ink was still wet. One should note that if the sheets had been piled up flat and not folded, the set-off of folio 1 recto would have appeared on 1 verso (that is, on the inner—not outer—forme; it is impossible to conclude that the wet sheets were invariably laid face to face and always with the printed surface opposite the blank

---

[14] It is noteworthy that Blades himself obtained, some time before 1879, a copy of the Boethius which was then "in the original stamped leather binding" (de Ricci 8.29). In the covers of this volume were found several leaves of the "so-called" second edition of the *Life of our Lady* (de Ricci 72). Thus at least two copies of this edition of Boethius are known which were not bound as soon as possible after printing. [Concerning these leaves see my papers *Three Notes &c.* (pp. 163-166) and *Two Caxton Problems*, in: *The Library*, December, 1939, pp. 268-271.]

[15] For further notes, see my paper *Caxton Studies, supra.*

page).[16] On the other hand, the copy of the *Cordiale* in the Pierpont Morgan Library may offer contradictory evidence. Here the inner forme of the third sheet of the fourth quire (27 verso-30 recto) shows a set-off from the outer (27 recto-30 verso). This certainly indicates that the sheets were at one time stacked flat but this may only have been a temporary condition prior to folding the sheets.

Contrary to what Blades suggests, we may thus safely deduce that Caxton did not send the sheets to the binders as soon as the book was off the press. As Goldschmidt has contended for the Continental presses, it seems certain that Caxton, following the usual fifteenth-century practice, had a few copies bound for immediate sale or for display and that the remaining sheets were stored until such a time as they were needed.

(From *PBSA* 38 (1944), pp. 1-8).

---

[16] Only in these two ways could the set-off of folio 1 recto appear on 2 verso, but the likelihood that it took place in the second manner described is so remote that it may safely be assumed that the set-offs are not the results of such happenings.

# CHAPTER B11

## THE FIFTEENTH-CENTURY EDITIONS OF PETRARCH'S *HISTORIA GRISELDIS* IN STEINHÖWEL'S GERMAN TRANSLATION

AMONG the recent acquisitions of the Pierpont Morgan Library, one of the most important was a copy of one of the two Ulm editions of Petrarch's *Historia Griseldis* in German.[1] In the course of cataloging the volume the present writer noted that, though much has been written not only about the various editions of this work but also about the press of the printer Johann Zainer, none of these accounts was accurate, and most, indeed, contained serious blunders. A correct list of the editions, together with a more detailed analysis of those printed in Ulm, thus seems desirable.[2]

## I

No fewer than ten[3] editions of Heinrich Steinhöwel's[4] translation of the *Historia Griseldis*[5] by Petrarch were printed in Germany in

[1] I wish to take this opportunity to thank Mr. Lessing J. Rosenwald for permitting his copy of this book (now forming part of the Rosenwald Collection in the Library of Congress) to be sent to New York for my perusal. This was a most thoughtful courtesy and greatly appreciated. Incidentally, the book is incorrectly listed in Margaret B. Stillwell's *Incunabula in American Libraries* (New York, 1940); Mr. Rosenwald's copy belongs to the edition listed as P 358, but this edition is not Hain 12815.

[2] The following are the sigla for references frequently made in the text: H—Ludwig Hain, *Repertorium bibliographicum* (Stuttgartiae, 1826-38); C—Walter Copinger, *Supplement to Hain's Repertorium bibliographicum* (London, 1895-1902); BMC—*Catalogue of Books Printed in the XVth Century Now in the British Museum* (London, 1908-35); GW—*Gesamtkatalog der Wiegendrucke* (Leipzig, 1925-38); Pr—Robert Proctor, *An Index to the Early Printed Books in the British Museum . . . . with Notes of Those in the Bodleian Library* (London, 1898-1903); Sch—Wilhelm Schreiber, *Manuel de l'amateur de la gravure sur bois et sur métal au XVe siècle* (Vol. V only; Leipzig, 1910).

[3] I have not taken into account, as not pertinent to the present study, the Low German edition (Sch 4920) printed at Lübeck, *ca.* 1483.

[4] For a useful short summary of Steinhöwel's career, see Karl Sudhoff's account in Arnold Klebs and Karl Sudhoff, *Die ersten gedruckten Pestschriften* (München, 1925), pp. 171-92.

[5] See Fr. von Westhenholz, *Die Griseldissage in der Literaturgeschichte* (Heidelberg, 1888).

the fifteenth century. They can be listed in the following order of appearance:

| I | H 12817 | Augsburg: G. Zainer, 1471 | Voulliéme-Berlin 4 |
|---|---------|---------------------------|--------------------|
| II | C 4716 | [Augsburg: G. Zainer, 1471/2][6] | BMC II:320 |
| III | H 12818 | Augsburg: J. Bämler, 1472 | Part of H 10005[7] |
| IV | C 4715 | [Ulm: J. Zainer, 1473] | Fiske, p. 53 (K 473)[8] |
| V | ....... | [Ulm: J. Zainer, 1473/4] | Fiske, p. 53 (KG 10) |
| VI | H 12819 | [Strassburg: H. Knoblochtzer], 1478 | Sch 4915 |
| VII | H 12815 | [Augsburg: J. Bämler, 1480] | Sch 4916[9] |
| VIII | C 4717 | [Strassburg: H. Knoblochtzer], 1482 | Sch 4917 |
| IX | H 12820 | Augsburg: J. Bämler, 1482 | Sch 4918 |
| X | H 12816 | [Augsburg: H. Schaur, 1497] | Sch 4919 |

The order of the editions can be determined with relative ease, since a printed date may be found in exactly half of them; and the others can be dated by typographical means and such other details as we are about to examine.

A mere glance at the bibliographical descriptions of these volumes will show that these editions fall into two distinct groups. In the first group, Nos. I–III, above, the text is headed by a note which reads in the first edition: "Diss ist ain epistel francisci petrarche / vō grosser stätikait ainer frowen. Grisel gehaissen."[10] The others all have a Prologue which reads (as in No. IV):

> So ich aber von stättikait / vnd getrüwer gemahelschafft / so manger frowen geschriben habe / vnd von kainer grössern v̄ber die grisel / von der franciscus petrarcha schrybet / doch vsz johañis boccacij welsch in latin! vnd von mir usz latin in tütsch gebracht! so bedunket mich nit vnbillich sȳn das sie ŏch bȳ andern erlüchten frowen / waren hystorien geseczet werde. Ob ŏch sölliche geschicht / in warhait beschenhē oder v̄m ander frowen manūg zů gedult geseczet werden

The explanation for this somewhat curious preliminary paragraph has been previously pointed out in the catalog of the Fiske Collec-

[6] Compare Ernst Voulliéme's notes in his facsimile edition of No. IV published in *Die Incunabel in ihren Hauptwerken* (Potsdam, n.d.).

[7] See *ibid.*; BMC II:331; and James F. Ballard, *A Catalogue of the Medieval and Renaissance Manuscripts and Incunabula in the Boston Medical Library* (Boston, 1944), pp. 120–21.

[8] Cornell University Library, *Catalogue of the Petrarch Collection Bequeathed by Willard Fiske*, compiled by Mary Fowler (Oxford, 1916). This is Sch 4914; for facsimile, see n. 6.

[9] According to Konrad Burger, *The Printers and Publishers of the XV. Century with Lists of Their Works* (London, 1902), p. 281, this is C 4714 but is attributed to Sorg's press.

[10] Quoted from the facsimile given on Tafel II of Klebs-Sudhoff, *op. cit.*

tion at Cornell. It seems reasonably certain that this edition was intended (in part at least) to be bound after and sold with Steinhöwel's translation of Boccaccio's *De claris mulieribus*, printed by Johann Zainer in the same year.[11] A certain number of copies were, apparently, reserved for separate sale,[12] and all subsequent editions of this work were taken from this edition. Thus, all these have this same preliminary note, though deprived of its connection with the Boccaccio and thus somewhat unsuitable. Since No. II, above, contains the earlier Introduction, the chronological position of this undated edition seems reasonably assured.

The Ulm edition (No. IV) was, as we have seen, intended to supplement the Boccaccio of 1473 and can thus be assigned to that year. The other Ulm edition, concerning which we shall have more to say later, was clearly printed subsequently to the one just mentioned. This is proved by the woodcuts, which in this edition show breaks not visible in the other, as well as by the state of the type. In the first state of Zainer's type 1:116, the *h* has a curve which ends on the line; this was gradually superseded by a tailed *h*, which, toward the end of 1473, replaced the original form.[13] The edition No. IV contains both forms of the *h*, while No. V has only the later (tailed) variety. Clearly, then, No. IV preceded No. V.

Number X is attributed to Schaur's press by Schreiber; since this printer was active in Augsburg (where, it is clear from the evidence noted by Schreiber, the book originated[14]) only after 1490, this is certainly the latest of the series. For No. VII the evidence is less

[11] Albert Schramm, *Der Bilderschmuck der Frühdrucke* (Leipzig, 1920–38), V, 3, believes the Petrarch was printed before the Boccaccio, an opinion also held by Ernst Weil, *Der ulmer Holzschnitt im 15. Jahrhundert* (Berlin, 1923), p. 24. Arthur M. Hind, *An Introduction to a History of the Woodcut with a Detailed Survey of Work Done in the Fifteenth Century* (Boston and New York, 1935), II, 305, suggests the Petrarch was printed "as a sort of epilogue" to the Boccaccio, which is also the belief of Erwin Rosenthal, "Zu den Anfängen der Holzschnittillustration in Ulm," *Monatshefte für Kunstwissenschaft*, VI (1913), 185–99. Whenever the cuts may have been made, it seems certain from the Introduction to the Petrarch just cited that this was designed to follow the Boccaccio and was probably printed later.

[12] Possibly the second Ulm edition only was meant for separate sale.

[13] For details concerning the type, see Voulliéme's notes in the facsimile; also BMC II:518 and Pr. I, 161.

[14] Cf. Sch 4919 and 3803. The latter book, *Somnia Danielis* (GW 7914), is signed in full by Schaur, Augsburg, 1497, and contains the same title-cut found in the Petrarch.

conclusive, though the date is given as 1480 by Brunet,[15] Schreiber, and Schramm;[16] and there seems to be no apparent reason to question this.

This, then, is the order in which the editions appeared. Since all the bibliographers who have written on the *Historia Griseldis* have omitted one or the other of these editions,[17] annotated them incorrectly,[18] or attributed them to the wrong press,[19] this summary may be found useful.

## II

Although Schramm (*op. cit.*, V, 3) refers to the two Ulm editions as "die wenig von einander abweichenden Johann Zainer'schen Ausgaben," these two editions differ from one another radically. They differ in these respects: the woodcut border on folio 1, the order in which the woodcuts appear, and the orthography throughout the texts. The second of these differences can be dismissed very briefly; in the second edition (No. V), the woodcuts listed in Schramm's work as Nos. 7 and 8 appear in the reverse—and, as the text proves, incorrect—order. The other two dissimilarities are considerably more interesting and important.

For the earlier of these two editions (No. IV), Zainer used the woodcut border which is reproduced by Schramm (Pl. 3, No. 5) and which also adorns the first printed leaf of his Latin edition of the *Historia Griseldis* (H 12814). In the foliage of this border may be found the coat-of-arms of the city of Ulm and that of Heinrich Steinhöwel.[20] The later edition, however, presents quite a different

[15] Jacques-Charles Brunet, *Manuel du libraire et de l'amateur de livres* (Paris, 1860–80), IV, 571; Hind, *op. cit.*, II, 306, gives the date as 1482.

[16] Schramm, *op. cit.*, III, 21.

[17] Schreiber, Hind, Sudhoff, Voulliéme, and Wegener (*Die Zainer in Ulm* [Strassburg, 1904], No. 33) did not know of No. V above; the Fiske Catalog omits No. II.

[18] Weil claimed the Ulm edition was the first in German; Schramm states that there are only slight differences between IV and V and that VII was Bämler's first edition; Elizabeth Mongan and Edwin Wolf, *The First Printers and Their Books* (Philadelphia, 1940), p. 32, suggest that No. V is earlier than No. IV, though Miss Mongan has since informed me that she, too, is now of the opinion that No. IV appeared first.

[19] Hain, Hind, Burger, and Brunet attribute No. VII to Sorg; Schramm, *op. cit.*, Vol. IV, lists no edition under Sorg in his bibliography.

[20] This coat-of-arms (hammers in saltire) has also been taken to be Zainer's; on this point see Hugh W. Davies, *Catalogue of a Collection of Early German Books in the Library of C. Fairfax Murray* (London, 1913), II, 526, No. 327. The appear-

border—that found also in the *De adhaerendo deo* (GW 582) of
Albertus Magnus.[21] This border does not contain either coat-of-arms;
it was probably selected for this very reason, as we shall have occasion to see later on.

The differences in the texts of the two editions can be shown most
easily by quoting the opening lines of the later edition; these can be
compared with those in the earlier edition already cited. In this
edition the preliminary matter reads:

¶ So ich aber von stätikait / vnd getreuwer gemahelschafft / so manger
frauwen geschriben habe / vnd von keiner grössern über die grisel / von der
frācisc⁹ petracha schreibet / doch ausz iohannis boccacij welsch in latein /
võ mir ausz latin in teutsch gebracht / so bedunket mich nit vnbillich sein
/ dz sie auch bei andern erleichten frauwen / waren hÿstorien geseczet werde.
Ob auch söliche geschicht / in warheit beschenhen oder vmb ander frauen
manug zů gedult geseczet werden [Morgan 38242].

Even this short extract will show that, though the first quotation is
rather Swabian (Alemmanic) in dialect and orthography, that cited
directly above is decidedly less so.[22]

In printing the following linguistic details the writer is well aware
that he thus exceeds the normal scope of a bibliographical paper, but
in this instance the matter is of such importance that it seems necessary to impose upon the reader's patience. In order to be as brief as
possible, only a few salient points will be noted.

The earlier edition, as we have seen, presents the text with the then

---

ance of Steinhöwel's portrait, together with this coat-of-arms, in the reprint of the
"tütsch Cronica" (1531), reproduced in Klebs-Sudhoff, p. 170, seems to prove that
the hammers in saltire (suitable for his name) belonged to Steinhöwel. See also
Voulliéme's note in the facsimile edition.

21 Schramm, *op. cit.*, Vol. V, Pl. 2, No. 4.

22 To my knowledge, only Weil (*op. cit.*, p. 104, n. 29) has noted this difference
in dialect between the two Ulm editions; he says: "Auch dialektisch ist der Text
leicht verändert." Wegener, *op. cit.*, pp. 8 ff., notes that the two Zainer editions
of the *Pestbuch* (Arnold C. Klebs, *Incunabula scientifica et medica* [Bruges, 1938],
No. 933.1 [1473] and No. 933.3 [1482]) differ in their orthography. Concerning the
later of these two editions, Victor Scholderer has said (Sir William Osler, *Incunabula
medica. A Study of the Earliest Printed Medical Books 1467–1480* [Bibliographical
Society, Illus. Mono. No. XIX (1923)], p. 99, No. 143): "As this edition is not in
the dialect of Ulm and therefore differs entirely from Zainer's 1473 edition (No.
29 above), it was perhaps printed at Augsburg or elsewhere. If it is really by
Zainer, it cannot be earlier than 1478-80." Since Klebs lists no edition of this
work as printed in Augsburg, it is not impossible that this book also was produced
in Ulm by Johann Zainer for sale in Augsburg.

current Swabian orthography; the later is more modern in this respect.[23] The following words may be specially singled out:

| No. IV | No. V | Shift |
|---|---|---|
| vsz, vff, husz | ausz, auff, hausz | u)au[24] |
| syn, din, lyb, wyb | sein, dein, leib, weib | i(y))ei[25] |
| ain, kain, haim[26] | ein, kein, heim | ai)ei[27] |
| och, ogen[28] | auch, augen | o)au |
| (i)uch | euch | iu)eu |

Thus, for the older orthography of No. IV, we find, with almost equal regularity, the newer in No. V.[29]

An examination of the fifteenth-century German books printed in Ulm and Augsburg (the principal Swabian places of printing) available in the Pierpont Morgan Library,[30] together with the ex-

[23] An analysis of the Swabian dialect and orthography found in early printed books is included in Friedrich Kauffmann, *Geschichte der schwäbischen Mundart im Mittelalter und in der Neuzeit* (Strassburg, 1890), pp. 293 ff. In the intervening fifty years since the publication of this work, many of the incunabula have been redated, so that in certain details Kauffmann's book needs supplementing. In general, however, his facts are quite clear.

[24] Kauffmann, *op. cit.*, p. 298: "Ausserhalb Augsburg's ist der entwicklungsgang genau derselbe gewesen, nur dass die drucker von Ulm . . . um ein paar jahre zurückbleiben. Johann Zainer . . . . lässt die neuen diphthonge nicht zu." Cf. also Paul-Gierach, *Mittelhochdeutsche Grammatik* (Halle, 1929), p. 23, § 21, Anm.

[25] *i(y)* is usual, though in city ordonnances of Augsburg (1276) one occasionally finds *ie*; *i* before *r* often became *ie* (thus, No. IV sometimes has *ier* where No. V prints *ir*). Cf. Kauffmann, *op. cit.*, p. 64.

[26] Once No. IV has "hain." For the characteristic change in the Swabian dialect from *m* to *n*, see Otto Mausser, *Mittelhochdeutsche Grammatik* (München, 1932), p. 25.

[27] Kauffmann, *op. cit.*, p. 88: "Die schreibung *ai* ist in den denkmälern schwäbischer herkunft constant." In Augsburg the *ei* forms begin to appear *ca.* 1276. See also the interesting note by Niclas von Wyle (1478), who states that, though his predecessors wrote *ai*, it was now customary in chancery writing to use *ei*. Occasionally one finds in the Ulm books *ein*, *-heit*, etc.; for this form in Swabian, see Paul Gierach, *op. cit.*, p. 78, § 110, Anm.

[28] Cf. Mausser, *op. cit.*, p. 27. The letter *u* sometimes appears as *o* in Swabian, and thus No. IV occasionally has "wonder," "sonder," etc.; for this, see Kauffmann, *op. cit.*, p. 75.

[29] To quote another example, No. IV, f. 7, has: "du macht mit dÿnen dingen dÿne recht gebruchen / on mÿnen willen. wañ als ich an dem ÿngang in dÿn hus mÿn alte klaider abdet! also zoch ich ŏch ab mÿnen frÿen willen vnd aigen begierd!" For this, No. V, f. 6ᵛ, prints: "du magst mit deinen dingen dein recht gebruchen on meinen willen! wan als ich an dem ÿngang in dein hausz mein alte kleider abdet! also zoch ich auch ab meinen freien willen vñ eigen begird!"

[30] These are listed in Ada Thurston and Curt Bühler, *Check List of Fifteenth Century Printing in the Pierpont Morgan Library* (New York, 1939), pp. 26–34 and 41–43.

tensive numbers of facsimiles, bibliographical descriptions, and re-productions of specific pages found in many books of reference, reveals certain interesting and significant facts. Practically all the Ulm books printed in the 1470's preserve the old forms; it was not until the middle 1480's[31] that the new spelling gained ascendancy—and even then it did not entirely replace the older, and more characteristically Swabian orthography. On the other hand, those printed in Augsburg show quite a different tendency. Although the earliest books in German, such as the *Apollonius* (GW 2273) and the *Historia Griseldis* (No. I above) of 1471, present the old spellings, these tend to disappear and the modern High German forms are gradually introduced. Probably the fact that Augsburg lay on the borders of Bavaria, where a different dialect prevailed, and that this city was rather more progressive than Ulm accounts for this trend. After 1473 the typically Swabian forms are quite unusual in the Augsburg books.[32] Thus the second Ulm edition of the *Historia Griseldis* is, from a dialectal point of view, much closer to the books produced at that time in Augsburg than to those printed in its own place of origin. One may well ask why this change was made in this edition.

It is, of course, a matter of common knowledge that the two Zainers —Johann of Ulm and Günther of Augsburg—were probably kinsmen;[33] some authorities have even represented them as brothers.[34] Whatever their relationship may have been, it could hardly have been much closer than that which existed between their respective printing houses. Günther, it is known, not only provided Johann with the models for his types but also with the "Boccaccio Meister," who supplied the latter with woodcuts—if the historians of the fine arts are correct.[35] In turn, each reprinted, with the utmost fidelity, works previously produced by the other press. Finally, Steinhöwel

[31] The appearance of two new printers, Holle and Dinckmut, takes place (perhaps significantly) about this time.

[32] As Kauffmann (*op. cit.*, p. 294) points out, the process of diphthongization was practically completed at Augsburg by 1473.

[33] Wegener, *op. cit.*, p. 1; Schramm, *op. cit.*, V, 3; Lawrence C. Wroth, *A History of the Printed Book* (New York, 1938), p. 67.

[34] Mongan and Wolf, *op. cit.*, p. 29; so also Albert Schramm, "Günther Zainer, Augsburgs erster Drucker," *Werden und Wirken, ein Festgruss Karl W. Hiersemann zugesandt* (Leipzig, 1924), p. 363. The Augsburg "Steuerbuch" of 1471 shows that Günther had a brother living with him that year, and it is not unreasonable to presume that this may have been Johann.

[35] Cf. Weil, *op. cit.*, pp. 27 ff.; Hind, *op. cit.*, II, 287 ff. and 304 ff.; Hellmut Lehmann-Haupt, *Schwäbische Federzeichnungen* (Berlin and Leipzig, 1929), p. 130.

himself provides a link between the two Zainers, as this translator sometimes chose one, sometimes the other, to be the first to print his texts.[36]

The facts that we have been examining may be summarized as follows: As we have seen, the earlier edition of the Ulm *Historia Griseldis* was printed with the local Swabian orthography and decorated with a woodcut connecting this book with Ulm. The text of the later edition, in turn, indicates that the book may not have been printed for the purpose of selling it in Ulm. Since the books produced there both before and after the appearance of this edition of Petrarch's work preserved their local character, at least as far as the spelling was concerned, we have a very good indication that this was what the citizens of Ulm demanded. Of further significance is the fact that the woodcut border with the Ulm coat-of-arms was replaced in the later edition (No. V) by one not containing this tell-tale device. If we combine these details with our knowledge of the close relationship existing between the two Zainers, we can come to an interesting and quite plausible hypothesis. I suggest that it is quite possible that Günther saw the first Ulm edition and that he was so pleased with it that he commissioned Johann to reprint the text for him for sale in Augsburg. Doubtless in order to make this work more attractive to the burghers of Augsburg, this edition was printed with the new spelling then already in vogue at that city. Further, to avoid any more trouble with the local guilds than Günther had previously been obliged to face,[37] he may very well have suggested that the border with the Ulm arms be replaced by one not so likely to stir the animosity of the woodcutters' guild. This seems a likely explanation for the curious changes in the border and dialect in the second Ulm edition, and no other equally satisfactory explanation has presented itself to me. If I am right in this reconstruction, this would make the second edition of the German *Historia Griseldis* printed by Johann Zainer one of the earliest books produced solely for export.

(From *The Library Quarterly* 15 (1945), pp. 231-236).

[36] Rosenthal, *op. cit., passim*: Klebs-Sudhoff, *op. cit.*, pp. 174–83.

[37] Georg W. Zapf, *Augsburgs Buchdruckergeschichte* (Augsburg, 1788–91), I, vii ff.; Lehmann-Haupt, *op. cit.*, p. 134.

# CHAPTER B12

## SOME DOCUMENTS CONCERNING THE
## TORRESANI AND THE ALDINE PRESS

THOUGH half a century has passed since publication of the diary of Marino Sanuto was first undertaken (*I Diarii di Marino Sanuto*, Venice, 1879–1903), these volumes do not seem to have been carefully searched for items of interest to the history of printing in Venice. It is not surprising, therefore, to find that the diary contains several notations of importance concerning Andrea Torresano di Asola, his family, and the Aldine press.[1] These are here reprinted together with explanatory notes in order to make them more readily available to students of early printing.[2]

In three instances, Rinaldo Fulin ('Documenti per servire alla storia della tipografia veneziana' in *Archivio veneto*, xxiii, 1882, pp. 84–212) has cited parallel extracts from official documents concerning Torresano. The comparable statements in Sanuto's diary have nevertheless been printed here, not only because they are short and add some incidental information but also because they complete the notations in the diary[3] concerning the press subsequent to the death of Aldus and offer evidence for the accuracy of Sanuto's notations.

[1] For full bibliography, see *Der Buchdruck des 15. Jahrhunderts, eine bibliographische Übersicht*, Berlin, 1929–36, under the headings Venice (pp. 269–73), Aldus Manutius (pp. 281–7), and Andreas Torresanus (pp. 291–2). The following books have been chiefly consulted: Antoine Augustin Renouard, *Annales de l'imprimerie des Alde*, Paris, 1834; Ambroise Firmin-Didot, *Alde Manuce et l'hellénisme à Venise*, Paris, 1875; Mario Ferrigni, *Aldo Manuzio*, Milan, 1925; Domenico Bernoni, *Dei Torresani, Blado e Ragazzoni, celebri stampatori a Venezia e Roma nel XV e XVI secolo*, Milan, 1890. I have been unable to see the article by P. Molmenti on 'La famiglia di Andreas Torresanus' in *Illustrazione bresciana* (v. 1906) but his later work (*Storia di Venezia nella vita privata*, 1910–18) gives no additional information. Indeed, in this work (ii. 270) Molmenti states that Torresano died in 1521.

[2] I should here like to thank two of my former teachers, Professors Alfred R. Bellinger and Angelo Lipari of Yale University, for the generous way in which they have invariably replied to all queries I have put to them not only in the preparation of the present paper but on every other occasion that I have consulted them. I am also obliged to Dr. Arthur E. Neergaard of New York City for kindly placing at my disposal his splendid collection of Aldines.

[3] There are several notations in Sanuto's diary about the Torresani (chiefly records of payments) which are of no interest to us. These may be found in the following places: xxii. 677; xxxviii. 179; xlvii. 555; l. 270; lii. 331.

That Sanuto's entries are correct in every detail cannot be questioned. Not only have we the official confirmations as cited by Fulin, but it is known that Sanuto was not only a personal friend both of Aldus and Torresano but also that he was, in all probability, a member[4] of the 'Aldi Neacademia'.

Although the biography of Andrea Torresano has been the subject of special studies,[5] it may be useful to review briefly the chief facts about his life. Andrea was born on 4 March 1451 in the town of Asola not far from Mantua. It is believed that he came to Venice about the year 1475, shortly after his marriage to Lambertina Battaglia[6] by whom he had three children: Maria, Giovanni Francesco, and Federico. His first appearance as a printer occurred in October 1479, as a partner of Petrus de Plasiis and Bartholomaeus de Blauis.[7] From 1481 he worked in collaboration with Bartholomaeus and Thomas de Blauis and Maphaeus de Paterbonis, while after 1486 he is found working mostly alone either as a printer or publisher. After his daughter Maria married Aldus Manutius in 1499, Andrea continued to carry on his own business as a separate undertaking until 1508, when, to all intents and purposes, he appears to have merged his firm with that of his son-in-law's.[8] Upon the death of Aldus (6 February 1515),[9] Torresano with the assistance of his sons

[4] See Renouard, p. 385; Ferrigni, p. 144; Firmin-Didot, pp. 469–70; Bernoni, p. 91; so also A. J. V. Le Roux de Lincy, *Researches concerning Jean Grolier*, New York, The Grolier Club, 1907, p. 33.

[5] Since the appearance of the works by Renouard and Bernoni, little search seems to have been made in the archives for facts concerning Andrea Torresano. For example, Ester Pastorello, *Tipografi, Editori, Librai a Venezia nel secolo XVI*, Florence, 1924, p. vii, states: 'Per i Manuzi e i Torresani, sarebbe stata infatti fatica 'troppo ardua, e quasi sicuramente inutile, quella di cercare nuovi contributi all' 'opera del Renouard e dei suoi integratori.'

[6] Apostolo Zeno, in his preface to the *Epistole di Cicerone*, Venice, 1732, p. x, states that her epitaph read: 'Lambertinae—uxori optimae et castissimae—cum qua vixit annos XL sine lite—Andreas Turrisanus ab Asula—librariae artis instaurator—P. M. MDXX idibus julii.'

[7] The *Catalogue of Books Printed in the XVth Century now in the British Museum*, vol. v, p. xxv, states that 'we know nothing of his work before August, 1480'. However, the *Gesamtkatalog der Wiegendrucke* lists under no. 5132 a *Breviarium Romanum*, which was printed on 12 October 1479 by Andrea Torresano and the two printers above named, according to the colophon.

[8] The Pliny *Epistolae* of November 1508 is the first book to contain the phrase 'In aedibus Aldi et Andreae Asulani Soceri' and this was regularly used thereafter, even after the death of Aldus. After the death of Torresano, it was changed to read 'In aedibus haeredum Aldi et Andreae Asulani Soceri'.

[9] On 8 February 1515 Sanuto made the following entry in his diary (xix. 425): 'In questa matina, hessendo morto zà do zorni qui domino Aldo Manutio romano,

undertook the management of the Aldine press until his own death, which is generally stated—incorrectly, as we shall see—to have taken place in 1529. With these historical facts in mind, we may turn to the documents themselves.

I

25 February 1517 (Diary, vol. xxiii, col. 604):

In questa mattina fo pubblichà in Rialto una termination fata per la Signoria, autor sier Jacomo Simitecolo cao di XL amator di dotrina e di lettere greche: come hessendo compita la gratia fu concessa a Aldo stampador, tutti possano stampar in greco e portar libri grechi in questa terra, senza pena alcuna a venderli.

Though Fulin (no. 213) cites the official decree, this includes no note of the part played by Giacomo Semitecolo. Semitecolo was a man of considerable prominence in the first quarter of the sixteenth century being not only a 'capo dei quaranti' as noted but also a 'savio agli ordini', a member of the Quarantia Criminale, a bursar of Padua, and a captain in the Venetian fleet. As a lover of learning he is not particularly noted, though Sanuto does enter on 20 February 1517 (vol. xxiii, col. 593) the following notice, apparently a part of the proceeding for the revocation of the privilege:

Item, sier Jacomo Semitecolo cao di XL, fe' lezer un' altra parte, che si stampi i libri greci per cadauno, nè se li possi far gratia, aziò quelli hanno tal gratie non li tengano in gran precio, ut in parte.

As Fulin has suggested, the privilege which was cancelled is probably the one for which Aldus applied on 25 February 1496 (Fulin, no. 41—a twenty-year concession for printing in Greek) rather than the more general one which he obtained on 17 October 1502.[10] Although

'optimo humanista et greco, qual era zenero di Andrea d'Asolo stampador, il 'qual ha fato imprimer molte opere latine et greche ben corrette, et fate le epistole 'davanti intitolate a molti, tra le qual assai operete a mi Marin Sanudo dedicoe, 'compose una gramatica molto excelente, hor è morto, stato molti zorni amalato. 'Et per esser stà preceptor dei signori de Carpi et fato di la casa di Pii, ordinò il suo 'corpo fosse portato a sepelir a Carpi, e la moglie e figliuoli andasseno ad habitar 'ivi, dove queli signori li deteno certe possessioni. Et il corpo in chiesa di San 'Patrinian posto, con libri atorno ivi fo fato le esequie e una oration in soa laude 'per Rafael Regio lector publico in questa cità in humanità; et il corpo posto poi 'in uno deposito, fino si mandi via.' See also Firmin-Didot, pp. 396–7.
[10] See the notation in Sanuto's diary (iv. 369): 'Fu posto, per li consieri, me 'fauctore, la gratia di Marco [sic] Aldo, romano, fa stampar libri, opere e cosse 'e letere nove, niun non stampi per X anni etc. Ave tuto il conseio.' Marco appears

the printing of Greek texts was thus made possible for all printers
in Venice by this act of the Signoria, there is little indication that
other printers hurried to avail themselves of this right.[11] In order to
keep control of this branch of the printing business, Torresano made
use of a different expedient, namely by taking out patents for the
exclusive right to print specified books.

## II

### 30 July 1520 (Diary, vol. xxix, col. 71):

Fu posto, per li Consieri e Cai, una gratia di Andrea di Axola stampador di
libri, qual vol stampar le Deche di Tito Livio, et le opere di Cicero corettissime,
che per anni 10 altri che lui nel dominio nostro non li possino far stampar,
soto pena *ut in gratia*. Ave 127, 20; fu presa.

Fulin (no. 224) states that Torresano applied for a fifteen-year patent
because of the trouble and expense he had been put to ' per haver
mandato in diverse parte del mondo per haver libri vechii et corretti ' ;
the patent was granted '127 favorevoli, 20 contrari ed uno dubbio',
but only for ten years.

The Livy for which Torresano had sought the monopoly appears
to be the folio edition which was brought out in that same year
(Renouard, pp. 89–90). It is not certain, however, what Torresano
meant when he referred to the ' opere di Cicero '. *The Opera omnia*
were not printed as a single undertaking by Andrea, though he did
produce the *Rhetorica* and the *Epistolae ad Atticum etc.* in 1521
(Renouard, p. 93) and the *Epistolae familiares* in the following year
(Renouard, p. 94). The privilege may, of course, refer only to the
*Opera philosophica* (Renouard, pp. 97–8) printed in two volumes in
1523. However, to his description of this edition, Renouard adds the
following comment:

Ces deux volumes complètent l'ancien Cicéron donné avant Paul Manuce,
soit qu'on veuille le former absolument des premières éditions, soit qu'on y
admette les secondes ou les troisièmes, données jusqu'en 1522.

---

to be a misreading of the editors, since Renouard (p. 505) prints M°. apparently
a contraction for Maestro. Renouard dates the entry as 17 October 1501, but this
is an error for 1502.

[11] Frank Isaac (*An Index to the Early Printed Books in the British Museum*,
Part II, MDI–MDXX, Section II—Italy, London, 1938) lists no book printed in
Greek at Venice by any other printer than the Aldine press between 1517 and 1521.

Though Torresano may have felt—as Renouard did—that his edition of the *Opera philosophica* completed the Aldine edition of the *Opera omnia*,[12] we can scarcely believe that the Signoria would grant a privilege for books that had already appeared and for which patents had been previously issued. The *Orationes* of 1519 (Renouard, p. 86), for example, has the printed privilege as granted by the Signoria and by Pope Leo X on the title-pages. On the whole, it seems more likely that Torresano was only referring to works not previously printed by the Aldine press or to whatever new editions were then in preparation.

### III

2 June 1524 (Diary, vol. xxxvi, col. 382):

Fu posto, per li Consieri, concieder licentia ad Andrea di Axola stampador, di poter far stampar tutte le opere di Galien greco che più non è stà stampade, sotto pena a chi stampasse, etc. et questo per anni 10 *ut in supplicatione*. Fu presa. Ave: 137, 6, 1.

Extracts from Torresano's application were printed by Fulin (no. 242). Torresano had applied not only for permission to print the Galen because it was 'molto necessarie et utile a gli corpi umani per esser il principe de la medicina' but also for all the unprinted 'comenti greci in logica et in philosophia et in medicina' as well as the 'comenti greci in humanità et altri authori greci non più stampati'. The celebrated edition of Galen's *Works* in five volumes,[13] the largest single production of the Aldine press, appeared the following year (Renouard, pp. 101–2). Torresano also printed a number of the other works applied for in his petition: Hippocrates in 1526 (Renouard, p. 102); Paulus Aegineta in 1528 (Renouard, p. 106); commentaries on various Aristotelian works by Simplicius, Joannes Grammaticus (Philoponus), and others (Renouard, pp. 102–4); and commentaries on Demosthenes by Ulpianus (1527, Renouard, p. 104) and on Homer by Didymus (1528, Renouard, p. 105).

[12] Renouard (p. 86) points out that to complete the *Opera* the *Libri Oratorii* printed in 1514 (Renouard, pp. 65–6) must be included in order to secure all first editions. This work was, as we have seen, reprinted by Torresano in 1521.

[13] The privilege on the title-pages reads: 'Ne quis alius impune, aut Venetiis aut 'usquam locorum hos Galeni libros imprimat, & Clementis VII. Pont. Max. & 'Senatus Veneti decreto cautum est.' In each volume there is printed a copy of Pope Clement's letter granting to Torresano's sons the privilege to print the Galen; this letter bears the date, 27 January 1525.

## IV

29 February 1528 (Diary, vol. xlvi, col. 656):

Fu posto per li Consieri, poi leto una gratia di heriedi del qu. missier Aldo romano, qual a requisition del reverendo episcopo di Baius vol stampar il *Cortesano*, opera del reverendo missier Baldissera Castion. *Item*, la medicina di Vegetio, la medicina di Cornelio Celso, la medicina di Quinto Sereno; et havendo trovato alcuni fragmenti di le oration di Tulio non più stampade voleno farle stampar con tutte le opere de Tulio in foglio grando e grossissima lettera et *etiam* tutti li simplicii latini; però per anni 10 altri che loro li possino stampar, *sub poena in parte*. Fu presa. Ave: 127, 3, 6.

This is, in several respects, the most interesting document relating to Torresano noted by Sanuto. It reveals, for instance, that Andrea undertook the printing of the *editio princeps* of the *Cortegiano* not at the request of Pietro Bembo as is usually stated[14] but on the urging of Ludovico di Canossa,[15] bishop of Bayeux and the expositor of the ' perfetto cortegiano ' in the first book of this work. The printing of the Celsus and Quintus Serenus must have been well under way at the time of the petition since the edition is dated March 1528 (Renouard, p. 105).[16] The other works referred to were not published by the Aldine press; doubtless this may be attributed to Torresano's death not long after and the subsequent suspension of the activities of the firm.[17] The medical work by Vegetius noted here is no doubt the *Ars veterinaria* by Publius Vegetius Renatus, published

[14] The *Enciclopedia Italiana*, ix (1931), p. 375, says: 'Fortunatamente il Castiglione, ' durante il suo soggiorno in Spagna, aveva provveduto ad assicurare, con l'aiuto di ' Pietro Bembo, la stampa del suo *Cortegiano*.' On the title is the privilege: 'Hassi ' nel priuilegio, & nella gratia ottenuta dalla Illustrissima Signoria che in questa, ' ne in niun' altra Citta del suo dominio si possa imprimere, ne altroue impresso ' uendere questo libro del Cortegiano per .x. anni sotto le pene in esso contenute.' This is repeated in the 1533 edition of which the Morgan Library possesses one of Grolier's own copies (PML 15498). Speaking of the first edition, Bernoni says (p. 307) that the title-page contains 'il privilegio, ch' è fra i primi, se non il primo, ' che vedesi sui libri veneziani'. There seem to be plenty of earlier examples.

[15] He had previously been Bishop of Tricarico and was in 1526–7 French ambassador at Venice. He was a close friend of Castiglione's and appears frequently in Sanuto's diary.

[16] The Celsus was printed a month earlier than the Castiglione and bears on the title the note: 'Venetorum decreto, ne quis aliquo in loco Venetae ditionis hos libros imprimat, impressos' ue alibi uendat, cautum est.'

[17] The same thing happened on the death of Aldus, according to Francesco Torresano's preface to the *Decamerone* of 1522. Here it is stated that 'not only this one [the Boccaccio] but also many other works worthy to be printed' were left unprinted.

in Basle in 1528, while the 'simplicii latini' probably refers to the
various herbals rather than to a work on simples. The fragment of
the unpublished *Orationes* by Cicero is of particular interest. The
1519 edition by the Aldine press contains nearly all the speeches now
known, and neither the Elzevir edition of 1642 nor the one produced in Paris in the following century (J. B. Coignard and others,
1741) added any further speeches. It seems not impossible that Torresano may have seen the fragments—or copies of them—subsequently discovered in palimpsests at Milan by Mai in 1814,[18] in other
manuscripts at Turin and Milan by Peyron,[19] and at the Vatican by
Niebuhr[20]—or the fragments known to have been in the possession
of Nicolaus Cusanus about the year 1451.[21]

## V

In Renouard's bibliography of the Aldine press (p. 107), the death
of Andrea Torresano is entered under the year 1529 while Bernoni
(p. 76), citing from an unprinted *Spogli di storia patria* by Gian
Carlo Tiraboschi (concerning which see Bernoni, p. 6, n. 1), adds
that the day was March 15.[22] Though most of the bibliographies and
biographies[23] agree that the year of Andrea's death was 1529, we
find the following record in Sanuto's diary for 21 October 1528 (vol.
xlix, col. 79):

[18] Angelo Mai, *M. Tullii Ciceronis sex orationum fragmenta inedita*, Milan, 1814.
[19] Vittorio Amedeo Peyron, *M. Tullii Ciceronis Orationum pro Tullio, in Clodium
. . . fragmenta inedita*, Leipzig, 1825. See also A. C. Clark, *The Descent of Manuscripts*, Oxford, 1918, pp. 138–56.
[20] Barthold G. Niebuhr, *M. Tullii Ciceronis Orationum pro M. Fonteio, et pro C.
Rabirio fragmenta*, Rome, 1820.
[21] Josef Klein, *Ueber eine Handschrift des Nicolaus von Cues, nebst ungedruckten
Fragmenten Ciceronischer Reden*, Berlin, 1866.
[22] Bernoni (p. 76) says: 'Quindi avendo voluto nel 1529 intraprandere di pieno
'inverno un viaggio ad Asola (non è noto se a scopo di finire qui in tranquillità i
'suoi giorni, o se con l'intendimento di restituirsi ancora a Venezia), appena giunto
'in patria, venne colto da fiero malore, che lo trasse prestamente al sepolcro; il
'che avvenne a' di 15 marzo 1529 nell' età di 78 anni.' This is also the date given
by the *Enciclopedia Italiana*, xxxiv. 68.
[23] The year 1529 is given for Torresano's death by Ferrigni, op. cit., p. 245; Firmin-
Didot, op. cit., p. 398; Fulin, op. cit., p. 195; *Enciclopedia universal ilustrada*
(Espasa), lxii. 1458; *Lexikon des gesamten Buchwesens*, iii. 412; Renouard, p. 107;
Giuseppe Fumagalli, *Lexicon typographicum Italiae*, Florence, 1905, p. 466; Theodore
L. de Vinne, *Notable Printers of Italy during the Fifteenth Century*, New York,
1910, p. 114; John E. Sandys, *A History of Classical Scholarship*, Cambridge, 1908,
ii. 100; &c.

Morite in questa nocte Andrea di Axola stampador, grandissimo ricco, di
età di anni . . . qual fo garzon di stampar.

As there is no reason to doubt the accuracy of Sanuto's statement,[24]
the date of Torresano's death must henceforth be set down as the
night of 20–1 October 1528.

## VI

Since Renouard stated that Torresano's death brought about 'la
'fermeture de l'Imprimerie, dont tous les travaux furent suspendus
' pendant quatre années entières, jusqu'en 1533, qu'elle fut rouverte
' sous la direction de Paul Manuce' (p. 107), it is clear that he believed
that the *Recognitio Veteris Testamenti ad hebraicam veritatem* by
Augustinus Steuchus (1529) was printed while Andrea was still
alive; with this belief Bernoni concurred.[25] The document cited
above shows that Torresano could not have printed this work and
another entry in the diary reveals that the petition for the privilege
to print the *Recognitio* was made by his heirs. On 23 March 1529
(vol. l, col. 81) it is noted:

Fu letto una suplication di heriedi di Andrea di Axola, vol gratia di poter
stampar una opera *Anotation sopra il Testamento vechio et Pentateuco* fatta
per domino Augustin d'Augubio, per anni 10, *ut in parte*, sotto pena a chi la
stampasse. Et li Consieri messe conciederli *ut supra*. Ave: 169, 7, 7.

The *Recognitio* is thus not the last book printed by Torresano[26] but
the first one produced by his heirs. The document also proves that
the printing house did not close its doors directly after Andrea's
death, but that an effort was made to continue the press. It was

---

[24] That Andrea was a man of considerable wealth can best be judged from the
records of his tax payments and the advances he made to Aldus, recorded by
Bernoni and others. One may also recall the well-known comment made by Erasmus
in his *Opulentia Sordida*, which is unquestionably a satire on Andrea's miserly
habits. 'Arbituor censum illius non fuisse infra octoginta ducatorum millia. Nec
'ullus erat annus, quo non accederet lucrum mille ducatorum, ut dicam parcissime'
(*Colloquiorum Desiderii Erasmi Roterodami familiarium opus aureum*, London,
1740, p. 466).

[25] 'Alla morte di Andrea Torresano restò per alcuni anni sospeso il lavoro della
'stamperia a cagione dei dissensi sorti fra la famiglia Torresani ed i Manuzi per la
'duplice eredità di Andrea e di Aldo', Bernoni, p. 97. It may also be pointed out
that Renouard (p. 107) enters the notice of Torresano's death *after* his description
of the Steuchus.

[26] This may be taken as further evidence that Andrea did not die on 15 March
1529, since it would be most unlikely that his heirs would apply for this privilege
scarcely a week after his death.

probably directly after the appearance of this book that legal steps were undertaken on Paul Manutius's behalf to ensure that he should succeed at least to his father's share in the ownership of the press.

## VII

Bernoni (pp. 112 ff.) has suggested that to Federico Torresano, Andrea's younger son, fell the management of the family affairs both in Venice and in Asola,[27] while the father and his elder son, Francesco, attended to the transactions of the press. This accounts, according to Bernoni, not only for the fact that Federico's name[28] is rarely mentioned in the productions of the press prior to 1538 but also for his frequent absences from Venice. Sanuto's diary contains certain entries which may explain why Federico played a very minor role in the workings of the printing house and why he found it expedient to absent himself from Venice from time to time. Relative to the events which were brought before the ' Quarantia Criminale ' on 28 March 1523 (vol. xxxiv, col. 52), we find the entry:

*Item*, preseno de retenir Ferigo di Andrea di Axola per haver barato molti in la dita caxa con carte false, et *maxime* sier Piero Zivran qu. sier Francesco. Il qual Ferigo inteso questo, mandò a inebir per il Legato, dicendo è prete etc.

The Pietro Civran whom Federico had cheated at cards[29] was a member of a well-known patrician family and is recorded in May 1526 (vol. xli, col. 411) as a part-owner of the ' Osteria del Sturion '. Federico, it will be noted, did not plead innocent to the charge, but based his defence on the fact that he was a ' priest '. This does not necessarily imply that Federico actually was a priest—which he certainly was not—but rather that he enjoyed the ' benefit of clergy ' and could not, therefore, be tried before a secular court. This line of de-

[27] 'Già dissi che Federico, senza rimanere affatto estraneo alla stamperia, era stato ' dal padre più particolarmente adibito alla gestione economica; in conseguenza di ' che gli era necessario alternare la sua residenza fra Asola e Venezia per attendere ' agli interessi delle due case', Bernoni, p. 113; see also ibid., p. 90.

[28] He is mentioned in the prefaces to the Pomponius Mela and Aeschylus of 1518 by his brother, Francesco. He also wrote the preface for the second volume of the Galen, for which see below.

[29] That Andrea's sons were fond of playing games of chance is noted by Erasmus in his *Opulentia Sordida* (ed. cit., p. 466): ' Jacobus.—Sed juvenes illi quibus haec ' parabantur, num eadem utebantur parsimonia? Gilbertus.—Utebantur, sed domi ' duntaxat; foris liguriebant, scortabantur, ludebant aleam: cumque pater in gratiam ' honestissimorum convivarum gravaretur teruncium impendere, juvenes interdum ' una nocte sexaginta ducatos perdebant alea.'

fence seems to have availed him little for on 10 July 1523[30] he was sentenced to pay a heavy fine and was banished for four years from Venice, Padua, and Treviso, and the territories under their control. On 30 December 1524 (vol. xxxvii, col. 377), Federico, though he was by this time ' absente ', again entered a petition still maintaining that, since he was ' in sacris ', he could only be tried by an ecclesiastical court, but he announced that he was willing to furnish 1,000 ducats to the Signoria.[31] Civran, however, opposed any such arrangement and demanded his money. On 7 January 1525 (vol. xxxvii, col. 412) Federico again attempted to have his case brought before the ecclesiastical court, where, it would appear, he hoped to meet with more liberal treatment. His credentials for his claim to the ' benefit of clergy ' were presented, and it is stated that he was now willing to 'prestar ducati 1000 per do anni'. The Signoria, however, considered that he had been ' intrigata ' (implicated) and refused the dismissal of the suit. Later in the same year (1525) Federico was apparently in Rome, judging from his dedicatory epistle to Alberto Pio in the second volume of the Galen, the only preface from the hand of Federico to appear in an Aldine book prior to the death of his father. In this dedication Federico acknowledges Pio's kindness to him ' nuper*que* mihi Romæ agenti pro tua humanitate nulla no*n* in re magno præsidio fueris ', from which one may deduce that Pio helped him materially during his exile. It is quite natural that Federico should have turned to the prince of Carpi for support in this crisis. Federico had married Aldus's sister Paola,[32] and Pio may have

---

[30] 'Da poi disnar, fo audientia di la Signoria et Colegio di Savii, et in Quarantia 'Criminal. Per il piedar di sier Donado da Leze *olim* avogador di comun e li 'compagni presenti Avogadori in opinione, fu processo contra Ferigo fio di Andrea di 'Axola absente, qual fu preso retenir per zuogo et bararie fate a sier Piero Zivran 'qu. sier Francesco, et preso di tutto il Consejo il procieder, fu condanato che in 'termine di zorni 15 el ditto pagi ducati 400 d'oro a . . . et passadi, ne pagi ducati '800; sia bandito per anni 4 di Venetia e suo destreto, Padoa et Trevixo e soi 'terltorl, con tala dl llre 1000 a chi quello prenderà in li dlttl confini, qual pagi 'la taia, stagi uno anno in la preson forte e torni al bando, et pagi il dito sier 'Piero Zivran et uno genoese di quello li hanno barato et vadagnato, come sarà 'iustifichà per li Avogadori etc. et sia publichata su le scale.' Sanuto, vol. xxxiv, col. 294.

[31] This is quite a substantial amount as we learn from Erasmus in the quotation already cited, being the sum which Andrea added to his capital each year as the result of his thrifty habits. According to Aldus's will (Firmin-Didot, pp. 487 ff.), his wife Maria had brought him a dowry of 460 ducats and Aldus left a bequest to his daughter Alda of 600 ducats for the same purpose.

[32] Bernoni (p. 112) states: 'Federico, fratello minore a Francesco, prese in moglie

been willing to do what he could for the brother-in-law of his old tutor, for whom he maintained throughout his life such genuine affection and interest. Two years later (3 April 1527—vol. xliv, col. 413) 'Ferigo di Axola bandito' again appealed either to have the case dismissed or the banishment lifted, offering to give 600 ducats to the Signoria and 'obligandosi pagar quelli li dimanderà danari per conto di zuogo'. Two ballots were taken but Federico's petition was not granted. Finally on 13 April 1527 he made a successful appeal; though the entry is incomplete or illegible (vol. xliv, col. 496), it is clear that Federico made a cash payment and was ' asolto del bando '. By the 11 January 1529 Federico was once again reinstated in Venice,[33] since on that day he advanced 200 ducats towards the payment of the duty on wine (vol. xlix, col. 411).

It may thus be deduced that Federico's interests lay elsewhere than in the operation of a printing press, and this may account for his small contribution to the success of the Aldine press. It seems somewhat unlikely that Federico, as Bernoni suggests, should have been the one chosen to manage the family affairs, at least in the 1520s. There are no further notes on Federico Torresano in Sanuto's diary, which extends through the 30 September 1533. He is known to have been thereafter an occasional printer of books and Bernoni states (p. 124) that he died in Asola on the 24 January 1561.

(From *The Library* (1945), pp. 111-121)

---

'la sorella di Aldo Manuzio a nome Paola, diventando così doppii cognati. Nel 'testamento di quest' ultimo è fatta menzione di una sorella; ma non vi è detto 'il nome: però siccome avverte che la medesima dimorava a Carpi, resta escluso 'potesse questa essere la moglie del Torresano.' I do not know where Bernoni obtained his information about Paola. It is clear from the following provision in his will (Firmin-Didot, pp. 489-90) that Aldus had more than one sister: ' Insuper 'lego et ordino duodecim puellis ducatorum viginti quinque singulis, ex quibus 'sex sint ex filiabus sororum mearum, sex vero ex aliis quae sunt Carpi sicut videbitur 'principibus praedictis.'

[33] Bernoni (p. 113) points out that, in November 1529, Federico served on a commission appointed by the Venetian Senate: 'per ottenere riparazione di arbitrii 'e atrocità commesse in Asola dalla guarnigione militare.'

# CHAPTER B13

## THE MARGINS IN MEDIAEVAL BOOKS[1]

ONE of the most difficult and elusive problems which confronts the historian of the written or printed word is that which concerns itself with what the early printer or scribe intended his book to look like when work on it had been completed. As far as the type or script page is concerned, we are tolerably well informed by the countless manuscripts and incunabula which have been preserved to us in immaculate condition. In most instances, however, the intervening centuries have taken their toll of the margins as the books passed through the hands of the binder (to whom—and, no doubt, in jest—William Morris once referred as "that enemy of books") or successive rebinders. When a book has once been bound, it is no longer possible to determine with complete accuracy what margins have been cropped and how much has been cut off; indeed, the size of the book may well have been cut down, considerably and deliberately, to suit the tastes or needs of the individual purchaser. When the book has gone through several rebindings and has been subjected to similar successive modifications of its original shape, the possibilities for arriving at erroneous conclusions as to the size of the original margins are proportionately greater. It was against just such pitfalls as these that the late Alfred W. Pollard warned in his two interesting studies entitled *Margins*; the earlier of these appeared in *The Printing Art* (Cambridge, Mass., 1907), X:17-24, and the later in *The Dolphin: A Journal of the Making of Books* (New York, 1933), I:67-80. Bearing Pollard's experiences in mind and complying with his expressed hope that others might continue his researches, I have thought it might be of somewhat more than passing interest to analyze what the scribes and the printers of earlier days believed the margins should measure in the light

---

[1] This paper is dedicated to my friend and colleague of the past dozen years, Mark D. Brewer. For a long time I have wanted to acknowledge publicly the great debt I owe him for his willing assistance wherever his special knowledge of science and mathematics could be of use in the study of mediaeval manuscripts and early printed books. Without his help much that I have written would have been incorrect and valueless. It is singularly fitting, I think, that this paper (which is more practical than theoretical) be dedicated to him.                                           C. F. B.

of three bits of evidence unknown to Pollard and of unquestionable integrity.

For very logical reasons, as Pollard pointed out, it is usual to find in modern books as well as in those of earlier centuries that the inner margin is the smallest, then the upper, next the outer and finally (and largest of them all) the lower. Whether a book is held in one hand or by both hands, as the case may be, it is the lower and the outer margins which the thumbs will grasp. Thus it is perfectly natural that we should here find the greatest amount of white paper, so that the hand holding the book need not cover the text in any way and thus impede the progress of the eye. Again, as William Morris maintained, it is not the single page but two contiguous pages (the opening, as it is generally called) which forms the unit of the book. The inner margin thus becomes a double expanse of white and to avoid making the gutter (as, I understand, printers call this space between the two text-pages) so wide as to be out of all proportion to the other white margins, each inner one is naturally the smallest. Finally, in order to achieve balance, the top margin is fitted to the size of the inner in a proportion somewhat similar to that which the lower margin bears to the outer. It has been stated, but on no very secure grounds, that printers normally adopt a proportion of $1:2:3:4$; this, as Pollard showed, is rather too extreme and he suggested the proper proportion might be $2:3:4:5$. The actual measurements in the best modern books, however, display a wide choice of modifications according to the taste of the printer, the size of his type and the book, illustrations, and other conditions over which he has no control.

The proportions throughout this study are all based on their relationship to the height of the paper, not only because Pollard employed this criterion and the resulting figures are simple to handle but also (as we shall see) because such proportions have been recognized as suitable means of comparison since very early days. As Pollard has rightly said, it is necessary to compare the inner and outer margin to the height, not to the breadth, of the paper "if we are to advance from the relations of one margin to other margins to the still more important point as to the proportion they should bear to the page of type." As an illustration of what the proportions of the margins to the height of the paper in modern fine printing amounted to, Pollard cited the following figures obtained from several of the Kelmscott editions and from the Doves Bible:

|                  | Lower | Upper | Outer   | Inner |
|------------------|-------|-------|---------|-------|
| Kelmscott Press  | 23%   | 9%    | 17-18%  | 7%    |
| Doves Press      | 19%   | 10%   | 18%     | 7%    |

For a rough estimate, then, we can conclude that the lower margin should be about one-fifth of the total height with the upper margin approximately half that much; the outer margin ought to be nearly four-fifths of the lower while the inner, in turn, just less than half the outer. A modern fine book, Pollard thought, would afford the following approximate percentages:

| Page         | Type-page    | Lower | Upper | Outer | Inner |
|--------------|--------------|-------|-------|-------|-------|
| 100% x 70%   | 68% x 45%    | 23%   | 9%    | 18%   | 8%    |

In such a book, it is interesting to note, the height of the type-page is roughly that of the breadth of the paper and its breadth is approximately two-thirds that of the height of the type-page.

So much for modern books. Previous estimates as to the space left for margins in the books of an earlier epoch have been based on examples which the investigator hoped were in their original condition, though it is obvious that many copies, if not all of them, had been cut down, no matter how slight and uniform this reduction may have been. Morris quoted a librarian-friend whose estimate, based on a study of the books in his care, was that "the mediaeval rule was to make a difference of 20 per cent from margin to margin." In figures this would mean that, if the inner margin measured 10 millimetres, the upper would be 12mm., the outer 14.4mm., and the lower 17.28 mm., roughly 10:12:14⅖:17¼.

The exceptionally large Bodleian copy of the 1459 *Psalter* shows extraordinary variations from page to page in its several dimensions; these may be found in Pollard's paper in *The Dolphin*. On the average we find that the approximate percentages work out to be the following:

| Page          | Type-page   | Lower  | Upper | Outer | Inner |
|---------------|-------------|--------|-------|-------|-------|
| 100% x 69½%   | 70% x 43%   | 20½%   | 9½%   | 17%   | 9½%   |

The three handsome fifteenth-century books noted in his earlier paper yielded on the average these percentages:

| Page          | Type-page   | Lower | Upper | Outer | Inner |
|---------------|-------------|-------|-------|-------|-------|
| 100% x 69¾%   | 68% x 41%   | 23%   | 9%    | 20%   | 8¾%   |

while the books printed early in his career by Anton Koberger with their unusually large margins averaged:

| Page | Type-page | Lower | Upper | Outer | Inner |
|------|-----------|-------|-------|-------|-------|
| 100% x 67% | 59% x 35% | 27% | 14% | 18% | 14% |

If we except the Koberger books with their over-ample margins (a proportion which this printer gradually reduced and finally corrected), the percentages for page, type-page and margins do not greatly differ from those estimated for a modern fine book. All these figures, however, have been compiled from books which have already been bound. Though it is likely that, while these books may have been slightly cut or trimmed here and there, the law of averages would tend to reduce the margin of error, we cannot be entirely certain that these figures are precisely the same as those which the scribe or printer had in mind when he began his work. We may, therefore, now turn to the new evidence to which reference has already been made.

I am greatly obliged to the late Edward K. Rand for his kindness in bringing to my attention the first piece of concrete evidence regarding the mediaeval concept of what the page proportions should be. This evidence is a marginal note found on folio 2 verso of the ninth-century manuscript Lat. 11884 of the Bibliothèque Nationale in Paris. Although this note has long been known to palaeographers, having first been noticed in the *Neues Archiv* of 1898, it seems to have escaped the notice alike of those bibliographers and of those practitioners of fine printing who have written about the sizes of margins. The text, as printed in Professor Rand's *Studies in the Script of Tours* (II:88), reads:

Taliter debet fieri quaternionis forma, quinta parte longitudinis, quarta latitudinis. Quintam partem da inferiori vel anteriori margini, et ipsam quintam partem diuide in .III. et dabis .II. superiori. subtracta .I. Rursus ipsas .II. partes divide in tres, dabisque duas posteriori margini subtrahendo unam. Huic compar erit si media interfuerit. Lineas vero iuxta rationem scripturae divides, quia maior scriptura latioribus, minor autem strictioribus lineis indiget.

The meaning of this notation is quite clear. Omitting those details which do not concern us, we find that the height of the whole page should be to its breadth as 5 to 4; the lower and outer margins were to be one-fifth of the height, the upper margin two-thirds of this figure and the inner margin two-thirds that of the upper. In percentages this would work out to be:

| Page | Script-page | Lower | Upper | Outer | Inner |
|------|-------------|-------|-------|-------|-------|
| 100% x 80% | 66⅔% x 51⅑% | 20% | 13⅓% | 20% | 8⁸⁄₉% |

The proportion of both the breadth of the leaf and that of the script-page to the overall height is noticeably greater than that for the modern fine book. In the ninth century, then, the page was intended to appear a good deal more "squat" than what is accepted as the standard now. In contrast we may note the approximate average percentages of the three later British Museum manuscripts which Pollard quoted in his second paper; they are:

| Page | Script-page | Lower | Upper | Outer | Inner |
|------|-------------|-------|-------|-------|-------|
| 100% x 68% | 65% x 38% | 24% | 11% | 19% | 11% |

The remaining sets of figures will be obtained from two fifteenth-century printed books which, incredibly enough, for almost half a millennium somehow or other escaped the hand of a binder. These two books (the only ones known to me in this condition) are preserved as the original sheets, unopened at the top and uncut at the sides and bottom; they show no marks of ever having been sewn or otherwise encased in a binding. One of these books, if one may speak of these sheets as such, belongs to Mr. Albert Ehrman, through whose kindness—and with the patient endurance of Mr. H. R. Spandel—I was enabled to examine it and make the necessary measurements; the other happens to be mine (Plate 8).

In order that the reader may see at a glance what these sheets look like, I reproduce (Plate 8) the first one from my copy. The book is of no particular consequence or value; its sole interest is in the condition in which it has been preserved. It is the *Oratio in laudem sancti Leopoldi* by Johannes Franciscus de Pavinis, apparently printed in Rome by Eucharius Silber at some unspecified time, but probably not long after the oration was delivered on November 20, 1484. This edition is listed under No. P 211 in Margaret B. Stillwell's *Incunabula in American Libraries* where the pertinent bibliographical references may be found. It is a quarto volume made up of three sheets and the side of the one here reproduced contains the text found on folio 1 recto, 2 verso, 11 recto and 12 verso, i.e., pages 1, 4, 21, and 24. The over-all dimensions of the sheet are 450 x 300mm. Though it may not be possible to detect this in the reproduction, the four pages are not perfectly centered on the sheet. The two type-pages each measure 87mm. in width and the space between them (the gutter) is 38mm.,

making a total width from the first character on the left-hand side
to the last character on the right-hand side of 212mm. and leaving
88mm. for the outer margins. On two sheets, however, one of the
outer margins measures 48mm., while the other but 40mm. To make
a perfect book with all the edges even, it would have been ultimately
necessary to trim the outer margins of all pages so as to leave a uniform outer margin of no more than 40mm.

Again for the height, a full page of 33 lines measures 145mm.,
ascenders and descenders included, for a total of 290mm. of printed
matter. The space between the pages is a constant 46mm. in height.
Thus the space enclosed by the type-pages is 336mm. in height,
leaving 114mm. for the lower margins. Here, also, the actual measurement varies between a maximum 62mm. and a minimum 52
mm., showing that the pages were not correctly set to the dead center of the sheet. If the edges were to be even, then, the sheet would
have to be trimmed to a lower margin no greater than 52mm.

We do not, of course, know with absolute certainty whether the
printer expected to leave the greatest possible margins or planned to
trim them to some previously determined size. As a practical measure, though, it seems likely that the printer would want to make the
maximum use of his sheet, particularly for such a strictly commercial
venture as the present book, with its contents of ephemeral interest,
represents. Since paper must have been a very considerable item in
the mediaeval printer's costs of production (the numerous cancels
in place of reprinting whole sheets found in many early printed
books certainly indicate a strict economy of paper), it does not seem
reasonable to presume that the early printer deliberately used a sheet
producing larger margins than was desirable for the bound volume.
Such margins would simply have had to be trimmed off and unnecessary wastage of paper would be the only result. It is difficult to
come to any other conclusion than that the printers of all ages,
mediaeval as well as modern, sought to make the best possible use
of the paper they had in hand and would plan their books to such
proportions that the smallest waste would be incurred. Again, one
may also argue, I think, that, for pleasing effect and to conform to
manuscript usage, the early printer (contrary to the practice of some
modern fine presses) would not favor uneven margins and that he
therefore probably trimmed the paper the smallest amount possible
under the given circumstances without leaving jagged edges.

The size of the book we have been discussing would then, after trimming and folding, have been 220 x 146mm.; actually the British Museum copy now measures 208 x 143mm., the Harvard copy 185 x 132mm. and the Huntington copy 217 x 141mm. The measurements and approximate percentages of the finished product would have been:

| Page | Type-page | Lower | Upper | Outer | Inner |
|------|-----------|-------|-------|-------|-------|
| 220 x 146 mm. | 145 x 87 mm. | 52 mm. | 23 mm. | 40 mm. | 19 mm. |
| 100% x 66% | 66% x 40% | 24% | 10% | 18% | 8% |

By one of those coincidences which are so incredible that they have to be seen to be believed, Mr. Ehrman's volume (if such it may be called) is another edition of this identical work, printed at Passau by Johann Petri. That it is later in date than my edition seems quite certain, since the Rome edition was probably issued in connection with the canonization of St. Leopold in 1485 and the Passau edition was only a reprint of this. Indeed, Petri is not known to have worked at Passau before 1485 and the type with which he printed Mr. Ehrman's book is his fourth, probably cut about 1489. This edition is listed by Miss Stillwell as P 212. The size of the sheet in this case is 430 x 320mm. and, making the smallest possible allowance for the essential trimming, the folded leaf would have measured 215 x 160 mm. The actual size of the British Museum copy is 188 x 137mm., while the copy in the Library of Congress measures 196 x 140mm. Thus the approximate measurements and percentages for Mr. Ehrman's book would have been, when bound:

| Page | Type-page | Lower | Upper | Outer | Inner |
|------|-----------|-------|-------|-------|-------|
| 215 x 160 mm. | 150 x 97 mm. | 40 mm. | 25 mm. | 40 mm. | 23 mm. |
| 100% x 74% | 70% x 45% | 18½% | 11½% | 18½% | 10½% |

What, then, can we deduce from all these figures? Chiefly, it seems to me, that for the mediaeval book as well as for its modern counterpart no hard and fast rule was observed by the scribes or the master printers of their day. A gradual increase in the proportionate size of the type-page to that of the leaf, as Pollard showed occurred in the work of the Venetian presses, is also discernible in the two books we have had under consideration. In almost all books, save for the ninth-century manuscript and Koberger's early works, the height of the type-page is approximately equal to the width of the page itself. Again, and this holds good for every example cited, the outer and lower margins are always larger than the other two. It is particularly interesting, to me at least, to note that the marginal proportions of the Rome incunabulum are almost identical with those found in the Kelmscott books, being just one per cent greater for each margin. Apparently Silber and Morris saw eye to eye in the matter of margins if in nothing else, since the former was one of the most mediocre printers of his day and the latter one of the greatest of the nineteenth century. The Passau volume achieves a different balance, since the lower and outer margins would have been the same and the inner and upper practically alike. A fair summary of the size of margins in early printed books would confine itself to these facts: the lower margin was usually between a fifth and a quarter the size of the total height of the page; the margins at the foot and the side of the page formed one pair and those at the top and in the gutter another; each member of one pair bore to the other member of that pair a proportion closely parallel to that found between the members of the second pair, while the greatest proportionate increase is that found between the two pairs themselves. Beyond these general estimates, it would, I believe, be hazardous to venture very far. It is remarkable evidence of the astuteness of the greatest bibliographer of all, Alfred W. Pollard, that his figures, based on books that had been bound, find full confirmation from these sheets which have never known the trimming-knife.

The question that naturally follows this examination of the page proportions in early printed books is whether or not these figures can have any practical application. To this the answer must be a hesitant "yes" though they may have a greater value for one whose mathematical training is less rudimentary than mine. We may take one simple example. Let us assume that a unique copy of a book is preserved with the upper, outer and lower edges trimmed close to the text. The type-page measures 136 x 90mm. and the inner margin is 17mm.; from such figures it may be possible to arrive at the original size of the book as it came from the press. The average usual size of the type-page may be estimated at 68% x 45% of the total height of the paper; consequently the original book may have been 200mm. tall. This is confirmed by the size of the inner margin, 17 mm. (or 8½%) being a good average figure. Again, the height of the type-page was approximately equal to the breadth of the paper so that the paper was probably at least 136mm. wide in its first state.

We may estimate the lower margin at 44 mm., a bit more than one-fifth of the total height. The approximate original dimensions of the book would thus have been:

| Page | Type-page | Lower | Upper | Outer | Inner |
|------|-----------|-------|-------|-------|-------|
| 200 x 140 mm. | 136 x 90 mm. | 44 mm. | 20 mm. | 33 mm. | 17 mm. |
| 100% x 70% | 68% x 45% | 22% | 10% | 16½% | 8½% |

The importance of the measurement of the inner margin must not be overlooked in such a book, for, taken together with the type-page, it alone can show whether the book had normal or exceptionally large margins. If in this case the inner margin had measured 30mm. (or much more than 10% of the assumed height of the paper), one would have to conclude that all the margins were proportionately greater and that the type-page represented a much smaller percentage than 68% x 45% of the height; in short, a book with exceptionally large margins. For such a book, our figures would be of no avail.

From these averages it may also be possible to determine whether or not a certain copy, now much trimmed, could at an earlier date have been encased in a particular binding or formed part of some miscellaneous collection. If the proportions prove that the book was never sufficiently large to have fitted comfortably into the binding, we may be reasonably certain that it was never bound in it; if it could have been larger, of course, one could make no such deduction. The same theory may be applied to a book now contained in a binding rather too large for it; if the proportions indicate that it was always a good deal smaller than the binding, we may be quite sure that the book was "placed" in it. There are, no doubt, other uses to which these percentages could be applied.

I trust that these figures may not only be of some interest to the student of fine printing but also of use to the bibliographer in general. It is my fervent hope that I have not erred in my mathematical computations, a subject which at best I approach with fear and trepidation.

(From *PBSA* 40 (1946), pp. 32-42).

# CHAPTER B14

## AN EPITHALAMIUM ON THE MARRIAGE
## OF CHARLES III OF SAVOY AND
## BEATRICE OF PORTUGAL

ONE of the earliest of the major political moves[1] initiated by the Emperor Charles V after his coronation at Aix-la-Chapelle, 23 October 1520,[2] resulted in the marriage of Charles III, Duke of Savoy, and Beatrice, second daughter of King Manuel "the Great" of Portugal and sister-in-law to the Emperor himself. This match was one of momentous and unhappy importance for the Duchy of Savoy and even less happy for Italy itself. The object of the Emperor in promoting this marriage was, of course, to detach Savoy from France, and in this Charles V was successful, though the consequences for the ducal family were indeed disastrous.[3] Savoy was naturally of great geographical significance in the wars between Francis I and Charles V and the Duchy was thus a vital factor in the Emperor's plans for establishing the Spanish rule over Italy.

The arrangements for this important marriage, as is usual in such matters, were somewhat protracted. Negotiations were begun in November 1520 and the Duke of Savoy's ambassadors reached Portugal the following February.[4] An agreement on the dowry having finally been reached, the marriage by proxy took place in Lisbon on 26 March 1521,[5] accompanied by festivities worthy of the occasion.

[1] For their kind assistance in the preparation of this paper, I am obliged to Mr. Richard Breaden, Mr. Bruce Rogers, Mr. John Bianchi, Miss Clara Penney, and Professor Alfred Bellinger.

[2] Charles was elected to the imperial crown on 28 June 1519; compare Edward Armstrong, *The Emperor Charles V*, London, 1910, I, 67.

[3] Cf. Armstrong, *op. cit.*, I, 270, 299 *et passim*.

[4] See A. Segre, "La politica sabauda con Francia e Spagna dal 1515 al 1533," *Memorie della Reale Accademia delle Scienze di Torino*, ser. 2, tomo L (1901), pp. 249-348. An early account may be found in H. Osorio, *De Rebus Emmanuelis Regis Lusitaniae*, Olysippone, Apud Antonium Gondisaluum, 1571, lib. XII.

[5] This date is given by Samuel Guichenon, *Histoire généalogique de la royale maison de Savoye*, Turin, 1778-80, II, 228; by De La Chenaye-Desbois and Badier, *Dictionnaire de la noblesse*, Paris, 1863-76, XVIII, 354; and by Cais de Pierlas, "Chronique Niçoise de Jean Badat," *Romania*, XXV, p. 56, n. 3. As Easter fell on

Beatrice and her attendants sailed from Portugal aboard a magnificent fleet on August 9th and she was greeted by her husband at Villefranche on September 29th.[6] On the first of October the nuptial mass was celebrated at Nice.[7]

In honor of this marriage, there was printed in Milan on 30 July 1521 a work entitled:

Petri Leonis Vercellensis Diuę Marię scalarum / Mediolani Canonici in Illustrissimorum / Karoli Principis Sabaudiae Ducis: / & Beatricis Portugallensis / auspicatissimis nuptijs / Epithalamion.

A bibliographical description sufficiently accurate for our purposes, save for some minor slips and the omission of typographical details, will be found in G. Carbonelli, *Bibliographia Medica Typographica Pedemontana*, Rome, 1914, pp. 193-4, no. 167. On the basis of the types used, it seems likely that the work was printed by Alexander Minutianus.[8] Two copies of the book are found in The Pierpont Morgan Library—one printed on paper and the other, intended as a presentation copy for King Manuel, on vellum (Plates 9 and 10).

As Sander[9] has noted, the Epithalamium contains several woodcuts: on the title-page are found the coats-of-arms of Charles of Savoy and of Beatrice of Portugal and a cut, showing the four-year old Veronica Lucia Leone presenting the book (perhaps reading out of it) to the ducal couple, appears on folios 2 and 16 verso. In the Morgan vellum copy the woodcuts were not inked in and the blank spaces thus left were filled in by manuscript illumination. The presentation scene is reproduced from both the paper (Plate 9) and vellum (Plate 10) copies and it will be observed that the illuminator

---

March 31st in 1521, this day was Tuesday in Holy Week. Anselme de Saint Marie, *Histoire généalogique et chronologique de la maison royale de France*, Paris, 1726-33, I, 603, incorrectly states that Beatrice was married by proxy on Easter Day, 8 April 1520.

[6] The fleet touched at Marseille on September 21st. An unfortunate consequence of this visit was the epidemic brought by the sailors, which ravaged the whole of Provence; see Pierlas, *op. cit.*, p. 34.

[7] Cf. Max Bruchet, *Marguerite d' Autriche*, Lille, 1927, p. 79 and Segre, *op. cit.*, p. 263. Anselme, *loc. cit.*, states that the wedding took place 29 September 1520.

[8] The types used seem to be 111 R (text), 78 R (marginalia) and 111 Greek. Minutianus apparently obtained type 111 R from Guillermus Le Signerre, for whom he acted as editor about 1500. Le Signerre had printed Leo's *Leonaea* in 1495 (Hain 10017) as the first recorded product of this press; see BMC VI: 788-791. [The British Museum's *Short-Title Catalogue* (of Italian books, 1958, p. 374) names Giovanni da Castiglione as printer. CFB]

[9] Max Sander, *Le livre à figures italien*, New York, 1941, II, no. 3933.

has followed the spirit of the woodcuts, though altering the proportions of the cut and supplying a background for the scene.[10] Again,
in the paper copy the coat-of-arms of Charles, as that of the husband,
appears on the left of those of Beatrice, while in the copy designed
for King Manuel the illuminated arms of Beatrice occupy the place
of honor at the left. The presentation copy contains an additional
vellum leaf with a manuscript dedication, in which are mentioned
the Portuguese voyages of exploration so significant for the reign of
Manuel. The discoveries are also noted in the text of the Epithalamium where we read (on folio 5 verso):

Dicant dicant quaeso isti scioli: & sibi tantum sapientes quis maiores Emanuelis soceri nunc tui: & subinde eum exciuit ut cum ualidissima classe inter
herculis quas columnas uocitant: Oceanum transfretaret: & ignoratas nostro
huic orbi Insulas: gentes barbaras: populos bello strenuissimos contunderent:
adque orthodoxam fidem hanc nostram perducerent? certe deus.

This work is not listed by Harrisse[11] or Sabin[12] and it is questionable
whether these slight notices (if, indeed, they refer to the West Indies—and not, as seems more probable, to those in the East) would
warrant the inclusion of the book among the true Americana. The
dedicatory address reads:[13]

[10] In the vellum copy, sig. D4 with the repeated woodcut has been cut away but
that this was also illuminated is shown by the off-set.

[11] Henry Harrisse, *Bibliotheca Americana Vetustissima*, New York, 1866.

[12] Joseph Sabin, *A dictionary of books relating to America*, New York, 1868-1936.

[13] The inscription is enclosed within a flowered border and the style of handwriting is such as to imitate closely the printed pages. A rough translation might
read:

To the most exalted Manuel, King of Portugal, the well-deserving. A little letter
from Petrus Leo of Vercelli, a canon of Blessed Mary of the Stairs at Milan.

I have had sent to you [this] copy of an epithalamium which I recently composed in honor of your most beloved daughter Beatrice and of Charles, best of the
Dukes of Savoy. Not, of course, because I deemed it worthy of you—you, indeed,
who yield to none in justice, temperance, bravery, modesty, generosity, learning, character, power, riches and wealth, and finally in knowledge of war and in counsel—
but also that you may know that you are cherished, reverenced and esteemed by me.
For since I feel that you are the most deserving King of Portugal and the wisest
in the opinion of everybody on account of your outstanding virtues, and your signal
achievements are celebrated throughout the entire world, and I feel [thus]—I may
say—because of the islands unknown to our world which you have taken, the infidel cities which you have converted to this our orthodox faith, the peoples and
the savages and wild barbarians whom you have conquered in combat. Really I cannot refrain from exalting you to the heavens for this manly deed, to eulogize you,
to cherish you fervently and to love you greatly. Since, in short, you deserve the
highest praise from the learned, I feel you will support them liberally and protect
them and be concerned most humanely with them. I both know you and it is

Ad Serenissimum Emanuelem Lusitanię Regem benemerentem. Petri leonis Vercellensis diuę Marię Scalarum Mediolani Canonici Epistolium.
Epithalamij exemplum quod nuper composui tua de Beatrice filia ualde dilecta: et de Karolo Sabaudię ducibus optimis: ad te mittendum duxi. Non sane quod Id te dignum putem, quippe qui Iusticia: Temperantia: Fortitudine: Modestia: Liberalitate: Doctrina: moribus: potentatu: diuitijs: et auro: re denique bellica: & consilio cędis nulli: Sed ut scias te a me diligi: coli: et obseruari Cum enim sentio portugallię meritissimum te Regem Sapientissimumque una omnium uoce insignes tuas ob uirtutes: et praeclarissima gesta toto orbe celebrari Etiam sentio Inquam quas Insulas orbi nostro incognitas cęperis: quas Infidelium urbes ad orthodoxam fidem hanc nostram perduxeris: quos populos: et eosdem barbaros efferos: et immites bello domueris: Non possum profecto non te pro virili parte ad cęlos efferre: prędicare vęhementerque diligere: et summopere amare. Cum denique de doctis mereri te quam optime: liberaliter fouere illos: tuerique: et cum his humanissime uersari sentio: simul et cognosco te et perquam doctum ut credam necesse est. Quemadmodum enim nemo satis laudat: quod non cognoscit: sic admittit quisquam non inuitus quę probat omnia: utque ueteri in adagio est. pares cum paribus facilime congregantur. Enim uero Scipionem: et Lęlium doctissimos suę ętatis uiros: non aliud quam similitudo quędam morum: et paria (Vt Cicero edocet in Lęlio) studia coniunxere. Quamobrem qualicumque munusculum hoc nostrum: quo datur animo: hoc est lętissimo capias obsecro: legasque (si dignum duxeris) quum per publica maximaque negotia feriari contigerit opere autem precium fuerit: quod tua preconia: et filię laudes tuę Singularesque uirtutes pro parte hoc in opusculo nostro recognosces: Valeat tua sine fine Maiestas: sibique de Petro leone cuncta despondeat.

The exact day upon which the Epithalamium was delivered seems uncertain. From the colophon we may conclude that it was delivered before the book went to press in July 1521. On the other hand, the early genealogist Samuel Guichenon (1607-1664)[14] states that the oration was presented at a reception given by the Duke in March

---

necessary that I believe you to be exceedingly learned, for, as no one praises enough what he does not know, so one is not unwilling to admit what he approved altogether. And as it is in the old saying—equals convene most readily with equals. For example Scipio and Laelius, the most learned men of their day, nothing other than a certain similarity of character and similar interests drew them together (as Cicero points out in his Laelius). Therefore this small gift of ours, of whatever worth it may be, is given with this intention—that is, I beg that you may accept it most agreeably—and that you may read it (if you find it worthy) since it touches upon the public and very great occasion of the festival; and it will be worth the trouble because you will recognize your commendations and the praises of your daughter and her extraordinary virtues set forth to the best of my ability in this little work. May your Majesty prosper without end and may your Majesty promise himself everything from Petrus Leo!

[14] *op. cit.*, p. 229.

1522, while the Portuguese historian Antonio Caetano de Sousa[15] maintains that the occasion took place in the following May. Since Manuel was certainly dead by this time[16] and Leo very probably so,[17] these dates are clearly incorrect; however, if we assume that Guichenon was mistaken by one year, it is not impossible that the address was delivered in March 1521 in connection with the marriage by proxy.

There is one further point about the printed work which seems worth noting. The printing of the Epithalamium was not, despite the importance of the occasion it celebrates, a particularly satisfactory piece of work as numerous misprints disfigure the text. Some of these have been corrected in ink in both Morgan copies, such as *quo* to *quos* (A3), *uos* to *quos* (D1) and *humi* to *humo* (E2 verso). Being apparently written by the same hand, the emendations were probably made in the printing office, though other misprints have been left uncorrected.[18] In addition the two copies contain a number of different readings. The marginal notes on folios 3 verso and 4 in the paper copy include the words *Decrops, Decropide* and *Domulus* where the vellum copy correctly has *Cecrops, Cecropide* and *Romulus*. Again, on folio 7 the paper copy prints:

Quod si principes alij omnes ita facerent aequabilius: atque constantius sese res humanae haberent: neque aliud alio ferri neque inuitari: ac misceri (ut ait crispus) omnia cerneremus.

Here the vellum copy supplies "immutari" for "inuitari," the correctness of this reading being confirmed by the text of Sallust.[19] It is quite apparent, therefore, that the vellum copy contains a cor-

---

[15] *Historia genealogica da casa real portugueza*, Lisbon, 1735-49, III, 297.

[16] Osorio, *ed. cit.*, p. 477, states: ". . . in morbum subito incidit, ex quo post dies nouem, decima tertia die mensis Decembris ex hac vita migrauit. Quinquaginta duobus annis & sex mensibus vixerat: è quibus viginti sex annis & mense cum dimidio regnauit." The year was 1521.

[17] Ph. Argelati, *Bibliotheca Scriptorum Mediolanensium*, Milan, 1745, II, 2123-4, says Leo died, as an octogenarian, in 1521. Tiraboschi, *Storia della litteratura Italiana*, Florence, 1809, VI, 1087, notes "Pietro Leone vercellese, professor d'eloquenza in Milano" as one of the lesser writers at the close of the fifteenth century. The author appears as Petrus Leo in the British Museum catalogue and as Pietro Leone in that of the Bibliothèque Nationale.

[18] For example, "seperbia" (B3), "snbinde" (C1 verso), and "suut" (D3).

[19] *Bellum Catilinae*: "Quodsi regum atque imperatorum animi uirtus in pace ita ut in bello ualeret: Aequabilius atque constantius sese res humanę haberent neque aliud alio ferri neque mutari ac misceri omnia cerneres," [Italy: Unidentified press], 1470, f. 1. Leo, of course, is adapting, not quoting, Sallust and uses an intensive form.

rected text and that the paper copy with the misprints and errors left uncorrected represents an earlier issue.[20] Thus it is self-evident that the vellum copy must have been printed after the paper one now in the Morgan Library had been struck off. It is often the practice nowadays to print the vellum copies first, while the type is still quite clean and sharp, but here for some reason or other the procedure was reversed. It would be interesting to see if the other extant paper copies[21] contain the same errors found in the Morgan example. If all the paper copies preserve these misprints, one must conclude that the entire issue was printed before the vellum copy was produced. On the other hand, if the other paper copies still extant contain the corrections as found in the vellum example, this would indicate that the Morgan paper copy was merely a trial or proof copy.[22] Unfortunately the present state of the world makes such a comparison impossible.

(From *To Doctor R. Essays here collected and published in honor of the seventieth birthday of Dr. A.S.W. Rosenbach* (1946), pp. 55-60).

[20] As in his earlier *Leonaea* (Carbonelli, *op. cit.*, p. 215), the author warns the reader in the colophon against the printer's possible errors: "Si quid erroris uel mutatione litterarum uel punctorum Impressoribus ascribatur."

[21] The only other copies known to the writer are in the Biblioteca Nazionale in Turin and in the British Museum.

[22] This is the procedure, I am informed, of one of our leading printers. When necessary, proof copies on paper are circulated with the purpose of discovering errors, but in the final printing the vellum copies are printed before the paper ones. On the other hand, another famous printer of our day always prints the special copies (such as those on vellum) last, so that it is impossible to make a hard and fast rule for contemporary practice.

# CHAPTER B15

## SOME REMARKS ON A
## NINETEENTH-CENTURY REPRINT

IT is, of course, a matter of common knowledge to booklovers that the famous sale of the Duke of Roxburghe's library in May, 1812,[1] stimulated many forms of interest in antiquarian books. One such manifestation was the founding, in the same year, of the Roxburghe Club,[2] which has continuously issued books esteemed by collector and scholar alike. As another example one may cite the practice of reprinting earlier monuments of typographic or literary excellence as a purely commercial venture which also received a decided impetus thereby.

Among those who apparently sought to capitalize on the suddenly increased popularity of early books was William Upcott (1779-1845), at that time the assistant librarian of the London Institution. Upcott had served his apprenticeship as a bookseller by working for R. H. Evans and John Wright in his early years. As the natural son of Ozias Humphry, the portrait-painter, he inherited his father's collections of correspondence and books both of which he greatly extended, leaving at his death an enormous mass of some 32,000 letters and a great number of printed works. He is today perhaps best remembered as the author of *A Bibliographical Account of the Principal Works relating to English Topography*, published in 1818 (London, R. and A. Taylor).

In 1814 Upcott undertook to edit, perhaps at the instigation of the printers, a reprint of Andrew Borde's *The fyrst boke of the Introduction of knowledge*, a work well calculated to attract the interest of potential buyers. This edition was set up from William Copland's second edition, printed by him "at London in Lothbury ouer agaynste Sainct Margarytes church" probably about the year 1562; the original is listed in the *Short-Title Catalogue*[3] under num-

[1] For a contemporary account, see T. F. Dibdin, *The Bibliographical Decameron* (London, Printed for the Author by W. Bulmer & Co., 1817), III: 49ff.

[2] A history of the club and a list of its publications is given by C. Bigham, *The Roxburghe Club, its History and its Members, 1812-1927* (Oxford, The University Press, 1928).

[3] *A Short-Title Catalogue of Books Printed in England, Scotland, & Ireland and*

ber 3385. The reprint consists of two leaves of preliminary matter and fifty-four for the text; nine woodcuts (twelve by repetition)[4] appear as decoration. The printers of the volume were Richard and Arthur Taylor of Shoe Lane, London, who enjoyed a deserved reputation for careful printing. Richard Taylor, moreover, was a man of broad learning and antiquarian tastes, as is evidenced by his fellowships in the Society of Antiquaries and in the Linnean and Philological societies.

The reprint of Borde's work was to be an edition of one hundred and twenty copies on paper and four on vellum, one of the latter now being in The Pierpont Morgan Library (PML 5853). The Morgan copy was, apparently, Upcott's own and a letter relating to the costs of printing the work is now bound in the volume. Though unsigned, it was certainly written at the instance of the printers; it is stamped "7 o'Clock 22 Ju. 1814 N$^t$." and is addressed to "Mr. Upcott London Institution Kings Arms Yard Coleman S$^t$." The letter reads as follows:

D$^r$ Sir:

This is I believe a Correct Statement of Expenses. There will be 3 Copies to give away, which should be overplus above the 120 Copies as there are generally 2 or 3 extra taken off at press.

The Price for the boarded ones which will afford a handsome Profit—£1.11.6.

The Vellum Copies—12.12.0 each.

The advertisements & boarding will probably not be so much.

The expence of your Sheet shifting Press is 8/6$^d$.

---

*of English Books Printed Abroad, 1475-1640* (London, The Bibliographical Society, 1926). A reprint of the first edition, with all the cuts of this edition and those of the second edition which differ, was issued by Frederick J. Furnivall, Early English Text Society, Extra Series X (London, 1870); this edition contains valuable notes on the text and a biographical sketch of Borde. The section devoted to Wales only was printed by E. Vincent Evans, *Andrew Boorde and the Welsh People*, in: *Y Cymmrodor* (London, 1919), XXIX: 44-55. Other chapters may be found in Sir Egerton Brydges and Joseph Haslewood, *The British Bibliographer* (London, T. Bensley for R. Triphook, 1810-1814), IV: 19-30, and in *The Retrospective Review* (London, J. R. Smith, 1853-1854), I: 163-173.

[4] In his introduction, Upcott states that two woodcuts (showing a Scotchman and a Frenchman) were taken from the *Recueil de la diversité des habits* (Paris, Richard Breton, 1562).

### Paper Copies

| | |
|---|---|
| Woodcuts | 10.13.0 |
| 3 Reams & ½ laid Post. 45/ | 7.17.6 |
| Boarding 120 Copies—say 2/0 | 12. 0.0 |
| Printing—as p. Acc. | 32. 7.6 |
| Coach Hire from Reading to Oxford & Back to Reading | 1.10.0 |
| | 64. 8.0 |
| Advertisements say | 4.12.0 |
| | 69. 0.0 |

or 120 Copies. P. Cost 11$^s$/6$^d$ pr. Copy.

### Vellum Copies

| | |
|---|---|
| Printing | 5.12.0 |
| Vellums | 14. 0.0 |
| ½ Binding 4 say | 2. 0.0 |
| | 21.12.0 |

say P. Cost Per Copy £5.5$^s$.0$^d$.
Will you have a Copy of Sir Egerton's Poems.

To what extent Upcott risked his own capital in this venture—and whether the original belonged to him, the Taylor brothers or to a third party—cannot be determined from the letter itself. The introductory note only states that the reprint was made from an original "in the publishers' hands" but who, in the absence of any further particulars, the publishers were, it is impossible to say. In view of the fact that Upcott was given a detailed statement of costs, it seems unlikely that he was acting only in a salaried capacity, and it is thus quite possible that both the book and the reprint were his property.

Which of the extant copies of this edition served Upcott is a doubtful problem; the matter is further complicated by the confusion, in the works of earlier bibliographers,[5] of the several editions and by the incorrect notations as to the present whereabouts of the established copies. In view of these circumstances, it seems necessary to set the facts aright.

[5] For example, the *Hand-Lists of Books Printed by London Printers, 1501–1556* (London, The Bibliographical Society, 1896-1913), IV, under William Copland, lists only the Pepysian copy of the first edition and identifies the Chetham copy as belonging to the second edition. In the catalogue of the Pepysian Library (*vide infra*) it is stated that the only other known copy of the first edition was in the Britwell collection (now British Museum). Ames-Herbert-Dibdin, *Typographical Antiquities* (London, W. Miller, 1810-1819), III: 160, gives the wrong collation.

The *Short-Title Catalogue* (Nos. 3383-3385) lists three early editions in all. The second of these (STC 3384), reputedly printed by Richard Tottell in 1555, is a "ghost" and does not exist; it is recorded through an error in the Bodleian Catalogue, as I learn through the courtesy of William A. Jackson. For the first edition (STC 3383), there are listed copies in the British Museum, Jesus College Cambridge, and Chetham Library at Manchester; the first of these is the West-Pearson-Bindley copy known to Upcott and obtained by the Museum at the Britwell sale (February, 1922), while the Chetham copy was already in that library at the time the reprint was made. There is no copy, however, in the library of Jesus College, according to the Librarian, but one is found in the Pepysian Library at Magdalene College and is listed in its printed catalogue.[6] The error in the *Short-Title Catalogue* seems to be the result of a misprint in the symbol ($C^8$ appearing for $C^6$).

Under No. 3385, the *Short-Title Catalogue* records two copies, viz. Bodleian and Huntington. In this case it happens that there are two copies in the Bodleian Library, one in the Selden collection ($4^0$ B 56 Art. Seld.) as noted by Upcott and the other from the collection of Anthony Wood (Wood 336); I owe this note to the kindness of Mr. C. J. Hindle of the Bodleian. The Huntington Library copy comes from the Britwell Library and the printed *Handlist*[7] of this collection states that it also belonged to James Bindley; it is not, however, recorded in the Bindley sale catalogue. Thus there are three copies of this edition, from which Upcott made his reprint, now known to us.

It is clear from Upcott's preface that the Selden copy was not used for the making of the reprint. Anthony Wood's copy, in turn, was bequeathed by him, together with the rest of his library, to the Ashmolean Museum in 1695 and thus came into the Bodleian through the transfer of the Wood collection to that library in 1860.[8] It is unlikely, I am told, that the Ashmolean would have lent their copy to Upcott and besides this copy lacks signature $D_4$. It may, of course,

---

[6] *Bibliotheca Pepysiana, a Descriptive Catalogue of the Library of Samuel Pepys* (London, Sidgwick & Jackson, 1914-1923), II: 12-13.

[7] *The Britwell Handlist* (London, Bernard Quaritch, 1933), I: 111. The Bindley sale catalogue (1818), Part 1, item 895, lists a copy of Borde's *Introduction of knowledge* but this is certainly that of the first edition as noted by Ames-Herbert-Dibdin, *loc. cit.*

[8] See *A Summary Catalogue of Western Manuscripts in the Bodleian Library at Oxford* (Oxford, Clarendon Press, 1895-1937), V: 86.

be possible that the reprint was made from the copy in the Huntington Library, but this volume has sheet C in facsimile;[9] unless these
leaves were present in the book in 1814 or the facsimile was supplied
before that year, it is difficult to see how Upcott could have used it
for his reprint. One cannot, naturally, ignore the possibility that a
copy was used by Upcott, and perhaps even owned by him, which has
since disappeared.

Whatever may have been the exact circumstances relating to the
making of the reprint, it is certain that some one expected to make
a very handsome profit of no less than 150 per cent in this undertaking. The estimate for the expenses of producing the reprint
amounted to £90. 12. 0 and it was proposed to dispose of the copies
thus:

| | |
|---|---|
| 120 paper copies at £1. 11. 6 | £189. 0. 0 |
| 4 vellum copies at £12. 12. 0 | £ 50. 8. 0 |
| Total | £239. 8. 0 |

The profit was thus expected to be £148. 16. 0. Whether it was realized or not is, of course, another matter, but Borde's work "which
doth teache a man to speake parte of all maner of Languages and
to knowe the usage and fashion of al maner of countreys" may
reasonably have been expected to appeal to the antiquarian tastes
of the early nineteenth century. There is, however, no mention of
the reprint in the *Gentleman's Magazine* or in the *Edinburgh* or
*Quarterly Reviews* for the years 1814-1815, nor does it appear in
R. A. Peddie's *The English Catalogue of Books 1801-1836* (London, Sampson Low, Marston & Co., 1914).

The subsequent history of the commercial value of this work is
not very encouraging for those who buy the reprints now being
published. Allowing for the bookseller's usual profit, the market
value of Upcott's reprint quickly depreciated; for example, a paper
copy was priced at only 14 shillings (just a little more than the
estimated cost of printing) in the Willis and Sotheran catalogue of
25 January 1859. In October 1929, at the very peak of the stock market boom, a copy was sold at auction in this country for $8, approxi-
mately the same price at which, it is suggested in the above letter, the

---

[9] This is not noted in the sale catalogue (Sotheby, 6 February 1922, lot 61) but
*Book-Prices Current* (London, E. Stock, 1922), p. 109, adds the note: "sheet C in
facsimile." Mr. Herman R. Mead of the Huntington Library has suggested to me
that the facsimile may have been made about the same time as Upcott's reprint.

book was to be sold in 1814. The vellum copies fared just as badly. Sir Mark Masterman Sykes's copy was sold at his sale (13 May 1824, lot 444) for £7. 7. 0, while Toovey purchased the copy now in the Morgan Library[10] for £5 at the Robert Samuel Turner sale in June 1888 (lot 719). On 9 November 1936, a copy was sold at auction for only £4. 5. 0, a pound less than the estimated cost of producing it a century and a quarter earlier.[11] Whatever profit may have accrued to those who invested their capital in the production of the Borde reprint, it is certain that the original purchasers fared rather badly if they bought their copies at the price set forth in the letter to Upcott.

(From *PBSA* 41 (1947), pp. 53-59).

[10] *Catalogue of a Collection of Books Formed by James Toovey . . . the Property of J. Pierpont Morgan* (New York, Privately Printed, 1901), p. 89.

[11] It is interesting to note that the Bindley first edition brought only thirteen guineas at his sale (not much more than the vellum copies of the reprint were expected to cost). By 1922 the market value of this book had reached £210, which it fetched at the Britwell sale.

# CHAPTER B16

## THE STATISTICS OF SCIENTIFIC
## INCUNABULA

IN that learned and fascinating analysis of the Italian book production in the fifteenth century with which Victor Scholderer
prefaced the seventh volume of the British Museum's incunabula
catalogue,[1] there is a summary of that country's contribution to the
period's scientific printing which is of singular importance to the
historians of science and culture. On page xxxii of his discussion,
Scholderer made some interesting observations on the relative importance, in this field of book production, of those Italian cities where
the new art flourished. It was with the intention of supplementing
this survey, and extending it so as to include those other parts of
Europe where the printing press was introduced prior to the year
1501, that the present study was taken in hand.

A word must be said about the methods of obtaining the statistics
which will be found in this paper. The listing for the scientific incunabula is handily available in the very useful work by Arnold C.
Klebs[2] which, whatever its sins of omission or inclusion may be,[3]
is universally recognized as a reference work sufficiently adequate
for any estimates of the sort we are about to make. On the other hand,
the information about the total book-production in all countries
where the art was practised in the fifteenth century is still to be assembled and tabulated. For certain countries (England and Spain
may here be cited)[4] and for such cities as Cologne[5] and Naples,[6]
our information is tolerably complete but an all-inclusive summary

---

[1] Catalogue of Books Printed in the XVth Century now in the British Museum,
London, 1908-35.

[2] Incunabula scientifica et medica, Osiris, vol. IV, 1938.

[3] See George Sarton, The Scientific Literature Transmitted through the Incunabula
(Osiris, vol. V, 1938). On p. 53, Prof. Sarton suggests that Klebs' list is "a good
approximation which is quite sufficient for my purpose."

[4] Compare E. Gordon Duff, Fifteenth Century English Books, Oxford, 1917, and
Konrad Haebler, Bibliografía Ibérica del siglo XV, La Haya, 1903-17.

[5] Ernst Voulliéme, Der Buchdruck Kölns bis zum Ende des fünfzehnten Jahrhunderts, Bonn, 1903.

[6] Mariano Fava and Giovanni Bresciano, La stampa a Napoli nel XV secolo,
Leipzig, 1911-12.

is wanting at the present—and will continue to be so until the monumental *Gesamtkatalog der Wiegendrucke*[7] is finished (when, and if, that may be). This study must, then, fall back upon the perennially indispensable *Index* by Robert Proctor.[8] Though the *Index* is, of course, only an account of the holdings of the British Museum and Bodleian libraries, it unquestionably records the most fully representative collection of fifteenth-century books from all parts of civilized Europe ever assembled. As Alfred W. Pollard so aptly observed:[9]

> Whether the British Museum possesses fewer or more numerous different incunabula (i.e., excluding duplicates) than some other great libraries is at present a matter of conjecture. But that the examples which it possesses cover the widest field and are most truly representative of the course of printing in the 15th century, no one who has used Robert Proctor's Index will be likely to deny.

The *Index* can therefore be regarded as listing a satisfactory cross-section of the book-production of the fifteenth century and the statistics given below relative to this aspect are based on Proctor's work.

Table I gives, as listed by Klebs, in the first column (A), the number of scientific books printed in each country, then, in the second column (B), the approximate percentages of each country's contribution, and, finally, in the last column (C), the percentage of the total number of books printed in each country in relation to the entire output of incunabula (based, of course, on Proctor).

It will be noted, at a glance, that four countries (Italy, France, Belgium and the Iberian peninsula—for the sake of convenience Spain and Portugal are listed together) show a higher percentage of scientific books to over-all production than do the others. As some 75 percent of all incunabula were issued by the presses of Italy and Germany, it is interesting to observe that Italy's gain in the percentages is largely at Germany's expense. England, if one may judge from the above table, held printed scientific works in but slight esteem, for whereas this country produced some two percent of the

[7] Seven volumes are usually cited (Leipzig, 1925-38). The first fascicle of Volume VIII was printed during World War II but few copies have reached this country.

[8] *An Index to the Early Printed Books in the British Museum: from the Invention of Printing to the Year MD. with Notes of those in the Bodleian Library*, London, 1898-1903. The interest of both these libraries in English books may make the percentages for these books slightly greater than they should be.

[9] *Catalogue of Books mostly from the Presses of the First Printers . . . Collected by Rush C. Hawkins, catalogued by Alfred W. Pollard, and deposited in the Annmary Brown Memorial at Providence, Rhode Island*, Oxford, 1910, p. xxxi.

TABLE I

| | Klebs (3155 books) | | Proctor (9841 books) |
| | A | B | C |
|---|---|---|---|
| Italy | 1445 | .458 | .422 |
| Germany[10] | 1003 | .318 | .337 |
| France | 387 | .123 | .101 |
| Belgium | 115 | .036 | .027 |
| Spain & Portugal | 74 | .023 | .014 |
| Switzerland | 62 | .020 | .039 |
| Holland | 46 | .015 | .038 |
| England | 23 | .007 | .021 |
| | 3155 | 1.000 | .999[11] |

total fifteenth-century output, the average for the scientific books printed in the British Isles falls to less than half of this figure; with but 23 such books, Great Britain issued not one percent of the editions known to Klebs.

If we now turn to the figures for certain representative towns, the second table gives, in the first column (A) the number of scientific books printed in each place, in the second (B) the percentage of that total to the country's entire output of such works and, lastly, in the third column (C) the percentage of the total number of books published in each city to the aggregate of that country's book-production:

TABLE II

| | A | B | C |
|---|---|---|---|
| *Italy* | | | |
| Venice | 567 | .392 | .411 |
| Padua | 85 | .059 | .019 |
| Pavia | 66 | .046 | .016 |
| *Germany* | | | |
| Leipzig | 188 | .186 | .075 |
| Cologne | 152 | .151 | .218 |
| *France* | | | |
| Lyons | 137 | .354 | .217 |

[10] Books printed in the former Austro-Hungarian empire are here included.

[11] The very few books printed during this period in Scandinavia and elsewhere, and not included in the list, account for the remaining .001.

Surprisingly enough, one notes in Table II that, despite its preponderant position and the high scientific merit of its publications, Venice as a publisher of books on science fails to hold its relative place—that is, though the Republic produced 41 percent of all the incunabula printed in Italy, it put out just 39 percent of the scientific works issued in that country. This proportional decrease struck me as quite unexpected. For any reader of Scholderer's preface, it will hardly prove astonishing that Padua and Pavia make such a creditable showing—nor do these percentages, as we shall see, tell the whole story. Although it does not (strictly speaking) come within the purview of this paper, one may note in passing the almost complete decline of printing in Padua after the close of the fifteenth century. The continuation of Proctor's *Index* by Frank Isaac[12] reveals only one Paduan book printed between 1501–1520 in the British Museum (No. 13836[13]—it is, to be sure, a scientific work). Conversely, the British Museum possesses 35 books printed at Pavia in the same period, approximately half of which are scientific if we include, as Professor Sarton rightly allows,[14] those works dealing with witchcraft.

In Germany, the figures for Leipzig and Cologne are even more significant than it was at first believed they might prove to be. According to Voulliéme, the Rhenish capital produced 1272 incunabula, over half of which are in Proctor. It was certainly to be expected that the ultra-conservative (to speak kindly of it) University of Cologne would have exercised a restraining hand upon any innovations that might have occurred to the members of the printing trade but hardly to such an extent that Cologne, which produced over a fifth of the German incunabula, accounted for barely 15 percent of the books dedicated to science. Leipzig, by contrast, published not eight percent of Germany's output, but of German scientific editions its total easily exceeds 18 percent. In connection with the activities of the printing presses in this German city, Pollard has shrewdly remarked:[15]

[12] *An Index to the Early Printed Books in the British Museum* (Part II, section II), London, 1938.

[13] *Divi Thome Aquinatis in libros physicorum Aristotelis interpretatio et expositio*, Padua, Convent of S. Joannes de Viridario, 25 Aug. 1506.

[14] *Op. cit.*, p. 51.

[15] Quoted from vol. III, p. xxv, of the work cited in note 1.

While here [Erfurt] and in several other towns the influence of the Universities on the German book-trade was mainly restrictive, at Leipzig it seems to have been unusually favourable. Towards the end of the eighties the University was exceptionally prosperous, and whereas the first Leipzig press had been singularly unproductive, from 1487 onward there was a large output of books obviously intended for students, and these seem to testify to a good deal of activity within the University, though on old-fashioned lines.

In France, the high percentage of scientific books printed at Lyons, obtained almost certainly at the expense of Paris and its fashionable liturgical trade, is very significant.

In a sense it is, perhaps, not entirely fair to make comparisons on the basis of the total number of editions known to Klebs. Surely works reprinted time and again—and presumably, such as the 39 editions of the *Somnia Danielis*, in sufficient current demand to be deemed "best-sellers"—reflect little credit on a printer or his city. With the *editiones principes*, however, it is another matter, since each first edition was necessarily a speculative venture for the publisher. Klebs lists 1058 such editions, which first saw the light of day in 95 different towns. Table III lists the fifteen places which produced the greatest number of first editions. Following the name of the city, there are given in order: (A) the number of editions, (B) the percentage of the Klebsian total, (C) the percentage of the town's book production to Proctor's 9841 incunabula and finally (D) the change in the relative position of a city (plus or minus) in the order of rank as the producer of scientific works:

## TABLE III

|    |             | A   | B    | C    | D    |      |
|----|-------------|-----|------|------|------|------|
| 1  | Venice      | 161 | .152 | .173 | (1)  | —    |
| 2  | Rome        | 72  | .068 | .074 | (2)  | —    |
| 3  | Padua       | 55  | .052 | .008 | (14) | + 11 |
| 4  | Augsburg    | 53  | .050 | .043 | (6)  | + 2  |
| 5  | Bologna     | 50  | .047 | .016 | (12) | + 7  |
| 6  | Leipzig     | 47  | .044 | .025 | (10) | + 4  |
| 7  | Paris       | 45  | .042 | .068 | (4)  | − 3  |
| 8  | Nuremberg   | 42  | .040 | .037 | (7)  | − 1  |
| 9  | Pavia       | 41  | .039 | .007 | (15) | + 6  |
| 10 | Milan       | 37  | .035 | .033 | (9)  | − 1  |
| 11 | Cologne     | 36  | .034 | .073 | (3)  | − 8  |
| 12 | Lyons       | 33  | .031 | .022 | (11) | − 1  |
| 13 | Florence    | 32  | .030 | .037 | (8)  | − 5  |
| 14 | Strassburg  | 25  | .024 | .059 | (5)  | − 9  |
| 15 | Naples      | 22  | .021 | .008 | (13) | − 2  |

As might have been expected, Venice and Rome easily head the list, though in each case the percentages of scientific books are smaller than for the total production. These two cities, then, had lost to the others a portion of the trade in such books which should, by rights, have been theirs.[16] Padua, with a share of less than one percent of the total trade, accounts for over five percent of the first printings of scientific texts—a really surprising proportion; Pavia, in this respect, stands somewhat below the satellite of Venice, Padua. The rest of the list offers few elements of surprise in regard to the order or the percentages—but the omission of some prominent cities from this tabulation merits attention. One looks in vain for Mainz, the birthplace of the new art, which, with 141 books noted by Proctor, exceeds the number there listed for Naples, Padua or Pavia. Speier, with almost the same total as Mainz, is also not listed. Among the Italian towns, Brescia (with its 110 books in Proctor) is conspicuously absent, as well as Deventer (173 books), and Louvain and Antwerp (113 each), important trade centers of the Low Countries.

Finally, if one turns to the true "cradle-books" of medical printing, i.e., those produced before 1481 and listed by Osler-Scholderer,[17] a real surprise is (I think) in store for the reader. There are 217 such editions listed in the bibliography and 139 texts are recorded as first editions. These may be tabulated in the following manner (Table IV), though for reasons of convenience it is possible to list only those towns which produced five or more such works. The table lists in the first column the cities with the number of books (A) and percentage of the total (B), and then (C) the number of first editions only, together with appropriate percentages (D) and the numerical position of the town in this respect (E).

The importance of the smaller Italian towns in this field of printing, which had attracted the notice of Scholderer, is here especially pronounced. That Venice should yield the primacy to Padua in the printing of medical books before 1481, and that Augsburg should precede Rome in the list, may surprise many. Perhaps the most unexpected name to appear in Table IV is that of Santorso, a town not especially renowned in the annals of printing. According to the

---

[16] In Rome, the printers of the first two decades of the sixteenth century followed the lead set for them by Plannck and Silber late in the preceding century by placing their presses in the service of the Curia. Of the 318 books listed by Isaac, only twenty were of scientific interest (.063)—if we exclude the twelve items relating to discovery and exploration (Vespucci—1, Barthema—2, and King Emmanuel—9).

[17] *Incunabula medica*, London, 1923.

TABLE IV

| | | Editions | | | First texts | |
|---|---|---|---|---|---|---|
| | | A | B | C | D | E |
| 1 | Padua | 31 | .143 | 24 | .173 | (1) |
| 2 | Venice | 26 | .120 | 20 | .144 | (2) |
| 3 | Augsburg | 23 | .106 | 11 | .079 | (3) |
| 4 | Rome | 15 | .069 | 8 | .058 | (4) |
| 5/6 | Milan | 12 | .055 | 5 | .036 | (9) |
| 5/6 | Naples | 12 | .055 | 7 | .050 | (5) |
| 7 | Bologna | 10 | .046 | 6 | .043 | (6) |
| 8 | Pavia | 8 | .037 | 5 | .036 | (10) |
| 9 | Strassburg | 7 | .032 | | [unlisted] | |
| 10 | Cologne | 6 | .028 | 5 | .036 | (8) |
| 11 | Lyons | 6 | .028 | | [unlisted] | |
| 12 | Nuremberg | 5 | .023 | | " | |
| 13 | Mantua | 5 | .023 | | " | |
| — | Santorso[18] | [unlisted] | | 6 | .043 | (7) |

Proctor averages, this Alpine village produced a mere .07 percent of the books published in Italy in the fifteenth century and less than one and one-half percent of those included by Osler-Scholderer, but its three medical volumes of the year 1473 account for six first editions (of separate texts) and for the prominent position accorded to Santorso in this list. Five of these are very short hydrotherapeutic tracts; the sixth, perhaps of this nature also, is the slightly longer *Quaestio de restauratione humidi* by the Italian physician Sigismondo Polcastro, who died in this same year.

These, then, are the statistics concerning the production of scientific books in the fifteenth century. While, in the main, they confirm the general impression which even a casual acquaintanceship with incunabula makes upon the student, the figures provide information of a definite and fundamental nature. Certain statistics are, nevertheless, quite unexpected—at least to one who can, perhaps, claim some familiarity with the history of early printing. In any case, it is the hope of the compiler that these tables may provide the historians of science, or of culture in general, with figures suitable for a more detailed evaluation along regional lines of the fifteenth-century production of scientific books.

(From *Isis* 39 (1948), pp. 163-68).

[18] Only the three medical books cited later on in the text were printed at Santorso in the fifteenth century. This makes Santorso's percentage of the total books cited by Osler-Scholderer equal to .014.

# CHAPTER B17

## THE FIRST ALDINE*

THE book that is the subject of this study is not, as might be suspected from the title, the first book issued by the Aldine Press but rather the first work which, it is believed, Aldus Manutius wrote and caused to be printed—the *Musarum Panagyris*. It might appear to be strange that a book which has been known to the world of bibliography for nearly a century and a half, which was reprinted in its entirety early in the nineteenth century by Morelli[1] and which was listed by Renouard[2] should never have received—so far as can be determined—a full-dress bibliographical description, any sort of typographical investigation, or a modern discussion of its contents. The explanation for this appears to be relatively simple. Only four copies of the original edition were known to the distinguished bibliographer of Aldus, and one of these four is now in The Pierpont Morgan Library.[3] Even Morelli's reprint of 1806 is seemingly nearly as hard to find. There is no copy of it in any of the great New York libraries and the Union Catalogue knows of but one example in America (at Harvard), so that the reprint—in this country, at least—seems to be as scarce as the original. As for the discussions of the literary contents of the work, the accounts given by Morelli, Renouard, Firmin-Didot[4] and Schück[5] are textually quite correct, but they need supplementing. In particular, these scholars

---

* Read at the meeting of the Bibliographical Society of America in Philadelphia, June 5, 1948.

[1] *Aldi Pii Manutii Scripta tria longe rarissima a Iacobo Morellio denuo edita et illustrata* (Bassani, Typis Remondinianis, 1806).

[2] A. A. Renouard, *Annales de l'imprimerie des Alde* (Paris, Jules Renouard, 1834), p. 257, no. 1.

[3] Ada Thurston and Curt F. Bühler, *Check List of Fifteenth Century Printing in the Pierpont Morgan Library* (New York, The Pierpont Morgan Library, 1939), no. 904. This was Renouard's own copy. The copy owned by the Biblioteca Queriniana (Brescia) is presumably still there, while one of the two examples formerly in private hands is now in the John Rylands Library; compare the *Catalogue of the Printed Books and Manuscripts in the John Rylands Library* (Manchester, J. E. Cornish, 1899), II: 1145.

[4] A. Firmin-Didot, *Alde Manuce et l'Hellénisme à Venise* (Paris, Firmin-Didot, 1875), pp. 9-11.

[5] J. Schück, *Aldus Manutius und seine Zeitgenossen in Italien und Deutschland* (Berlin, Dümmler, 1862), pp. 107-115.

have failed to observe the curious inconsistencies and contradictions which are inherent in the text of the volume and their conclusions upon it. Finally, no one, it would seem, has asked himself the very pertinent questions—why and when was the work written and when and why did Aldus have it printed?

The bibliographical annotations are equally scanty and incomplete. Morelli assigned the *Musarum Panagyris* to a press with which Antonio Moreto was connected and Renouard has styled this press "apud Antonium Moretum Brixiensem." No such printing-house, however, is listed by modern bibliographies, though Moretus[6] is known as an occasional publisher who employed various presses to print for him. The two books[7] cited by Morelli as publications by Moretus are now believed to have been printed with the types of Damianus of Gorgonzola, but the earliest work known to have been produced by this printer is dated 29 March 1493. The *Musarum Panagyris*, as we shall see, must have been printed several years before that. The detailed bibliographical description[8] of this book is as follows:

MANUTIUS, ALDUS. Musarum Panagyris. [Venice: Baptista de Tortis, after March 1487 and before March 1491.]

Renouard, p. 257; Morgan *Check List* 904; *Census* M 195.

Quarto. 8 leaves, the first blank. a[8]. 29 lines. Type-page (f. 5): 162 x 99 mm. Types: 1*:114R* (with Q/u), 78 Gk.

f. 1, blank. 2-a2: Musarū Panagyris per Aldum Mannucciū Bassianatē || latinum cū exasticho & parænesi eiusdē ad Albertū || Pium Magnificum: atq[3] inclytum Carpi principem. || Exastichon. || Carmina delectant pueros: en carmina princeps: || Dant ad te faciles ex Helicone deæ. || . . . [ends 8ᵛ-a8ᵛ, l. 25]: Hunc ubi tu scieris longe maiora dabuntur || Dona tibi: pro te quæ tuus Aldus habet. || FINIS. ||

Contents: Musarum Panagyris (a2-a3 verso, l. 6); Parænesis Aldi Mannuccii ad eundem principem (a3 verso, l. 7-a4, l. 17); Hesiodus in Theogonia de nominibus Musarum [3 Greek lines with Latin translation] (a4, ll. 18-25); Aldus Mannuccius Bassianas latinus Catharinæ Piæ Principi clarissimæ ac prudentissimæ. S. P. D. [Letter from Aldus to Caterina Pio] (a4, l. 26-a8, l. 25); Aldus Mannuccius Bassianas latinus Alberto Pio principi Carpensi. S. P. D. [Verse epistle from Aldus to Alberto] (a8, l. 26 - a8 verso, l. 26).

First edition. The copy in The Pierpont Morgan Library (PML 22035) measures 215 x 150 mm. and is bound in nineteenth-century blue morocco, gilt.

---

[6] Compare BMC VII: 1142/1143.

[7] Sabellicus, *De situ urbis Venetae* (H 14056; BMC V:544) and Leonardus Aretinus, *Epistolae familiares* (H 1567; BMC V:512).

[8] The form of this description is that which I outlined in the Rosenbach lecture of 1947.

From the collection of Antoine Augustin Renouard. Other copies are in the John Rylands Library (Manchester) and in the Biblioteca Queriniana (Brescia).

Turning first of all to the literary contents—the why and when of the work's composition—it can be conveniently summarized as follows. The work contains two poems by Aldus in honor of his pupil Alberto Pio, an extract in Greek and Latin from Hesiod,[9] a letter from Aldus to Alberto's mother Catherine, and concludes with another poem for Alberto. The verse portions of the work may be consulted in Renouard's book[10] so that they need not occupy much of our time. The sentiments and exhortations found therein were obviously set down for some one quite young—and the Latin is sufficiently simple so that anyone familiar with the language can read it without benefit of dictionary or grammar. It may be added that the last poem is clearly a preface to a grammatical work which Aldus had written[11] and which, he says, he had presented to Alberto shortly before writing the letter to the boy's mother. It is certain, therefore, that the *Musarum Panagyris* was written by Aldus at Carpi where he resided as tutor to the young princes of Carpi between 1483 and 1490.[12]

It is, however, the letter from Aldus to the mother of Alberto and Leonello Pio which deserves a closer scrutiny than that bestowed on it by earlier bibliographers and students of Aldus. True enough, the bare outlines of the contents were analyzed by Firmin-Didot, but this analysis tells us little more than may be found in the text as reprinted, according to the standards of the early nineteenth century, by Morelli.[13] This faulty version was subsequently reprinted by Julius

---

[9] Lines 77-79 of the *Theogony*. The whole *Theogonia* appears for the first time in Aldus's own edition of Theocritus, February 1495/1496 (Hain 15477).

[10] *Op. cit.,* pp. 538-540.

[11] Aldus says:

Accipe nunc igitur paruum: mea munera: librum
Conscriptum nuper: compositum*que* mihi.

[12] These are the dates given by Schück and accepted by the *Enciclopedia Italiana* (XII: 182). Some authorities believe that Aldus went to Venice in 1488/1489 but this seems too early. The letter from Pico to Aldus with date 11 February 1490 (Schück, pp. 115-116) speaks of a Homer which Aldus had requested and which Pico was sending from Florence. It is likely that Aldus would have had greater difficulty in getting the Homer in Carpi than he would have had if at that time he was in Venice. It seems reasonable to infer, therefore, that this letter was sent to Aldus when he was still in Carpi.

[13] Spelling and punctuation are modern, while misprints have been corrected. There are occasional misreadings.

Schück. In brief, Aldus explains in the letter to Catherine the precepts he is following in the education of her sons and expends much time in emphasizing the importance of a thorough grounding in Greek and Latin. Why did he write the letter? Surely the elder sister of Pico della Mirandola was in no need of a lecture from a young scholar on the value of a classical training. The letter contains a number of classical clichés drawn from various sources, including the lines from Horace which (then as now) must have been familiar to anyone at all acquainted with the classics:[14]

> Graiis ingenium, Graiis dedit ore rotundo
> Musa loqui, praeter laudem nullius avaris.

And again Aldus quotes:

> . . . Vos exemplaria Graeca
> Nocturna versate manu, versate diurna.

The epistle to Catherine also includes two Greek passages borrowed from Aulus Gellius.[15] The first quotation is a letter from King Philip to Aristotle announcing the birth of Alexander and expressing the hope that the child might be taught by him; the second is a letter from Alexander to Aristotle[16] concerning the publication of certain of the philosopher's lectures. Oddly enough (and this is another point that escaped both Morelli and Schück) Aldus did not use the Latin translation which Gellius thoughtfully provided for the first extract but supplied one of his own. On the whole Aldus' rendering is better —in any case more Ciceronian, and consequently easier Latin—than Gellius'. This may offer a clue as to the very reason for the composition of the letter—namely that it was intended to show the boy's mother that Aldus knew his business, that he was capable of writing a good Ciceronian style and that he was fully acquainted with the works of classical antiquity. Further citations from scholars of his own era were meant to indicate that Aldus was equally aware of more recent trends in thought and education. Among those of his contemporaries whose learning and wisdom he praised were the boy's uncle, Pico della Mirandola, Zacharias Barbarus and his distinguished son Ermolao, and Federigo, Duke of Urbino, "qui pariter et armorum et liberalium disciplinarum gloria excelluit."

[14] *Ars poetica*, lines 323-324 and 268-269 (ed. R. Bentley, Cambridge, 1711, pp. 304 and 302).
[15] *Noctes Atticae*, IX. iii. 6 and XX. v. 11 (Venice, Aldus, 1515, ff. 120 and 284).
[16] This letter is also cited in Plutarch's "Life of Alexander." It is probable, however, that Aldus took both excerpts from Gellius.

As we have seen, the *Musarum Panagyris* must have been written before Aldus went to Venice, but to limit the date any further offers serious complications. The earliest date for a *terminus a quo* is that which is given by Schück by implication. Hermolaus Barbarus is referred to in the text as an "eques." In explanation of this, Schück[17] points out that the Italian was knighted by the Emperor Frederick III in August 1486 following a laudatory address which Ermolao presented at Bruges in his rôle as Venetian ambassador. Since, however, Ermolao's father is also spoken of as an "eques"—and since Zacharias, the procurator of St. Mark's, is not known to have received the accolade—it does not follow that Aldus in using this term was necessarily referring to Ermolao as a German "Ritter." August 1486 does not, therefore, serve as a critical date.

Morelli, in turn, believed that the letter to Catherine was written at some time after May 1487 when Pietro Barozzi was translated from the see of Belluno to that of Padua, since Barozzi is here cited as Bishop of Padua. Schück, however, following Cardinal Quirini, maintained that Barozzi became Bishop of Padua in 1488—but in this he is not supported by the *Series episcoporum* of Gams[18] who also gives the date as May 1487.

But all these dates involve a contradiction which Morelli and Schück failed to note. Aldus' letter is specifically addressed to Catherine Pio—but by May 1488 (or 1487), or even by August 1486, Catherine was no longer the widow of Leonello Pio but the wife of Rodolfo Gonzaga. The exact date of this marriage[19] has so far eluded me (the Gonzagas for good and sufficient reasons seem to have destroyed all the pertinent records) but an approximate one can be

---

[17] *Op. cit.*, p. 114, note 2.

[18] P. B. Gams, *Series episcoporum* (Leipzig, K. Hiersemann, 1931), pp. 777 and 798. According to Conrad Eubel, *Hierarchia catholica medii aevi* (2 ed., Münster, 1913-1923), II: 210, Barozzi became Bishop of Padua on 14 March 1487.

[19] No date is given in the standard work by Pompeo Litta, *Famiglie celebri Italiane* (Milan, 1819–1910) under the tables for Pio (I. xii. 3), Pico (I. x. 3) or Gonzaga (III. xxxiii. 16). According to Aglauro Ungherini, *Manuel de bibliographie biographique et d'iconographie des femmes célèbres* (Turin, 1892-1905), Suppl., col. 433, the marriage took place in 1477; this, however, is an impossible date as her first husband was then still alive. Through the courtesy of the Centro Nazionale di Informazioni Bibliografiche in Rome, I learn that G. Silingardi states in his *Caterina Pico. Cenni storici* (Modena, 1876) that Catherine was married to Rodolfo "negli ultimi giorni del 1484" but that it was impossible to confirm this statement.

determined.[20] During the Christmas festivities of 1483 Rodolfo conveniently and under somewhat mysterious circumstances "liqui-
dated" his first wife—Antonia or Anna, the daughter of Sigismondo
Malatesta of Rimini—and it must have been just a year later that he
espoused Catherine Pio. The Archivio di Stato at Mantua[21] contains
a letter written on 3 January 1485 wherein Rodolfo Gonzaga informed his chancellor (Leonardo di S. Gemeniano) that with the
consent of the Marquis of Mantua and the "consiglio dei maggio-
renti" he had married "Caterina da Carpi" who was furnished with
a dowry of 12,000 ducats; furthermore, he asked that the news be
kept confidential. Again Rodolfo wrote the Marchese himself on
January 15 of the same year that he was now married to Catherine;
this probably was an official announcement. Other records indicate
that Rodolfo was quite ill in November of the previous year, so that
one would not be far wrong to infer that the wedding had taken
place towards the end of December 1484. Why, then, if the letter was
written to Catherine after August 1486, or May 1487 (as the case may
be) was it not addressed to her as Catherine Gonzaga?

The contradictions into which Schück's own arguments led him
are curious. The German scholar assumed that the *Musarum Panagyris* was written in 1488 but, as he himself acknowledged, the last
poem to Alberto speaks of a grammatical work which Aldus had
recently presented to the young Prince of Carpi. The literary allusions in the text clearly show that the presentation took place about
the time of the great pagan festival of the Saturnalia—and the grammar might well have been intended as Aldus' "strena" to Alberto.
Aldus, furthermore, expressly stated that the work he thus presented was a treatise on accents; in short, it was an elementary tract
for a beginner in Greek. Is it conceivable that Aldus, coming to Carpi
about the year 1484, should wait four years before beginning his instructions in that tongue? It seems hardly likely. In 1484 Alberto was
nine years old; would Aldus have waited until the boy was thirteen
before beginning to teach him the language of Homer? In the second decade of the twentieth century, an average and none too bril-

[20] The date of the wedding is not given in the exhaustive study by Felice Ceretti,
*Biografie pichensi*, in: *Memorie storiche della città e dell'antico ducato della Mirandola* (Mirandola, 1872-1916), Vols. XVII-XX, nor in his numerous papers in the
various *Atti e memorie* for the provinces of Emilia, Modena, and Parma.

[21] I am deeply obliged to Dr. Giovanni Praticò, the Director of the Archivio di
Stato in Mantua, for supplying me with this information from the Gonzaga archives.

liant student like myself was subjected at the age of ten to "amo, amas, amat." A year or two later I can remember acquiring (somewhat informally, it is true—I was even then a book collector) a Greek Grammar with the strange notion that if I had once mastered the alphabet I should forthwith be able to read Greek. The disillusionment was complete! In any case, it is altogether likely that an Italian boy of the Renaissance began to learn Greek before he was ten.²² Politian, it will be recalled,²³ was sent to Florence at that age to study under Callistus and Argyropoulos. Even the daughters of the nobility were occasionally taught Greek in their early youth, for it is a matter of record that Cecilia Gonzaga²⁴ was already studying Greek grammar at seven and Damigella Trivulzio²⁵ was proficient in that tongue at fourteen. In view of Aldus' inclinations and the brilliance of his pupils it is reasonable to assume that their instruction in Greek began immediately upon the arrival of their new tutor in Carpi. It seems certain that we must set down the *Musarum Panagyris* as belonging to the first year of Aldus' stay with the young Princes. One may well suppose, therefore, that the work was written probably not long before the end of December 1484. We shall have more to say about this later on.

²² Compare, for example, the letter from Ambrogio Camaldolese to Niccolo Niccoli printed by Edmund Martène and Ursin Durand, *Veterum scriptorum et monumentorum, historicorum, dogmaticorum, moralium, amplissima collectio* (Paris, 1724-1733), III:554-555: "Posteaquam scripseram & obsignaveram litteras, profectus ut viserem Victorinum, graecamque ipsius discuterem bibliothecam, occurrit ille nobis cum filiis principis, maribus duobus, & puella septem annorum. Major ex his XI. minor V. annorum est. Duo item alii pueri X. ferme annorum singuli dominorum aliorum filii. . . . Principis filios & puellam graecas docet litteras, omnesque graece scribere didicerunt. Novem sunt ferme pueri, qui scribunt adeo venuste, ut miratus sim. Vidi Chrysostomi traductionem ab uno ex discipulis ejus factam, satisque placuit." Ambrogio, of course, is speaking of the famous school of Vittorino da Feltre at Mantua; compare also his letter to Cosimo de' Medici (cols. 451-454).

²³ John A. Symonds, *Renaissance in Italy, The Revival of Learning* (London, John Murray, 1929), p. 350: "At the age of ten he came to study in the University of Florence, where he profited by the teaching of Landino, Argyropoulos, Andronicus Kallistos, and Ficino. The precocity of his genius displayed itself in Latin poems and Greek epigrams composed while he was yet a boy."

²⁴ William H. Woodward, *Vittorino da Feltre and other Humanist Educators* (Cambridge, University Press, 1897), p. 50: "But Cecilia Gonzaga was already learning the [Greek] grammar at the age of seven; and rapidly became proficient; and possibly her brother Gianlucido had begun even earlier." Compare also pp. 31 and 54-55.

²⁵ Jacobus Philippus Foresti [Bergomensis], *De claris selectisque mulieribus* (Ferrara, de Rubeis, 1497), sign z4: "et grecarum breui tempore acquisiuerit non vulgarem noticiam: adeo vt iam concine grecum proferat sermonem."

The name of the printer and the *terminus ad quem* for the printing of the *Musarum Panagyris*, though somewhat easier to determine, were not established by the scholars already mentioned. Upon the evidence of the types, the book was certainly printed at Venice at the press of Baptista de Tortis; it is equally clear that this volume must have been produced before the middle of March 1491. The celebrated Humanist, Hermolaus Barbarus, is cited in the text of Aldus' letter as "the glory and ornament of the most powerful and illustrious Venetian Senate." On the seventh of March, 1491, Ermolao was created Patriarch of Aquileia.[26] Barbaro's acceptance of this appointment was a direct violation of the laws of the Republic which forbade an ambassador to accept any major honor or reward without first securing permission to do so.[27] Barbaro's dispensing with this formality proved so offensive to the Venetian government that he was promptly banished from the Republic and never saw his native city again. It is scarce likely that a Venetian printer would have compromised himself by printing such glowing praise of anyone who had recently incurred the displeasure of the Senate; one may, therefore, assume that the volume was printed before this event had taken place. The *Musarum Panagyris* can thus be confidently dated as having been printed not later than March 1491 nor before March or May 1487 since (as we have seen) Barozzi is cited as Bishop of Padua.

Nor is the selection by Aldus of Baptista de Tortis as the printer for his booklet a matter of surprise. Although more than 150 different presses produced books in Venice during the fifteenth century, only thirty-one were in active operation between 1486 and 1491, and but seven of these could be considered prominent presses if judged by the quantity and quality of their output.[28] Aldus would naturally have been most familiar with the names of those houses specializing in classical publications; this, in turn, narrows the field down to three firms, those of Joannes and Gregorius de Gregoriis, Bonetus Locatellus, and Baptista de Tortis. Since Locatellus was a comparative newcomer (and printed no classics before 1490) and since the de Gregoriis firm seems to have experienced financial difficulties between 1486 and 1489[29] and did very little publishing in

---

[26] Gams, *op. cit.*, p. 774.    [27] Compare Schück, p. 114, note 1.
[28] These figures are obtained from Konrad Haebler, *Typenrepertorium der Wiegendrucke* (Halle & Leipzig, 1905-1922) and Konrad Burger, *The Printers and Publishers of the XV. Century with Lists of their Works* (London, Sotheran, 1902), supplemented by the more recent bibliographies.
[29] See BMC V:xxix.

these years, it seems almost inevitable that Aldus should have turned for the printing of the *Musarum Panagyris* to Baptista de Tortis (half of whose production prior to 1490 had been of a classical nature).

At this point one must pause and survey the answers to the queries that have been posed. So far we have been able to give a likely date (1484) for the composition of the work and have been led to believe that the letter to Catherine was written with a view towards reassuring her as to Aldus' capabilities. It has also been established where, by whom, and approximately when the pamphlet was printed. A reason for the printing of the volume must still be supplied. At first glance, there seems to be no particular reason *why* it should ever have been printed. Aldus' arguments for the necessity of a classical education are certainly not "dangerously original" and the verse is neither sufficiently elegant nor suitably polished to have commanded the attention of his scholarly colleagues. It is easy to believe that Aldus wrote the poetry for the entertainment of his young pupils, but this in itself is not sufficient reason for explaining the printing of this text. Again it seems hardly likely that Aldus wrote the letter merely to convince the sister of Pico of the importance of studying the classics. Finally it is *highly* unlikely that Alberto and Leonello Pio would have had any choice in the matter anyway—so they needed no convincing. Whatever their tastes may have been at that time, Aldus was certainly going to teach them Latin and Greek—of that one can be very sure!

However speculative it may be, only one explanation presents itself to me, namely that Aldus printed the letter to Catherine for the primary purpose of providing himself with a sort of propaganda booklet. Aldus had for long been planning to establish his own press and he was clearly in need of some form of advance publicity before invading the highly competitive publishing business at Venice. Surely it is no coincidence that shortly after the appearance of this volume, Aldus began printing exactly those books which were suitable for the purposes he had outlined in the letter to Catherine. If he actually did send the epistle to Catherine—and there is nothing to indicate that he did not send it—the address would prove that he wrote it in 1484 before her marriage to Rodolfo Gonzaga, and this date, as we have seen, is confirmed by the literary contents of the volume. That Barozzi appears in the printed version as the Bishop of Padua and not of Belluno presents no particular difficulty. At the time he revised the manuscript and sent it to de Tortis, Aldus may simply have corrected what he took to be a slip on his part; that is, when he forwarded the manuscript to the printer he knew Barozzi as Bishop of Padua and did not recall that, when the letter was originally written, Barozzi was still Bishop of Belluno. Aldus must here have corrected what he believed to be an earlier mistake. He would not, however, have dared to tamper with the heading of the letter and would have preserved it in the form in which it was originally written. This would explain why the letter is addressed to Catherine Pio (it was written or sent prior to Catherine's marriage to Rodolfo Gonzaga) and that it was both written and printed as a form of self-promotional literature.

Such evidence as we have, then, leads one to believe that Aldus wrote the contents of the volume now known as the *Musarum Panagyris* in 1484 and that he had it printed by Baptista de Tortis between 1487 and 1491 as a bit of advance publicity for the distinguished career which was subsequently to be his at Venice.

Before closing I should very much like to make one further comment. Dr. W. W. Greg has made the somewhat startling suggestion —a curious slip, it seems to me, on the part of the foremost bibliographer of our day—that "bibliography has nothing to do with the subject-matter of books."[30] Indeed I have always felt rather strongly that the contents of a book often give us information absolutely invaluable to the bibliographer and that the subject-matter cannot —and should not—be lightly dismissed as of no bibliographical significance. In the case of the *Musarum Panagyris*, for example, the literary content is of signal importance since it tells us not only when and why the book was written but also when—and most probably why—it was printed.

(From *PBSA* 42 (1948), pp. 269-80).

[30] "Bibliography—an Apologia" in: *The Library* (Oxford University Press, 1932-1933), 4th ser., XIII:114.

[Note: since publication of this study, four more copies have come to light— Bologna, Biblioteca Universitaria (Caronti 529); Naples, Biblioteca Universitaria (IGI 6140); Sélestat, Bibliothèque Municipale (Walter 1821); and Cracow, Bibljoteka Jagiellońska (Inc. 2718a; Neolat. 855). CFB]

# CHAPTER B18

## STOP-PRESS AND MANUSCRIPT CORRECTIONS IN THE ALDINE EDITION OF BENEDETTI'S *DIARIA DE BELLO CAROLINO*

THE productions of the Aldine press, at least those issued by the founder of the firm himself, have been listed so often and have been so thoroughly described according to various bibliographical standards that new additions to the canon are hardly to be expected.[1] For well over a century, the world of books has been provided with a detailed list of the Aldine classics,[2] and these volumes have served classical scholarship as important prime sources for textual research practically since the day they came off the press. Under these circumstances, it seems almost unbelievable that the surviving copies appear to have escaped investigation for the purpose of discovering variant settings.

A study of several of the earliest Aldines recently undertaken by the present writer in the chief European and American libraries has brought to light certain new facts which should claim the attention not only of bibliographers but also of classicists and of editors of Renaissance texts in general. For the one, it is a matter of some moment to determine what the "ideal" copy of any Aldine may be, while, for the others, it is supremely important to know how the final and correct text (as Aldus intended to present it to his readers) should be read in order to make it possible to utilize such an edition for *variae lectiones*. Stop-press corrections will, of course, be readily identified by a line-for-line comparison of many copies against a control. But there are other corrections made by hand in many early Aldines which have been ignored both by the bibliographers and by

---

[1] It is my pleasant duty to acknowledge, with grateful thanks, the kind help of my good friend and colleague, Dr. George K. Boyce, not only in the preparation of the material for this paper but also in the reading of the final article both in manuscript and in proof. Furthermore, my obligation to him extends far beyond the present paper and applies equally to whatever I have written for the past several years. Naturally it would be most improper to attribute any possible errors of judgment or fact to anyone but the present writer.

[2] The standard reference work is the bibliography by A. A. Renouard, *Annales de l'imprimerie des Alde* (Paris, Jules Renouard, 1834).

the several editors, though it is my contention that such manuscript alterations *made by the printer or in his shop in several copies*[3] form an integral part of the book. Since it is clear that such corrections were considered by Aldus as essential in the presentation of the text as he wished it to appear, these emendations are as much a part of the book as, for example, inserted slips or texts supplied by means of stamping. Unfortunately, eighteenth- and nineteenth-century bibliophiles demanded that many such Aldines be washed and cleaned, with the unfortunate result that manuscript corrections were often obscured or made undecipherable. Such books require the use of ultra-violet rays, or possibly infra-red photography, both of which multiply the task—and deplete the purse—of the twentieth-century scholar. Earlier classicists ignored these manuscript alterations, even when they could read them; for example, among the variants admitted to the text of Musaeus by the eighteenth-century editor Röver (Lugduni Batavorum, 1737) there are at least two which Aldus repudiated by means of manuscript entries. The Aldine edition of *Hero and Leander* still requires further investigation before a summary can be offered the reader, but another Aldine of the same period illustrates the points which I have made.

The *Diaria de Bello Carolino* by Alessandro Benedetti (GW 864; H 807; *Census* A 355) has been described in bibliographies too numerous to list here in full, but I have seen no mention anywhere either of the stop-press corrections or of the manuscript emendations commonly found in the several copies. The fifteen that have been studied for this purpose may be identified by the following sigla:

a – New York, The Pierpont Morgan Library, PML 365 (*partly washed*)
b – "     "     "     "     "     " PML 442
c – Vatican City, Biblioteca Apostolica Vaticana, Inc. Ross. 9
d – "     "     "     "     " Inc. IV. 203
e – Rome, Biblioteca Casanatense, Inc. 826
f – Venice, Biblioteca Marciana, no. 38487

---

[3] Since the corrections are always identical in form, written in at the same time and with the same ink, and many are certainly supplied by just one hand, it is certain that these alterations are not the diligent corrections of individual scholars but "wholesale" emendation made at the printing house. Of course, individual copies also contain specific corrections made by an industrious reader; thus, for example, the copy in the New York Public Library contains extensive marginal notes found only in that copy, while in Morgan 365 "iunt" in the last line of sign. h5 recto has been corrected to "aiunt." This emendation is found in none of the other copies. Only in the Bibliothèque Nationale copy has "indignatiois" on h5ᵛ, l. 19, been corrected to "indignationis."

g – Milan, Biblioteca Ambrosiana (only partly checked)
h – Paris, Bibliothèque Nationale, Rés. K. 511
i – London, British Museum, Grenville 6202 (*much washed*)
k – "        "        "    C. 8. h. 14 (vellum)
l – New York, New York Public Library, Reserve
m – Baltimore, Walters Art Gallery, Inc. A 355[4]
n – San Marino, Henry E. Huntington Library (Mead no. 3297)[5]
o – Cleveland, Army Medical Library[6]
p – Washington, Library of Congress, Inc. x. B 46
D – Lodovico Domenichi's Italian translation (Venice, 1549)
E – J. G. von Eckhart's Latin edition in his *Corpus historicum medii aevi* (Leipzig, 1723, Vol. II)
G — P. Giustiniano's Latin text in his *Rerum Venetarum historia* (Strassburg, 1611-1612, Appendix, pp. 74-101)

Listed below are five stop-press corrections, followed by seventeen cases of manuscript emendations; in each instance the earlier (incorrect) form of the text is given first. Following this list, one example of each type of correction will be subjected to a more detailed analysis in order to show why Aldus felt obliged to correct his text in this fashion.

### Stop-press Corrections

a6$^v$, l. 5: golli - dfi; a (MS. cor. to "galli")[7]    galli - bceghklmnop; EG
c7$^v$, l. 14: eneæ - bceghln    aeneæ - adfikmop; EG
d7$^v$, ll. 18/19: eos fugientes persequi statuerunt. Ac ad inces-||sendos à tergo, remorandosq;. Petrum duo-|| [so: an]

eos fugientes persequi statuerunt: miserūtq; ad || incessendos à tergo, remorandosq; Petrū duo-|| [so: bcdefghiklmop; DEG]

d7$^v$, l. 22: præde - an    prædæ - bcdefghiklmop; EG
g7, l. 15; uerinatum insigna uiderūt: quæ oppidanis im-|| [so: bcdfgilmnop]
uerinatum insignia uiderūt: quæ oppidanis im|| [so: aehk; DEG]

---

[4] Miss Dorothy Miner has kindly supplied the readings of the Walters' copy.

[5] For the presence or absence of corrections in the Huntington copy (from the collection of the Duke of Sussex), I am obliged to Mr. Herman R. Mead.

[6] Dr. Dorothy M. Schullian has not only provided me with the citations from the copy in the Army Medical Library but has most graciously permitted me to draw upon her own full knowledge of this text. Dr. Schullian has in preparation a critical edition of the *Diaria* together with an English translation, which will present the text in a definitive form. This copy will be listed as incunable no. 97 in Dr. Schullian's forthcoming *Catalogue of Incunabula and Manuscripts in the Army Medical Library* (at press).

[7] Curiously enough this is the only instance where a misprint was set aright both by means of stop-press and of manuscript correction. In the cases of the other variant readings, the printed errors have not been corrected by hand in the pertinent copies.

## Manuscript Alterations*

a4, l. 11: Alph - k*; EG     phʳ (for Ferdinandum)[8] - abcdefhlmnop

a6, l. 13; decreuisse - k* ; EG     decreuisse ? - abcdefhlmnop

    16: foedera - k* ; EG     foederae - abcdefhlmnop

a8ᵛ, ll. 10/11: se||sedem - k*o     se (deleted) - abcdefhlmnp

b1, l. 2: Temporariũ - k*o ; E     Teporariũ - abcdefhlmnp; G

    l. 4: adeo - hiklop; E     à deo - abcdefmn; G

b4ᵛ, ll. 1-5 uncorrected - see below - k* ; DE

    corrected - see below - abcdefghlmnop; G

c5ᵛ, l. 2: Angelo sctī angeli - ko

    Angelo de scto angelo[9] - abcdefhilmnp; DEG

d1, l. 6: capte - abcdflop     capti - eh; EG

e1, l. 22: Tortonam[10] - k*; EG     Dertonam - abcdefhlmnop

    l. 24: soederatis - k*     foederatis - abcdefhlmnop; EG

e6ᵛ, l. 12: sueuiorum - k     sueuorum - abcdefhilmnop; EG

g5, last line: diributorium - k*     distributorium[11] - abcdefhlmnop; EG

g6, l. 13: seditionémq; - k     seditionéq; - abcdefhilmnop; EG

h3ᵛ, l. 9: prætentarũt - k; G     nunciarunt - abcdefhilmnop[12]

i1ᵛ, l. 13: restitueret ac - k*; DE

    reuocaret restitueretq; - abcdefhlmnop; G

i2ᵛ, l. 1: noluerit - ko; E     nolueritis[13] - abcdefhilmn; D

---

* The symbol * denotes that this is the reading in the BM Grenville copy, but since this has been thoroughly cleaned, it is uncertain whether or not the manuscript corrections were also once found in this copy.

[8] The printed text refers to "Alphonsum et Elisabetham Hispaniae reges." The King of Spain at that time was, of course, Ferdinand the Catholic; this explains the necessity for the manuscript correction.

[9] Angelo de Sancto Angelo was a Venetian of some distinction and appears frequently in the diary of Marino Sanuto (Venice, F. Visentini, 1879-1903).

[10] Tortona is the Italian name for the city, while Dertona is the correct Latin form. In some copies the name appears to be emended to Dartona.

[11] Emendation is uncertain; this reading is supported by Eckhart and Giustiniano. Domenichi (*op. cit.*, f. 45ᵛ) has: "Elle [le lettere] diceuano, come i Proueditori s'erano lamentati, che .CC. huomini d'arme delle genti Milanese contra il uolere del generale s'erano partiti per difetto di dinari & che assaissimi fanti Vinitiani hauuta la paga s'erano fuggiti."

[12] In many cases the "praetentarunt" is heavily obliterated and the "nunciarunt" difficult to read. Eckhart (II: 1622), taking his editorial duties lightly, made no attempt to discover what Aldus had in mind and resorted to the simple expedient of printing a series of dashes.

[13] This emendation was quite unclear to me until suggested as a possible reading by Dr. Schullian, even though this correction is not in the Army Medical Library's copy! Eckhart reproduced the text as it was originally printed and Giustiniano has "volueritis." This leaf is wanting in the Library of Congress copy.

## Analyses

Turning first to the stop-press corrections we find on d7 verso that the text in the earlier version reads:[14]

Legati Veneti cognita tandem hostium fuga convocatis Ducibus eos fugientes persequi statuerunt ac ad incessendos à tergo remorandosque Petrum Duodum Praefectum militum Graecorum levis armaturae cum equitibus suis ac comitem Acaiazanum cum Italis leviter armatis.

Since Pietro Duodo was one of the Venetian officers in charge of the fierce Albanian *stradiotti* and the Count of Caiazzo was the chief Milanese officer, it is clear that the legates planned something for them to do on behalf of the League—but *what* is not exactly clear from this text. When Aldus realized that a verb was wanting after "ac," he stopped the press, supplied "miseru*ntque*" for "ac" and made the necessary modifications in order to fit this word into the lines. It thus becomes clear that at this stage of the battle of Fornovo (July, 1495), Duodo and Caiazzo were sent to assist those harassing the French from the rear. The purpose of the stop-press corrections thus becomes perfectly evident.

The manuscript corrections on b4 verso, in turn, can only be satis-factorily explained by means of the illustration (compare Plate 11). According to the text as originally printed, Charles VIII (who was travelling North from Naples for his encounter with the army of the League upon the banks of the river Taro) proceeded from Naples to Siena, from there to Rome and thence to Pisa—geographically a most curious way to travel North. The manuscript marks, however, indicate that the text should be read probably in this fashion:

[Rex] Gallus interea ad Calendas Iunias Romam uenit. Amissa opportunitate frustratus intacta Roma, Senas uenit: & a factiosis ciuibus in urbem exceptus est. & arcem occupauit. Pisas deinde uenit. . . .

Other contemporary accounts (such as those supplied by Francesco Guicciardini and Philippe de Comines)[15] and modern historical stud-ies[16] prove that Charles left Naples on May 21, entered Rome on

---

[14] For the sake of clarity, the spelling and capitalization have been given in mod-ern form.

[15] Compare Guicciardini, *Storia d'Italia* (Pisa, Niccolò Capurro, 1822-1824), I: 297 ff., and De Comines, *Mémoires* (English version by Thomas Danett, London, Samuel Mearne, 1674), pp. 286-290.

[16] John A. Symonds, *Renaissance in Italy: The Age of the Despots* (London, John Murray, 1934), pp. 451-453, and *The Cambridge Modern History* (New York, The Macmillan Company, 1902-1912), I: 115-116. See especially H. Fr.

June 1, arrived at Siena on June 13, and that he left that city on June 17 for Pisa which he seems to have entered two days later. It is clear that the text as printed was altogether too incorrect for Aldus to accept and that he was thus obliged to make the manuscript emendations in thirteen of the copies examined, possibly in *all* the paper examples consulted.

So much for the stop-press and manuscript corrections in the various copies of this book. Certain further deductions may perhaps be ventured. For example, the British Museum vellum copy (C. 8. h. 14) presents a text incorporating all the stop-press corrections. This indicates that the printing of the vellum leaves was accomplished after at least a majority of the paper copies had been produced. This is shown by the stop-press emendation on g7 where eleven of the fourteen paper copies preserve the misprint; the vellum copy, of course, has the emended text.[17]

It should furthermore be pointed out that the Museum's vellum copy was probably the presentation copy to the Admiral Melchior Trevisano, one of the chief officers of the Venetian forces at the battle of Fornovo.[18] This copy contains no manuscript corrections, perhaps because Aldus feared that they might disfigure the vellum leaves. Allowance must therefore be made for the many cases where this vellum copy is the only example exhibiting no manuscript corrections.

One further point of historical value—if of no bibliographical significance—is that the presence (or absence) of certain manuscript emendations may indicate when a particular copy was sold. The fact that not all corrections are found in every copy may indicate that misprints were eliminated as they were discovered. It may, therefore, be argued that those copies lacking certain manuscript altera-

---

Delaborde, *L'Expédition de Charles VIII en Italie* (Paris, Firmin-Didot, 1888), pp. 611-620.

[17] I have a notation to the effect that in four copies (Ambrosiana, Casanatense, and Vatican) the misprint "ffuuiorum" on signature e1v, line 9, has been reset to read correctly "fluuiorum." There is a grave doubt in mind, however, that this is actually the case and it is quite impossible, for obvious reasons, to verify the matter now. It is likely that my eye slipped, when examining these copies, to line 6 on the same page where "fluuiorum" appears correctly. *If* this correction is actually present in the four copies, it represents another stop-press emendation. If this be true, it also proves that the vellum copy in the British Museum was printed after the majority of the paper copies had been printed but that still others were produced after the vellum leaves had gone through the press.

[18] The arms of the Trevisano family appear in the lower margin of folio 2 verso.

tions were perhaps sold by Aldus before the slips requiring these emendations came to his attention. However, it may also be argued that the absence of a manuscript correction may be due to simple negligence at the press. At the present stage of our investigations into Aldus' methods of publication, it would not be advisable to show a preference for either of these arguments, though it should be borne in mind that both these possibilities provide satisfactory explanations for the absence of manuscript corrections in some copies.

(From *PBSA* 43 (1949), pp. 365-73).

[A critical edition of this text, with English translation, has now been published by Dr. Dorothy M. Schullian (New York: The Renaissance Society of America, 1967). CFB]

# CHAPTER B19

## ALDUS MANUTIUS:
## THE FIRST FIVE HUNDRED YEARS*

IT has been determined, by that happy mixture of deductive reasoning and intuitive inspiration which characterizes those kindred occult disciplines of bibliography and history, that the year of our Lord 1949 marks the 500th anniversary of the birth of that great Venetian printer, Aldus Manutius. The line of argument which established the anniversary year would not, I believe, meet the most elementary demands of the Rules of Evidence in any court of law on this side of—or including—the Kremlin, but the validity of this year as the proper one to celebrate this birth need not, I am equally convinced, disturb us unnecessarily. Some time in the late 1440's or in the early 1450's, the infant Aldo Mannucci first saw the light of day in the hamlet of Bassiano, a part of the Duchy of Sermoneta.

The verifiable dates that we possess in connection with Aldus' life and career are few, but even at that we know a great deal more about him than we do of most of his contemporaries. He certainly received his early education in Rome and studied under Gaspar of Verona and Domitius Calderinus. Our future printer is next found at Ferrara, studying Greek with Battista Guarino, the learned son of the great Guarino da Verona; shortly thereafter he had settled in Mirandola, under the patronage of his renowned friend, the scholarly humanist Pico. In 1483 or thereabouts, Pico obtained for Aldus (then aged 34) the position of tutor to his two young nephews, Alberto and Leonello, the sons of his sister Caterina Pio. For the next half-dozen years, Aldus remained at their palace at Carpi, eleven miles from Modena, teaching the lads both ancient tongues and the works of classical antiquity.[1] Thence he seems to have journeyed directly to Venice (probably in 1490) there to begin the new career which was to reward him more in terms of a lasting fame than with good Venetian ducats. The year 1495 saw the appearance of the first product of

---

* This paper is a slightly revised version of the Trumbull Lecture given at Yale University, October 27, 1949.
[1] Curt F. Bühler, *The First Aldine, supra.*

his press (the Greek grammar by Constantinus Lascaris), the beginning of that long series of distinguished publications for which his name has ever since been revered wherever "men of parts" gather together. In 1505, Aldus was relieved by the Pope from a vow to take Holy Orders (a vow which he had sworn to fulfill—not unnaturally, considering the medical skill of his day—when he lay critically ill of the pest); thereupon, he married (at the age of 56) Maria Torresano, the twenty-year-old daughter of the printer, Andrea of Asola. By her, Aldus had five children: Letizia, who died shortly before or shortly after Aldus' own demise; Manuzio, who enjoyed an ecclesiastical benefice at Asola till 1568; Antonio, who was exiled from Venice for some unspecified "boyish prank" (or worse) and who fled to Bologna where he became a bookseller; Paolo, the printer who fell heir to his father's business; and a daughter Alda, who married a Mantuan gentleman and had one son by him, named Julio Catone. Aldus himself died on the 6th of February, 1515; his body lay in state, surrounded by his books, at the church of San Paterniano in Venice, where a laudatory oration was delivered by the humanist Raffaele Regio. Aldus was buried, at his own request, at his foster home of Carpi, for the kind Prince Alberto had showed deep affection for his former tutor all the days of his life—and had even permitted the printer to make his family name (Pius) part of his own. These, then, are the facts of his life.

In any of the innumerable histories of printing written in the last century, and in any of the numberless works compiled for the benefit of collectors, one will find voluble and highly inaccurate accounts of Aldus' achievements as a printer. It is, of course, because he was a printer—and a very great one too—that we pay tribute to his memory; but it is not for those aesthetic reasons about which so much nonsense has been written and spoken. Aldus was not a great printer in the sense that Nicolaus Jenson or Erhard Ratdolt, or even his own father-in-law Torresano, were masters of the art and technique of book-making. His presswork was indifferent and his types were poor. It has been said—I believe, with all possible justification—that his Greek types set back the study of that tongue by three hundred years. His type-cutter, Francesco Griffo of Bologna, has been described too enthusiastically as "one of the leading designers in typographical history"—and Aldus himself penned the lines (with that complete lack of modesty typical of the Renaissance) in praise of his italic fount:

Qui graiis dedit Aldus, en latinis
Dat nunc grammata scalpta daedaleis
Francisci manibus Bononiensis

("The same Aldus, who gave the types to the Greeks—behold now he gives them to the Latins fashioned by the skilled hands of Francis of Bologna.") But fortunately his Greek type ultimately fell into discard, and the italic fount has, by this time, found its natural and proper habitat among the footnotes of learned periodicals. Psychologically, both styles of type were unsound, since they were modelled upon the hurried hand-writing of his day. For the Greek type, it is self-evident that whatever virtue quasi-stenographic shorthand may have had for Marcus Musurus while he was taking notes or writing informally, characters based on such scribblings were no benefit for the leisured reader and a handicap for those untutored in the current Pitman or Gregg. Again, in regard to the italic fount, it is just as easy to set upright characters as to set slanting type, so that whatever was gained by way of speed through cursive writing was not carried through to the printed book by the use of this style of letter. As a craftsman, then, Aldus cannot, I believe, be listed among the truly great—and if anyone should ask me about the *Hypnerotomachia Poliphili*, I shall insist that this is the exception that proves the rule.

It was not, therefore, as a printer that Aldus achieved greatness but rather as a publisher and as an innovator—and primarily as a publisher of the first printings of the Greek authors and as a purveyor of editions, both accurate and cheap, of classical texts in general. Secondly, Aldus is distinguished as a great innovator in the development of typographical designs. Of his types I have already spoken—and if his experimentations were not altogether happy, they were at least significant in their own day and showed that Aldus' mind was actively on the move in fields other than classical antiquity. The italic type (the "Testo d'Aldo") achieved such popularity that it soon found imitators, despite the exclusive rights which Aldus managed to wrest not only from the Venetian Senate but also from three Popes (Alexander VI, Julius II and Leo X). These monopolies were of little use to him, however, as Aldus' characteristic fount was counterfeited by Giunta at Florence and the Soncini in Fano—not to mention the extensive counterfeiting of entire Aldine editions which were made at Lyons and which Aldus bitterly denounced. By 1570 italic had become *the* fashionable vernacular type for Italian and French books, but thereafter its popularity declined rapidly.

Much more important than these type-innovations were his experiments with the formats of books, leading ultimately to his "forma enchiridii"—the portable, small octavo now associated in our minds with the typical "Aldine." It was a real departure from tradition to issue the classics in small handy volumes rather than as the stately folios which his predecessors had produced, and the popularity of the small pocket book has never declined. It is, perhaps, due almost as much to its handy size as to the comfortable presence of the parallel English translation that the Loeb Library has enjoyed its astonishing success; but then, this may be too optimistic a view.

And lastly, Aldus was the man who first introduced the good book, sturdily produced and reasonably priced. Before his time there had been a sufficiency of "de luxe" printing for the moneyed trade—volumes printed on vellum and illuminated by celebrated craftsmen—and an even greater amount of the "cheap and nasty" had already run through the presses; but of good books solidly built and comparatively cheap there had been precious few, at least so far as we know today. Students interested in the economics of printing will find the necessary details concerning the prices of Aldines set forth in Renouard's great bibliography. Here will also be found an estimate of what the Venetian coins of Aldus' day were worth as compared with the French franc of Renouard's time. The first edition of Musaeus, we learn, could be purchased in 1495 at the price of one "marcello"—worth 68 centimes in 1834 and perhaps a quarter-dollar (certainly less than fifty cents) of our present money. In 1947, be it noted, a copy of this book was offered for sale at $1,600! Although Aldus did occasionally print examples on vellum and the firm put out (from time to time) special copies on the blue paper called "charta caerulea," the Aldine press at no time sought to cater primarily to the "large-paper racket." Aldus was interested in producing good texts of the great masterpieces of literature, clearly printed on substantial paper, at a price at which poor scholars could afford to buy them. In short, Aldus was busily producing exactly the sort of book for which, we may surmise, he searched in vain in his own student days.

Since Aldus' reputation rests so largely on his activity as a publisher, we should turn now to the output of his press. If I have counted aright—an hypothesis not to be lightly accepted without careful check—the Aldine press issued 132 books in the twenty years of activity under the personal direction of the founder of the firm. Of this total 73 are classical works (34 Latin and 39 Greek) as compared with but eight in the vernacular and twenty contemporary works in Latin. Eighteen items are schoolbooks, exactly two-thirds of which are in Greek. Contemporary science with five Latin texts, and religious books with a total of eight, played a very minor role at the Aldine press. Indeed, there was practically no liturgical printing done and little (if any) work was undertaken for the Papal curia (the staple for the Roman presses of the day). This, I think, will hardly surprise anyone acquainted with the history of the period—and with Venice's peculiar attitude towards the Papacy. In some respects, indeed, this parallels the position taken by that other great maritime power some years earlier. When the great Turk sat before the walls of Constantinople and the Pope was proffering help to the beleaguered city, the citizens of Byzantium are reputed to have cried: "Better the turban than the tiara."

But to return to Aldus. His real interest lay, of course, in the classics, and of these he printed an almost identical number in Latin and Greek. However, it is for his publications in the Greek tongue that he chiefly deserves our admiration. In his valuable and handy list of *editiones principes*, Sir John Edwin Sandys informs us that, prior to the death of Aldus, 68 Latin first printings were produced. The only works there credited to our printer are the first appearances of two fifth-century Christian poets, Sedulius and Prosper of Aquitaine. When we turn to the list of Greek first editions, however, we find the situation quite different. Of 49 such works, Aldus printed no fewer than 30—or well over fifty per cent. Nor were these the works of obscure writers such as are met with in the case of the Latin *editiones principes*—for the roster includes such "firsts" as Aristotle, Demosthenes and Thucydides, as well as Aristophanes and Sophocles among the dramatists.

When one examines the career of Aldus Manutius, one must always bear in mind that the printer was producing his volumes in a period of the greatest unrest and uneasiness throughout the Italian peninsula, a period as ill-suited to the pursuit of literary studies and philosophical speculations as our own day. Wars were constant and foreign invasions almost continuous. After long years of freedom from transalpine aggressions, Charles VIII invaded the peninsula in 1494; though the French were driven out two years later, this afforded only a temporary relief. In 1498 Louis XII succeeded to the throne of France and shortly thereafter Italy was invaded again by French troops. Once more the French were driven out, but peace again proved fleeting for all. In 1508 the League of Cambrai was founded, partly on the theory that Venice had committed treason against Christendom by coming to terms with Islam. The offensive of the allies was completely successful; though the Venetians capitulated to the Pope in 1510, the terms were hard and bitter for the citizens of the Republic. Venice never recovered from this blow.

These could hardly be described, then, as times excessively propitious for a new venture in so competitive a trade as the publishing business then was. The events of the day are mirrored in the activity at the Aldine press. The "big" years of production were those of peace—1497 with thirteen books and 1502 with sixteen top the list, closely followed by 1501 and 1513 through 1515—each year with eleven items. Prior to 1506, Aldus printed 89 books and from 1512 until his death three years later no fewer than thirty-two. In the years 1506 through 1512 he printed exactly eleven.

Not only were his presses stilled, but Aldus fled—or found it advisable to absent himself—from Venice for long periods during these troubled years. Was this because he was a citizen of the Papal states and proudly signed himself: Aldus Romanus? However that may be, he was certainly arrested—apparently by mistake—at Mantua on the 16th of July, 1506, and was only released by the Gonzaga at the insistence of the French Ambassador, Geoffroy Carles. He was in Ferrara in 1509 and 1510, and in June of that year found himself in Mantua where he was summoned to call upon Isabella d'Este. Aldus was back in Ferrara in 1511 and there he executed a last will and testament. By 1512, he had returned to Venice and his presses were once again humming after a two-year period of inactivity.

Nor were the external troubles of the Republic the only ones to plague Aldus. His shop was, apparently, one of the "sights" of Venice for the visiting yokels and the incredulous from the great hinterland—a sixteenth-century precursor of the Murano glass works which are today such a major attraction for tourists. "Veniunt igitur frequentes et sedent oscitabundi." "They come, then, in hordes"— Aldus complains—"and sit there gaping." To the problems inevitably incident to the operation of a press, we must add those which apparently revolved about his domestic life. The picture that Erasmus drew in his famous account of the living conditions in the Aldine home is not very reassuring—and one can easily see that Aldus' brothers-in-law were sporting lads of the worst sort. Quite obviously the young men were given to excessive gambling and to such villainies as the age permitted, and these were considerable. One may recall that, after the death of Aldus, Federigo Torresano was finally caught cheating at cards and promptly banished from the Republic. At a later date Aldus' son Antonio was similarly compelled to flee from justice. At the time of his father's death he was, of course, only a slip of a lad, but one may well suppose that he was even then zealously perfecting himself in those paths of unrighteousness in which his uncles excelled. Troubles at home and troubles at the press, the Republic besieged and his books counterfeited—it can hardly be said that Aldus' life moved in an even, uneventful course.

This much for the historic Aldus. Let us see what he and his work mean to us nowadays, for there are some who will question their importance. Have not these books been catalogued for years, are they not minutely described in standard bibliographies, have not the professors and learned scholars of the past 450 years extracted from these volumes every scrap of information likely to be of value? Nevertheless I affirm that we stand at the very threshold of a new era of discovery among Aldine imprints. The productions have been listed, it is true—and they have been consulted by scholars—but neither bibliographers nor literary students have examined these volumes with that careful attention to bibliographical niceties which is considered standard procedure in these later days. To cite one example: the diary of Alessandro Benedetti (the *Diaria de Bello Carolino*), a work of great importance and interest to the medical historian, is one of the chief scientific incunabula printed by Aldus. For years the syphilologists have been clamoring for a reprint—preferably, of course, accompanied by an English translation. Yet I do not believe that many medical bibliographers are aware that one cannot simply reprint the text as it appears in *any* copy of the original. There are stop-press corrections, some of major importance, which appear in some copies and not in others. But not even when all these stop-press corrections have been accounted for does one possess the text as Aldus wished it to be issued forth. What Aldus printed, alas, was not always exactly what he wanted to say. For example, according to Aldus' printed text and to the reprint of it as supplied by Eckhart as late as 1723, Benedetti is made to state that Charles VIII, in moving his army north to meet the enemy at Fornovo, marched his troops from Naples to Siena to Rome to Pisa—clearly an impossible route for anyone not

entirely bereft of his senses. That is what the printed text says, however—yet every one of the twenty-three copies that I have seen contains manuscript notations (occasionally very faint, it is true) which
correct the text. For over four hundred years no scholar seems to have
taken the slightest notice of the numerous manuscript corrections of
this nature which appear in the pages of the earliest Aldines. In this
case the manuscript marks simplify our problem, for they tell us that
the text needs correction here and that what Benedetti had written
(and what Aldus wanted to say) was that the army had moved from
Naples to Rome to Siena to Pisa. There are numerous other emendations.[2] Corrections of similar nature are certainly to be found in the
Musaeus and in Bembo's *De Aetna*, both printed by Aldus before
the turn of the century. Stop-press corrections are also known for the
Aldine Pliny of 1508, as George Parker Winship and Arthur E.
Case have previously pointed out. Other inquirers may wish to determine whether or not emendations of this sort are also to be found
in the later productions of the Aldine press. Of one thing we may be
quite certain. Aldus would have been as pleased as he would have
been incredulous had anyone foretold him that half a millennium
after his birth such scholars as Dr. Dorothy Schullian would now be
laboring to re-establish the purity of his texts so that we might have
his books in the form he wished his readers to have them.

As Aldus lay dying in his house in the Campo di San Agostino
many thoughts and reminiscences must surely have crossed his mind.
The boy from the foothills beyond Rome had come a long way! His
friends were numbered among the great and powerful of the land:
Federigo Gonzaga (Duke of Mantua), Pico Prince of Mirandola,
Andrea Navagero and Daniello Rinieri (Senators of the Republic),
Jean Grolier (the French ambassador in Italy), and, of course, Alberto Pio, Prince of Carpi. The printer had been accepted as a peer
by the greatest scholars of his day—Desiderius Erasmus, Giovanni
Battista Egnazio, Giovanni Gregoropoulos, and Thomas Linacre (to
name a varied group)—*all* of whom had worked for him. Distinguished members of the Church were pleased to join him in the
Aldi Neacademia: Pietro Bembo, secretary to Pope Leo X and a future cardinal, and Marcus Musurus, who became Archbishop of Mal-
vasia shortly after Aldus' death (to be exact, on the 26th of May,
1516, as my colleague Dr. G. K. Boyce has recently discovered).

---

[2] Curt F. Bühler, *Stop-Press and Manuscript Corrections in the Aldine Edition of
Benedetti's "Diaria de Bello Carolino," supra.*

Aldus' reputation as a scholarly printer had spread far beyond the limits of the Republic—and if imitation be the sincerest flattery, then the printers of Lyons gave adequate proof of the high regard in which they held him. Though the Aldine press had been profitable, it was not (it is true) an outstanding financial success in that great commercial metropolis which Aldus had chosen to make his home. Nevertheless, it provided a living for him and his family, and after his death for his children and grandchildren. For a full century the printing shop provided a competence for three generations of Manuzii. It had been a good life for him, Aldus must have felt as he lay there dying—and what may well have been the greatest satisfaction of all was the sure knowledge that he had been a publisher "il qual ha fatto imprimer molte opere Latine et Greche *ben corrette.*"

(From *PBSA* 44 (1950), pp. 205-15).

[Note: Dr. Dorothy M. Schullian's edition of Benedetti's work was published in 1967 under the auspices of the Renaissance Society of America as No. 1 in its Renaissance Text Series. CFB]

# CHAPTER B20

## OBSERVATIONS ON TWO CAXTON VARIANTS

THE two Caxton variants which provide the topic of discussion for the present investigation are by no means recent discoveries; quite to the contrary, they have been noted for many years in the standard books of reference. It is most strange, therefore, that these well-known variant states have been subjected neither to critical study nor to thorough technical analyses, especially since, as distinct from many other Caxton variants, it is absolutely certain in each instance which is the earlier state and which the later. This circumstance further permits the investigator to ascertain specific details as to the workings of Caxton's printing office, with special reference to the resetting of copy previously printed at the same press.[1] The two variant states to be discussed here are found in: Lydgate, *The Pilgrimage of the Soul*, Westminster, 6 June 1483 (Duff 267) and Christine de Pisan, *The Book of the Fayttes of Armes and of Chyvalrye*, [Westminster], 14 July 1489 (Duff 96). The separate states are identified by the fact that one sheet in each book appears in two different settings of type.

### PILGRIMAGE OF THE SOUL

In E. Gordon Duff's *Fifteenth Century English Books* (Bibliographical Society, Illustrated Monograph No. XVIII, 1917), one finds the following note appended to his description of No. 267:

There are two issues of this book: in the original issue (B.M.) the two inner pages of sheet f3 have been imposed wrongly, so that what should be on f3$^b$ is on f6$^a$ and what should be on f6$^a$ is on f3$^b$, and the whole book is in type 4. In the second issue (Britwell) this whole sheet has been reprinted in type 4*, so as to read correctly.[2]

Of the six copies that have survived to our day,[3] the British Mu-

---

[1] It is a great pleasure to record once again my hearty thanks for the kind help of Professor Fredson Bowers. In this case, as always whenever he has been consulted, he has been ever ready to offer advice and criticism.

[2] The Britwell copy is now in The Pierpont Morgan Library (Accession number 20892; *Check List* 1778). Under no. 6474, the *STC* states: "Sheet f reprinted" and cites only the Morgan copy.

[3] Five copies are cited in Seymour de Ricci's *Census of Caxtons* (Bibliographical Society, Illustrated Monograph no. XV, 1909, pp. 78-79). The sixth copy was formerly

seum is the only one to have sheet f3.6 in the original state,[4] the remaining copies all belonging to the later "issue" (contrary to the opinion expressed in *STC* 6473).

Since it is absolutely certain that the Museum copy belongs to the earlier state, one may well ask how it compares with the "corrected" later form of sheet f3.6? The ready answer to this query is that the resetting (though corrected so far as the imposition is concerned) is much the more inferior text. Not only does the reprint contain eleven misprints to seven found in the original setting[5] but it also omits nineteen words found in the original—a fact of much greater significance. To be exact, twenty words are omitted by the reprint but, by way of partial compensation, one word[6] not found in the first setting is added by the second.

Almost half the words wanting in the later sheet are clearly omitted because of careless type-setting. The compositor of the reprint, although he was setting type from printed copy, did not follow his original line for line.[7] On the verso of signature f3 (of the reprint) he departed so far from his copy that when he reached the bottom of the page he found that he had less than half a line to accommodate a full line of the original text. By making radical omissions, the compositor succeeded in having his page end at the proper place but not without doing violence to the text. In the original state (f6) the passage in question reads:

... And leue || it wel y^t though the passiō of crist profite not these innocēts to their || ful saluaciō yet it profiteth them so moch y^t sathanas lyeth loken in || the depthe of helle / so that he ne may not ne none of his mynystres || [f4] annoyen ne tormenten none Innocent / as their malyce wold / ne || harmen none persone / but by his owne assent ...

In the reprint, the same text (f3 verso) appears as:

... & || leue hit wel that thonӡ (*sic*) the passion of Jhesu crist prouffite not || these innocentes to their sauacion / yet it prouffiteth them soo || moche y^t

---

in the possession of the firm of William H. Robinson Ltd., and was described by W. Loftus Hare in his study: "A Newly Discovered Volume Printed by William Caxton," *Apollo*, October, 1931 (11 page reprint published by the firm). Details as to this copy I have as the courtesy of the present owner.

[4] Leaf "f iij" appears to be signed "f ij" in the Morgan copy, but this may be the result of improper inking.

[5] On f6, line 27 of the BM copy, is found the word "lauement" ("lauament" in the reprint); the earliest occurrence of this word noted by *NED* is 1597.

[6] See below, where the reprint has "Jhesu crist" for the "crist" of the first setting.

[7] On f6 verso, 27 lines of the first setting have been expanded to 28 lines in the second.

sathanas lyeth lokē in helle y$^t$ none of his mynystres || [f4] annoyen ne tor-
menten none Innocent / as their malyce wold / ne || harmen none persone /
but by his owne assent . . .

In making these omissions the compositor succeeded in having his
text end with the correct word, but in order to achieve this both sense
and grammar were sacrificed to expediency.

Apart from this instance, the textual differences are slight and occasionally reflect no more than the spelling habits of two different
compositors;[8] for example, the British Museum state has "nought"
eight times where the reprint has "not." In those cases where a choice
can be made, however, the British Museum setting is always the better. Thus where the soul *asks* the body "how hast thou lost al thy
queyntyse" (BM, f3$^v$, l. 33), the reprint offers "how thou hast lost al
queyntyse." Clearly then, instead of seizing upon the opportunity
to improve the text, a careless compositor has permitted the text of
the reprint to deteriorate.

Curiously enough, the reprint exhibits a technical—as well as a
textual—deterioration. Concerning the use of "guide-letters" or "directors," Konrad Haebler[9] observes that in order "to lighten the rubricator's work, the custom was gradually adopted of printing in small
type (usually in lower-case), in the space left to be filled in by hand,
the initial which the rubricator was to add in colors." This had been
common practice on the Continent from as early as 1471-2, and directors appear in books printed at Caxton's press even in the days of
its activity at Bruges.[10] In the *Pilgrimage*, guide-letters were used
throughout the volume including the first setting of sheet f3.6, but
directors are not present in the reprint of this sheet. Thus the reprint
demonstrates the return to a more primitive practice of type-setting
where such reminders were not considered necessary for the benefit
of the rubricator.

[8] For discussions of this problem, see Charlton Hinman, "Principles Governing
the Use of Variant Spellings as Evidence of Alternate Setting by Two Compositors," *The Library*, 4th ser., XXI (1940), 78-94, and Philip Williams, "The Compositor of the 'Pied-Bull' *Lear*," *Papers Bibl. Soc. Univ. Virginia*, I (1948), 61-68.

[9] *The Study of Incunabula*, trans. by Lucy E. Osborne (New York, 1933), p. 112.

[10] Guide-letters are found regularly in the *Recueil des histoires de Troie* (Duff
243) and occasionally in the English version of this work (Duff 242). They appear
regularly in the *History of Jason* (Duff 245), which both Blades and Proctor considered the first large English book printed in England. Blades (no. 9) dates it as
belonging to the "early part of 1477."

## BOOK OF THE FAYTTES OF ARMES

To its description of this edition (No. 6648), the *Gesamtkatalog der Wiegendrucke* adds the note: "Das Doppelblatt 140 u. 143 ist neu gesetzt worden." This appears to be the first notification that sheet S2.5 is known in two different settings, a fact that (apparently) escaped the attention of the editor of this work for the Early English Text Society's edition.[11] Of the twenty-one copies of this book known to me, only four have the variant sheet specified by the *Gesamtkatalog*—Göttingen, Bibliothèque Nationale, Bodleian (S. Selden d 13) and the Grenville Kane copy now at Princeton University Library.[12] Thirteen copies have the text as printed in the Early English Text Society series, while three copies want (among others) the pertinent leaves—Windsor, Bodleian (Auct. QQ supra l. 25) and the York Minster copy now in the collection of Phyllis Goodhart Gordan and Howard L. Goodhart of New York. Seymour de Ricci informs us that the Sion College copy lacks S5, but I have been unsuccessful in my attempts to obtain information as to the state of S2 in this copy.

Although the *Gesamtkatalog* simply assumes without further proof that the Göttingen state is that which was "neu gesetzt," there is plenty of evidence to prove that this is certainly the case.[13] In this instance, positive proof is supplied by the different systems of punctuation employed by the two compositors. As will be seen from a perusal of the modern reprint, the enormously preponderant punctuation mark used in the *Fayttes* is the virgule (/). For example, on

---

[11] Original Series 189 (1932), edited by A. T. P. Byles. In the re-issue with corrections (1937), Mr. Byles takes note of the two states (p. xxxi) but no variant readings are given in his text. Volume VI of the *Gesamtkatalog*, which contains the description of the *Fayttes*, bears the date 1934.

[12] This is the former Huth copy, listed by Seymour de Ricci under no. 28.2.

[13] The first line on folio B7 recto normally reads: "swīmyīg ouer a gret ryuer / and thurghe thees waye of swī- || mīg . . ."; in the Yale copy the same line reads: "swimyn oer a gret ryuer / and thurghe thees waye of swīs- || mīg . . ." . This may represent a variant setting caused by a desire to improve the text or it may be no more than a mechanical variant brought about by having the type pulled out by the ink-ball and incorrectly restored. Another minor variant indicating stop-press corrections may be found on N6; here the "Capytulo" should be numbered 16 but no copy seems to have this number. Some copies (for example: Morgan, Columbia, Yale, Queens [Oxford], etc.) have "Capytulo xiiij" while others (Huntington, Princeton, Bodleian, University Library Cambridge, etc.) have the number "xv." It is not clear which is the earlier setting in this case.

signatures S1, S3, and S4 (six pages common to all copies), there are 164 punctuation marks of which 163 are virgules, the remaining one being a semi-colon. In the first setting as represented by the copy in The Pierpont Morgan Library (PML 781), there are 118 instances of punctuation on S2 and S5; of these 117 are virgules and the remaining one is a semi-colon.

For the other setting, the Kane-Princeton copy shows (on sheet S2.5) 105 cases of punctuation, of which 96 are periods, 6 are semi-colons and only 3 are virgules. Obviously the text of this sheet was set by a different compositor—one following his own rules of punctuation—than the one who had composed all the rest of the volume. Thus it is quite certain that sheet S2.5 of the Morgan copy belongs to the original setting and that the Princeton one is the reprinted sheet.

Again we may enquire what a comparison of the two states reveals and again we will note that the reprint shows a deterioration of text. The state of the Morgan copy has six misprints, while the total in the Princeton setting amounts to some seventeen such errors; two misprints are common to both states.[14] Characteristic of the better text of the first is the reading "Consules of Mountpellyer" (S2, l. 4) where the reprint specifies "Consules Mountpollyer." Conversely, however, the second setting has the more correct last lines in the colophon which read: ". . . he may || atteyne to euerlastyng lyf in heuen. whiche god graunte to || hym and to alle his lyege peple. AMEN. || Per Caxton ||". The first contained the misprints "euerlastpng" and "gaunte." However, since the far greater number of misprints is found in the form as represented by the Princeton copy, we must consider this second setting as the more inferior text.

A most singular peculiarity of the Princeton volume requires special mention. The blank last leaf (S6 recto) in this copy shows a distinct off-set of the text of S5 verso, a condition often encountered among Caxton imprints. But the startling fact here is that the Princeton leaf shows an off-set of the original setting, *not* of the resetting which now faces it in the volume. There seem to be only two logical explanations for this phenomenon, either that the copy was "made up," perhaps when it was rebound by Bedford,[15] or that the off-set-

[14] On S2, l. 22, both settings have "theunto" for "therunto" and on S5ᵛ, l. 6, "hyeues" for "hyenes."

[15] Neither Seymour de Ricci nor the Huth Catalogue (I, 310) indicate that any leaves have ever been added to the copy. According to the sale catalogue (p. 444,

ting took place in Caxton's workshop. If the latter assumption be the correct one, we would have certain evidence that the copies of the *Fayttes* were not bound up as soon as printed but that the sheets were stored unbound.[16] Thus it would have to be argued that the Princeton sheet S1.6 came into contact soon after printing (possibly by being gathered with it) with a sheet of the earlier setting of S2.5, but that, in the long run, it was not bound up with this particular sheet.

Turning to the other alternative, it seems highly improbable that the blank leaf was added to this copy,[17] since no one would ever have considered it necessary to supply such a leaf in order to create a "perfect and complete" example. Again one cannot assume that only leaf S5 was supplied, since S2 is its proper conjugate; therefore, if anything was added to the Princeton volume, it must have been the whole sheet (S2.5). Furthermore, if the blank be the original one, as we have good reason to believe, it seems unlikely that the important printed leaf just ahead of the useless blank could have been missing from this copy at any time; surely, if S5 was lost, S6 would have disappeared too. One must believe, then, that if the volume is not in the same condition as it was when sold by Caxton (at least, as far as the identity of leaves is concerned), one must assume that the Princeton book was so "made up" that S1.6 was supplied from one copy and S2.5 from another. This seems to be so highly improbable a hypothesis that the first explanation for the presence of the off-set in the Princeton *Fayttes* appears the more acceptable.

In conclusion, a word should (I think) be said on the subject of the origin of these two variant settings. In the case of the *Pilgrimage*, of course, the sheet was reprinted in order to correct an error of imposition;[18] a similar technical error[19] occurs in the very first

---

lot 1570), the copy is "perfect and large" and was described as being in a binding by Riviere.

[16] For a discussion of when Caxton volumes were presumably bound, see my "The Binding of Books Printed by William Caxton," *supra*.

[17] The modern binding makes it impossible to be entirely certain, but S1 and S6 appear to be conjugates. Whether conjugacy can be proved or not is immaterial, since it is shown above that no one would supply a blank leaf anyway. Accordingly it is reasonable to assume that S6 is the conjugate of S1.

[18] A similar error of imposition occurs in the *Fayttes* where O3 verso contains the text which should be found on O6 recto and vice versa. All the copies seen by the writer contain this error. An example of an error of imposition which led to the

book credited to Caxton's press—the *Recuyell of the Histories of Troy*, [Bruges, *circa* 1475]. The cause for the reprint of sheet S2.5 in the *Fayttes* is less obvious. It illustrates, however, a phenomenon previously noticed in several volumes printed by England's proto-typographer. Since the second setting contains more misprints than the first, it was probably not called into being through a desire to improve the text. True enough, two glaring errors in the colophon were corrected by the second setting, but this improvement could have been achieved by simple stop-press corrections and certainly would not have required the resetting of four entire pages.[20] It seems likely that the reprinting was necessitated either because something happened in Caxton's workshop which required the resetting of sheet S2.5, or that Caxton failed to print the correct number of sheets to complete the copies in hand and was thus obliged to make good the deficiency after the original formes had been distributed.

One must, then, assume that the reprinting of sheet S2.5 was the result either of an accident in the printing office or of a short count when the sheet was being machined. If an accident necessitated the reprint, it is scarcely probable that this took place during the print-ing of the sheet since it would be an incredible coincidence for both

---

suppression of the sheet is cited in my note "Caxton's *Blanchardin and Eglantine*: Notes on the Leaf Preserved in the British Museum," *PBSA*, XXXIX (1945), 156-61.

[19] For a discussion of the classification of variants, see my paper "Variants in Eng-lish Incunabula," *supra*.

[20] It has been suggested to me that Caxton might have suppressed the first setting of S2.5 because of the errors in the colophon (representing the printer's official statement) and that the incorrect sheets were withdrawn from the made-up copies and the new sheets substituted for those suppressed. Thus the off-set in the Prince-ton copy could have come from the first sheet S2.5 before the corrected one was substituted for it. However, this seems to me an untenable theory in view of the fact that only four copies of the second setting are known against the thirteen of the first. If Caxton reprinted and substituted sheet S2.5 in order to correct the colophon, one would (I should judge) expect the *majority* of copies to have the second (official) setting and only the occasional (overlooked) example to preserve the original reading. If, however, extra sheets of the second setting of S2.5 were printed because of an original short count, it may be argued that these were sub-stituted (because of the superior colophon) for sheets of the first setting to the extent that these correct sheets were available; this also would explain the presence of the "wrong" off-set in the Princeton copy. But one should observe that errors in the colophon did not seem to disturb Caxton unduly; note the many instances of such misprints cited by W. J. B. Crotch, *The Prologues and Epilogues of William Caxton* (Early English Text Society, Original Series 176, 1928). Other Caxton edi-tions with errors in the colophons include: *Ars moriendi* (Duff 33), two *Chronicles of England* (Duff 97-8), *Doctrinal of Sapience* (Duff 127), etc.

inner and outer formes to "pie" at approximately the same stage in the course of production.[21] If sheet S2.5 was not reprinted because a short count made this necessary, one must believe that some accident took place at the press *after* the full number of sheets had been printed and the formes distributed, for the loss of a sufficient number of sheets would have compelled Caxton to reset the text and supply the necessary number in a new setting. While this would be a perfectly reasonable explanation for the reprinting of sheet S2.5 in the *Fayttes*, one can only with difficulty credit a theory which assumes that Caxton permitted such accidents to happen again and again. There are reprinted sheets of precisely this sort in the *Dictes and Sayings of the Philosophers* (Duff 123), the *Morte d'Arthur* (Duff 283), the *House of Fame* (Duff 86), and probably elsewhere, for aught I know.[22] Surely these could not all be the results of physical accidents. On the other hand, contemporary accounts prove beyond question that short printing was a common enough occurrence to be a source of annoyance and trouble to both printers and publishers. Neither of these explanations for the presence of the variant setting in the *Book of the Fayttes of Armes and of Chyvalrye* is completely convincing, but if there be a more satisfactory one, it is not apparent to me.

(From *Studies in Bibliography* 3 (1950/51), pp. 97-104).

[21] Furthermore one would then be obliged to assume that Caxton employed two presses, one to print one forme and the other to perfect the sheets. In that case it is easy enough to believe that one forme might go to pie but that both should do so about the same time passes the bounds of credibility.

[22] Such reprintings are not peculiar to Caxton. See, for example, the case cited in my article "Notes on Two Incunabula Printed by Aldus Manutius," *PBSA*, XXXVI (1942), 18-26.

# CHAPTER B21

## ALDUS MANUTIUS AND HIS FIRST EDITION
## OF THE GREEK MUSAEUS

IT is generally held to be certain, by students of early Venetian printing, that the *editio princeps* of Musaeus was the second book to be printed by Aldus Manutius,[1] even though the printer's own priced list of his productions (issued in October 1498)[2] places the Greek *Hero and Leander* in eighth place. Though this edition has been described in numerous bibliographies and has been almost invariably cited by the many editors of the Greek text, the reader of the present account may be somewhat surprised to learn that the group of facts set forth below appears for the first time in this study. The Musaeus has often been acclaimed as one of the rarest of the early Aldines, yet the present writer has noted more than a score of copies, twelve of which have passed under his personal scrutiny while another three have been examined for him through the good offices of colleagues and the owners of the books.[3] The copies thus available for this study are the following:[4]

[1] See, for example, Robert Proctor, *The Printing of Greek in the Fifteenth Century* (Bibliographical Society, Illustrated Monograph No. VIII, 1900), pp. 94-97, and the *Catalogue of Books Printed in the XVth Century now in the British Museum* (London, 1908-1935), V, 552-553. Cardinal Quirini would fix a later date for the Musaeus than that set down here (before November 1495), believing that the *Hero and Leander* may have been printed just before the final volume of Aristotle's *Opera* had been issued in June 1498; see the letter from Angelo Maria Quirini to Giuseppe Antonio Sassi (Saxius) added as a supplement at the end of volume II of Filippo Argellati's *Bibliotheca scriptorum Mediolanensium* (Milan, 1745). Thomas F. Dibdin, *An Introduction to the .... Greek and Latin Classics* (London, 1827), II, 237, believed that the Musaeus was « the first work which ever issued from the press of Aldus ».

[2] A facsimile of this may be found in Henri Omont, *Catalogues des livres grecs et latins imprimés par Alde Manuce à Venise* (Paris, 1892), plate I; see also the account in Proctor, *op. cit.*, pp. 93-94.

[3] For details of the Yale copy and for other suggestions, I am deeply obliged to Professor Alfred R. Bellinger, while Mr. Herman R. Mead has earned my thanks for his report on the Huntington copy. Mr. Scheide kindly sent me notes on the example in his library.

[4] In order that the copies containing only the Greek text may be identified at a glance, these have been assigned minuscule letters; those examples with both Greek and Latin texts have been given capital letters.

New York, The Pierpont Morgan Library, PML 264          — A
New York, The Pierpont Morgan Library, PML 362          — B
London, British Museum, IA 24387 (Grenville copy)        — C
London, British Museum, IA 24386 (Royal copy — Greek only) — d
Paris, Bibliothèque Nationale, Rés. Yb 335              — E
Paris, Bibliothèque Nationale, Rés. Yb 336              — F
Paris, Bibliothèque Nationale, Rés. Yb 480              — G
Milan, Biblioteca Ambrosiana                            — H
Venice, Biblioteca Marciana, no. 38472 (Greek only)      — i
Vatican City, Biblioteca Vaticana, Ross. 411            — K
Vatican City, Biblioteca Vaticana, Inc. IV. 662 (Greek only) — 1
San Marino, Henry E. Huntington Library, Mead no. 3289  — M
Washington, Library of Congress (Rosenwald Collection)   — N
New Haven, Yale University Library (Greek only)          — o
Titusville, Penn., Collection of William H. Scheide      — P

The theory that two distinct issues of the Musaeus have come down to us was intimated not long ago by the distinguished bibliographer of early Italian illustrated books, Max Sander.[5] This scholar called attention to the fact that the Ferrara copy of the Musaeus did not contain the two woodcuts, which constitute the book's chief claim to fame, but that this copy was decorated by « une ornementation d'arabesques. » Clearly Sander was contenting himself with citing, in too abbreviated a form, the account given by Essling, who made the following notation:[6] « La Bibl. Communale de Ferrare possède une édition s. d., qui ne comporte que le texte grec (10 ff. n. ch. s.: a 20 vers par page), et dont le colophon est identique à celui de l'édition décrite ici. Les deux bois ne s'y trouvent pas: l'ornementation ne consiste qu'en une bordure d'arabesques au trait, en tête du r. $a_{ii}$ et une in. o. E du même genre au commencement du texte. »

Since Essling affirms that the Ferrara copy contains only the Greek text, this example could not possibly provide the two woodcuts which are included in the Latin part of this work. The arabesques, moreover, are present in all copies in the places designated by Essling. The Ferrara copy does not, then, provide us with proof as to the existence of variant issues for the first edition of the Greek Musaeus.[7]

---

[5] Le livre à figures italien depuis 1467 jusqu'à 1530 (New York, 1941), II, 842, no. 4912.

[6] Essling, Les livres à figures vénitiens de la fin du XVᵉ siècle et du commencement du XVIᵉ (Florence, 1907-1914), part II, p. 22, no. 1296, note 1.

[7] Since the Latin text was issued later than the Greek, it might be argued that

That such is actually the case, however, and that two distinct issues of the Latin text have been preserved has not, to my knowledge, been previously pointed out. The third sheet of the Latin portion offers an example of stop-press correction which is instructive for our knowledge of Aldus' methods of book production. The different settings can be simply and speedily identified, for that one with the signature letter « c » is the earlier (incorrect) state and that with the signature « b$_{iii}$ » is the later, corrected version.[8] Significantly enough, in the eight copies known to me having the signature « c », this index letter has been changed to « b$_{iii}$ » by manuscript correction in every instance. The two issues were occasioned by the circumstance that Aldus wished to correct line 9 of the text on the recto of the third Latin leaf which, in the earlier state (as exemplified by signature « c »), reads:

Haec quidem Sestū habitabat, uero oppidū ille Abydi
[Copies: ACEFHKMP]

This text was reset for the later issue to read:
Haec quidem Sestū habitabat, ille uero oppidū Abydi
[Copies: BGN]

In each case, the copy having the text with the earlier reading was corrected by manuscript emendation to provide the reading of the later setting.[9] The chief reason—and, indeed, the only apparent one —which compelled Aldus to make this alteration seems to have been a desire to improve the metre of the line. This line reappears in the corrected form in the Aldine reprint of 1517 as well as in several later printings, including such eighteenth-century ones as the editions of 1737, 1742, and 1795/6.[10]

In addition to this stop-press emendation, no fewer than six manuscript corrections appear in enough copies to warrant the assumption

---

the copies with both versions constitute a later issue. It is, however, just as likely that Aldus sold the Musaeus with or without the Latin text as the purchaser wished, so that those copies having only the Greek do not necessarily belong to an earlier « issue ». Curiously, the second Vatican copy (1) contains the first Latin leaf with title-page, as a preface to the Greek text.

[8] Antoine Augustin Renouard, *Annales de l'imprimerie des Alde* (Paris, 1834), p. 257, cites only « c » as the signature letter for this leaf.

[9] The Grenville copy (G) has been heavily washed but apparently contained this emendation.

[10] Lugduni Batavorum, 1737 (ed. Math. Röver); Leovardiae, 1742 (ed. Joh. Schrader); and Paris, « L'an quatrième » [1795/6], (ed. J.-B. Gail).

that these improvements were made at the printing house, either by Aldus himself or (rather more probably) by one of his resident assistants. For reasons which I have set forth in my discussion of the manuscript corrections found in Alessandro Benedetti's *Diaria de bello Carolino*,[11] which was printed by Aldus in the next year, it seems certain that such corrections as these must be treated as integral parts of the book—indeed, as much a part of the volume as the more frequently encountered insertions achieved by means of hand stamping. Briefly the corrections are the following:

Folio 2; signature: « α »
    line 3: παλαίοτατον altered to παλαιότατον (i. e., accent shifted)
    line 5: ἐντυπησομένοις altered to ἐντυπωσομένοις
Folio 3; signature « b »
    line 17: « inuidiam » corrected to « iniuriam»
Folio 6; signature « a_{iij} »
    verso, line 14: Ὥς ʽοι corrected to Ὥς ἡ (line 67 of Greek text)
Folio 15; first word: Λείανδρος
    verso, line 9: Οἱ μὲν corrected to Ἡ μὲν (line 224 of Greek text)
Folio 16; first words: Sed cara
    line 12: « Hanc » corrected to « Haec » (cf. line 227 of Greek text)

The first of these instances, it must be admitted, was previously noted by Robert Proctor (*op. cit.*, p. 154), but only in the case of the British Museum's Grenville copy and not as a general observation applicable to all examples.[12] This alteration is found in every copy which I have noted and requires no further comment. Proctor, however, missed the Aldine correction in line 5 of the same page,[13]

---

[11] *Supra.*

[12] The uncorrected form reappears in the 1517 edition of the Aldine press and is also printed by Dibdin. *Bibliotheca Spenceriana* (London, 1814-1823), II, 177, no. 316. However, Michael Maittaire, *Annales typographici ab artis inventae origine ad annum MD* (Hagae-Comitum, 1719-1741), I, 70, places the accent in the proper position.

[13] The form as originally printed is quite impossible, since the future middle participle requires the *omega*, not the *eta*. The incorrect form is printed in the 1517 reprint, by Maittaire (*loc. cit.*), and by Ambroise Firmin-Didot, *Alde Manuce et l'Hellénisme à Venise* (Paris, 1875), p. 55. The emended reading is cited by the British Museum's incunabula catalogue (V: 553), by Proctor (*op. cit.*, p. 95), and by Beriah Botfield, *Praefationes et epistolae editionibus principibus auctorum veterum praepositae* (Cantabrigiae, 1861), p. 182; none of these works, however, points out that this reading is the result of manuscript correction. The second Morgan copy (B) has been badly washed, but it is likely that it too once contained this emendation. All the other copies have this correction.

though it is certainly present in both copies preserved in the British Museum; a careful scrutiny will reveal this correction even on plate XV of Proctor's classic study *The Printing of Greek in the Fifteenth Century.*

The two other Greek corrections are desirable for grammatical reasons,[14] and yet so recent a scholar as Arthur Ludwich failed to take notice of Aldus' manuscript emendations. For example, Ludwich credits the Aldine edition (following Codex Estense III A 17) with the reading Ὣς ʽοι for line 67 in his edition of *Hero and Leander* issued in 1929, though all but three of the copies known to me bear the correction noted above.[15] The edition of 1737 already cited similarly paid not the slightest heed to either of these manuscript emendations.

The Latin corrections are of a similar nature and occur in all the copies which were examined by the writer.[16] The « inuidiam » of the Latin version of Marcus Musurus' poem on Musaeus is clearly incorrect as a translation for ʽυβριν and « iniuriam » is wanted, as is proved by the 1517 reprint put out by the Aldine press after the death of the founder. However, in order not to disfigure the text too much, Aldus here contented himself with merely changing the « d » into an « r » and hoped, apparently, that the eye would read « iniuriam » rather than the impossible « inuiriam » which is actually present. The correction of « Hanc » in line 227 to « Haec » was adopted also by the 1517 reprint but does not seem to have pleased editors Schrader (1742) and Gail (1795) as they emended the text further to read « Ea ».

These, then, are the corrections, both those in manuscript and those resulting from the resetting of type, which are to be found in the *editio princeps* of Musaeus. Even though these happen to be of relatively slight importance, they are nevertheless significant as material evidence for the care with which Aldus supervised not only the actual printing but also the publication of his texts. Since Aldus took such pains to correct his books by making manuscript improvements in the several copies before permitting them to be sold to the public, it is certainly not too much to require that the modern editor pay

---

[14] The 1517 edition prints the corrected reading in both these instances.

[15] Only copies EiK do not seem to have this correction. These same examples also lack the second Greek emendation.

[16] Mr. Scheide informs me that these corrections are present in his copy, and Mr. Mead says they are also found in the Huntington example.

close attention to these manuscript emendations. It is obviously unjust to credit Aldus with a reading which he had deleted from his edition or repudiated by means of manuscript alterations. The corrections which we have noted for the Musaeus should serve as a reminder that editorial duties demand more than the casting of a fleeting glance at the text of any Aldines (where these editions are consulted for the purpose of preparing critical editions) and no unhappy variant reading should be ascribed to the great Venetian scholar-printer unless it is manifestly obvious that this reading had received Aldus' final approval. If a text has been emended in manuscript, a comparison with other copies will speedily reveal whether the corrections were made in Aldus' printing house or not—and if they were made in his office, such corrections should be accepted as an integral part of the official Aldine text.

This is the chief lesson which is brought home by a study of the manuscript corrections in the first edition of *Hero and Leander*. There is, however, another small point which may be touched upon, although collectors now-a-days are better informed in such matters than their predecessors of the eighteenth and nineteenth centuries. Many of the extant Aldines were carefully cleaned and washed by the fastidious owners of an earlier day, who thereby hoped to improve the appearance of these early volumes. In the process of removing the honorable scars of time, however, the Aldine emendations were often almost obliterated as well, though these can sometimes be made legible once again by the aid of an ultra-violet lamp. One may express the hope that book-lovers of the future will keep their books as they find them; it is fairly certain that the false attempts to enhance the value of copies by attempting to improve their appearance will in the long run have quite the opposite result.

(From *La Bibliofilia* 52 (1950), pp. 123-27).

ADDITIONAL NOTE TO ALDUS MANUTIUS
AND HIS FIRST EDITION OF THE GREEK MUSAEUS

To the issue of *La Bibliofilia* devoted to the « Centenario Aldino » (vol. LII, 1950, pp. 123-127), the present writer contributed a study on the manuscript and stop-press corrections found in the first Aldine edition of the Musaeus. Since the appearance of this discussion, it has been my good fortune to be able to examine eight more copies of this book. The fact that four of these volumes contain stop-press variants not found in any of the fifteen copies previously consulted suggests the desirability of adding this supplementary note to my original paper. The following are the additional copies seen by me:

Vienna, Nationalbibliothek, 3. H. 23
Munich, Staatsbibliothek, Rar. 303
Modena, Biblioteca Estense, .S. 7. 15
Milan, Libreria Antiquaria Hoepli
Florence, Biblioteca Laurenziana, D'Elci 986
Madrid, Biblioteca Nacional, Inc. 1322
Cambridge, Mass., Harvard University Library, William K.
    Richardson Collection
Geneva, Martin Bodmer Library

These eight copies all have the manuscript corrections to the Greek text noted in my earlier study, except that the Laurenziana volume does not appear to have those found on folio 2 recto though it does show the Greek emendations on folios 6 verso and 15 verso. The Latin correction by means of pen and ink on folio 3 recto (« inuidiam » altered to « iniuriam ») does not occur in the Hoepli and Modena copies though present in the other six examples. The stop-press corrections on folio 5 recto, discussed on page 125 of my paper, occur in all copies except the Bodmer, Laurenziana, and Madrid volumes; these contain, however, the manuscript corrections to the text common to the eight other copies previously cited which belong to the earlier setting of the Musaeus.

The new stop-press variants are found on folio 16 recto. Here it had been previously observed (page 126) that in line 12 the first word (« Hanc ») had in every case been corrected in ink to read « Haec ». This is also true in the case of the Bodmer, Madrid, Munich, and Laurenziana copies, but in the other new examples the correction is achieved by means of resetting of type; thus in these four examples, « Haec » is the first *printed* word of that line. Furthermore line 19 of the same page usually reads:

Sed multifremi apud lirora maris

The misprint « lirora » for « littora » appears not to have received manuscript correction in any of the copies hitherto examined. However, those four copies (Vienna, Modena, Hoepli, and Harvard) which have the stop-press emendation to « Haec » in line 12 of this page also have the additional stop-press correction of « littora » for the incorrect « lirora ». Apparently this misprint was discovered only after the great majority of copies had already been printed off; though pen-and-ink emendation for this slip might be expected in the copies of the earlier (incorrect) state, no such examples came to my notice, perhaps indicating that most of these had been sold before this error came to light.

(From *Scritti sopra Aldo Manuzio* (1955), pp. 106-107).

# CHAPTER B22

## MANUSCRIPT CORRECTIONS IN THE
## ALDINE EDITION OF BEMBO'S *DE AETNA*

ON two previous occasions,[1] the present writer has commented upon the manuscript corrections found in incunabula printed by Aldus Manutius; these one may credit, with almost absolute certainty, to the press itself. The present study will discuss editorial emendations of a similar sort found in the first edition of Pietro Bembo's *De Aetna* (GW 3810); for this purpose, a score of copies scattered between Los Angeles and Vienna have been examined. Through the study of this book, one may obtain not only some very interesting particulars as to the Italian Cardinal's familiarity with the Classics and his method of literary composition, but also, I think, one may discover a pattern by which it will be possible to determine if certain copies were sold by Aldus shortly after they had come off the press or if they had remained unsold upon his shelves for some time. Any unexamined copy may be fitted into this analysis, and thereby it may readily be discovered whether such a copy was sold sooner or later, relatively speaking. With these objectives in view, it will first of all be necessary to enumerate thirteen instances of manuscript corrections which have been checked in all twenty copies; these examples will be cited in as brief a form as possible, just enough detail being given so that the checking of other copies may be facilitated:

1. A1$^v$, line 12: "nos" interlineated after "tuorum."
   line 13: "nos" deleted after "Angele."
2. A2, line 8: "interrogaremus" altered to "interrogaremur."
3. A2, line 18: "ripam" altered to "ripa."
4. A4$^v$, line 11: "sibi" altered to "tibi."
5. A6$^v$, line 21: "debeamus" altered to "debebamus."
6. A8$^v$, line 5: "Socratem modo aut" added after "non."
   line 6: "modo aut Aristotelem" deleted after "Platonem."
7. B1, line 10: "es" altered to "esses."
8. B1$^v$, line 18: "aquila" altered to "aquula."
9. B4$^v$, line 19: "feritate" altered to "fertilitate."

[1] For Benedetti's *Diaria de bello Carolino* (GW 863), and the corrections in the Musaeus (HC 11653), see *supra*.

10. C8ᵛ, line 17: "subiit" altered to "subit."
11. D1, line 4: "inocuparunt" altered to "inoccuparunt."
12. D3ᵛ, line 10: "natura" altered to "naturae."
13. D6, line 8: "Antinoiq3" altered to "Alcinoique."

In addition to the above instances, three more "points" may be listed. The first of these is a stop-press emendation checked in all copies; the other two are pen-and-ink alterations which came to light late in the course of my investigations and could not, accordingly, be verified in those copies previously inspected.[2] These are cited here in order to complete the list of manuscript corrections as it is known to me and so as to provide still further criteria for future comparison:

A. B2, line 3: "qnia" corrected to "quia."
B. D2ᵛ, line 6: "usq3" altered to "ususque."
C. D2ᵛ, lines 5 & 7: "meminit Strabo" altered to "Plinius et Strabo meminere"; "illius" altered to "illorum."

The table on page 172 sets forth the readings as they are found in twenty copies of the first edition; for the sake of confirmation, two later printings of the *De Aetna*[3] are also cited. The 1530 edition, issued while Pietro Bembo was still very much alive, differs materially from the Aldine text; one may reasonably presume, however, that it represents a revision authorized by the future Cardinal himself. It is most significant that, save for a single instance, the 1530 text accepts all the manuscript emendations found in the copies of the 1495 edition. A check mark (√) indicates that the manuscript alteration is present in the cited copy, while a dash (—) implies that the necessary details are not known to me; a blank space, correspondingly,

---

[2] It is almost impossible to check such variants by correspondence, unless one has absolute confidence in the judgment and ability of one's correspondents. In the first place, the corrections are often so skillfully made that they defy identification unless one knows exactly what to look for. Secondly, many copies have been "cleaned" and these pen-and-ink emendations more or less obliterated, making it difficult (on occasion, without the use of ultra-violet rays, impossible) to determine whether or not the corrections ever existed in such copies. Certain readings in the British Museum copies have, however, been checked for me by Mr. F. C. Francis, who has thereby earned my deep gratitude.

[3] The 1530 edition forms part of the *Opuscula* of Bembo which was printed by the firm of "Joannes Antonius et Fratres de Sabio" at Venice in that year. The later text is included in the edition of *Aetna* (sometimes attributed to Cornelius Severus) printed at Amsterdam, Henricus Schelte, 1703. The copies checked belong to the present writer and have been confirmed by those in the Boston Public and New York Public Libraries.

| | 1 | 2 | 3 | 4 | 5 | 6 | 7 | 8 | 9 | 10 | 11 | 12 | 13 | Total | A | B | C |
|---|---|---|---|---|---|---|---|---|---|---|---|---|---|---|---|---|---|
| New York, The Pierpont Morgan Library, PML 364 | ✓ | ✓ | ✓ | ✓ | ✓ | ✓ | ✓ | ✓ | ✓ | | | | ✓ | 10 | ✓ | | |
| New York, The Pierpont Morgan Library, PML 431 | ✓ | ✓ | ✓ | ✓ | ✓ | ✓ | ✓ | ✓ | ✓ | ✓ | ✓ | ✓ | ✓ | 13 | ✓ | ✓ | |
| New York, Dr. Arthur E. Neergaard | ✓ | ✓ | ✓ | | | | | | | | | | ✓ | 4 | | | — |
| San Marino, Henry E. Huntington Library, Mead 3295 | ✓ | ✓ | ✓ | ✓ | ✓ | ✓ | ✓ | ✓ | ✓ | ✓ | ✓ | | ✓ | 12 | ✓ | ✓ | — |
| Paris, Bibliothèque Nationale, Rés. 946 | | | ✓ | | | | ✓ | | ✓ | ✓ | ✓ | | ✓ | 6 | ✓ | | — |
| Paris, Bibliothèque Nationale, Rés. 1249 | | | ✓ | | | | ✓ | ✓ | ✓ | ✓ | ✓ | ✓ | ✓ | 9 | ✓ | | — |
| London, British Museum, IA. 24413 | | | ✓ | | | | ✓ | | | | | | ✓ | 4 | | | — |
| London, British Museum, IA. 24412 | | | ✓ | | | | ✓ | ✓ | ✓ | ✓ | ✓ | | ✓ | 9 | ✓ | | — |
| London, British Museum, IA. 24411 | | | ✓ | | | | ✓ | ✓ | | | | | ✓ | 6 | ✓ | | — |
| London, British Museum, IA. 24410 | ✓ | ✓ | ✓ | | | ✓ | ✓ | ✓ | ✓ | FN | | | ✓ | 10/11 | ✓ | | — |
| Milan, Biblioteca Ambrosiana, Rossi 1258 | | | | | | | | | | | | | ✓ | 1 | | | — |
| Milan, Biblioteca Braidense, AN. XI. 46 | | | | | | ✓ | | | | | | | ✓ | 2 | ✓ | | — |
| Florence, Biblioteca Laurenziana, D'Elci 96 | | | | | | ✓ | ✓ | | | | | | | 2 | | | — |
| Florence, Biblioteca Nazionale, Inc. Nenc. 76 | | | | | | ✓ | ✓ | ✓ | ✓ | ✓ | ✓ | | ✓ | 7 | ✓ | | — |
| Venice, Biblioteca Marciana, Aldine 380 (41402) | | | | | | | | | ✓ | | ✓ | | | 2 | ✓ | | |
| Venice, Biblioteca Marciana, Aldine 335.1 (76217) | ✓ | ✓ | ✓ | ✓ | ✓ | ✓ | ✓ | ✓ | ✓ | ✓ | | | ✓ | 10 | ✓ | | ✓ |
| Modena, Biblioteca Estense, α. Z. 2. 15 | ✓ | ✓ | ✓ | | ✓ | ✓ | ✓ | ✓ | ✓ | ✓ | ✓ | ✓ | ✓ | 11 | ✓ | | |
| Rome, Biblioteca Universitaria | ✓ | ✓ | | | ✓ | ✓ | | ✓ | | ✓ | ✓ | ✓ | ✓ | 9 | ✓ | | |
| Munich, Staatsbibliothek, 4°. Inc. s.a. 1180 | | | | | | | | | | | | | ✓ | 1 | ✓ | FN | FN |
| Vienna, Nationalbibliothek, 11 H 84 | ✓ | ✓ | ✓ | ✓ | ✓ | ✓ | ✓ | ✓ | ✓ | ✓ | | ✓ | ✓ | 12 | ✓ | FN | FN |
| **Total** | 13 | 20 | 13 | 9 | | 7 | 12 | 13 | 13 | 10 | 8/9 | 7 | 8 | | 13 | | |
| Venice, J. A. & Fratres de Sabio, 1530 | ✓ | ✓ | ✓ | ✓ | ✓ | ✓ | ✓ | ✓ | ✓ | ✓ | ✓ | | ✓ | 11/12 | ✓ | ✓ | |
| Amsterdam, H. Schelte, 1703 | ✓ | ✓ | ✓ | ✓ | ✓ | ✓ | ✓ | ✓ | ✓ | ✓ | ✓ | ✓ | ✓ | 11 | ✓ | ✓ | ✓ |

will assure the reader that the text remains as originally printed by Aldus.[4]

If we turn first of all to the literary implications of the pen-and-ink emendations, we will note that Bembo had a faulty recollection of at least two classical allusions.[5] One must assume, naturally, that the author was relying upon his memory, for if he had the original texts before him it is difficult to see how he could have made these slips. Again, the misquotations are of such nature that they can only be attributed to Bembo; it is impossible to place the blame for these upon Aldus or any of his employees.

The first instance is represented by example 6 cited above; here Bembo's text may be freely translated as follows:[6]

Bembo Senior: Is that so, then; these shores do have plane-trees?
Bembo Junior: Indeed yes, most beautiful ones and lots of them, so that they could entice not only Plato and Aristotle and all the more gentle disciples to philosophize in their shade but indeed even those most austere men, and thorough devotees of the sun, the Gymnosophists.

The Latin text, as we have seen, has been so emended that it alters "ut non Platonem modo, aut Aristotelem, scholasque" to read "ut non Socratem modo, aut Platonem, scholasque." This was a most necessary correction, since it was Socrates, not Aristotle, who was enticed into the shadow of the plane-tree, as Plato relates (*Phaedrus* 229A and 230B). However, it is perhaps even more likely that Bembo had in mind not the original Greek text but rather Cicero's observation in the *De oratore* (Lib. I, cap. vii. 28), as the Modena copy of the *De Aetna* suggests. On the page in question, the Estense example preserves a scribal note which, though difficult to make out, apparently reads:

Unde Sceuola in oratorem ita ad Crassum loquitur: Cur non imitamur, Crasse, Socratem illum qui est in phedro platonis? Nam hec [*Cicero*—me haec] tua

---

[4] For the citation "FN" in the list, the following further notations are necessary: no. 5, the 1530 edition omits the entire phrase containing "debeamus"; no. 11, the British Museum's Cracherode copy has leaf D1 in facsimile; nos. B and C, the Munich copy has leaf D2 mutilated and these readings are lost.

[5] The eleven other emendations involve stylistic improvements or corrections of orthographic or grammatical slips.

[6] The Aldine edition (A8ᵛ, lines 3-10) prints: "B. P. Ain'tandem, Platanos illae habent ripae? B. F. Pulcherrimas illas quidem, et multissimas; ut non Platonem modo, aut Aristotelem, scholas*que* omnes mitiores suis umbris inuitare possint ad philosophandum; sed etiam Gymnosophistas durissimos illos quide*m* homines, et sole admodum delectatos."

platanus admonuit quae non minus ad optandum [?; *Cicero*—opacandum][7]
hunc locum patulis est diffusa ramis quam illa cuius umbram secutus est Socrates.

Whichever classical allusion one may believe that Bembo was pointing to, it is obvious that the editorial emendation to this passage is
vitally necessary.

The second example is number 13 of our list, where Bembo cites
Horace (*Epistolae*, Lib. 1, Epist. 2. 27-31) in these words:

> Nos numerus sumus, et fruges consumere nati,
> Sponsi Penelopes, nebulones, Antinoique
> In cute curanda plus aequo operata iuuentus;
> Quis[8] pulchrum fuit in medios dormire dies, et
> Ad strepitum citharae cessantum ducere curam.

Clearly, as the editorial correction indicates, "Alcinoique" is wanted,
for Horace here refers to the gracious host of Odysseus and king of
the Phaeacians, Alcinous, and not to the chief of Penelope's suitors,
Antinous. Thus, in these two instances, Bembo made classical "slips"
which demanded corrections[9]—and, in a number of copies, got them.

What, in turn, can be deduced, in a strictly bibliographical sense,
from these pen-and-ink alterations? It seems to me quite likely that
a general idea of the order in which the misprints were discovered
can be detected from the frequency table. Thus, example 2 shows that
the correction was made in each copy examined; therefore one may
argue that this slip was discovered soon after the sheets had come off
the press. Conversely, one might infer, in the case of the two literary
problems discussed above, that these errors did not come to the attention of Bembo (or Aldus, as the case may be) till after a good
number of copies had already been sold and only seven or eight
copies in a score remained available for correction.

The stop-press correction, consisting in the righting of a turned letter, affords certain information of its own. Since thirteen of the
twenty copies consulted have this correction, it indicates that the text
was "proofed" before half the edition-sheet had been run off. The
fact that the appearance of the stop-press variant has absolutely no
relation to the occurrence of the manuscript emendations shows that

---

[7] Some of the earliest editions, including the *editio princeps* [Subiaco, Sweynheym
and Pannartz, 1465], here print "occupandum."

[8] The usual reading here is "Cui."

[9] In example C, Bembo has added to the authority of Strabo that of Pliny. This,
then, is supplementary information, not correction of an error.

the corrected sheets were scattered at random through the entire edition. For example, the second Morgan copy with all its manuscript emendations has the uncorrected misprint, while the example in the Ambrosiana Library has but a single scribal alteration and yet the typographical error has here been eliminated.

The several copies themselves seem to disclose the relative order of sale. Thus, the second Morgan copy, containing all the pen-and-ink corrections, as well as the Vienna and Huntington examples (each with twelve emendations) must have been sold after a considerable lapse of time (that is, when all the errors here listed had been discovered). The Munich copy, on the other hand, has only one correction, and here the inference is, of course, that it had been disposed of by Aldus before he knew of the other misprints. In conclusion one must observe that Aldus' correctors worked in a somewhat slipshod manner, so that a particular correction will be found in one copy and not in another, whereas the second example will exhibit a different emendation unknown to the first. Again, it may be possible to show that a misprint not corrected at the press might have come to the attention of a diligent reader who then made the necessary alteration on his own account. Such considerations naturally preclude the possibility of determining absolutely the order of sale of the several examples. In general, however, it seems obvious that (to choose at random) the Laurenziana and the first Marciana examples were sold by Aldus shortly after having come off the press, while the Modena copy was one upon which Aldus did not realize his profit too quickly. Such editorial emendations, then, as those found in the first edition of the *De Aetna* have a bibliographical as well as a literary significance and, if treated with necessary caution, do provide us with some useful information as to editorial practices and bookselling problems in the closing years of the fifteenth century.

(From *PBSA* 45 (1951), pp. 136-42).

# CHAPTER B23

# THE LAYING OF A GHOST?

## OBSERVATIONS ON THE 1483 RATDOLT EDITION

## OF THE *FASCICULUS TEMPORUM*

EVER since the middle of the eighteenth century, a 1483 edition of the *Fasciculus temporum* from the press of Erhard Ratdolt has appeared in the annals of Venetian printing history. We have it on the excellent authority of Georg Wolfgang Panzer,[1] who quotes Georg Wilhelm Zapf's notation[2] that this edition was listed in the *Bibliotheca historicocritica librorum opusculorumque rariorum* (Nürnberg, 1736) by Georg Jacob Schwindel,[3] writing under the pseudonym of Theophilus Sincerus. If Schwindel actually saw the book, he appears to have been the first and last person who ever examined such an edition. There is, however, an exceedingly persuasive suggestion that, in this case, Schwindel (either consciously or otherwise) was simply living up to his name. The 1483 edition by Ratdolt was nevertheless duly noted by Hain, Pollard, Essling, Diehl and the British Museum's incunabula catalogue;[4] furthermore it is listed with reservation by Redgrave and Sander.[5]

---

[1] *Annales typographici ab artis inventae origine ad annum, MD* (Nuremberg, 1793-1803), III, 189, no. 667; "Zapf. p. 163. ex Catal. Schwindelii p. 15. ubi tamen nomen typographi non indicatur. Adesse tamen hanc editionem, eamque esse tertiam Ratdolti, puto."

[2] *Augsburgs Buchdruckergeschichte* (Augsburg, 1788-91), I, 163, no. II of 1483: "S. Theoph. Sinceri oder Ge. Jac. Schwindelii Bibliotheca p. 15. n. 177. Sonst hab ich von dieser Ausgabe nichts entdecken können."

[3] This is apparently the work referred to by Zapf, though I have been unable to confirm this reference.

[4] Ludwig Hain, *Repertorium bibliographicum* (Stuttgart, 1826-38), no. 6933; Alfred W. Pollard, *Italian Book Illustrations* (1894), p. 28; Victor Masséna, Prince d'Essling, *Les livres à figures vénitiens de la fin du XVᵉ siècle* (Florence, 1907-14), I, 269, no. 279, n. 1 ("Hain [6933] cite une édition de Venise, 1483, imprimée par Ratdolt, qu'il nous a été impossible de découvrir; elle n'est pas mentionnée par Panzer"); Robert Diehl, "Erhard Ratdolt," *Philobiblon*, VI (1933), 126; and *Catalogue of Books Printed in the XVth Century now in the British Museum*, (1908-49), V, 289 & 290.

[5] Gilbert R. Redgrave, *Erhard Ratdolt and his Work at Venice* (Bibliographical Society, Illustrated Monograph No. 1, London, 1894), p. 38, no. 39 ("The [citation]

Yet it is curious beyond measure that no copy of this edition has ever been located! Through the kind offices of Dr. Elisabeth von Kathen, I have recently been informed that not even the manuscript of the unprinted sections of the *Gesamtkatalog der Wiegendrucke* records the existence of a single example of Ratdolt's 1483 *Fasciculus temporum*.

If this Schwindel notation were the only evidence for such a production, one would quite properly set down this edition as an error (perhaps a misreading by the cataloguer of the roman date "M.cccc.lxxxiiij" of a known Ratdolt printing). But, as the BMC duly points out,[6] there is a statement made by Ratdolt himself which postulates an edition no copy of which has survived to our day. At present there are four extant editions credited to Ratdolt: those of 24 November 1480 (Hain 6926), 21 December 1481 (Hain 6928), 28 May 1484 (Hain 6934) and 8 September 1485 (Hain 6935). In the 1484 edition (PML 334, folio 1ᵛ),[7] Erhard Ratdolt remarks, in his dedicatory letter to Niccolò Mocenigo "il grande", as follows:[8]

> In these circumstances, since I have undertaken to print with greater care and labor the *Fasciculus temporum*, which thrice before this I alone have printed in these parts of Italy having set figures and images in their due order, I have decided to dedicate this work and my labors to you.

In the following year, Ratdolt speaks of the 1485 edition as having been preceded by four earlier printings.[9]

Since this statement was made by the printer himself, one is certainly required to believe that Ratdolt printed three editions before that of 1484, though only his editions of 1480 and 1481 are evidenced by actual copies. While this appears to point directly to a 1483 print-

---

is perhaps due to an error in reading the date of No. 43 [1484]"); and Max Sander, *Le livre à figures italien depuis 1467 jusqu'à 1530* (New York, 1941), III, 1133, no. 6528 ("L'existence d'une édition de 1483 est supposée par Essling . . . mais on n'en connaît aucun exemplaire.").

[6] BMC V:289: "This confirms the existence of the edition of 1483 quoted with an obelus by Hain."

[7] Ada Thurston and Curt F. Bühler, *Check List of Fifteenth Century Printing in the Pierpont Morgan Library* (1939), no. 858.

[8] The original reads thus: "statui impresentia cum temporum fasciculum quem ter solus ego his in partibus italie impositis ordine suo figuris & signis ante hac impressi cura & opera diligentiori imprimendum sumpserim: opus ipsum laboresque meos tibi dicare."

[9] On folio 1ᵛ the text reads: "fasciculum quem quater . . . ante hac impressi."

ing, it is indeed amazing that, in the past 215 years, no one has seen an example of such a production. The other Ratdolt editions may, without exaggeration, be called quite common works, and some edition by this printer is almost certainly to be found in even the most modest collection of fifteenth-century books. Such large European libraries as those in Berlin, Florence, London, Madrid, Munich, Oxford and Venice (among others) possess all four Ratdolt printings. For North America alone, Miss Margaret B. Stillwell[10] lists no fewer than sixteen copies each for the 1480 and 1484 editions, fifteen of that of 1485, and twenty-one for the 1481 production. And yet no one can find a copy of the 1483 Ratdolt edition anywhere in the wide world! Is there another explanation for Ratdolt's very explicit statements?

In order to present a possible (and plausible) solution for these somewhat contradictory pieces of evidence, it will be necessary to review briefly some biographical details which may not be too familiar to the reader.[11] Erhard Ratdolt of Augsburg seems to have arrived in Venice about the year 1476, and shortly afterwards formed a partnership with Bernhard "Maler" (a native of the same Swabian city) and Peter Löslein of Langenzenn (near Fürth in Bavaria). Ratdolt was apparently in charge of the press, while the painter Bernhard may have been the head of the firm and its art director;[12] Löslein was certainly the "corrector et socius."[13] This press had a successful career until 1478 when Löslein dropped out and shortly thereafter Maler and Ratdolt dissolved their partnership. Following the dissolution of the firm, Ratdolt's name disappears from our sight until 1 April 1480, on which day he completed and signed (by himself) a *Breviarium Benedictinum congregationis S. Iustinae* (GW 5181).

Shortly after the disappearance of the house of Maler, Ratdolt, and Löslein in 1478, a new press made its appearance in Venice

[10] *Incunabula in American Libraries* (1940), nos. R253, R256, R262, and R263. Of the Walch edition which will shortly be referred to, Miss Stillwell (R252) also records sixteen American copies.

[11] For further details, compare Konrad Haebler, *Die deutschen Buchdrucker des XV. Jahrhunderts im Auslande* (München, 1924), pp. 107-110; BMC:xvii-xviii; and Redgrave, *op. cit.* Haebler too (p. 109) speaks of Ratdolt's five editions of the *Fasciculus temporum.*

[12] Compare Leo Baer, "Bernhard, Maler von Augsburg, und die Bücherornamentik der italienischen Frührenaissance," *Monatshefte für Kunstwissenschaft*, II (1909), 46-57.

[13] He is cited thus, for example, in the colophon of the *Gesta Petri Mocenici* (1477) by Coriolanus Cepio (Hain 4849; copy in PML, *Check List*, no. 848).

under the sponsorship of yet another German, Georg Walch.[14] This press employed a gothic type very similar to one subsequently found in the hands of Ratdolt (his type 4:76G). The woodcut capitals used by Walch were not unlikely the identical ones employed by Ratdolt before 1479 and after the reopening of his own press. In all Walch printed but four books known to us, the last of which (the *Rationale divinorum officiorum* by Guillelmus Duranti—GW 9124) is dated 18 May 1482. But it is surely worthy of note that the very first of these four productions is a *Fasciculus temporum*, dated 1479, which, the colophon assures us, was "printed with the extraordinary diligence and expense of Georg Walch, a German."[15] This book, among the earliest of Venetian illustrated works,[16] is one which must have required considerable technical skill.[17] Is it reasonable to suppose that Walch, as his very first venture, could turn out such a work without the assistance of outside and experienced help? Or could we be justified in assuming that Ratdolt had a hand in this undertaking, as the practical printer; that his were the labors which actually produced the 1479 *Fasciculus temporum* while Walch's contribution was limited to supplying the text and the very necessary capital?

This *Fasciculus temporum* with its numerous technical difficulties was obviously produced by a professional and can hardly have been the trial effort of a novice.[18] Moreover, it was printed with equipment certainly forming part of Ratdolt's stock-in-trade and was taken in hand just about the time that Ratdolt disappears from our view. To

[14] Haebler, *op. cit.*, 113-114. The BMC (V:xxii) has this interesting comment: "Georgius Walch, a German whose name points to Italian ancestry, appears to have been connected in some way with Ratdolt, but the precise relation is obscure. His first recorded book, Rolewinck, Fasciculus temporum, belongs to 1479, when Ratdolt had severed his connexion with Maler and Löslein but had not yet resumed printing on his own account. Its type closely resembles one which Ratdolt employed in the following year for an edition of the same work evidently modelled on that of Walch, while its woodcut capitals are even more like those used by Ratdolt both before and after this date and may possibly form part of the same sets."

[15] The colophon (PML 324, f. 72) reads: "*impressa* Venetijs singulari industria atq*ue* impensa Georij Walch almani. *an*no *do*mini 1479. Sixto quarto pontifice maximo: finit feliciter."

[16] See Arthur M. Hind, *An Introduction to a History of Woodcut* (1935), II, 456.

[17] The difficulties of composition are noted by Margaret B. Stillwell, "The Fasciculus Temporum: A Genealogical Survey of Editions before 1480," *Bibliographical Essays; A Tribute to Wilberforce Eames* (1924), pp. 409-440.

[18] Neither Haebler nor BMC knows anything of Walch's career prior to his appearance in Venice with the printing of the *Fasciculus temporum*. Haebler (p. 114) surmises that he is the same person as the Jorg Walich listed as a citizen of Vienna in 1493, where he is described as a "Buchführer."

this investigator anyway, it seems an altogether likely solution for the conflicting evidence cited above to assume that Ratdolt was employed by Walch to print the *Fasciculus temporum* for him, though he received no credit for his share in the work in the colophon of the 1479 edition. Perhaps this irked Ratdolt, though so long as Walch was still in Venice, Ratdolt made no mention of his part in the production of this first Italian printing and no statement to that effect is found in Ratdolt's 1480 and 1481 editions. But Walch probably left Venice for his homeland some time after May 1482—and in his first printing of the *Fasciculus temporum* subsequent thereto (28 May 1484), Ratdolt made the claim set forth above.

Until a copy of the 1483 printing can actually be produced, it is my belief that one may treat this edition as a "ghost." The *five* editions printed by Ratdolt can be identified as the four issued on his own initiative, plus the 1479 printing for which Walch allowed him no credit. The theory set forth here would completely set at rest the problems discussed in this study and explain the known facts relative to the editions now credited to Erhard Ratdolt. It does not seem essential, to the present writer anyway, to postulate the existence of a 1483 Venetian *Fasciculus temporum*; this can be deferred until such a time as a copy may be presented for the inspection of the bibliographical world.

(From *Studies in Bibliography* 4 (1952), pp. 155-59).

# CHAPTER B24

## A GERONA INCUNABULUM AND THE PRESS
## OF DIEGO DE GUMIEL

ALTHOUGH the edition of the Catalan *Fiore di virtù* printed at Gerona in the fifteenth century has been listed in most of the standard bibliographies of Spanish incunabula, it is a curious fact that no full description of this book is available to date. Konrad Haebler[1] was unable to see a copy of this edition, and Martin Kurz[2] even expressed a doubt as to its existence ("nicht nachweisbar"). Similarly, Francisco Vindel[3] could not give full details, although he did reproduce the title-page and the colophon in his new bibliography; these reproductions seem to be recuttings of the illustrations found in a bookseller's catalogue of some years past.[4] The Vindel cuts, however, have been so "touched up" that they no longer properly represent the original; those in the Maggs catalogue are much more honest and accurate in this respect. The only extant copy of this edition of the *Flor de virtuts e de costums* was obtained by The Pierpont Morgan Library in February, 1938, and the book was duly listed in the library's *Check List* of incunabula published in the following year.[5] It is, one supposes, a result of the recent war that a book, recorded as being in public ownership in 1939, was not

---

[1] *Bibliografía Ibérica del siglo XV*, La Haya, 1903, p. 126, no. 276. Haebler adds the note: "Mis investigaciones ulteriores no me han dado noticias ni de este (copy reported in the library of San Juan de Barcelona) ni de otro ejemplar y con gran sentimiento mio no me es posible dar una descripción exacta ni un facsimile de los caracteres con que fué compuesto".

[2] *Handbuch der iberischen Bilddrucke des XV. Jahrhunderts*, Leipzig 1931, p. 90, no. 181. The book is, however, listed under no. 1874 in Mariano Aguiló y Fustér, *Catálogo de obras en lengua catalana impresas desde 1474 hasta 1860*, Madrid 1923, pp. 479–480.

[3] *El arte tipográfico en España durante el siglo XV. Cataluña*, Madrid, 1945, pp. 201–202, no. 121.

[4] *Seventy-five Unique or Rare Spanish & Portuguese Books*, London, Maggs Bros. (Catalogue No. 589, c. 1933).

[5] Ada Thurston and Curt F. Bühler, *Check List of Fifteenth Century Printing in the Pierpont Morgan Library*, New York, 1939, p. 164, no. 1748. The book was also listed in the American "Second Census" (Margaret B. Stillwell, *Incunabula in American Libraries*, New York, 1940, p. 200, no. F 166).

fully described in an official government publication half a decade later.

The complete description of this book follows:[6]

Fiore di virtù. In Catalan.

*Flor de virtuts e de costums.* Gerona: Juan de Valdes, 9 November 1497.

Haebler 276; Kurz 181; Vindel 121.

4°. 52 leaves. a—f⁸ g⁴. Type-page (f. 3, 29 lines): 145 x 93 mm. Types: 1:99 G (text) and 2:136 G (title). Woodcut border on title and woodcut initials; some capital spaces. Rubric.

f. 1 [title within border]: Flor de virtuts || e de costums. || 1ᵛ: ¶Aquests son los capitols cōtenguts enlo pre-||sent libre e apres de cascun capitol hi ha molts e||xemplis los quals redueix e porta a preposit del || natural de certs animals cascu en sa condicio. || [below, table of contents in two columns]. 2 [preface]: (S⁶) I stimar volem per raho: auctori-||tat: e exemple la miserable creatu-||ra quant sia dejecta perduda: e de-||cayguda:... 2ᵛ, line 8 (text begins): (A⁴)Mor beniuolēcia d'lectacio e caritat || sō q̃si vna cosa segōs la vniuersa e cōu||na doctrina d'ls sagrats theolechs ... 9—bl: les dones bones: e moltes lo qual nos pot negar|| ... (ends 52—g4, line 28): ... iuuenal diu la breu || paraula trespassa lo cel||52ᵛ (explicit):(D⁴)Onant fi al tractat: prech als legidors || que tenguen sment a les paraules que || yo he scrites:... (ends line 12): ... La qual obreta es sta||da treta del tosca enla present lengua cathalana. || (colophon): ¶Migençant la diuina gracia fonch stampat lo || present tractat enla insigna ciutat d'Gerona per || Johan de valdes esturiano. Fon acabat en lany|| de nostre senyor Mil. cccclxxxxvij. a. viiij. de Noē||bre.||

The only recorded copy is in The Pierpont Morgan Library (Check List no. 1748). It measures 167 x 119 mm. and is bound in stiff vellum. The present edition appears to have been set up from the edition printed at Barcelona by Diego de Gumiel, 3 January 1495 (Haebler 275). The types and initials seem to have been acquired from the same printer, as well as the woodcut on the title-page. This consists of a shield (to enclose the title) framed by two juxtaposed lions with floreated tails, shown menacing one another. In the present copy, the

---

[6] The description follows the methods suggested by the present writer (cf. *Standards of Bibliographical Description*, Philadelphia, University of Pennsylvania Press, 1949, pp. 3–60).

initials are rubricated and there are a few manuscript scribblings of no importance.

In the past, it has usually been assumed that three printers were at work in Gerona in the fifteenth century,[7] to each of whom a single book is credited in the excellent bibliographies of Haebler and Vindel. The books are these:

Felipe de Malla, *Memorial del pecador remut.*[8] Gerona: Mateo Vendrell, 17 November 1483. Haebler 389; Vindel 31.

*Paris e Viana.*[9] Gerona: [Diego de Gumiel], 5 June 1495. Haebler 516; Vindel 102.

*Flor de virtuts e de costums.*[10] Gerona: Juan de Valdes, 9 November 1497. Haebler 276; Vindel 121.

Despite the traditional attribution, Francisco Vindel[11] nevertheless strongly supported the argument that Gumiel never actually owned a press in Gerona. He maintained that the *Paris e Viana* printed there with Gumiel's equipment was not really produced by that printer, but that this book too came from the press of Juan de Valdes. On this point Vindel remarks (p. 202): "Yo creo, como apunto en el núm. 102 (Paris y Viana), que en realidad Juan de Valdes fué el único impresor que tuvo Gerona en esta última época del siglo XV, y que trabajaba protegido por Gumiel y con sus materiales, lo que justifica que el escudo de los leones lo usaran ambos tipógrafos."

It is, of course, a historic fact that Diego de Gumiel operated a press in Barcelona from 27 October 1494 onwards,[12] his firm being credited with a total output of at least a dozen books before the end of the century; eight of these books proudly proclaim his name. Again, the only two books known to Vindel which were printed at Gerona in

[7] Only two presses (Vendrell and Valdes) were, however, listed by Robert Proctor in his *An Index to the Early Printed Books in the British Museum . . . with Notes of those in the Bodleian Library*, London, 1898, p. 708.

[8] Copy examined at the Biblioteca Nacional at Madrid (*Catálogo de Incunables*, 1945, p. 311, no. 1216).

[9] The only recorded copies are in the Royal Library at Copenhagen and in the possession (1904) of D. Mariano Aguiló. This collection is now owned by the Biblioteca Central of the Diputación Provincial, Barcelona. I am grateful for the kind permission to make use of this great library on the occasion of my visit to Barcelona in November, 1951.

[10] Neither this book nor its printer (Juan de Valdes) is cited by Konrad Haebler, *Geschichte des spanischen Frühdruckes in Stammbäumen*, Leipzig 1923.

[11] See also his comments on page 175, relating to the *Paris e Viana* of 1495.

[12] Compare Haebler, *Geschichte*, pp. 269–274.

the last decade of the fifteenth century were produced by identical types, each having the same framing-cut on the title. Since one of these volumes is silent as to its printer while the other cites Valdes and since Gumiel is found at work in nearby Barcelona both before June 1495 and after February 1497, it was very logical for Vindel to assume that both books were printed by Juan de Valdes, who had (apparently) succeeded to the types, initials and title-cut previously used by Gumiel in Barcelona.

Vindel's plausible theory must, however, be abandoned in view of the existence of a book not recorded by him. This may be identified as the only known fifteenth-century edition of the *Psalterium lauda-torium* by Francesch Eximeniç (Franciscus Ximenes),[13] in the Catalan translation made by Guillem Fontana; the colophon of this book reads:[14]

¶ Migençant la diuina gracia fon || stampat lo present tractat enla ciu-||tat de gerona per Diego de gumiel || castella. Fon acabat enlany de no-||stre senyor .M.ccccxcv. a .xx. de març.||

It now becomes evident that Diego de Gumiel actually did move his press from Barcelona to Gerona in the spring of 1495.[15] It was only after he had printed at least two books[16] in this Catalan town that Gumiel disappears from Gerona and returns to Barcelona;[17] his

---

[13] The only known copy was in 1909 in the possession of Mr. Narcís J. de Linan of Madrid. Subsequently the book was owned by Mr. José Gallart Folch and is now in the library of Mr. Santiago Espona. I am under the deepest obligation to His Grace, the Duke of Alba, for helping to locate the present whereabouts of this incunable, and to Mr. José Porter for introducing me to the owner of it. It is indeed a great pleasure to record here my grateful thanks to Mr. Espona for his kind hospitality in receiving me in his home and for his generosity in putting both his library and his time at my disposal.

[14] Compare J. Massó y Torrents, "Les obres de Fra Francesch Eximeniç (1340?–1409?). Essaig d'una bibliografia" (*Institut d'estudis catalans, Anuari*, vol. III, 1909–1910, pp. 588–692). The book is described as no. 186 on pp. 675–676, with cuts of the title (border as Valdes) and colophon on p. 673. The book is also cited by Kurz, op. cit., p. 75, no. 133.

[15] The last dated book printed (but not signed) by Gumiel in Barcelona is the *Usatges de Barcelona e Constitucions de Cathalunya* of 20 February 1495 (Vindel 99), while the first book with a full date printed upon his return there was the *Tirant lo Blanc* of 16 September 1497.

[16] I am strongly inclined to leave the *Paris e Viana* with Gumiel rather than to assign it to Valdes. In the present state of our information, we know that Gumiel was printing in Gerona in the spring of 1495, and we have no record of printing by Valdes before Gumiel was back once more in Barcelona, in the summer of 1497.

[17] Compare Haebler, *Geschichte*, p. 270. It seems reasonable to conjecture, from the evidence in hand, that Gumiel was not able to compete successfully with the

equipment, as we have noted above, is subsequently found in the hands of Juan de Valdes. Thus it is quite certain that Gerona can make the proud claim to have had three presses operating there in the last quarter of the fifteenth century.

(From *Gutenberg-Jahrbuch* (1952), pp. 64-66).

---

experienced press of Pere Miguel and that, as a consequence of this, he left Barcelona some eight months after the completion of his first venture. Upon the death of Miguel in the winter of 1496/7, Gumiel returned to Barcelona and succeeded to this business. On 18 February 1497, Gumiel signed a contract to finish the printing of the *Tirant lo Blanc* within six months, a venture which Miguel had begun and Gumiel then completed, as the colophon explains (Vindel 119). Haebler, however, suspects that an epidemic of the pest drove Gumiel to Gerona in the spring of 1495—but if he did flee Barcelona for this reason, he took all his equipment with him (a strange circumstance!).

# CHAPTER B25

## PAULUS MANUTIUS AND HIS
## FIRST ROMAN PRINTINGS

HAVING determined, upon the urging of no less a personage than Pope Pius IV, to quit Venice in favor of Rome, Paulus Manutius left the Republic in the early days of June, 1561. By September, Aldus' third son (the successor to his business) had established his residence at the Palazzo d'Aragonia not far from the famous Trevi fountain, sacred to all tourists for its (reputedly) miraculous power of guaranteeing them a return visit to the Eternal City. On the sixteenth of the same month, Paolo Manuzio (as the Italians prefer to call him) had already obtained his Roman citizenship (cittadinanza). Since it is a matter of record that he issued books from his new firm early in 1562, we can well believe that Paolo wasted no time in setting up his press and outlining a publication schedule. The very first books put out by the "Aldine press" in Rome (probably in February, 1562) were two issues of great historical and political importance and interest, being closely connected with contemporary England, the Tudors, the Reformation and its attendant Counter-Reformation. These first productions were the *De Concilio* and the *Reformatio Angliae* by Cardinal Reginald Pole, former Archbishop of Canterbury, and it is some new information about these two books which provides the material for the present study.

I

The fact that Paulus Manutius printed more than a single edition of the *De Concilio* in 1562 has long been known and is cited by such bibliographers as Renouard, Lowndes and Barberi. In their accounts, however, both Continental scholars make such curious bibliographical statements that these notes apply to no known edition of the *De Concilio*. Renouard (*Annales de l'imprimerie des Alde*, Paris, 1834, p. 490) asserted that, following folio 64, the first edition had "dix feuillets d'*errata*," while Francesco Barberi (*Paolo Manuzio e la stamperia del Popolo Romano*, Rome, 1942, p. 112, n. 7) claimed that "l'esemplare da me esaminato ha una sola riga di *errata*." Further-

more, Barberi misquoted, on the same page, the English bibliographer: "Il Lowndes registra due differenti ristampe, ambedue da-
tate: Roma, 1562 'la prima avente 10 righe di *errata* dopo la parola
*finis*; la seconda corretta e pertanto senza di esse.'" Lowndes, however, did not affirm that there were two *reprints* (ristampe) of 1562
making a total of three editions for the year, but only that two editions in all were produced that year in Rome; for this point, compare his *The Bibliographer's Manual of English Literature* (London,
1857-1864), IV, 1905.

Barberi's insistence that the copy of the *De Concilio* seen by him
had but a single line of *errata* rather than the ten lines actually present in copies of the first edition may well have a very simple explanation. What the Italian scholar probably saw was a copy of
the *De Concilio* which had (as is often the case) the *Reformatio Angliae* bound after it. The first edition of this latter tract, as we shall
see, does indeed have a single line of *errata* at the end, and if Barberi had only hastily glanced at the last printed page of a volume
containing both works, he might easily have concluded that the single line of *errata* (proper for the *Reformatio Angliae*) applied to
the *De Concilio*. The two works by the Cardinal are typographically
very similar and they were obviously designed to be sold either separately or together. Indeed, the three copies of the *Reformatio Angliae* personally examined by this writer are all bound behind the
*De Concilio*, where they can easily be overlooked and taken as part
of the first tract. Thus the copy of the *De Concilio* in the Biblioteca
Nacional at Madrid has the *Reformatio Angliae* bound with (and
after) it, though the card catalogue of the library, in October 1951,
failed to indicate that a copy of the second tract was to be found in
the national library of Spain.

It is clear that the demand for and the sale of the 1,700 copies,
which Paolo had printed, was far greater than anticipated, so that
a reprint of the *De Concilio* was necessary in the same year. The
printer took the occasion, of course, to correct in the second edition
the slips noted in the *errata* of the first printing. The reprint, however, seems to be much scarcer than the original edition, and the only
copy which the present writer has come across is in the Pierpont
Morgan Library (no. 1549.1). This copy has been minutely compared with the example of the earlier printing also in the Morgan
Library (no. 1548.1) and the results tabulated. From this comparison
one learns that the second edition is a page-for-page (though not in-

variably a line-for-line) reprint of the first as far as folio 61. Thereafter the reprint has one less line per page; at this point it becomes a
line-for-line (but not page-for-page) reprint, the change being apparently made to fill the room occupied by the *errata* in the earlier
edition. The *errata* notes were, naturally, no longer necessary and
were therefore deleted, since the reprint made all the corrections
directly in the text; in addition it incorporated in the printed text
all the improvements which were made in the copies of the first edition by manual means.

In this respect, Paulus Manutius closely followed a practice which,
as the writer has shown, was quite usual in his father's shop; like
Aldus himself, Paulus continually made corrections in the copies
of his earliest Roman productions, both while printing was still in
progress and after the sheets had gone through the press. Fourteen
such "post impression" corrections have been noted in the nine
copies whose readings are known to me: Chicago, Newberry and
University Libraries; Madrid, Biblioteca Nacional; New Haven,
Yale University Library; New York, Pierpont Morgan and New
York Public Libraries; Oxford, Bodleian Library; Providence, John
Carter Brown Library; and San Marino, Henry E. Huntington Library. The alterations to the printed text are the following:

(1) Sig. B3$^v$, line 16: "ipse" has been corrected to "ipsę" (ipsae) in ink.
(2) Folio 1, line 23 (of text): text reads "id unquam" by erasure from "id
nunquam."
(3) Folio 15, marginal note: note "Heb. 1" has been removed by pasting a
slip of paper over it.
(4) Folio 21, marginal note: note "Marc. 10" has been corrected to "Marc. 16"
by ink.
(5) Folio 26$^v$, line 8: a comma has been supplied after "Ephraim" in ink.
(6) Folio 33$^v$, line 19: "quæ" has been corrected to "qua" in ink.
(7) Folio 45: misnumbered (? 47) and corrected to 45 in ink.
(8) Folio 47: misnumbered (? 45) and corrected to 47 in ink.
(9) Folio 48, line 4: "securitate" has been emended to "securitati" in ink.
(10) Folio 59, line 13: "Conciliorum" has been altered to "Consiliorum" in ink.
(11) Folio 59$^v$, line 15: by erasure behind "a" (of original "ante") text now
reads "iam a te dictum est."
(12) Folio 59$^v$, line 27: a period has been supplied after "dedit" by means of
ink.
(13) Folio 60, line 17: "eadem" has been corrected to "eādem" in ink.
(14) Folio 60$^v$, line 11: "acta" has been corrected to "actæ" by means of ink.

These alterations are present in all nine copies except in the case of
the last item. Here the example in the New York Public Library

differs, as the result of an eye-slip, in its manuscript emendation from all its fellows. Instead of correcting the "a" at the end of line 11 to give the reading "actæ," the corrector altered the "a" at the end of line 9 to give the impossible reading "fæ‖miliares."

Finally, a fifteenth ink-cancellation is found in all copies except those in the Bodleian, Newberry and New York Public Libraries. This involves the ink-deletion of the incorrect first *errata* note (Pag. 2. b. 1. Cum ii, pro, Cur ii). The printer seems to have been able to eliminate this error by means of a stop-press emendation, since all copies read "cum ii" on folio 2ᵛ, line 1, which the *errata* specifies as the correct reading.

Stop-press corrections too are found in this Aldine, just as they may be discovered in the work of Aldus himself. The last heading on folio 28 reads "ESPONSIO" in six copies, while the other three (Biblioteca Nacional, Chicago University Library and Huntington Library) offer the correct form "RESPONSIO." Again, the Yale example (folio 43, line 20) has "Concila" which has been corrected to read "Concilia" by means of ink; the Morgan and New York Public Library copies both have "Concilia" correctly printed, an obvious stop-press emendation. Thus, as with his father's productions of the previous century, Paolo's first Roman impression shows both stop-press emendations and corrections made by manual means after the printing had been completed.

## II

Although, as we have seen, it has long been known that more than one 1562 edition of the *De Concilio* was printed by Paulus Manutius, it appears not to have been pointed out previously that precisely the same situation prevails for the *Reformatio Angliae* of the same year. Of this work too, Paolo printed two editions in the first year of his activity in Rome, the second printing being a page-for-page (but not always a line-for-line) reprint of the earlier. Again the only copy of the second edition which the present writer could discover is in the Pierpont Morgan Library (no. 1549.2); examples of the first printing, in addition to one in the same library (no. 1548.2), were noted for Madrid (Biblioteca Nacional), New Haven (Yale), San Marino (Huntington) and British Museum (2 copies). The reprint can easily be identified as it does not have the line of *errata* already referred to, the correction having been made directly in the text.

Furthermore, a comma is found after "ANGLIAE" on the title-page of the reprint; this does not appear there in the original edition.

Upon comparison, the texts of the two Morgan copies of the *Reformatio Angliae* show the same relationship to each other as do the two printings of the *De Concilio*, the later edition making a few corrections and modifications. Here too, manual corrections make their appearance in the earlier printing; the Madrid, Morgan and Yale copies (folio 11ᵛ, line 29) have "cupientes" corrected in ink to read "capientes." On folio 18ᵛ, line 24, of the original edition there is an erasure at the end of the line (following "purgati, &") in the same three copies, while the reprint here offers the reading "purgati, & ea,".

\* \* \* \*

From this study we may conclude that, for his first ventures in Rome, Paulus Manutius exercised the same care—and employed the same means to achieve accuracy—as his father had done before him in Venice. A tradition of exact scholarship and an unwillingness to compromise with anything less than the best was a heritage which Aldus bequeathed to his son; this is amply demonstrated in the care bestowed on the editions of the *De Concilio* and the *Reformatio Angliae* which, in 1562, Paulus Manutius issued from his Roman press.

(From *PBSA* 46 (1952), pp. 209-14).

# CHAPTER B26

## THE WALTERS *POLYCRONICON* OF 1495

THE Walters Art Gallery, in acquiring its first English incunable, has obtained a most interesting example of a fifteenth-century printed book. The new acquisition is an early printing of the well-known English version of the *Polycronicon* by Ranulf Higden (died 1364), as translated into the vernacular for the fourth Baron Berkeley by his chaplain, John of Trevisa (1326-1412). This book was put into print three times by the earliest English printers:[1] the first edition was produced at Westminster by William Caxton in 1482; the second by Caxton's ex-foreman and the successor to his business, Wynkyn de Worde, in 1495; and the third at Southwark (a suburb of the City of London famous even then for its ale)[2] by Peter Treveris in 1527. The Walters copy of the De Worde edition, recently added to the Gallery's library, is an exceptional example in that it differs materially from the eighteen other copies[3] with which the present writer is acquainted.

[1] The editions are listed in the *Short-title Catalogue of Books Printed in England, Scotland & Ireland and of English Books Printed Abroad, 1475-1640* (London, The Bibliographical Society, 1926), nos. 13438-13440.

[2] See for example the Miller's Prologue in the *Canterbury Tales* [F. N. Robinson, *The Complete Works of Geoffrey Chaucer* (Boston and New York, 1933), p. 56]. By 1665 we find the couplet:

> The nappy strong ale of Southwirke
> Keeps many a gossip fra the Kirke.

Compare Käte Heidrich, *Das geographische Weltbild des späteren englischen Mittelalters mit besonderer Berücksichtigung der Vorstellungen Chaucer's und seiner Zeitgenossen* (Freiburg, 1915), p. 62.

[3] London, British Museum; Manchester, John Rylands Library; Cambridge, University Library and King's College Library; Edinburgh, National Library of Scotland; Copenhagen, Det Kongelige Bibliotek; New York, Pierpont Morgan Library and New York Public Library; Washington, Library of Congress; San Marino, Henry E. Huntington Library; Chicago, Newberry Library; New Haven, Yale University Library; Boston, Public Library; Chapel Hill, University of North Carolina Library; Los Angeles, Clark Library; and the private libraries of the Duke of Devonshire, Phyllis Goodhart Gordan-Howard L. Goodhart, and Dr. A. S. W. Rosenbach. Five copies are sometimes listed as belonging to the De Worde edition but actually belong to the Treveris printing; they are: Chichester Cathedral Library; Hereford Cathedral Library; Bibliothèque Royale de Belgique; Boston Athenaeum; and the Library Company of Philadelphia. The Treveris edition may be easily distinguished from De Worde's by the fact that Treveris printed 44 lines to the column; in addition, the headline of the 1527 edition includes the word "Fo." before the folio number, while the De Worde edition simply prints the number.

The De Worde edition of this famous chronicle is a work of 398 leaves and these are gathered into 52 quires (2a$^8$ 2b-2h$^6$a-y$^8$ z$^6$ A-S$^8$ T$^6$ V-X$^8$).[4] The text of the volume as it appears in the usual copy is printed throughout with De Worde's type 4, with his second type appearing in the headlines. While the new Walters incunable seems to agree with the other copies[5] cited above for some 376 leaves, the first three gatherings of text[6] in this copy (save for the innermost sheet of the third quire) differ entirely from those found in the "standard" copies. Thus, with the exception of sheet c4.5, all the leaves of gatherings a-c in the Walters example are printed from different settings of type than those which were composed at the printing office of Wynkyn de Worde during the spring of 1495. This edition, as the colophon informs us, was "Ended the thyrtenth daye of Apryll the tenth yere of the regne of kyng Harry the seuenth. And of the Incarnacyon of our lord: M. CCCC. lxxxxv. ¶ Enprynted at Westmester by Wynkyn Theworde /". This very explicit statement, as we shall shortly discover, is not entirely true of the Walters copy.

Although quire a in the Walters *Polycronicon* is printed with the same fount of type (De Worde 4) as the normal quire a of the "standard" (Plate 12a) copy,[7] it is certainly printed from different settings of that type. The outermost sheet (a 1.8) (Plate 12b) in the Walters incunable was composed with 42 double-column lines to the page while all the other leaves (a2-7) contain but 41 such lines; in the standard example, all the pages of this gathering have 42 lines. In the reprint the compositor normally shortened the text of one column from 42 lines of his prototype to 40 lines, brought over one line from the other column (thus creating 41 lines for his column) and retained for his second column the remaining 41 lines of the original. The outer sheet

---

[4] A full bibliographical description of this edition will be found in E. Gordon Duff's *Fifteenth Century English Books* (London, The Bibliographical Society, 1917, no. 173).

[5] As in most fifteenth-century books, "stop-press" corrections may be found in the several copies. Thus the Morgan example has "couutree" on sign. k1, col. 1, last line, while "countree" is correctly printed in such copies as NYPL, BM, LC, HEH, Yale, BPL, Clark, Gordan-Goodhart, etc. Similarly on sign. E1 verso, col. 2, line 1, Morgan has "cfter" where the other copies cited above read "after."

[6] The text proper is, of course, preceded by the "Tabula," an alphabetical index to the eight books. It was normal practice to print such a table last, since it would only be possible to determine on which folio the reference appears after the whole text had been printed; in many cases, however, the table would be *bound* before the text.

[7] The Library of Congress copy is the only other copy known to me which also contains the reprinted gathering a.

(a l.8) of the reprint,[8] although it has the same number of lines as the first setting and agrees with it page-for-page, does not agree with it line-for-line, as Plates 12a & 12b make evident. Thus it is obvious that it too was printed from different formes of type than the comparable sheet of the "standard" issue.

While quire a of the Walters copy thus shows a close visual correspondence to the comparable quire in the other copies, this is not true of the two succeeding gatherings.[9] Here b and c (except sheet c4.5) are not printed with De Worde's type 4, but with his type 8 as modified after 1500 (Plates 13a & 13b).[10] The state of the type, in turn, indicates that these sheets were probably printed in the first decade of the sixteenth century.[11] The innermost sheet (c4.5), on the other hand, was produced with type 4; since it corresponds completely with that found in the standard copies, one may safely assume that this sheet belongs to the original issue.

The conclusions that may be drawn from the Walters *Polycronicon* are most interesting since they give us an insight into the publishing methods of the earliest English printers. The marketing of the volume from the De Worde printing office apparently proceeded along these lines: after having completed the printing of his book, the printer placed the volume on sale in the spring of 1495 and continued to offer it as still "in print" for at least a decade thereafter. It is self-evident that the books were not bound directly after the completion of the printing, but that the sheets were stored separately and not as complete copies. It is likely that the books were bound "to order"; possibly De Worde kept on hand a few copies in a simple leather binding for immediate sale.

At some unknown time after the printing of gathering a had been

[8] Both because of the differing number of lines and because the proportion in the surviving copies indicates this, it seems reasonably certain that the gathering a represented by the Walters copy is the re-issue and not the original setting. Furthermore one must also note that this setting is found in the same volume which contains the reprinted quires b and c, a further strong argument against the assumption that the Walters quire represents the first issue.

[9] The Library of Congress copy here has the quires of the first setting and thus represents a state between the "standard" copy and that of the Walters volume.

[10] The headlines in the reprint are in the type listed by Frank Isaac, *English & Scottish Printing Types 1501-35*1508-41* (London, Bibliographical Society, 1930), as "Textura 116 mm." This was in use in 1508-10 and again in 1513-15.

[11] The lower-case s found in the volume is Isaac's second sort (s[2]), used from 1503 until 1518; w[2] (small) is the usual lower-case letter, this being employed from 1506 onwards. Other characteristic sorts found in the Walters *Polycronicon* include v[3] and y[2].

completed (and the type had been distributed) and before the year 1503 (this is predicated upon the fact that the use of type 4 was discontinued in that year),[12] Wynkyn de Worde discovered—for one reason or another[13]—that he did not have enough leaves of the first gathering to complete the copies he had on hand. He was, therefore, obliged to reprint these leaves, thus creating the variant settings resulting in the issue represented by the Walters and the Library of Congress copies. Then, towards the middle of the first decade of the sixteenth century, our printer was once again faced by such a shortage and was compelled to reprint the entire gathering b and three of the four sheets of quire c.[14] Since by this time he had discarded his fourth type, it was necessary for him to use a different fount and he thus employed the modified type 8, by that time his favorite. Fortunately for our printer, this fount was of a tolerably similar appearance to that found in the rest of the book and both types were of almost exactly the same size, each measuring 95 millimetres for twenty lines of print.

For no very good reason, as we shall see, it is often assumed that a reprint (a second issue or edition, as the case may be) will be more correct than the original. This belief is apparently based on the erroneous notion that a later compositor would benefit from the mistakes of his predecessor and, by correcting the slips of the earlier printer, he would arrive at a purer text. This, alas, seems to be the exception rather than the rule. While it is quite true that the second compositor often corrected the misprints found in his original, he

[12] The state of the type is exactly the same as that in plate XIV of Duff (*op. cit.*). Isaac (*loc. cit.*) states that type 4 "lasted only a short time and is found in no dated book after 1502."

[13] This most perplexing problem still requires a satisfactory explanation. It is, however, familiar knowledge that not only De Worde and his predecessor Caxton, but also such skilled Italian printers as Aldus Manutius were compelled to reprint certain leaves in order to complete the copies on hand. It seems difficult to believe that the piles of printed sheets were miscounted time and again—yet no other likely solution presents itself. On this point, compare my notes: "Variants in English Incunabula" in *Bookmen's Holiday, Notes and Studies Written in Tribute to Harry Miller Lydenberg* (New York, 1943), pp. 459-474, and "Notes on two Incunabula Printed by Aldus Manutius" in *Papers of the Bibliographical Society of America*, XXXVI (1942), pp. 18-26. Whatever the correct explanation may be, this is certain evidence that all the copies of the *Polycronicon* were not bound as soon as they had been printed, since shortages were only discovered after a lapse of several years following the completion of the original printing.

[14] At least one headline, characterized by a peculiar capital L (showing damage in the lower left corner where the foot meets the right perpendicular stroke) appears in both quires b and c, proving that they were printed at the same time.

frequently—with regret one must say, usually[15]—contributed an even greater number of slips of his own.

If my eye chanced to note all such instances, at least 132 misprints (excluding turned letters) are found in the two states of gatherings a–c of the *Polycronicon*. Of this total, 34 are found in the original issue, as represented by the copy in the Pierpont Morgan Library,[16] and 98 in the reprint, of which the Walters copy is the only recorded example. If these slips are tabulated according to their position in the book, one notes a progressive deterioration in the quality of the text belonging to the second settings. In quire a, the number of misprints in each issue is fairly equal (21 in the original and 25 in the reprint). The compositor of the reprint of quire b was, however, very much more slip-shod and about two-thirds of the total errors in this gathering are found in the later setting (9 in the original and 20 in the reprint). Though only 12 pages of gathering c were reset (as against 16 in the other two quires), the number of misprints is much the greatest here, 57 instances being recorded for this quire (4 in the first issue and 53 in the second); in this gathering, the second compositor contributed no less than 93 percent of the slips. Thus it will be seen that, so far as accuracy is concerned, the first issue was more dependable than the re-issue.

One may further note that, in addition to these misprints, there are 67 cases where the text of the reprint departs from that of its original.[17] Mostly this disagreement represents no more than a change in tense, number, preposition or type of pronoun; in some few cases, the divergencies are material from a literary point of view; in no case, however, does the alteration in the text affect the facts (or supposed facts) set forth in this chronicle. It will be found both interesting and instructive to discuss these variant readings in connection with the text as found in the third edition (that of 1527).

[15] For a further discussion of this problem, see my paper "Observations on Two Caxton Variants" in *Studies in Bibliography* (*Papers of the Bibliographical Society of the University of Virginia*), III (1950-51), pp. 97-104.

[16] Ada Thurston and Curt F. Bühler, *Check List of Fifteenth Century Printing in the Pierpont Morgan Library* (New York, 1939), no. 1805.

[17] In a few cases, not counted in the summary, Treveris agrees with the reprint by having "Plinius" and "Priscianus" where the Morgan copy consistently uses "Plenius" and "Prescianus." It is uncertain whether these are misprints or orthographical variants of their day—in any case, it is likely that Treveris agrees with the reprint merely by accident. This situation is further compensated for by the several instances (also not counted) where Treveris agrees with the Morgan copy by printing "occean" against the "occian" of the reprint.

The third edition of the *Polycronicon* was printed, as we have had occasion to record, by Peter Treveris; it may further be remarked that this edition was quite obviously set up from the one printed by De Worde and not from that produced by William Caxton. Oddly enough, however, it is equally certain that in 1527 Treveris obtained for his compositor a copy of the first issue (that of 1495) and not a copy representative of the state in which the book was offered for sale some ten years or more later. In 65 of the 67 recorded instances, Treveris has exactly the same wording as that found in the Morgan *Polycronicon*, while the Walters copy offers a different reading. The two instances where Treveris agrees with the text as found in the Walters example do not require one to believe that Treveris also consulted the later issue. The first example will be found in line 17 of the second column of signature a2 verso; here the Morgan copy has: "The epystle syr of Johan Treuysa" while Treveris and the Walters *Polycronicon* print: "The epystle of syr Johan Treuysa." Clearly these are identical, though not necessarily interdependent, emendations of a compositor's slip. Again (b4ᵛ, second column, line 31), the Walters copy and Treveris have "the holy wrytte" where the Morgan example merely prints "holy wrytte." In such a case as this, it is not difficult to conceive that two compositors might independently arrive at the same reading. There are, however, no fewer than eight cases where Treveris perpetuates the misreading we find in the Morgan copy.[18] This can hardly be coincidence!

It is occasionally quite obvious that the compositor of the second De Worde issue miscalculated the amount of his text; he was thereupon obliged either to drop a word or two or to expand the text in order to bring his page into agreement with his original. Only one such emergency has left its own impress on the text; it will be seen fully illustrated in Plates 13a & b. By the time the compositor had reached line 39 (column 1) of the folio numbered "xii," he found that he was left with a line and a half of space to accommodate but a single line of the original text. He handled this difficulty with the easy freedom characteristic of the early printer: he simply expanded "hit is an hylle of helthe and plente" into reading "it is a fayre and a plenteuos hylle and a holsome."

With its first English incunabulum, the Walters Art Gallery has

---

[18] Thus, for example, the Morgan *Polycronicon* has "shouto" instead of "shoute" (a4, col. 1, line 9) and "transmygurycion" (a6, col. 1, line 14) for "transmygracion." In both cases Treveris has the identical misreading as the first printing.

acquired a book not only of significant literary and historical value but also a volume of the greatest typographical interest.[19] Though this copy of the *Polycronicon* may not belong to the (often so wrongly prized) first issue of its edition, it represents to the bibliographer a noteworthy and important new discovery. The Walters volume provides the historian of books with some further details as to the problems which confronted the early printer and publisher, in those days still one and the same person, and the means whereby he overcame the difficulties with which he was beset. However one may want to view this point, it is obvious that the Walters *Polycronicon*, as the only recorded copy, can certainly lay claim to the distinction of belonging to the very rarest issue of this historic work.

(From the *Journal of the Walters Art Gallery*
13-14 (1950/51), pp. 39-43, 74).

[19] A further point of interest is noted by the *Catalogue of Manuscripts and Early Printed Books . . . now Forming Portion of the Library of J. Pierpont Morgan* (London, 1907), III, 206: "this is the first book printed in England which contains musical notes. These occur here in the form of a small diagram relating to the consonances of Pythagoras. In Caxton's edition the space was left blank."

# CHAPTER B27

## THE TWO ISSUES OF THE FIRST EDITION
## OF THE *MANIPULUS FLORUM*

THE third book printed in Piacenza, the ancient city of Emilia on the banks of the Po, and the only volume issued by the second printer working there, is the editio princeps of that excellent reference work, useful alike for the mediaeval writer and for the modern scholar, the *Manipulus florum* by Thomas de Hibernia.[1] According to the colophon, the printing was completed by Jacobus de Tyela on 5 September 1483.[2] Though the book was put out by a small provincial press, it is not as uncommon as such books normally are; copies are to be found in most large libraries and several remain in private hands. Despite this circumstance, so favorable for comparison of copies, no one has previously shown, I believe, that there are two issues of this first edition. These are distinguished from one another by the first two quires which occur in two entirely different settings. Apparently when Tyela commenced the printing of the third signature, he decided to enlarge the size of the edition; in order to complete the now greater number of copies, he was obliged to reset and to reprint the first two quires, probably because the type for these had already been distributed. The two issues may easily be identified by the following variant settings:

| sig. | col. | line | A<br>Madrid copy | B<br>Writer's copy |
|------|------|------|------------------|--------------------|
| a1   | β    | 2    | igit'            | igitur             |
| a2ᵛ  | α    | 1    | liberat          | libēat             |
| a3   | β    | 4    | Ibidem           | Ibidē              |

[1] In addition to my own copy, I have personally inspected the examples at the Barcelona, Harvard, Madrid and Morgan libraries. For reports on the other copies, I should here like to express my thanks to: Bernhard Bischoff (München), Frederick R. Goff (Washington), Stanley Pargellis (Chicago), Miss Margaret B. Stillwell (Providence) and to my good friend and colleague, George K. Boyce, who most kindly checked the Huntington copy for me. Derek A. Clarke, of the British Museum, has earned my particular gratitude not only for reporting on the Museum's copy but also for many another chore that he has willingly consented to do for me both in London and in Oxford.

[2] References: HC 8542; BMC VII: 1072; Stillwell Census H 137.

| sig. | col. | line | A<br>Madrid copy | B<br>Writer's copy |
|---|---|---|---|---|
| a4 | $a$ | 1 | Bernardus | Bernar. |
| a5 | $a$ | 1 | fomentum | fomētū |
| a6ᵛ | $\beta$ | 1 | confuto | cōfuto |
| a7 | $\beta$ | 2 | incendio | īcendio |
| a8 | $\beta$ | 1 | ibidem | ibide3 |
| a9ᵛ | $a$ | 4 | Amici | Aīci |
| b1 | $\beta$ | 3 | Seneca | Sen. |
| b2ᵛ | $a$ | 2 | īquā | inquā |
| b3 | $\beta$ | 4 | sciētem | sciēte3 |
| b4 | $a$ | 1 | rōnale3 | rōnalē |
| b5ᵛ | $a$ | 1 | Isido. | Isidor' |
| b6 | $a$ | 1 | ambrosium | ambrosiū |
| b7 | $\beta$ | 1 | enim | enī |
| b8 | $\beta$ | 2 | patitur | patit' |

Comparable to the example in the Biblioteca Nacional at Madrid are those in the British Museum, Harvard, Morgan and München libraries, while the copies at Barcelona (University Library),[3] Chicago (Newberry Library), Providence (Annmary Brown Memorial), San Marino (Huntington Library), and Washington (Library of Congress) have the text as in my own copy.

This much having been established, it seemed desirable to examine the two issues with the object of determining whether the issue represented by the Madrid example or that exemplified by my copy was the earlier. This study can be based on technical considerations and on textual study, and both investigations, I believe, lead to the same conclusion.

In the course of the examination of the physical structure of the volume, a curious irregularity in the presswork becomes apparent. The collation for the volume is as follows: $a^{10}$ b-m$^8$ n$^6$ o$^8$ p$^6$ q-r$^8$ s-x$^{6.8}$ y-z$^6$ &$^8$. Setting aside, for the time being, the first two quires, one discovers that each page of the volume has 47 lines with these exceptions:

46 lines: r3 and r6, recto and verso
         t4 verso — t5 recto
         &4 verso — &5 recto, column 1[4]

48 lines: c5 verso
         d3 verso
         d6 recto and verso

[3] The first quire is wanting in the Barcelona copy.
[4] Column 2 has the full number of lines, or 47 in all.

d7 recto and verso
d8 recto

i4 verso — i5 recto
r4 verso — r5 recto
z3 verso — z4 recto

Now, apart from r3 and r6 which are exceptional and may represent an unusual miscount of lines or a miscalculation of text, a definite pattern of printing technique becomes apparent. In quires c and d, when an error in estimating the amount of text to be printed made this necessary, Tyela simply added a line wherever required, however irregular the resulting appearance of the volume might be. Beginning with the fifth quire, the printer shows himself more practised in his art; when he needed an extra line or had to dispense with one, Tyela did so in the innermost opening, the place where such irregularity would be least noticeable.

Now in the first two quires, my *Manipulus florum* has 47 lines on some pages and 48 lines on a2$^v$, a3$^v$, a4$^v$, a5, a5$^v$, a6, a6$^v$, and a7; the Madrid copy, on the other hand, has 47 lines on every page except in the innermost opening of the first quire (a4 verso — a5 recto), where 48 lines are found. Thus the Madrid issue (A) exhibits a printing technique comparable to that found in the later quires of the volume, while the issue represented by the writer's copy (B) shows the same irregularities peculiar to the earlier quires c and d. This fact, it seems to the present investigator, is very strong evidence indeed for the priority of issue B. If A were the earlier, one cannot but wonder as to why the printer would reset the type so as to create irregularities when all he had to do was to follow his copy line-for-line to attain regularity in the number of lines. Assuming the priority of B, it is interesting to observe the typesetter at work. For example, in order to reduce a5 verso and a6 to 47 lines, the compositor of the text for the Madrid issue worked as follows. He compressed the text of the first column on a5$^v$ from the 48 lines of the writer's copy to 45 and brought over two lines from the second column. To the resulting 46 lines of the latter he added one line from the first column of a6, thus having 47 lines in each of these columns. For the second column of a6, the compositor compressed the first eleven lines into ten, and thereby obtained 47 lines for issue A. Tyela was thus able, with very little trouble, to improve the quality of his presswork for the first two quires which had originally been so irregular.

When the texts of the two issues are compared, the presence of numerous small differences between the issues becomes quite evident; sometimes issue A has a misprint where B is correct, at other times the contrary holds true. There are nevertheless four important instances where the textual differences between A and B are such as to allow a reasonable conclusion to be made as to the priority of one issue over the other. They are these:

Sig. a3$^v$, col. β, lines 13-16, example "g" of Adiutorium. B prints: "Necessitates aliorum quantum possumus iuuemus: & plus interdum quam possumus. etc."

A has "invenimus" instead of "juvemus".

Sig. a6, col. α, lines 3-5 (of B), example "l" of Advocati. B prints: "Irritare a canibus tractum est. quorum latratibus .r. sonat plurimum. Cassiodorus super illud psalmus [sic] 73. Irritat aduersarius nomen tuum." (See Migne, LXX, 530).

So in A, though this omits the last four words.

Sig. a9, col. β, lines 4-7, example "by" of Amicitia. B prints: "Nihil eque egrum reficit. sicut amicorum affectus. non iudico me mori: quum illos superstites reliquero. puto inquam me victurum non cum illis: sed per illos. Seneca. 79 epistola."

So in A, though there attributed to Epistle 76.

Sig. b3$^v$, col. α, l.45 — col. β, l.3, example "ab" of Angelus. B prints: "Adest vnicuique nostrum etiam minimis qui sunt in ecclesia dei angelus bonus. angelus domini. qui regat. qui moneat. qui gubernet. qui pro actibus nostris corrigendis & miserationibus exposcendis quotidie videat faciem patris qui in celis est. Origenes super librum numerorum homilia. lxvj." (See Migne, XII, 733).

So in A, though there attributed to Homily 71.

In each case, the issue represented by my copy (B) has the correct text and that issue characterized by the Madrid example (A) is at fault.

Now the question naturally arises: does issue B represent a corrected re-issue of A, or is issue A a faulty resetting of the earlier issue B? Assuming A to be the earlier, one must argue that the compositor (or the proof-reader) who set the text of B was a remarkably careful and competent scholar in the instances just cited and equally careless elsewhere. For example, he has permitted such misprints to creep into the text as: aliteri (for alteri — a4, α, 35); Hero (for Hiero — a4$^v$, α, 36); vtilitate (for vilitate — a6, β, 28); non non metuit (for non metuit — b8$^v$, α, 39-40). These misprints are not present in issue

A. Furthermore the question arises: why did this "scholarly" corrector fail to supply fuller references for the frequent, and excessively vague, citations, such as "in quadam epistola" or "in quodam sermone"?

Before turning to the examples cited above, let us examine a characteristic instance where issue A has the correct text and B is wrong. On sig. b4$^v$, col. $\beta$, lines 9–12 (example "b" of Antichristus), we find in A: "quo*rum* inter*pr*etatio*n*em no*minu*m cognouim*us* esse: got tectu*m*: magot de tecto. ta*nquam* dom*us* & ip*s*e *qui* *pr*ocedit de domo."[5] Issue B agrees exactly with A except that it incorrectly prints "decto" for "tecto". Now if we still assume that A is the earlier, we must conclude that the compositor of issue B was not the careful man we believed him to be but, instead, somewhat slipshod. Further he is evidently not the scholar we thought he must be, for he failed to realize that this quotation (as well as the two succeeding ones)[6] comes not from Book 12 of St. Augustine's *City of God*, as stated in both issues, but from Book 20 of the same work. This line of argument seems to lead us into irreconcilable contradictions.

If we now glance at the four examples set forth above, we can, I believe, come to the only correct conclusion. For the first example, if we assume that issue B is the earlier, then A must illustrate the case of a simple and hasty misreading of the contraction "iuuem'" found in B. On the contrary assumption that A is the earlier, one must argue that B necessarily represents a scholarly correction to the text. (Both versions are quite translatable but only the one in issue B makes logical sense). But, one wonders, how can it be possible that the compositor was such a scholar as to catch this slight slip and yet fail to realize that the citation itself is apparently at fault, for this passage does not seem to be present in St. Ambrose's *De officiis*. Such a contradiction does not exist if issue B is taken to be the earlier.

For the second case, the line omitted represents part of the reference citation but is not essential to it; consequently it is easier to conclude that it was accidentally dropped out of issue A rather than that it was unnecessarily inserted in issue B. In the third example, epistle 79 is certainly the correct citation and 76 is wrong;[7] again it is simpler

---

[5] Compare Migne, XLI: 676.

[6] Ibid., col. 668.

[7] This is an adaptation, rather than a strict quotation, from a Senecan letter. In fifteenth-century editions, this letter bears either the number 79 (thus in the editions of Treviso: Bernardus de Colonia, 1478, and of Naples: Mathias Moravus,

to assume that 76 resulted from a turned letter (9 → 6) rather than to attribute the change to the scholarship of a corrector whose competence we have already called into question.

A situation similar to the last is shown in the final example. It is certain that Homily 66 is the correct reference, and not Homily 71. Actually, Origen wrote only 28 homilies on the Book of Numbers so that the reference seems very curious indeed.[8] It is, however, clear that Thomas de Hibernia listed all the homilies on the Old Testament by Origen in one numerical sequence (Genesis = 17; Exodus = 13; Leviticus = 16; and Numbers = 28). Our quotation is found in Homily 20 of Numbers (66 of the series) and not in Homily 25 (71 in the total numeration). Obviously it is far easier to believe that issue A was set from B, and that "lxvj" degenerated to "lxxj", than to assume that the compositor of B, realizing a mistake in A, read through the homilies of Origen in order to find the correct location. Here again, as in the other three cases, it seems more logical to assume that issue A was set from B than that the reverse situation prevailed.[9]

The examination of the two issues of the Piacenza *Manipulus florum* both from a textual as well as a bibliographical point of view leads, it seems to me, to the same conclusion. In both cases the issue exemplified by the Madrid copy appears to be the later. The printing technique observed in the first two quires of this copy is similar to that characteristic of the later sections of the same book, while in the other issue the presswork in quires a and b is just as primitive and irregular as in the adjacent quires c and d. We have also noted an

---

1475) or number 78 (in the editions of Strassburg: R-Printer, circa 1474, and of Venice: Bernardinus de Choris, 31 October 1492). To my knowledge, this letter is never found as number 76.

[8] The citation in Thomas de Hibernia comes, of course, from the translation of Origen's homilies made by Rufinus.

[9] As the British Museum's catalogue points out (BMC V: 420), the edition printed at Venice by Joannes Rubeus (on 20 December, year uncertain) is based on the Tyela edition ("The phraseology of the colophon is as in the edition of Tyela, Vicenza (sic), 1483"). Through the courtesy of Miss Dorothy Miner, I have been able to consult the copy owned by the Walters Art Gallery, Baltimore. It is quite obvious that the Venetian printing was set up from the Piacenza one; indeed, it is clear that it follows the text of issue B. This is made evident by the fact that the Rubeus edition has "decto" and "utilitate" for "tecto" and "vilitate" which, as we have seen above, are characteristic readings of the first issue. The Venetian edition also agrees with issue B of the Piacenza printing in regard to the four examples cited in the text above and does not have the errors which occur in issue A.

equally strong argument based on textual study for believing the Madrid issue to be the later one, for it seems far more reasonable to assume that issue A represents a deterioration of the text of issue B rather than to believe that B is the corrected re-issue of A. It is, therefore, entirely logical to assert that issue B (to which the writer's copy belongs) is the first issue of the first edition of the *Manipulus florum*, which Jacobus de Tyela printed at Piacenza.

(From *Gutenberg-Jahrbuch* (1953), pp. 69-72).

# CHAPTER B28

## THE FIRST EDITION OF *THE ABBEY* *OF THE HOLY GHOST*

IN the Spring of 1952, the Pierpont Morgan Library acquired the only known copy of a previously undescribed English incunable. Such an event, especially in the case of a work of literary interest written in the vernacular, is not one of routine occurrence; it has consequently been thought proper that this new "find" be given a somewhat more extensive discussion than the familiar "previously unknown" incunabulum normally deserves. The results, it is believed, will not only fix the approximate date and the proper order in which the several editions appeared, but will also indicate to bibliographers the value of textual study in the solution of bibliographical problems.

In the form advocated by the present writer (*Standards of Bibliographical Description*, 1949, pp. 3-60), the new incunable may be described in these terms:

The Abbey of the Holy Ghost. Westminster: Wynkyn de Worde, [1496].
  Apparently the first edition.
  4°. 20 leaves. a-b⁶ c-d⁴. 28-29 lines. Type-page (f. 4, 28 lines): 132 x 87 mm. Type: 4:95G. Woodcut initial (I) on a2. Two woodcuts (Hodnett 313 on title; Hodnett 325 on a1ᵛ).
  f. 1 [title-page]: [woodcut] || ¶ The abbaye of the holy Ghost || 1ᵛ: [woodcut]. 2—a2: ¶ Here begynnyth a matere spekynge of a place þᵗ || is namyd the abbaye of the holy ghost. that shalbe || foūdyd or groñdyd in a clene conscyence. in why-||che abbaye shall dwelle. xxix. ladyes ghostly. || (I⁶)N this abbaye Charyte shall be Ab||besse: Wysdom Priouresse: Mekenes || Suppryouresse. And thyse ben in þᵉ || Couent: Pouertee Clennesse . . . 7—b1: And to them that be his true seruauntes he gyueth || . . . [ends 20ᵛ—d4ᵛ, line 15]: . . . And calle || ye to your counsell Reason & Dyscrecōn: Pacyence || & Peas. And go ye forth to Oryson / & crye ye in so||ule to the holy ghost. And inwardly pray hym that || he come & defende charyte. That he thorugh his || gracyous helpe kepe you fro euyll chaunce. And he || that made vs all wyth blysse vs auaunce. Amen. || ¶ Enpryntyd at Westmestre by || Wynkyn the Worde. ||
  Signature c4 is missigned c iij, and d4 is missigned d iij. Only c1ᵛ, d2ᵛ and d3 have 29 lines. Hodnett does not explain that the cut on the title (his no. 313) is a pictorial representation of the Allegory of the Four Daughters of God.
  The only recorded copy is in the Pierpont Morgan Library (*Check List*, no. 1816A). It measures 193 x 138 mm. and is stitched in the remains of the con-

temporary half-vellum binding. Obtained by the Library in March, 1952 (Accession no. 43328).

Two other fifteenth-century editions of *The Abbey of the Holy Ghost* have long been known and are described by E. Gordon Duff[1] under his numbers 1 and 2. I have been able to consult the edition identified as Duff 1 by using the facsimile prepared from the copy in the University Library Cambridge by Francis Jenkinson (published by the Cambridge University Press in 1907), while the Folger Library has kindly supplied me with a microfilm of their copy of the remaining edition (Duff 2). With a view towards determining the order and approximate date of the editions, it will be necessary to subject these not only to a strict bibliographical scrutiny but to a thorough textual examination as well. We may best begin by considering the physical "make-up" of the editions which, for the sake of convenience, will hereafter be cited as C (Cambridge), F (Folger) and M (Morgan).

As we may see from the description given above, M was printed with only one column to the page while the other two editions were each set up with double columns. One fount of type only (Wynkyn de Worde no. 4) was used in the printing of M, whereas two different sizes of type are found in both other editions (types 2 and 4 in C; types 4 and 6 in F). Furthermore, C and F have a constant number of lines (29) to the page; M usually has 28 though thrice 29 lines were needed to accommodate the text. Similarly, on signature a4 verso of M, de Worde miscalculated the amount of text he could crowd onto a page and was obliged to set a portion of the word "ravisheth" in the position normally occupied by a catchword; thus, by printing "ra||uyssheth||", he was able to get all the text on that page. Again, while c4 and d4 are missigned in M as noted in the above description, there are no errors in the signing of the other editions. Finally, the text of M ends on the verso of the last leaf, whereas in both other editions the narrative concludes on the recto and is followed in each case by a printer's device. All these points suggest that M is the most primitive (and consequently the earliest) of the three editions.

The evidence of the woodcuts, while inconclusive, at least con-

[1] *Fifteenth Century English Books* (Bibliographical Society, Illustrated Monograph no. XVIII, 1917).

firms the belief that C was printed before F. The woodcut of the Crucifixion (Hodnett 374)[2] has suffered greater material damage at the top of the block in F than in C; in addition, the Folger copy shows the loss of a border-line at the top and another at the bottom of this cut.

If we now turn to the textual examination, it is clear that six different arrangements for the successive order of appearance of the editions are possible. Two series (C→M→F and F→M→C) can be eliminated immediately, both for typographical and for textual reasons. Since C and F were each printed with double columns and always agree page-for-page (and mostly line-for-line), it is self-evident that the one was set from the other with no single-column edition intervening. The text too corroborates this theory, as one example will suffice to indicate. In line 4 of sig. c4$^v$, M has the text "þ$^t$ were callid Merci & Pyte," while both C and F omit the word "callid". Now one will find it difficult, probably impossible, to believe that the second compositor could supply a needed word which in a third printing was then again omitted, thus accidentally duplicating the reading of the editio princeps. Yet one would be obliged to accept this coincidence if the order of appearance was either of those given above. No; one can only conclude, on the basis of reasonable probability, either that C was set from F or that the contrary took place.

The next two possibilities (C→F→M and M→F→C) are equally unacceptable, for C and M often have the identical text from which F alone departs. For example, in M (b1, line 4) one reads: "For no man I trowe myght al fully it fele"; with this C completely agrees. In F (a6$^v$, β, 17-18), however, we find: "for I trowe þ$^t$ no man myght all fully it fele". To cite another example, M (a6$^v$, lines 14-19) prints the following:

Our lorde Jhū Cryste sendyth them the oyle of comforte & of mercy that gyueth the lyghte of & shewyth his heuenly preuytees þ$^t$ he hydeth fro men that ben full of flesshly lustes.

---

[2] Edward Hodnett, *English Woodcuts 1480-1535* (Bibliographical Society, Illustrated Monograph no. XXII, 1935). No certain conclusions can be drawn from the impressions of the cut of the Trinity (Hodnett 313), the only cut common to all three. Hodnett also notes that the block of no. 374 had suffered a diagonal crack through the entire length of the block by the time it was used for Duff 2. This cut also appears in the three editions of Alcock's *Mons perfectionis*, which will be discussed below.

While C offers this same text, F (a6ᵛ, α, 16), sensing an omission, alone supplies the word "understanding", giving the reading "lyght of vnderstandynge".

That M and C are textually related—and that the one was set from the other—is convincingly demonstrated (if further proof be needed) by a curious slip common to both; this does *not* occur in F. On b6ᵛ, lines 2-5, M reads:

Therfore he was take & put in to the pryson of hell. & there hathe be now. M. yere &. vi. C & more. & that is grete pyte.

With this reading C agrees, while F, in accordance with tradition, correctly asserts that, before the coming of Christ, Adam had languished in Hell 4,600 and more years ("and there hath be now .iiij. M. yere and .vi. C. and more"). Thus, if we assume that F intervenes between C and M, we must believe that the error in time was corrected for the Folger text only to have the third edition, by sheer coincidence, make the identical error found in the first printing.[3] The points here made surely eliminate these two possibilities.

We thus arrive at the last two alternatives.[4] The series F→C→M seems improbable for typographical reasons. The state of the woodcuts assures us that F is the latest of the three, and the typographical "set-up" of M is certainly more primitive than the sophisticated presswork of the other two editions. Textually too, this is unlikely, for M and C exhibit older dialectal and orthographic variants ("her", "syndre", and the habitual use of "wol") where F offers the more modern forms ("theyr", "sondry", and usually "wyl").[5]

---

[3] A similar instance can be cited from a quotation from Isaiah (64.1). In M (b5ᵛ, line 15), the citation incorrectly reads: "Vtinam dirumperam celos et descenderes." With this C agrees while F more correctly has: "Vtinam disrumperes celos et descenderes" (b5, β, 20-21). If F intervenes between M and C, it is difficult to account for these two editions having the same mistake ("dirumperam" for the Biblical "dirumperes").

[4] It is, of course, mathematically possible (if unlikely from a logical point of view) that one edition might have served as the original for the other two, independently composed. This line of argument too can be dismissed for these reasons: C and F could not have been set up independently from M because their identical "make-up" shows obvious dependence of the one upon the other; M and C could not have been separately produced from F since they are textually related; and, finally, M cannot have been set up from C for reasons we shall now set forth in the text.

[5] M contains certain anachronisms in orthography which can best be accounted for by assuming that it was composed from a much earlier manuscript. Thus M (b2, line 9) has "pine of hell" where both other editions print "payne". In the

By this process of elimination we arrive at the conclusion that the order M→C→F is the only possible one for the appearance of the three editions of *The Abbey of the Holy Ghost*. Furthermore, there are an adequate number of pieces of evidence to support this contention. In illustration of this, the text in M (d3, lines 11-14) may be cited:

Whan they wolde haue naylyd his fete to the crosse: all his body was so shronke vp togyd⁾ for payne þᵗ it was to shorte to þᵉ hole þᵗ they had made by a large fote.

The term "too short to the hole" had been used a few lines earlier in very similar circumstances; in that case, all three editions employed this same phrase. In the instance previously cited, however, both C and F substitute (d2ᵛ, β, 3) "to short for þᵉ hole", an apparent modernization introduced by the later printings.

The gradual deterioration of the text (M→C→F) is amply demonstrated by one enlightening example.[6] In M (a6, lines 15-19) one reads:

Medytacyon is thoughte in god / of his werkes: of his wordes / & of his creatures / & of his paynes that he suffryd. & of his loue þᵗ he louyd vs wyth / For ofte a good thoughte is better than many indeuowte prayers.

This appears in C (a6, *a*, 17-24), where the omission is clearly due to haplography, as:[7]

Medytacōn is thought in god / of his werkes / of his wordes / & of his creatures / & of his paynes þᵗ he loued vs with. For oft a good thought is better than many Indeuowte prayers.

The compositor of F, sensing a corruption of text, set about "correcting" it, and with this in mind he substituted "losyd" for "loued" (loved). In the special Biblical sense of "to loose" (NED vb. 1ᵉ) this emendation gave meaning to the passage though it did not result in a return to the original sense. The explanation for the texts of C and F can only be made evident by assuming the priority of M. Surely it is clear, from this lengthy analysis, that the newly discovered copy

---

inflectional endings too, M often has "-is", "-yth", and "-yd" where the other editions have the more modern forms "-es", "-eth", and "-ed".

[6] A quotation from the Bible ("Vae misero mihi!"—Jeremiah 45.3) undergoes strange mutations. In M one finds "Ve michi mis*ero*"; in C, "Ve michi miser*e*"; and in F, "Ve michi miser*i*"!!

[7] While both M and C here have "indeuowte", F (a6, *a*, 23) prints "vndeuowte". This is a further indication that F cannot intervene between M and C.

of the *Abbey* now in the Morgan Library belongs to the earliest known printed edition of this text.

A fortunate set of circumstances makes it possible to supply a likely date for the several editions of *The Abbey of the Holy Ghost*. As we have seen, the Morgan copy of the *Abbey* was printed in a single column with de Worde's type 4; Duff 1 was set up in two columns with types 2 and 4; and Duff 2 was issued with double columns using types 4 and 6. Now the first edition of Bishop John Alcock's *Mons perfectionis* (Duff 12) was also printed in one column with de Worde's type 4, while the second edition (Duff 13) has double columns with types 2 and 4; a third edition was issued by de Worde after he had left Westminster (STC 281). Are we not justified in assuming that the *Abbey* and the *Mons perfectionis*, being similar tracts of devotional literature, were issued as companion pieces and that they were designed to be sold either separately or together?[8] Since the first edition of the *Mons perfectionis* has the printed date 22 September 1496, and the second bears the date 23 May 1497, it is with some confidence that one may assert that the first two editions of the *Abbey* were also produced, respectively, in September 1496 and May 1497.

The third edition of the *Mons perfectionis* presents an added complication in that it was printed after 1500, at a time when Wynkyn de Worde had left Westminster and had moved to "the City." According to Sayle (no. 144),[9] the volume states that it was printed in London "and fynysshed the xxvii. daye of þe moneth of Maye" 1501. We may well suppose that this book was intended to go on sale together with the third edition of *The Abbey of the Holy Ghost*; consequently it is likely that little time had elapsed between the printing of these two volumes. On the basis of this reasoning, there is some justification for believing that the third *Abbey* (Duff 2) may well have been the last book printed by Wynkyn de Worde at Westminster, just as the third *Mons perfectionis* is judged to be the first

[8] That Wynkyn de Worde followed this practice in other cases seems certain from his *Treatise of Love* (Duff 399), most copies of which are still bound together with the *Chastising of God's Children* (Duff 85). It is also known that Richard Pynson too issued some of his books in series of this sort; compare the present writer's "Notes on a Pynson Volume," *Library*, 4th ser., XVIII (1937-38), 261-267.

[9] Charles E. Sayle, *Early English Printed Books in the University Library, Cambridge* (1900-07), I, 37.

one issued by his new press in London; in any case, no earlier book with a London imprint has yet been discovered.[10]

This discussion, then, offers what seems to be fairly conclusive evidence in support of the contention that the Morgan copy of *The Abbey of the Holy Ghost* belongs to the first printed edition of this work (at least, of those that are now known to us) and that this work was probably printed by Wynkyn de Worde not much later than 22 September 1496. In concluding this somewhat lengthy account, one further observation may be made. If Duff's bibliography (or if the *Gesamtkatalog der Wiegendrucke*) should ever be reprinted, the present edition of the *Abbey* will head the list of entries as the very first number, with the Morgan copy cited as the only known example.

(From *Studies in Bibliography* 5 (1953), pp. 101-06).

[10] "At the end of the year 1500, De Worde moved from Westminster into Fleet Street at the sign of the Sun, the earliest book from the new address being dated May, 1501." [E. G. Duff, *The Printers, Stationers and Bookbinders of Westminster and London from 1476 to 1535* (1906), p. 33].

# CHAPTER B29

## AUTHORS AND INCUNABULA

IT is surprising to note—in view of the fact that researches and investigations into books printed in the fifteenth century have been growing both in intensity and in perplexity these past hundred years—that there are exceedingly few general observations available as to the nature of these "fifteeners." There is a profusion of special studies on various bibliographical problems peculiar to this period, but nowhere can one find the answers to such simple questions as: who was the most popular author in the fifteenth century? to what century did most of the incunabula authors belong? what was the proportion of Latin books to those printed in the vernacular languages? which "vulgar tongue" appeared in print most frequently during this century? etc. To queries of this nature, it is hoped, the present study will supply some answers—tentative though these must necessarily be.

The reasons that such analyses have not been repeatedly made in the past are probably twofold. First of all, bibliographers have been handicapped by the absence of any single reference work listing all the books printed in that period. It is most unlikely that this need will ever be satisfied unless the monumental *Gesamtkatalog der Wiegendrucke*[1] be completed; without such a list, a total survey is, of course, impossible. Again, where partial surveys are available and figures can be compiled, it is the sheer toil of counting, dividing, averaging, and comparing—grueling and unrewarding tasks as every compiler of such figures well knows—which has (perhaps) restrained bibliographers from embarking upon quests of this nature. There are some special studies which point the way—Ernst Voulliéme in regard to the Cologne incunabula[2] and George Sarton on the scientific works printed in this era,[3] to which the present writer (im-

---

[1] Seven volumes have appeared up to now, Leipzig 1925-1938. These cover the letters A-Eig of the alphabet.

[2] Ernst Voulliéme, *Der Buchdruck Kölns bis zum Ende des fünfzehnten Jahrhunderts*, Bonn 1903, especially pp. lxxix-lxxx.

[3] George Sarton, "The Scientific Literature transmitted through the Incunabula" in *Osiris*, v (1938), pp. 41-245.

modestly) might add two short listings of his own[4]—but this seems to be the sum total of studies along these lines.[5]

In the present state of the listing of fifteenth-century books, then, it is impossible to obtain a complete, over-all view of the output of the presses of that day. No one knows for certain how many editions of Savonarola were produced in the fifteenth century nor which books were actually the most frequently printed during this period. If one were to hazard a guess, it seems likely—from the evidence now in hand—that schoolbooks were the most often put to press, for the *Gesamtkatalog* lists no fewer than 356 editions of the *Ars minor* of Donatus and more than 280 separate printings of the *Doctrinale* by Alexander de Villa Dei. These numbers may be compared with the 128 Bibles and 173 editions of the *Legenda aurea* which were printed in the fifteenth century according to Professor Robert F. Seybolt's compilations.[6] Yet both the Bible and Voragine's informative and entertaining account of the lives of the Saints have been repeatedly cited as the most frequently printed books in the first half-century of printing.[7] Naturally, a final count and a complete tabulation must await the completion of the *Gesamtkatalog der Wiegendrucke.*

Certain preliminary and tentative facts may, however, be determined from the seven volumes already printed by the *Kommission* entrusted with the publication of this enormous bibliography.

[4] "English Incunabula in America" in *The Library Quarterly*, xi (1941), pp. 497-502, and "The Statistics of Scientific Incunabula" in *Isis*, xxxix (1948), pp. 163-168, *supra.*

[5] Excellent surveys of the output of the German and Italian presses only, based largely on the holdings of the British Museum, will be found in the Introductions to the third and seventh volumes of the *Catalogue of Books Printed in the XVth Century now in the British Museum*, London 1908-1935. [Since the present essay was written, the eighth volume of this same catalogue has appeared (London 1949). Dr. Scholderer here discusses the Museum's French incunabula in similar vein. Mr. George D. Painter analyzes the Dutch and Belgian incunables in volume IX of the catalogue (London 1962). The present writer would like to take this opportunity to thank the Editor, Miss Dorothy Miner, for permission to use some of this material in an address delivered before the Grolier Club of New York. This was subsequently printed in the Club's publication *Fifteenth Century Books and the Twentieth Century*, New York 1952.]

[6] "Fifteenth Century Editions of the *Legenda aurea*" in *Speculum*, xxi (1946), pp. 327-338.

[7] Compare the citations given by Robert F. Seybolt, "The *Legenda aurea*, Bible, and *Historia scholastica*" in *Speculum*, xxi (1946), pp. 339-342.

In these volumes are described 9,255 editions—perhaps a quarter of all the editions printed before the year 1501 and for which evidences of their existence have reached our own day.[8] Let us turn first of all to the authors listed in these volumes of the *Gesamtkatalog*. These number, if I have counted aright, exactly 680 writers; of this total 12 are not classifiable and the remainder may be divided by the periods to which they belong into the following groups:

| PERIOD | NUMBER |
| --- | --- |
| Classical | 48 |
| Christian to 700 | 15 |
| 701-800 | 2 |
| 801-900 | 3 |
| 901-1000 | 3 |
| 1001-1100 | 5 |
| 1101-1200 | 5 |
| 1201-1300 | 42 |
| 1301-1400 | 64 |
| 1401-1500 | 481 |
| TOTAL | 668 |

It will, I feel sure, surprise many students (even as it surprised the writer) to find that the authors living in the century which saw the introduction of printing throughout civilized Europe so heavily outnumber all the other writers whose books were printed in this century. Some 72 per cent of the authors of incunabula were actually contemporaries of Johann Gensfleisch, otherwise known as Gutenberg. With this high percentage for the writers of the fifteenth century in mind, it will come as no surprise that those authors living in the century just prior to this era form the second largest group (9.5 per cent). That classical authors with 7.2 per cent should hold third place against the 6.2 per cent turned in by the writers of the thirteenth century—"the greatest of centuries" as Dr. James Walsh has chosen to call it[9]—may prove unexpected to many students of the period. Curiously enough, the early Fathers fared badly at the hands of the fifteenth-century printers, for a mere 5 per cent of the authors published in the infancy of printing lived between the era of classical antiquity and the year 1200. The facts set forth above

[8] The preface to the seventh volume of the *Gesamtkatalog* gives an estimate of 40,000 for the editions produced in the fifteenth century.

[9] James J. Walsh, *The Thirteenth, Greatest of Centuries*, New York 1909.

buttress to an amazing degree the statements made by Professor Sarton in connection with the scientific incunabula:

The majority of the incunabula authors [of scientific books] were contemporaries, and most of these were mediocre. A great many are entirely unknown. Indeed the very high proportion of worthless publications among incunabula is appalling. However, if the printed literature of any time were examined in the same way that we were able to examine the total printed [scientific] literature of the fifteenth century, mediocre publications would swamp the others in the same manner, for the simple reason that mediocre authors are always more numerous than distinguished ones, and each of them on the average more prolific.[10]

This judgment—harsh as it may seem on first sight—is quite justified; indeed it is not confined to the printing of scientific texts, but is equally applicable to the total book production of the fifteenth century, as the already published volumes of the *Gesamtkatalog* adequately prove.

Once the authors of fifteenth-century books have been fixed chronologically, it is a natural corollary to enquire as to the countries of origin of these men. In five instances it has proved itself impossible to determine the nationality of the writer with any degree of confidence; the rest may be listed thus:

| | | | | | |
|---|---|---|---|---|---|
| Italian | 345 | (.511) | Hebrew | 9 | |
| German | 85 | (.126) | Arabic | 8 | |
| French | 65 | (.096) | Swiss | 4 | |
| Spanish | 46 | (.068) | Dalmatian | 4 | |
| Roman | 26 | (.038) | Polish | 2 | (.047) |
| Netherlandish | 24 | (.036) | Czech | 2 | |
| Greek | 22 | (.033) | Russian | 1 | |
| English | 18 | (.027) | Swedish | 1 | |
| Byzantine | 12 | (.018) | Hungarian | 1 | |
| | 643 | | | 32 | |

Probably the reader would have expected the Italians to head the list, followed (at a respectable distance) by the Germans and the French. But this compiler would certainly not have hazarded the guess that Italy would have supplied over 50 per cent of the writers whose works were printed in the fifteenth century, as the present figures would tend to indicate—nor that the Peninsula, joined by Germany, France, and Spain, would account for 80 per cent of the authors of incunabula. Classical authors, totaling 7 per cent, actually

[10] *Op. cit.*, p. 84.

outnumber the writers from the Iberian peninsula, while England—remote from the centers of culture and handicapped by a relatively small population—turns up with a very creditable 2.7 per cent.

Turning now to the linguistic distribution of the books printed in the fifteenth century, Professor Sarton has observed:

It would be interesting to find out on the basis of Klebs' list [of scientific incunabula] how many books were printed in each of many languages. Of course the overwhelming majority were in Latin which was then and remained until the seventeenth century, and even until the eighteenth, the international language of scientists and scholars.[11]

The following table shows in what languages the 9,255 books now listed by the *Gesamtkatalog* were printed:[12]

| LANGUAGE | | | | | | | | | |

| | *Gesamtkatalog* VOLUME | | | | | | | | PER-CENT-AGE |
| LANGUAGE | 1 | 2 | 3 | 4 | 5 | 6 | 7 | TOTAL | |
| Non-Latin | | | | | | | | | |
| German | 80 | 269 | 86 | 109 | 45 | 86 | 56 | 731 | 7.9 |
| Italian | 67 | 120 | 84 | 111 | 32 | 177 | 136 | 727 | 7.9 |
| French | 56 | 38 | 57 | 41 | 5 | 110 | 115 | 422 | 4.6 |
| Spanish | 34 | 30 | 5 | 15 | 3 | 22 | 30 | 139 | 1.5 |
| Dutch | 12 | 16 | 13 | 19 | 3 | 21 | 24 | 108 | 1.1 |
| English | 16 | 4 | 4 | 11 | 2 | 28 | 10 | 75 | .8 |
| Greek | 3 | 5 | — | — | — | 10 | 10 | 28 | .3 |
| Hebrew | 2 | — | 4 | 3 | — | — | 5 | 14 | |
| Czech | 1 | 5 | — | 2 | — | 2 | — | 10 | |
| Croatian | — | — | — | — | 1 | 1 | — | 2 | .3 |
| Danish | — | — | — | — | — | 1 | — | 1 | |
| Swedish | — | 1 | — | — | — | — | — | 1 | |
| | 271 | 488 | 253 | 311 | 91 | 458 | 386 | 2258 | 24.4 |
| Latin | 985 | 994 | 1086 | 712 | 640 | 1088 | 1492 | 6997 | 75.6 |
| Total | 1256 | 1482 | 1339 | 1023 | 731 | 1546 | 1878 | 9255 | |

As we had every reason to believe, the number of Latin books easily exceeds the total of those printed in all the other languages—but that this sum should prove to be three times the number of those in the

---

[11] *Ibid.*, p. 80.

[12] Where a book is printed in two languages (Latin and another), the edition is listed as a vernacular work. For the sake of convenience, Portuguese books are included under Spanish and Flemish under Dutch.

vernacular seems greater than anticipated. The only other item of real surprise to the compiler was the fact that the German books exceeded in number—if not in quality and size—those printed in Italian; the remainder of the list performed rather as one might have expected it to do.

Having viewed the total figures for the Latin and the vernacular books listed to date by the *Gesamtkatalog der Wiegendrucke*, we may once again refer to an observation made by Professor Sarton:

Indeed the use of a vernacular in printed books was a function of the importance attached to that vernacular, but also of social factors (the group of readers for which a particular book was intended) and of knowledge (or ignorance) of Latin. . . . We might thus expect a larger proportion of Latin incunabula (vs. the vernacular) in Italy than in England. I do not know whether the facts agree with my conjecture.[13]

The facts do indeed bear out Professor Sarton's conjecture. In the seven published volumes of the *Gesamtkatalog*, the number of items printed in Italy appears to reach a total of 3,501—approximately 38 per cent of the entire number described in these volumes. While this figure is somewhat lower than the estimate I drew from the holdings in the British Museum and Bodleian libraries,[14] one would not be far wrong in estimating that Italy produced two-fifths of all books printed in the fifteenth century, while German production probably totaled a third. Of the 3,501 items printed there, as we have seen, 727 are in Italian—about 21 per cent. Since fewer books were produced in Germany than in Italy and yet more books seem to have been printed in German than in Italian,[15] the proportion of vernacular books put out by the northern country must have been considerably higher than that which prevailed south of the Alps. Italy, the *fons et origo* of the Renaissance culture, actually produced, in proportion to total production, a much smaller number of books in its national language than a Germany which was still, in the main, purely medieval. This once again underlines the fact that, for the country of its origin, the Renaissance was more a return to an an-

---

[13] *Op. cit.*, p. 81.

[14] *Statistics*, p. 164. There the figure amounted to 42 per cent, but these libraries have, of course, specialized in classical books with the inevitable increase in holdings of Italian printings.

[15] In all fairness, it must be pointed out that not all German books were printed in Germany, but that some were printed in Switzerland, Austria, France and even Italy. These relatively few books cannot have a very great influence on the percentages.

cient culture rather than the creation of an entirely new form of civilization.

Oddly enough, it seems that the further one gets away from the Peninsula the greater becomes the proportion of the books printed in the vernacular. In his standard bibliography of the books printed in the Low Countries during the fifteenth century, Marinus Campbell counts 1,794 editions,[16] of which no fewer than 477 (over 26 per cent) were printed in the three national tongues current in this part of Europe. Again, according to the studies of E. Gordon Duff,[17] 359 books were run off by the English presses before the year 1501. Almost two-thirds of these books were in the vernacular, including 207 (58 per cent) in English and 29 (8 per cent) in French. The 123 books in Latin represent just a shade more than 34 per cent of the total output. These high figures for the printing of non-Latin books in the British Isles may seem surprising—but the proportion of Latin books produced on the Iberian peninsula would seem to approximate closely the figure reached in England. Of the 720 numbers enumerated in the original volume of Haebler's bibliography,[18] over 400 are non-Latin books, for a total of nearly 60 per cent of the entire output.[19] Whatever may have been the reason which impelled the cultured reader of Italy to buy these early printed volumes (whether he read them or not is, of course, another matter), it is certain that in Spain and England the demand was for books printed in the national languages. The figures we have been examining amply demonstrate

[16] *Annales de la typographie néerlandaise au XVᵉ siècle*, La Haye 1874.

[17] *Fifteenth Century English Books*, Oxford 1917. Seventy-two books there listed were printed on the Continent for sale in England; these have been disregarded.

[18] Konrad Haebler, *Bibliografía Ibérica del siglo XV*, La Haya 1903.

[19] With the appearance of Francisco Vindel's *El arte tipográfico en España durante el siglo XV*, Madrid 1945-1951, further comparisons are made possible. Vindel lists 984 Spanish incunables, of which 533 (or just over 54 per cent) are printed in languages other than Latin. Again it may be noted that, the further away from Italy, the lower the percentage of Latin books becomes. In Catalonia, nearly two-thirds of the books printed there (112 of a total of 180) are in Latin; in Andalusia, on the other hand, 106 non-Latin books were printed in Seville and Granada as against 52 in Latin, giving the vernacular books a percentage of two-thirds of the total. In Portugal, only 7 (or 30 per cent) of the 24 books printed in the fifteenth century were in Latin; compare Raúl Proença and António Anselmo, "Bibliografia dos incunábulos portugueses," *Anais das bibliotecas e arquivos*, ser. II, I (1920), 186-191. Significantly enough the first eleven books produced in Portugal were in Hebrew. The proportion of Hebrew books, which outnumbered those in Latin (7) and Portuguese (5), would doubtless have been much greater but for the expulsion of the Jews from that country in 1497.

this fact—for the printers of all ages have been primarily concerned with producing books for which the sale could be assured. The fifteenth-century printer, as much as his successors in the following centuries, was engaged in the task of making a living from his press and it is certain that then (as now) his shop was busily turning out the sort of books most in demand. One can assume, then, with some confidence that the figures and proportions listed in this study tell us facts of importance and interest for our knowledge of the book trade of the fifteenth century.

(From *Studies in Art and Literature for Belle da Costa Greene* (1954), pp. 401-06).

# CHAPTER B30

## ALDUS MANUTIUS AND THE PRINTING
## OF ATHENAEUS

THE *editio princeps* of the *Deipnosophistae* by Athenaeus is generally admitted to be the edition printed by Aldus Manutius in Venice and issued by him in August 1514. However, to his description of this edition, Antoine Augustin Renouard adds the following note[1]:

> "*M. Schweighaeuser, p. 25 de la préface de son édition d'Athénée, parle d'une page d'essai in-fol., specimen d'une édition de ce livre, mais qui n'a pas eu lieu; et il croit cette page d'impression Aldine. Elle se trouve dans mes mains, faisant partie du Recueil de lettres et autres pièces grecques manuscrites et imprimées, que j'ai déjà mentionné plusieurs fois en ces Annales, et que j'ai acquis de M. Schweighaeuser le fils. J'ai examiné avec attention cette feuille, et j'ai reconnu qu'elle n'est point d'édition Aldine, mais qu'elle a été imprimée à Bâle chez Froben ou chez Oporin.*"

So far as I am aware, no further discussion of the leaf has appeared either in editions of Athenaeus subsequent to the Aldine[2] nor in the numerous bibliographical notes on the activities of the Aldine Press[3].

In his edition of Athenaeus[4], Johannes Schweighaeuser made this comment which, as we have seen, Renouard disputed:

> "*Caeterum* ante hanc Editionem [1514] *Venetiis ab Aldo Musuroque curatam, iam* aliam (*nescio an Florentiae*) tentatam Athenaei Editionem *video; quae tamen ultra primum tentamen non progressa videtur . . . Is codex olim Beati Rhenani fuerat, qui propria manu pluribus locis nomen suum inscripsit. In illarum schedarum numero unum est folium, cuius prior pagina exhibet luculentis typis, qui minime similes Aldinis sunt, excusum initium Epitomes Athenaei, hoc titulo:*" (*etc.*).

---

[1] *Annales de l'imprimerie des Alde*, Paris, 1834, pp. 67–68.

[2] Johann Grässe (*Trésor de livres rares et précieux*, Dresde, 1859–69, vol. I, p. 244) summarizes the statements of Schweighaeuser and Renouard without expressing his own opinion.

[3] Although Ambroise Firmin-Didot (*Alde Manuce et l'Hellénisme à Venise*, Paris, 1875, p. 379) cites the edition by Schweighaeuser, there is no mention anywhere in the book of this « trial leaf » for the Athenaeus. No article on this subject is cited by Lamberto Donati, "Bibliografia Aldina", in: *La Bibliofilia*, vol. LII (1950), pp. 188–204.

[4] *Athenaei Naucratitae Deipnosophistarum libri quindecim*, Argentorati, 1801–07, vol. I, pp. xxv–xxvii, note «t».

Schweighaeuser went on to cite the inscription ("Beati Rhenani sum. Nec muto dominum. AN. M.D.XIII. Basileae") and listed the readings which in this text differed from those in the 1514 Aldine edition.

There is reproduced on Plate 14 a leaf acquired not long ago by the Pierpont Morgan Library (MA 1346–230). It is printed only on one side (the other being blank) and contains the opening lines of the Epitome of Book I of Athenaeus. The inscription, which may be read in the reproduction, is precisely the same as that cited by Schweighaeuser from the hand of Beatus Rhenanus (Bild von Rheinau, 1485–1547). The library of this celebrated humanist, still preserved at Schlettstadt[5], contains a number of books with exactly this same form of inscription; thus one may cite the Arrianus of 1508 (dated Basel, 1512), the Cortesius of 1513 (dated Basel, 1514), the *Novum Instrumentum* of Erasmus of 1516 (dated Basel, 1516) and others. There can, therefore, be no doubt; the inscription in the Morgan leaf is in the handwriting of Beatus Rhenanus and this leaf is the same as that formerly belonging to Johannes Schweighaeuser.

Although Schweighaeuser expressed some hesitation in ascribing the leaf to Aldus, it is readily apparent that the printing of it was done by this great Venetian press. The type measures 114 mm. and thus corresponds exactly to Proctor type no. 7[6], a type not used after 1500 according to Proctor-Isaac and certainly one never employed by the firm of Amerbach-Froben[7]. Contrary, too, to Renouard's suggestion, it is self-evident that Johann Oporinus could not have been the printer of this little piece, since this estimable printer to be was but seven years old when Rhenanus inscribed the « trial leaf ». Furthermore, both the head-piece and the large initial A belonged to Aldus' typographical equipment; the former may, for example, be found in the fifth volume of the Aristotle (GW 2334[5]), folios 157 and 185, while the latter is present on folio 44 of the Theophrastus and on signature N 2 of the Aristophanes.

[5] Compare Adalbert Horawitz, "Die Bibliothek und Korrespondenz des Beatus Rhenanus zu Schlettstadt", in: Akademie der Wissenschaften, Philosophisch-historische Classe, *Sitzungsberichte*, vol. LXXVIII (Wien, 1874), pp. 313–340, and Joseph Walter, *Catalogue général de la Bibliothèque Municipale* [de Sélestat], *Incunables & imprimés du XVIme siècle de la Bibliothèque de Sélestat*, Colmar, 1929.

[6] See Robert Proctor, *The Printing of Greek in the Fifteenth Century*, The Bibliographical Society, 1900, plate XVI, and the *Catalogue of Books Printed in the XVth Century now in the British Museum*, London, 1908–49, vol. V, p. 551.

[7] On these points, see Frank Isaac, *An Index to the Early Printed Books in the British Museum*, Part II, Sections II & III, London, 1938, especially pp. 47 and 221.

It is certain, then, that Aldus Manutius had contemplated an edition of Athenaeus before 1501 but that, for one reason or another, he laid the text aside and did not return to it for more than a decade. The trial leaf of the Athenaeus is therefore somewhat similar to that for a polyglot Bible which Aldus apparently printed about this same time[8]; the only known « sample leaf » for such an edition is preserved in the Bibliothèque Nationale in Paris. In a letter to Conrad Celtes of July 1501, Aldus referred to the Bible as not yet printed ("nondum impressi, sed parturio"), a statement which is corroborated by the preface to the undated Greek Psalter (HCR 13452). An Athenaeus of 1499-1500 may thus be added to the list of projected Aldines. Contrary to the history of the polyglot Bible, however, this project was not completely abandoned by Aldus; rather it was successfully issued from the press a scant six months before death terminated the career of this great Venetian printer.

(From *Gutenberg-Jahrbuch* (1955), pp. 104-06).

[8] Compare Renouard, op. cit., pp. 388, 389 and 516.

# CHAPTER B31

## THE EARLIEST EDITIONS OF JUVENAL

A CENTURY and a quarter ago, there seemed to be no doubt concerning the chronological order of appearance of the earliest printed Juvenals. Dibdin had established this in his bibliographical account of the classics,[1] and his decisions were accepted without question by his contemporaries.[2] In the century following Dibdin's death in 1847, however, the chronology of the first printings of the great Roman satirist became, curiously enough, remarkably confused and beclouded. Not long ago, Professor Gilbert Highet,[3] in his excellent book on Juvenal, set forth the present doubts as to the proper order of appearance of the earliest editions and expressed the opinion (p. 317) that "an expert typographical investigation of the earliest printed editions of Juvenal's satires remains to be made". Since I had some part in creating the hesitation expressed by Professor Highet, it is desirable, I believe, to seek to disentangle the confusion that now exists. The occasion which caused the present writer to review the problem of the earliest printed Juvenals was the acquisition by the Pierpont Morgan Library just two years ago of one of these editions.[4] According to Dibdin, the first printings of Juvenal were the following: (1) [Rome: Ulrich Han, undated];[5]

---

[1] Thomas Frognall Dibdin, *An Introduction to the Knowledge of Rare and Valuable Editions of the Greek and Latin Classics* (London, 1827), II, 141–143.

[2] For a recent appraisal of Dibdin as a bibliographer, see A. N. L. Munby, *The Formation of the Phillipps Library up to the Year 1840* (Cambridge, 1954), p. 113.

[3] *Juvenal the Satirist* (Oxford, 1954), p. 206; one finds here the entirely correct statement that "Juvenal's satires were first printed by Ulrich Han, probably in Rome between 1467 and 1469". In the note attached to this quotation, Professor Highet has confused the two Han printings.

[4] The Andrew Fletcher copy of Hain 9660; compare Frederick B. Adams, Jr., *Fourth Annual Report to the Fellows of the Pierpont Morgan Library* (New York, 1953), pp. 24–26.

[5] Dibdin (*loc. cit.*) cites only two copies, that in the collection of Count D'Elci of Florence and the one "in the Magliabecchi library in the same city". The first is now in the Biblioteca Laurenziana (D'Elci 981), but there is no copy in the Biblioteca Nazionale Centrale in Florence, which includes the Magliabecchi library. Apparently Dibdin was misled by the notice in Ferdinando Fossi's catalogue (*Catalogus codicum saeculo XV impressorum qui in publica bibliotheca magliabechiana Florentiae adservantur* [Florence, 1793–95], III, 91). This does not, however, refer to a Magliabecchi book but to a volume belonging to the Duke of Cassano. See note 11 below.

(2) [Venice: Vindelinus de Spira,] 1470;[6] and (3) Rome: Ulrich Han, [undated].

The present uncertainty concerning the *editio princeps* of Juvenal seems to have its beginning, as odd as this may be, with Robert Proctor's *Index*.[7] It is not often that the origin of a bibliographical problem can be laid to Proctor's door; more often it was he who resolved doubts. In his *Index*, however, the Bodleian Library was credited with a copy of the edition listed as Hain 9661.[8] But when I requested a microfilm of this book from the Bodleian Library, the Keeper of Printed Books in that institution, Mr. L. W. Hanson, informed me that Proctor had erred in crediting the Oxford library with that edition and that the Bodleian actually owned a copy of Hain 9660. Within a decade after the appearance of the *Index*, Isak Collijn had issued his catalogue of the incunabula at Uppsala,[9] basing his typographical assignments upon Proctor; that university's copy of Hain 9661 was accordingly described (no. 914) as: "[Roma: Ulrich Han, c. 1470.] 8°. Hain 9661. Proctor 3344."

A dozen years after the appearance of Proctor's work, Mariano Fava and Giovanni Bresciano published their *La stampa a Napoli nel XV secolo* (Leipzig, 1911–12). Under no. 237, they gave a bibliographical account of the edition identified as Hain 9661; it was there credited to the press of Ulrich Han largely on the strength of Proctor's determination for his no. 3344,[10] though the Italian bib-

[6] The *Catalogue of Books Printed in the XVth Century now in the British Museum* (London, 1908–49), v, 582, maintains that neither Johannes nor Vindelinus de Spira printed this edition, but that it is the work of an anonymous press.

[7] *An Index to the Early Printed Books in the British Museum: from the Invention of Printing to the Year MD. with Notes of those in the Bodleian Library* (London, 1898–1903).

[8] Ludwig Hain, *Repertorium bibliographicum* (Stuttgart, 1826–38). The numerical order, of course, implies that Hain considered his no. 9660 as the earlier; he assigned his no. 9661 either to Riessinger at Naples or to Han at Rome. Hain 9661 was printed with Han's second type and Hain 9660 with the same printer's third type. Proctor (p. 226, no. 3344) incorrectly notes that Hain 9661 was printed with Han's type 3.

[9] *Katalog der Inkunabeln der kgl. Universitäts-Bibliothek zu Uppsala* (Uppsala, 1907). On p. XI, Collijn explains: "Ferner sind überall Verweise auf Proctors Index gegeben worden, sofern die betreffende Inkunabel dort verzeichnet ist, und seine Bestimmungen sind benutzt worden, wenn nicht meine eigenen Untersuchungen zu abweichenden Ergebnissen geführt haben."

[10] "Il Fossi (III, 92) aveva assegnato ad Ulrico Han quest' edizione . . . Gli studii recenti hanno mostrato che il Fossi s' era bene apposto (Pr. 3344)" (II, 189).

liographers failed to note that the volume which they were describing was not printed with the same type as that used in the production of the book listed as Proctor 3344. Since it subsequently became clear that Proctor 3344 did not correspond to Fava-Bresciano 237, there was then no bibliographical evidence, apart from the statement of Ferdinando Fossi, to connect the printing of this work with the press of Ulrich Han in Rome.

In 1906, and again in 1926, the John Rylands Library at Manchester held special exhibitions of the *editiones principes* of the classics.[11] In both exhibitions, and in the catalogues issued in connection with them, the Juvenal displayed was the library's copy of Hain 9660.[12] The catalogues added the further decisive note:[13] "Of extreme rarity. This impression may be earlier than the Venetian one, dated 1470, printed by Vindelinus de Spira, of which the library possesses a copy."

The next significant pronouncement concerning the earliest editions of Juvenal came in 1938 from the pen of Professor George L. Hendrickson. In his study of the Marston collection of Juvenals at Yale, Professor Hendrickson wrote:[14]

The Juvenal which commonly bears the title of *editio princeps* (not in our collection) is attributed to Ulrich Hahn, printer at Rome. It is without date, but is generally assigned to 1470. Unless evidence can be adduced for assigning

---

[11] The Rylands copy of Hain 9661 was the copy formerly belonging to the Duke of Cassano (see note 5 above). Compare the note in *The John Rylands Library Manchester: A Brief Historical Description of the Library and its Contents, with Catalogue of the Selection of Early Printed Greek and Latin Classics Exhibited . . . MCMVI* (Manchester, 1906), pp. 9–10: "The three books in the [Cassano] collection that had special attractions in Lord Spencer's eyes were an unique edition of Horace, printed by Arnoldus de Bruxella at Naples in 1474, an undated Juvenal, printed by Ulrich Han at Rome before 1470, and an Aldine Petrarch of 1501, on vellum, with the manuscript notes of Cardinal Bembo. Could he have obtained these three volumes, there is reason to believe he would have been willing to forgo the rest of the Cassano Library, fine as it was, but the fates decreed otherwise."

[12] "Of the fifty principal Greek and Latin authors, we are fortunate in being able to show the first printed edition." *The John Rylands Library Manchester: Catalogue of an Exhibition of the Earliest Printed Editions of the Principal Greek and Latin Classics* (Manchester, 1926), p. v. The prefatory note is signed by Henry Guppy.

[13] 1906 Catalogue, p. 56, and 1926 Catalogue, p. 32. Ironically enough, the edition displayed was not that represented by the Cassano copy, one of the three prized items of this collection, but Lord Spencer's copy of Hain 9660 (cf. Dibdin, *Bibliotheca Spenceriana* [London, 1814–15], II, 117–119).

[14] "The Marston Juvenals", *Yale University Library Gazette*, XII (1938), 76.

it to an earlier time, there seems to be no reason why our [Venetian] edition, bearing the date of 1470, should not dispute with it the title of *editio princeps*. It was in fact so designated by Moss (Vol. II, p. 142).

Whether Hain 9660 or Hain 9661 was here referred to as the Han edition is not self-evident; in any event, Professor Hendrickson took cognizance of only a single Han printing of Juvenal.

The most recent setting forth of the chronological order of the earliest Juvenals is that contributed by the Italian *Indice generale*.[15] Here are the first five editions as there listed:

5564. [Rome: Ulrich Han, c. 1469]. Hain 9661. Fava-Bresciano 237.
5565. [Venice: unassigned], 1470. Hain 9665. BMC V:582.
5566. [Venice: Vindelinus de Spira, c. 1471]. Hain 9672. BMC V:164.
5567. Fivizzano: Jacopo da Fivizzano, [c. 1472]. Hain 9662. BMC VII:955.
5568. [Venice: Printer of Duns Scotus, c. 1472]. Hain 9676. BMC V:212.

The Han edition with the poetic colophon (Hain 9660) is now listed in tenth place, under no. 5573. This order too seemed to this writer in need of revision. With this in view, microfilms of the copies of Hain 9661 in the Biblioteca Nazionale at Naples[16] and of the Fivizzano edition at the Huntington Library[17] were procured, the copies of the four earliest Venetian editions at Yale[18] were consulted, and a new survey of these editions (including, of course, the Han edition with the metrical colophon, Hain 9660) was begun, conducted with complete independence of previously published bibliographical views.

### I

If we turn first to the two editions described by Hain under the numbers 9660 and 9661, we find that the former proclaims Han's

[15] Teresa Guarnaschelli and Enrichetta Valenziani, *Indice generale degli incunaboli delle biblioteche d'Italia* (Rome 1943–54), III, 203–04.

[16] This and the copies at Florence, Manchester, and Uppsala seem to be the only survivors of this edition. The copy at Naples bears the press-mark: S. Q. IX B 19. [A copy is now also in the Morgan Library, PML 60173. CFB]

[17] Herman R. Mead, *Incunabula in the Huntington Library* (San Marino, 1937), p. 169, no. 3946.

[18] A copy of Hain 9676 (*Indice generale* 5568) is also found, and has been consulted, in the Pierpont Morgan Library; cf. Ada Thurston and Curt F. Bühler, *Check List of Fifteenth Century Printing in the Pierpont Morgan Library* (New York, 1939), p. 70, no. 806. Yale now also has a copy of the Fivizzano edition.

name in its verse ("anser") colophon; Alfred W. Pollard[19] brilliantly rendered the Latin stanza into English in these words:[20]

> Bird of Tarpeian Jove, though died the Gaul
> 'Gainst whom thou flap'dst thy wings, see vengeance fall.
> Another Gallus comes and thy pen-feather
> Goes out of fashion, beaten altogether.
> For what a quill can write the whole year through,
> This in a day, and more, his press will do.
> So, Goose, give over: there's no other plan;
> Own yourself beaten by all-conquering man.

Hain 9661, though silent as to the printer's name, was certainly produced at the same press; it was printed in Han's type 2 "cum spatiis interlinearibus" as Fossi had correctly observed. It is easy to demonstrate that the edition *sine nota* is unquestionably the earlier, and that the one with the "anser" colophon is the later. Hain 9661 was printed with Han's second type which was in use, according to the British Museum's incunabula catalogue, "in 1468 and 1469"; Hain 9660, on the other hand, displays the third Han type, known to have been employed in 1470 and 1471.[21] Finally, only Hain 9660 has the Greek passages printed (albeit not very correctly) in that tongue, while Han's other edition leaves blank spaces where Greek words should appear.[22] The Greek type used by Han seems to have been a new fount of type introduced in 1471, and was therefore not available for an edition printed before 1470.[23]

---

[19] *An Essay on Colophons* (Chicago, 1905), p. 89.

[20] In PML 44865, the colophon reads:

> Anser Tarpei custos Iouis: unde quod alis
> Constreperes: Gallus decidit: Vltor adest
> Vdalricus Gallus: ne quem poscantur in usum
> Edocuit pennis nil opus esse tuis.
> Imprimit ille die: quantum non scribitur anno
> Ingenio haud noceas: omnia uincit homo.

[21] Thus *BMC*, iv, 18: "In use in 1470 and 1471".

[22] The famous phrase "Know thyself" (Juvenal, Satire XI, l. 27) is printed in Hain 9660 as: νωθι σε αυτον. The Naples copy of Hain 9661 has the following text supplied in manuscript: γνωσ ῖ σε αυτων. The longer Greek passage in Satire IX, l. 37, reads in Hain 9660: ηθους Γαρ Γλυκεοσ ανδρα κιναιδον; in the blank space of the Naples copy (of Hain 9661), there is written: ηθους γλυκεισ ανδρα κηρα ιδον. This should read: αὐτὸς γὰρ ἐφέλκεται ἄνδρα κίναιδος.

[23] According to *BMC*, iv, 18. Robert Proctor (*The Printing of Greek in the Fifteenth Century* [Bibliographical Society, 1900], p. 29) was of the opinion that the Greek type "seems to occur for the first time in the Tortellius of 1471".

In 1471, Han took as partner one Simon Nicolai Chardella of Lucca, and this partnership continued until October 1474. Since Chardella is not mentioned in the colophon of Hain 9660 and since books printed during the partnership bore either both names or were *sine nota*, the inference is that the Juvenal with the colophon was printed either before the partnership was formed or after it was dissolved.[24] The type, however, points to a period earlier than the partnership, and one concludes both from Burger[25] and from the British Museum's catalogue that the "anser" colophon was also characteristic of this earlier period. In any event, no book with the verse colophon produced after the dissolution of the firm is recorded. The edition described by Hain 9660 should therefore be dated as "not after 1471"; it may well have been printed early in that year. The date assigned to this edition by the *Indice generale* (ca. 1474) is obviously much too late for the bibliographical reasons set forth above.

From a textual study, too, one obtains the impression that Hain 9660 must be the later printing. Numerous slips, typographic as well as editorial, are common to the two editions, so that it seems quite plain that one edition was set from the other. Thus in Satire VII, both editions print lines 128–131 in this order, Hain 9661 reading:[26]

> Eminus. & statua meditatur prelia lusca.
> Tongilli magno cum neroceronte lauari
> Sic pedo conturbat. matho deficit. exitus hic *est*
> Qui solet & uexat lutulenta balnea turba.

Here lines 129–130 are reversed, though the Naples copy of this Han edition contains the usual mediaeval sign for inversion (a letter B having been placed before the line beginning "Tongilli", while the line beginning "Sic" has an A prefixed).[27]

[24] No example of a book printed in type three during the life of the partnership is known to BMC, nor was it used by Han after the partnership had lapsed.

[25] Konrad Burger, *The Printers and Publishers of the XV. Century with Lists of their Works* (London, 1902).

[26] The correct order is found in the 1470 Venetian and Fivizzano editions, as well as in that by the printer of Duns. In the Naples copy, "neroceronte" has been corrected in manuscript to read "rinocerote" (rhinocerote—Duns), while Hain 9660 prints "kinoceronte". The first Venetian edition has "rinocerunthe", and the two Vindelinus de Spira editions, as well as the Fivizzano printing, give "rinoceronte".

[27] Professor Edward Robertson, librarian of the John Rylands Library, kindly informs me that their copy has been washed and that it is impossible to tell whether or not such marks were once there. For the use made of these letters by early printers, compare my "Stop-press and Manuscript Corrections in the Aldine Edition of Benedetti's *Diaria de Bello Carolino*", PBSA, XLIII (1949), 365–373, and my "Corrections in Caxton's *Cordiale*", PBSA, XLVIII (1954), 194–196.

However, Hain 9661 contains gross errors not found in the other Han printing; this may be regarded as evidence of editorial care in the production of the later edition. Thus, the closing lines of Satire XIV read in Hain 9661:[28]

> Si nondum impleui gremium: si panditur ultra.
> Nec cresi fortuna nunqu*am* nec persica regna
> Sufficiens animo: nec diuitie narcisci
> Paruit imperiis uxorem occidere iussus.

This, of course, makes incomplete sense, the penultimate line having been omitted, which in Hain 9660 reads:[29]

> Indulsit cęsar cui claudius omnia: cuius

Again, lines 219–227 of Satire VII appear thus in Hain 9661:[30]

>     . . . cede palemon
> [220] Et patere inde aliquid decrescere. non aliter qu*am*
> Institor hiberne tegetis niueiq*ue* cadurci
> Dum modo no*n* pereat: totidem olfecisse lucernas
> Sedisti qua nemo faber. qua nemo sedebat
> Qui docet obliquo lanam deducere ferro
> [225] Dum modo no*n* pereat: medie q*uo*d noctis ab hora
> Quot stabunt pueri. cum totus decolor esset
> Flaccus & hereret nigro fuligo maroni.

Here, lines 222 and 225 have changed place, again to the detriment of the sense; the correct order is observed by Hain 9660.[31]

In themselves these facts do not necessarily prove that Hain 9660 is a later, corrected edition; the contrary could equally be true, and Hain 9661 might be a careless reprinting of the text of an earlier edition. In still other circumstances, however, one observes what appears to be a deterioration of text which can only be accounted for by assuming that Hain 9660 was set up from Hain 9661;[32] in illustration

[28] Fivizzano prints "cresi" as Han, while the "Duns" and 1470 Venetian editions have "croesi" and Vindelinus offers "cresci". In the Naples copy "sufficiens" (also found in the second Han printing) has been corrected by hand to read "sufficient", thus agreeing with all the other editions. "Narcisci" is also corrected to "narcissi" in the Naples volume.

[29] The line appears thus in all the other early editions. The Naples copy of Hain 9661 supplies the following text in manuscript: "Induxit cęsar cui claudi*us* om*n*ia: cui*us*".

[30] In line 226, Hain 9660 also reads "stabu*n*t". This has been corrected in the margin to "stabant", the reading of the other texts.

[31] The other Juvenals here discussed also have the correct order.

[32] See, for example, the "rhinoceros" of note 26 above. Then, too, the edition of Hain 9661 lacks the printed Greek words found in Hain 9660. One would hardly

of this we may cite the following example. Lines 86–89 of Satire XI read in a modern text:

> cognatorum aliquis titulo ter consulis atque
> castrorum imperiis et dictatoris honore
> functus ad has epulas solito maturius ibat,
> erectum domito referens a monte ligonem.

In line 87 of Hain 9661, the battered type makes "imperiis"[33] look much like "imperus". The compositor of Hain 9660 apparently read the word in his "Vorlage" as "imperus" and, realizing that this was impossible, emended this reading to "impetus". That the reading "impetus" in Hain 9660 arose in this fashion seems evident, especially since no other way to account for this unique variant is at hand. Though occasionally the edition described by Hain 9660 has some errors not found in the other,[34] it must be admitted that, taken all in all, it presents a better text than Hain 9661.[35] In view of these findings, it is quite apparent that Hain 9660 is a corrected and improved version of the earlier Han printing, listed as Hain 9661.

## II

Turning now to the other early Juvenals, we may note with relief that the first Venetian edition (V) has the printed date 1470;[36] with this statement we have no reason or desire to quarrel. In connection with these north Italian editions, one point is most curious: the

---

expect a printer to revert to a more primitive practice once he possessed the technical equipment for a more perfect product.

[33] Without exception, the other editions have "imperiis".

[34] In Juvenal VII, 233, the Morgan copy reads: "Dum petit aut termas phebi balnea dicat". Hain 9661 has the second "aut" before "phebi" as required. Again, in line XI, 103, the second edition prints: "Vt phaleris gauderet equs. celataque cassis". Here the "equs" is doubtless a misprint for "equus" (as the other editions). It seems most unlikely that the "equs" is a graphic variant for the "ecus" preferred by Housman (*Saturae,* Cambridge, 1931, p. 105).

[35] For Ulrich Han's career, compare also Konrad Haebler, *Die deutschen Buchdrucker des XV. Jahrhunderts im Auslande* (München, 1924), p. 18 ff. Haebler stresses the fact (p. 20) that "klassische Texte sind seit dieser Zeit [partnership with Chardella] aus der Werkstatt des Ulrich Han fast gar nicht mehr hervorgegangen". This is still another reason for believing that the Juvenal (Hain 9660) appeared before the partnership began. In that case, too, one must assume that the first appearance of the Greek type was not, as Proctor had stated, in the Tortellius of 1471 (a product of the partnership) since it is used in the second Han Juvenal.

[36] For convenience in citing examples, sigla have been assigned to the several editions. The printer of V is discussed in note 6.

Italian *Indice* lists only a single Vindelinus de Spira edition (*Indice* 5566; Hain 9672), whereas two printings were certainly produced by the brother of Venice's prototypographer. The second edition (Hain 9672; $V^2$) was set up from its predecessor and closely resembles this edition.[37] It is possible, therefore, that among the dozen copies recorded by the *Indice* under no. 5566, there may be some which are actually the edition Hain 9673 ($V^1$). In order to arrange these two Juvenals chronologically, we are obliged to fall back upon the evidence of the types. The Juvenal represented by Hain 9673 was printed, according to *BMC*, v, 164 (IB. 19590), in Vindelinus's type 110 R in its second state.[38] This same authority states that "the first use of this state is perhaps seen in the Malermi Bible (IC. 19527), 1 Aug. 1471" (*BMC*, v, 152). In this condition, the type was certainly in use as late as January 1473 when Vindelinus printed with it an edition of Boccaccio's *De montibus* (*BMC*, v, 162, IB. 19561). The second Juvenal put out by Vindelinus de Spira (Hain 9672) has some gatherings printed in the third state of this type (with a *v* of the round-topped gothic variety), and this edition must, consequently, be of still later date. With the collapse of his business in the autumn of 1473, Vindelinus practically ceased printing,[39] so that we may assume that his second Juvenal was printed certainly no later than this period and, equally probably, not much earlier. The year 1472, finally, marks the earliest date connected with the presses operated by the "Printer of Duns, Quaestiones" (D) in Venice and by Jacobus de Fivizzano (F) in the town of the same name.[40] This is, consequently, the earliest date that one may safely ascribe to the Juvenals issued by these printers.

The textual examination of these editions has not, unfortunately, been very rewarding. It is well to bear in mind that, in studies of this sort, one can never be absolutely certain whether a printer used a corrected copy of some earlier edition or printed from some manuscript preserving the same *variae lectiones* as those in the manuscript

---

[37] Concerning the curious repetitions of lines in $V^1$ and $V^2$, compare the BMC's annotations.

[38] Since the publication of Miss Margaret B. Stillwell's *Incunabula in American Libraries* (New York, 1940), the Huth-Ascherson copy has been acquired by the Yale University Library. It is a pleasant duty to acknowledge the kind help cheerfully rendered by the staff of that library, particularly the interest taken in this study by Mr. Thomas E. Marston.

[39] Compare Haebler, *op. cit.*, p. 27, and *BMC*, v, ix.

[40] For further particulars, see *BMC*, v, 212 and vii, l-li.

to which his predecessor had access. A few points may, however, be reasonably assumed to be of value.

The first Venetian Juvenal gives no evidence of being descended directly from the Han printing. As we have remarked (note 26), this edition has Satire VII, 128–131 in the correct order (as also D and F).[41] On the other hand, Vindelinus de Spira, in both his editions, has here the curious line-sequence of the Roman Juvenals, which may indicate that Vindelinus either used the first Han printing[42] or that he employed a manuscript closely related to that used by his Roman colleague.[43] It seems certain that Vindelinus could hardly have set up his Juvenal from V and by sheer accident have inverted the lines, thus to arrive at the same order as printed by Ulrich Han.

Another possible connection between the first de Spira and Han printings may be seen in Satire VII, 206 ("nil praeter gelidas ausae conferre cicutas").[44] Here the earlier Han edition has "aut se" for "ausae"; with this slip both de Spira printings concur. The Naples copy, however, emends this by manuscript correction to read "ause" and thus agrees with all the other editions here discussed.

A third significant passage will be found in Satire IV, line 26. In a modern text, this reads: "piscator quam piscis emi; provincia tanti" and with this the second Han and the Fivizzano printings agree. However, V and D omit "emi", while the two Juvenals issued by Vindelinus de Spira leave out "quam". By what is certainly more than coincidence, the first edition put out by Ulrich Han also omits the "quam" (though it is present in the Naples copy by manuscript insertion). These three instances give some grounds for believing that Vindelinus may possibly have used the first edition by Ulrich

[41] Edition V has its own share of errors, which do not reappear in the other editions. Thus in the lines comparable to VII, 142–145 of a modern text, V omits line 144 (sardonyche, atque ideo pluris quam Gallus agebat); this line is present, however, in the later printings. The Yale copy had the line supplied in manuscript, but this volume has been thoroughly washed and cleaned so that the readings are now partly obliterated.

[42] In place of the proper name Iunco (at XV, 27), all Han and de Spira editions have "vinco"; V prints "iunio", a variant admitted by Housman; F has "iunco" and D offers "iuno".

[43] The de Spira editions do not invariably follow the Han readings. Thus, at VII, 59, the word "enim" is omitted (from: "fontibus Aonidum. neque enim cantare sub antro") by both Han editions and by V and D; the de Spira and Fivizzano editions have the "enim".

[44] In order to save space, lines have been quoted whether they provide complete sense or not. If not, the reader is referred to the Loeb edition (New York, 1930), which has provided the modern quotations.

Han in the preparation of his own first Juvenal, though the Venetian edition is no slavish follower of the Roman text. Vindelinus either possessed a corrected copy or corrected one against other manuscripts, if there be any truth to the supposition that he used the Han edition.[45]

On occasion, F corresponds with V and D; for example, the first word of VII, 13 is "Hoc" in FVD, while the two German printers have "Hec" (the latter being corrected to "Hoc" by manuscript emendation in the Naples example). Edition D sometimes has readings found otherwise only in V; here are a few examples:[46]

> componis dona Veneris, Telesine, marito (VII, 25)
> [V and D have "componis"; all the other editions have "conscribis", a good variant according to Housman, p. 64]

> hi sunt qui trepidant et ad omnia fulgura pallent (XIII, 223)
> [only V and D have "fulmina" for "fulgura"]

> invidiam facerent nolenti surgere Nilo? (XV, 123)
> [only V and D have "nolenti"; the other editions all have "uolenti", though the Naples copy has a manuscript correction in ink]

Again, F has an occasional variant in common with D, though the other Venetian editions differ:[47]

> gaudia longa feras. tamen ima plebe Quiritem (VIII, 47)[48]
> [F and D—and the second Han printing—alone have "ima"; the other Venetian texts and the first Han edition offer "una"]

> te veto nec plana faciem contundere palma (XIII, 128)
> [the same misprint "te uero" is found only in F and D]

However, no certain pattern emerges from this textual study; the editions now form one group, and now display other affinities.

In fine, then, it is possible, though by no means absolutely certain, that Vindelinus de Spira had access to the *editio princeps* of Juvenal

---

[45] Occasionally, all the Venetian editions have the same reading. Thus in XIII, 62 ("prodigiosa fides et Tuscis digna libellis"), the last two words are "digna tabellis" in V V¹ V² D, while the Han and Fivizzano editions provide the standard text.

[46] V and D have the same error ("Has pariter") in XIII, 208 ("has patitur poenas peccandi sola voluntas"); the other editions give the correct word.

[47] In VII, 138 ("sed finem inpensae non servat prodiga Roma"), the Han and Fivizzano editions have "obseruat non" for "non servat". In the Naples copy this has been corrected in ink to "non seruat" and the text thus corresponds to that found in all the Venetian Juvenals.

[48] The copies of F at the Huntington and Yale libraries have the misprint "longfa eras". In VIII, 79, only F and D (and the Han editions) have "esto" in the line "esto bonus miles, tutor bonus, arbiter idem"; the reading is "est" in V, V¹ and V².

issued by Ulrich Han when he was preparing his own first edition. The 1470 Venetian edition, since it does not depend on the Han printing, must derive from a manuscript source. Beyond these observations it would be hazardous to venture.

## III

We may now conclude by summarizing our findings.[49] It seems certain beyond reasonable doubt that the *editio princeps* of Juvenal is the edition put out by Ulrich Han at Rome "sine ulla nota" (Hain 9661). The printing of this work may be judged to have taken place "not after 1469". In the following year there appeared in Venice the second printed Juvenal; the printer of this edition is unknown, but the work is dated 1470 (Hain 9665). The third edition of the works of the Roman satirist is the second printing by Ulrich Han;[50] this (Hain 9660), on the evidence of the types and of the historical facts relative to the press which are known to us, must be dated "before the autumn of 1471". This edition was followed by the first

---

[49] The problems that have here been investigated, although based upon a classical text, belong wholly to the Renaissance. It is through the study of printings such as these that we may come to a realization of the numerous difficulties and obstacles which beset the Renaissance printer, as well as the means that he found to solve and eliminate them. By investigations of this sort, we may arrive at a full knowledge of the nature of book-production and the means of distribution of printed books in Italy in the fifteenth century.

[50] Although we now have reason to believe that the use of the Greek type by Ulrich Han anticipated the date (August 1471) set by Proctor, it seems doubtful that the fount came into Han's possession as early as 1470. It is therefore not likely (though not, of course, impossible) that the second Han printing preceded the first Venetian one. In any event, this second edition by Han is the first to include the text of Persius, and this is the true *editio princeps* of that work (Morris H. Morgan, *A Bibliography of Persius* [Cambridge (Mass.), 1909], no. 1). Professor Morgan, however, added his small contribution to the confusion surrounding the earliest Juvenals which was just then growing. In describing the first Persius, he stated (p. 1): "Printed in Rome by Udalricus Gallus (Han) in 1469 or 1470, in the same type as his Juvenal, and the two are sometimes found bound together, whence it has been wrongly thought that they were so published." Morgan referred, of course, to the second Han Juvenal, not the first (no copy of which contains a Persius). The date for the first edition of Persius, therefore, is not "Rome, 1469 or 1470" (as Morgan asserted), but [Rome, summer 1471]. Incidentally, Morgan's second edition of Persius is that issued with the second Juvenal by Vindelinus de Spira (Hain 9672); this should now be dated in the summer of 1473. Morgan no. 3 appeared with the first de Spira Juvenal (Hain 9673); this is now the second Persius, printed "after 1 August 1471".

printing of the text by Vindelinus de Spira (Hain 9673) at Venice.[51] For typographical reasons, the date of this edition is set as "after 1 August 1471". It may never be determined whether the edition of Juvenal by Jacobus de Fivizzano or that by the shadowy "Printer of Duns" holds fifth place. If any evidence should ever be wanted as to the priority of the one or the other edition, it must be looked for in the archives of Venice and Fivizzano. I have not the slightest hesitation in assigning the second Vindelinus de Spira Juvenal (Hain 9672) to the spring or summer of 1473. Perhaps, then, this contribution may, in its small way, serve to provide that investigation of the earliest printed Juvenals which Professor Gilbert Highet hoped for not long ago.

(From *Studies in the Renaissance* 2 (1955), pp. 84-95).

[51] The Greek words in VI, 195 (ζωὴ καὶ ψυχή) are printed in V² while a blank space is left in V¹. This is still another bit of evidence pointing to the conclusion that V¹ preceded V². The Greek words are printed in the second Han edition and are supplied in manuscript in the Naples copy of the *editio princeps*. For the significance of these details, compare note 32 above.

# CHAPTER B32

## STUDIES IN THE EARLY EDITIONS
## OF THE *FIORE DI VIRTÙ*

PROBABLY the most popular of all the books printed in Italian during the fifteenth century was an anonymous work entitled the *Fiore di virtù*.[1] Prior to the year 1501, no fewer than 57 editions in the vernacular of Italy were put out by the presses of the Peninsula; to this should be added the nine editions in Catalan, French and Spanish which were also published in these years.[2] This makes a very respectable total of editions for a popular text of the late Middle Ages; this it essentially is, though in point of time the work belongs to the period of the High Renaissance in Italy. The popularity of this tract continued throughout the following centuries and the text survived in countless editions, chiefly as a chap-book or as a "courtesy book" for the moral education of the young.[3]

Since the influence of the *Fiore di virtù* was not only continuous but equally widespread, the following notes on various bibliographical details of a number of the very earliest editions and on the textual transmission as evidenced by them will, it is hoped, be of general interest. From a literary point of view, of course, the printed editions are late products and a "textus receptus," if one were ever wanted, would necessarily have to be based on a thorough study of the multitude of earlier manuscripts. Nevertheless, since each generation made use of whatever text came to hand, it is not inevitable that the received text will alone be of value for literary research. The *Fiore*

[1] For particulars concerning this text, see my note "The *Fleurs de toutes vertus* and Christine de Pisan's *L'Epître d'Othéa*," and the supplemental notice, both reprinted on pp. 423-427.

[2] The text has been discussed and the fifteenth-century editions listed by Lessing J. Rosenwald in his foreword to *The Florentine Fior di Virtu of 1491* (Washington, D. C., The Library of Congress, 1953). Most of the Italian editions are also listed by T. M. Guarnaschelli and E. Valenziani, *Indice generale degli incunaboli delle biblioteche d'Italia* (Rome, 1943-1954), II, 222-227, nos. 3927-3970. For a great many of these editions, only a single copy is recorded as being in Italian public libraries. The extreme scarcity of these early editions is further attested by the fact that twelve editions listed by Mr. Rosenwald are not represented in the *Indice*.

[3] The *Fiore di virtù* was continuously printed into the nineteenth century, the British Museum having a copy printed at Venice in 1803. By 1895, a new edition based on manuscript texts was put out by G. Ulrich and printed in Leipzig.

*di virtù* text was extensively quoted and pilfered, as a useful source for homely citations, by many generations of writers of note. It will be of unquestioned value, consequently, to establish for the guidance of literary historians a few of the main groups and the chief lines of textual connection of the earliest editions. The purely bibliographical notations, it may be judged, will be of particular interest to the historians of printing.

## I

Under no. 838 of the *Check List of Fifteenth Century Printing in the Pierpont Morgan Library* (New York, 1939, p. 73), the writer added the following note to the listing of the edition of the *Fiore* printed in Venice, at the press established in the Beretin Convento della Ca Grande, in 1474: "f. 3 is from the 1477 edition." This is a masterpiece of understatement!

The unsigned edition of 1474 collates: [*² a-h⁸ i-k⁶], while the 1477 printing[4] put out by the same press is signed: [*²] a-i⁸ k⁴. When two editions are printed with the same type and one is a page-for-page reprint of the other, substituted leaves from one edition "planted" in the other are rarely suspected at once and, even when doubt arises, are not always easy to detect with certainty. Where the text runs on without a break, when the typographical design is the same and the leaves are unquestionably of genuine antiquity, then one normally assumes that the book is what it pretends to be— a complete example. If the watermarks and other tell-tale indications point to the suspicion that the book has been "perfected," one would hardly jump to the conclusion that the book was "imperfectly" perfected; one would normally expect that the supplied leaves were obtained from some other copy of the same edition. Without the opportunity to compare a presumably "sophisticated" copy with a perfect example of the same printing, it becomes extremely difficult, if not impossible, to be certain of the nature of the supplied leaves. The Morgan copy of the 1474 "Nel Beretin Convento" edition is the only one in America—and such a comparison has been impossible.

However, a closer examination of the book than was feasible in 1938 was recently undertaken, including a comparison with the 1477 reprint which was acquired by the present writer in the past year. This reveals the unhappy truth that the following fourteen leaves are

---

[4] Compare the *Catalogue of Books Printed in the XVth Century now in the British Museum* (London, 1908-1949), V, 238-239. This work is hereafter cited as BMC.

supplied in the Morgan volume from some copy of the 1477 edition: a1, a2, b5, d3, e3, e4, e8, f1, f5, f6, f8, k1, k2 and k4.[5] That the substitution was done by an earlier owner with full knowledge of *what* was being done and with the deliberate intention of deceiving is made evident by one circumstance. Where the signature marks were present in the leaves substituted from the 1477 edition, these were very carefully and skilfully removed. This is not evident at first glance—but when one is suspicious enough to look for them, then there is no question but that the printed signatures were once present. The removal of them was a patent act of dishonesty.[6]

## II

In one respect, certainly, my copy of the 1477 "Nel Beretin Convento" edition of the *Fiore* differs from the other copies of which I possess the necessary information, viz.: Florence (Biblioteca Nazionale and Biblioteca Riccardiana), London (British Museum), Milan (Biblioteca Ambrosiana), New York (The Rosenbach Company), Rome (Biblioteca Vaticana) and Verona (Biblioteca Comunale).[7] The outer sheet of the second signature (quarto: b1.2.7.8) in my copy differs from that of the other seven.[8] The differences between the two "states" are slight but constant, and reveal the fact that the type was completely reset during the course of publication. In the vast majority of points (40 of a total of 48, or over 83% of the cases) at which the two states display textual variation, the state typified by the Vatican example corresponds to that in the 1474 edition while my copy departs from this agreement. In three specific cases, it seems certain beyond reasonable doubt that the text of the Vatican state was set up directly from the 1474 edition and not through the intervention of that state represented by my copy. These are the significant points:

[5] Signatures k1, k2 and k4 of the 1474 edition correspond to i7, i8 and k2 of the 1477 printing.
[6] For a very similar case, compare the article ("The Creation of a Ghost") by Dr. M. E. Kronenberg (*PBSA*, XLIX [1955], 249-252). This concerns the "manufactured" edition of the *Geestelijke Minnebrief* [Schoonhoven, Canonici apud S. Michaelem, 1500] in the Pierpont Morgan Library (PML 660).
[7] The *Indice* (no. 3931) lists copies at Velletri and Vicenza which I have not seen. The copy credited to Torino is not a Beretin Convento edition at all, but is an example of Mr. Rosenwald's edition 8.
[8] It was the search for an explanation for these leaves (the reprinted ones in my 1477 *Fiore*) that first caused me to examine all the editions claiming to have been issued at the press Nel Beretin Convento della Ca Grande. The definition "Vatican state" is used (for convenience) to identify the copies of this issue.

(1) On signature [b1] of the 1474 edition, line 9 ends a sentence with the word "conuieni"; line 10 is indented and the first word is "Aristotile." The same situation prevails in the Vatican "state" of the 1477 edition,[9] while my copy has line 10 beginning "uieni. Aristotile . . ." Now it may (perhaps) be possible that by sheer accident the line endings of the 1474 edition and the Vatican state might agree even though not directly related—but how can one account for the exceptional indentation at exactly the same place unless one assumes that the Vatican text was set up from the 1474 print?

(2) At line 17 on the verso of the same leaf, one reads in the 1474 text: "Capitulo viii de le done:". In both states of the 1477 edition the chapter is correctly numbered "six,"[10] but the Vatican copy offers "Capitulo vi de le donne.", while my copy has "Capitulo. vi. De le donne." If the Vatican text were a reprint of mine, then one would expect the same punctuation and capitalization, and not the accidental return to an earlier style.

(3) In lines 11-12 on the seventh leaf (recto) of the second quire in the 1474 print, one reads the words: "e questa se chiama propria tristeza." For "propria" the Vatican state has a contraction which looks very much like "pprīa". While the abbreviation for "pro" is the standard one for the period, the dot over the *i* seems to have been damaged and the character now looks like an *i* with a nasal bar (*m*-stroke) over it. This could certainly account for the reading in my copy, where "p prima" is found to the utter confusion of the sense. In any case, no other explanation for this curious text occurs to me.[11]

The inference to be drawn from these examples is certainly that the 1474 edition was the immediate predecessor of the standard (or Vatican) text of the 1477 printing, and that the state in my copy is a later resetting. The question that now presents itself concerns the reason for the existence of the two states. The reprinting of such sheets is of relatively common occurrence among the fifteenth-century books. The only satisfactory explanation for their presence that I have ever been able to think of is that, in such instances, not enough sheets were available (for one reason or another) to complete the copies on hand; when such a shortage became evident, the printer would simply reset the type and run off the number of copies

[9] The edition 2 *bis* (shortly to be discussed) also has the line ending and the subsequent indentation as the 1474 text.

[10] Edition 2 *bis* reads: "Capitulo vi de le done:" indicating that the number "eight" is peculiar to the 1474 edition.

[11] In b2, line 9, the 1474 edition and Vatican text have "Salamon" while my copy offers "Salamone." In b2^v, l. 2, the same two texts have "sotieza" where mine has "sotileza." My text has "de lalegreza" at b7, l. 8, where the other two print "dalegreza." In line 21 of the same page, my copy has "Poeta" while the other two have "Profeta." Such examples as these serve to emphasize the fact that the Vatican text descends directly from the 1474 edition and is not dependent on the state found in my copy.

needed.[12] This seems to be the only theory that will satisfactorily explain the existing facts.

## III

An edition of the *Fiore di virtù* has long been known in the annals of bibliography which contains the rhymed colophon of the Beretin Convento text,[13] though it is certain that this edition was not even printed in Venice. The great incunabula catalogue of the British Museum assigns the printing to another monastic press, that established in the Convent "Apud Sanctum Jacobum de Ripoli" in the Via della Scala in Florence. To its bibliographical description, the BMC adds the note:[14]

The colophon shows that this is reprinted from one of the two editions printed nel Beretin Convento at Venice in 1474 and 1477. If its model is that of 1474 (IA. 20412), the date 1477 here given in the colophon must be that of printing, otherwise the date 23 October 1477 of the second Venetian edition (IA. 20424) supplies a terminus post quem only. The alterations in type 117 R. made in this book presumably preclude its being earlier than the concluding months of the year 1477, but two editions of the Fior di virtù are recorded for the year 1483, the later, finished by 23 September, being printed on paper watermarked with a cross, and as this is the watermark found in the present book, it may perhaps represent a revival in 1483 of type 117 R. slightly modified. The present book is Reichling 180, while Hain 7100 apparently records another reprint of the same nature.

It was with the hope of settling this problem that the present writer cheerfully set off on a quest which has led into many by-ways. One of the methods of approach was necessarily a textual one, and this gradually became more and more extended. In the long run, the eleven earliest editions were examined in regard to a variety of specific examples where the editions gave evidence of falling into distinct groups or "families"; a number of other fifteenth-century editions, and a few later printings that were conveniently at hand

[12] I have discussed this problem on a number of occasions; compare my "Variants in English Incunabula," "Observations on Two Caxton Variants," and "The Walters *Polycronicon* of 1495," all printed *supra*.

[13] The text here reads: "Delle uirtu ison chiamato el fiore Le feste almeno leg|| gimi per amore. Fu rinnouato nel mille quattro cen||to Septanta septe nel beretim [*sic*] conuento. Della chasa || grande sichiama la chiesa. Grande ornamento della || alma uinesia." The compositor had apparently failed to realize the verse form of the prototype.

[14] BMC VI:621. The *Indice* (no. 3932) dates this edition as "dopo il 23 X 1477."

were occasionally drawn upon for their readings.[15] The twenty-four editions thus consulted were the following:[16]

| *Rosen-wald*[17] | *Imprint* | *Reference* | *Copy consulted* |
|---|---|---|---|
| 1 | [Venice: Adam of Ambergau, 1471] | 3927 | Florence N |
| 2 | Venice: [Jenson], 29 April 1474 | 3929 | Morgan |
| [2 bis] | Venice: Nel Beretin Convento, 1474 | [R 7098] | Venice M |
| 3 | Venice: Nel Beretin Convento, 1474 | 3928 | Morgan |
| 4 | Vicenza: [Achates], 1475 | 3930 | Florence N |
| 6 | Venice: Nel Beretin Convento, 23 Oct. 1477 | 3931 | Bühler |
| [6 bis] | Venice: Nel Beretin Convento, 1477 | H 7100 | [Not seen] |
| 7 | [Florence: Ripoli Press, 1477] | 3932 | London BM |
| 8 | "Venice: Nel Beretin Convento, 1477" | Pell 4804 | Paris BN; Torino N |
| 9 | Florence: Ripoli Press, [1477] | 3933 | "    " |
| 10 | [Rome: Bulle, 1478] | H 7092 | Morgan |
| 11 | [Rome: Guldinbeck, 1478] | BMC IV:70 | Bühler |
| 24 | [Rome: Plannck], 30 June 1484 | 3943 | Huntington |
| 30 | Florence: Bonaccorsi & Francisci, 1488 | 3949 | Bühler |
| 32 | Treviso: Manzolus, "1489" | 3951 | Bryn Mawr |
| 39 | Florence: [Libri], 1491 | — | Rosenwald |
| 59 | Florence: [Compagnia del Drago], 1498 | 3965 | Florence N |
| A | Milan: Turate, 20 Nov. 1502 | | Morgan |
| B | Milan: Vimercato, 1524 | | Bühler |
| C | Treviso: Righettini, 1666 | | " |
| D[18] | Padua: Comino, 1751 | | " |
| E | Udine: Murero, 1756 | | " |
| F | Bologna: Sassi, 1772 | | " |
| G | Bologna: Nella Stamperia di S. Tommaso d'Aquino, 1782 | | " |
| H | Florence: Brazzini, 1818 | | " |

[15] With the exception of no. 24, I have seen either the originals or photocopies of all the volumes here discussed. For full particulars of the Huntington copy of no. 24, I am much obliged to Mr. Carey S. Bliss. Mr. George D. Painter has, as always, been kindness itself in replying to my many queries regarding books in the British Museum. I am also obliged to Dr. Elizabeth Mongan for details relative to the 1491 edition, and to Miss Janet M. Agnew and Miss Pamela Reilly for giving me such ready access to the Goodhart-Bryn Mawr copy of no. 32 and for specific details relating to this book.

[16] Two other bibliographies will be repeatedly cited in this study under the sigla H (Ludwig Hain, *Repertorium bibliographicum* [Stuttgart, 1826-1838]) and R (Dietrich Reichling, *Appendices ad Hainii-Copingeri Repertorium bibliographicum* [Munich, 1905-1914]). Also occasionally cited (as Pell) is Marie Pellechet, *Catalogue général des incunables des bibliothèques publiques de France* (Paris, 1897-1909). Unless otherwise noted, the reference number refers to the *Indice*.

[17] Mr. Rosenwald's no. 5, being one of the French texts about which I have written (compare note 1), will here be omitted since it clearly has nothing to do with the Italian texts.

[18] Edition D, according to the preface in that volume, is an attempt to establish a

Only three editions require special comment here; these are 2 *bis*, 6 *bis*, and 8. The edition 2 *bis* has not been previously identified as a separate printing, though it is listed by Hain-Reichling 7098. This is not the same as Hain 7098, which (no. 3 above) is also identified as BMC V:238; so far as I am aware, the only copy known is in the Biblioteca Marciana at Venice (no. 40231). It also has the rhymed colophon indicating that it was printed at the Beretin Convento in 1474; for reasons shortly to be set forth, it is certainly the earlier of the two editions with this date. I have not seen, nor indeed located, a copy of 6 *bis*, but its existence is attested under Hain 7100.[19] It shares the following particulars with nos. 7, 8, and 9, and would seem to be responsible for their having: (1) the rhymed colophon of the 1477 edition (but without mention of month and day) and (2) the line "Lodato sia Iesu e la sua dolze Madre Vergine Maria", which occurs in no other (genuine) Beretin Convento edition.[20] Under 8, we find a pseudo-Beretin Convento edition. The copy in the University Library at Cambridge was recently assigned by Mr. J. C. T. Oates to the Venetian press of Erhard Ratdolt.[21] The present writer has set forth elsewhere his reasons for assigning this edition to Eucharius Silber at Rome.[22] In any case, as we shall see, this edition is not textually related to the Venetian printings but adheres to the Ripoli tradition.

The only certain way to arrive at a possible relationship between the several editions is to examine a number of specific passages where (relatively) important differences occur. It may seem that the varia-

---

pure text based on manuscripts and is thus not related to the other editions here noted. The title-page of edition H makes it clear that the work was now (1818) primarily a children's book ("utilissimo a' Fanciulli").

[19] See also the statement from BMC VI:621 cited above. The fact that this edition may have disappeared since Hain's day need cause no surprise. The rarity of the copies of the early editions has already been stressed. Only the Morgan copy of no. 10 is recorded and, until recently, the British Museum appeared to own the only copy of edition 11. The copy of this printing which I recently secured has somewhat literally been "read to pieces" and is incomplete at the end. The British Museum's example is also imperfect.

[20] This appears below the verse colophon where the details of the exact date appear in edition 6.

[21] J. C. T. Oates, *A Catalogue of the Fifteenth-Century Printed Books in the University Library Cambridge* (Cambridge, 1954), p. 311, no. 1765.

[22] See my review of Oates's catalogue in *PBSA*, XLIX (1955), 82-84. As I am kindly informed by M. Jacques Guignard, Conservateur à la Bibliothèque Nationale, the copy at Paris is also assigned by them to the press of Eucharius Silber. A third copy is found at Torino (see note 7 above).

tions are of the slightest sort—but such slight *variae lectiones* are all one can expect to find in a text so well distributed and popular. There is cited below the "exempio" of the Beaver from the chapter on Peace (XI).[23] It will speedily be seen that the first three quotations are quite independent of one another and that the first, judging from the style and orthography, was apparently based on a manuscript of considerably earlier date than 1471.[24]

E puose apropiare la uirtu de la paxe alo chastorno che una bestia che sa per natura perche li chazadori lo ua chazando zoe per li suo parechi che sono da zerte medesine si che lo uien a tanto che lo non possa fuzere e lo si li prende conli denti e tiraselli fuora del chorpo: e lasali chazere in terra a zoe che li chazadori li abiano e lasino andare lui a zoe che lo possa uiuere in paxe. (1)

Et puossi apropriar la pace al castoreo il quale intende per natura perche i cacciatori il uanno cacciando & persequendo zoe per hauer li suoi coioni iquali son boni ad certe medecine: Et uedendo esser persequitato & che non possi scampare se gli caua cum gli denti & zetali in terra & lassali stare accio che li cacciatori l'habbiano: Et chel possa doppo uiuere in pace. (2)

Et puose apropriare la pace al Castorio che e uno animale che sa per natura: per che li cazadori lo ua perseguendo cioe per li suo testicoli: per che sono medicinali a certe infirmitade: si che quando lo e perseguito e uede che non possa piu scampare: lo se piglia li parechi cum li denti e taiaseli uia a cio che li cazadori li habia: e che ello possa scampare uia e uiuere in pace. (2 *bis*)

The remaining editions are, however, closely related to 2 *bis*—but with a few significant variants. In place of the first "testicoli," one finds "coglioni" in 3, 4, 6, 7, 8, 9, 24, and 32, while "testicoli" occurs in 10, 11, 30, 39, 59, A, B, C, E, F, G, and H. Only 11 has "li parechi" as 2 *bis* (E and H simply have "gli"); editions 3, 4, 6, 7, 8, 9, 24, and 32 have "coglioni", while "testiculi" is reported by 10, 30, 39, 59, A, B, C, F, and G.[25]

[23] Although the numbering of the chapters varies in the several editions, that number found in the Library of Congress edition (based on no. 39) has always been used in order to simplify the location of the excerpt.

[24] Since many of the arguments here presented are based on misprints, misread contractions, irregular punctuation, broken characters, etc., the texts are printed as they appear in the volumes without correction or emendation. Occasionally when a particularly obscure or impossible reading needs emphasizing, a "*sic*" has been added. It is, of course, largely on the recurrence of errors that the opinions here set forth are based, so that it is of prime importance that these be preserved in the passages cited.

[25] This is one of the relatively few instances where editions 30, 39, and 59 depart from the "Ripoli tradition." The shifting from one word to another may here be attributed to the desire to find an expression "meno indecente" rather than to any dialectal tendency.

In the well-known "keenings" over the bier of Alexander ("Tris-teza"—Chapter X), this saying is recorded:[26]

e dal fino dise chi uedea Alexandro temea de lui e mo quelli chel uede no*n* nano [*sic*] tema. (1)

Dalphino disse quegli che non uedeuano Alexa*n*dro haueuano paura d*e* lui: Et hora quelli chel ued*e*no nol timeno niente. (2)

Delfino dice: queli che non uideano Alexandro haueano paura de lui E hora queli che lo uedeno no*n* lo temeno niente. (2 *bis*)

Again 1 is outside the tradition of the other printings, but 2 is reason-ably close to 2 *bis*. However, only 10 and 11 have the text precisely as in 2 *bis*; all the others differ in one material point.[27]

Now it happens that in 2 *bis* the last line on signature [b8] verso contains the words: "hora queli . . . niente." When the second 1474 Beretin Convento edition (3) was printed, this line (except "hora" which had been absorbed into the penultimate line) was omitted[28] and the text now read: "Delfino dice: queli che no*n* uideano Alexan-dro haueano paura di lui e hora ‖ Prisia*n*o dice . . ." Although this made incomplete sense, this text was repeated by 4, 6, and 32. The Rome edition of 1484 (no. 24) sought to correct this awkward text by ending the sentence very simply at "de lui"; with this A and B concurred.[29] The first Ripoli printing (9),[30] sensing an omission,

---

[26] In the *editio princeps*, this saying is found at the end of the quote attributed to "Barbaricon," not as a saw attached to a philosopher named Delfino.

[27] In the example of the Beaver, edition 11 has the exact same text as no. 2 *bis*, while no. 10 shows a small emendation. This proves that no. 11 could not have been set from no. 10.

[28] The reason for the omission of this line is plainly evident and most curious. In edition 2 *bis*, we find that on signature [b8$^v$] the compositor forgot to leave a blank line between the end of a paragraph and the heading for the next (reading "Capitulo viiii de la tristeza" in error for "Exempio"). When edition 3 was com-posed, the printer inserted the blank line where needed. This, of course, left him with an extra line for that page. We shall never know whether he intended to carry this line over to the next page and then forgot about doing so, or whether he simply con-cluded that no one would note the difference; why, then, should he bother to squeeze an extra line into a page which he could so easily follow line for line at little trouble and no complication!

[29] Since edition 24 differs from no. 8, it is clear that the Roman editions are not directly related. In editions C, F, and G, the text is reduced to: "Vn' altro disse. Quelli, che non vedeuano Alessandro, haueuano paura di lui." The philosophers are not identified in these texts. Possibly because the saying was so obviously corrupt, it was omitted by editions E and H. Edition D prints: "Dalfino dice: Quegli che non vedeano Alessandro, aveano tema di lui; ora quegli che'l veggono, nol temono ni-ente."

[30] For the order of the Ripoli editions, see below.

emended the passage to read: "Delfino dice. Quegli che no*n* uedeano alexandro haueuano paura di lui: & hora quegli che lo ueggono no*n* ha*n*no paura. Prisiano . . ." This is also the text of 7, 8, 30, 39, and 59.

From these two examples a pattern begins to emerge which resolves itself into the stemma given below for the earliest editions. Certain relationships still remain to be justified in individual analyses.

IV

We may next examine the two Roman printings that derive directly from the first Beretin Convento edition. That this printing (2 *bis*) was the direct ancestor of these two has already been suggested by the examples previously cited and will be further demonstrated in instances yet to be examined. The problem that now remains to be solved is to determine how the Guldinbeck and Bulle texts relate to each other.

A number of passages (only one need be cited here) prove that the two printings are indeed related and have not come separately from the Venetian edition. In the "exempio" on Ira (Chapter XII), one finds in edition 2 *bis*: "Sancto Gregorio dice tre remedii se fano contra lirato *etc.*" Both Roman editions here have the same misprint;[31] thus Guldinbeck has: "santo Gregorio tre dice remedii se fano co*n*tra lirato *etc.*" This was also the text as printed by Bulle, though the Morgan copy has been corrected by manuscript emendation. Clearly, both editions could not have made the same slip at this place quite independently.

Since these editions reveal that they are related, we must now inquire into the nature of this relationship. Fortunately, this too can be settled with certainty.[32] In the section on Superbia (Chapter XXXVI), the Venetian prototype has: "Job dice se la superbia andase fina ale nuole e tocase el cielo: ala fine retorna in niuula." With this statement Bartholomaeus Guldinbeck agrees, but Johann Bulle concludes his text with the words: ". . . e ala fine retorna in uilamento."[33]

---

[31] It would be an impossible coincidence to suppose that both editions, set independently from the same Venetian edition, could make the same slip at this place.

[32] One may here recall the example, cited above, from the account of the Beaver where only edition 11 follows no. 2 *bis* in having "li parechi" and edition 10 prints "li testiculi."

[33] Here the editions fall into a number of distinct groups. The first two editions, as usual, stand completely outside the orderly arrangements of the groups. Edition 1 has: "Job dise se la superbia a*n*dasse ale nole el so chore tochase lo zielo ale fin torna

It is apparent that the compositor of the Bulle edition either misunderstood his "Vorlage" or wished to improve on it, and thus substituted his own wording. The Guldinbeck printing is therefore certainly the earlier, for one could hardly believe that a compositor would accidentally return to the original reading when he had another, equally suitable, variant before him.[34] This makes it apparent that the Guldinbeck edition could not have been set from the Bulle text.[35] Since, however, we have seen that the two are related, we must conclude that Bulle's compositor worked directly from the Guldinbeck edition.

## V

From the example of the philosophers at the bier of Alexander, we learned in what manner the second 1474 Beretin Convento edition differed from the first; also that editions 4, 6, and 32 omit the identical words wanting in no. 3. Other instances may be cited to prove that the texts are descended from the same original.

Under "Humilita" (Chapter XXXV), the *Fiore* lists four virtues stemming from humility. The last of these is described by edition 2 *bis* as: "La quarta sie gratification*e*. cioe a meritar e recognoser lo

in negota." Number 2 prints: "Job dice. se la sup*er*bia montasse fino ale nuuole & toccasse il cielo: a la fine tornerebbe i*n* niente." Editions 3, 4, 6, 24, 32, A-D, and F-G also follow the order: nuvole - cielo - nuvola; the saying is wanting in E and H. Nos. 24, 32, A-C, and F-G print "sopra le nuole." The first Ripoli edition (9) offers: "Job dice se la superbia andassi infino al cielo & toccassi le nuuole alla fine ritornasi in nuuola." With this order, numbers 7, 8, 30, 39, and 59 agree, though for "ritornasi" all the others print "si ritorna." Editions 30, 39, and 59 offer the further variant reading "la mia superbia." Edition D has: "Giobbe dice: Se la superbia andasse infino a' nugoli, e toccasse il cielo, alla fine tornerebbe in terra" with the variants "neente *or* incotta" for the last word.

[34] In the *exempio* of Largato given under the chapter on "Joy" (IX), edition 2 *bis* describes the result of the autopsy in these words: "Et facendo aprire per mezo el corpo: Trouaro || [folio b7] no scrito i*n* lo suo cuore: dolce amor mio Iesu cristo." Edition 10 prints: "e facendo aprire per mezo el corpo trouarono scritto || in lo suo cuore. dolce amor mio Iesu cristo" while no. 11 has: "et face*n*do aprire p*er* mezo el corpo. Trauaro [*sic*] no scrito || in lo suo cuore. dolce amor mio Iesu cristo." Now it is perfectly evident how Guldinbeck might have arrived at his text because of the division of the words and the capitalization in edition 2 *bis*, but if he was setting up his text from Bulle's edition it is difficult to see how he arrived at his text and the use of upper case "T."

[35] In the example at the tomb of Alexander, editions 2 *bis* and 11 both name the philosopher as "Barbalico" where number 10 has "Barcalico." If edition 11 was set from 10, one would expect to find the same name in both editions.

seruitio che se receue."[36] The second 1474 edition put out by the Beretin Convento press (3) inserts the word "grato" between "recognoser" and "lo seruitio." This insertion is found only in the Vicenza (4), Treviso (32),[37] and the two Milanese editions (A and B) of our list. The Ripoli editions and the texts dependent on them (7, 8, 9, 30, 39, and 59) here offer: "La quarta e gratificatione cioe a meritare & ricognoscere el seruigio e beneficio che si riceue."[38]

The *Fiore di virtù*, under "Constantia" (Chapter XXXI), quite properly provides a story concerning King Constantine; here the King, as related in 2 *bis*, asks his people to await the verdict of their gods which he will go to seek ("*in questo mezo io andare a parlare ali nostri dei*").[39] Instead of the first person singular future (*andaro* = modern *andrò*) as required by the sense, 2 *bis* misprints the infinitive (*andare*). Editions 3 and 4 perpetuate this slip, and this also appears in Guldinbeck's text (11). Johann Bulle (10) corrected the infinitive (or rather, miscorrected it into "*endaro*"), while the Treviso (32), Rome (24), and Milanese (A & B) editions have "andaro." The 1477 Beretin Convento printing (6), noticing the grammatical slip in its *Vorlage*, altered the text into reading: "*in questo mezo io uoglio andare a parlare a li nostri dei.*" This revision was accepted by all texts of the Ripoli tradition (7, 8, 9, 30, 39, and 59).[40]

The Treviso *Fiore di virtù* (32)[41] has its own problem of dating. The colophon states that the book was printed by Michael Manzolus: "Nel anno MCCCCLXXXViiii a di xv di Ienaro. Principe di Viniegia Lo inclyto & magnanimo huomo Ioanni Mozenico." Despite the presence of these precise and comforting particulars, it is absolutely

---

[36] The first two editions again differ sharply from the standard text. No. 1 has: "e la quarta sie la gratificazione che e acognoscere e ameritar li seruisi che lie fato." Edition 2 offers: "La quinta [4 is omitted] sie gratitudine cioe a cognoscer & remunerar altri de' beneficii receputi."

[37] The word "grato" is also found in the dependent edition no. 24 (on which, see below) but is omitted by nos. 6, 10, and 11. For "gratitude," editions A and B have "significatione;" these two texts also insert "grato."

[38] Edition 9, actually—as we shall see—the earliest of the Ripoli texts, here observes a slightly different arrangement: "La quarta e gratificatione cioe a meritare e ricognoscere el benefitio & seruigio che si riceue."

[39] Edition 1 has: "& io in questo mezo andaro: e parlaro con li nostri dei." The second edition reads: "& in questo mezo io parlero ali nostri dei."

[40] Editions 7, 8, and 9 have "io uoglio andare & parlare," while nos. 30, 39, and 59 have "io uoglio andare a parlare."

[41] A full descripton of this edition is given by Reichling under number 515 from the Naples copy, though he failed to realize that the date as given in the book was impossible.

certain that the book, contrary to the position it occupies in Mr. Rosenwald's list and in the Italian official *Indice* (no. 3951), could not have been printed on 15 January 1489, for on that date the Doge of Venice was Agostino Barbarigo.[42] Since Giovanni Mocenigo was Doge from 18 May 1478 to 4 November 1485, the only possible way to account for the date of the colophon is that an extra "X" found its way into it. Consequently, this Manzolus edition can be dated with some certainty as having been printed on 15 January 1479.[43]

The Treviso volume, then, is later than the Vicenza one, with its printed date of 1475, and it now becomes necessary to discover whether the Treviso text was set from this edition or whether they both descended independently from their common ancestor (edition no. 3). Though the Vicenza edition bears the earlier date, we need not rely solely on this to prove that it could not derive from the Treviso *Fiore*. Through the frequent error of haplography, Manzolus prints in the chapter on "Vanagloria" (XXX):

Sancto Augustino dice: non iudicar mai alchuno per el dire de le parole: ma per el far de le opere: perche la magior parte de le persone: sono uane & piene de parole: ma per li facti: non porai falire.

The other fifteenth-century editions of our list (with one exception)[44] all attribute this saying to Seneca, while attaching to St. Augustine the proverb: "Sancto Augustin dice: adir bene: e far male: non e altro che inganar si insteso" (edition 3). If the Vicenza edition had developed from Manzolus's, one would expect to find the same "omissio ex homoeoteleuto" (from "Sancto Augustin *dice*" to "Seneca *dice*") therein.

It can also be proved, however, that the text of the Treviso edition goes straight back to the Venetian source, and not through the inter-

[42] Succeeding to the rule of Giovanni Mocenigo was Marco Barbarigo, who was elected Doge on 19 November 1485 and died 14 August 1486. He was succeeded by his brother Agostino (ruled 30 August 1486-20 September 1501), this being the only example in Venetian history where a Doge was immediately followed by another member of the same family. Compare A. Cappelli, *Cronologia, cronografia e calendario perpetuo* (Milan, 1952), p. 347, and the *Enciclopedia italiana* (Rome, 1929-1939), VI, 131.

[43] It seems unlikely that the wrong date can be accounted for by the supposition that the "V" was accidentally added. The last known book produced by Manzolus in Treviso is dated 27 March 1482 (BMC VI:886), so that it is unlikely that the *Fiore* was completed after an interval of almost two years (15 January 1484).

[44] The significance of edition 32 is stressed by the fact that it is not only the source for the other Treviso editions but also for nos. 24, A-C, and F-G, at least for some readings (cf. note 33). Here these editions have the text as in no. 32.

vention of the Vicenza printing. There are omissions and errors which clearly establish this. In the study of "Prudentia" (Chapter XIX), the Venetian prototype preserves two sayings:[45]

anchora dice: alo seruo sauio: serui liberalme*n*te: a*n*chora dice i*n* la tua zo-ue*n*tu i*m*para scie*n*tia e dotrina e mai no [*sic*] manchare fine ali cauelli canuti:

The Vicenza *Fiore* omits the first proverb, but it is present in the Treviso edition. So also in the example of the Basilisk ("Crudelitade," Chapter XIV), who scorches everything "per lo suo crudelissimo fiado: che uiene fuora del suo uenenoso corpo," the Vicenza text differs from its contemporaries. There the land is laid waste simply "per lo suo uene*n*oso corpo." In this case, it is clear that the eye of the compositor of the Vicenza edition traveled from the first "suo" to the second, and we thus have another omission as the result of identical readings. In both instances, the Treviso *Fiore di virtù* gives the full text, thus providing adequate proof for the fact that it is directly descended from the second Beretin Convento edition of the year 1474.[46]

## VI

We come now to the problem which was the *fons et origo* of the investigation into the nature of the Ripoli text—namely, from which Beretin Convento edition did the Ripoli series derive? A considerable number of minor variants makes it perfectly certain that editions 7, 8, and 9 were based on no. 6; two examples will suffice to establish this fact.

[45] Two curious variants may here be noted. Edition 1 reads: "e anchora el scriuano sauio scriue liberame*n*te," and Edition D has: "Ancora: Il servo savio sappia servire liberamente."

[46] A broken piece of type here offers interesting evidence. In the story under Misericordia (XIII), the pirate says to Alexander (edition 3): "Et tu per che uai cum gran || de multitudine de gente: sei chiamato signore:". The second "i" in "multitudine" is here badly broken and the character looks very much like a colon. In the Vicenza edition (4) the text reads: "Et tu || per che uai cum gran de multitudine: ne de gente: sei || chiamato signore:". It is clear what happened in this case. The compositor of 4, having edition 3 before him, set "gran de multitudine" due to the line-ending of his prototype. He then picked up again at the colon, but his eye wandered to the broken character rather than to the true colon; hence he printed the otherwise senseless "ne de gente." Edition 32 has "multitudine de gente." Again, under Cruelty (XIV), edition 3 has: "La terza si e no*n* uolere perdonare lizurie," while 4 offers: "La terza sie non uolere perdonare luzurie." Clearly the compositor here misread the abbreviation. The other editions agree with no. 32 in having: ". . . perdonare le iniurie."

Under "Ira" (Chapter XII), the first Beretin Convento text (2 *bis*) quotes Saint Augustine to the effect that five conditions make war permissible: "Per la fede: per la iustitia: per hauer pace: per stare in liberta: Et per fugire forza." The 1477 edition (6), on the other hand, numbers these reasons in this fashion: "Prima per la fede. Seconda per la Iustitia. Terza per hauer pace. Quarta per stare *in* liberta. Quinta per fugire forza." These reasons also remain unnumbered in the editions: 1-4, 10-11, 24, 32, A-D and F-G.[47] The Florentine editions together with Silber's text (viz. nos. 7-9, 30, 39, and 59) supply the numeration.[48]

A second, and most instructive, example will be found in the chapter on "Corectione" (XVII). Here are listed the ten scourges which God visited upon the Egyptians (as related in Exodus).[49] Disregarding in this case the first two printings, we may note that the first Beretin Convento edition offers for the eighth scourge: "La otaua fo mortalita de tuti li primogeniti de egito."[50] Due to misnumbering, this scourge becomes "La nona" in edition no. 3, and with this the Vicenza text (4) agrees. The next Beretin Convento printing (6) partly corrects the error, and the text now appears as: "La ottaua mortalita de tutti li primogeniti de egipto."[51] The texts of the Ripoli tradition (nos. 7-9) similarly omit the copulative verb ("fo") at this place, though they have it in the other scourges where needed. Thus we may be certain that editions 7-9 are related. The first and third of these are, despite the evidence afforded by the verse colophon (here printed as prose) which claims the edition for the Beretin Convento, the products of the Florentine press established in the

[47] This passage is omitted by the shortened versions E and H.

[48] In the story of the wild ass who will drink only clear water ("Abstinentia"— XXXVII), edition 1 has: "& selo ua al flume e ueda chel sia torbado," while 2 prints: "& sel ua a riuo o a fiume che sia turbido." In 2 *bis*, 3, 4, 10, 11, 24, 32, A, and B, we find "al fiume o ala fontana;" in 6, 7, 8, 9, 30, 39, and 59, one finds "al fiume o ala fonte." In editions C-H, there is simply "al fiume."

[49] The crickets of the seventh scourge appear as "cavalete" in nos. 2 *bis*, 3, 4, 6, 10, 11, 24, 32, A-C and E-H; in the texts of the Ripoli tradition (7, 8, 9, 30, 39, and 59) as well as in edition D the name is "grilli." This appears to be the word preferred by the Florentines. We may recall that to this very day the *Festa del Grillo* is celebrated in Florence on Ascension Day. The *editio princeps* has "locuste."

[50] This is also the reading in nos. 10, 11, 24, 32, E, G, and H.

[51] In edition 1, one reads: "e la nona si fo mortalita de tuti li primigieniti de egypto." In no. 2, it is: "La septima si fu mortalita de tutti suoi animali," which appears as scourge six in edition D. Editions A-C and F have: "la octaua fu la mortalita de tutti gli primogeniti di egypto."

nunnery "Apud Sanctum Jacobum de Ripoli" in the Via della Scala. Edition no. 8, as was stated above, was printed in Rome by Eucharius Silber, though the colophon (in verse form) also proclaims the book as from the Venetian press.[52]

That neither of the Ripoli editions could have been copied from Silber is proved by a number of omissions peculiar to this faulty text. In the chapter on Liberality (XV) alone, there are two omissions "ob homoeoteleuton." One of the sayings proper to this chapter is given by edition no. 6 as: "Anchora dice: se tu domandi adaltri domanda cosa iusta: per che e pacia a domandar cosa che se posa negar cum rasone." Silber omits "domandi adaltri," though this is present in the Ripoli editions.[53] The anecdote anent King Antigonus further illustrates this point; it reads in the Beretin Convento (6) text:[54]

lo contrario de questo fece lo Re Antigono: lo quale per trouar casone de non fare lo seruitio che iera domandato: che siandoli domandata una cosa picola: respose che non se conuenia alui de dare una picola cosa: siando Re: Et siandoli poi domandata una gran cosa Respose: non se conuiene ati domandare: ni receuere cosi gran cosa.

The Silber printing skips, obviously the result of an eye slip, everything between the first "non se" and "conuiene." Both Ripoli editions have the text substantially as in the Venetian prototype; thus

[52] In 1515, Marcello Silber, the son of Eucharius Silber (alias Frank) of Würzburg, also put out an edition of the *Fiore di virtù*. The colophon there reads:

Delle virtù io son chiamato el Fiore,
E son composto a darti documento.
Le feste almen leggemi per amore;
Se tu il fai ti troverai contento.
Nel mille cinquecento del Signore,
E quindici anni, se io ben ramento,
Fu rinovato in la città di Roma,
La qual del mondo tiene la corona.

Compare Fernanda Ascarelli, *La tipografia cinquecentina italiana* (Florence, 1953), pp. 62-63, and edition D, p. 11.

[53] All the other editions have the full text. This again suggests that Stephan Plannck (24) did not utilize the printing of the text by Silber.

[54] The edition by Stephan Plannck does not have the omission. Edition C (similarly F and G) prints: "Il contrario fece il Rè Antigono, ilquale per ritrouare cagione di non fare il seruigio, che li era dimandato à quello, che li domandaua vna gran cosa, rispose. Non conuiene à te dimandare questa cosa così grande." Editions E and H have: "Il contrario fece il Re Antigono, il quale per trovar cagione di non far il servigio a quello, che gli dimandava una gran cosa, rispose: Non conviene a te dimandare, nè ricevere cosa così grande."

it is as certain as bibliographical truth can be that the Silber edition is the last of the three.[55]

Equally, as shown in the chart, there can be no doubt that edition no. 9 is earlier than no. 7. In Chapter XVIII ("De le losenge"), all Beretin Convento editions include a saying attributed to Hermes; it may be found just before that by Varro at the end of the first "Exempio." In edition 9 the saying reads (comparable to the text in no. 6): "Hermes dice: lo cane ama losso infino che ui truoua da piluchare: e le pechie amano e [sic] fiori infinche sono begli." In similar form, the saying is also given to Hermes by editions 1-4, 10-11, 24, 32, and D; nos. A-C and E-H assign it to Esopo. However, the saying is omitted by nos. 7, 8, and the later Florentine printings (30, 39, and 59).

In "Lusuria" (Chapter XL), the gradual corruption of the text becomes plain. The Beretin Convento edition (no. 6) cites the fourth variety of Lust as: "Lo quarto sie īcesto [sic]: che e quando sono parenti." The compositor for edition 9 misread the abbreviation[56] and produced the reading: "Lo quarto sie questo: che e quando sono parenti." To the next compositor, this must have seemed to be merely a circumlocution, for he cut the text to: "Lo quarto sie: quando sono parenti." This, then, is the reading of editions 7 and 8.[57]

Finally,[58] under "Castita" (Chapter XXXIX), the unexpected in-

---

[55] According to BMC IV:xiv and 103, the earliest book printed by Eucharius Silber in Rome bears the date 20 May 1480. The first appearance of his type 2:88 R², with which the *Fiore di virtù* is printed, is set as late 1484, and this edition may safely be assigned to this period. For the Ripoli editions, a curious bibliographical point may be noted. It was normal for a printer, in his reprints, to reduce the number of printed pages and thus lessen his paper costs. In this case, however, the earlier edition (9) is printed on 46 leaves and in double columns, while the reprint (7) is in single columns and occupies 58 leaves. The colophons of editions 2 *bis*, 3, 6, 6 *bis*, 7, 8, and 9 (no matter where these were printed) all state that the book was produced in Venice, the last line reading: "Grande ornamento de lalma Venesia." In editions 30, 39, and 59, the last line points to "Firenze bella gratiosa & degna." For the same line, no. 4 has: "Vincenza dico ni la cita benigna." Edition B here prints: "Milano bello grarioso [sic] e degno." See also note 52.

[56] Since we do not have the reading of edition 6 *bis*, it is not certain whether the misreading is the fault of the compositor of edition 9 or of its predecessor. In no. 1, we find: "E la terza sie inzesto chie quando uno parente se zonze con la parente," which is closely paralleled by no. 2: "La terza sie incesto zoe quando uno parente si coniunge con una sua parente." Edition D (and H) print: "e la seconda è detta incesto, e questo è usando con propria parente." The full text of the first Beretin Convento edition is: "Lo quarto si e incesto: che e quando sono parenti."

[57] It is also the reading of editions 30, 39, and 59.

[58] See also note 33, where 7 and 8 agree in having "si ritorna" and only 9 has

sertion of a phrase shows the reverse process. Edition no. 6 gives the fourth danger to be avoided by the chaste as: "La quarta sie guardarsi da le rufiane: e da persone che conforti de lusuriare." With this text, edition 9 more or less conforms.[59] However, the compositor who set edition 7 must have read the ampersand and the following "da" twice, for the second Ripoli edition has: "La quarta si e guardarsi dalle ruffiane & etiam dio dalle persone che confortino di Luxuria."[60] This text is also found in the edition put out by Eucharius Silber but not elsewhere outside the "Ripoli group," and it is therefore clear that Silber must have prepared his *Fiore di virtù* from edition no. 7.[61] From the arguments that we have examined above, there is every reason to accept as correct the *stemma* as given.

## VII

It is also possible to date many of the Ripoli editions with full confidence, since the day-book of the press has come down to us.[62] Two editions of the *Fiore di virtù* are mentioned there. The earlier (Nesi LXXIX) was listed as being for sale on 2 January 1483 (f. 104 of the manuscript).[63] A further entry (f. 117) reads: "Ricordo che a di 25 dagosto 1483 incominciamo 300 fior di virtu." This is apparently that edition concerning which the British Museum Catalogue's comment has already been quoted; it is entered as Nesi LXXXV.[64] Since number 9 of Mr. Rosenwald's enumeration has been proved to be the earlier, this must now be dated as having been printed "before 2 January 1483." The later printing, represented by

---

"ritornasi." If 9 were the latest, one would expect the subsequent editions (30, 39, and 59) also to have "ritornasi" but they agree with nos. 7 and 8.

[59] "La quarta sie guardarsi dalle ruffiane & da persone che confortino di luzuria."

[60] Editions 30, 39, and 59 also have the insertion. However, of all the editions descended from 2 *bis*, only 7-9 and G-H have "luzuria," the remainder (including the three Florentine editions, otherwise belonging to the Ripoli tradition) have "lusuriare."

[61] As we have seen, editions 7 and 8 are related. Since it has been shown that no. 7 could not have been set from no. 8, it follows that the contrary must be true.

[62] This day-book has been discussed and excerpted by: Vincenzio Fineschi, *Notizie storiche sopra la stamperia di Ripoli* (Florence, 1781); Pietro Bologna, *La stamperia fiorentina del Monastero di S. Jacopo di Ripoli e le sue edizioni* (Turin, 1893); and Emilia Nesi, *Il diario della stamperia di Ripoli* (Florence, 1903).

[63] According to Nesi (p. 11), the manuscript is: Magliabechiana $\dfrac{6}{x - 143^*}$.

[64] Nesi, p. 96: "Ricordo che a di 23 di detto [Settembre] si fornirono di stampare 300 fiori di virtu."

the British Museum copy IA. 27030, should bear the date "23 September 1483."

We are now in a position to rearrange the earliest editions here under discussion in accordance with those dates and lines of descent which we have established. The new list would be:[65]

| New no. | Rosen- wald no. | Imprint | Reference |
|---|---|---|---|
| I | 1 | [Venice: Adam of Ambergau, 1471] | Indice 3927 |
| II | 2 | Venice: [Nicolas Jenson], 29 April 1474 | H 7091 |
| III | [2 bis] | Venice: Nel Beretin Convento, 1474 | R [not H] 7098 |
| IV | 3 | Venice: Nel Beretin Convento, 1474 | H 7098 |
| V | 4 | Vicenza: [Achates], 1475 | H 7099 |
| VI | 6 | Venice: Nel Beretin Convento, 23 Oct. 1477 | R [not H] 7100 |
| VII | [6 bis] | (?) Venice: Nel Beretin Convento, 1477 (?) | H 7100 |
| VIII | 11 | [Rome: Guldinbeck, 1478] | BMC IV:70 |
| IX | 10 | [Rome: Bulle, 1478] | H 7092 |
| X | 32 | Treviso: Manzolus, 15 January "1479"[66] | R 515 |
| XI | 9 | Florence: Ripoli Press, [b. 2 Jan. 1483] | Pell 4802 |
| XII | 7 | [Florence: Ripoli Press, 23 Sept. 1483] | BMC VI:621 |
| XIII | 8 | [Rome: Silber, after 23 Sept. 1483] | Pell 4804 |

In conclusion, some interesting deductions and general observations may be set forth. We can, first of all, correct an observation in the British Museum's incunabula catalogue (V:238) under the entry for the press "Nel Beretin Convento della Ca Grande"; here it is stated that "the entire known output of this press appears to be catalogued below and includes one book dated 1474, two dated 1477, and one dated 1478." This is not, however, a complete list, since the very first edition of the *Fiore di virtù* by this press, and possibly a second printing of the year 1477, are not here recorded. There is also no mention of the variant issue of that 1477 edition which is described by the catalogue.

[65] The present re-arrangement of the numbers is not meant to reflect any discredit upon the great usefulness of Mr. Rosenwald's list. He relied, of course, upon the records of the Kommission für den Gesamtkatalog der Wiegendrucke, modifying these to suit his purposes. The results of my own investigation are due to research extending over many years and in many different libraries; they are useful chiefly in supplementing Mr. Rosenwald's excellent list, so far as bibliographical details are concerned.

[66] Since the Ripoli editions are no longer assignable to 1477, a number of editions in Mr. Rosenwald's list now intervene between my numbers X and XI. There are seven such editions all dated 1480-1482 (Rosenwald nos. 12-19; no. 15 is a French text, and thus lies outside the scope of this discussion).

This analysis will, almost certainly, provide the bibliophile with some sobering thoughts; he must come to the reluctant conclusion that, for the history of the printed text of the *Fiore di virtù*, the *editio princeps* is quite valueless. Indeed, even the second edition is (relatively speaking) unimportant. An obscure third edition, on the other hand, assumes prime significance as the ancestor of a long line of printed texts, running into the scores of editions. It will give many a bookman, one hopes, pause to reconsider the special significance that we have attached to that "sacred cow"—The First Edition. For here certainly, the importance of the text is totally unrelated to the date of its production. I am equally sure that the case of the *Fiore di virtù* is far from being the sole instance of this perhaps revolutionary concept in the evaluation of early printed books.[67]

It is instructive, too, to note that so prolific a printer as Eucharius Silber neither pirated the text of his Roman predecessors (Johann Bulle and Bartholomaeus Guldinbeck) nor "borrowed" the *Fiore di virtù*, at that very moment on sale in Rome, as printed by his great competitor, Stephan Plannck.[68] How and why, one wonders, did Silber acquire a Florentine imitation of a Venetian edition? The Plannck *Fiore* of 1484 is (presumably) only a reprint of earlier printings by the same press (1481 = Rosenwald no. 16; 1482 = no. 18; and 1483 = no. 20); the evidence at hand suggests that all the Plannck editions descended from the text as printed by Michael Manzolus in Treviso (Rosenwald no. 32).[69] It comes as quite a surprise to discover that Plannck turned to one of the most northerly of Italian presses for his prototype.[70] Why did he not choose one printed nearer to the Eternal City? If neither printer chose to copy any of the Roman editions available to him, why—one may well ask—did he not make use of any of the numberless manuscripts of the *Fiore di virtù* then in circulation?[71]

[67] Compare, for example, the present writer's "The Earliest Editions of Juvenal," *supra.*

[68] The Parisian printers of the early sixteenth century had no scruples about stealing each other's texts; see my "The Edition of the *Ditz moraulx des philosophes* Printed at Paris by Michel Le Noir," *Gutenberg-Jahrbuch*, 1950, 182-185.

[69] See especially notes 33, 37, and 44.

[70] It is possible, of course, that the Bologna edition of 15 August 1480 (Rosenwald no. 13) may be the direct ancestor of the Plannck text and may thus intervene between the two Treviso editions (15 January 1479 and 14 April 1480) and the first Plannck printing. This problem still needs to be investigated.

[71] The number of manuscripts of the *Fiore di virtù* still extant is legion and must have been even greater in the fifteenth century. For the Florentine libraries alone,

After 1491 practically all the editions of this text were illustrated,[72] as befits a book intended (more and more, as the years went on) for the moral guidance of the young and consequently in need of something to hold the children's flagging attention. These woodcuts, too, were used over and over again; they were copied and even re-copied. Further, one can see the blocks passing from the hands of one printer into those of another. The illustrations, too, have an enlightening story to tell—but an investigation of the *Fiore di virtù* along these lines we must necessarily leave to the art historian.

For us, the examination of the texts in the printed volumes of the *Fiore di virtù* has underlined once again the basic principle that a student of literature cannot content himself with examining merely the earliest manuscript or the first printed edition of any given text. Every manuscript and each edition may have its own importance in the history of the transmission, growth, and metamorphosis of a literary artifact; all such literary documents must, therefore, be minutely and properly evaluated by those scholars competent to perform this service.

(From *PBSA* 49 (1955), pp. 315-339).

---

T. Casini lists thirty-eight such volumes ("Appunti sul Fiore di virtù," *Revista critica della letteratura italiana*, III [1886], 154-159).

[72] The edition printed in Florence in 1491 (Rosenwald no. 39) is the first North Italian one that was fully illustrated. For a full list of the other early illustrated editions, cf. Max Sander, *Le livre à figures italien depuis 1467 jusqu'à 1530* (New York, 1941), I, 477-483, nos. 2720-2758 plus five unnumbered entries.

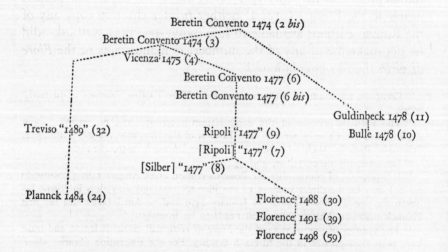

Beretin Convento 1474 (2 *bis*)
Beretin Convento 1474 (3)
Vicenza 1475 (4)
Beretin Convento 1477 (6)
Beretin Convento 1477 (6 *bis*)
Guldinbeck 1478 (11)
Treviso "1489" (32)
Ripoli "1477" (9)
Bulle 1478 (10)
[Ripoli] "1477" (7)
[Silber] "1477" (8)
Plannck 1484 (24)
Florence 1488 (30)
Florence 1491 (39)
Florence 1498 (59)

# CHAPTER B33

## WATERMARKS AND THE DATES OF
## FIFTEENTH-CENTURY BOOKS

NEARLY half a century ago, a landmark now famous in the annals of historical research made its memorable appearance; this was Charles M. Briquet's *Les Filigranes* (Paris, 1907), a work to which many students in varied fields of scholarship still turn daily with gratitude. The value of Briquet's contribution in its broadest implications cannot be questioned, whatever reservations one may entertain in regard to the more precise information to be gleaned from its pages.

For the students of "prototypographica" in 1907, one of Briquet's summaries seemed to hold the greatest potential significance.[1] This concerned the appearance of "filigranes identiques" in the ordinary fifteenth-century formats of paper; according to Briquet's findings (vol. I, p. xx), the extreme limits of their first and last datable occurrence could be determined in this fashion:

> Within 1 to 5 years: 512 instances
> " 6 to 10 " : 255 "
> " 11 to 15 " : 115 "

Thus, 882 of the 978 examples used for this calculation (or 90% of the total) made their initial and final appearance within the limits of fifteen years, the longest recorded extent of duration being 85 years.

Briquet's table further indicated that the use of over half the pa-

---

[1] Compare E. J. Labarre, *Dictionary and Encyclopaedia of Paper and Paper-making* (Oxford, 1952), p. 358: "His general conclusion was that the *probable* employment of a given mark fell within a period of about 30 years at most. In the collection of his data Briquet paid attention almost solely to Mss., paper for which, unless they extended to many sheets, was far more likely to have a long currency than that used for books, since *small* quantities might remain long on hand, while again the varieties of sorts and sizes was great, and the use of paper was not quite so general nor the sorts used so standardized as in later times." This is not quite true since Briquet certainly cited many examples of watermarks from incunabula, as we shall see. Further, the use of paper for the press between 1450 and 1470, must have been insignificant as compared with that used in the production of manuscripts. First of all, the proportion of printing on vellum was then at its highest rate. Secondly, we may recall that prior to 1470 only fourteen presses (established in ten cities) had begun to print, the total production of four of these being quite slight.

pers was confined to a maximum period of five years.[2] Despite these ascertained facts, the theory that "les filigranes" could supply evidence for the dating of incunables was not heartily endorsed by incunabulists. In respect to this, the comment of the British Museum's great catalogue may be cited:

By the aid of M. Briquet's facsimiles it might be possible, according to the method he describes, to use this multiplicity of marks as a means of determining dates. But the method is laborious and not free from uncertainty, so that other kinds of evidence are almost always preferable.[3]

In more recent years, especially since the founding of the Paper Publications Society in 1948, the attention of scholars has again been directed towards the significance of watermarks for the determination of date. It has even been suggested that Briquet's estimates were much too liberal and that the normal elapsed time between the manufacture and the final use of a run of paper was three years, frequently less but sometimes as much as ten years.[4] Naturally enough, such assertions have not gone unchallenged, though one need not, perhaps, go so far as to echo the words of a scholarly Keeper of Printed Books at the British Museum, who publicly stated: "I have no use for watermarks." Sir Henry Thomas was, of course, mildly jesting here, though he was serious enough in his reservations as to their use for dating.[5] Nor can one entirely ignore, in this connection, the statement made (in 1923) by the dean of American experts on paper:[6]

[2] Conversely, we may note that, according to these findings, over 47% of the examples were in use for a period longer than five years, while 96 watermarks (nearly 10% of the total) continued in use for more than fifteen years.

[3] *Catalogue of Books Printed in the XVth Century now in the British Museum* (London, 1908-1949), I, xv.

[4] See, for example, Allan H. Stevenson's estimates in *Briquet's Opuscula* (Hilversum, 1955), p. xxxix. A more hesitant view was expressed by Edward Heawood, *Watermarks mainly of the 17th and 18th Centuries* (Hilversum, 1950), p. 31: "The idea that paper moulds had a fairly long life has been pretty generally held, and the currency of a given mark (in identical form) therefore fairly long—30 years or so according to Briquet. If correct for early periods it is to be questioned as regards later ones."

[5] "Watermarks," *Edinburgh Bibliographical Society Transactions*, II (1946), 449-450. Sir Henry also observed that watermarks "may be able, during certain later periods, to suggest a date (or at any rate a *terminus ante quem non*, as in the simple instance [a dated mark] mentioned above) but rarely a place."

[6] Dard Hunter, *Old Papermaking* ([Chillicothe, Ohio], 1923), p. 65. He also states: "The sheets might have been dated in the watermark and then remained in the mill a great time before the paper was sold, and after being purchased the paper might have been held for years in the warehouse of the printer before being printed upon."

A great deal has been written on watermarking from a historical point of view but their value as a means of determining the dates of paper, books, and prints or the locality where the paper was made, is to be questioned.

The information that watermarks can supply for purposes of dating is beset with several difficulties. First of all, the employment of averages for specific purposes is always hazardous—as observers of scientific facts are well aware. We all recall the story of the man who, in wading through a river, drowned in a channel seven feet deep, having been assured that the average depth was only two feet. Special circumstances may always be present to contradict averages; two such instances are conveniently at hand to illustrate this point. My whole correspondence relating to this article has simply been dated by month and day, and I have suggested to my correspondents that the year can easily be deduced from the watermark in the paper: this happens to provide 1909. In 1956, the Morgan Library issued, as a gift to its Fellows, a facsimile of a previously-unknown Dickens letter; entirely by itself, however, the watermark present in the facsimile would suggest that the edition had been printed forty years ago. The "filigrane" in the Dickens facsimile is—at least so far as I can judge—in the identical state as that found in the printed *Archives of the General Convention* [of the Protestant Episcopal Church in the U. S. A.], New York, 1911-12. It certainly *should* be identical since all the paper (Kelmscott Handmade) comes from a single purchase made prior to 1911. The Library has, from time to time, made varied use of this paper—but there is still enough on hand to print a sizable edition of some reasonably-sized text. These facts relate, of course, to special circumstances. Nevertheless, it would manifestly be impossible, five hundred years after the event, to single out the special circumstances from those which were entirely usual.

There are, obviously, two prime elements of uncertainty in regard to the use of watermarks for purposes of dating; first, no one is quite certain for how long any particular mould could be used (i.e., how long was it possible to make paper with the same watermark) and, secondly, it is not clear how successful the methods for speedy distribution were—or even if this was considered essential or desirable in those days. Estimates for the "life" of a mould vary between half a year and four years;[7] but how can one ever be sure of the value of

---

[7] According to Alfred W. Pollard (*Shakespeare Folios and Quartos* [London, 1909], p. 93), Briquet believed that a device "had a life of about two years before it

such figures in determining the life of any *particular* mould? It could as well be asked: how long will the machine last upon which the present study is being typed? Clearly, the reader will want to know: (1) who made the type-writer (i.e., question of quality); (2) how is it looked after (problem of maintenance); and (3) how much is it used? This last query is certainly as crucial for a mould for making paper, as Alfred Schulte was quick to recognize, as it is for a type-writer. This scholar[8] preferred to estimate that the average pair of moulds could produce half a million sheets before they became unfit for further use, rather than to speculate on the conjectural life of a mould.[9] We know, too, from contemporary records that early paper-makers were not particularly reliable as a source of supply:[10] plagues, floods, droughts, and other inconveniences played havoc with the productivity of the makers and frequently curtailed the essential water-supply for the mills or made it unfit for use.[11]

The dubious facilities for distribution in those days create another factor for uncertainty in the estimates under consideration. As BMC (I:xv) reminds us:[12] "we have to reckon with the existence of middlemen, such as Adolf Rusch, who bought paper from the makers and sold or bartered it to other printers." A most significant time-lag[13] is noted by Adolf Tronnier:

---

lost its shape altogether." Various estimates are given by Alfred Schulte, "Papier-mühlen- und Wasserzeichenforschung," *Gutenberg-Jahrbuch 1934*, p. 22.

[8] Schulte, *op. cit.*, p. 24. The same writer also remarked (in his contribution "C. M. Briquet's Work and the Task of his Successors," *The Briquet Album* [Hilversum, 1952], p. 56): "If, for instance, it is assumed that a paper-mill manufactured only one size and one sort of paper, it would every year require a new pair of moulds. If, however, it made several sorts and sizes, as was nearly always the case, then this single year of possible usage was extended into several or even many calendar years."

[9] Assuming that a certain folio of 200 leaves, in an edition of 200 copies (fairly large for those days), contained equal amounts of three sorts of paper, then the entire edition consumed only 7,000 sheets, or less than 2% of the 500,000 sheets a pair of moulds could produce. An early printer, then, would require in a year's time only a very slight amount of the total production of a mould.

[10] Cf. Oscar Hase, *Die Koberger* (Leipzig, 1885), pp. 71-72. On 17 December 1501, the dealer Friedrich Brechter asked the printer Johann Amerbach to take compassion upon the papermakers ("eyn mytliden haben des bapires halben") with regard to their products (Hase, letter 42, p. XLVIII).

[11] Compare the letter from Anton Koberger to Hans Amerbach (31 Dec. 1498) and that from Thomas Anshelm to Hans Koberger (7 Jan. 1518) printed by Hase, pp. XIX and CXXVII. See also Hans H. Bockwitz, *Papiermacher und Buchdrucker im Zeitalter Gutenbergs* ([Leipzig], 1939), pp. 9-10.

[12] On Rusch, compare also Hase, *op. cit.*, pp. 64-65.

[13] In the Koberger correspondence, we find continuous complaints as to the qual-

Es ist höchst eigentümlich, wenn auch wohl kein Zufall, dass alle die genannten und noch zu nennenden Marken sich ausnahmslos auch in den Strassburger Inkunabeln finden. Auffällig ist dabei, dass sie in Strassburg fast stets ein oder zwei Jahrzehnte früher vorkommen als in Mainz, fast nur in den sechziger und siebziger Jahren.[14]

If one accepts this statement, set forth by an eminent and reliable scholar, it is apparent that the same paper might be available for purchase in two cities, joined together by the easiest means of communication known to the Middle Ages (the river Rhine), at intervals of ten and more years.

We may now particularize and inquire how palaeographers and art historians view the evidence afforded by watermarks for the purpose of dating. One may cite such views as those of Arthur M. Hind ("the date of manufacture [of paper] is only certain as a *terminus a quo*")[15] and Arthur E. Popham[16] ("But in few cases can a watermark, even when it actually contains a date, afford more than an approximate indication of period *post quem*").[17] Palaeographers display similar caution. Regrettably enough, there seems to be no adequate (modern) handbook in English on "Handschriftenkunde,"[18] so that we are obliged to fall back upon the recent judgments of two German scholars:

---

ity of the paper (letters, 7, 8, 49, 50, etc.), much of which was returned by the printer. This contributed an extra delay in the ultimate marketing of some papers.

[14] *Die Missaldrucke Peter Schöffers und seines Sohnes Johann* (Mainz, 1908), p. 81.

[15] *An Introduction to a History of Woodcut* (Boston and New York, 1935), I, 26. On p. 79 he remarks: "Moreover, the uncertain period during which stocks of paper might be kept adds a further limitation in regard to the conjectured dating of woodcuts on the same basis." In his *A Short History of Engraving & Etching* (London, 1908), p. 17, we find: "the manner in which paper must have been transferred from one country to another, and the uncertainty of interval between manufacture and use, necessitate many reservations and qualifications in accepting this type of evidence."

[16] *A Handbook to the Drawings and Water-colours in the . . . British Museum* (London, 1939), p. 9.

[17] Commenting on the use of watermarks for dating, Joseph Meder stated "dass man noch wenig Nutzen aus dem Studium derselben habe ziehen können" (*Die Handzeichnung* [Wien, 1923], p. 695). Elsewhere he endorses the view that watermarks are useful in dating "freilich nicht auf das Jahr, so doch auf Dezennien"; Meder also remarks "doch bleiben sie immer nur ein Behelf, der in dem einen Falle rasch zur Entscheidung führt, in dem anderen alle Vorsicht gebietet" (*Dürer-Katalog* [Wien, 1932], pp. 8 and 293). Some watermarks occur in Dürer prints throughout his lifetime, while the posthumous editions of the *Marienleben* show the same watermarks in use 1540-65 and 1550-80.

[18] On this point, see my review of Sir Hilary Jenkinson's *Domesday Re-Bound* (London, 1954) in *Speculum*, XXX (1955), 118-119.

Aber auch wenn alle diese Feststellungen lückenlos gemacht sind und das Wasserzeichen einwandfrei erkannt ist, muss noch grosse Vorsicht obwalten, dass daraus nicht zu sichere Schlüsse auf Zeit und Heimat gezogen werden. . . . Alle diese Gründe erklären, warum die grossen Hoffnungen, die man zunächst auf die Wasserzeichenforschung gesetzt, nicht in dem Umfang sich erfüllt haben, wie man sich in der ersten Begeisterung versprochen hatte.[19]

Gewiss, als alleiniges Kriterium für die Datierung einer Handschrift reicht das Wasserzeichen nicht aus.[20]

The significance of all these remarks will not fail to impress itself upon the reader. Palaeographers and art historians are accustomed to assign material which cannot be identified with an individual, school, or related group of artifacts to quarter-centuries;[21] those scholars who willingly fix such items within specific decades are often considered rash by their colleagues. It is suggested by scholars in these disciplines, then, that watermarks as evidence even for such broad datings must be treated with caution.[22]

Among bibliographers, the incunabulists—whether directly or by inference—also suggest that such evidence as "filigranes" afford

[19] Karl Löffler, *Einführung in die Handschriftenkunde* (Leipzig, 1929), pp. 57-58. Compare also the same writer's remarks in Fritz Milkau, *Handbuch der Bibliothekswissenschaft* (Leipzig, 1931-40), I, 296: "Dafür bieten die Papierhandschriften durch ihre Wasserzeichen mancherlei Mittel zur zeitlichen und örtlichen Festlegung, freilich nicht in dem Umfang und mit der Sicherheit, wie die Wasserzeichenforschung in der ersten Begeisterung gehofft hatte."

[20] Joachim Kirchner, *Germanistische Handschriftenpraxis* (München, 1950), p. 13. A French view is expressed by Maurice Prou, *Manuel de paléographie* (Paris, 1910), p. 33: "Ces marques de fabrique considérées comme éléments chronologiques ne sauraient donner qu'un *terminus a quo*, car il est arrivé que des écrits ont été consignés sur des papiers beaucoup antérieurs à la date de transcription."

[21] If objects can be so identified, there will, of course, be external pieces of evidence at hand. It must, however, be recalled that, though printed on paper, the date of production of the blockbooks is still a matter of controversy, these being variously dated between 1420 and 1475.

[22] Literary historians express a similar hesitation. "As a rule the utmost that we can do is to determine whether in a particular book or group of books the watermark is the same throughout or not, a point which indeed may be of great importance as indicating whether or not the whole was printed at or about the same time: it is seldom that we can go further and infer anything from the watermark as to the actual date of printing" (Ronald B. McKerrow, *An Introduction to Bibliography* [Oxford, 1949], pp. 101-102). Lawrence C. Wroth warns us on the "pit-falls" of dating by means of watermarks in *Imago Mundi*, XI (1954), 94. See also Rossell H. Robbins, "A Middle English Diatribe against Philip of Burgundy," *Neophilologus*, 1955, p. 132, n. 3, where he refers to the manuscript as being dated "1436-1456 from the watermarks, but the hand is certainly later ['Second half XV century']. Watermarks are evidence for establishing a *terminus a quo*, but not such reliable evidence for a *terminus ad quem*."

for establishing dates cannot be employed with precision. Paul Heitz (art historian, palaeographer, and incunabulist) found the same watermarks appearing over wide intervals of time in the incunabula,[23] as well as in documents belonging to the archives,[24] of Strassburg. This fact was further emphasized by Karl Schorbach in his study of the press of Johann Mentelin:

In 16 Druckwerken unseres Meisters ist das Ochsenkopfpapier vertreten, und zwar sowohl in seinem ersten [1460] als auch in seinem letzten [1477] Verlagswerk.

Erwähnenswert ist noch, dass das bei Mentelin vorliegende Turm-Wasserzeichen [in use 1472-73] auch im Mainzer Catholicon von 1460 vorkommt und später (1480 ff.) oft in Nürnberger Inkunabeln.[25]

Similar reservations as to the validity of the evidence of watermarks for dating—whether made directly or implied in practice—can be traced even to experts on the making of paper, its history and use.[26] In connection with this, the above-quoted statement by Dard Hunter may be recalled. We are further reminded that watermarks are "a kind of circumstantial evidence to be used with great caution by bibliographers."[27] Finally, so recently as 1952, the director of the Forschungsstelle Papiergeschichte in the Gutenberg Museum at Mainz,[28] accepted Briquet's judgments in regard to the dating of

---

[23] *Les filigranes des papiers contenus dans les incunables strasbourgeois de la Bibliothèque Impériale de Strasbourg* (Strassburg, 1903). "Le n° 54, représenté ici par le filigrane d'un imprimé de 1477, se retrouve dans des documents beaucoup plus anciens appartenant aux archives de la Ville, et remontant à 1351 et 1399" (p. 9) and p. 10, no. 168: "Ce filigrane a été relevé par Keinz à Munich dans un Codex de 1422. Il se retrouve dans un manuscrit des archives de Strasbourg, remontant à 1438. Nous l'avons copié dans un imprimé sans date de chez Eggesteyn [active 1466-1482]."

[24] *Les filigranes des papiers contenus dans les archives de la Ville de Strasbourg* (Strassburg, 1902). The "Tête de boeuf" mark (Plate V, no. 55) is found in use for 42 years (1413-1455), the "Léopard" (Plate XV, no. 182) for 53 years (1422-1475), and the "Lettre Y" (Plate XIV, no. 154) for 27 years (1455-1482). It will be noted that these years cover the period of the prototypographica.

[25] *Der Strassburger Frühdrucker Johann Mentelin* (Mainz, 1932), pp. 72 and 81. Compare also the table on p. 87.

[26] Labarre, *op. cit.*, p. 358: "If it is true that paper-moulds quickly wore out—as they would especially if used for sorts in common use—the value for dating purposes of the marks they bore would be much enhanced." The use of a conditional clause is certainly significant here.

[27] Cf. K. Povey's review of Jean-Marie Janot's *Les moulins à papier de la région vosgienne* (Nancy, 1952) in *The Library*, 5th ser., IX (1954), 274.

[28] August W. Kazmeier, "Wasserzeichen und Papier der zweiundvierzigzeiligen Bibel," *Gutenberg-Jahrbuch 1952*, pp. 21-29.

certain watermarks (nos. 13034-43) "dass einige derselben 50-60 Jahre ohne Veränderung bestanden." Dr. Kazmeier,[29] moreover, cites Briquet without hesitation as the authority for the fact that the Gutenberg Bible's watermark (no. 13040) was used in documents from 1440 to 1495. Solely on the basis of the "filigranes," one wonders, how would this Bible be dated? In the *Gutenberg-Jahrbuch* for the previous year (1951, p. 36), this German scholar expressed the belief that "durch längere Benutzung einzelner Formen, als auch durch Lagerung von Papieren können entsprechende Wasserzeichen um Jahrzehnte verschieden in der Zeit auftreten." This would imply considerable hesitation on the part of a most distinguished "Papier-Forscher" as to the value of the "evidence" which watermarks could furnish for purposes of dating.[30]

What value, then, have watermarks for the dating of prototypographica? It seems certain that a "filigrane," without external controls or confirming evidence from other sources, cannot be regarded as a sure guide for the dating, within narrow limits, of mediaeval documents or early printed books. Equally, I am sure, no one will deny that watermarks can, *and do*, provide essential and valuable pieces of evidence for this purpose; they certainly have a corroborative—though not an absolute—value in arriving at an approximate date for an early printed book. Allan H. Stevenson, for example, has shown that the watermarks in a certain Caxton volume can supply

---

[29] See especially pages 23-26. The Ochsenkopf mark (Briquet 15093) is assigned to Lyons 1400-1409 and to the 42-line Bible. For the Traube mark (Briquet 13008), the given range is Cologne 1427 to Wiesbaden 1458 (and Swiss and French localities of 1437-1466). Dr. Kazmeier seems to find nothing remarkable about these wide spreads of time in the use of these (and other) watermarks.

[30] In this connection, see Armin Renker's comment in the new edition of Milkau's *Handbuch* (Wiesbaden, 1952, I, 1065): "Da fast jedes Stück Papier seinen Ursprungsvermerk in Gestalt eines Zeichens in sich trägt, sollte man annehmen, dass es leicht sein müsste, Zeitpunkt und Ort der Entstehung hieraus zu erkennen. Die Forschung lehrt aber, dass es schwer ist, diese Ursprungsmerkmale zu deuten. . . . Verfügungen über Verleihungen geben zuweilen Anhaltspunkte, weniger das Datum der Dokumente, da ja das Papier bedeutend älter sein kann. Erfahrungsgemäss nimmt man als längsten Spielraum zwischen Anfang der Herstellung und Ende des Verbrauchs eines mittelalterlichen Papiers zehn bis fünfzehn Jahre an; bei grossen und ungewöhnlichen Papieren kann er sich bis zu dreissig Jahren ausdehnen." The recent expressions of even shorter estimates do not seem to have changed Herr Renker's opinion, for these are almost the identical words he printed in his *Buch vom Papier* (Leipzig, [1934]), p. 107. Compare also Alfred Schulte's opinion cited in note 8.

a date for it[31]—and it so happens that this date is one that is made probable by other evidence.[32] But what, one wonders, would the decision have been if the evidence had been contradictory? Relying only upon a watermark with a 1608 date[33]—and with no other evidence to go upon—it would clearly have been impossible to prove that a Shakespeare quarto with the printed date "1600" was actually produced in the year 1619 and at no other time. The watermark would certainly cast suspicion on the year 1600, but it could never have pointed to 1619 as the one likely year of publication.[34]

In conclusion, then, it may be stated that watermarks, instead of suggesting a date based on an approximate maximum of three years between manufacture and ultimate use, do furnish the student of fifteenth-century books with an additional (and important) tool for the dating of an incunabulum "sine ulla nota," possibly within a score or so of years as Briquet intimated. It has not been demonstrated, however, that watermarks provide the incunabulist with that absolute criterion which some filigranologists believe to see in them.

(From *Studies in Bibliography* 9 (1957), pp. 217-224).

---

[31] *Historie of Jason* [Westminster, 1477]. Cf. *Briquet's Opuscula* (Hilversum, 1955), p. xlii. This year [1477] is also assigned to the *Jason* by Aurner, Bennett, Blades, Crotch, De Ricci, Duff, Guppy, Hittmair, Plomer, Winship, and the *STC* (no. 15383).

[32] In any event, Caxton's work falls into the last quarter of the fifteenth century. After 1470, the demand for paper by the printing presses must have suddenly become enormous, and the paper-makers hard put to it to supply the demand. In the 1450s and 1460s the requirements of the press would have made no great demands upon the available supply.

[33] See Allan H. Stevenson's informative paper "Shakespearian Dated Watermarks," *Studies in Bibliography*, IV (1951), 159-164.

[34] Dard Hunter, *op. cit.*, p. 66, cites a paper made in 1859 with the date 1810 in the watermark; it was made in Pennsylvania at the Ivy Mills. See also Agnes Mongan and Paul J. Sachs, *Drawings in the Fogg Museum of Art* (1940), I, 418; here the following comment is made on watermark 45: "The date [as in the reproduction] is given, following a tariff decree of 1741 which ordered that all paper printed after the first of the following January should be dated 1742. The wording of the law was not clear, so that many papermakers continued for years to date their papers '1742'." These examples may serve to alert scholars against "the traps that await the unwary, even in the case of dated watermarks" (Sir Henry Thomas, *op. cit.*, p. 450).

# CHAPTER B34

## LITERARY RESEARCH AND
## BIBLIOGRAPHICAL TRAINING

IT appears both strange and unhappy that, despite the tremendous progress made in bibliographical knowledge and practices since the middle of the last century, it should still be necessary to plead for a greater understanding, by the practitioners of sister disciplines, of the functions and possibilities in the study of books *per se*. It would seem self-evident to some of us that an acquaintanceship with bibliographical methods was a necessity for the literary student even as a knowledge of palaeography or handwriting must be for the historian, at least for the student of original documents. This is not to argue that every investigator of literary material should be equipped with the full panoply of bibliographical technique or that it be necessary for such a scholar to have mastered the intricacies of the *Principles of Bibliographical Description* so brilliantly set forth by Professor Fredson Bowers.[1] But one should at least expect that those scholars who conduct investigations in the history of literature would know a good deal about the book as the "material vehicle of the living word."[2] In short, and as a minimum requirement, a literary investigator ought to have some knowledge of the works listing the editions pertinent to his research and should know in what bibliographies to seek information covering the field of his interest. Unfortunately, this does not always seem to be the case. Two articles—excellent in themselves, but not so complete and accurate as they might have been if the proper bibliographical tools had been employed—illustrate the point I wish to make; these are found in the current number of *Medievalia et Humanistica* (Volume XI, 1957).

### I

In his article "The Manuscript Tradition of the *De vita et moribus philosophorum* of Walter Burley" (pp. 44-57), Mr. John O. Stigall

[1] Princeton University Press, 1949.

[2] [Sir] Walter W. Greg, "Bibliography—a Retrospect," *The Bibliographical Society, 1892-1942, Studies in Retrospect* (London, 1945), p. 27.

includes, as Appendix II, a list of early printed editions of his text. Selecting only the items listed as incunabula from this list, we obtain the following twenty entries:

1. Köln: Ulrich Zell, c. 1470
2. — G. B., 1472
3. Köln: Arnold ter Hoernen, 1472[3]
4. Köln: Printer of the "Flores Sancti Augustini," 1473
5. Köln: Conrad de Homborch, 1475
6. — G. B., 1477 (?)
7. — W. B., 1477
8. Louvain: Johannes de Westfalia, c. 1477
9. Nürnberg: Anton Koberger, 1477
10. Nürnberg: Friedrich Creussner, 1479
11. Louvain: Johann de Paderborn, 1479-82
12. Köln: Konrad Winters de Homborch, 1479
13. — G. B., 1479
14. Toulouse: J. Parix, c. 1480
15. Speier: Johann and Conrad Hist, 1483
16. Köln: Johann Koelhoff, the Elder, c. 1486
17. Augsburg: Anton Sorg, 1490 [in German]
18. France: ——, 1495
19. Paris: Georg Mittelhaus, 1496[4]
20. Eustadt: Reyser, [without date]

On the one hand, the compiler does not explain whence he obtained his list; on the other, the standard bibliography of incunabula (the *Gesamtkatalog der Wiegendrucke*)[5] lists a total of only thirteen such editions. Let us consider Mr. Stigall's entries seriatim.

No. 1: this is GW 5781. No. 2: no printer with the initials G. B. used in a colophon and no printer identifiable only by these initials is known to me. Konrad Burger knew of two printers identified by these initials in the reverse order (B. G.—Bartholomaeus Girardinus of Venice and Bartholomaeus Guldinbeck of Rome), neither of whom published an edition of the *De vita et moribus philosophorum*.[6] This entry quite baffled me until I turned to the old "general

---

[3] Apparently as the result of a misprint, Mr. Stigall gives the name as Arnold ter Hoeren. For this printer, see Ernst Voulliéme, *Die deutschen Drucker des fünfzehnten Jahrhunderts* (Berlin, 1922), pp. 42-43.

[4] This printer, an Alsatian, usually signed his name Mittelhus, occasionally Mittelhuss. Compare Konrad Haebler, *Die deutschen Buchdrucker des XV. Jahrhunderts im Auslande* (München, 1924), pp. 191-192, and Anatole Claudin, *Histoire de l'imprimerie en France* (Paris, 1900-1914), II, 5-12.

[5] Leipzig, 1925-1938, V, 681-689, nos. 5781-93.

[6] *The Printers and Publishers of the XV. Century with Lists of their Works*, (London, 1902), p. 32.

catalogue" of the British Museum, where several editions of the work are briefly listed under Burleus, Gualterus as "[By G. B.]". This seems to be the ultimate source for the entry in Mr. Stigall's list. The G. B., of course, stands for the author and not for the printer. The British Museum's press-mark (C. 14. b. 7/2) indicates that this edition corresponds to GW 5785 and the book should be assigned thus: [Nürnberg: Anton Koberger, c. 1472].[7] No. 3 = GW 5783. No. 4 = GW 5784. No. 5 = GW 5782. No. 6: see also remarks under no. 2. The incipit, according to the BM general catalogue, suggests that this edition is the same as no. 8 (see GW 5788). No. 7: no printer W. B. (or B., W.) is listed by Burger. This entry too seems to stem from the old BM catalogue, where the incipit suggests that this is the same as no. 9, the only one dated 1477. The W. B., of course, represents Walterus Burlaeus (or Walter Burley). No. 8 = GW 5788. No. 9 = GW 5786. No. 10 = GW 5787. No. 11: this is the same edition as the one listed under no. 8.[8] No. 12: this is the identical edition as that listed under no. 5.[9] No. 13: see also remarks under no. 2. The incipit as cited by the BM general catalogue indicates that this is the same edition as no. 10, the only one dated 1479 (compare GW 5787). No. 14 = GW 5789. No. 15 = GW 5790. No. 16 = GW 5791. No. 17 = GW 5793. Nos. 18 and 19: the *Gesamtkatalog* asserts that no edition was printed in France before the sixteenth century.[10]

[7] *Catalogue of Books Printed in the XVth Century now in the British Museum* (BMC), (London, 1908-1949), II:411 (IB. 7140).

[8] John of Westphalia was a native of Paderborn and was known both as Johannes de Westfalia and as Johannes de Paderborn. Two editions were listed by Marinus F. A. G. Campbell, *Annales de la typographie néerlandaise au XVᵉ siècle* (La Haye, 1874), p. 106, nos. 387 and 388, though no. 387 has since been rejected as a separate edition by several authorities (cf. Maria E. Kronenberg, *Campbell's Annales de la typographie néerlandaise au XVᵉ siècle, Contributions to a new Edition* (The Hague, 1956), p. 71).

[9] GW 5782 is signed by "Conradus de Homborch," who is identical with Konrad Winters de Homborch (see Voulliéme, *op. cit.*, p. 48). Only one edition of Burley's *De vita et moribus philosophorum* is credited to his press by the standard bibliography of Cologne incunabula (Ernst Voulliéme, *Der Buchdruck Kölns bis zum Ende des fünfzehnten Jahrhunderts* (Bonn, 1903), p. 135, no. 297).

[10] Compare GW V:col. 688. Four editions are here relegated to the sixteenth century which were listed as incunabula by Marie Pellechet, *Catalogue général des incunables des bibliothèques publiques de France* (Paris, 1897-1909), nos. 3089 and 3091-93. Some of these also appear in Mr. Stigall's list of XVIc editions, although there may well be some duplication here. Thus, Joh. Parvus (Jean Petit) printed an edition of which some copies have the device of De Marnef as publisher. The two editions credited to Mittelhus may also represent a single original, since no incunable edition by him is known.

Accordingly, these two editions should be dated *post* 1500. No. 20: noted by Mr. Stigall on p. 57 as "printed by *Reyser* at Eustadt, but without date." Apparently, this entry comes from Hain 4117[11] or Brunet I:1407[12] (both assign the edition to: Eustadii, Reyser). The press of Michael Reyser at Eichstätt is not known to have produced such a work.[13] Hain 4117, according to GW 5790, corresponds to no. 15. One edition not listed by Mr. Stigall is described by the *Gesamtkatalog* under no. 5792.[14]

In revised form, and with the usual practice of placing all inferred information into square brackets, the fifteenth-century editions of the *De vita et moribus philosophorum* may be chronologically listed thus:

| GW | Imprint | Stigall |
|---|---|---|
| 5781 | [Köln: Ulrich Zell, c. 1470] | 1 |
| 5783 | [Köln]: Arnold ter Hoernen, 1472 | 3 |
| 5785 | [Nürnberg: Anton Koberger, c. 1472] | 2 |
| 5784 | [Köln: Printer of Flores S. Augustini, n.a. 1473] | 4 |
| 5786 | Nürnberg: Anton Koberger, 6 May 1477 | 7,9 |
| 5782 | [Köln]: Konrad Winters, [a. 18 Mar. 1479] | 5,12 |
| 5787 | Nürnberg: Friedrich Creussner, 30 June 1479 | 10,13 |
| 5788 | Louvain: Johann de Paderborn, [c. 1479/82] | 6,8,11 |
| 5789 | [Toulouse: Johann Parix, c. 1480] | 14 |
| 5790 | [Speier]: Johann and Conrad Hist, [c. 1483] | 15,20 |
| 5791 | [Köln: Johann Koelhoff, the Elder, c. 1486] | 16 |
| 5792 | [Belgium: Printer of Mensa philosophica, 1486/90] | — |
| 5793 | Augsburg: Anton Sorg, 31 August 1490. [German] | 17 |

## II

The article by Mr. John N. Hough, "Plautus, Student of Cicero, and Walter Burley," follows next in the journal (pp. 58-68). In the course of his analysis, Mr. Hough cites the *Mer des histoires*, quoting from the edition printed at Lyons by Jean Dupré in 1491. He there observes that this work was certainly descended from Burley's treatise but that, in regard to the added material, "*La Mer* evidently expanded at whim. Whether these are original or not is not possible

---

[11] Ludwig Hain, *Repertorium bibliographicum* (Stuttgart, 1826-1838).

[12] Jacques-Charles Brunet, *Manuel du libraire et de l'amateur de livres* (Paris, 1860-1880).

[13] See Voulliéme, *Die deutschen Drucker*, p. 58, and Burger, *op. cit.*, p. 245.

[14] Listed as: [Südliche Niederlande? Drucker der Mensa philosophica (Hain 11076), um 1486/90].

to determine, but some are certainly Gallic in nature."[15] It should
have been relatively easy to determine the true extent and the exact
nature of the expansions.

Such reference books as the BMC,[16] Polain,[17] Oates,[18] and others[19]
plainly state that the *Mer des histoires* is an adaptation of a work first
published in Northern Germany,[20] the *Rudimentum novitiorum*
printed by Lucas Brandis at Lübeck on 5 August 1475. The first
edition of the French text was issued in Paris from the press of
Pierre Le Rouge in 1488. In the prefatory matter, the author himself
states:

Par quoy en ce present liure qui peult estre nomme La fleur ou la mer des
histoires: & en latin est appelle Rudimentum nouiciorum | Cest adire en francois
le Rudiment des nouices | ou lenseignement des nouueaulx. Nous raconterons
par ordre. de degre en degre la greigneur partie des hystoires & des grandes
choses dignes de memoire | qui sont aduenues depuis la creation du monde
iusques a present.

Thus it would have been possible to determine exactly the part contributed by the French compiler through a comparison of copies of

[15] P. 61, note 18.

[16] In the comment on the first edition (VIII:109), it is stated that "Le Rouge had
before him the editio princeps of the Rudimentum nouitiorum . . . but decorated his
own book more effectively." Compare also the note in Robert Proctor, *An Index to
the Early Printed Books in the British Museum* (London, 1898-1903), p. 579, no.
8092.

[17] M.-Louis Polain, *Catalogue des livres imprimés au quinzième siècle des
bibliothèques de Belgique* (Bruxelles, 1932), III, 169-171, no. 2673, and 640-642,
no. 3404.

[18] J. C. T. Oates, *A Catalogue of the Fifteenth-Century Printed Books in the
University Library Cambridge* (Cambridge, 1954), p. 504, no. 3007, and p. 538,
no. 3207.

[19] Margaret B. Stillwell, *Incunabula in American Libraries* (New York, 1940),
p. 439; [Sir Henry Thomas], *Short-title Catalogue of Books Printed in France and
of French Books Printed in Other Countries from 1470 to 1600 now in the British
Museum* (London, 1924), p. 83; Alfred W. Pollard, *Early Illustrated Books* (London, 1893), p. 162; etc.

[20] It is interesting to recall Mr. Stigall's comment (p. 50) to the effect that "no
MSS of the *De vita* have as yet been traced in north Germany." Burley's treatise
was, in any case, known there. Similarly, Mr. Stigall (p. 49) knew of only one
manuscript (Trinity College, Cambridge, MS O. 2. 50) of English origin though
written in a Flemish hand (in his catalogue, Dr. Montague Rhodes James merely
states "clearly written, perhaps in Flanders"), and not a single English edition of
the Latin text is listed by the *Short-Title Catalogue of Books Printed in England,
Scotland, & Ireland and of English Books Printed Abroad 1475-1640* (London,
1926). Nevertheless, so fastidious a scholar as Sir Thomas Elyot (1490?-1546)
knew and quoted Burley's work; on this point, see my note "Diogenes and *The
Boke named The Governour*," *Modern Language Notes*, LXIX (1954), 481-484.

the two editions,[21] such as are to be found, for example, in the library with which the present writer is connected.[22]

Mr. Hough also makes the following observation in connection with the account of Plautus (pp. 67-68):

> La Mer offers still another, perhaps supplementary, hint as to the origin of the connection [of Plautus] with Cicero. The entry following *Plautus* in *La Mer* is: Plaucius armacius disciple de Ciceron fut grand orateur, etc. and notes his foundation of Lyons (with pardonable Gallic addition of explanation as to why *Gallia comata* is so called). This is identical with Burley (ch. 100, only two "lives" totalling six lines intervene between this and Plautus, ch. 103).

The *Mer des histoires* is here simply following the arrangement in the *Rudimentum novitiorum* (f. 270), where "Plaucius armacius" (in the identical words as in Burley)[23] follows Plautus and is separated from it by this short passage not found at this place in the French text: "Item hoc anno. plaucius apud tharentum. seipsum interfecit."

Still another bibliographical handbook might have suggested a further additional note of considerable interest.[24] Although not a single printed edition of the *De vita et moribus philosophorum* was produced by Italian presses in the fifteenth century, the work was not without influence on Italian literary history. As I pointed out in the reference just cited, the Italian version of the *Vitae et sententiae philosophorum* claiming to be a translation of the work of Diogenes Laertius is nothing of the sort.[25] To a remarkable extent, it is little more than a translation into Italian of Burley's text.[26] One may best

---

[21] The French sentences cited at the foot of p. 61 and in note 21 (p. 62) have no counterparts in the *Rudimentum novitiorum*.

[22] Listed in Ada Thurston and Curt F. Bühler, *Check List of Fifteenth Century Printing in the Pierpont Morgan Library*, (New York, 1939), nos. 507 and 1458; see also the listing on p. 326.

[23] Without the full explanation for *Gallia comata*, which is, therefore, a French addition (as Mr. Hough thought probable).

[24] Curt F. Bühler, James G. McManaway and Lawrence C. Wroth, *Standards of Bibliographical Description* (Philadelphia, 1949), p. 36, n. 34.

[25] The *Gesamtkatalog der Wiegendrucke* lists ten editions (GW 8385-8394) under Diogenes Laertius, with the note "ist eine gekürzte, freie Bearbeitung der lat[einischen] Vorlage."

[26] This was pointed out in my article "Greek Philosophers in the Literature of the Later Middle Ages," reprinted later in the volume (especially pp. 346–347). In the same study (pp. 331–337), the textual relationship of the *De vita et moribus philosophorum* to the *Rudimentum novitiorum* and the *Mer des histoires* is also discussed at length.

illustrate this by quoting the passage on Plautus (not to be found at all, of course, in the Greek original of Diogenes Laertius)[27] which may then be conveniently compared with the Latin passage from Burley as printed by Mr. Hough (p. 58):

Plauto poeta fu gran maestro di comedie o uer tragedie: & discipulo di Tullo. Fu eloquentissimo & per po[u]erta[28] scriuea historie & fauole & uendeuale & per sustentar la uita non si uergogno far el mestier del pistor Soleua dir chi non crede esser meritato del ben che fa ad altri singana lui stesso Non torre amicitia de pazzi Con gli huomini peruersi e piu facil cosa hauer odio che familiarita Non si debe far lhuomo troppo amico daltri Diceua ancora lhuomo esser el piu fiero animale & el piu nuouo del mondo imperoche chi gli e alpari di se non lo puo soffrir: se gli e minore elo spreza: se e magiore li ha inuidia: se gli e equale non si concorda seco. Vixe a Roma al tempo di Pompeio.[29]

This, one might suggest, is about as "unhumanistic" a volume as the Italian Quattrocento produced; it is entirely in the mediaeval tradition!

A few literary points might also be raised. In the ter Hoernen edition of Burley (GW 5783), the description of Plautus opens with the words: "Plautus Poeta Comicus Tulij discipulus Rome claruit." This is the precise wording also found in the *Rudimentum novitiorum*, the *Mer des histoires*, the German translation,[30] and the Italian "Diogenes" (with very minor changes). The Koberger (GW 5785) and Winters (GW 5782) editions have the text as given by Mr. Hough: "Plautus, comicus, philosophus, Tullii discipulus, Rome claruit." Again, the first group, which refers to Plautus as a poet, sets forth a section "De sentencijs eius moralibus," while the texts which describe Plautus as a philosopher refer to his sayings as being notable rather than moral. These details, as presented above, once more emphasize the fact that it is not only the words as written by the author (the "official" text) that have value; just as often the altered (even

---

[27] Nor was an account of Plautus added to the Latin version (by Ambrosius Traversarius), at least in the edition of Venice: Nicolas Jenson, 14 August 1475 (PML 309).

[28] The original has the misprint "ponerta."

[29] Quoted from the first edition, Venice: Bernardinus Celerius, 9 December 1480 (GW 8385; PML 36049), sign. h3, cap. CI. With very minor differences, the same text is found in the edition, Florence: Francesco Bonaccorsi and Antonius Francisci, 5 July 1488 (GW 8387).

[30] "Plautus der poet Comicus tulius junger ist zů Rom erschÿnen" (Sorg, f. 132ᵛ).

corrupt) version is more important in the development of a literary tradition than that authenticated by the writer himself.[31]

These, then, are some details which might have been set forth more accurately or more fully in the two articles under discussion. The present study was not undertaken with the purpose of casting aspersions on either of the studies. Both are extremely interesting and useful contributions to scholarship. It is equally true, however, that a greater acquaintance with bibliographical reference works would have made both essays even more interesting and more useful.

(From *PBSA* 51 (1957), pp. 303-11).

[31] On this point, see also the conclusions reached in my article "Studies in the Early Editions of the *Fiore di virtù*," *supra*.

# CHAPTER B35

## A LETTER WRITTEN BY ANDREA ALCIATO
## TO CHRISTIAN WECHEL

THE autograph collection of Alfred Bovet, formed in the second half of the nineteenth century, contained a letter written by Andrea Alciato, the learned Italian jurist of emblem fame, to the Parisian printer, Christian Wechel.[1] The description given in the catalogue of that collection, where the letter is dated 'Bourges (où il professa de 1528 à 1532), III des calendes de février (29 janvier 1529)', includes the following note:

Intéressante lettre dans laquelle Andrea Alciati envoie à Wechel un opuscule composé dans ces dernières années et où il a expliqué par ordre alphabétique la plupart des termes de droit. Il lui propose d'imprimer cet ouvrage.—(Il s'agit probablement dans cette lettre du livre d'Alciati intitulé *De verborum significationibus*, composé en 1521 et imprimé en 1529.)

When, some threescore years later, Gian Luigi Barni was preparing his edition of the correspondence of Alciato,[2] he was unable to provide the text of Alciato's only letter to Wechel, and had to content himself with supplying this summary, based (of course) on the Bovet catalogue:[3]

Questa lettera è citata in: *Lettres autographes composant la collection de M. Alfred Boret* [*sic*], Paris, 1887, p. 440, n. 1199, catalogo preparato da Etienne Charavay per la vendita all'asta. Di questa lettera non siamo riusciti a trovare nè copia nè autografo.

Con questa lettera l'Alciato invia al Wechel un suo opuscolo composto negli ultimi anni e nel quale egli ha spiegato in ordine alfabetico la maggior parte dei termini di diritto, proponendogliene la stampa. Può trattarsi del *De verborum significatione* stampato appunto nel 1529. Avignone, 1529 gennaio 30.

---

[1] See *Lettres autographes composant la collection de M. Alfred Bovet décrites par Étienne Charavay, ouvrage imprimé sous la direction de Fernand Calmettes* (Paris, 1887), p. 440, no. 1199. For an account of this collection, see Simon Gratz, *A Book about Autographs* (Philadelphia, 1920), pp. 143–6.

[2] *Le lettere di Andrea Alciato giureconsulto* (Florence, 1953), p. 81, no. 46.

[3] Barni adds the following note to his description: 'Dobbiamo la notizia di questa lettera, come pure dell'altra in data 20 agosto 1533, alla cortesia di S. E. Federico Patetta, Accademico d'Italia, maestro indimenticabile. La lettera nel catalogo è così indicata: *Lettre à Chrétien Wechel, Bourges, III des calendes de février (29 janvier 1529)*, correggiamo però la data in 30 gennaio, poichè questa corrisponde alla data indicata secondo il calendario romano.'

While Barni was still at work on this edition, the Pierpont Morgan Library purchased one of the former C. Fairfax Murray collections of autographs,[4] a group of 296 letters and documents, including this particular letter by Alciato (MA. 1346-3). Unfortunately, the Library was not aware of Barni's projected edition and was thus unable to supply the text for his volume.

Since both previous accounts of Alciato's letter to Wechel give erroneous information, a full transcript of the original is printed below:[5]

[Address, on verso]: Domino Christiano Wechel negotiatori librario Parisijs. ad signum scuti basileiensis.[6]
Superioribus mensibus cum huc se contulisset quidam ex institoribus tuis, ei libellum grecum tradidi, quo per ordinem alphabeti pleraque uocabula iuris nostri explicabantur. feci hoc libentissime tum ut morem tibi gererem, tum ut studiosis consulerem si forte in mentem tibi uenisset, ut eum typis tuis publicares. ceterum quid de eo factum sit nihil ultra intellexi. Quare uelim mi christiane abs te certior fieri an eum ut[7] sis editurus. quod si alia tibi cura animum subijt, cuperem eum libellum ad me mitteres. ego si quid habeo quod e re tua esse existimes libentissimo animo sum communicaturus. emblematum edendorum curam arbitror tibi excidisse, que ratio facit ut ea de re interpellandum te non putem. tu tamen non ideo uereare me interpellare si quid est quod possim, repulsam a me non feres. Vale. Biturigibus III Kal. Febr.                                                      Andreas alciatus.

Though the letter is clearly dated Bourges, 30 January (year unspecified), and though Bovet had correctly pointed out that Alciato cited Bourges as the place of writing, Barni chose to place this letter with those written from Avignon (nos. 39-49; 30 October 1527-1 March 1529). According to his biographer, Paul Émile Viard,[8] Alciato began his lectures at Bourges on 23 April 1529, and his earliest

---

[4] Compare Frederick B. Adams, Jr., *Second Annual Report to the Fellows of the Pierpont Morgan Library* (New York, 1951), pp. 49-52.

[5] For help with the transcription and interpretation of the document, I am greatly obliged to Professors Paul O. Kristeller and Chester F. Natunewicz.

[6] In Pierre Larousse, *Grand dictionnaire universel du XIXᵉ siècle* (Paris, 1865-90), xv, p. 1295, it is stated that 'il a pris pour marque l'écusson de Bâle'. No such printer's mark is recorded by Louis C. Silvestre, *Marques typographiques* (Paris, 1853-67), or by Philippe Renouard, *Les Marques typographiques parisiennes des XVᵉ et XVIᵉ siècles* (Paris, 1926-8). The note in Larousse is apparently due to a confusion with the printer's residence 'at the sign of the shield of Basel'.

[7] The 'ut' is cancelled by a stroke of the pen.

[8] *André Alciat, 1492-1550* (Paris, 1926), p. 73. In his *Andreas Alciatus* (Basel, 1934), pp. 10-11, H. de Giacomi similarly asserts that Alciato began his work in Bourges in April 1529 and that he was lecturing in Pavia in 1533, without specifying the month.

surviving letter from there (Barni, no. 51) bears the date: 7 May 1529. The letter to Wechel cannot, therefore, be dated earlier than 30 January 1530. It is equally certain that this letter must have been sent prior to January 1534. On 20 August 1533 Alciato wrote from Bourges to the Duke of Milan (Barni, no. 85),[9] thanking him for the professorship at Pavia, which he planned to assume about 1 November. By 7 October (Barni, no. 86) Alciato was already addressing letters from Milan.

Both Bovet and Barni were mistaken in assuming that the booklet referred to in the text of the letter to Wechel was Alciato's *De verborum significatione*. The present writer has not come across the 1529 edition cited by these scholars; nevertheless, even the 1530 edition (Lyons: Sebastianus Gryphius—BM.501.h.2.[1]) must have been taken in hand before Alciato sent to Wechel the letter now in the Morgan Library. As we have seen, this cannot be dated before 30 January 1530, and the 1530 *De verborum significatione* has a dedication to the future Cardinal François de Tournon,[10] Archbishop of Bourges, dated 'Kal. maii 1529'.[11] It is, therefore, not unreasonable to assume that, by 1 May 1529, the text of the *De verborum significatione* was completed and in the hands of the printer. Furthermore, in his letter, Alciato specifically refers to 'a little book in Greek in which, according to the order of the alphabet, very many words of our law were explained'. Under no circumstances could this description be applied to the treatise of which we have spoken, since this work is almost exclusively in Latin and is not alphabetically arranged.

Alciato's comment to the effect that 'I believe that the task of editing the Emblems has fallen to your lot' is of added interest, as it clearly indicates that the Paris printing of the *Emblems* was then already under way. Wechel's first edition of this work appeared in 1534. If, then, one allows a year for its production (two years seems

---

[9] According to Adriano Cappelli, *Cronologia, cronografia e calendario perpetuo* (Milan, 1930), p. 331, Francesco II Sforza became Duke of Milan on 29 November 1529 and died on 1 November 1535.

[10] For a sketch of his life, see Jacques Paul Migne, *Dictionnaire des cardinaux* (Paris, 1857), cols. 1572–86.

[11] Consult the bibliographical description given by Henri Louis Baudrier, *Bibliographie lyonnaise* (Lyons, Paris, and Geneva, 1895–1952), viii, p. 54. The same date is given in the 1617 *Opera omnia*, iv, pp. 753–6. According to De Giacomi (p. 7), the *De verborum significatione* (in lecture form) was already well known to the scholarly world in the winter of 1520/21.

somewhat excessive, even for an author as meticulous as Alciato is known to have been), it would seem probable that the letter to Wechel should be dated: 30 January [1533].

A quarter-century ago Eustace F. Bosanquet pointed out,[12] for the first time, that Wechel actually produced two editions in the year 1534. He suggested two possible reasons for the double issue, either 'that the first edition was a comparatively small one, so that a second was called for in the same year', or that Wechel, 'having produced what is admitted by everybody to be a far superior edition to Steyner's [of 1531], he submitted it to Alciat, who was then at Bourges,[13] for his commendation; and the latter would have at once called his attention to the mistakes [therein]'. Bosanquet's own conviction is expressed in these words: 'Wechel therefore, either on his own initiative or at Alciat's request, at once withdrew the first edition and hurriedly printed a new one, substituting a new cut that met with Alciat's approval and with the typographical errors corrected.'

This may, indeed, be the correct explanation for the two editions of 1534, but it must be recalled that, in that year, Alciato was no longer living a mere 122 miles south of Paris but was already settled, across the Alps, at Pavia. At such a distance, it would have been difficult for Alciato to make his (possible) complaints effective to the point where Wechel was willing to undergo the financial loss of 'withdrawing' an entire edition. To this writer, anyway, it seems far more plausible to argue that the successful sale of the first edition enabled Wechel to print a second, in which he made the emendations apparently suggested to him by Alciato.

The identity of the 'libellus graecus' remains unsolved.[14] No such book appears under Alciato's name in any of the numerous bibliographies or library catalogues which I have consulted. No work, or

[12] 'The First Paris Edition of the Emblems of Alciat, 1534', The Library, 4th series, iv (1923-4), pp. 326-31.

[13] Bosanquet adds the note (p. 331, n. ii): 'He left Bourges for Pavia sometime in 1534.' Bosanquet is here following the biography supplied by Henry Green, Andreae Alciati Emblematum fontes quatuor (London, 1870), p. 2: 'From Bourges, about 1534, just after Christian Wechel, the printer, of Paris, had prevailed on him to issue a more correct and better ornamented edition of his Emblems than Steyner's Augsburg edition of 1531, Alciat was recalled by his sovereign, Francis Sforza, Duke of Milan, who bestowed senatorial rank on his now famous subject, and commanded him to lecture on law in Pavia.'

[14] No such work is cited by Viard (op. cit.), or by Ernst von Moeller, Andreas Alciat (1492-1550), ein Beitrag zur Entstehungsgeschichte der modernen Jurisprudenz (Breslau, 1907).

part of any work,[15] corresponding to the précis furnished in the letter is to be found in the 4,118 folio columns of the four volumes of his *Opera omnia* (Frankfurt, 1616–17; BM. 501. k. 4, 5). The special 'fichiers'[16] concerning sixteenth-century Parisian printing record no Wechel imprint which could be identified with Alciato's description of the booklet. In these circumstances, it seems probable that the author could find no publisher for this 'libellus' and soon abandoned any thought of having it printed.

(From *The Library* (1961), pp. 201-05).

[15] Perhaps this work may be identified as one of the other little works, of which Alciato wrote to Bonifacius Amerbach on 12 March 1531 (Barni, p. 124, no. 68): 'Ego aliquid edendi causa ad Frobennios mittere non possum, priusquam in Italiam accedam, hoc est ante proxima vulcanalia: recognoscam ibi in bybliotheca mea Parergorum libros III pauculaque quaedam alia.' See, also, Alfred Hartmann, *Die Amerbachkorrespondenz* (Basel, 1942–58), iv (1953), p. 30, and Emilio Costa, 'Andrea Alciato e Bonifacio Amerbach', *Archivio storico italiano*, 5th series, xxxvi (1905), p. 122, n. 2.

[16] I am much obliged for the help of Mr. Charles A. Foster, who kindly searched the files in Paris on my behalf. Professor Matthias A. Shaaber has had the great kindness to look through the files of the 'Check List of the Works of Sixteenth-Century Latin Authors', begun by Professors Leicester Bradner and Don Cameron Allen. This work is being continued under the auspices of the Renaissance Society of America, with Professor Shaaber as editor. This file provides no entry under Alciato which can confidently be identified with his work cited in the letter to Wechel. The *Glossemata de stipulationum diuisionibus* (Bologna, 1544; copy in the Bayerische Staatsbibliothek, Munich) is both too late and apparently not in Greek.

# CHAPTER B36

## THE PUBLICATION OF SEBASTIAN BRANT'S
### *VARIA CARMINA*

A
T an auction sale in London nearly thirty years ago, the present
writer obtained a copy of Sebastian Brant's *Stultifera Navis*,
Basel: Johann Bergmann de Olpe, 1 March 1498 (GW
5062). Bound with this work was the first edition of the same writer's *Varia Carmina*, Basel: Johann Bergmann de Olpe, 1 May 1498
(GW 5068), the auction catalogue calling attention to the fact that
12 leaves were missing[1] in the *Stultifera Navis* and to the possibility
that "the two books were probably originally issued together, as the
matter in the twelve missing leaves of the first book is included in
the second, sigs. a$^{1-8}$ and bc$^{1-3}$". This is a perfectly accurate statement—for, if the two works were sold together, then duplication
of text would be inevitable unless one set of the duplicating quires
were removed.[2] In view of the seemingly limitless number of surviving copies (the *Gesamtkatalog der Wiegendrucke* lists 62, before
adding "und zahlreiche andere", and the American *Census*[3] of incunabula of 1940 locates 9 more examples), it appeared reasonable to
assume that some other copy (possibly several others) might display
similar excision of duplicating text and thus justify the conclusion
that this had been done in the printing office. Though such copies
may exist, the 28 other specimens of this edition of the *Stultifera
Navis* that I have examined[4] failed to prove this point. Some exam-

---

[1] The volume wants quires t$^4$, v$^4$, and x$^4$.

[2] In the case of quire ſ, which was so printed that it could be inserted either in
the 1497 or the 1498 *Stultifera Navis*, the possible duplication of text in the earlier
edition was avoided by resetting. Cf. GW 5061, Anm.

[3] Margaret B. Stillwell, *Incunabula in American Libraries, a Second Census of
Fifteenth-Century Books owned in the United States, Mexico, and Canada*, New
York, 1940.

[4] These are: Basel, Universitätsbibliothek (Falk 2093, N. A. VI. 11, D. A. III. 4,
D. A. III. 4a); Cambridge, Mass., Harvard University (2 copies); Colmar, Biblio-
thèque Municipale (Inc. V 12634, Inc. XI 9820); Copenhagen, Det Kongelige Biblio-
tek (Madsen 864, Madsen 865); Frankfurt, Stadtbibliothek (Inc. oct. 40. nr. 2);
Freiburg im Breisgau, Universitätsbibliothek (E 4681d); Linköping, Stiftsbiblioteket
(Inc. 38); London, British Museum (IA. 37947); Mainz, Gutenberg-Museum; New
York, Columbia University Library, New York Academy of Medicine, New York
Public Library, Pierpont Morgan Library (PML 235, PML 27525. 1); Oxford,

ples do, indeed, suggest that Bergmann may have been a little careless in making up copies of his publication; for example, both the Colmar (Inc. XI 9820) and the Frankfurt Stadtbibliothek (Inc. oct. 40. nr. 2)[5] copies want quire v, and both the New York Academy of Medicine and the Basel Universitätsbibliothek (N. A. VI. 11)[6] ones want quire ſ (long s). But no copy seen by me was comparable to the volume in my possession.

The writer's copy of the *Varia Carmina* displayed a variant setting on signature $n^4$ verso, which is not recorded in any of the very many printed bibliographical descriptions of this book; it is illustrated in the accompanying plate (No. 15). To explain this variant and to discover other examples of this issue, the following 33 copies were consulted:

Baltimore, Walters Art Gallery – with m and n
Basel, Universitätsbibliothek, AN VII 18 – with m and n; FN VI 4ᶠ – with m and n
Brussels, Bibliothèque Royale, A 1323 – through m only
Cambridge, University Library, Oates 2854 – with m and n
Cambridge, Mass., Harvard University Library – with m and n
Cleveland, National Library of Medicine, Schullian 128 – through l only
Colmar, Bibliothèque Municipale, Inc. I. 5832 – through m only
Copenhagen, Det Kongelige Bibliotek, Madsen 869 – through l only
Frankfurt, Museum für Kunsthandwerk, LB 14 – with m and n
Frankfurt, Stadt- und Universitätsbibliothek, Inc. oct. 40, nr. 1 – with m and n
Freiburg im Breisgau, Universitätsbibliothek, D 8305 – with m and n
London, British Museum, IA. 37949 – with m and n; IA. 37950 – with m and n
Madrid, Biblioteca Nacional, Inc. 407 – through m only

---

Bodleian Library (Douce 69); Paris, Bibliothèque Nationale (Rés. Yh 55); Providence, R. I., John Carter Brown Library; Stockholm, Kungliga Biblioteket (Collijn 260); Strassburg, Bibliothèque Universitaire (K 949); Uppsala, Universitetsbiblioteket (Collijn 377); Washington, Library of Congress; and Williamstown, Mass., Chapin Library.

[5] In this copy, sheet $q^{8-6}$ is unprinted. Bound in a contemporary binding with the *Varia Carmina*, though here quires l–n are misbound after first quire K.
[6] This is in an early, probably contemporary, binding.

Munich, Bayerische Staatsbibliothek, Hain 3731 (ex. 1) – with m
    and n; (ex. 2) – with m and n
New Haven, Yale University Library – with m and n
New York, Library of Curt F. Bühler – with m and n
New York, Pierpont Morgan Library, PML 236 – with m and n
Oxford, Bodleian Library, Auct. II. Q. VI. 33 – with m and n
Paris, Bibliothèque Nationale, H 723 – through l only; m Yc 64 –
    through m only; m Yc 65 – with m and n; m Yc 66 – with m and n
Princeton, Princeton University Library – through m only
Seville, Biblioteca Colombina – through l only
Stockholm, Kungliga Biblioteket, Collijn 257 – through l only
Strassburg, Bibliothèque Nationale et Universitaire, K 929.1 – with
    m and n; K 929.2 – with m and n; K 929.3 – with m and n
Uppsala, Universitetsbiblioteket, Collijn 375 – with m and n
Washington, Library of Congress – through m only

The only copy found to have signature n$^4$ verso in the same state as
in my copy was Strassburg K 929.3.[7] On the title of this volume,
Charles Schmidt (great scholar and collector of Alsatian books) had
written: "Il paraît qu'on fit 2 tirages de cette édition. L'exempl. de
la biblioth. de Strasb.[8] n'a pas l'Exhortatio ad divum Maxim. qui
occupe la dernière page du présent exempl.; elle est remplacée par
la gravure du titre & des vers ad lectorem". Schmidt gave a long account of the publication of the Bergmann edition in his *Histoire
littéraire de l'Alsace à la fin du XV$^e$ et au commencement du XVI$^e$
siècle* (Paris, 1879, II, 351–352).[9] Nevertheless, the information there
provided is not wholly complete and, in addition, appears to have
escaped the notice of all subsequent bibliographers, not even being
recorded in the very long and detailed description in the *Gesamt-*

[7] This copy wants the unsigned quire of 4 leaves at the end.

[8] Copy K 929. 1. Copy K 929. 2, formerly in the Gomez de la Cortina collection,
came to the Strassburg library with Charles Schmidt's books.

[9] The problem is also treated by Sister Mary Alvarita Rajewski, *Sebastian Brant,
Studies in Religious Aspects of his Life and Works with Special Reference to the
Varia Carmina*, [The Catholic University of America, Studies in German, vol. XX],
Washington, D. C., 1944. This study seems to be based on the Cleveland copy
and Schmidt's account, with attendant confusion since the copy in the National
Library of Medicine went only through quire l. No reference is, therefore, made to
quire m, and a "ghost" is created by the listing of the "two editions printed by
Olpe", one in May and the other in September, 1498 (p. 16). These are described
as differing from each other, "if only slightly".

*katalog* (no. 5068). It would, therefore, seem useful to review the order in which the various states of the two fifteenth-century editions made their appearance.

The two editions are, of course, the Bergmann one previously referred to and the "pirated" edition issued at Strassburg by Johann Grüninger, 1 August 1498 (GW 5069). The history of their publication can best be followed by discussing the various states of the two editions in a single sequence[10]:

I Bergmann edition.
    IA – text (with register) through quire l only; dated 1 May 1498.
    IB – as IA, but with Errata leaf[11].
    IC – text enlarged by addition of quire m, and with register expanded to include the new quire.

II Bergmann edition (IC) issued together with Johann Reuchlin's *Scenica Progymnasmata* (HC 13882, issued by Bergmann not before 1 May 1498 [date of his letter to Johann von Dalberg, Bishop of Worms] nor after 1 August 1498 [date of Grüninger reprint]; thus British Museum IA. 37950 and Colmar Inc. I. 5832).

III Grüninger's reprint of II; dated 1 August 1498 (copies seen: British Museum IA. 1478 and Frankfurt Stadtbibliothek Flugschr. G. Fr. XIX, 90).

IV Bergmann's printing of the *Thurcorum Terror et Potentia* (with the Exhortation to Maximilian on the verso of the fourth leaf as here illustrated) to be added to IC as quire n; after 1 September 1498, date of Brant's *Responsio*.

V Bergmann becomes aware of Grüninger's reprint (III) and replaces Brant's Exhortation to Maximilian with the same author's

[10] Minor variants have also been noted. Thus on C[1], line 5, the Bodleian copy and the British Museum IA. 37949 have "festini", where most other copies correctly have "festini". At the foot of k[1] verso, the "Stützsatz" (Träger) had been inked and printed "Ad Campanā Basilee di" (from recto of the same leaf) in the copies: Basel (AN VII 18), Colmar, Frankfurt (both), Madrid, Morgan, and Yale. This "bearer" was not printed in copies: Basel (FN VI 4[r]), Bodley, British Museum (both), Bühler, Freiburg, Harvard, Seville, Stockholm, Strassburg (all 3), and Uppsala. Dr. Dorothy M. Schullian (*A Catalogue of Incunabula and Manuscripts in the Army Medical Library* [now National Library of Medicine], New York, [1948], p. 60) notes the variants "Wymmare" (for Wynmare) and "veterē" (for veterēqʒ) on the first leaf of the unsigned quire in that copy.

[11] Thus in the Paris (H 723) and Stockholm copies, as noted by GW 5068, Anm. 1. Also Seville and Colmar, though the latter has text through quire m and has the Reuchlin text bound in.

lines Ad lectorem (below the woodcut of the kneeling Brant, as on the title)[12]. Here he warns the prospective purchaser not to buy anything but the genuine Basel printings[13] if he wishes to get the authorized and corrected text[14]. This quire n also circulated separately; copy at Colmar (Inc. C. G. 11574)[15] in addition to Bonn and Nikolsburg as noted by the *Gesamtkatalog*.

VI Grüninger coolly reprints V (with the warning against the piracies)[16] and adds this to his edition (III); thus British Museum IA. 1478.

If the above synopsis is consulted in connection with the full descriptions given in the *Gesamtkatalog der Wiegendrucke*, the various stages in the publication of these editions of Sebastian Brant's Poems will be clearly outlined in succinct form.

(From Gutenberg-Jahrbuch (1962), pp. 179-82).

[12] That only n⁴ verso was reset and that the other seven pages are identical in both states is made evident by the same broken characters appearing in both states at the same places. For example, a wrong-fount (gothic) v appears in "unanimi" in both states at n³, line 18.

[13] Brant strongly urges that "no one should buy copies which lack the name of Olpe", and Grüninger simply repeats this warning.

[14] The Stockholm copy of the *Carmina* is bound with the Grüninger *Stultifera Navis* of 1497 (GW 5057). The Morgan *Narrenschiff*, Basel: Bergmann, 1494 (GW 5041) is also bound with a copy of GW 5057, and the second Morgan copy of Bergmann's 1498 *Stultifera Navis* with Grüninger's first printing of *Das neue Narrenschiff* (GW 5048). All are in early, or contemporary, bindings—and one wonders how Bergmann would have felt about having his books bound up with Grüninger's!

[15] Schmidt (p. 352) writes: "Au mois de septembre Brant publia: Thurcorum terror et potentia . . . Ce poème reçut la signature n pour être ajouté aux exemplaires des carmina non encore vendus, mais fut aussi débité séparément. La dernière page est occupée par une Exhortatio ad divum Maximilianum regem. Un exemplaire du Thurcorum terror est à la Bibl. de Colmar, un des carmina avec l'Exhortatio à Maximilien, dans la mienne". This seems to suggest that the Colmar copy of the *Thurcorum Terror* had the *Exhortatio* – but it actually has Brant's distichs "Ad lectorem". The Colmar *Thurcorum Terror* is bound in a contemporary pig-skin binding with still another copy of Grüninger's 1497 *Stultifera Navis* (GW 5057) and two other incunables.

[16] This must have been printed well after September 1st (date of Bergmann's first issue) and could not have formed part of the original August 1st edition (III).

# CHAPTER B37

## ROMAN TYPE AND ROMAN PRINTING
## IN THE FIFTEENTH CENTURY

ANY discussion of roman type must necessarily include a brief consideration of the sources from whence it stemmed.[1] Though this may be familiar ground for some readers, a short survey of the antecedent history of this variety of letter may prove to be generally useful. In the hundred years between 1365 and 1465, the humanists became increasingly more dissatisfied with the current hand, gothic or black-letter, which reminded them forcefully of the barbarity of the North. Burckhardt points out that, as late as the papacy of Nicholas V (1447-1455), the copyists in Rome were still mostly Frenchmen and Germans—"barbarians" in the eyes of the humanists—for whose culture and traditions the future members of the Roman Academy had nothing but contempt.[2] "Antiquam exquirite matrem" Vergil had urged;[3] and in their new enthusiasm for the ancient world, the humanists too would search out their ancient mother—Rome, the fount from which flowed all language, literature and art, the source of all government and law. Stanley Morison would even have us believe that Byzantium, too, had a hand in this cultural urge for scribal reform—and that the capital of the Eastern Empire contributed to the creation of the humanistic majuscules.[4]

So far as capital letters were concerned, the scribes did not have to search far and wide for just the sort of characters they wanted; such capitals were present wherever Roman inscriptions were to be found. For the lower case, however, there were no such classical precedents; nevertheless, the incipient calligraphers ultimately found precisely what they were looking for in the Carolingian hand of half a mil-

[1] The present article is based upon an address delivered before the Philadelphia Graphic Arts Forum on 8 March 1960.

[2] Jacob Burckhardt, *The Civilization of the Renaissance in Italy* (Vienna & New York, [c. 1938]), p. 100.

[3] Aeneid, III, 96.

[4] *Byzantine Elements in Humanistic Script illustrated from the Aulus Gellius of 1445 in the Newberry Library* (Chicago, 1952).

lennium earlier. These minuscules reached the acme of their perfection in the hand written in Tours in the ninth and tenth centuries.[5] The humanist-scribes adapted these two sizes of letters to
each other, and thus the neo-Caroline hand was born, probably in
Florence. Whether it was invented by Poggio Bracciolini, as Professor
Berthold L. Ullman sets forth,[6] or was first regularly employed by
Coluccio Salutati or Niccolò Niccoli as Morison suggests,[7] is immaterial for our purposes. The earliest surviving manuscript written
in the new humanist hand is, perhaps, the 1429 Valerius Flaccus
from the pen of Antonio di Mario now preserved in the Biblioteca
Laurenziana in Florence.[8] It is certain, in any event, that the 'littera
antiqua' (as the humanists themselves liked to call it) was created
about the turn of the century and that, early in the fifteenth, Niccolò Niccoli, by enforcing it upon his school of copyists,[9] firmly established the new hand as the 'correct' one for the disciples of the new
cult of the antique. At the same time, especially in the chancery offices of the Curia, the informal, sloping variety of the *lettera anticha*
—the *corsiva* or *cancelleresca*—became the proper and necessary
hand for the documentary and archival material; this form of writing, in turn, ultimately fathered the 'italic'. By 1465, when the Germans had first brought the press into Italy, the humanistic script
had entered (calligraphically speaking) its 'perfected style,' as Professor J. P. Elder has described it,[10] a period which continued (according to the same authority) to about the year 1490. This was the
hand, inspired by Antonio Sinibaldi, which the early type-cutters in

[5] See especially Edward K. Rand, *A Survey of the Manuscripts of Tours* (Cam-
bridge, Mass., 1929), and (with Leslie W. Jones) *The Earliest Book of Tours* (Cambridge, Mass., 1934).
[6] 'Pontano's Handwriting and the Leiden Manuscript of Tacitus and Suetonius,'
*Italia medioevale e umanistica*, II (1959), 328. Since the present paper was written,
Professor Ullman's important study *The Origin and Development of Humanistic
Script* (Rome, 1960) has been published. [See especially his Chapter II 'The
Inventor—Poggio Bracciolini']. This thorough and detailed monograph amplifies
and corrects the short account given above.
[7] 'Early Humanistic Script and the first Roman Type', *The Library*, 4th ser.,
XXIV (1943), 1-29, especially p. 6.
[8] MS. Laur. 39, 35; cf Stanley Morison, *Four Centuries of Fine Printing* (London,
1924), p. xiii.
[9] See Morison's 'Printing Type', *Encyclopaedia Britannica* (14th edition; London,
1929), XVIII, 508.
[10] 'Clues for dating Florentine Humanistic Manuscripts', *Studies in Philology*,
XLIV (1947), 127-139.

Italy took as their model.[11] Is it surprising that they succeeded in cutting such impeccable types, the outstanding excellence of which have left their mark on much of the best typography of our own day?

If the known facts regarding the introduction of printing into the Italian Peninsula are recalled, it will be remembered that the palm for this achievement is awarded, for no well-documented reasons whatever, to Conrad Sweynheym and Arnold Pannartz.[12] No one knows for certain that it was Sweynheym and Pannartz who established Italy's first press at Subiaco, some fifty miles by road from Rome—but, in the absence of any other logical contenders, we may as well assume that it was the clerics from (respectively) Mainz and Cologne who performed this immensely significant job. Certain it is, in any case, that the Benedictine monastery of Santa Scolastica provided the quarters for the machinery of the press—and there printing began with the first movable type, suitable for this sort of work, ever cut south of the Alps. What sort of type was this? Here opinions differ—and differ radically! Alfred W. Pollard, then Keeper of Printed Books at the British Museum, remarked of the Subiaco books that they were 'printed in a light and pleasing gothic.'[13] In 1924,[14] the eminent designer, Stanley Morison, could write of the 'semi-gothic "Subiaco" type'; twenty years later, he would flatly assert that this same type was 'the first humanistic or roman type.'[15] Daniel Berkeley Updike,[16] a distinguished expert on type-design, maintained that Sweynheym and Pannartz, finding themselves in a country where the humanistic hand was the fashionable one, cut a type that 'appears to us gothic, but which they probably considered roman.'

No matter how one views it, the name 'roman' for the *antiqua* type is clearly a misnomer. As we have seen, the type is based on

---

[11] As E. P. Goldschmidt (*The Printed Book of the Renaissance*, [Cambridge, 1950], p. 59) pointed out, roman types originated 'in the humanistic script of Italian scholars'. Similarly, Daniel Berkeley Updike (*Printing Types; their History, Forms, and Use* [Cambridge, Mass., 1922], I, 70) remarks that 'the best roman types. . . . were modelled on Humanistic characters, which were in turn revivals of the Carolingian book-hands.'

[12] Compare Konrad Haebler, *Die deutschen Buchdrucker des XV. Jahrhunderts im Auslande* (München, 1924), p. 8 ff.

[13] *Fine Books* (New York & London, 1912), p. 88.

[14] *Four Centuries of Fine Printing*, p. xxiv. On p. xiv, he refers to it as 'a beautiful transitional type'.

[15] *Early Humanistic Script and the first Roman Type*, p. 26.

[16] *op. cit.*, p. 71.

Florentine calligraphy; if not first used in Subiaco, it made its initial appearance in Strassburg;[17] and it reached final perfection in Venice. If any type deserves the epithet 'roman', then it is the italic—*the* Roman type *par excellence*. But a discussion of that style of letter, a product of the sixteenth century, cannot be fitted into the announced limits of the present study.

In the summer of 1467, Sweynheym and Pannartz established their press at Rome in the palace of the Massimi. If they were the same printers who had issued the books from Subiaco (as seems extremely likely), then they did not bring their Subiaco type with them. Instead, they began to print 'in domo Petri de Maximo' an edition of Cicero's *Epistolae ad familiares* with quite a fine and pure roman letter.[18] Roman type had—at last—come to Rome!

At this point, it may be well to recall that roman type was not the only type used in fifteenth-century Italy. The gothic letter, too, was not unfamiliar to contemporary Italians. Indeed, the ultra-conservative professions of the Church and the Law continued to prefer this form of character for their liturgical and legal volumes. Some years ago, Alfred W. Pollard maintained:[19] 'That gothic type was used at all in Italy was due partly to the difficulty found in cutting very small roman type, so that gothic was used for economy, partly to the advantages of the heavy gothic face when a contrast was needed between text and commentary.' But this clearly overlooks the powerful force of tradition, which required the use of gothic face for those classes of books to which reference has just been made. Again, one must be on guard against such oversimplification as to assume that classical texts were invariably printed with the humanistic founts and that legal textbooks had to be printed in gothic letter —in Rome or elsewhere in the Peninsula. Leaving apart the Subiaco Cicero (whose type may be classed as semi-gothic or fere-humanistica, depending on one's *point de départ*) and some classics printed by Ulrich Han in a fount concerning which Updike has said:[20]

---

[17] Cf. Konrad Haebler, *Handbuch der Inkunabelkunde* (Leipzig, 1925), pp. 84-85; E. Miriam Lone, *Some Noteworthy Firsts in Europe during the Fifteenth Century* (New York, 1930), p. 19; Erich von Rath, 'Adolf Rusch und die Anfänge der Antiqua', *Beiträge zur Inkunabelkunde*, II (1938), 130-131; and Victor Scholderer, 'Adolf Rusch and the earliest Roman Types', *The Library*, 4th ser., XX (1939), 43-50.

[18] *Gesamtkatalog der Wiegendrucke* (Leipzig, 1925-38 = GW), VI, 563, no. 6799.

[19] *Fine Books*, p. 88.          [20] *op. cit.*, p. 72.

'whether it was a roman letter under Gothic influence, or a gothic letter under Roman influence, it is hard to say', we may note that the British Museum's incunabula catalogue[21] discusses no fewer than nine classical incunabula from Rome printed with gothic type. And these are no obscure books by obscure printers, either! Included here are five books printed by Stephan Plannck,[22] who was (after Heinrich Quentell of Cologne) probably the most prolific issuer of incunables; according to Pollard, Plannck 'had some good types' and the British Museum Catalogue asserts that, typographically, his work was better than much other Roman printing.[23] In comparing another fount with Aldus's Poliphilus type, Pollard also states that[24] 'a far finer fount is the large text type used by the Silbers at Rome, on both sides of 1500. This is well proportioned and beautifully round, and it is surprising that it has not yet been imitated by any modern typecutter.' Yet on 10 January 1492, Eucharius Silber issued a Lucan, printed entirely in gothic types.[25] The 'catch' here is that this is a translation into the vulgar tongue, and Silber may have thought that vernacular translations of the classics did not require roman types. It is curious to note that Plannck produced a gothic-type edition of Caesar's *Oratio Vesontione ad milites habita* about the same time that Bartholomaeus Guldinbeck issued one in roman;[26] the latter printer, in turn, put out an edition of three of Seneca's shorter tracts printed in a gothic fount.[27]

Conversely, law books were issued in roman type from the presses of Georgius Lauer, Sixtus Riessinger, Johannes Gensberg, Johannes Reinhardi, and others—seven in all, so far as books in the British Museum bear witness. These, too, were not just unimportant and trivial textbooks, but included such standard treatises as the *Constitutiones* of Pope Clement V, Gratian's *Decretum*, and Johannes

[21] *Catalogue of Books Printed in the XVth Century now in the British Museum* (London, 1908-49). Volume IV deals with the Roman books. Cited as BMC:IV.

[22] Two editions of the *Epistolae* of Phalaris (IA. 18747 and IA. 18745), an oration by Caesar (IA. 18610), the *De historia Romana* by Sextus Rufus and the *De viris illustribus* by Sextus Aurelius Victor, both of January 1492 (IA. 18503-4). Besides the Lucan and the Seneca, one may point to the Horace and the Manilius, both printed by the 'Printer of the Manilius' (BMC IV:133).

[23] Pollard, *Fine Books*, p. 68, and BMC IV:xiv.

[24] *Fine Books*, p. 90.

[25] BMC VII:1131-2 (IA. 18927).

[26] BMC IV:89 and GW 5098. The GW enters the edition under the name of the editor, Andreas Brentius.

[27] BMC IV:73 (IA. 18185).

Andreae's *Novellae* on the sixth book of the *Decretales*. These three volumes are all from the press of Lauer, a 'good craftsman' who owned more different types than any other fifteenth-century firm at Rome could boast.[28] The British Museum claims that Lauer possessed fourteen different founts, four of which are gothic types. Konrad Haebler,[29] on the other hand, asserts that Lauer owned, exclusive of Greek faces, some thirteen types, seven being roman and six gothic. Obviously, Lauer had a variety of types to choose from, and his choice of a roman fount in which to print these works is significant. A curious case is that of the press operated in the house of Anthony and Raphael de Vulterris, which produced a series of important legal works, using as its text-type a single roman fount.[30] The landlords, and probably the press's financial backers, were papal notaries. One would have expected such worthies to prefer law books to be printed in a more traditional letter. Of course, it took another quarter of a century before Aldus Manutius could produce a type based on the Roman chancery hand, the famous italic type cut for him by Francesco Griffo,[31] but gothic type—one would suppose —would have been more suited to the tastes of these 'scriptores apostolici'. It almost seems as though the early Roman printers were still quite uncertain as to what the public wanted.

One thing is crystal clear. When the German printers had crossed the Alps and established themselves in Italy, they felt that they had excellent expectations of reaping a handsome profit from their profession in their adopted country. The field seemed limitless: here was a land blessed with an abundant literate population and one where the supply of books had historically been incapable of meeting the demand. These high hopes were quickly dashed!

In Rome, Sweynheym and Pannartz became obsessed with an irrepressible enthusiasm for printing classical texts. By the summer of 1472, they were bankrupt. The pitiful petition to the Pope, set forth on their behalf by the bishop of Aleria, describes their predicament in no uncertain terms: 'our house', they assert, 'sufficiently commodious as it is, is full of printed quires, empty of the necessities

[28] BMC IV:35-42, and Pollard, *Fine Books*, p. 68.

[29] *Typenrepertorium der Wiegendrucke* (Halle & Leipzig, 1905-24), II, 90-91, and V, 93.

[30] Cf. BMC IV:46-48.

[31] Compare Stanley Morison, *A Tally of Types* (Cambridge, 1953), pp. 30-32, and Arundell Esdaile, *A Student's Manual of Bibliography* (London, 1932), pp. 136-138.

of life.'[32] Disheartened by lack of success with the press, Sweynheym soon withdrew from the business and turned his hand to engraving.[33] Although Pope Sixtus IV re-established the Roman Academy which his predecessor Paul II had suppressed—and appointed the humanist, Bartolommeo Sacchi of Piadena (commonly called Platina after his birthplace), as librarian of the Vatican[34]—the publication of classical texts in Rome did not flourish to any noteworthy extent after the great crash of the 1470s.

In Naples and Florence, those who could afford to buy books wanted manuscripts, and the press had a difficult time taking root. One notes with interest that Florence, the home of the most prized humanistic handwriting, never produced anything but rather mediocre founts of type. In Venice, on the other hand, roman type reached the highest state of its development in the hands of that grand master of the roman letter, Nicolaus Jenson. He produced what has been widely acclaimed as 'the most beautiful of all the letters of the fifteenth century.'[35] The Venetian script, though, is of no conspicuous merit. Consider, for example, the diary of Marino Sanuto which this member of the Maggior Consiglio of the Republic kept between the years 1496 and 1533.[36] The fifty-eight large volumes of the modern printed edition which contain this chatty and informative account display many lacunae, obviously because the learned editors could not decipher what Sanuto had written down. Somehow one doubts if a contemporary Florentine of similar social rank and official position would have been guilty of such slipshod writing. So far as book production was concerned, the old law of supply and demand still held good. Where a beautiful manuscript was wanted, it was written; where the preference was for a handsome incunable, it was printed. Florence's contribution to printing lay chiefly in the influence which its manuscripts exerted upon the lay-

---

[32] "Et ementes non esse nullum est gravius testimonium quam quod domus nostra satis magna plena est quinternionum, inanis rerum necessariarum" (Beriah Botfield, *Praefationes et epistolae editionibus principibus auctorum veterum praepositae* [Cambridge, 1861], p. 66).

[33] For a short note on the printers, see the *Catalogue of Manuscripts and Early Printed Books from the Libraries of William Morris, Richard Bennett, Bertram, Fourth Earl of Ashburnham, and other Sources, now forming Portion of the Library of J. Pierpont Morgan. Early Printed Books* (London, 1907), II, 2-3.

[34] See Vittorio Rossi, *Storia letteraria d'Italia. Il quattrocento* (Milan, 1953), p. 313 ff., and the article on Pope Sixtus IV in the *Enciclopedia Italiana*, XXXI, 923.

[35] Morison, *Tally*, p. 25.

[36] *I diarii di Marino Sanuto* (Venice, 1879-1903).

out of the well-printed book whenever produced, whether in the world of its own day or in the one more familiar to us.

Let us turn, now, to the roman types themselves and examine their status in the city whence they derived their name (if little else) and, for comparison's sake, their popularity in some other Italian communities, chosen at random. The learned book-seller, Mr. E. P. Goldschmidt,[37] once remarked that it was not necessary to give statistics—that 'they would be laborious to establish and tedious to read.' With the statement that it was laborious to compile them, I can heartily agree—but I trust that they will not be equally tedious to peruse. It is easy enough to make generalizations, but these are quite meaningless when not supported by facts. For example, what percentage of the total number of founts used in Rome in the fifteenth century would one judge to be roman—and what, if anything, does this figure prove? The writer's compilations show that the forty-one Roman presses which produced incunabula owned 131 different founts,[38] of which sixty-eight (not 52 per cent) were roman; consequently, sixty-three were gothic. I would never have believed, were the statistics not there to prove it, that the amount of Roman gothic type would have come so near equalling the total for the roman faces. But statistics, we need hardly be reminded, can be as misleading as they may be accurate! Since the types were nearly half roman and half gothic, were the books printed with them in Rome in the same proportion? By no means!

It should here be explained that this account of the Rome incunabula is based on the British Museum's holdings only, which I judge to be a fully representative group. According to Konrad Burger's listing, Rome produced about 1,400 different incunables, of which approximately a half are in the Museum.[39] It would certainly have been possible to compile a nearly complete list from other sources—but Panzer, Hain, Copinger, and others do not always provide us with essential particulars as to types, and these details it would have been extremely difficult, in many cases, to determine with

---

[37] *Printed Book of the Renaissance*, p. 8.

[38] The *Typenrepertorium* names forty-three presses. However, Arnoldus de Villa and the Printer of Philelphus have to be deleted from this list for reasons given in BMC VI:xxv and 734 and BMC VI:xxii and 703. Also, Hebrew and Greek founts have not been included in the total.

[39] This estimate is given in BMC IV:xvi as based on the lists provided by Konrad Burger, *The Printers and Publishers of the XV. Century with Lists of their Works* (London, 1902).

accuracy. Consequently, all the figures concerning the Roman incunabula given in this study will be based on the British Museum's
incunable catalogue.

Half the books issued from Rome prior to 1501 were *not* put out
with gothic as their *basic* text-type. By actual count (excluding the
three Subiaco books), of the 680 Roman incunabula in the British
Museum, 426 display roman, and 254 gothic, text-types. In short,
just a bit more than a third of the total (*not* half) may be classed as
gothic books.

Again, let us examine the prevalence of roman types in several
other centers of incunabula printing which have been selected by
lot: Florence, Modena, Naples, Pavia, Reggio Emilia, and Siena.[40]
In these six places, 92 presses used 261 types, of which 110 were roman and 151 gothic. It is almost incredible that this predominance
of gothic founts should exist in Roman Italy, yet there are the figures!
But here too, statistics can be misleading. For instance, seven gothic
founts were used in Siena, and not a single roman one was employed
in the city which was the Tuscan rival to the humanist glories of
Florence. Similarly, 89 of the 95 types used in Pavia are gothic. An
explanation for these figures we shall seek later. On the other hand,
27 of the 49 Neapolitan types were roman—and, in Florence, 55 roman founts leave the 22 gothic ones far behind in the competition
for popularity. Neighbouring towns can show exactly opposite traditions, so that 16 of the 19 types employed in Reggio are roman—
while nearby Modena displays a slight preference for the gothic letter, eight to six.

The answer as to which fount prevailed in the several towns lies
in the nature of the book-production of these centers. The Law and
the Church, as we have seen, had a traditional preference for the
gothic face; scientific books,[41] too, tended to appear in the same letter. In the case of the latter, economy may also have played a significant role, for not only was it easier to cut a smaller gothic letter
than a roman one but, as against roman, gothic saved space both in
width and in depth. More words, in short, could be put on the same
page with gothic than with roman letter. As a result of these circum-

---

[40] The figures here cited are taken from the *Typenrepertorium*. Printing in
Reggio di Calabria was confined to Hebrew books.

[41] For the scientific books issued in some of these cities, see my 'The Statistics
of Scientific Incunabula,' *supra*.

stances, Goldschmidt could assert that 'no law book, no medical book, no sermons, no Prayer Books or missals, no Bibles (as far as I know) exist, which are written in the "antique" letters.'[42]

This circumstance, of course, accounts for the overwhelming predominance of the Fraktur in Siena and Pavia, whose schools of law and medicine were well served by the local press. The influence of production on the choice of type may, perhaps, be best seen in Jenson's publications.[43] Of the 27 works printed by him before 1474 found in the British Museum, exactly two-thirds are of classical or humanist concern—and all 27 were printed in roman. With the collapse of the book-market in 1472/3, Jenson turned his attention to other classes of literature—and to other types. A third of the 30 later books found in the Museum are legal tracts, thirteen are religious works, and only seven are classical by nature. Thus, more than two-thirds of the books issued after 1473 were anything but classical—and more than two-thirds of the books issued by the Jenson press in that period were printed with gothic types. Actually, Jenson (whose roman founts were extolled by William Morris, Emery Walker, Cobden-Sanderson, Bruce Rogers, Updike and others)[44] possessed seven gothic types against only two roman.[45] On the other hand, Aldus Manutius, appearing on the scene late in the Quattrocento, had no gothic type at all. But it must be remembered that Aldus eschewed legal works; though he printed scientific books, these were mostly classical in origin and current texts were hardly represented in his 'list'.

Well then, it may well be asked, in the capital of Christendom there must have been a great demand for religious works; why did the total of gothic types and books in gothic letter not exceed those in roman? As I have counted them, 307 books of Roman origin[46] were items of religious or devotional character or connected, in one way or another, with the activities of the Papal Court. Yet books in

[42] *Printed Book of the Renaissance*, p. 2.

[43] 'At first, Jenson's production, also, was influenced by humanism; then, no doubt on account of a stagnating market, his main effort was transferred to legal treatises, elegantly executed and textually impeccable' (*A History of the Printed Book* [ed. L. C. Wroth; New York, 1938], p. 71).

[44] Cf. Morison, *Tally*, p. 25.

[45] According to BMC V:165-166. The *Typenrepertorium* (II, 117) credits Jenson with six gothic and three roman founts.

[46] Approximately 45 per cent of the total Roman editions in the British Museum.

roman type, it will be recalled, accounted for two-thirds of total Roman production. How can this apparent contradiction be reconciled?

To those who may have contemplated the nature of Roman book-production in the fifteenth century, the explanation may come as no surprise. Pollard has observed:[47] 'At first also there seems to have been some doubt as to whether printed service books were suitable for use in church, and liturgical printing did not begin to flourish until the end of the century.' In Rome, printing of liturgical texts (a specie of religious book preponderantly in the gothic letter) did not flourish at all in the early days of the press.[48] Of some 182 characteristic liturgical texts (*Agendae, Directoria, Ordinarii*, and so forth) issued before 1501, only a single one was printed in Rome; Venice alone issued 18 *Diurnalia*. The fifteenth century saw the production of over 350 *Missals*, just seven of which were put out by Roman presses; indeed, between 1496 and 1551, Weale-Bohatta could not discover a single *Missal* printed in the city of the Popes. *Breviaries* to the number of 418 were turned out in the fifteenth century, exactly one of which was Roman in origin. Only one *Bible* was produced in Rome prior to 1501,[49] of 127 recorded such editions of Holy Writ. Of the more than 1,700 *Horae* ever printed, precisely two can be assigned to Rome, and one of these is in Greek, a version rather more exotic than practical.[50] In the related *Officia*, Rome fared slightly better, contributing six of the more than 236 editions. Of the 130 *Indulgences* checked in the German bibliography of broadsides, many of which

[47] *Catalogue of Books mostly from the Presses of the First Printers . . . . collected by Rush C. Hawkins* (Oxford, 1910), p. 110.

[48] Besides the GW, the following works have been used in compiling the figures here cited: Hanns Bohatta, *Bibliographie der Livres d'heures* (Wien, 1924) and his *Liturgische Bibliographie des XV. Jahrhunderts mit Ausnahme der Missale und Livres d'heures* (Wien, 1911); W. H. J. Weale and H. Bohatta, *Bibliographia liturgica. Catalogus missalium ritus latini ab anno M.CCCC.LXXIV. impressorum* (London, 1928), and *Einblattdrucke des XV. Jahrhunderts . . . . hrsg. von der Kommission für den Gesamtkatalog der Wiegendrucke* (Halle, 1914).

[49] This edition was printed by Sweynheym and Pannartz in 1471 with their roman type (GW 4210). Oddly enough, the only other *Bible* printed with this style of letter (GW 4209) was that produced by Adolf Rusch in Strassburg, before 1470, with the type that was formerly thought to be the earliest roman fount. Hans Volz (*Bibel und Bibeldruck in Deutschland im 15. und 16. Jahrhundert*, [Mainz, 1960], p. 17) points out that, after the edition of 1471, the press in Rome published "für mehr als hundert Jahre keinen einzigen weiteren lateinischen Bibeldruck".

[50] Printed by Zacharias Callierges, *circa* 1515 (Bohatta 1483). The other edition was produced by Georgius Herolt, about 1480 (Bohatta 440).

were issued to raise money for the war against the Turks and for the defense of Rhodes and Cyprus against the attacks of the infidels, only a single one was printed in Rome. Some 102 papal broadsides were issued in the fifteenth century and have come down to our day, but only 15 of them were put out in the papal city itself. Such liturgical and ecclesiastical texts were precisely the ones most commonly printed in black-letter—and Rome supplied exactly 34, of the 3,245 editions which I have enumerated—just one per cent! The other classes of books most frequently printed with gothic types could not compensate for the lack of liturgical printing in Rome, since scientific books numbered only 68 (10 per cent) and legal works totalled but 91 (or 13.3 per cent). These figures may be astounding—but they certainly explain why books printed in Fraktur were not more common in Rome.

What sort of books, then, comprise the category of ecclesiastical printing which accounted for such a large proportion of Roman-printed incunabula? The printed versions of the orations delivered at the papal court (138 of them in the British Museum) apparently formed 45 per cent of this class—and 20 per cent of all the Roman incunabula. But, as often as not, these were printed in the antiqua rather than in the competing letter. Stephan Plannck, for example, 40 per cent of whose output was devoted to such speeches,[51] habitually used a small gothic type for printing them in the decade following August 1482. Then he suddenly switched to Roman types, though this change coincided with a dropping off in his output, until he finally ceased printing altogether at the turn of the century. His great competitor, Eucharius Silber, appears to have preferred antiqua for his printed orations, though he also used black-letter. It is interesting to note that, in the spring of 1494, Silber issued with gothic types two orations delivered by Martinus de Viana before Pope Alexander VI. Exactly two years later, he printed two other orations by the same doctor of Sacred Theology, but this time Silber used roman type.[52] Even more arresting is the fact that, in the autumn of 1492, Silber printed the oration 'on the election of a new pope' by the future Cardinal Bernardino de Carvajal in two (apparently simultaneous) editions, one roman and the other gothic. Another gothic-

[51] Of the 158 editions listed by BMC, no fewer than 62 are orations. If these are added to the other books printed for the benefit of the Curia, the total rises to 98 (or 62 per cent of Plannck's total output as recorded in BMC).

[52] Cf. BMC IV:116 (IA. 18999 and 19000) and IV:117 (IA. 19012 and 19016).

letter edition was issued by Plannck, and a roman one by an unde-
termined press, perhaps also working in Rome.[53] Similarly, Andreas
Freitag put out both a roman and a gothic-letter edition of the oration
which Niccolò Tegrimi of Lucca delivered before Alexander VI on
25 October 1492 on behalf of his fellow citizens.[54] Competition between presses may be the explanation for the two editions of the
oration, bringing the respectful greetings of the Republic to the new
Pope, which the patrician Sebastiano Badoer of Venice delivered
before the same Pope on 17 December 1492. Freitag printed this
with gothic type, while Plannck put out his edition with roman
letter.[55]

Enough of such figures and statistics. What, it is proper to inquire, do these prove—or, more accurately, suggest? So far as printing
in Rome is concerned (for that matter of fact, in other communities
in Italy too), it is evident that the new 'antique' type did not wholly
and completely capture the field. Once the great spate of classical
texts had been absorbed, this was followed by a renewal of interest
in the older alphabetical forms. In Venice as in Rome—in Milan and
in Florence—in Bologna and in Naples—Roman type came first, but
the press was quick to discover that money was also to be made from
black-letter printing. There was, perhaps, a more assured and more
generous (if less spectacular) source of income from this type of
business than from the issuing of the glamorous classical and humanist texts, the publication of which entailed fierce competition.
For example, Octavianus Scotus of Venice, both as printer and as
publisher,[56] built a successful career largely on the production of
books printed with gothic type. So, too, did the brothers De Gregoriis
of the same city, who owned the astonishing total of 48 different
founts, 36 of which were Fraktur.[57]

The essential difference between the scriptoria and the press, it
seems to me, is that the scribe was interested in beauty, the printer
in accuracy of text. For a thoroughly qualified appraisal of the manu
scripts sold by the firm of Vespasiano da Bisticci, I should like to cite

[53] BMC IV:113 (IA. 18940 and 18941). The other two editions are listed by
GW 6150 and GW 6149.
[54] BMC IV:135 (IA. 18946) and IV:137 (IA. 19326).
[55] BMC IV:137 (IA. 19329) and IV:97 (IA. 18524); cf. GW 3159 and 3160.
[56] Consult BMC V:xxii-xxiii and 275-279.
[57] Compare BMC V:xxviii-xxix and 336-352. The types are listed in the *Typenrepertorium*, II, 131-134 and V, 102-104.

E. P. Goldschmidt's comment:[58] 'They are all magnificently written in splendid *litera umanistica* on the finest vellum. Many are beautifully decorated with initials and borders in the purest Florentine Renaissance style. They are, indeed, the best examples of artistic craftsmanship. . . . However, it is only too evident that these books were produced to be admired, to be shown, to be treasured, but not to be read. From the textual point of view Vespasiano's admirable masterpieces of calligraphy are written with extraordinary slovenliness. Whole lines are left out, mistakes abound, repetitions are left uncorrected rather than spoil the beautiful page. Vespasiano's manuscripts are written for people who wanted to possess these books, not to read them, and the scribes knew it and were much more attentive to the evenness of their letters than to the sense of what they were writing.' Now let Aldus Manutius speak for himself:[59] 'It is hard,' he allowed, 'to produce a good Latin text, harder still a correct Greek one, and hardest of all, a text free from error.' Aldus, then, was chiefly concerned with accuracy of text—and this is but one of many such comments which could be cited.

That the Roman printers were somewhat indifferent to the unities and were not at all averse to using both gothic and roman face on the same page is a further indication that the fifteenth-century press was more concerned with purity of text than with aesthetic appeal. Indeed, one instance affords a splendid example of curious insensitivity on the part of one Roman printer. In 1477, Johannes Schurener from Boppard on the Rhine issued, as perhaps his very last production, an edition of the *Facetiae* by Poggio,[60] printed with his roman type, 20 lines of which measure 85 millimetres. Some time later, Johannes Bulle de Bremis (whose first dated and signed book appeared on 18 November 1478)[61] must have acquired the remaining unsold stock of this printing. When the new owner received the unbound sheets, he could not help but note that leaves 47 to 50 (forming the two inner sheets of the last quire) were missing; they had either been lost or destroyed, or a sufficient quantity of them had

[58] 'Preserved for Posterity', *The New Colophon*, II (1950), 331.

[59] See his preface reproduced in *Aldus Manutius and his Thesaurus Cornucopiae of 1496* (Syracuse University Press, 1958).

[60] BMC IV:58 (IA. 17790).

[61] BMC IV:xiv and 78. For the English printer, also called Joannes Lettou, see E. Gordon Duff, *The Printers, Stationers and Bookbinders of Westminster and London from 1476 to 1535* (Cambridge, 1906), pp. 41-47.

never been printed, a common-enough mishap in the early days of printing.[62] Without hesitation, Bulle made good the deficiency by reprinting these leaves to replace the wanting originals—but he reprinted them with his *gothic* type of about the same measurement, 20 lines measuring 83 millimetres. This press did not, indeed, own a roman type; nevertheless, it seems significant that the printer apparently made no attempt whatsoever to acquire or borrow suitable characters from any of his colleagues. His gothic type is strikingly similar to that used by John Lettou of London, and some scholars like to think that the Roman printer was the same person who later worked in England. What name could be more appropriate for the first printer to open shop in the City of London than—John Bull?

In the long run, of course, roman type almost completely replaced the gothic, which today survives in occasional phrases in legal documents and resolutions and as greetings on our Christmas cards. But Rome itself had no hand in this victory, for, between 1473 and 1501, the Eternal City 'took no very important part' in the development of typography.[63] It had to wait a further quarter-century before achieving typographic fame through the italic type of Ludovico degli Arrighi, whose type came from the hand of Lautizio de Bartolomeo dei Rotelli—'the great Lautizio', as Cellini called him.[64] Nor did Rome distinguish itself in the quality of its book-production in the Quattrocento. Pollard rightly summarized this in these words:[65] 'much of the work of Plannck, the most prolific of the Roman printers, was ephemeral and unimportant, whether we regard it from a literary or a typographical standpoint, and it cannot be said that printing at Rome either fulfilled the promise of its enthusiastic beginning or produced a total output worthy of so great a city. When the first torrent of classics and the succeeding, but much smaller, torrent of law-books were exhausted, no books of any distinction took their place, and the scantiness of the vernacular literature committed to the press speaks eloquently of the lack in Rome of the well-to-do burghers for whom printers at Venice catered with such success.'

(From *Bibliotheca Docet: Festgabe für Carl Wehmer* (1963), pp. 101-110).

[62] See, for example, the discussion in my article 'The Walters "Polycronicon" of 1495', *supra*.
[63] Pollard, *Fine Books*, p. 68.
[64] *History of the Printed Book*, p. 122, and Morison, *Tally*, p. 27.
[65] BMC IV:xvi.

# CHAPTER B38

## ALDUS'S *PARAENESIS* TO HIS PUPIL, LEONELLO PIO

A VOLUME in the Bibliothèque Humaniste at Sélestat (no. 1171) once formed part of the great library formed by the justly celebrated humanist, Beatus Rhenanus. This collection was bequeathed by Rhenanus's nuncupative will to his native city on his death at Strassburg, 20 July 1547. The 'Sammelband' here noted contains the following items as listed in Joseph Walter's catalogue of the early printed books at Sélestat:[1]

(*a*) no. 2066. Plutarchus, *Moralia*. Venice, Bernardinus Venetus, de Vitalibus, [*a*. 1 May 1505]. Proctor–Isaac 12744; British Museum 1481. c. 17.

(*b*) no. 2068. Plutarchus, *Regum et imperatorum apophthegmata*. Venice, Georgius de Rusconibus, 2 October 1508. Pr. 13034; British Museum 609. h. 3 (2).

(*c*) no. 2069. Plutarchus, *De his qui tarde a Numine corripiuntur*. Nürnberg, Friedrich Peypus, 30 June 1513. Pr. 11111; British Museum 720. e. 31.

(*d*) no. 1635. Isocrates, *Oratio Isocratis pulcherrima in qua praecepta a iuvenibus observanda continentur*. Bologna, Benedictus Hectoris, 5 April 1502. Pr. 13720; British Museum 11391. e. 1.

(*e*) no. 1821. Manutius, Aldus, *Musarum Panagyris*. '(Aldus, Venise).' Renouard, p. 257.

(*f*) no. 1696. Leonicenus, Nicolaus, *De Tiro, seu Vipera*. [Venice, Aldus Manutius, *c*. 1498]. Klebs 600. 1; *B.M.C.* V. 563—1A. 24477.

(*g*) no. 1593. Hyginus, *De mundi et sphaerae declaratione*. Venice, Melchior Sessa, 15 September 1512. Pr. 13166A; British Museum 1395. f. 41.

This volume's chief claim to fame obviously rests on the exceedingly rare Aldine imprints contained therein.[2] Of the Leonicenus,

---

[1] *Incunables & imprimés du XVIᵐᵉ siècle de la Bibliothèque de Sélestat* (Catalogue général de la Bibliothèque Municipale, Iᵉ série, IIIᵉ partie), Colmar, 1929.

[2] Though the works are undoubtedly incunables, Walter has listed them with the sixteenth-century imprints.

Renouard[3] knew only of the copy belonging to Lord Spencer. Lord Gosford's annotations in his copy of Renouard (now in the Pierpont Morgan Library) listed, besides his own (Morgan) and that belonging to Lord Spencer (John Rylands Library), the copies owned by Thomas Grenville (now in the British Museum) and, with a query, by Samuel Butler, Bishop of Litchfield.[4]

The *Musarum Panagyris*, which the present writer has discussed elsewhere,[5] is no less scarce. To the three copies previously identified, one may now add the example cited above and the one in the Biblioteca Universitaria in Bologna (Caronti 529).[6]

But the most interesting item in the volume is surely one which Walter either overlooked or believed, wrongly, to form part of the *Musarum Panagyris*, to which it is appended in the volume. This consists of a single sheet of paper, the heading and opening lines of verse on the recto of the first leaf reading:

Aldi Manuccii Bassianatis latini ad Leonellum pium Magnificū || præstantiq3 ingenio pueŘ: atq3 ad eos q boni eē cupiūt: sibiq3 aditū: || & ad uirtutem: & ad caelum parere expeditissimum Paraenesis. || Uirtuti: & magno callem: qui affectat olympo || Haec legat: & seruet: quæ mea scripta sonant || …

The text ends on folio 2 recto, line 35, with:

Tu quoque si uitia effugies: Christumq3 sequerere:[7] || Virtutemq3 coles: ibis ad astra puer. || DEO GRATIAS AMEN: || (2ʳ, blank)

This is the work described by Renouard on p. 257, no. 2; a reprint of the complete text appears on pages 540–1. Renouard remarked (p. 257): 'On ne connoît jusqu'à présent de cette pièce que ce seul exemplaire'—but he did not state, here or elsewhere, where the only known copy was preserved. Moreover, it is not at all certain that Renouard ever saw the original,[8] since he annotated his reprint with

[3] A. A. Renouard, *Annales de l'imprimerie des Alde*, 3ᵉ éd. (Paris, 1834), p. 259.

[4] No copy is listed in the *Indice generale degli incunaboli delle biblioteche d'Italia*, Rome, 1943–54, nor in the microfilm continuation of Marie Pellechet [and M.-Louis Polain], *Catalogue général des incunables des bibliothèques publiques de France*, Paris, 1897–1909.

[5] Curt F. Bühler, 'The First Aldine', *supra*.

[6] Andrea Caronti, *Gli incunaboli della R. Biblioteca Universitaria di Bologna* (Bologna, 1889), p. 314.

[7] Renouard (p. 541) and, following him, Firmin-Didot (p. 11) print 'sequere', but the transcript made by the writer (2 June 1961) has the second person singular, imperfect subjunctive of 'sequor'.

[8] It should be pointed out, however, that Renouard does observe (p. 257) that the *Paraenesis* 'est imprimée en lettres rondes un peu plus petites que celles du

the remark that 'imprimant d'après une copie manuscrite, je dois
la reproduire telle que je l'ai reçue, avec la ponctuation et les abbrévia-
tions de l'original' (p. 540, note). If he had had access to the original,
would Renouard have been content with a manuscript copy? Ambroise Firmin-Didot,[9] too, referred to this work 'dont on ne connaît
qu'un seul exemplaire', without locating it.[10] It is quite possible, of
course, that the Beatus Rhenanus 'Sammelband' provided the text
for Renouard; if not, one must argue that two copies were certainly
extant in the first half of the nineteenth century.

Unfortunately the library at Sélestat is not very well provided with
bibliographical reference books, which made it impossible to determine on the spot who the printer of the leaflet may have been.
Such details as could conveniently be noted (single Qu, Haebler's
type G, measuring 78 mm., together with a Greek type of the same
measurement, apparently identical with that found in the *Musarum
Panagyris*, &c.) suggest that Baptista de Tortis was the printer of
this work also, as he had been of the similar piece dedicated to Alberto Pio, in this case using his second roman type together with the
matching Greek fount.[11]

The probable date of printing would seem to be *c.* 1490 (corresponding to that of the *Musarum Panagyris* and to the period in
which De Tortis made use of these types). This would place the
printing shortly after the close of Aldus's tutorship of the young
princes of Carpi (1483-90), during which time the *Paraenesis* was
certainly written. It is unlikely, under any circumstances, that it
could have been printed much later than 1490, since in that year
Leonello (elder brother to Alberto) was certainly over sixteen years
old.[12] How much older, we do not know, but two years later Leonello
was already a married man.[13] The somewhat youthful character of

*Panagyris'*. This information could, of course, have been supplied to him by the
person who provided the manuscript transcript.

[9] *Alde Manuce et l'Hellénisme à Venise* (Paris, 1875), p. 10.

[10] Julius Schück, *Aldus Manutius und seine Zeitgenossen in Italien und Deutschland* (Berlin, 1862), p. 5, simply cites Renouard's reprint of the text without locating
the original. He calls the *Paraenesis* 'eine poetische Zuschrift des Aldus an Leonellus'.

[11] See the details in the British Museum's incunabula catalogue (*B.M.C.* V, pp.
319-20 and plate xxix*).

[12] Cf. Pompeo Litta, *Famiglie celebri Italiane* (Milan, 1819-1910), under the tables
for Pio di Carpi (1. xii. 3). Leonello is there listed as the second son of Lionello
(d. 1480) and Caterina, sister of Pico della Mirandola. No date of birth is given,
though his death is placed in 1535. The youngest son (Alberto) was born in 1475.

[13] He was married in 1492 to Maria di Bernardino Martinengo.

Aldus Manutius's admonitions[14] to his pupil would hardly have been suitable for printing at a much later date. In sum, it seems likely that the *Paraenesis* for Leonello Pio was both written and printed as a companion piece for the *Musarum Panagyris*, dedicated to Alberto, and that both pamphlets were produced at Venice by Baptista de Tortis about the year 1490.

(From *The Library* (1962), pp. 240-42).

[14] Schück (p. 5, note) states: 'Die Paränese an Leonellus enthält gut abgefasste Lebensregeln'. However, such examples as he cites ('Amandos esse moderatores: gnatonicos uero fugiendos. || Qui te corripiunt monitus audito libenter. || Pagina: castigo quos amo: sacra refert.') are hardly very sophisticated.

# CHAPTER B39

## COMMENTS ON A BELGIAN "SAMMELBAND" OF THE EARLY SIXTEENTH CENTURY IN THE PIERPONT MORGAN LIBRARY

A COMPOSITE volume in the Pierpont Morgan Library (Accession No. 18720) provides the investigator with fascinating and unusual insights into the characteristics and traditions peculiar to its period. This volume contains a number of tracts, all of them printed in Paris in the first decade of the sixteenth century. The first and longest item therein is the Aulus Gellius, *Noctes Atticae*, Paris: Jean Marchant for Jean Petit, 22 Mar. 1508. This work is followed by editions of nine pamphlets written by the Bolognese humanist, Philippus Beroaldus, a scholar whose writings had recently become extremely popular, and (consequently) frequently printed, in France.

The binding of the volume is of contemporary, stamped leather over wooden boards. In the center of both upper and lower covers, one finds a stamp reading "Gruenendale." On the title of the Aulus Gellius is the early note of ownership which, with contractions expanded, reads: "Liber monasterij Viridisvallis in Zonia Ordinis Canonicorum Sancti Augustini Episcopj" (i.e., "This book belongs to the monastery of the Austin Canons at Groenendale in the forest of Soignies").[1] These facts demonstrate that the book not only belonged to, but was very probably bound in, the Augustinian monastery of Groenendale, not far from Brussels. Finally, it is important to note that the volume consists of a collection not of the traditional theological tracts suitable for a monastic library (as might be expected) but of the "new learning" then just becoming popular north of the Alps.

I

One of the tracts bound in this "Sammelband" is the *Orationes, prelectiones et prefationes* [etc.] of Beroaldus, printed by Jodocus Badius Ascensius in Paris and dated 13 Nov. 1505 (for sale both by

[1] Concerning books bound at, or for, this monastic library, see E. Ph. Goldschmidt, *Gothic & Renaissance Bookbindings* (London, 1928), I, 198, no. 87 and Plate CV.

Jean Petit and himself). This is a quarto, the collation of which is: a-g⁸ h⁴ i⁸ k⁴. There is nothing very unusual about the printing of this work save for the second sheet in the sixth quire, at least in the copies in the Morgan and Yale University libraries.² In quire f of these copies, the pages must be read in the order: 5, 10, 11, 8, 9, 6, 7, and 12, if the text is to make sense. This is a variety of error rarely to be encountered in the work of so skilled and estimable a printer as Josse Bade was.

When one seeks for an explanation for this phenomenon, one turns immediately, of course, to *An Introduction to Bibliography for Literary Students* by Ronald B. McKerrow (Oxford, 1949). As usual, a number of explanations for precisely this sort of confusion is set forth here. McKerrow remarks (pp. 260-61): "This may seem a strange muddle, but it is due to a very simple cause, namely, to the sheets, after being printed on one side, having been turned the wrong way round when being perfected; or, alternatively, to the second forme printed having been placed the wrong way round on the bed of the press." The present example, however, is not exactly covered by either of these alternatives. This is proved by the existing foliation and signature mark, which here continue to run in the correct sequence. The recto of the fourth leaf in this quire, therefore, is signed "fiiii" and is foliated xliiii (though it provides the text proper to f6 and xlvi); conversely, the recto of folio xlvi has the text properly found on f4 (and should be numbered xliv). McKerrow says (pp. 259-60):

We may, I think, say that the wrong arrangement of pages of type in a forme is, in ordinary work, extremely rare. The correct imposition for the various sizes of books is so elementary a part of a printer's training that such an error could hardly occur save by most extraordinary carelessness or misunderstanding; and if it did, it would almost certainly be corrected in proof.

What may have happened here is that the type-pages were placed the wrong way around while the correct order was maintained in supplying the headlines and foliation (plus the signature mark). Alternatively, it is possible that the wrong folio numbers (and signature) were attached to the two pages and that the pressman, working solely from the foliation, placed these on the bed of the press in the traditional manner (with the two unfoliated versos in *their* tra-

² Yale no.: Gr12 B538 A1 1505.

ditional order relative to the numbered leaves). In either case, the result of such faulty procedure would be that the foliation continues correctly while the text is upset. If the proper folio number had been attached to the pages in the first place and the whole laid the wrong way round and printed thus, then the foliation would have been confused in the same manner as the text. Subsequent editions printed by Badius (in 1508 and 1511) and another Parisian one by Bonnemere for Roce in 1509, as well as the Basel editions of 1513, 1515 and 1517,[3] have the correct order.

In the Morgan copy, this typographical error was noted by some contemporary reader,[4] who made the following guide-notes for the correct reading of the text:

> foot of f3 recto: folio xlvj. prima pagina lege documenta
>     "    "   f4   "    : folio xlvij. prima pagina lege obarmauerat
>     "    "   f5   "    : folio xliiij. prima pagina lege comiter accipiunt
>     "    "   f6   "    : folio xlv. pagina prima lege nobili genere &c.

Normally, one would expect (for example) that "folio xlvj. prima pagina" would refer to the recto of leaf 46—but it does no such thing! This notation refers to the verso of leaf 45. Apparently, here (and similarly in the three other instances) the early corrector thought of "folio 46" as referring to the *opening* (45ᵛ-46ʳ) and that the "first page" would be the first page of the opening or folio 45 verso. I have met with no other instance of such an interpretation of "prima pagina."

## II

Also included in this "Sammelband" is an edition of the commentary of Beroaldus on the *Symbola Pythagorae*, Paris: Marchant for Petit, 14 July 1505. Here one finds that almost an entire page (c4 recto) has been so heavily inked over, that the text is quite illegible. On examining other printings of this text,[5] one discovers

---

[3] Bade's editions are page-for-page reprints of his 1505 production but with the correct order in quire f. The Paris printings (as here listed) may be consulted in the British Museum: 12301.e.39(1); 1073.l.1; and 1073.l.4. The Basel edition of 1515 is also in the BM (1073.l.6), the other two being at Yale (Zi 9477 and Gr12 B538 A1 1517).

[4] In the Yale copy, another reader has sought to set the text in order by supplying the pages with numbers from 1-8.

[5] The text begins: "Non tamen credamus in totum nobis concubitu interdictum esse & venere: quod pernitiosum magis esset quam salutare: Nam concubitus sicut

that this chapter deals with the topic "concubitus" in a manner which did not precisely conform to the rather rigid views on that subject which characterized the official attitude of the Austin Canons living under the Windesheim rules. This, then, is a fine example of monastic and mediaeval censorship in a humanistic treatise.

(From *PBSA* 58 (1964), pp. 154-56).

---

frequens soluit corpus: ita rarus excitat. Et sicut veneri si modus absit nihil pernitiosius: ita bonae valitudini nihil pene utilius si modice rarenterque exerceatur . . ." (Basel, 1513, folio 109).

# CHAPTER B40

## THE FIRST EDITION OF FICINO'S
## *DE CHRISTIANA RELIGIONE*: A PROBLEM
## IN BIBLIOGRAPHICAL DESCRIPTION[1]

THE first edition of the *De christiana religione* by Marsilius Ficinus[2] was produced at Florence, some time within the month following 10 November 1476, by Nicolaus Laurentii,[3] a German printer who had emigrated to Italy from his native diocese of Breslau. The book itself is an unsigned quarto, and the collation given in the British Museum's monumental incunabula catalogue reads: [a b$^{10}$ c-f$^8$ g$^{6+1}$ h-p$^8$ q$^{10}$; *$^2$]. A manuscript entry in the Museum's own "working copy" of this catalogue[4] notes that "[g]1 was occupied by the same text as [g]2 in a different setting-up & was cancelled. The Phillipps copy (Sotheby sale cat. 25 Nov. 1946 no. 122) contained both leaves. Sold to Harvard Univ. Lib." Accordingly, it would seem proper to emend the collation of this copy so that the seventh quire would be described as [g]$^{8-1}$.

A thorough consideration of the problem presented by this irregular quire poses such questions as to WHY the duplication of text came into being, WHAT would be the true make-up of an ideal copy of this printing, and HOW should the seventh quire be properly listed?

Turning, then, to the redundant text, a close comparison of the two settings shows that for fifty lines the two agree, line for line;[5]

---

[1] Once again it is my pleasant duty to acknowledge, with my most sincere thanks, the very real help provided by the critical comments of Professor Fredson Bowers. "Numquam ad eum accedo quin abeam doctior"!

[2] References: HCR 7069; *Indice* 3857; Stillwell *Census* F133; Proctor 6125.

[3] Konrad Haebler, *Die deutschen Buchdrucker des XV. Jahrhunderts im Auslande* (München, 1924), pp. 159-160, gives a good short account of this printer's activity.

[4] *Catalogue of Books Printed in the XVth Century now in the British Museum* (Lithographic Reprint; London, 1963), VI, 625. From his study of a copy then in the possession of the antiquarian bookseller Leo S. Olschki, Enrico Rostagno ("Di un esemplare del *De christiana Religione* di Marsilio Ficino," *La Bibliofilia*, II [1900/01], 399) was aware of the repetition in the seventh quire but offered no explanation for the presence of the repeated text.

[5] If the text had twice been set from the manuscript quite independently, then there surely would have been some differences in the line-endings through the differing use of contractions.

the only difference between the two occurs in lines 5-6 of the verso, where [g]1 divides "criſti‖ana" and [g]2 has "chriſtia‖na." Such agreement can hardly be accidental![6] Of even greater significance, at least in the opinion of the writer, is the fact that both settings offer the identical misprints or errors: in line 4 (recto), both copies have "ſactio" where "ſanctio" is required; in line 12, "elegi" for "elegit"; in line 12 (verso), "denu(m)ptiat" for "denunciat"; and in line 14, both read "permictit" where "permittit" is wanted.[7] Of course, the archetype itself might have been corrupt at these several places—but it seems strange that no emendation was attempted for these rather obvious mistakes by the compositor of either setting. Then, too, neither setting is any real improvement on the other; on the verso, setting [g]1 has the slip "exrahi" for the "extrahi" on [g]2, while [g]2 incorrectly has "ſeruari" where "ſeruare" is preferable.[8] In any event, minor corrections of this sort could have been made in the forme without the necessity of resetting two entire pages of type. Significantly enough, the two rectos display only orthographic variations,[9] so that it cannot very well be argued that the printer reset the type in order to correct his text and then, by some mishap, used both settings in the printing.

Before analyzing our chief problem, it would be best to examine briefly Laurentii's printing practices at this time, which marked the very outset of his career as an independent printer.[10] His two earliest productions appear to be the work under discussion and an Italian version of this same text (HCR 7071; Stillwell *Census* F135), both being quartos. The evidence of the watermarks suggests that these

[6] Proper names are either capitalized or not in identical fashion in both settings, and both have identical major contractions at the same places. The chapter-heading on the verso is entirely in capitals in both settings, whereas elsewhere (save for that of chapter 18 on [e]2) the headings are in upper and lower case. All this could scarcely be the result of simple coincidence.

[7] I have consulted the Columbia University Library copies of the editions of Venice, 1518 (878 F44 P5); Basel, 1561 (B 878 F44 I); and Basel, 1576 (facsimile reprint, Torino, 1959—878 F44 I3). The text of the Venice: Otinus de Luna, 1500, edition has been made available through photostats of the copy in the Walters Art Gallery (*Census* F134). All these copies have *sanctio, elegit, denunciat* and *permittit*.

[8] The four later editions all have *servare*.

[9] In line 20, recto, of [g]2, a turned "n" provides the misprint "uudecies," this being the only major difference between the two texts.

[10] That Laurentii was still quite inexperienced at his trade is shown by the fact that, in these books, he made no use of signatures or register, foliation or pagination, title-page and colophon, running-heads, etc.

books were printed by half-sheet imposition, for in some five quires of two copies,[11] watermarks are found in six of the eight leaves. Again, it is clear that Laurentii possessed at least two presses; the BMC (VI:625), for example, remarks that, in the Italian version, "a miscalculation of the length of ch. 28 has resulted in the greater part of 81ᵇ and the whole of 82 (end of quire [k]) being left blank. Possibly the book was set up on three presses, ending with quires [e], [k] and [o] respectively." That quire [l] was probably printed before [k] seems reasonable enough, and two presses may, therefore, be postulated. However, a third press could hardly have started with quire [f], since this begins in the middle of the word "[absti]nen-tia." Finally, it seems certain that Laurentii was not printing from cast-off copy but that he was setting type seriatim by pages. Of the 27 quires in the two volumes which come into consideration, 10 begin in the middle of a sentence and 16 in the middle of a word.[12] Since he was following this practice (in effect, printing as in folio), it is likely that he was working "from inside out"; that is, in the order: [g]4-[g]5, [g]3-[g]6, [g]2-[g]7, and [g]1-[g]8.

Only one explanation for the redundant text—and not a very good one at that—has occurred to the writer. For the printing of the two innermost sheets, there was, of course, no problem, but either with the third or with the outermost one, Laurentii may well have suddenly discovered that, by some miscalculation, he did not have enough pages to fill out the formes. Clearly, there was some excellent reason for his not being able to use two pages from the next quire as type-high supports—and one may consequently assume that quire [h] was then either printing or had already been printed off. Thus, one may again assume that Laurentii was working with at least two presses.

Now if the printer did not realize that he was short of type-pages till he was machining [g]2-[g]7, then it is self-evident that [g]2 must be the earlier setting. For some reason not clear to us, Laurentii apparently had no standing type [or blocks, furniture or quads] to make up the two pages necessary to fill the formes. His compositor was, therefore, obliged to supply him with two duplicate pages, which he set up quickly from the already printed copy. If, how-

---

[11] The Morgan copy (Accession number 397) of *Census* F135 and the writer's example of *Census* F133.

[12] Only one quire—the second one in the Latin version—begins with a new sentence.

ever, Laurentii was working with more than one press, he might
have been machining the two sheets simultaneously, in which case
it would be impossible to determine whether [g]1 or [g]2 was set
first.

The purpose of these two reset pages was, of course, to act as
"bearers" which were probably never meant to be inked but simply
to serve as a support during the printing. Normally, they would
have provided a blank leaf, subsequently to be cut out. Here, however, they were inked and printed, and thus escaped excision.[13]
Examples of accidental inking and printing of "bearer" type, and
the consequent survival of such, are not unknown in the incunabula
period.[14] In any case, one cannot assert with any degree of certainty
which pages were set first or which leaf was supposed to have been
excised.[15]

For the descriptive bibliographer, of course, the perplexing problem is what will here constitute an "ideal copy" and what index
number shall be given to the seventh quire. According to Professor
Fredson Bowers[16] (and all will agree with him on this), "an ideal
copy is not a redundant copy." With this in mind, one may well
argue that [g]⁸ would not be, in the least, acceptable. Equally, any
bibliographer of the Greg-Bowers school would argue that an "index
figure should represent the number of conjugate quired leaves in the
original gathering, with all abnormalities accounted for by other
means."[17] An uneven index-number is repugnant to this school of
bibliography,[18] and for very excellent reasons too, since a sheet could
not very well be machined with an odd number of leaves. There-

[13] In my article "Caxton Studies" (*supra*), I set forth reasons for suggesting that
Caxton, for his smaller folios, might have been able to print two pages with but
one pull of the lever—and that thereby bearer-type might have received ink by
mistake. Similarly, Laurentii could certainly have printed two quarto pages with a
single pull—and a careless press-man might have inked the type where he should
not have done so. [Unfortunately, due to the outbreak of war and the consequent
break in communications, the figures which were meant to illustrate the points I
was seeking to make were never printed with the Caxton article. They are, however, reproduced here, and a few gross misprints are also corrected.]

[14] Compare also my articles: "A Note on a Fifteenth-Century Printing Technique," *The Library Chronicle*, XV (1949), 52-55 and "A Misprinted Page in a
Fifteenth-Century Book," *ibid.*, XXI (1955), 3-5.

[15] If he were printing page by page (a most unlikely circumstance at this late
date), why would he have reprinted on his second leaf the texts which he had
just printed on the first one?

[16] *Principles of Bibliographical Description* (1949), p. 115.

[17] Bowers, p. 227.                              [18] Compare Bowers, p. 488 ff.

fore [g]⁷, too, is inadmissible. One could, of course, write [g]⁸ (-g1) if one were positive that the publisher wished the first leaf to be cut out, or [g]⁸ (-g2) if it were the second which Laurentii might have wished to suppress.

Since the ideal copy is that which represents the "most perfect state of the book as the printer or publisher finally intended to issue it,"[19] one turns to the surviving copies to see if a clue as to what Laurentii's intention was might be discovered there. The make-up of the seventh quire in the sixteen copies known to the writer provides the following information:

Four copies have only [g]1:

> Florence, Biblioteca Nazionale Centrale [A.7.8]
> Oxford, Bodleian Library [Auct. 1 Q 5.59]
> San Marino, Huntington Library [Mead 3578 and 3579][20]

Four copies have only [g]2:

> Bryn Mawr, Bryn Mawr College Library [Goodhart, p. 59][21]
> Florence, Biblioteca Nazionale Centrale [D.7.6.6]
> London, British Museum [IA. 27111]
> Venice, Biblioteca Marciana [Incun. 903]

Eight copies have both:

> Cambridge, Mass., Harvard University Library
> Florence, Biblioteca Nazionale Centrale [B.5.18]
> Milan, Biblioteca Ambrosiana
> Naples, Biblioteca Nazionale Vittorio Emanuele III [S.Q.V.C.9]
> New York, Curt F. Bühler
> Oxford, Bodleian Library [Auct. 1 Q inf. 1. 7]
> Rome, Biblioteca Corsiniana
> Rome, Biblioteca Vaticana [Stamp. Ross. 1026]

What can be deduced from this? Perhaps the not unreasonable assumption that Laurentii may have been quite indifferent to [possibly even ignorant of] the true state of affairs. It is certainly unclear whether such excisions as there are were made in the shop or by the individual purchasers. That one or the other leaf should have been deleted is quite self-evident, but this does not get us very far. One may still wonder (1) whether the publisher [as distinct from the press-man or compositor] was aware of the repetition, (2) whether,

---

[19] Bowers, p. 113.

[20] Herman R. Mead, *Incunabula in the Huntington Library* (1937), p. 151.

[21] Phyllis W. G. Gordan, *Fifteenth-Century Books in the Library of Howard Lehman Goodhart* (1955), p. 59.

being aware of it, he had any interest in what the purchaser did about it, or (3) whether he himself cut out one or the other of the offending leaves in those copies still unsold when he discovered the duplication, without caring very much which of the leaves he removed. In view of such uncertainties as these, how can the ideal copy be identified and what should be the index number of the seventh quire?

(From *Studies in Bibliography* 18 (1965), pp. 248-252).

Plates

nūc ē supra retulimus formosissimū ab Homero p̄dicari b°ħ.u.
pipενσ αρ συμηθϵρ αιϵρ τρϵισ ρ ηασ ϵιϝασ.
pipϵνσ αγλαιησ υιοσ χϵροποιο ταρ αρτοσ.
pipϵνσ οσ κλλιτοσ αρηρ υπ ιλιορ ηλθϵ·
τωρ αλλωρ δ̄αραωρ μϵταμνμορα πιλιωρα.
Heu translatosalio merebis amoref·ingemescit iā vicē illinsq̄
reliqui meruit·Ast ego vicissim risero·modo coniunctiuo dicit
tpe futuro vt ē illud Terētianum vxore op⁹ est duxero·

**❡ In mores prēsentis ētatis**

Ltera iā terrē bellis ciuilib⁹ ētas
Suis & ipsa roma viribus ruit
Q̄uā neq̄ finitimi valuerūt pdeꝝ marsi
Minacis aut hetrusca porsenē manus
Aemula nec capuē ͛otus nec sptaculsacer
Nouisq̄ rebus infidelis allobrox
Nec fera cerulea domuit germaia pube
Parentibusq̄ abominatus hannybal
Impia pdemus deuoti sanguinis ētas
Feris & rursus occupabitur solum
Barbarus heu cineres insistet victor &
Eques sonate ͛ berabit vngula   ꝝvrbē
Queq̄ caret ventis & solib⁹ ossa quirini
Nefas videri dissipabit insolens
Forte qd expediat cōiter aut melior ps
Malis carere quēritis laboribus
Nulla fit hac potior sententia phoceoꝝ
Velut ꝑfugit exsecrata ciuitas
Agrosatq̄ laresꝑprios habitādaq̄ pha/
Aoris reliquit & raptorib⁹ lupis   ꝝna
Ire pedes q̄cunq̄ ferunt q̄cunq̄ ꝑvndas
Notus vocabit aut proteruus aphricus
Sic placet an meli⁹ qs hᴣ suadeꝝ secunda
Ratem occupare quid moramur balite

Plate 1.  Horatius. Opera. [Rome: Wendelinus de Wila (?),
circa 1475]. PML 27321

nouiſſimo die⌋Tho.ſ.de morte advitā glorioſã.⌊Hec eſt
autemvoluntas patris mei qui miſit me:vt ois quividet fi-
liū⌋Tho.ſ.paſſibilem et mortalē:et cū hoc miracula faciē
tem⌊et credit in eū⌋id eſt adheret ei ſicutvnivero deo per
miracula ductus ād fidem⌊habeatvitā eternā⌋Ly.Si pſe
ueret.qd eſt in fallibiliter very in pdeſtinatis de quibus hic
xp̄s loquiſ⌊et ego reſuſcitabo eū in nouiſſimo die⌋quo ad
corpus:ut ſimul gaudeat in corpore et in anima zc̄.

¶Finit poſtilla ſup euangelia dn̄icalia/ et ſuper euangelia
de ſanctis:fm ſenſū litteralem collecta/ Anno dn̄i milleſi-
mo quadringenteſimo triceſimo ſeptimo: ex poſtillis et ex
ſermonibus illory ſacre pagine doctory.ſ. ex poſtilla Nicolai de ly. ſup quattuor euāgeliſtas.et ex poſtilla Nicolai de
Gorrā.ſup quattuor euangeliſtas.et ex poſtilla ſancti tho.
de acquino ſup Io.Et ex ſermonibusvuilhelmi lugdunenſis
de tempe.Et ex ſermonibus Iacobi ianuenſis de tempe. Et
ex aliis quory tituli infra ꝑtinenſ de modo legendi doctory
titulos:cū ſubiūctione poſt qdlibet dn̄icale euāgeliū quorū-
dam notabiliū ad maiorē euangelii declaratōne ꝑcernenti-
um/extractory ex ſermonibus eximii doctoris Hugonis de
prato de tpe.Et ſi quid in pn̄ti poſtilla minus bene poſui:in
hoc me correctioni ſancte matris eccleſie/et cuilibet carita-
tiuo correctori ſubiicio ac ad emendā offero.¶Impreſſūꝗ
eſt hoc opus piſius p Magiſtrū Vdalricū Cering/pariter et
Guillermum maynyal.Anno.M.cccc.lxxix.29.Marcii.

Modus legēdi noīa doctory abbreuiata i iſto libro.ly.i.Ni
colaus de lyra doctor ſacre theologie ordinis minory.
Gor.i. Nicolaus de gorram doctor ſacre theologie ordinis
predicatorum.                                     p̄dicatory.
Tho.i. ſanctus thomas de aquino doctor eximius ordinis
Vuilh.i.vuilhelmus lugdunēſis doctor ſacre theologie ordinis predicatorum
Ia.vel Iaco.i.iacobus ianuenſis doctor ſacre theologie ordinis predicatorum.
Ior.i.iordanus doctor ſacre theologie de ordine auguſtinē
ſium. ¶Raba.i.Rabanus

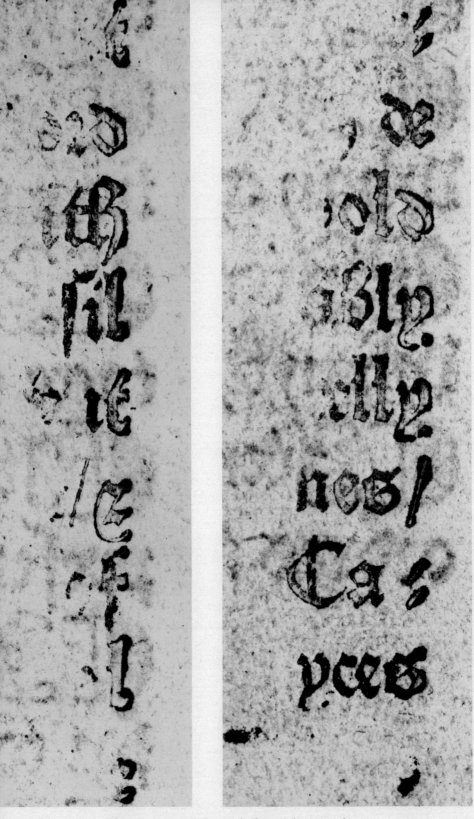

Plate 3. Caxton's Type 6 (enlarged four times)

Fac tibi proponas mortem non effe ti
Que bona fi non eft tamen finio illa n

Hou ougffiff not fo boughe the
that foweƶꝛ / thif is to thee the
Bot bona fi non eſt bergꝛaꝛ

4b, PML 690. The Book called Caton

Fac tibi proponas mortem non effe t
Que bona fi non eft tamen finio illa n

Hou ougffiff not fo boughe the
that foweꝛ / thif is to thee the
Bot bona fi non eſt bergꝛaꝛ

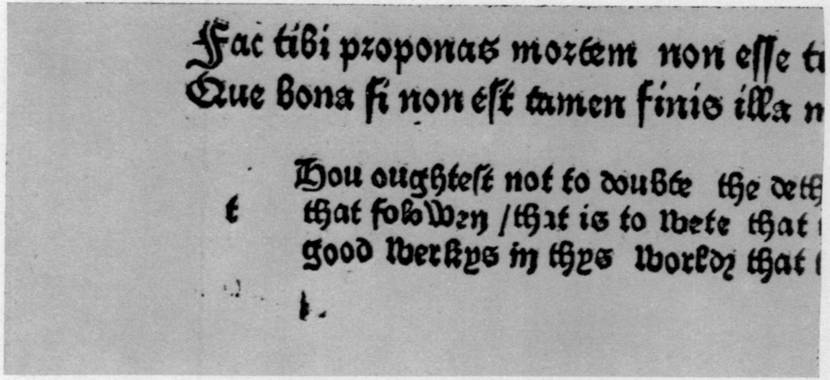

4b, PML 691. The Book called Caton

ou haſt not fo moch of rentes andƺ
s wonte to haue / or of marchaundꝛ;
/ ffor the goodes of this worldꝛ
az waƺ erꝛ Socrates
dz / and now poure / Socrates
qꝛaxiunus waƺ communus ſcoleꝛ
quaxiunus waƺ communus ſcoleꝛ
To Socrates anſebꝛing ſuch ꝺꝛ

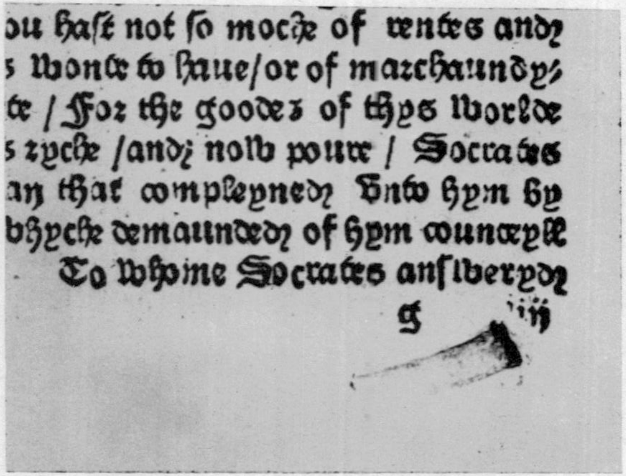

4a, PML 690. The Book called Caton

ou haſt not fo moch of rentes andꝛ
s wonte to haue / or of marchaundꝛ;
/ ffor the goodes of this worldꝛ
az waƺ erꝛ Socrates
dꝛ / and now poure / Socrates
quaxiunus waƺ communus ſcoleꝛ
To Socrates anſebꝛing ſuch ꝺꝛ

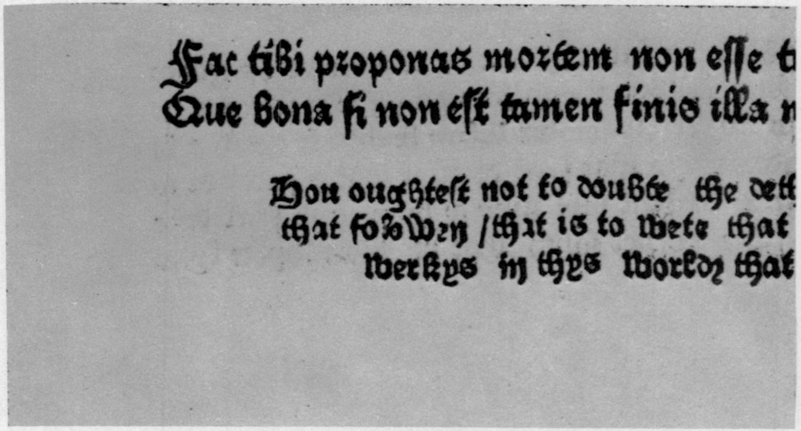

4a, PML 691. The Book called Caton

Plate 4. The Book called Caton

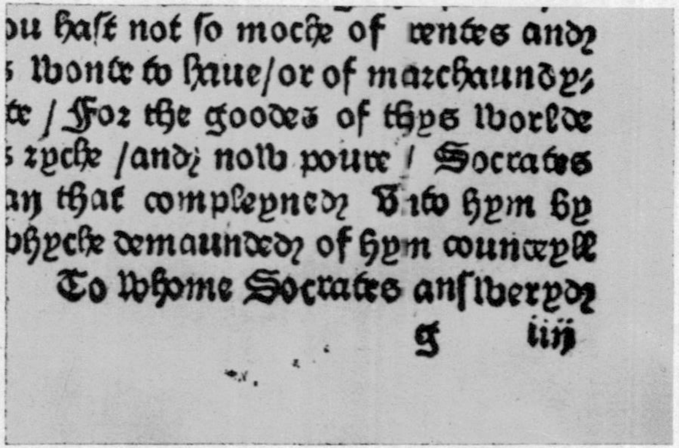

graui m̄? Dʒ ſi ꝑ rectores ⁊ vic̄a ⸗
rios ecclesiaꝝ hm̄i ſpēno ide nō ꝑ⸗
cernetur ad votum ipſos laboꝛib⁹
beꝛantes queſitis coloꝛib⁹ et cauſis
confictis⸗infeſtant grauiter et mo
leſtant. Propter que et alias iuſtas
cauſas⸗preſentis ſtatuit⁹ declara
ciōne꜀ciū ꝓ hm̄oi ꝓhiſtoꝛia ſigula
leſſiones et capitula in locis iuris⸗
dictionū et decanatuū predictoꝛ
magis in ſingulis bel ſalte ī quib⁹
pictualia ꝛmuniter baleant inue⸗
niri benalia de cetero celebrentur.
Dꝺꝫ officiales et ceteri oꝛdinarij⸗
oꝛ miniſtri ſuoꝝ ſuꝑtib⁹ dñoꝛ taꝫ
in hm̄oi celebꝛacione cōſiſtoꝛioꝝ꜀
ſeſſionū et capituloꝝ ꝙ ī alijs acci
bus⸗quos pꝛo ſuis exercent dñs fa
ctunt que in cunbit. ¶ Citaciones
aūt et ꝓhiſtoꝛia leſſiones ⁊ capitu

ahm̄oi in alijs locis ꝙ expꝛeſſis ſu
petus celebꝛanda et proceſſus quos
ſu eis cōtigerit impoſteꝝ fieri Jꝓo
iure decernimus fore nullos ac oſ⸗
ficiales pꝛedictos ꝑ ſuoꝝ dominoꝛ
expediendis negocijs ſumptus a di
ctis ſuboꝛis exigentes ſeu ipſos oc
caſione nō pꝛefacionis ſumptuum
hm̄oi infeſtantes eo ipſo ab officio
⁊ ingreſſu eccleſie ſuſpenſos bolu
mus remanere.     Dephant

¶ Dimaꝝ ſaluti pꝛoſpicere · cū
pientes inicium oꝛdinauir de
fontib⁹ ſaluatoꝛis. ¶ Statuimus
itaꝗ ⁊ oꝛdinam⁹ vt dies illa ſac̄a
paraſcaues qua ſaluatoꝛ dñs nr̄e
ſus chriſtus pꝛo ſalute hominū pre
cioſa animā ſuā poſt multa flagel
la poſuit in cruce⸗Scd̄m rituū et
cleſie in lectione cūſuec̄o in oꝛōne

Plate 5. Lyndewode. Constitutiones provinciales. 1496. Huntington Library, Mead 5258

grauius. Dd si per rectores ⁊ vica-
rios ecclesiay hmoi splendoide non
procurent ad vctu ipsos laboribus
berantes. quesitis coloribus ⁊ causis
conficttis. insestant grauiter ⁊ mo-
lestant. propter que ⁊ alias iustas
causas. presentis statuum9 declaratione ⁊cliy. q hmoi ⁊historia singula sessiones ⁊ capitula in locis un-
uisdictionu ⁊ decanatuu preducto2
magis insignibus. bel saltem iqb9
victualia comuniter valeant inue-
niri venalia decreto celebrentur.
Ddq3 officiales ⁊ ceteri ordiario2
ministri. suo2 sumptib9 domino2
tam in hmoi celebratioe ⁊historio2
sessionu⁊e capitulo2. q in alijs acti
bus. quos vo suis exercet dominis
faciut que incubunt. Citationes
aut ad ⁊historia. sessiones ⁊ capitu

la huiusmodi. ⁊ alijs locis q expensis
superius celebranda. ⁊ pressus quos
in eis ptigerit imposter fieri. Ipso
iure decernimus fore nullos. ac officiales predictos p suo2 domino2
expediendis negocijs. sumptus a di
ctis subditis exigentes seu ipsos oc
casione non prefatationis sumptuum
hmoi infestates. eo ipso ab officio
⁊ ingressu ecclesie suspensos volu-
mus remanere. ¶ Depham.

Animay saluti prospicere cupientes. inicium ordinauit de
funitibus saluatozis. ¶ Statuimus
itaq3 ⁊ ordinam9 vt dies illa sacta
parasceues. qua saluator dns nr Je
sus christus. pro salute hominu pre
ciosam anima sua post multa sla-
gella posuit in cruce. scdm ritu ecclesie ⁊ lectione cu silentio. in ordne

grauius. Dd si per rectores e vica-
rios ecclesiar hmoi splendide non
procurent ad botu ipsos laboribus
berantes. quesitis colorib9 e caufis
confictis. infestant grauiter e mo-
lestant. propter que e alias iuustas
caufas. presentis statuim9 declaratione pciliy q hmoi pstoria singula. lectiones e capitula in locis ui-
cisioctioni e decanatuu predictoz
magis insignibus. vel faltem iqb9
victualia comuniter valeant inue-
niri vernalia decetero celebrentur.
Dodq3 officiales e ceteri ordiariox
ministri. luoz sumptib9 dominox
eam in hmoi celebatioe psistoriox
sessioniq capitulox. q in alijs acti
bus. quos pro luis exercet dominis
faciut que incubunt. ❡Citationes
aut ad pistoria.sessiones e capita

a huiusmodi alijs locis q expssis
uperi us celebranda. e pcessus quos
in eis pntigerit impostern fieri. Ipso
'iure decernimus fore nullos.ac officiales predictos p luoz dominox
expediendis negocijs.sumptus a di
ctis subditis exigentes. feu ipsos oc
cafione no prestationis sumptruum
hmoi intestates. eo ipso ab officio
e ingressu ecclesie suspensos volu-
mus remanere. ❡Depham.

N Dimaz saluti prospicere cupientes. inicium ordinatur de
fortibus saluatoris.❡Statuimus
itaq3 e ordinam9 vt dies illa sacra
paraseues.qua saluator dns nr Je
fus christus.pro salute hominu pre
ciolam animã tuã post multa fla-
gella poluit in cruce. Scom ritu ecclesie i lectione cu filentio in ordine

Plate 7. Lyndewode. Constitutiones provinciales. 1496. PML 733

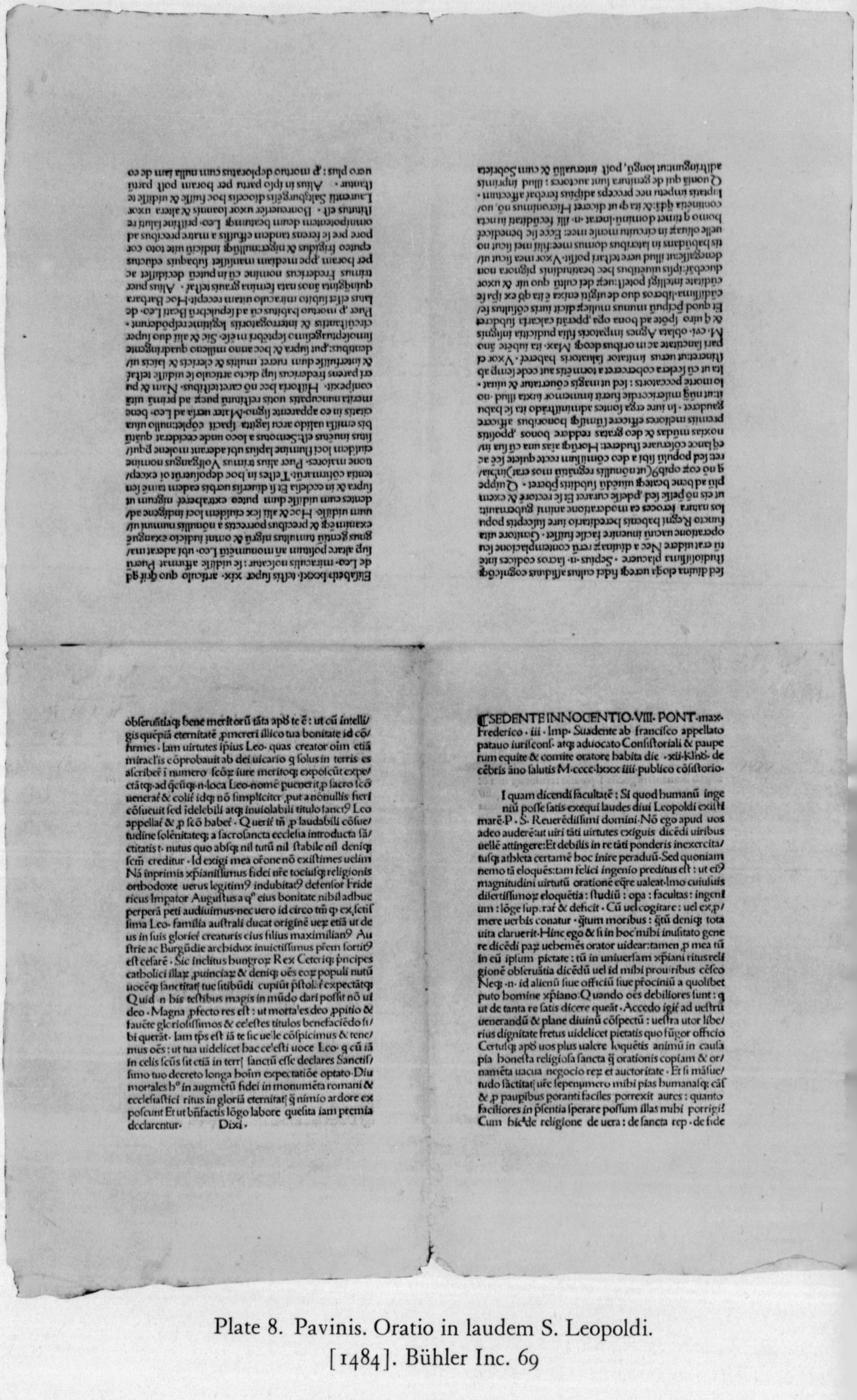

obſeruātiaq; bene meritorū tāta apð te ē : ut cū intelli/
gis quēpiā eternitatē ꝓmereri illico tua bonitate id cō/
firmes · Iam uirtutes ipius Leo· quas creator oīm etiā
miracl'is cōprobauit ab dei uicario q ſolus in terris es
aſcriberī i numero ſcōꝝ iure meritoq; expoſcūt expe/
ctātq;·ad q̄cūq;·n·loca Leo·nomē pueneritꝑ ſacro ſcō
uenerať & colit idq; nō ſimpliciter ꝓut a nōnullis fieri
cōſueuit ſed īdelebili atq; inuiolabili titulo ſanct9 Leo
appellať & ꝓ ſcō habeť · Q uerit tn̄ ꝓ laudabili cōſue/
tudine ſolēnitateq; a ſacroſancta eccleſia introducta ſā/
ctitatis t· nutus quo abſq; nil tutū nil ſtabile nil deniq;
ſcm̄ creditur · Id exigi mea oȓone nō exiſtimes uelim
Nā inprimis xp̄ianiſſimus fidei nr̄e tociuſq; religionis
orthodoxe uerus legitim9 indubitat9 defenſor Fride
ricus Impator Auguſtus a q° eius bonitate nihil adhuc
perperā peti audiuimus·nec uero id circo tm̄ ꝙ ex ſctiſ
ſima Leo· familia auſtrali ducat originē ueꝝ etiā ut de
us in ſuis gloriet creaturis eius filius maximilian9 Au
ſtrie ac Burgūdie archidux inuictiſſimus pr̄em ſortit9
eſt ceſarē · Sic inclitus hungroꝝ R ex Ceteriq; p̄ncipes
catholici illaꝝ ꝓuinciaꝝ & deniq; oēs eoꝝ populi nutū
uocēq; ſanctitat tue ſitibūdi cupiūt p̄ſtolaꝛ expectātq;
Q uid ·n· his teſtibus magis in mūdo dari poſſit nō ut
deo · Magna ꝑfecto res eſt : ut mortales deo ꝓpitio &
fauēte glorioſiſſimos & celeſtes titulos benefaciēdo ſi/
bi querāt · Iam tp̄s eſt iā te ſic uelle cōſpicimus & tene/
mus oēs : ut tua uidelicet hac celeſti uoce Leo· q cū iā
in celis ſcūs ſit etiā in terr ſanctū eſſe declares Sanctiſ/
ſimo tuo decreto longa hoīm expectatiōe optato·Diu
mortales h° in augmētū fidei in monumēta romani &
eccleſiaſtici ritus in gloriā eternitat q̄ nimio ardore ex
poſcunt Et ut bn̄factis lōgo labore queſita iam premia
declarentur·                Dixi ·

¶ SEDENTE INNOCENTIO·VIII· PONT·max·
Frederico · iii · Imp· Suadente ab franciſco appellato
patauo iuriſconſ· atq; aduocato Conſiſtoriali & paupe
rum equite & comite oratore habita die ·xii·Klnð· de
cēbris āno ſalutis M·cccc·lxxx iiii·publico cōſiſtorio·

I quam dicendi facultatē : Si quod humanū inge
niū poſſe ſatis exequi laudes diui Leopoldi exiſti
marē·P · S· Reuerēdiſſimi domini·Nō ego apud uos
adeo auderē:ut uiri tāti uirtutes exiguis dicēdi uiribus
uellē attingere:Et debilis in re tāti ponderis inexercita/
tuſq; athleta certamē hoc inire peraduū·Sed quoniam
nemo tā eloquēs:tam felici ingenio preditus eſt : ut ei9
magnitudini uirtutū orationē eq̄re ualeat·Imo cuiuſuis
diſertiſſimoꝝ eloquētia : ſtudiū : opa : facultas : ingeni
um : lōge ſup·rať & deficit · Cū uel cogitare : uel exꝓ/
mere uerbis conatur · q̄tum moribus : q̄tū deniq; tota
uita claruerit·Hinc ego & ſi in hoc mihi inuſitato gene
re dicēdi paꝝ uehemēs orator uidear:tamen ꝓ mea tū
in cū ipſum pietate : tū in uniuerſam xp̄iani ritus reli
gionē obſeruātia dicēdū uel id mihi prouiribus cēſeo
Neq; ·n· id alienū ſiue officiū ſiue p̄ſociniū a quolibet
puto homine xp̄iano:Q uando oēs debiliores ſunt : q
ut de tanta re ſatis dicere queāt · Accedo igiť ad ueſtrū
uenerandū & plane diuinū cōſpectū : ueſtra utor libe/
rius dignitate fretus uidelicet pietatis quo fūgor officio
Certuſq; apð uos plus ualere loquētis animū in cauſa
pia honeſta religioſa ſancta q̄ orationis copiam & or/
namēta uacua negocio reꝝ et auctoritate · Et ſi māſue/
tudo ſāctitat ur̄e ſepenumero mihi pias humanaſq; cāſ
& ꝓ paupibus poranti faciles porrexit aures : quanto
faciliores in p̄ſentia ſperare poſſum illas mihi porrigi
Cum hic de religione de uera : de ſancta rep · de fide

Plate 8. Pavinis. Oratio in laudem S. Leopoldi.
[1484]. Bühler Inc. 69

Petri Leonis Vercellensis Diuę Marię scalarum
Mediolani Canonici in Illustrissimorum
Karoli Principis Sabaudiæ Ducis:
& Beatricis Portugallensis
auspicatissimis nuptijs
Epithalamion.

N Hac summa omniũ lætitia Inclytissi-
me Princeps:& quasi cuiusdam optimo
sæculi ueluti renascētis initio minime de-
futuros arbitror:qui me:quem semper
antea inter eos:qui excultas:bonisq̃ eué-
tibus plenas habuerunt orationes:Silétem compressis

A ij

Plate 9.  Leo. Epithalamium. Milan: [Minutianus], 30 July 1521
First text page of paper copy (PML 24150)

Petri Leonis Vercellensis Diuę Marię scalarum
Mediolani Canonici in Illustrissimorum
Karoli Principis Sabaudiæ Ducis:
& Beatricis Portugallensis
auspicatissimis nuptijs
Epithalamion.

I N Hac summa omniũ lætitia Inclytissi-
me Princeps : & quasi cuiusdam optimo
sæculi ueluti renascẽtis initio minime de-
futuros arbitror : qui me : quem semper
antea inter eos:qui excultas:bonisq; euẽ-
tibus plenas habuerunt orationes:Silẽtem compressis
A ij

Plate 10. Leo. Epithalamium. Milan: [Minutianus], 30 July 1521
First text page of vellum copy (PML 24149)

Gallus interea Senas uenit:& a factiosis ciuibus in urbem exceptus est.& arcem occupauit. ~~deinde~~ ad Calendas Iunias Romam
uenit. Amissa opportunitate frustratus intacta
Roma, Pisas uenit. ubi genuenses a fide Lu-
douici ducis& quasdam traspadanas urbes a-
uertere conatus est. ut liberam abeundi potesta-
tem haberet. Quod cum impetrare nequi-
ret: uiam saltem sibi ferro aperiendam esse pro
posuit. Spem dabat cæleritatis fiducia: ac segni-
or (ut sperabat) sociorum expeditio. Tum Au
riliensem ducem qui haste alpium fauces custo
diebat, excitauit. ut iure hæreditario res mediolanenses turbaret opem protinus laturus. Is no
uarienses quosdam optimates ut in Ludouicum cospirarent effecit: Forte mediolanenses
milites ad custodiendos ditionis suæ terminos
missi fuerant. Hos Auriliésis dux intercepit:
protinusq̃; in urbem Nouariam. iiii. Idus Iunias exceptus est a ciuibus quos clandestinis
consiliis sibi conciliauerat. cum eo eqtes. D. ar-
mati erant. Peditum. yiii. millia. Paucisq̃; diebus arcem male munitam occupauit. Pauor
ingens Ludouicum Ducem ne iperium subito

Sȳth the tyme that the grete ⁊ myghty toure of babylone was byl¬ ded men haue spoken with dyuerse conges. In suche wyse that dyuerse men be ſtrange to other and vnderſtode not others ſpeche. Speche is not knowen but yf it be lerned. co¬ myn lernyng of ſpeche is by heryng/ ⁊ ſo alwaye he that is deef is alway dombe / for he maye not here ſpeche for to lerne. So men of fer countrees and londes that haue dyuerſe ſpeches yef neyther of hem haue lerned others langage. nether of of hem wote what other meneth/though they mete and haue grete nede of informacyon and of loor in talkyng ⁊ of ſpeche be the nede neuer ſoo grete neyther of hem vnderſtondeth others ſpeche no more than gaglyng of gees. For Jangle þ one neuer ſoo faſt that other is neuer the wyſer/though he ſhrewe hym in ſtede of good morowe. This is a gre te myſchyef that foloweth now men¬ kynde. But god of his mercy ⁊ gra¬ ce hath ordeyned double remedye. One is that ſomme may lerneth and knoweth many dyuerſe ſpeches. And bytwene ſtrange men of the whiche neyther vnderſtandeth others ſpeche. ¶ Suche a man may be meane and tell eyther what other wyll meane. That other remedye is/that one lan gage is lerned vſed and knowen in many nacyons and londes. And ſoo latyn is lorned knowen and vſed ſpe cyally on this halfe grece in alle the nacyons ⁊ londes of Europe. Ther¬ fore clerkis of her goodnes and curto ſye make and wryten theyr bokes in

latyn. For her wrytyng ⁊ bokes ſhol¬ de be vnderſtonde in dyuerſe nacions and londes. ¶ And ſoo Ranulphus monke of Cheſtre wrote in latyn his bokes of Cronycles that deſcryupth the worlde aboute in lengthe and in brede. And maketh mencyon ⁊ myn de of doynges and dedes of meruay¬ les and of wondres. and rekeneth the yeres to his laſt dayes / fro the fyrſte makyng of heuen and of erthe. And ſoo there in is grete and noble Jnfor¬ macyon ⁊ loore to hem that can the¬ re in rede and vnderſtande. ¶ Ther fore J wolde haue theſe bokes of Cro nycles tranſlated out of Latyn in to Englyſſhe / for the moo men ſholde hem vnderſtande ⁊ haue therof con¬ nyng informacōn ⁊ lore ¶ The clerke anſwerth. Bokes of cronycles bē wri ten in latyn. And latyn is vſed ⁊ vn¬ derſtanden on this halfe grece in alle the nacyons and londes of Europa. ¶ And comynly Englyſſhe is not ſo wyde vnderſtonde vſed ne knowen. And thenglyſſhe tranſlacyon ſholde nomay vnderſtande but Englyſſhe men allone. Thenne how ſholde the moo men vnderſtonde the Cronycles though they were tranſlated oute of latyn that is is ſoo wyde vſed ⁊ kno wen. in to Englyſſhe that is not vſed ⁊ knowen but of englyſſhe men allo ne. The Lorde ¶ This queſtyon and doubte is eaſy to aſſoyle. ¶ For yf the ſe Cronycles were tranſlated oute of Latyn in to Englyſſhe / thenne by þ ſoo many the moo men ſholde vnder ſtande hem. as vnderſtonde englyſſhe ⁊ no latyn. ¶ The clerke. ye can ſpe ke rede ⁊ vnderſtande latyn/thenne it nedeth not to haue ſuche an engliſſhe

a i

12a. Higden. Polycronicon. Westminster, 1495. PML 731

Sith the tyme that the grete & mygthy toure of babylone was byl/ded men haue spoken wyth dyuerse tonges. In suche wyse that dyuerse-men bee straunge to other and vnderstonde not other speche. Speche isnot knowen but yf it be lerned. co/myn lernyng of speche is byhenyng/ & so alwaye he that is deef is alwaye dombe/ for he maye not here speche for to lerne. So men of fer countrees and londes that haue dyuerse speches yf neyter of hem haue lerned others langage. nether of theym wote what other meneth/though they mete and haue grete nede of informacion and of loor in talkynge & of speche be the nede neuer soo grete neyther of them vnderstondeth others speche no more than gagelyng of gees. for jangle p one neuer soo fast that other is neuer the wyser/though he shrewe hym in stede of good morowe. This is a gre te myschyef that foloweth now man kynde. But god of his mercy & grace hath ordeyned double remedye. One is that somme man lerneth and kno weth many dyuerse speches. And by/ twene straunge men of the whiche neyther vnderstandeth others speche. ¶Suche a man may be meane and telle eyther what other wylle meane That other remedye is/that one lan gage is lerned vsed and knowen in many nacyons and londes. And soo latyn is lerned knowen and vsed spe cyally on this halfe grece in alle the nacions & londes of Europe. Ther/ fore clerkis of her goodnes and curto sye make and wryten theyr bokes in

latyn. for her wrytyng & bokes shol/ de be vnderstonde in diuerse nacions and londes. ¶And soo Ranulphus monke of Chestre wrote in latyn his bokes of Cronycles that descryueth p worlde aboute in lenghthe and in bre de. And maketh mencion and mynde of doynges and dedes of meruaples and of wordes. And rekeneth the ye/ res to his laste dayes/ fro the fyrste makyng of heuen and of erthe. And soo there in is grete and noble Infor/ macyon & loore to them that can the/ re in rede and vnderstande. ¶There fore I wolde haue these bokes of Cro nycles translated out of latyn in to en glysshe/ for the moo men sholde them vnderstande and haue therof conpyng Informacion and lore. ¶The clerke answereth. Bokes of cronycles be wri ten in latyn. And latyn is vsed & vn/ derstanden on this halfe grece in alle the nacions and londes of Europa. ¶And comynly Englysshe is not so wyde vnderstonde vsed ne knowen. And the Englysshe translacion shold noman vnderstande but Englysshe men allone. Thenne how sholde the moo men vnderstande the Cronycles thought they were translated oute of latyn that is soo wyde vsed and kno/ wen. in to Englysshe that is not vsed & knowen byt of Englisshe men allo ne. The Lorde. ¶This question and doubte is easy to assoyle ¶For yf the se Cronycles were translated oute of latyn in to Englysshe/Thenne by p soo many the moo men sholde vnder stande hem. as vnderstonde englysshe & no latyn. ¶The clerke. ye can spe ke rede & vnderstonde latin/thenne it nedeth not to haue suche an englysshe

a i

Plate 12b. Higden. Polycronicon. Westminster, 1495. Walters Art Gallery

tour was fyue myle and almooſt two hondred paas hyghe and foure myle brode.⊂Arabia is ſette by south Caldea / and hath iy the eeſt ſyde Perſida/and iy the weſt the reed ſee. Jy Arabia is ſtoor myrre and Caneil/ and a byrde that is called phenir. The northeeſt porciou of Arabia is named Saba/and is called Saba after Saba Chus ſone.This Saba is beclypped iy three ſydes with the reed ſee. ⊂Joſephus libro primo.Jy this Arabia iy the contree of Madyay is the mount of Syna/the mount Oreb is a partye of the mount of Syna/ e is hyghe and hath grete plente of gras and of leeſe.But it is harde to come therto / for hyghe Rockes and ſcarres. Moyſes was the fyrſt may that ladde thyder beeſtes / hit is named alſo the mount of Couenaunt and of drede.for god almyghty ther vpoy made thondryuge and lyghteuynge and gaf the lawe to the folke of Iſraell that were at the hylle foote/loo that noman durſt approche to it but he were purefyed and made clene.⊂Treuyſa.fenir is a wonder byrde/for of all that kynde is but one a lyue. ⊂R.Jy the contree of Arabye towarde Cyrcius is the hylle that is called mons Libani/that hylle departeth thre londes a ſonder.Arabia Jude/and fenis/that hylle is full hygh ſoo that ſnowe lyeth alwaye iy ſome ſyde of that hylle.And it is a certayy marke and token to ſhypmey that ſaylley iy the grete ſee and ledeth hey to dyuerſe mouthes and hauens hit is ay hylle of helthe and plente. for Cypreſſe Cedre trees and herbes growey theroy that droppey gôme e ſmelle ſwete/by the whiche trees gôme and ſwetnes leke mey bey heled/ and venyy deſtroyed. ⊂Suria hath the name of Cyrus Abrahams neuew And lyeth bytwene the water Eufrates iy the eeſt ſyde / and the grete ſee iy the weſt ſyde/and hath iy p northe ſyde Armenia and Capadocia / and iy the ſouthe ſyde the ſee that is named Arabicus/and conteyneth many prouynces/that bey Comagena.paleſtina.fenys.Chanaay.Joumea.e Judea/that is the Jurye.Damalcus was ſomtyme the chyef Cyte of that prouynce. Eleazar Abrahams ſeruaunt bylded and made that Cyte Damalcus.Ralpy kynge of Damaſke helpe awaye the tey lygnages of Iſrahell the kynges of Juda. Damalcus as moche to ſaye as thedynge of blood. for there Chapiy ſlowe Abell and hydde hyty iy the londe.

De Regione Judee.     Capſ iy.riiii.

Jodea is a kyngdome of Siria/a parte of paleſtina and hath the name of Judas Jacobs ſone / and was ſomtyme called Cananea of Chay Noes ſone/eyther of the tey maner of people that the Jewes put oute of that londe. ⊂petrus.Judea is takey iy many maner otherwhyle for the londe of byheſte. And thenne it hath the name of the Jewes and of Judas. And ſoo it is takey iy this ſpeche.The grete pompeus made Judea trybutaryes.And otherwhyle it is takey for the Royame of Juda/and ſoo it is wrytey of Joſeph / that whay he herde that

b iiii

Plate 13a. Higden. Polycronicon. Westminster, 1495. PML 731

tour was fyue myle and almoste two
hondred paas hyghe and foure myle
brode. ¶Arabia is sette by south Cal-
dea/and hath in the eest syde Persi-
da/and in the weste the reed see. In
Arabia is stoor myrre andCanell.and
a byrd that is called Phenix. The nor
theest porcion of Arabia is named Sa
ba / And is called Saba after Sa-
ba/ Thus sone. This Saba is beclyp
ped in three sydes wyth the reed see.
¶Iosephus libro primo. In thys A-
rabia in the contree of madyan is the
mount of Syna/ The mounte Oreb
is a partye of the mounte of Syna/
and is hyghe and hath grete plente of
gras and of leese. But it is harde to
come therto / for hyghe Rockes and
scarres. Moyses was the fyrste man
that ladde thyder beestes/it is named
also the mounte of Couenaunt and of
drede.for god almyghty there vpon
made thondrynge and lyghtenynge
and gaue the lawe to the folke of Is-
raell that were at the hylle fote/ so that
noman durste approche to it but he
were purefyed and made clene/
¶Creuisa. Fenix is a wonder byrde
for alle that kynde is but one a lyue/
¶R. In the contre of Arabye toward
Cyrcius is the hyl that is called mons
Libani/that hylle departeth thre londes asonder. Arabia Iude/and Fenis
that hylle is fulle hyghe soo that sno-
we lyeth alwaye in some syde of that
hylle: And it is a certeyne marke and
token to shypmen that sayllen in the
grete see and ledeth theym to dyuerse
mouthes and hauens it is a fayre
and a plenteuos hylle and a holsome.
For Cypresse Cedre trees and herbes
growen theron that droppen gome &

smelle swete / by the whyche trees gó-
me and swetnesse seke men ben heled/
and venyme destroyed. Syria hathe
the name of Cyrus Abrahams neuew
And lyeth bytwene the water Eufrates in the eest syde / and the grete see
in the west syde/and hath in the north
syde Armenia and Capadocia/and in
the southe syde the see that is named
Arabicus/and conteyneth many pro-
uynces/that ben Comagena. Palestina: Fenis Chanaan. Idumea and Iu
dea/that is the Iurye/ Damascus
was somtyme the chyefe Cyte of that
prouynce. Eleazar Abrahams seruaunt bylded and made that Cytee
Damascus.Rasyn kynge of Damas-
ke helpe awaye the ten lynguages of Is
raheli the kynges of Iuda. Damascus as moche to saye as shedynge of
blood/ For there Chayme slowe his
broder Abell and hydde hym in the
sonde.

¶De Regione Iudee. Capt[']m. xiiii.

Iudea is a kyngdome of Syri-
a /a parte of Palestina and hath the name of Iudas Iacobs sone/
and was somtyme called Cananea of
Cham Noes sone / eyther of the ten
maner of people that the Iewes put
oute of that londe. ¶Petrus. Iudea
is taken in many maner wyse otherwhyle for the londe of beheste.
¶And theunne it hath the name of the
Iewes and of Iudas/ And soo it is
taken in this speche. The grete Pom
peus made Iudea trybutaryes. And
otherwhyle it is taken for the Royame of Iuda / and soo it is wryten of
Iosephe/ that whanne he herde that
b iiii

---

Plate 13b.  Higden. Polycronicon. Westminster, 1495. Walters Art Gallery

# ΤΩΝ ΑΘΗΝΑΙΟΥ ΝΑΥΚΡΑΤΙΤΟΥ ΔΕΙΠΝΟ
## ΣΟΦΙΣΤΩΝ ΠΡΟΛΕΓΟΜΕΝΑ.

Ἀθήναιος μὲν ὁ τῆς βίβλου πατὴρ ποιεῖται δὲ τὸν
λόγον πρὸς Τιμοκράτην. Δειπνοσοφιστὴς δὲ ταύτῃ
τὸ ὄνομα. ὑπόκειται δὲ τῷ λόγῳ Λαρήνσιος ῥωμαῖος
ἀνὴρ τῇ τύχῃ, περιφανής· τοὺς κατὰ πᾶσαν παιδείαν ἐμπειροτάτους ἐν τοῖς ἑαυτοῦ δαιτυμόνας
ποιούμενος, ἐν οἷς οὐκ ἔσθ' ὅντινα τῶν καλλίστων ἐκ
ἐμνημόνευσεν. ἰχθῦς τε γὰρ τῇ βίβλῳ ἐνέθετο καὶ
τὰς τούτων χρείας, καὶ τὰς τῶν ὀνομάτων ἀναπτύ-
ξεις. καὶ λαχάνων γένη παντοῖα. καὶ ζῴων παντο-
δαπῶν. καὶ ἄνδρας ἱστορίας συγγεγραφότας καὶ ποιητὰς καὶ ὅλως σοφούς. ἢ ὄργανα
μουσικὰ καὶ σκωμμάτων εὐφημεία καὶ ἐκπώματα διάφορα. καὶ πλοῦτον βασιλέ-
ων διηγήσατο. καὶ ῥαῶν μεγέθη. ὧ ὅσα ἄλλα οὐδὲν ἂν ἰχθρῶς ἀπεμνημονεύσαιμι. ἢ ἐπι-
λείποι με ἡ ἡμέρα κατ' εἶδος διερχόμενον. Καὶ ἔστιν ἐν τῷ λόγῳ οἰκονομία μιμη-
μα τῆς τοῦ δείπνου πολυτελείας. ὧ ἡ τῆς βίβλου διασκευὴ τῆς ἐν τῷ λόγῳ παρα-
σκευῆς. τοιοῦτον τὸν θαυμαστὸν οὗτος τὸν λόγον οἰκονόμει Ἀθήναιος ἄριστος λόγων δει-
πνον εἰσηγηται. κρείττων αὐτὸς ἑαυτοῦ γινόμενος ὥσπερ οἱ ἀθήνησι ῥήτορες ὑπὸ τῆς
ἐν τῷ λέγειν θερμότητος, πρὸς τὰ ἑπόμενα τῆς βίβλου βαθμηδὸν ὑπεραλλεται. οἵδε
τῷ δείπνῳ δὴ δι' ἐπιδημήσαντες δειπνοσοφισταὶ ἦσαν Μασούριος ὁ νόμων ἐξηγητὴς
ἐν πᾶσης παιδείας οὐ παρέργως. ἐπιμελῶς ποιούμενος μόνος ποιητὴς ἀνὴρ καὶ κατὰ
τὴν ἄλλην παιδείαν οὐδενὸς δεύτερος. καὶ τὴν ἐγκύκλιον οὐ παρέργως ἐζηλωκώς.
ἕκαστον γὰρ ὧν ἐπεδείκνυτο ὡς μόνον τοῦτο ἠσκηκὼς ἐφαίνετο. τοιαύτη πλύμα
θεία ἐκ παίδων συντεθραμμένη, ἰάμβων δὲ ἦν ποιητὴς οὐδενὸς δεύτερός φασι τῶν με-
ταρχέλοχον ποιητῶν. παρῆν δὲ ὧ Πλούταρχος ὧ Λεωνίδης ὁ ἠλεῖος ὧ Αἰμιλιανὸς
ὁ μαυρούσιος ὧ Ζωίλος γραμματικῶν οἰκειότατοι. φιλοσόφων δὲ παρῆσαν Ποντι-
ανὸς ὧ Δημόκριτος οἱ νικομηδεῖς, πολυμαθείᾳ πάντας ὑπερηκοντικότες. ὁ φιλά-
δελφός τε Πτολεμαῖος, ἀνὴρ ὁμοίου ἐν φιλοσόφῳ θεωρίᾳ τεθραμμένος, ἀλλ' εἰς κατὰ τὸν ἄλλον βίον ἐξητασμένος. τῶν δὲ κυνικῶν, ὃν ἂν ὁ κυνάλκον καλεῖ· ὧν οὐ
μόνον δύο κύνες ἀρτὶ ἐπηγρὸς τῷ Τηλεμάχῳ ἐκκλησιάζουσιν, ἀλλὰ τῶν πλείους.
νος πολὺ πλείονες. ἢ κρατυντῶν ἢ αἱ ρετῶν τῶν κυνικῶν οὐδὲν ἀπολειπομένη. ὧν κατὰ
τρέχει μετὰ δὲ τῶν ἄλλων ὅσοι τι ἐφθέγγοντο. Οὐλπιανός ὁ τύρειος. ὃς διὰ τὰς συνε-
χεῖς ζητήσεις ἃς ἀνὰ πᾶσαν ὥραν ποιεῖται, ἐν ταῖς ἀγυιαῖς, περιπάτοις βιβλιοπω-

Plate 14. Athenaeus. Deipnosophistae. [Venice: Aldus, c. 1499]. MA 1346-230

Ad diuū Maximilianū regē &c. Exhortatio. S.B.
Aspice quanta tuis rex inuictissime / Thurci
   Sacrilegi faciant iam mala christicolis:
Hęc tibi carminibus pręscripsimus optime Cęsar
   Nomine sub Thurci quę prius edidimus.
Decretum a superis est feliciffime Cęsar
   Res fidei lapsas te reparare sacrę:
Adcȝ Theodosii / Conftantinicȝ beata
   Tempora / romanum te reuocare ftatum.
Relliquias regni rex Clementiffime solus
   Colligere: & solus tu retinere potes.
Tu potes imperium: populū quocȝ morte redēptū
   Conferuare dei: te fine nemo poteft·
Quid nam agitare putas gentē populūcȝ nefandū
   Barbaricū: aduentum q̄ timuiffe tuum?
Namcȝ his increbuit fi quando Maxmiliani
   Nomen: & aduentus fi tuus intonuit:
Continuo cuncti metuūt: trepidantcȝ / timentcȝ:
   Atcȝ fuis rebus confulere incipiunt.
Nempe fciūt: fuerit quis Karolus: & Gothofredus
   Quis Conftantinus: Iuftinianus item.
Se quocȝ cognofcunt chrifti patrimonia: pręter
   Ius retinere: mala continuata fide.
Vaticinantur item fcriptis: multum nec abeffe
   Ab Mahumętani nominis interitu:
Id quod noftri etiā vates: facręcȝ Brigittę: &
   Methodii: atcȝ alia fcripta probata canunt.
Vade igitur Cefar: hoftefcȝ euince fuperbos:
   Ne dubites turbam colligere innumeram.
Et tibi fortunam tribuat deus optimus illam·
   Traiano dederat: q̄ pri⁹ atcȝ Tito.
       Vale rex fęculi decus·

Plate 15. Brant. Varia carmina. Basel: Bergmann, 1498. Bühler Inc. 59

# IACOBVS DEI GRATIA REX

## SCOTORVM SERENISSIMO PRINCIPI

ALBERTO eadem gratia Archiduci Austriæ, Duci Br̃-
bantiæ, Burgundiæq̃ consanguineo Et fratri nostro charissimo, Salutem Et perpe-
tuum fœlicitatis omnis incrementum. Serenissime Princeps consanguinee Et frater c̃-
rissime, cum anno superiore captus esset à naui Dunkerkensi subditus noster Ioann̄-
Smelius ciuis Edinburgensis, commendatitias nostras obtinuit, quibus faciliorem ad Ser̃
vestram aditum inueniret, faciliusq̃ impetraret vt bona tam ipsi quam alijs subditis nostris
eadem naui à Dunkirkensibus ablata restituerentur. Verum cum singula reliquis adem̃
demonstrare non posset ab eorum petitione abstinuit, earum tamen mercium quas ad se pertin̄
docuit estimationem tanta facilitate obtinuit vt damni accepti compensationem omnino clemen̄
estre acceptam ferat. Reuerso in patriam Smelio supplices a nobis petierunt ROBER̃
WALDEGRIVIVS Typographus noster, Et ROBERTVS BARNETTVS ejus
ner, quorum bona (aureis mille estimata) in eadem naui cum Smelio fuerant dirept̃
vt causas suas Ser̃.ti vestræ commendare dignaremur, quod quia ob virorum probitatem̃
recusare non potuimus primum omnium Ser̃.ti vestræ gratias agimus quantas possumus
ximas tam ob ipsum Smelium, quam ob singularem in nostros omnes animi propension̄
petimusque, vt eadem clementia WALDEGRIVIVM generumq̃ suum, eorumque
curatorem Gulielmum Morauium mercatorem Edinburgenum tractet qua erga reliq̃
subditos nostros hactenus est vsa. Et quia Ser̃.ti vestre non leuiter deuinctos nos exi-
mamus, dabimus operam vt nostram vicissim gratiam Et fauorem vbi occasio tulerit
vestris comprobemus, Deus Opt. Max. Ser̃.tem vr̃am seruet incolumen. Datæ
Regia nostra Sancruciana septimo die mensis Iannarij Anno salutis humanæ 1603.

S: V. Frater amantiss̃

Iacobus R

Plate 16. Letter of James I regarding Robert Waldegrave. PML, R. of E., James I, 6

actīt-e ·Contupiennbus· mīrum· est· et· ſummo· eʒtollendum· Laudis·
preconio: potuiſſe·a·tot·tamquam· diuerſis· urbium· et· oppidorum· po
pulis· oditam· ciuitatem: per· annos· mille· cum· tali· incremento· acglo
rie·ſplendore· unanimiq̔· ſagacitate· Conſeruare·· ͠

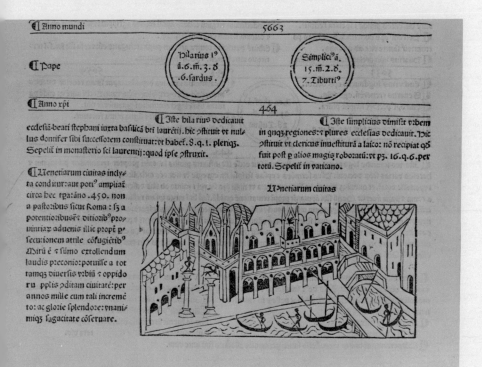

Plate 17a.  Rolewinck. Fasciculus temporum. M 801, f. 30

---

¶ Anno mundi                                          5663

¶ Pape          ⟨Hilarius 1⁹  / ñ.6.m̄.3.d̄. / .6.ſardus .⟩        ⟨Simplic⁹ñ. / 15.m̄.2.d̄. / 7.Tiburti⁹⟩

¶ Anno xp̄i                                           464

¶ Iſte bila rius dedicauit
eccleſiā·beati ſtephani iuxta baſilicā br̄i laurētij. hic pſtituit vt nullus donrifer ſibi ſucceſſorem conſtituat:vt habeř.S.q.1. pleriq̔.
Sepelit̄ in monaſterio ſci laurentij:quod ipſe pſtruxit.

¶ Venetiarum ciuitas incly-
ta condiuit:aut pon⁹ ampliat̄
circa hec tpa:āno .450. non
a paſtoribus ſicut Roma : ſ3 a
potentioribus:t ditiorib⁹pro-
uintiaz aduenis illic prope p̄-
ſecutionem attile cōfugiērib⁹
Mirū é t ſūmo extollendum
laudis preconio:potuiſſe a tot
ramq̔ diuerſis vrbiū t oppido
ru pplis oditam ciuitate:per
annos mille cum tali incremē
to: ac glorie ſplendore:vnani-
miq̔ ſagacitate cōſeruare.

¶ Iſte ſimplicius dimiſit vrbem
in qnq̔ regiones:t plures eccleſias dedicauit. Hic
pſtituit vt clericus inueſtiturā a laico: nō recipiat qd̄
fuit poſt p alios magis roboratū:vt p3. 16.q.6.per
totū. Sepelit̄ in vaticano.

Venetiarum ciuitas

Plate 17b.  Rolewinck. Fasciculus temporum. Venice: Ratdolt, 1481. PML 326, f. 37ᵛ

ditur arte.....

I ſte deus dedit fuit uir ſciſſimus dum quendam Leproſum oſculare
ntur ſtatim mundatus eſt multa bona ſtatuit ·:·

M archometus deceptor orbis propterea falſus nuncius ſatane percu
ſſor ante chriſti. Complementum hereſum ac tocius falcitatur pro
dignum circha hec tempora ueſaniam ſuam oſtentare incepit fuit. eni mo
onus et mercator uiliſſimus et factus princeps Latronum ſubtiliter
arabes ſibi attraxit qui tunc ualde ab erodio grauabantur per ſas ui

Plate 18a. Rolewinck. Fasciculus temporum. M 801, f. 36

gregorio detrahere nõ timebat
ab eo percuſſus interijt: ⁊ hic eſt
tertius de toto cathalogo ponti-
ficũ: qui formidabili morte ⁊ cul-
pabili vita notatus ẽ vſq̃ huc.

pann⁹ſuper
altare pone
retur.

ex malis inſtitutis paganoꝝ ſcit eligere ſanctum
exercitium deuotionis: quaſi medicina fiat ex ve
neno: vbi impſi colebãt omnes vemones: ibi chri
ſtiani colũt oẽs ſcõs ſic ars vcludit arte.

oſcularef: ſtati mã
datus eſt: m̃ta bo
na ſtatuit.

Pantheon Templum omnium deorum latine.

Plate 18b. Rolewinck. Fasciculus temporum. Venice: Ratdolt, 1481. PML 326, f. 41ᵛ

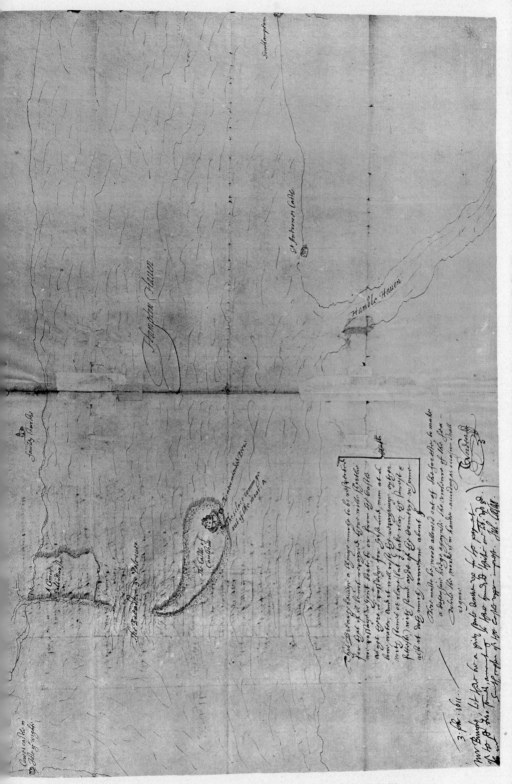

Plate 19. Calshot Castle and Surroundings. PML, R. of E., James I, Treas., 52

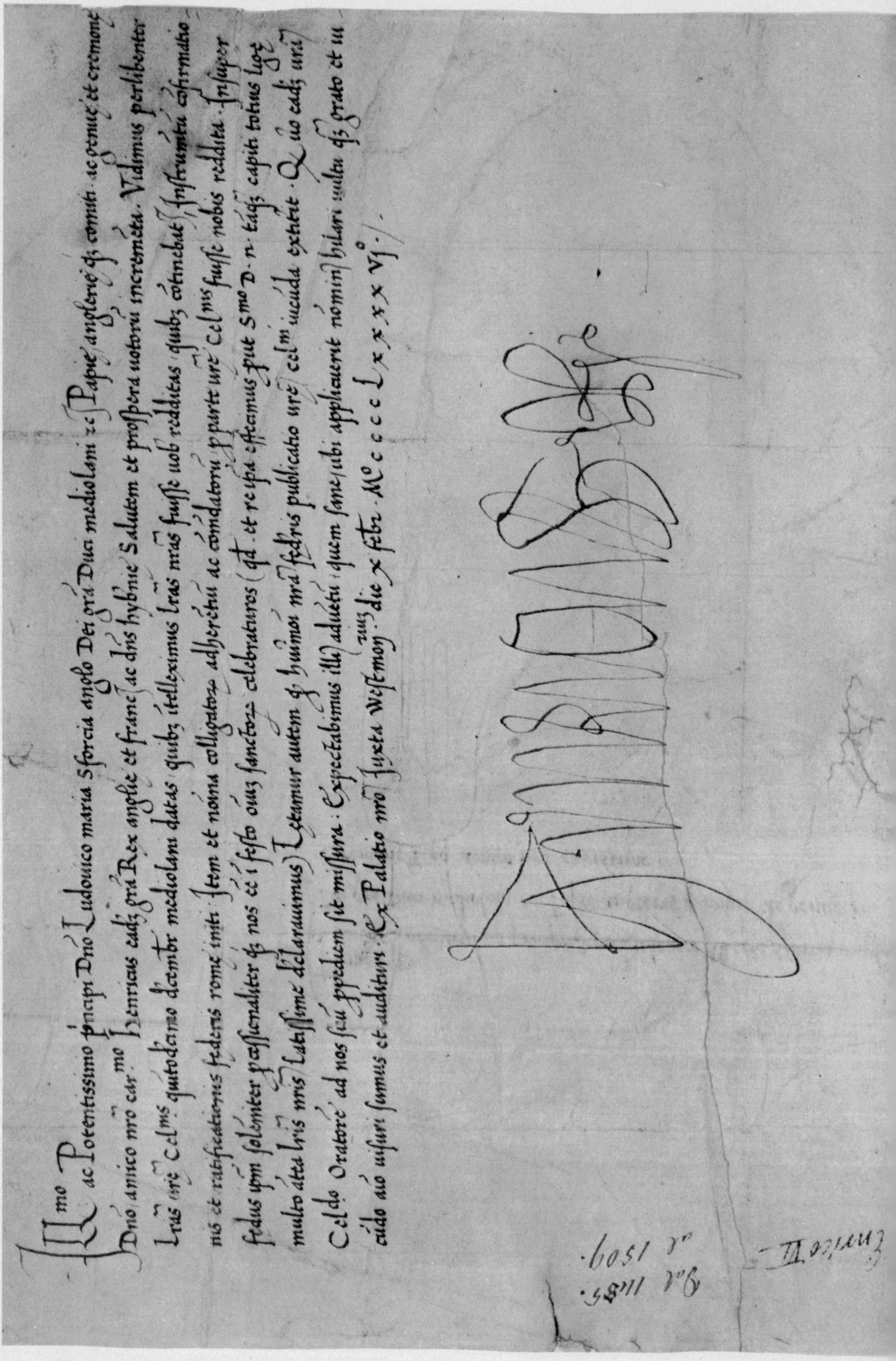

Plate 20. Henry VII to Lodovico Maria Sforza. PML, R. of E., Henry VII, 40

# CHAPTER T1

## "KYNGE MELYZYUS" AND *THE PASTIME*
## *OF PLEASURE*

THE identity of the character described as "Kynge Melyzyus" in *The Pastime of Pleasure* presents an interesting problem. In his edition of Hawes's poem, Dr. W. E. Mead,[1] confessing that he is puzzled, makes the following observation,

> Melyzyus appears rather frequently in *The Pastime*: cf. ll. 430, 998, 2484, 3257, 3278, 3305, 3346. But it is not altogether clear why Hawes makes so much of him. According to the *Courte of Sapyence*, c. iiii (ed. 1510), Millesius was "one of the sages seven in grece," but his name is not found in any of the lists of the sages that I have examined. According to Smith's *Dictionary of Greek and Roman Biography and Mythology*, Melisseus was "an ancient king of Crete who by Amalthea became the father of the nymphs Adrasteia and Ida, to whom Rhea entrusted the infant Zeus to be brought up." Hawes evidently drew upon material of a different sort.

What is this "material of a different sort"? As the various dictionaries of classical mythology offer no further assistance, we are forced to conclude that Hawes either invented this personage to serve his needs or that he had some definite classical figure in mind. "Kynge Melyzyus" represents the perfection of knighthood and has a correspondingly important role in *The Pastime*. Hawes refers to him thus:

> In whose tyme reygned / also in Thessayle
> A parte of Grece / the kynge Melyzyus
> That was ryght stronge / and fyerce in batayle
> By whose labour / as the story sheweth vs
> He brake fyrst horses wylde and rygoryous
> Techynge his men / on them ryght well to ryde
> And he hymselfe / dyde fyrst the horse bestryde." (ll. 218-24.)

> Bycause Mylyzyus / with his worthynesse
> Dyde fyrste attame / and breke the wyldnes
> Of the ryall stedes / and ryght swyftly
> His men and he / rode on them surely" (ll. 998-1001).

[1] Early English Text Society, 1928. Note to l. 218.

Than forthe he wente vnto the mageste
Of Kynge Melyzyus the myghty conqueroure
Saynge O power so hye in dygnyte
O prynce vyctoryous and famous Emperoure
Of Iustynge truely the orgynall floure (ll. 3277–81).

"Melyzyus," king of "Thessayle," is represented as an able horse-man, a victorious jouster, and a valiant soldier. As we can see from the frequent and specific references to him that Hawes was very proud of his knowledge of "Kynge Melyzyus," the supposition that he is merely an invention of Hawes's can, I believe, be dismissed. We must, therefore, come to the conclusion that this character is what he is represented to be, a definite classical figure and should ap-pear in Greek literature. Although it may be a bold conjecture, I suggest that the origin of the character may be found in the works of Pindar. The third Isthmian Ode was written to celebrate the victories of *Melissus* of *Thebes* at the Isthmian and Nemean games, and Pindar[2] says:

And he bringeth no disgrace on the manliness inherited from his fathers. Ye know, I ween, the olden glory of Cleônymus in the chariot-races: and, being on their mother's side akin to the Labdacidæ, they walked in the ways of wealth with toilsome training of their teams of four horses.

These men verily are spoken of as honoured of old in Thebes, as patrons of the neighbour-towns, and as untainted by boisterous insolence; and, as for the memorials of men now dead or of men that live, the memorials of bound-less fame that fly through all the world—all of these did they attain in all their fulness. And by far-reaching deeds of native valour, did they touch the pillars of Heracles; and let none pursue prowess that passeth beyond that bound! Aye, and they became breeders of horses, and were the joy of the mail-clad Arês.

The Cleonymidæ were a wealthy Theban family, particularly noted for their devotion to horse-breeding and honoured as the "patrons of the neighbour-towns" and as "the joy of the mail-clad Arês." Melissus, the winner of the pancratic games on the Isthmus, was certainly a "myghty conqueroure," and, owing to the success of his "stedes" at Nemea, an equally famous horseman. The achieve-ments of these two champions are so similar as to be more than a mere coincidence.

There is no reason to presume that Hawes could not have been acquainted, possibly only indirectly, with Pindar's Odes. It is certain

[2] Sir John Sandys, *The Odes of Pindar*, London, 1915, pp. 457–61.

that Hawes was familiar with the Classics, though, according to Mead, "there is no convincing proof that he knew Greek." Pindar was not unknown to the early Humanists. As early as 1427, Francesco Filelfo[3] possessed a manuscript of Pindar; even more important is the fact that, in a letter dated the "XIII, KAL. Maias 1461," Filelfo[4] quotes from the ninth Olympian Ode, giving a Byzantine version of

> τὸ δὲ φυᾷ κράτιστον ἅπαν·
> πολλοὶ δὲ διδακταῖς
> ἀνθρώπων ἀρεταῖς κλέος
> ὥρουσαν ἀρέσθαι
> ἄνευ δὲ θεοῦ σεσιγαμένον
> οὐ σκαιότερον χρῆμ' ἕκαστον

Politian, under whom Grocyn and Linacre studied, refers to Pindar in the *Silvæ*,[5] although there is no definite evidence that he had read the odes.

I am not attempting to prove that Hawes knew Greek; indeed, if we are to assume that "Kynge Melyzyus" is the Melissus of the third Isthmian Ode, it presupposes that Hawes was not a student of Pindar, the two characters being similar but not the same. It is probable that Hawes was at Oxford during the closing years of the fifteenth century, at which time Erasmus, Linacre, and Grocyn were arousing interest in the study of Greek. Did he obtain his information concerning "Melyzyus" in his Oxford days or on his later Continental travels? At all events, Melissus of Thebes is apparently the only classical figure that approximates Hawes's "Melyzyus" and must represent the earliest instance of Pindar's influence on English literature.

Dr. Mead, in his valuable introduction (to *The Pastime of Pleasure*), omitted to remark on the peculiar rhyme-scheme of the following passage. The rhyme-words of each stanza reappear as the initial words of each successive stanza, with the curious result that there is a first word rhyme-scheme. The lines are:

[3] L. Mehus, *Ambrosii Traversarii . . . Latinæ Epistolæ*, Florence, 1759, Liber XXIV, Epist. XXX.

[4] F. Filelfo, *Liber Epistolarum*, Venice, 1502, Lib. XVII, Epist. VII. See also Lib. XXIV, Epist. I, etc., for references to Pindar.

[5] The passage consists of twenty-six lines, beginning:

> "Aerios procul in tractus et nubila supra
> Pindarus it, dircaeus olor, cui nectare blandae," etc.

Mesure / mesureth / mesure / in effecte
Mesure / mesureth / euery quantyte
Mesure / mesureth / all way the aspecte
Mesure / mesureth / all in certayne
Mesure / mesureth / in the stabylyte
Mesure / mesureth / in euery doutfull case
And mesure is the lodesterre of all grace

Affecte of mesure is longe contynuaunce
Quantyte without mesure is nought
Aspecte of mesure deuoydeth repentaunce
Certayne wolde weye all thynges thought
Stabylyte vpon a perfyte grounde is wrought
Cace doutfull may yet a whyle abyde
Grace may in space a remedy prouyde

Countenaunce causeth the promocyon
Nought auayleth seruyse without attendaunce
Repentaunce is after all abusyon
Thought afore wolde haue had perceueraunce
Wrought how sholde be by dede the myschaunce
Abyde nothynge tyll thou do the dede
Prouyde in mynde how thou mayst haue mede

Promocyon groweth after good gouernaunce
Attendaunce doth attayne good fauoure
Abusyon is causer of all varyaunce
Perceyueraunce causeth the grete honoure
Myschaunce alway is rote of doloure
Dede done can not be called agayne
Mede well rewarded bothe with Ioye and payne (ll. 2633–60).

Stanza 1, l. 4 and stanza 2, l. 4. For "certayne" read "Certaynte" as edition of 1509. Stanza 2, l. 1. For "Affecte" read "Effecte" as stanza 1, l. 1.

(From *The Review of English Studies* 10 (1934), pp. 438-41).

# CHAPTER T2

## ON THE DATE OF THE
## LETTER WRITTEN BY SIR PHILIP SIDNEY
## TO CHRISTOPHER PLANTIN[1]

I N his edition of Sidney's *Complete Works* (Cambridge University Press, iii. 134), Professor Albert Feuillerat printed the following letter sent by Sir Philip Sidney to Christopher Plantin:

> Les mappes de lortelius en la plus nouvelle édition.
> Le livre en flaman descripvant les havres de leurope.
> La description des villes et forteresses

> Je vous prie Mons. Plantin que je puisse avoir ces livres et ne faudray point de vous les remburser et en récompense demeure.
> Vostre affectionné ami pour vous faire plaisir et service.
> 
> Ph. Sidney.

Professor Feuillerat apparently considered the letter to have been written in 1580/1, as he printed it among the correspondence of that period, but it is quite certain that Sidney's letter cannot be dated before 1584 and, in all probability, even somewhat later.

As we shall see that the first two books can be positively identified as books actually printed by Plantin, it seems reasonable (in the absence of any contradictory note in the letter) to suppose that the third book would have had Plantin's imprint—if, indeed, it was not actually printed by him. If Sidney was referring in the case of the third book to a work not bearing the imprint "Ex officina Plantiniana" and the first two were from that press, it is difficult to see how he could have expected Plantin to know precisely what book he wanted. I have no doubt that Sidney really had three books of Plantin's in mind; for if he was not ordering such works, he would most certainly have been more specific in recording the title of the books he wanted, or he would at least have given some indication of the printer of the various works.

The publications of the Plantin press are known not only through the occasional "hand-lists" issued by that press (*Catalogus Librorum a Christophoro Plantino excussorum*, Antwerpiae 1575, 1584, 1596,

---

[1] The original letter is in the Pierpont Morgan Library, New York.

etc.) but also through modern bibliographies (C. Ruelens and A. de Backer, *Annales Plantiniennes*, Paris, 1866, etc.) so that it is comparatively easy to identify the books Sidney wanted. The first is, of course, Abraham Ortelius's well-known *Theatrum Orbis Terrarum*, of which the first edition printed by Plantin appeared in 1579. An edition in German of 1580, copies of which are in the British Museum and in the National Library in Warsaw, or more probably a Latin one of 1584 would represent the "newest edition" referred to by Sidney. (The "editio princeps" of this work, incidentally, was issued by Gilles Coppens de Diest, Antwerp, 1570, the book meeting with such success that at least ten separate editions were printed before Plantin's appeared.[2])

The second item should have suggested to Feuillerat the approximate date of this letter. The only book that corresponds to Sidney's "Les havres de leurope" is the famous *Speculum Nauticum*, the first book containing printed maritime charts, published by Plantin in 1584.

"De Spieghel der Zeevaerdt, vande navigatie der Westersche Zee, innehoudende alle de custen van Vranckryck, Spaignen ende t'principaelste deel van Engelandt, in diversche zee Caerten begrepen, met den gebruycke van dien, nu met grooter naersticheyt by een vergadert ende ghepractizeert door Lucas Jansz. Waghenaer, piloot ofte stuyrman residerende inde vermaerde zeestadt Enchuysen. Ghedruct tot Leyden by Christoffel Plantyn voor Lucas Janssz. Waghenaer van Enckhuysen. MDLXXXIV."

The third volume is, however, more difficult to identify. It has been shown that the first two books were issued by Plantin so that one would naturally expect the third work also to have been printed by him. No single book, however, appears to have been issued by the Plantin press (prior to 1586) that corresponds exactly to Sidney's description. The following *two* Plantin books most nearly approximate Sidney's title; in as much as Pasino's book is in quarto and Guicciardini's in folio, the tempting suggestion that Sidney saw these two works bound together must, unfortunately, be dismissed; it is not impossible, however, that Sidney merely confused the two.

"Description de touts les Païs-Bas, autrement appelés la Germanie inférieure, ou Basse-Allemagne, par Messire Louis Guicciardin, gentilhomme florentin: maintenant revue et augmentée plus que de la moictié par le mesme autheur. Avec toutes les cartes geographicques desdicts païs, et plusieurs pourtraicts

---

[2] See J. Denuce, *Oud-Nederlandsche Kaartmakers in betrekking met Plantijn*, Uitgaven der Antwerpsche Bibliophilen 27–28, Antwerp, 1912–13.

de villes tirés au naturel. Avec Indice tres-ample des choses les plus memorables. A Anvers, de l'imprimerie de Christophle Plantin. MDLXXXII."[3]

Sidney's reference to a book on fortresses,[4] a much more uncommon item in the contemporary booksellers' stocks than those having only descriptions of cities, leads me to believe that he had another work in mind.

"Discours sur plusieurs poincts de l'architecture de guerre, concernant les fortifications tant anciennes que modernes. Ensemble le moyen de bastir et fortifier une place de laquelle les murailles ne pourront aucunement estre endommagées de l'artillerie. Par M. Aurelio de Pasino Ferrarois, architecte de très-illustre seigneur, Monseigneur le duc de Buillon. A Anvers, de l'imprimerie de Christofle Plantin, imprimeur de sa Majesté. MDLXXIX."

Sidney was, of course, one of the strongest advocates of the theory that the Spanish advance in the Netherlands could best be checked by attacking the Spanish seaports and destroying their trade on the high seas, thereby forcing them to withdraw at least a part of their forces from the Netherlands. In the summer of 1585 he enthusiastically welcomed the preparations made by Drake for the equipment of a great fleet, and in August of that year he travelled secretly to Plymouth with the obvious intention of joining the expedition. Drake, apparently fearing that the Queen might be angry if he permitted Sidney to participate in this undertaking, prevented his doing so. It is my opinion that Sidney wrote to Plantin before August 1585, while he was planning to join Drake's expedition. The books he ordered were ideally suited to such an enterprise; the first two works[5] became at this time the indispensable maritime reference

[3] An Italian edition of this work had been issued the previous year. An English translation appeared in 1593 (*S.T.C.* 12, 463) under the title "The Description of the Low countreys and of the Prouinces, thereof, gathered into an Epitome."

[4] Only on one occasion does Guicciardini describe a fortification at length, *i.e.* in the case of Antwerp (Plantin, 1588, p. 88 and following). Usually the military defences are briefly dismissed; so Deventer ". . . è citta molto forte & ben' munita, di bonissima muraglia, oue fra le altre, è la porta chiamata Brinconi, opera bella & eccellente." The important seaport, Gravelines, with its new fortifications is described thus: "Gravelinghe—sarà forse la piu forte terra di tutti questi paesi, con vn' buon' Castello & baluardi marauigliosi."

[5] I am indebted to Dr. R. B. McKerrow for the following information. In 1585 the Lord Admiral of England, Lord Charles Howard, drew the attention of the Privy Council to Waghenaer's book. Sir Anthony Ashley was commissioned to translate it into English and the work appeared in the latter part of 1588 (*S.T.C.* 24, 931). The title of this work is described in the *D.N.B.* (ii. 170) as: "The Mariners Mirrour—of Navigation, First made and set fourth in divers exact Sea Charts by that famous Navigator Luke Wagenar of Enchuisen, and now fitted with necessarie

books, and, if we can identify this book with Sidney's request, the inclusion of Pasino's work may possibly indicate Sidney's views on naval strategy. Drake's expedition developed into a mere punitive voyage, with the principal object of obtaining booty and of destroying Spanish cities and trade. To judge from this third request, it would appear that Sidney's plans included not only the capture of Spanish seaports but also the fortifying and holding of them, with the expected result that the Spaniards, harassed in their own country, would be forced to abandon their plans of expansion elsewhere. It is interesting to recall that Monson, writing several years later, concurred with this opinion,

"But it seems our long peace made us inexperienced of advice in war; for had we kept and defended those places when in our possession and provided to have been relieved and succoured out of England, we had diverted the war from this part of Europe into America. For at that time there was no comparison betwixt the strength of Spain and England by sea, by means whereof we might have better defended them and encroached upon the rest of the Indies, than the King of Spain could have aided or succoured them" (*The Naval Tracts of Sir William Monson*, Naval Records Society, 1902, i. 123).

No other books of the period were of more practical value in formulating plans for extensive naval operations than these, and it is surely no bold conjecture to suggest that it was for this purpose that Sidney ordered the three volumes from Plantin.

For the sake of completeness, I must point out that the letter *might* possibly be assigned to a later period, even though the internal evidence points so decisively to the summer of 1585. On November 7, 1585, Queen Elizabeth signed a patent appointing Sidney governor of Flushing, and only eleven days later he had already arrived at his new post. As the Spaniards held the nearby Antwerp, it was essential for a governor of the Dutch seaport to be acquainted with the latest methods of defending the city against a possible siege and to be thoroughly familiar with the neighbouring coastline. In that case, of course, both Guicciardini's and Pasino's books would have proved most useful, but surely the coast and harbours of Zeeland would have been more accurately displayed and therefore better suited to Sidney's immediate needs, in a local *portulan* than

---

additions for the use of Englishmen by Anthony Ashley. Heerin also may be understood the exploits lately atchived by the right Honorable L. Admiral of England with her Ma^{ties} Navie, and some former services done by that worthy knight S^r Fra. Drake." The title thus connects this work directly with Drake's expedition.

in the books by Waghenaer and Ortelius, the charts of which are necessarily on a smaller scale as they cover the entire coastline of Western Europe.

Did Sidney send his request to Plantin with the idea of acquainting himself with his new duties as governor of Flushing? The evidence that may be deduced from the contents of the letter points almost certainly to the summer of 1585 rather than to the winter of that year. The departure of Drake's fleet (September 14, 1585) realized, to some extent, Sidney's plans for a direct attack on the Spanish coast and we may take it for granted that, with the departure of the expedition, Sidney's expectations of participating in a naval manœuvre vanished, and whatever need of maps he had after that time was limited to local charts of the Netherlands. This need, as I have shown above, would have been more adequately filled by the *portulans* than by the larger atlases printed by Plantin. The attack on Axel (July 6/7, 1586) was made "by night and in boats," but can scarcely be made to represent a naval undertaking so extensive that the Plantin charts were essential to the success of the venture. It was, indeed, only a small local encounter and was doubtless planned with the assistance of a native "stuyrman" perfectly familiar with the mouth of the West Schelde and more to be relied upon than any small-scale map.

(From *The Review of English Studies* 12 (1936), pp. 67-71).

[Note: Dr. William H. Bond has shown (*Harvard Library Bulletin*, viii [1954], 233-235) that the letter was probably written in March or early April of 1586. CFB]

# CHAPTER T3

## *LONDON THOW ART THE FLOWRE*
## *OF CYTES ALL*

FOUR manuscripts of the poem *London thow art the Flowre of Cytes All* are extant, of which two are in the British Museum (MSS. Vitellius A. XVI and Lansdowne 762), one in the library of Balliol College, Oxford, and another in the Pierpont Morgan Library, New York. The Morgan manuscript is the only one of these that has not been previously printed.[1]

In MS. Vitellius A. XVI, "a chronicle of England containing the remarkable passages of what happened; together with the mayors and sheriffs of London, from A° 1215 to A° 1509,"[2] the poem *To London* is quoted (on f. 200) with a statement to the effect that it was presented at a dinner given by the Lord Mayor in Christmas Week, 1501. The occasion was a formal reception in honour of the Scottish mission sent to arrange the marriage (tentatively planned some years before by James IV and Richard Foxe, Bishop of Durham) between James and Margaret Tudor, when "sitting at dyner ane of the said Scottis giving attendance upon a Bishop ambassador, the which was reputed to be a Protonotary of Scotland and the servant of the Ld. Bishop, made this Balade."[3]

The Morgan manuscript of this poem (MA 717) is an important independent authority which was not consulted when the previous editions of this "balade" were prepared. The leaves on which the poem is found were originally bound in a copy of Caxton's *Cordiale*

---

[1] MS. Vitellius A. XVI was used for the text of this poem in the editions of Dunbar's *Works* by J. Schipper, J. Small, and W. M. Mackenzie. (For editions, see below.) The text of Lansdowne 762 was printed by T. Wright and J. O. Halliwell in *Reliquiæ Antiquæ*, London, 1841, vol. i., pp. 205-7. The contents of the Balliol MS. were printed by Dr. Roman Dyboski in *Songs, Carols, etc. from Richard Hill's Balliol MS.*, E.E.T.S., 1907. At the end of the poem in the Balliol MS. is the note "Explicit þe treatise of London made at Mr. Shaa table whan he was mayre" and in the table (f. 4ᵃ): "A litill balet made by London, made at Mr. Shawes table by a Skote." (John Shaa, goldsmith, was Lord Mayor of London in 1501). The texts of the Balliol and Lansdowne MSS. correspond closely to that in the Cotton manuscript.

[2] *A Catalogue of the Manuscripts in the Cottonian Library*, London, 1802, p. 381.

[3] Quoted by Dr. W. Mackay Mackenzie, *The Poems of William Dunbar*, Edinburgh, 1932, p. 240.

(finished March 24, 1479) formerly in the library of the Earl of Ashburnham. As the hand-writing appears to be of the first decade of the sixteenth century and the binding is certainly earlier, indeed it is, in all probability, one of the few books still extant which were bound in, or for, Caxton's printing-house,[4] we may assume that the Morgan manuscript represents an almost contemporary transcript. The Cotton manuscript, as we have seen, contains a list of the Mayors and Sheriffs of London to 1509, so that it is not unlikely that the Morgan text antedates that in Vitellius A. XVI. The poem in the Morgan MS. is preceded by the note:

"A balad mayde at London when my Lorde Prince Arthur was wed, by a Skotte hauyng muche money of dyuerse lordes for hys Indytyng."

The marriage referred to is that of Prince Arthur (eldest son of Henry VII) and Katherine of Aragon, which took place on November 14, 1501. The celebrations which preceded and followed the wedding were, of course, worthy of the international importance of this union, and there can be little doubt that the inevitable "ballads" were presented by the Court poets and visiting literateurs. John Stow, although not an eye-witness, describes the wedding in a most detailed manner.

The 9 of Nouember prince Arthur with a goodly companie came through Fleetstreet of London to S. Paules, and so to the wardrobe by the Blacke friers, and there was lodged. And the same day came the Lady Katherine Princesse vnto Lambeth, where she with her ladies was lodged, in the archbishops Inne of Canterbury: & upon the Friday next following about two of the clock at afternoone, the said lady princes accompanied with many lords & Ladies, in most sumptuous manner apparrelled, came riding from Lambeth into Southwarke & so to London bridge, where was ordeined a costlie pageant of S. Katherine and S. Vrsula, with many virgins: from thence shee rode to Grace streete, where was ordeined a second pageant, from thence to the condict in Cornehill, where was another pageant. The great condict in cheape ran with Gascoine wine, and was furnished with musick. Against Soperlane end was the fourth pageant. At the standard in cheape was ordeined the fift pageant. At Pauls gate was the 6 pageant: by which the princesse rode through Paules Churchyard vnto the bishop of Londons palace, where she and her people were lodged.

Now within the church of S. Paul, to wit, from the west gate of it vnto the vppermost greese or step at the going in of the quier, was made a pace

4 See the *Catalogue of Manuscripts and Early Printed Books from the Libraries of William Morris, Richard Bennett, Bertram Fourth Earl of Ashburnham and other Sources now forming portion of the Library of J. Pierpont Morgan,* London, 1907, vol. iii., p. 167.

of timber and boords to go vpon, from the sayd west doore vnto the fore-
named greese, of the height of 6 foote from the ground, or more: & foreanenst
the place where the commissaries court is kept within the said church, was
ordeined a standing, like vnto a mountaine, with steps on euery side, which
was couered ouer with red wusted, & in likewise was all the railes: against
which mountaine vpon the northside, within the foresaid place of the commissaries court was ordeyned a standing for the king, and such other as liked
him to haue: and on the south side almost, for against the kings standing
was ordeined a scaffold, whereupon stoode the Maior and his brethren.

Then vpon the 14 of Nouember being Sunday, vpon the aboue named
mountaine, was prince Arthur about the age of 15 yeeres, and the lady
Katherine about the age of 18 yeeres, both clad in white sattine, married by
the archbishop of Canterbury, assisted by 19 Bishops and abbots mitered.
And the K. the Queene, the kings mother, stood in the place aforenamed
where they hearde & beheld the solemnization which being finished, the said
archbyshop & Bishops tooke their way from the mountaine, vpon the saide
pace couered vnder foote with blew rey-cloth vnto the quier, & so to the
high altar, whom followed the spouse and spouses, the lady Cicile sister to
the Q. bearing her traine, after her followed 100 ladies & gentlewomen, in
right costly apparell, then the Maior in a gowne of crimson veluet, and his
brethren in scarlet, with the sword born before the maior, & sate in the quier
the masse while, the archb[ishop] of Yorke sate in the deanes place, & offred
as chiefe, and after him the duke of Buckingham etc. Woonderfull it was to
behold the riches of apparel worne that day, with the poisant chaines of gold:
of which, two were specially noted, to wit, sir T. Brandon knight, master of
the kings horse, which that day ware a chain valued at 1400 pound: and
the other W. de Riuers esquire, master of the king haukes, whose chaine was
valued at a thousand pound: many mo were of 200, 300 and so foorth, these
were not noted for length, but for the greatnesse of the linkes. Also the Duke
of Buckingham ware a gowne wrought of Needle worke and set vpon cloth
of tissue, furred with sables, the which Gowne was valued at 1500. l. & sir
Nicholas Vause knight ware a gown of purple veluet, pight with peeces of
gold so thicke & massie, that it was valued in golde, besides the silke and fur,
a thousand pounde: which chaines and garments were valued by goldsmithes
of best skill, and them that wrought them. The masse being finished, the
princesse was led by Henry duke of Yorke, and a Legate of Spain, by the
foresaid pace into the palace, going before her men of honor, to the number of
160 with gentlemen and other. There came vnto the Maior, sir Richard
Crofts steward of the Princes house, which brought him & his brethren the
aldermen into the great hall, and at a table vpon the west side of the hall,
caused them to bee set to dinner, where honorablie were they serued with
12 dishes to a messe at the first course, 15 the second course, and 18 dishes
the third course. In this hall was a cupboord of fiue stages height, being tri-
angled, the which was set with plate valued 1200 l. the which was neuer
mooued at that day: and in the vtter chamber where the princesse dined, was
a cupboord of gold plate, garnished with stone and pearle, valued aboue
20000 pound. The tuesday following the king & queene being all this season

at Bainards castle, came vnto Powles, and heard there masse and then accompanied with many nobles went into the palace, and there dined with the
princesse. This day sir Nicholas Vause ware a coller of Esses which weied, as
the goldsmithes that made it reported 800 pounde of nobles: And the same
day at afternoon, the said princes were conueied with many Lords and Ladies
vnto Powles wharffe, where the said estates tooke their barges, & were rowed
to Westminster, vpon whom the Maior attended, with the Aldermen & fellowships in barges, garnished with banners and other deuises, musick, etc.
Thus much for that marriage.[5]

The general description of London in the poem very closely resembles Stow's account of the wedding celebrations; on the other
hand, if we are to believe that the poem was written at that time, it
is indeed strange that there is no reference to the wedding anywhere
in the "balad."

The same is true, though to a lesser degree, if we consider the
manuscript attribution in the Cotton MS. The poem is appropriate
enough for a Lord Mayor's banquet in its eulogies of the "city"
and its Mayor, but it is strange that the reason for which these
"Scottis" came to London is not mentioned. "Conversations" were
still going on and the wedding "by proxie" did not take place till
"the day of the conuersion of S. Paule," so that the poet may have
considered it best not to refer to the "mission" at all. The marriage
conversations could hardly, however, be said to have been secret,
as they had been going on for upwards of three years. It is scarcely
probable that the real purpose of Bishop Blackader's visit was unknown to the citizens of London, although official circles may not
have discussed it publicly. The plenipotentiaries actually left Scotland early in October, so that they may have been in London for a
month before the poem *To London* was written. In view of the
circumstances, some delicate tribute to Margaret, however much it
might have been veiled, would, no doubt, not only have been welcomed but expected.

If, and the evidence of the manuscripts cannot very well be completely ignored, we consider these attributions, it is evident that the
poem was composed in the winter of 1501/2 by a "Skotte" who was
at that time in London. Whether or not the poem can be attributed
to Dunbar is doubtful. It appears that the main reason for ascribing
the poem to him is based on the rather circumstantial evidence that

[5] *The Annales or Generall Chronicle of England*, London, Thomas Adams, 1615,
pp. 483 and 484. See also Edward Halle's, *The Union of the two noble and illustre
famelies of Lancastre and Yorke*.

Dunbar was the only distinguished Scottish poet who was there at the time the poem was written. Professor Schipper[6] says that "the poem bears all the characteristics of Dunbar's style and metre etc.," while Mackenzie (p. 241) maintains that "the proposition that no one but Dunbar *could* have produced this poem is not at all self-evident, since it is clear that other clerkly people of the time were capable of turning out quite tolerable verses." The poem is included, however, in the critical editions of Dunbar's works and is ascribed to him without hesitation by *The Cambridge History of English Literature* and the *Oxford Book of English Verse*.

It has not been definitely established that Dunbar was a member of Bishop Blackader's mission. In the Scottish *Accounts of the Lord High Treasurer*, there is a record of the payment of £5 to Master William Dunbar (the "Master" implies that Dunbar was a Magister Artium) on December 20th, 1501, "quhilk wes payit to him eftir he com furth of England."[7] This presumably could not have been entered into the *Accounts* or have been paid to Dunbar, if he was in England at that time. Dr. Mackenzie, however, notes this interesting fact (p. 240):

> But an entry in the *Accounts* for 3rd January, 1501/2, records a payment to Lyon Herald "quhen he cum furth of Ingland," yet "Lyon King of Armes" is recorded among those who received gifts from King Henry on the Thursday after the conclusion of the treaty of marriage on 25th January, 1502. It would seem, then, that the inference as to Dunbar's return suggested by the entry in the *Treasurer's Accounts* does not necessarily follow.

According to the Morgan manuscript, however, the celebration at which the poem was presented was the wedding of Prince Arthur and Katherine of Aragon on November 14, so that if Dunbar really composed the "balad" for this occasion he might easily have been back in Scotland by December 20. Apart from the reference in the Cotton manuscript, there is no evidence that Dunbar was a member of the Scottish mission; although it is clear, from the *Accounts*, that he had been in England prior to December 20, 1501. It has been

---

[6] J. Schipper, "Poems of William Dunbar," in *Denkschriften der Kaiserlichen Akademie der Wissenschaften*, Philosophisch-Historische Classe, Wien, 1892–3 (vol. 40, p. 87, and vol. 42, p. 86). See also J. Small, *The Poems of William Dunbar*, Scottish Text Society, 1893.

[7] Concerning this entry, Dr. Mackenzie says: "This is plainly the amount of pension due to him at the previous Martinmas, and the entry would suggest that this was the later date of payment and that Dunbar by that time was therefore back in Scotland, in which case he could not have been at the Lord Mayor's dinner or been the writer of the poem."

supposed that Dunbar was occasionally entrusted with diplomatic missions; did he attend the royal wedding on behalf of King James? The Morgan manuscript does not set at rest these perplexing problems, but it does show how Dunbar might have written the ballad for an important celebration in London[8] and yet have been in Scotland on December 20 to receive his pension.

Dr. Mackenzie notes two further records: "On 31st December, 1501, there is a payment on behalf of Henry VII of £6 13s. 4d. 'to the Rhymer of Scotland in reward,' repeated on 7th January, 1502, as 'to a Rhymer of Scotland.' " If the "Rhymer of Scotland" was Dunbar, the question that arises is why Henry VII authorized these payments. Among the extant poems of Dunbar, there are only two which connect the Scottish poet with Henry VII; the ballad *To London* and *The Thrissil and the Rois*. In the Morgan Manuscript, we are expressly told that the poet had "muche money of dyuerse Lordes for hys Indytyng." Was Henry VII one of these Lords? But we can scarcely believe that King Henry patronized Dunbar for a poem presented at the wedding of the Prince of Wales in which neither the wedding nor the royal reception is mentioned. On the other hand, if the ballad was presented at the Lord Mayor's dinner and as it is little more than a eulogy of the "city" and its Mayor, it is not quite clear why the notoriously close-fisted Henry made Dunbar such comparatively handsome grants. The King presented to the "Scottish Rhymer" more than thirteen pounds, whereas the annual pension paid to Dunbar at this time amounted to only twenty pounds *per annum*. That Dunbar received these sums for writing *The Thrissil and the Rois* is possible, but there is no direct evidence for this. In that case, we must assume that the money represented an advance payment, which in a time when even a promised subsidy was paid late and reluctantly (if at all), is unusual. The date of this poem is confusing in any case; it was written, ostensibly, to commemorate the marriage of James IV and Princess Margaret Tudor, but the last two lines bear the date May 9.

> And thus I wret, as ye haif hard to forrow,
> Off lusty May upone the nynt morrow.

[8] Obviously one of the attributions is wrong. The two events took place little more than a month apart and were of a very similar nature, so that this may explain the two MSS. notes. As the gloss in the Morgan MS. speaks of "my lorde Prince Arthur" and not of "my Late Lorde," are we to suppose that the transcript was written before Arthur's death on April 2nd, 1502? In that case, the gloss in the Morgan MS. would probably be correct.

The marriage treaty was concluded on January 24, 1502, and on January 25, 1503, as we have seen, the espousal with the Earl of Bothwell as proxy took place. Margaret did not leave Richmond till June 27, arriving in Scotland towards the end of July (Henry VII had, indeed, stipulated that Margaret was to remain in England till September 1, 1503, but he yielded to James's request that she come earlier); the actual wedding was celebrated on August 8 at Holyrood. In view of these facts, why did Dunbar write *The Thrissil* on May 9? Possibly the answer may be found in the poem itself; May says to the poet:

> Thow did promyt, in Mayis lusty quhyle,
> For to discryve the Ros of most plesance.

The poem, although that may be expected in view of the special circumstances, is more friendly towards England than most of Dunbar's poems. Did Dunbar promise Henry VII that he would write some such poem and do the grants of December 31, 1501, and of January 7, 1502, represent Henry's payment for *The Thrissil*?

In both the Morgan and the Cotton MSS., *To London* is definitely ascribed to a Scottish poet, but the poem in the Morgan manuscript is no more Scottish than in Vitellius A. XVI. The Southern verb terminations for the present indicative predominate; *ben* (*be*) and *arte* for Sc. *ar* and *es*, the present participle in *-yng, churchys* (*c>ch*, not *k*), etc., are all Southern characteristics. Northern forms occur in: (1) the present indicative plural is *-s* (Stanza VI); (2) *mast* (*mast* is the normal form in the North and Scotland, *mæst>mast*); (3) *kelles* ("Kell. A Northern form corresp. to M.E. *calle, caul*; the difference in vowel is not easy to account for"—*N.E.D.*); (4) *apon* (mostly Scottish); (5) *beryall* (a Scottish form—so Dunbar, *Goldyn Targe*, l. 23 and Lyndesay, *Ane Satyre*, l. 132; but see the Southern form *byrall* in Stanza II); (6) *hore* (generally spelt *ar* in Scottish; it could not have been pronounced with a decided *o* here, as it rhymes with *compare*), etc. As in most late MSS. the *þ* has lost almost entirely its original character and is written like a *y*; the *o* is made with two strokes of the pen, so that it is sometimes difficult to distinguish it from an *a*. (In Stanza II, *flode* may be *flade*—a form not recorded by the *N.E.D.*—from the verb *flede* via *flæde>flade*?).

A balad mayde at London when my lorde Prince Arthur was wed, by a Skotte hauyng muche money of dyuerse lordes for hys Indytyng.

### I

London, thow arte of townes chefe of dygnyte,
And sowerent of all cytes, semlyste in syght,
Of hye renowne, ryches, and eke of ryalte;
Of lordes, barons, & many goodly knythe;
Of maste delectable lusty & ladys bryghte;
Of famos prelates in habytes clerly alle;
Of merchandes of svstans, & men of grete myght:
O London, thow arte the flowre of cytes alle.

### II

Now may thow reioy, thow lusty Troy meyyte;
Cyte þat som tyme clepyd was newe Troy;
In alle erthe imperialle as þou standythe;
Byralle of cytes, of plesure and joye,
A rychere restoryd vnder Crysten roye;
ffore manly powere, with craftes naturalle,
ffore there ware no feyerere sythe the flode of Noye:
London, thu art the flour of cytes alle.

### III

Gemme of alle joy, jasper of jocundite,
Maste myghty carbuncle of vert(u)es & valour;
(S)tronge Troy in vigore & strenuyte;
Of rialle cites rose & gerafloure;
Emperas of cytes, exalte to honour;
In bewte beryng the crowne imperyalle;
Swete paradyse precellyng in plesure:
London, thow art the flowre of cytes alle.

### IV

A-bowe alle reuerse, thy reuer hathe renowne,
Whos beryalle stremys, plesand & preclere,
Vnder thy lusty walles contynualy rynes a-downe;
Where many a swanne dothe swym with wyngges feyre;
Where many a barge dothe sayle & rowe with hore;
Where many a shyppe dothe reste with toppe ryalle.
O towne of townes, not to compare:
London, þou art the flowre of cytes all.

### V

A-pon thy lusty brygge of pyllors whyte
Bene merchandes fulle ryalle to be-hold;
A-pon the stretes gothe many a semly knythe
In welvet gowns & chenys of gold.

By Juli*us* Cesar*e* the towne foundy[t] of hold
May be the hows of Mars victoryall*e*,
Whos arttelery wit*h* tong may not be told:
London, thow art (the flowre of cytes alle).

## VI

Strong ben*e* the wallys þ*at* a-bowte the stond*es*;
Wyse be*n* the peple þ*at* in the dwellys;
Freshe ys the ryver*e* wit*h* hys lusty stremys;
Blythe be the churchys, well sowndy*ng* wit*h* bell*es*;
Ryche be the m*er*chaund*es* in substance þ*at* excell*es*;
Feyre be ther*e* wyves, ryght luf-som, ge*n*tyl & small*e*;
Cler*e* be the v*ir*gyns, lusty vnd*er* kell*es*:
London, þou art (the flowre of cytes alle).

## VII

The famos mayre, by pr*in*cely gou*er*nance,
Wit*h* swerde of justyce he rewlythe pr*u*de*n*tly.
No lord of P*ar*ys, Venys, or Florance
In dignite or*e* hono*ur* gothe hy*m* nye.
He ys exsampler*e*, lode-ster*e*, and guye,
Pr*in*cipall & rose oryginall*e*,
A-bow all*e* meyres ys moste wurthy:
London, þou art the flowre of cytes all*e*.

Stanza    I, l. 3 : eke of] *so by interlinear correction in MS.*
Stanza    II, l. 7 : ware] were? MS.
Stanza    III, l. 2 : vert(u)es] v*er*tes MS.
          l. 3 : (S)tronge] Tronge MS.
Stanza    IV, l. 3 : contynualy] *so by correction from* contynuly
          l. 3 : a-downe] *so by correction from* downe
          l. 6 : dothe reste] *so by correction from* restes
          l. 7 : to compare] *the* to *added interlinearly in* MS.
Stanza    V, l. 3 : semly] sem*l*y man *with* man *crossed out in* MS.
          l. 5 : towne] towre?
          l. 8 : MS. *reads* London thow art ut supra; *so also in Stanza* VI, l. 8.
Stanza    VI, l. 2 : dwellys] *so by correction from* dwellythe
Stanza    VII, l. 5 : lode-stere] *so by correction from* stere.[9]

(From *The Review of English Studies* 13 (1937), pp. 1-9).

[See also R. H. Robbins and J. L. Cutler, *Supplement to the Index of Middle English Verse* (Lexington, Kentucky, 1965), no. 1933.5 and Sydney Anglo, "The Court Festivals of Henry VII," *Bulletin of the John Rylands Library* 43 (1960), pp. 12-45.  CFB]

[9] [No attempt has been made by Dr. Bühler to compare the Pierpont Morgan text with that of other MSS., but it is evident that the relationship of the texts is not a simple matter, and requires investigation. Some of the readings of the Morgan MS. may perhaps be due to misreadings on the part of the scribe, but in others the divergence from the accepted text is so great that such an explanation is out of the question.—ED. *R.E.S.*]

# CHAPTER T4

## GREEK PHILOSOPHERS IN THE LITERATURE
## OF THE LATER MIDDLE AGES

### PART I

THE rôle played by the Greek Philosophers in later mediaeval literature is not without general interest. Almost all
the learned encyclopaedists of that time quoted them, generally with deference, so that their sayings, or at least the proverbs
reputed to be theirs, recur at frequent intervals. While it is true that
these are largely second-hand quotations and that references to what
may be called fundamental source-books are very rare indeed, this
does not detract in the least from the charm of these aphorisms. Nor
is it safe to dismiss these descriptions with the notion that they are
always mediaeval fantasies; the story of Socrates' death in the *Dictes*
is reasonably accurate and is told with genuine feeling and ability.
The proverbs of these philosophers, whether judged authentic or
merely apocryphal by modern scholarship, were part of the stock-in-
trade of almost every writer of the period, and they cannot fail to be
of interest to the mediaevalist.

In the preparation of an edition of the *Dictes and Sayings of the
Philosophers*, a number of mediaeval opinions on the Greek Philosophers were brought to my notice but, as they were not directly connected with the *Dictes*, they were temporarily put aside. The present
article is intended as a series of notes on the Greek Philosophers; it
will shortly be seen that the term mediaeval literature will be taken
in its broadest meaning, as a cultural state of mind rather than an
historical period, so that even a sixteenth-century English text is
included.

### I

On the fifth of August, 1475, there was completed by Lucas
Brandis in Lübeck a huge chronicle of 473 leaves entitled *Rudimentum Novitiorum*. Neither the author of the work nor the typographical points, interesting as they are, need detain us long. It will
suffice to say that the *Rudimentum Novitiorum* is 'a very splendid
and noteworthy book' (in the words of Professor Pollard), and as
for the author, it is probable that he was a Dominican, living 'in

nostra provincia Saxonia inferiori,' not unlikely in Lübeck itself.[1]
The work may be dated *ca* 1470–74.

That Brandis's magnificent edition achieved its merited success is
attested by the fact that the work was translated into French and
was published in Paris (1488) under the title *La Mer des Hystoires*,
not a few of the woodcuts of the French edition being modelled
upon the Lübeck ones.

Theodore Schwarz's investigations on the *Rudimentum Novitiorum* go to show that the author was a man of wide learning: for the
sources, Schwarz[2] names among others: Augustine, Aquinas, Ambrosius, Solinus, Bernard, Plato, Methodius, *Chronicon Slavicum*,
etc. It is probable, however, that many of these references were not
obtained from the original source-books, but were taken from the
larger chronicles and encyclopaedias which preceded the *Rudimentum Novitiorum*; chiefly those by Isidore, Hugo of St Victor, Vincent of Beauvais, etc.

For the sources of the statements on the Greek Philosophers,
Schwarz makes the following observation: 'Diogenes Laertius ist
in seinem Buche *de vita philosophorum* viel benutzt. Valerius Maximus ebenfalls oft in *sententia et effectu verborum* (libri ix); häufig
auch die *Noctes Atticae* des Gellius.' Besides these, Ovid, Vergil,
Horace, Terence, Cicero, Seneca, and Boethius appear, according to
Schwarz, to have been used. There can be no doubt that the authorities named by Schwarz are the ultimate sources for the statements in
the *Rudimentum Novitiorum*, but did the author of this work make
the compilations himself or did he literally borrow them from another's work?

The problem can most easily be solved by examining closely the
description of any philosopher. In the *Rudimentum Novitiorum*,
Empedocles is described thus:

Empedocles philosophus Athenis claruit tempore Ciri regis persarum. Hic, vt
ait Boecius in prologo de arte musica, adeo nouerat ex musica de arte canendi
quod, cum eius hospitem (iuuenis)[3] quidam furibundus inuaderet eo quod

---

[1] A contemporary manuscript note on fol. 473[r] of the copy preserved in The Pierpont Morgan Library reads:

> Nome Autoris Borcha(rdus)
> Sacre pagine professor

This is very probably a confusion with Brocardus, author of the *Descriptio terrae
sanctae*, a work much quoted in the *Rudimentum Novitiorum*.

[2] *Über den Verfasser und die Quellen des Rudimentum Novitiorum* (Rostock,
1888).

[3] *Text* inuenis.

patrem eius accusacione damnasset, ipse Empedocles adeo dulciter canendi modas (*sic*) dicitur flexisse (*sic*) quod adolescens iracundiam temperauit. Huius hec legitur sentencia vt habetur in prologo libri de vegetalibus (*sic*): tria sunt in tota rerum varietate precipua, scilicet mobilis affluencie contemptus, future felicitatis appetitus & mentis illustracio, quorum primo nihil honestius, secundo nihil felicius, tertio nihil ad amborum compendiosam adepcionem efficacius. Interrogatus Empedocles, vt ait Bernardus Siluestris, cur viueret ait: vt astra inspiciam; Celum subtrahe, nullus ero. Hic deum sic legitur descripsisse: Deus est spera cuius centrum est vbique & circumferencia nusquam. Hic animas immortales esse arbitrans Athenis se incendijs dedit & sibiipsi mortem intulit (fol. ccxLii).

Boethius, *De musica*, says (Migne, *Patr. Lat.*, LXIII, 1170):

Sed et Empedocles cum ejus hospitem quidam gladio furibundus invaderet, quod ejus patrem ille accusatione damnasset, inflexisse dicitur modum canendi, itaque adolescentis iracundiam temperasse.

It is clear that the description in the chronicle is ultimately derived from Boethius and similar sources, but the question is if the author of the *Rudimentum Novitiorum* was the compiler or if they were taken from some other work?

The transmission of Boethius through the earlier Middle Ages is of little interest to us; it is not till we come to that great work written some seven hundred years after Boethius, the *Speculum Historiale* of Vincent of Beauvais, that anything of peculiar interest is brought to our attention. Vincent writes:

Boecius in prologo de arte musica. Empedocles cum eius hospitem gladio quidam furibundus inuaderet quod eius ille patrem accusatione damnasset inflexisse dicitur modum canendi & ita adolescentis iracundiam temperasse. Aristoteles in libro de vegetabilibus. Tria sunt, vt ait Empedocles, in tota rerum varietate precipua, scilicet mobilis affluentie contemptus, future felicitatis appetitus, mentis illustratio: quorum primo nichil honestius, secundo nichil felicius, tercio nichil ad amborum adeptionem efficacius. (Then follows a quotation from the *Metaphysica*, Lib. II.) Bernhardus Siluestris. Querenti Empedocles cur viueret, inquit: vt astra inspiciam; celum subtrahe nullus ero. Actor. Hic est Empedocles qui sic deum legitur descripsisse; deus (inquit) est spera cuius centrum est ubique et circumferentia nusquam. Hic totum sese Athenis incendiis dedit (vt refert Lactantius) mortem sibi intulit eo quod eternas esse animas suspicabatur. (Then a quotation from Macrobius; Lib. IV, c. xliiii.)

It can be seen at a glance that with only a few minor changes (if the quotations from the *Metaphysica* and from Macrobius are omitted and the words *Actor* and *Lactantius* deleted) we have the text as it appears in the *Rudimentum Novitiorum*. The word 'Actor' in Vincent's works is familiar to all mediaevalists; it stands either for Vincent's own opinion or it is sometimes used, as he expressly states, for information imparted to him by his teachers. It will be found, on examining the *Rudimentum Novitiorum*, that the author was quite meticulous in quoting his authorities; if he quotes Vincent by name, why does he not mention the 'Actor'?

Turning, for the moment, from Empedocles, let us see what the *Rudimentum Novitiorum* says of Chilon, one of the Seven Sages of Greece:

Chilo, philosophus lacedemonius, Athenis claruit, vnus de septem sapientibus Grecie. Hic, vt dicitur in Pollitico libro primo, iungende societatis causa missus fuit Corinthum, vbi duces & seniores populi ludentes inuenit in alea, propter quod, infracto negocio, reuersus est, dicens, se nolle gloriam spartanorum quorum virtus, constructo Bisancio, clarescebat hac maculare infamia ut diceretur cum aleatoribus traxisse societatem. Hunc vt ait Laercius, interrogauit Esopus poeta; quid nam ageret Jupiter; respondit: alta humiliat, humilia vero exaltat. Interrogatus: in quo differunt dociles ab indoctis; ait, bona spe. Interrogatus: quid difficile; respondit: ineffabilia tacere, diligenciam bene disponere & iniuriam passim posse pacienter pati. Interrogatus: quid est fortuna; ait: ignarus medicus, multos enim execat. Docebat autem hec: dominari lingue & presertim in conuiuio. Non esse maledicendum proximis, alioquin oporteret audire ea quibus quis tristabitur. Item non esse minandum cuiquam, quoniam hoc muliebre est. Cicius ad calamitates amicorum quam ad prosperitates ire. Humiles nupcias facere. Non esse maledicendum mortuo. Senium honorare. Cauere sibiipsi. Damnum malle quam prauum lucrum, illud enim semel contristabit, hoc vsquequaque. Non irridere infelicem. Dominatorem mansuetum esse decet vt eum subditi magis reuereantur quam timeant. Discere bene preesse proprie domui. Linguam non preuenire intellectum. Ire dominari. Non cupere impossibilia. Non festinare in via. Loquentem non mouere manum. Non maniatum esse. Obedire legibus. Uti solicitudine. In hijs que dicuntur de aliquo ad propriam mentem recurrere; in lapidibus enim & cotibus aurum examinatur, virorum vero bonorum & malorum intellectus dedit examen. In iudicijs inimicum iudicare secundum leges vt saltem lex conser, uetur scilicet et amicus. Dicebat eciam tristia cuncta exuperari posse animo & amico. Item has duas affectiones, scilicet amorem & odium, licet fortissimas, sic dicebat esse coherendas (*sic*) vt amicos diligas quis tamquam forte quandoque odio habiturus & inimicos odit tamquam postea amaturus. Fuit autem Chilo breuiloquus, vnde & Aristogoras [hunc][4] loquendi modum chilum-colum vocat. Vixit autem annis LVI & mortuus est. Et iuxta sepulchrum eius erecta fuit statua. Scripsit autem notabilia multa inducentis carminibus eleganter, ut ait Laercius. Et claruit tempore Sedechie, regis Iude (fol. ccxxxiii).

[4] *Text* hnuc.

'Chilo' appears in Diogenes Laertius's *Vitae et Sententiae Philoso-phorum* as follows (Venice; Nicolas Jenson, 1475—only parallel passages are quoted):

Chilo lacedaemonius . . . . Fertur & Aesopum interrogasse: quidnam faceret Iuppiter; illumque respondisse; excelsa humiliat & humilia extollit. Rogatus quo differunt periti ab imperitis; bona, inquit, spe. Quid sit difficile; arcana, inquit, reticere & ocium recte disponere, iniuriasque tolerare posse. Praecipiebat & haec; linguam semper quidem, sed in conuiuio praesertim, continendam. Proximo non maledicendum, alioquin audituros quae nos moerore conficiant. Nemini intentandas minas, esse enim muliebre. Promptius ad amicorum aduersos casus, quam ad secundos successus accurrendum. Uxorem humilem apparatu modico ducendam. Mortuo non maledicendum. Honorandam senec-tutem. Obseruandum seipsum. Damnum potius quam turpe lucrum eligen-dum; id quippe semel tantum angere, hoc semper. Elato secundis rebus non irridendum.[5] Fortem mansuetum esse oportere, ut proximi non tam metuant quam reuereantur. Discendum domui suae rite praeesse. Linguam praeire animo non permittendam. Superandam iracundiam. Diuinationem non exe-crandam. Impossibilia non appetenda. In uia non festinandum. Interloquen-dum non agitandam manum; esse enim uaecordium. Obtemperandum legibus. Quietem adamandam. Inter caeteras eius sententias haec maxime placuit qua dixerat; lapideis cotibus aurum examinari & dare apertum sui documentum. Auro autem bonorum malorumque hominum mentem cuiusmodi sit, com-probari. Aiunt illum cum iam esset uetulus, dixisse; sibi nihil esse conscium in tota uita ingrate fecisse, una tamen re se modice moueri, quod cum semel inter amicos illi iudicandum esset, neque contra ius agere aliquid uellet, per-suaserit amico iudicium a se prouocare, ut sic utrumque,[6] legem scilicet ami-cumque, seruaret. . . . Erat in loquendo breuis, atque ob eam rem Aristagoras milesius, hunc loquendi morem Chilonium appellat.

It is apparent that the *Vitae Philosophorum* is largely responsible for the Chilon in the *Rudimentum Novitiorum*, but it does seem that the Latin translation of Diogenes Laertius is not the immediate source. If, however, we turn to the *Speculum Historiale* this time, we find that Chilon is hardly mentioned at all; he is called one of the Seven Sages, but the chapter (Lib. III, cap. cxix) in which he is no-ticed is almost entirely devoted to Thales. It is clear, therefore, that Vincent also is not the direct source.

It was shown by Hermann Knust, *Gualteri Burlaei Liber de Vita et Moribus Philosophorum* (Tübingen, 1886) that Burley's book is not entirely derived from classical sources[7] but is largely a rework-

[5] *Text* arridendum.    [6] *Text* utrunque.

[7] However, R. D. Hicks, in his edition of Diogenes Laertius for the Loeb Classical Library (1925), states (p. x): 'An Englishman, Walter de Burleigh (1275-1357) a disciple of Duns Scotus, endeavoured to satisfy this curiosity by a Latin work, *De*

ing (with some additions) of Vincent's compilations. Upon comparing Burley's text with the *Rudimentum Novitiorum*, it is immediately made clear that the two are identical and, as Burley's work is the earlier, it must be that the author of the *Rudimentum Novitiorum* did not actually derive his statements from the classical sources named by Schwarz but that he simply borrowed a large part of Burley's work. Burley's text (Nuremberg: Anthon Koberger, *ca* 1472), reads, with pertinent collations from the editions of ter Hoernen (Cologne 1472=*T*), Conrad Winters (Cologne 1479=*W*), and Knust (*K*), as follows:

Chilo,[8] philosophus lacedemonius, Athenis claruit, vnus de vii sapientibus Grecie. Hic, vt dicitur in Pollitico[9] libro primo, iungende societatis causa missus fuit Corinthum, vbi duces & seniores populi ludentes inuenit in alea, propter quod, in fracto[10] negocio, reuersus est, dicens; se nolle gloriam spartanorum quorum virtus, constructo Bisancio clarescebat hac maculare infamia vt diceretur cum aleatoribus traxisse[11] societatem. Hunc vt ait Laercius, interrogauit Esopus poeta: Quid nam ageret Jupiter; Respondit: alta humiliat, humilia vero exaltat. Interrogatus in quo differunt dociles ab indoctis; ait, bona spe. Interrogatus: quid difficile; Respondit: ineffabilia tacere, diligenciam bene disponere & iniuriam passim posse pacienter pati. Interrogatus: quid est fortuna; ait; ignarus medicus, multos enim excecat. Docebat autem hic: dominari lingue & presertim in conuiuio. Non esse maledicendum proximis. Alioquin oporteret audire ea quibus quis tristabitur. Item non esse minandum cuiquam quoniam hoc muliebre est. Cicius ad calamitates amicorum quam ad prosperitates ire. Humiles nupcias facere. Non esse maledicendum mortuo. Senium honorare. Cauere sibi ipsi. Dampnum malle quam prauum[12] lucrum, illud enim semel contristabit hoc vsquequaque. Non irridere infelicem. Dominatorem mansuetum esse decet vt eum subditi magis reuereantur quam timeant. Discere bene preesse proprie domui. Lingwam non preuenire intellectum. Ire dominari. Non cupere inpossibilia. Non festinare in uia. Loquentem non mouere manum. Non maniatum esse. Obedire legibus. Vti solicitudine. In hijs que dicuntur de aliquo ad propriam mentem recurrere. In lapidibus enim & cotibus aurum examinatur, virorum vero bonorum & malorum intellectus dedit examen. In iudicijs inimicum iudicare secundum leges vt saltem lex conseruetur scilicet & amicus. Dicebat eciam tristia cuncta exuperari[13] posse animo & amico. Item has duas affectiones, scilicet amorem & odium, licet fortissimas,[14] sic dicebat esse cohercendas vt amicos diligas[15] quis tamquam forte quandoque odio habiturus & inimicos odit[16] tamquam

---

*vita et moribus philosophorum*, drawing his materials principally from Diogenes Laertius.' My own findings seem to support Knust's contentions.
[8] Chilon *TWK*.  [9] Policrato *TWK*.  [10] Infecto *TWK*.
[11] contraxisse *WK;* construxisse *T*.  [12] malum *WK*.  [13] *Text* exuperrari.
[14] ferocissimas *TWK*.  [15] *MS. correction to* diligat; *so TWK*.
[16] oderit *TW;* odiat *K*.

postea amaturus. Fuit autem Chilo breuiloquus, vnde & Aristagoras hunc loquendi modum chilum-colum[17] vocat. Vixit autem annis LVI & mortuus est. Et iuxta sepulchrum eius erecta fuit statua. Scripsit autem notabilia multa inducentis[18] carminibus eleganter, vt ait Laercius. Et claruit tempore Sedechie, regis ude.

(The Koberger text corresponds closely to the R.N.)

The same is true, of course, in the case of Empedocles. As Burley's text corresponds almost word for word with the *Rudimentum Novitiorum*, there is nothing to be gained by reproducing these lines here.

If we take one more short example and print the two versions together with the text of the *Mer des hystoires* in parallel columns, the identical character of the three texts is most easily made evident.

| *Rud. Novit.* | *Burley* | *Mer d. H.* |
|---|---|---|
| Anaximenes Euristrati, philosophus milesius, asianus, Anaximandri philosophi auditor fuit & preceptor Permenidis & Anaxagore. Hic omnium rerum causas aeri infundo dedit. Nec deos negauit aut tacuit, non tamen ab ipsis dijs aerem factum, sed ipsos ex aere ortos credidit. Claruit autem tempore Cyri regis persarum. | Anaximenes Euristrati, philosophus milesius, asianus, Anaximandri philosophi auditor fuit & preceptor Permenidis & Anaxagore. Hic omnium rerum causas aeri infundo dedit. Nec deos negauit aut tacuit, non tamen ab ipsis dijs aerem factum, sed ipsos ex aere ortos credidit. Claruit autem tempore Ciri regis persarum. | Anaximenes, philosophe asian cestadire de asie, fut auditeur & disciple du philosophe Anaximander & maistre de Permenides & de Anaxagoras ou temps de Cirus roy des perses. Il dist que lair estoit cause de toutes choses. Et que non pas seulement les choses inferiores mais que aussi les dieux estoient procedez & fais de lair. |

## II

One of the most popular chronicles, if not the most popular, printed in the fifteenth century was Werner Rolewinck's *Fasciculus Temporum*. Hain's *Repertorium Bibliographicum* alone records over thirty different editions of this work. The connection and the interdependence of the various editions is extremely complicated; the question of these relationships, however, need hardly detain us as we are merely enquiring into the contents of a few of the editions for descriptions of Greek Philosophers.

Most of the earlier editions of the *Fasciculus Temporum* (such as: Cologne: A. ter Hoernen, 1474; H. Quentell, 1480; Louvain: J.

---

[17] chiluculum *T;* chilonculum *WK.*    [18] in ducentis *WK.*

Veldener, 1476; Venice: G. Walch, 1479; E. Ratdolt, 1481; etc.) hardly go beyond naming the Seven Sages and adding the following short note to Thales:

Thales milesius vnus de 7 sapientibus clarus habetur qui post theologos, id est poetas, sophi dicti sunt, id est sapientes. Iste Thales primus potuit predicere defectum solis & lune, ut dicit Augustinus de civitate dei.

A number of other Greek and Roman 'men of letters' are noted by name only or with a short note of description, rarely extending beyond a few words. In naming Democritus, Anaxagoras, Heraclitus, Pindar, etc., Rolewinck adds the note: 'Sententias horum floridas: vide in speculo historiali vincentij,' so that we may suppose that the *Fasciculus Temporum* is largely dependent on Vincent of Beauvais.

Whether ter Hoernen's 1474 edition of the *Fasciculus* is the *editio princeps* or not is still unsettled; at present it shares this distinction with Nicolaus Götz's first edition. ter Hoernen's colophon has the note 'sicut ab autore suo . . . edita est' which I should interpret as a 'slap' at Götz, even though the same note occurs in the *Paradisus Conscientiae* of the following year. The prefatory note to Rolewinck's *Sermo in Festo Praesentationis Beatissimae Mariae Virginis* testifies to the fact that ter Hoernen knew Rolewinck as early as 1470 and had been selected by him to print this work. The note to the *Fasciculus* does little more than affirm the authenticity of this edition, and would be unnecessary unless another work had appeared (or was appearing) without the author's assistance. However it may be, we need only turn to the part dealing with the Seven Sages of Greece to discover that, in this part at any rate, Götz's edition was printed from a completely different manuscript. Six of the Seven are given adequate descriptions (Pittacus only being omitted) and these descriptions are *not* taken from the *Speculum Historiale* but from Walter Burley's *Liber de Vita et Moribus Philosophorum*. Below are transcribed the lines on 'Chion':

Chion, philosophus lacedemonius, vnus de septem sapientibus Grecie; breuiloquus fuit in sentencijs suis. Hic docebat: dominari lingue et presertim ne quis in conuiuio maledicat proximo ne conuiuantes tristentur. Interrogatus: quid sit fortuna; respondit: humiliat alta et exaltat humilia. Docebat eciam; humiles nupcias facere; mortuis non malidicere; senium honorare; damnum malle quam paruum (*sic*) lucrum; infelicem non irridere; non festinare in via; legibus obedire; et plurima notabilia (fol. LXIII).

It was brought out in Part I that Vincent only mentioned Chilon by name, so that the *Speculum Historiale* could not be the source for this passage. If the text is compared to the *Burley-Rudimentum Novitiorum* quotation, it will be seen that the lines in Götz's *Fasciculus* are only a very condensed version of Burley's account. To take another example, Anaxagoras in Götz's edition corresponds to the closing lines in Burley:

Götz: Anaxagoras studiosissimus multa de motu celi et syderum cursu scripsit; tandem ab Athenij veneno extinctus est (fol. LXXV).

Burley: Hic studiosus fuit valde et multa de motu celi & cursu siderum & natura rerum scripsit. Vixit autem annis LXXIJ. In carcere enim ab Atheniensibus positus & multa inedia squalidus ab eis venenatus est quia solem dicebat lapidem ignitum esse quem illi pro deo colebant.

ter Hoernen, on the other hand, literally copies Vincent's short note in the *Speculum Historiale:* 'Hic Anaxagoras, vt dicit Augustinus, successorem habuit Archelaum qui fuit magister Socratis' (Lib. IV, cap. xxxiii). There are other differences between the two editions; the British Museum Catalogue of Incunabula (I, 238) notes that 'the author's introduction (in the Götz edition) differs widely from that in the original edition by ter Hoernen, and the table is much more elaborate.' There are numerous other dissimilarities; for example, if we examine the text on folio 13 (ter Hoernen's numbering), the following variations may be noted: for Salmanazar, there is no corresponding passage in Götz; the Seven Sages are listed only by ter Hoernen; Thales differs in the two editions; (folio 14) 'On false Gods' is omitted by Götz; the Sibilla Samia is longer in ter Hoernen, while Numa Maximus is described at greater length by Götz; etc.

Ernst Voulliéme (*Der Buchdruck Kölns* [Bonn, 1903] p. XVII, n. 1) writes: 'Indessen scheint es mir keinem Zweifel zu unterliegen, dass diejenige Arnold Therhoernens die editio princeps ist. Dieser war der Verleger des Rolevinck, dessen Schriften, soweit sie überhaupt gedruckt wurden, zuerst bei ihm erschienen.' On the other hand, it has also been maintained[19] that Götz's edition was at press while the ter Hoernen one was being prepared. As it has been demonstrated that these two editions were set up from different manuscripts, the assumption that the Götz edition is a pirated one can, I believe, be dismissed. A pirated edition usually corresponds closely to the genuine work which it is meant to duplicate. If, also, ter Hoernen's is the *editio princeps* and Götz's a revision, it is strange that Götz, for his

---

[19] M. B. Stillwell, 'The Fasciculus Temporum,' *Bibliographical Essays: A Tribute to Wilberforce Eames*, Cambridge, Mass., 1924.

second edition of the work, instead of reprinting this 'revised' copy, used ter Hoernen's throughout. On the whole, Miss Stillwell's suggestion that Götz's was a trial edition appears to be the most satisfactory solution, as this explains also why Götz used ter Hoernen's text for his second edition.

## III

Hartmann Schedel's famous *Nürnberg Chronicle* is the last of the chronicles to be examined here. Schedel's work appears to be little more than a reworking of other chronicles, one of the most important of these being the *Fasciculus Temporum*, which may even have served as a model. In describing the Seven Sages, the *Nürnberg Chronicle* combines the methods of the two 'first' editions of the *Fasciculus Temporum*. The Seven Sages are discussed separately as in Götz's edition and collectively as in ter Hoernen's. On fol. LIX$^r$ may be found the long description of 'Tales'; on fol. LX$^v$, the Seven Sages are listed as in ter Hoernen's edition, together with the following note, quite obviously borrowed from the *Fasciculus:*

Tales milesius vnus de vii sapientibus clarus habetur qui post theologos et poetas sophi dicti sunt, id est sapientes: iste Tales primus potuit predicere defectum solis & lune, vt dicit Augustinus. De his folia precedentia gesta ac dicta eorum manifestant.

For the rest of the Seven Sages as well as for a number of other classical philosophers, Schedel borrowed heavily from Burley's *De vita et moribus philosophorum*. The note on Chilon, for example, is longer than in the Götz *Fasciculus*, although it is also little more than a condensed account of the *Burley-Rudimentum Novitiorum* text:

Chilon, philosophus Lacedemonius, Athenis claruit, tercius de septem sapientibus Grecie qui ob eius profundissimam sapientiam breueloquus dictus est. Hic iungende causa societatis missus fuit Corinthum. vbi duces & seniores populi ludentes inuenit in alea, propter quod, infecto negocio, reuersus est: dicens se nolle gloriam spartanorum quorum virtus, constructo Bisantio, clarescebat: hac maculari infamia vt diceretur cum aleatoribus contraxisse societatem. Interrogatus; quid est fortuna. Respondit; ignarus medicus, multos enim excecat. Docebat autem Chilon; dominari lingue & presertim in conuiuijs. Non esse maledicendum proximis, alioquin audire oportet ea quibus quis tristabitur. Item non esse minandum cuiquam, quoniam hoc est muliebre. Cicius ad calamitatem amicorum quam ad prosperitatem ire. Humiles nuptias facere. Non esse maledicendum mortuo. Senium honorare. Cauere sibiipsi. Damnum malle quam prauum lucrum, illud enim semel contristabit hoc vsquequaque.

Non irridere infelicem. Dominatorem & fortem mansuetum esse decet, vt eum subditi magis reuereantur quam timeant. Ire dominari. Non cupere impossibilia. Et claruit tempore Sedechie regis. Vixit autem quinquagintasex annis (fol. LIX).

Empedocles is also taken from Burley's work and not from the *Speculum Historiale*, as may be seen by comparing Schedel's text with that in the *Rudimentum Novitiorum* printed above:

Empedocles philosophus Atheniensis his temporibus laudatur: qui adeo canendi pericia edoctus erat. Quod cum hospitem[20] eius iuuenis quidam furibundus inuaderet eo quod patrem eius accusatione damnasset: ita dulciter canendi modum inflexisse dicitur: vt iuuenis iracundiam temperarit. Huius autem hec fuit sententia. Tria sunt (inquit) in tota rerum varietate, scilicet affluentie mobilis contemptus, future felicitatis appetitus & mentis illustratio; quorum primo nihil honestius, secundo nihil efficacius; tercio nihil de amborum adeptione compendiosa efficacius. Descripsitque deum: Deus est spera cuius centrum est vbique & circumferentia nusquam. Arbitratus denique animas immortales se incendijs dedit (fol. LXXI).

That Schedel did not depend exclusively on the *De vita et moribus philosophorum* may be seen in the case of Pythagoras, but it is safe to say that Schedel's most important source for the Greek Philosophers was Burley's work with a few additions, possibly from more classical sources.

## PART II

### I

In the first section of this article,[21] a number of Latin chronicles have been discussed which were dependent, for the descriptions of the Greek Philosophers, on Walter Burley's *Liber de Vita et Moribus Philosophorum*. It is needless to add that the influence of Burley's work and what I call the 'Vincent tradition' extended far beyond the chronicles. In a great many works quotations can be found which could very easily have been borrowed from Burley but which, as was pointed out in the first part, may also have been extracted from other works; for example, Jacques Le Grand includes the following in his *Sophologium*: 'Iste est Empedocles qui sic descripsisse deum legitur. Deus, inquit, est spera cuius centrum est ubique et circum-

---

[20] *Text* hospotem.

[21] References to books in the Pierpont Morgan Library, New York, are noted PML., with the accession number following.

ferencia nusquam,'[22] but it will be recalled that, though this statement occurs in Burley's work, it also forms a part of Empedocles' sayings in the *Speculum Historiale* and elsewhere. As the attribution of such quotations is doubtful, we shall examine only those that can, with some certainty, be ascribed to a definite work.

Before turning to Burley's influence on the works written in the vernacular, we may note that, on the one hand, Burley's compilation was not the only work used as a source for fifteenth-century chronicles and, on the other, that the Renaissance did not entirely discredit the *Liber de Vita et Moribus Philosophorum* and that its influence extended well into the sixteenth century.[23] The *Supplementum Chronicarum* of Jacobus Philippus Bergomensis is a most interesting case. Solon is thus described:

Solon philosophus e septem sapientibus greciae secundus: patria atheniensis siue salaminus: his temporibus Gellio teste lib. s. 14 noctium atticarum: athenis floruit: et ibi leges multas: atque optimas instituit: quas sicut Valerius liber de ingratis ait: si athenienses perpetuo seruare uoluisset sempiternum habituri fuissent imperium. Constat namque ut Laertius scribit: ipsum leges et contiones scripsisse: et in semetipsum monita elegia: qui quum hominum omnium: ac oraculi iudicio sapientissimus haberetur: uino indulsisse fertur. De Solone autem isto Plato in Thimeo: et Aristotiles in 2 Politicorum multa scripsere. Tandem in cypro insula obiit octogesimo aetatis suae anno: quum mandasset suis: ut ossa sua Salaminam transferrent: atque ea in cinerem dissoluta: per omnem prouinciam disseminarent: sed eius iussis obtemperatum non fuit: quum ipsius sepulchro tale epigramma inscriptum sit: qua dudum rabidas medorum propulit iras legiferum Solonem pulchra tenet Salamis: ex sententiis autem eius plurimis: hanc solam hic habeamus: satietatem ex diuitiis nasci: et ex sacietate contumelias gigni: quae non posuisti non tollas: mentiri noli et cetera.[24]

If this passage is compared with the description given by Burley, it will be seen to be of quite a different origin. Philippus has drawn his statements from the *Noctes Atticae* of Aulus Gellius (incidentally

[22] [Cologne: Printer of Albertus Magnus de Virtutibus, *ca* 1473], Lib. 1, cap. 8 (PML. 21538).

[23] In the seventeenth century, the work was issued as an *original* compilation under the title: *Tractatus de Vita et Moribus Philosophorum Veterum Anastasii à Sala Mombellensis J. U. D. cum Sapientium Dictorum ac Indicis Adiectione Locupletissima*. Casali, 1603.

[24] Venice: Albertus de Lissona, 1503, fol. 94ᵛ (PML. 20977). In these quotations, punctuation has only been supplied where absolutely necessary. Contractions have been expanded without the use of italics, but typographical peculiarities, such as *u* for *v* and *e* for *ae*, have been retained.

the reference should read *Liber 17*), from Valerius Maximus, Plato, Aristotle and Diogenes Laertius. The latter writes:

Obiit autem in Cypro aetatis suae anno octogesimo: hoc suis mandans ut Salaminam eius ossa transferrent: atque in cinerem soluta per prouinciam disseminarent: . . . porro ipsius imagini in hunc sensum Epigramma scriptum est:

> Quae dudum rabidas medorum propulit iras.
> Legiferum Solona pulchra tenet Salamis.

. . . Satietatem ex diuitiis nasci: et ex satietate contumelias gigni, etc.[25]

It is clear that the Solon of the *Supplementum Chronicarum* is largely drawn from Diogenes Laertius, and as the epitaph in these two works agrees verbatim, it is certain that Philippus used the same translation as Jenson did for his edition, that by Ambrosius Traversarius.[26] Most of the philosophers are similarly described from various classical sources, but even in this work the Vincent tradition is at work, for we find that the description of Empedocles reads:

Empedocles philosophus atheniensis et ipse his temporibus laudatur: qui adeo canendi peritia edoctus erat: quod quum hospitem eius iuuenis furibundus quidam euaderet eo quod patrem eius accusatione damnasset: ita dulciter canendi modum inflexisse dicitur: ut iuuenis iracundiam temperarit. Huius autem haec fuit sententia. Tria sunt (inquit) in tota rerum uarietate: scilicet: affluentie mobilis contemptus, future felicitatis appetitus: et mentis illustratio. Quorum primo nihil honestius. Secundo nihil efficacius. Tertio nihil ad amborum compendiosa adeptione efficacius. Descripsit autem hic Deum sic. Deum est spera cuius centrum est ubique et circunferentia (*sic*) nusquam. Arbitratus denique animas immortales se incendiis dedit: ut habetur ff. de iniusto rupto testamento: lege Siquis filio. Parafo. Quod si quis tedio uite.[27]

With the exception of the last few lines, Empedocles has the same description as in Burley's work.

Albrecht von Eyb, in his great compilation, the *Margarita Poetica*, included a chapter which he called: 'Ex laercio de vita et moribus philosophorum autoritates incipiunt.' Although Eyb was to a cer-

[25] Quoted from the edition by Jenson, Venice, 1475 (PML. 309). The text has been slightly rearranged to conform to the text in the *Supplementum Chronicarum*.
[26] Only the Latin translation by Ambrosius Traversarius was published in the fifteenth century. The following editions will appear in the *Gesamtkatalog der Wiegendrucke*: Rome, Lauer, *ca* 1472; Venice, Jenson, 1475; Brescia, Brittanicus, 1485; Venice, Locatellus, 1490; Bologna, Ragazonibus, 1495; and Venice, Pincius, 1497.
[27] *Op. cit.*, fol. 109ʳ.

tain extent an early German humanist and had read extensively in the classics,[28] nevertheless this chapter has nothing to do with Diogenes Laertius, but consists of extracts from Burley's work. As an illustration, the following passage on Crates may be cited:

Crates thebanus philosophus. Hic, vt ait Hieronimus epistola tercia, magnum pondus auri proiiecit in mare dicens: abite pessime diuitie: ego potius vos submergam quam submergar a vobis. Non enim putauit se posse simul virtutes et diuitias possidere. Hic etiam, vt ait Seneca libro primo epistolarum: adolescentulum secreto ambulantem interrogauit: quid illic faceret? Solus mecum, inquit, loquor; cui Crates: caue ne cum homine malo loquaris.[29]

This passage follows Burley's text closely, and differs in detail from Vincent's description.[30] The fact that St Jerome is quoted is positive proof, if any more is needed, that this Crates has not been directly taken from Diogenes Laertius. Incidentally, the reference to Jerome is incorrect. In the letter 'Ad Paulinum Presbyterum de Institutione Clericorum,' he writes:[31] 'Crates ille Thebanus, homo quondam ditissimus, cum ad philosophandum Athenas pergeret, magnum auri pondus abjecit; nec putavit se simul posse et virtutes et divitias possidere.'[32] Burley's quotation is, however, drawn from another of Jerome's works, *Adversus Jovinianum* (Liber II, cap. 9): 'Unde et Crates ille Thebanus, projecto in mari non parvo auri pondere, Abite, inquit, pessum malae cupiditates: ego vos mergam, ne ipse mergar a vobis.'[33]

## II

If we now turn to the vernacular literature, we find that Burley's influence is by no means any less. Each of the works discussed in the previous section was translated into one or more of the national tongues; the *Rudimentum Novitiorum*, as we have seen, reappeared as the *Mer des Hystoires*; the *Nürnberg Chronicle* was issued in

---

[20] He quotes from Valerius Maximus, Cicero, Lactantius, Macrobius, Apuleius, Terence, Plautus, Seneca, Orosius, Quintus Curtius, etc.

[29] Nürnberg: Sensenschmidt, 1472, fol. ccxcvi, E (PML. 23552).

[30] Vincent omits the sentence beginning 'non enim' and the order differs slightly. The Seven Sages, in any case, are unquestionably borrowed from Burley.

[31] Migne, *Patr. Lat.*, XXII, 580.

[32] Compare, also, Brant's *Das Narrenschiff* (Basel: J. Bergmann von Olpe, 1494— PML. 25971):

> Crates syn gelt warff in das mer
> Das es nyt hyndert inn zur ler.

[33] Migne, *Patr. Lat.*, XXIII, 298. Quite obviously Jerome's two statements were combined into one at an early date.

German less than six months after its initial appearance in Latin; and the *Fasciculus Temporum* was translated into German, French and Dutch. As the *Buch der Chronik* is an accurate translation of the original, nothing more need be said about it, and although the *Mer des Hystoires* was discussed in the first part, one more point is worth noting. *MS.* 277 of The Pierpont Morgan Library is a collection of moral sayings of the philosophers, the title page of which reads: 'Si apres sensuiuent aulcuns moraulx dictz des philozophes que i'ay extraitz de la mer des ystoires et d'ailleurs.' These sayings are *all*, however, derived from the *Mer des Hystoires*, and do not include any statements not found in the original. Occasionally a passage is slightly rewritten; for example, the *Mer des Hystoires* attributes the following to Socrates: 'Le malicieux ouurier fait la chose bonne estre laide,'[34] which appears in the Morgan manuscript (under Ozocrates) as: 'Le meschant fait trouuer la chose bonne estre mauuaise.'

A number of the philosophers have changed their names, as Philo appears in place of Chilo in the Morgan text, and Platon for Anaxagoras; at least once (in Pittacus), the text was emended, possibly with an attempt at humour. The *Mer des Hystoires* has:

> Quelle chose est loyale / respondit la terre.
> quelle desloyale / respondist la mer.[35]

In *MS.* 277 the same saying reads: 'L'on luy demanda quelle chose est loyalle. Respondit, la terre. et quelle chose est desloyalle: la femme.'[36] The manuscript bears the autograph entry of Pierre Sala, apparently a member of the wealthy Sala family who had numerous manuscripts written and illuminated for them, and thus gives an interesting example of the literary taste of that period.[37]

Nor is there anything special to note in regard to the *Fasciculus Temporum*. The German, French, and Dutch translations represented by the respective editions of Strassburg 1492 (Hain 6940), Geneva 1495 (Hain 6943) and Utrecht 1480 (Hain 6946) were made

[34] Paris: Pierre le Rouge, 1488, Vol. II, fol. 23r (PML. 17593).
[35] *Op. cit.*, I, 256r.
[36] The two quotations from Morgan *MS.* 277 will be found, respectively, on folios 24r and 8v.
[37] See Léopold Delisle, *Le Cabinet des Manuscrits de la Bibliothèque Impériale* (Paris, 1868), I, 285. For identification of the manuscript with Pierre Sala and notes on the Sala family, I am obliged to Miss Meta Harrsen of The Pierpont Morgan Library.

from the normal text,[38] and thus have only short notes on the Greek philosophers instead of the long descriptions given in the Götz edition.

The influence of the Vincent tradition extends far beyond the translation of these dependent works. As early as the last quarter of the thirteenth century, a compilation of sayings of the philosophers extracted from the *Speculum Historiale* and translated into Italian appeared under the title *Fiori e Vita di Filosafi*.[39] Burley's work also appeared in the vernacular; it was printed in German by Anton Sorg (Augsburg, 1490; Hain 4125), the title of which reads: 'Das buch von dem leben vnd sitten der heydnischen maister;' a Spanish translation of this work was published by Hermann Knust;[40] and a manuscript of an Italian translation was mentioned by Mone.[41] In addition, a number of editions of a book entitled 'Il libro della vita de philosophi et delle loro elegantissime sententie extracto da D. Lahertio & da altri antiquissimi auctori' appeared in the last quarter of the fifteenth century.[42] Despite the title,[43] the book is little more than a translation of Burley's compilation to which a number of sayings were added, chiefly drawn from Valerius Maximus and Aulus Gellius. That this work was not dependent on Diogenes Laertius will be seen in the following passages on Empedocles:

Empedocle fu philosofo Agrigentino di Sicilia: & secondo Aristotile fu inuentore dell'arte oratoria. Costui era cosi buono musico secondo che dice Boetio, che una uolta un giouane elcui padre lui haueua accusato uenne per assaltarlo & fargli male. Empedocle comincio si dolcemente a cantare che il giouane si stette fermo & non hebbe mai animo doffenderlo. Dimandato Empedocle perche uiuesse Rispuose per guardare il cielo. Costui uedendo l'anime essere

---

[38] The Dutch edition is in The Pierpont Morgan Library (PML. 626). I have examined the copy of the German edition in the Union Theological Seminary, New York. For the French text, I am obliged to Mr Ernst F. Detterer of The Newberry Library, Chicago, who kindly sent me a transcription of the lines in question.

[39] Compare Hermann Varnhagen, *Über die Fiori e Vita di Filosafi* (Erlangen, 1893).

[40] *Bibliothek des litterarischen Vereins in Stuttgart*, Vol. CLXXVII.

[41] *Anz. f. Kunde d. deutsch. Vorzeit*, VIII, 323. Possibly there is also an early French translation of Burley's book; compare Brunet, *Manuel du Libraire*, II, 767.

[42] The *Gesamtkatalog der Wiegendrucke* will enter this work under Diogenes Laertius with the note: 'ist eine gekürzte, freie Bearbeitung der lateinischen Vorlage.' No less than twelve separate fifteenth-century editions are recorded.

[43] Burley's book was apparently known as the work of Diogenes Laertius at this time. This accounts for the title in the Italian edition as well as for Eyb's chapter previously noted.

immortali: & sperando di la essere miglior uita lui stessi sabrucio in Athene. Fu al tempo di Cyro Re di Persia.[44]

This is clearly enough only an extract made from Burley's work. Not all the philosophers are so closely copied from the *Liber de Vita et Moribus Philosophorum*; in the description of Anaximenes, only the first two sentences are from Burley, all the rest having been taken from Valerius Maximus:

Anaximenes philosopho Milesio discepolo di Anasimandro & maestro di Parmenide & di Anaxagora. Costui trouo la ragione di molte cose: ne credeua, ne negaua gli dei: & diceua l'aria non essere facta da gli dei: ma l'aria hauer facto gli dei. Diceua Valerio che sapendo Alexandro che Anaximenes doueua uenire dallui, egli giuro fare l'opposito di quello che adimandasse: laqualcosa conoscendo Anaximenes domando che Alexandro douesse disfare la cipta di Lampsaco: & cosi Alexandro per fare l'opposito della sua domanda la conseruo, et in quel modo fu liberata quella cipta. Costui fu al tempo di Cyro Re di Persia: & non pocho doppo che fusse disfacto Dario da Alexandro.[45]

### III

Turning now to the popular works in the various national languages, we can see that the Vincent tradition extended even into this field. In Hugo von Trimberg's *Der Renner*, we find the following lines:

> Wol hât uns bescheiden des
> Der wîse man Empedocles,
> Der wunders vil geschriben hât,
> Und sprichet alsô an einer stat:
> 'Swer werltliches guotes lützel ahtet
> Und nâch êwigen sêlden trahtet
> Und hât wol einen erliuhten muot,
> Diu driu dinc sint besunder guot:
> Vor dem êrsten ist niht êrlîcher,
> Vor dem andern ist niht nüzlîcher,
> Niht volbrengelîcher vor dem dritten
> Daz disiu zwei besliuzet mitten.'[46]

[44] Quotations are taken from the third edition (Florence: Francesco Buonaccorsi & Antonio di Francesco, 1488: Hain 6207). Compare the text with Burley (cap. XLVIII).

[45] Compare with Valerius Maximus (Lib. VII, cap. III) and with Burley (cap. LXIII). Since the Seven Sages are treated as in Burley, the Italian work cannot go back directly to Vincent.

[46] Gustav Ehrismann's edition, *Bibliothek des litterarischen Vereins in Stuttgart*, CCLII, 179, ll. 21257–68.

This is, of course, the passage beginning 'Tria sunt' and attributed to Aristotle's *De Vegetabilibus* by Vincent. It is amusing to note that this is the only passage omitted in the Pseudo-Laertius *Libro della Vita de Philosophi* and the only quotation preserved in the *Fiori e Vita di Filosafi*, where it reads: 'Empedocles filosafo disse che nele cose del seculo tre sono le principali, cio e despregiare abondancia di richece, desiderare beatitudine, chiararsi nell'animo di buone virtudi.'[47]

The opening lines of Albrecht von Eyb's *Ob einem Mann sei zu nehmen ein ehelich Weib oder nicht* read:

Socrates phylosophus ein natürlicher meister zu Athenas der do ist gewest zu den zeytten Assweri des künigs ward von einem Jüngling gefragt ob er ein weyb nemen solt oder nit. Antwurt der meister vnd sprach zu im. Wellichs du tust, das wirt dich reuen. Wann nymstu ein weyb so bistu allezeyt in sorgen vnd angsten, in stetem kriege mit dem weybe, mit der schwiger, mit iren freuntten, mit auffhebung des heirat guts, in verdechtlichkeit mit anndern mennern vnd in vngewisheit der kinder. Bleibest du aber on weybe, so wirt dich bekümern vnd peinigen allein on weyblich lieb vnd troste zuleben, der kinder berawbt zu sein, vnttergangk deines geschlechts, vnd eines fremden vngewisen erbens zu wartten.[48]

The origin of this story is surely to be found in Diogenes Laertius, who wrote: ἐρωτηθεὶς πότερον γῆμαι ἢ μή, ἔφη, ὃ ἂν αὐτῶν ποιήσῃς, μεταγνώσῃ.[49] The full story is found, however, in Valerius Maximus (Liber VII, cap. 11), in Vincent (*Spec. Hist.*, IV, cap. 58), in Burley (cap. 30) and in Eyb's own *Margarita Poetica*, in a section entitled: 'Ex valerio maximo historie et autoritates incipiunt.' There can be little doubt that Eyb took this passage from the classical source rather than from any of the mediaeval works; on the other hand, the name Assweri is unusual. I cannot recall that Assweri is found in any classical text, most certainly not in Aulus Gellius, Valerius Maximus or Diogenes Laertius, and he is also not found in Vincent.[50] In the passage Eyb extracted from Valerius Maximus, king Assweri is not mentioned, but he is noted in Eyb's *Ex laercio* chapter under Socra-

[47] Varnhagen, *op. cit.*, p. 2.
[48] [Nürnberg: A. Koberger, *ca* 1472]—(PML. 30060).
[49] Liber II, cap. 33.
[50] This name is not found in Pauly-Wissowa, *Real-Encyclopädie der klassischen Altertumswissenschaft*. Assweri is obviously the Biblical character Assuerus or Ahasuerus; the Book of Esther opens with the words 'In diebus Assueri qui regnavit ab India usque Aethiopiam etc.' The name *Assweri*, like *Athenas* above, was simply taken over in the original case.

tes: 'Mortuus est veneni poculo tempore assueri regis assiriorum anno vero etatis sue nonagesimo quarto.'[51] This is not exactly the same arrangement as in Burley's text (cap. 30) for it is a somewhat condensed account, but there can be no doubt that it was derived from that work. Vincent in a similar passage (IV, 66) omits king Assweri (Ahasuerus) and correctly states that Socrates was seventy when he died. Burley and Eyb (*Ex laercio*) both claim that Ysocrates also lived in the reign of king Assweri.[52]

In Middle English literature, the influence of the Vincent tradition is also not wanting. Hoccleve, in his *Regiment of Princes*, wrote:

> Demostenus his hondes ones putte
> In a wommans bosome japyngly,
> Of face faire, but of hir body a slutte;
> 'Withe you to dele,' seide he, 'what shalle I
> You yeve?' 'Fourty pens,' kothe she, 'sothely.'
> He seide nay, so dere he bye nolde
> A thyng for whiche he repent sholde.[53]

The story of Demosthenes and Lais goes back, of course, to a similar passage in the *Noctes Atticae* of Aulus Gellius:

Ad hanc ille Demosthenes clanculum adit et ut sui copiam faceret, petit. At Lais μύριας δραχμὰς id est decem drachmarum milia poposcit; hoc facit nummi nostratis denarium decemmilia. Tali petulantia mulieris atque pecunie magnitudine ictus expauidusque Demosthenes auertitur et discedens: ego, inquit, poenitere tanti non emo.[54]

A parallel passage is found in Burley's work:

Demostenes stomachum laydis nobilissime meretricis iocando subpalpitans et queritans quantum licet. Cum illa diceret pro mille denarys, respondit: ego penitere tanti non emo.[55]

It is readily apparent that the English lines in the *Regiment of Princes* are much closer to Burley's text than to the classical source.

---

[51] Eyb, *op. cit.*, fol. ccxcvii[v].

[52] Eyb, *op. cit.*, fol. ccxcvi[v]: 'Isocrates philosophus claruit in Grecia tempore Assueri regis'; so also in Burley (cap. 27).

[53] Edited by Thomas Wright, Roxburghe Club, 1860, p. 135. For other notes on Hoccleve's poem, see Allan H. Gilbert, 'Notes on the Influence of the *Secreta Secretorum*,' SPECULUM, III (1928), 93–98.

[54] Rome: [Sweynheym & Pannartz], 1469, Lib. I, cap. 8 (PML. 242).

[55] *Op. cit.*, cap. XXXVII.

One other stanza at least, Hoccleve borrowed from Burley's work; it reads:

> Smalle tendirnesse is hade nowe of our lawes;
> For yf so be that one of the grete wattes
> A dede do, whiche that ageyn the lawe is,
> Not at alle he punysshede for that is.
> Right as lop-webbes flyes smale and gnattes
> Taken, and suffren grete flyes go,
> For alle this world lawe is reulede so.[56]

This statement can be traced back to Diogenes Laertius (Solon) but as it is beyond probability that Hoccleve was acquainted with this Greek work and as the quotation may be found in the *Liber de Vita et Moribus Philosophorum* in the same words as in the marginal note in the manuscript, there can be little doubt that Hoccleve actually had some work of the Vincent tradition before him when he was writing the *Regiment of Princes*.

It remains to be pointed out that a few sources apart from those already noted can be traced. In the anonymous *Court of Sapience*, the history of Greek philosophy is summed up as:

> Millesius, oone of the sages seuyn,
> In Grece furst drew, as in the craft of kynde,
> By hys reasoun the causes of the heuyn,
> And of yche thyng the nature gan he fynde;
> Than came Plato, a worthy clerk of kynde;
> For naturall art sought out geometry,
> Arsmetryk, Musyk and Astronomy.
>
> Dame Ethica, pryncesse of polycy,
> Good Socrates furst found for gouernaunce,
> To know vertew and to lyue honestly;
> And fowre ladyes he sought, full of plesaunce,
> To serue Dame Ethyke wyth obeysaunce,
> Whos names byn Prudence and Ryghtwysnes,
> Dame Fortitude and Temperaunce I geas.[57]

This is a simple translation of a passage in St Isidore's *Etymologiae*:

Physicam apud Graecos primus perscrutatus est Thales Milesius, unus ex septem illis sapientibus. Hic enim ante alios caeli causas atque vim rerum naturalium, contemplata ratione, suspexit, quam postmodum Plato in quatuor

[56] *Op. cit.*, p. 101.

[57] Robert Spindler, 'The Court of Sapience,' *Beiträge zur englischen Philologie* (Leipzig, 1927), pp. 187–188, and my note in the 'Sources of the Court of Sapience,' *Beiträge zur englischen Philologie* (Leipzig, 1932), pp. 13 and 93.

definitiones distribuit, id est, arithmeticam, geometriam, musicam et astronomiam. Ethicam Socrates primus ad corrigendos componendosque mores instituit, atque omne studium eius ad bene vivendi disputationem perduxit, dividens eam in quatuor virtutes animae, id est, prudentiam, justitiam, fortitudinem et temperantiam.[58]

It is amusing to note also how the famous Greek proverb γνῶθι σαυτόν was transliterated in fifteenth-century French and English texts. Jacques Le Grand in *Le Livre de Bonnes Moeurs* wrote: 'Et ce mesmes dist Juuenal et tesmoigne que la dicte voix disoit, Notis elicos qui vault autant a dire comme cognois toy toy mesmes.'[59] When Wynkyn de Worde published the English translation of this work, it read: And the same sayth Juuenall and wytnesseth that the sayd voys sayd Gnoto solidos whiche is to saye knowe thy selfe.'[60] So far we have only traced the influence of the Vincent tradition on mediaeval literature. It is hardly necessary to add that other sources were used by mediaeval writers for the stories of the Greek philosophers.[61] The most important of all these sources, the *Liber Philosophorum Moralium Antiquorum* recently attributed to Johannes de Procida by Remigio Sabbadini,[62] will not be discussed at all. The text of this important work, as well as the sources and the early Spanish text have been admirably edited and investigated by Hermann Knust[63] and Ezio Franceschini.[64] The French and English translations will be more fully treated in my edition of the *Dictes and Sayings of the Philosophers* than is possible here, but it may be pointed out in passing that the importance of this work to the French

[58] Migne, *Patr. Lat.*, LXXXII, 141.

[59] *Morgan MS. 734*, fol. 6ᵛ. The printed edition (Lyons: Guillaume le Roy, *ca* 1487—PML. 24939) similarly has 'Notis elicos' (fol. 5ᵛ).

[60] PML. 747, sig. A₄ verso.

[61] A great many references to Greek philosophers are, of course, purely fictitious; so, for example, in *Die Vier Angeltugenden* [Strassburg: P. Attendorn, *ca* 1492— PML. 27818], Socrates quotes from Aristotle, St Gregory and St Augustine, while Aristotle is made to quote from Seneca, Nero, Theodosius, Solomon, etc. Such works do not, of course, come into the scope of this paper.

[62] 'Il Traduttore Latino del Liber Philosophorum,' *Atti del Reale Istituto Veneto di Scienze, Lettere ed Arli*, Anno Accademico 1932–3, Tomo XCII, Parte Seconda.

[63] 'Ein Beitrag zur Kenntniss der Escorialbibliothek,' *Jahrbuch für romanische und englische Literatur*, x and xi, and 'Mittheilungen aus dem Eskurial,' *Bibliothek des litterarischen Vereins in Stuttgart*, 1879.

[64] 'Il Liber Philosophorum Moralium Antiquorum,' *Atti del R. Istituto Veneto di Scienze etc.*, Anno 1931–32, Tomo XCI, Parte Seconda. The sources and influences of this work were treated by the same author in *Memorie della R. Accademia Nazionale dei Lincei*, Classe di Scienze Morali, Storiche, e Filologiche, Serie VI, Vol. III, Fasc. v.

and English literature of the period has not yet been fully appreciated. Over forty manuscripts of the French text and dependent versions, in addition to some ten early editions, are known to me; of the various English translations, I have seen twelve manuscripts and four early printed texts. The influence of Ausonius and the pseudo-Ausonius texts I hope to discuss in a subsequent essay.

(From *Speculum* 12 (1937), pp. 440-55).

# CHAPTER T5

## SOME NEW PASTON DOCUMENTS[1]

IN a collection of royal and historical documents apparently formed by the noted printseller and antiquary, John Thane (1748–1818), and now a part of the manuscript collection of The Pierpont Morgan Library, there are a number of letters and documents of the fifteenth and sixteenth centuries. Although none of these are letters written by the Pastons, some of them are addressed to various members of that family and others concern individuals who play a not inconspicuous part in that interesting series of letters known as the *Paston Letters*. The Morgan letters are here gathered together in the following manner: the two documents concerning Thomas Daniel, being apparently the most interesting ones, are printed in the first section; in the second part the remaining letters are printed in chronological order. Each letter is noted with a number followed by *bis*, which indicates where the letter belongs in James Gairdner's edition of the *Paston Letters* (6 vols., London and Exeter, 1904), and a discussion of the contents or the date follows the text in each case.

## I

### 150 *bis*
### HENRY VI. TO RICHARD WALLER, DAVID JOHN, WILLIAM NEEDHAM AND JOHN INGOLDESBY

#### Dated November 8, 1450

Henricus dei *gracia* Rex Angl*ie et* Franc*ie et* Domin*us* Hibern*ie* Dilect*is* sibi Ric*ardo* Waller[2] armigero, Dauid John, Willi*amo* Needham, *et* Joh*anni* Ingoldesby sal*utem*. Sciatis q*uod* cum quedam Nauis vocata le George de Prucia modo/no*m*inata Danyellis Hulke nup*er per* Thomam Danyell armige-*rum* sup*er* altum mare velando capta *et per* eundem Thomam *et* suos com-plices *per* nonnulla tempora detenta *et* occupata fuerit[3] Dilect*us*/tamen et fidelis n*oster* Joh*ann*es Fastolf miles p*ro* victualib*us et* aliis naui pred*icte* necessariis ad instanciam d*i*cti Thome ac ma*gis*tri *et* marinario*rum* eiusdem

---

[1] I am obliged to Dr. E. Silk, of Yale University, and to Professor A. Gold-schmidt, of Berlin, for their kind assistance in correcting my transcriptions of the two Latin documents.

[2] *The name* Ric*ardo* Waller *is interlineated.*          [3] fuit?

nauis quibusdam mercatorib*us* ciuitatis n*os*tre London*ie* in/centum libris in-debitatus existit Nos considerantes q*u*od d*ic*tus Thomas nullum ius in naui pre*dic*ta ha*b*et set ea nob*is* notorie dinoscit*ur* p*er*tinere volentes q*uia* prouide d*ic*tu*m* Joh*ann*em Fastolf de debito pre*dic*to/in vsum nauis pre*dic*te conu*er*so seruari indempnem vt est iustum vob*is* ad vendend*um* et alienand*um* igit*ur* vice *et* auctoritate n*os*tris nauem illam cum suis apparatib*us* melioribus viis *et* modis quib*us* sciu*er*itis aut/pot*er*itis *et* saltem plus offerentib*us* *et* pre*dic*to Joh*ann*i Fastolf de d*ic*ta su*m*ma vna cum expensis rac*i*onabilib*us* prout p*er* iudicem admirallitatis in forma iuris taxate existunt n*o*mine n*os*tro satisfacien-d*am* potestatem/c*om*mittim*us* spec*i*alem Ita q*u*od de residuo valoris nauis pre*dic*te nob*is* fidelit*er* respondeat*ur* vt est iustum Et ideo vob*is* mandam*us* q*u*od circa premissa diligent*er* intendatis ac ea fac*i*atis et exequamini in forma pre*dic*ta Dam*us* autem/vniu*er*sis et singulis vicecomitib*us* maiorib*us* Balliuis Constabulariis mag*is*tris et marinariis nauiu*m* et alior*um* vasor*um* quorum-cumq*ue* ac om*n*ibus aliis Officiariis ministris ligeis (sic) *et* subditis n*os*tris quibuscumq*ue* tam c*i*tra q*ua*m vltra/mare constitutis tenore presenciu*m* firmit*er* in mandatis q*u*od vob*is* in execuc*i*one premissor*um* consulent pareant obedeant *et* intendant in om*n*ibus diligent*er* quociens *et* quando p*er* vos ex parte n*os*tra fu*er*int requisiti. In cuius/rei testimoniu*m* has l*i*teras n*os*tras fieri fecim*us* patentes. T*e*ste me ip*s*o apud W*e*stm*o*nast*e*riu*m* viij die Nouembr*is* Anno r*e*gni n*os*tri vicesimo nono.

(signed at top R H)                                                     Hill

Although the name Richard Waller occurs only as a contemporary insertion, the letter was most probably intended especially for him. Waller was at this time apparently "joint-chamberlain of the ex-chequer with Sir Thomas Tyrrell" (*D.N.B.*, LIX. 130); as the others named in the letter are not noted in the *Paston Letters* or in the *Dictionary of National Biography*, these may be presumed to have been minor officials of the exchequer actually entrusted with the disposal of *The George of Prussia*. Richard Waller, on the other hand, had for many years been on intimate terms with Sir John Fastolf, having served under him in France in 1442–3; some years later (Paston Letter 264) Fastolf speaks of Waller as his "right well-beloved Brother."

The Thomas Daniel mentioned in the letter is familiar to all readers of the *Paston Letters*. Apparently a native of Norfolk, he belonged throughout his career to the more riotous element in control of that shire, and was a continual source of annoyance to the Pastons and their friends. Before the Duke of Suffolk's impeachment Daniel had been his faithful adherent, but even so he had at various times been "owth of the Kings gode grase," as Margaret Paston notes (Letter 75). The present letter, written some six months after Suffolk's death, clearly shows that Daniel stood in no great favour at Court, although some doubt may be expressed as to whether Fastolf actually recovered his money at this time. As late as 1452 (and also in 1455?) William Worcester records that "Fastolf lent to the voyage that Thomas Danyell made in to Breteyn, as it is notorily knowen, of which he ys not yhyt payd, the somme of C *li*" (Letter 309; also 310).[4] It is hard to believe that anyone so close-fisted as Fastolf notoriously was would have lent another £100 to Daniel after having had difficulty in recovering a previous loan. It is therefore quite possible that Fastolf was not repaid his £100 out of the sale of *The George of Prussia*, if such a sale actually took place.

The ship *The George of Prussia* is not noted in the *Paston Letters*. For some time before November 8, 1450, it is known that Daniel was involved in or had some connection with maritime affairs, probably mainly in the form of freebootery. In a letter written on May 25, 1449 (No. 90), Robert Wenyngton reported to Daniel that his ships had met with and taken a hundred "grete schyppys of Pruse, Lubycke, Campe, Rastocke, Holond, Selond, and Flandres". Was *The George of Prussia* one of these? In one of the *Paston Letters* reputed to have been written late in 1450 (No. 165), it is stated that "Daniel is amrel," and it may be possible that *The George of Prussia* came into Daniel's possession as his Admiral's share of the booty taken by Wenyngton.[5]

Before turning to the second document concerning Thomas Daniel, it is well to cast a brief glance at the political events that took place at this time. After Suffolk's death the country was disturbed by the rivalry between the Duke of York and the Duke of Somerset for the control of the government. Although the latter had proved himself incompetent in France and far from popular with the people in England, he gradually gained the favour of the King, and by the late summer of 1451 had nearly assumed the position that Suffolk once held. Daniel was not a man to let such an opportunity to re-establish himself at Court escape him, and he carefully cultivated the friendship of Somerset for a "quarter of this yere," as Richard Southwell informed John Paston in December 1451 (Letter 206).

Daniel had not, in the meantime, been inactive. In the spring of

---

[4] See also *Paston Letters*, II. 82, for the abstract from Hickling 104 (Magd. Coll., Oxf.) regarding a debt of £100 due to Fastolf from Daniel.

[5] Gairdner (II. 103) quotes a record from Joseph Stevenson's *Letters and Papers illustrative of the Wars of the English in France* (I. 489) showing that Robert Wynnyngtone of Devonshire was bound by an indenture "to do the King service on the sea."

1450 he had forcibly entered the manor of Brayston (Bradeston) in Norfolk, the property of one Osbert Mundford, but was dispossessed again by Mundford on September 7 of that same year. It is known that he once again entered this manor some time before February 9, 1452; the second Morgan document adds certain specific details to our knowledge of this wanton act.

## 207 *bis*

### RICHARD DUKE OF YORK. TO JOHN PAGRAVE, WILLIAM BOKENHAM AND OTHERS

### Dated February 9, [1452]

To oure right trusty and welbeloued (*space*) Pagraue, (*space*) Bokenham, John Wyndam, John Paston, William Calthorp, Thomas Gurney, William Norwich, and Nicolas Ovy, and to eu*er*y of thaim.[6]

The Duc of York etc.

Right trusty and welbeloued. We grete you hertily wel. And wol ye wit that the reuerend fader in God, oure right trusty and entierly welbeloued cousin, the Bisshop of Ely, hath rapported vnto vs this same day that Thomas Danyell vppon Tuesday last passed entred with force in the manoir of Braydeston, vppon Osborn Mountford and his son being at Calais in the Kyng oure souu*er*ain lord*is* seruice, and dispoylled thaire goodes. Sayeng and affermyng for maintenance of his saide presumptueux and vnlawful entree, that oth*re* lordes and we stode enfeffed in the saide manoir to þe vse of him and of his wyf t*er*me of thaire lyves, and þat hit was the wille of þe saide lordes and of vs þat he shuld soo entre, & þe same lordes and we forto assiste him in keping of his possession. Wherfore in somuch as the same suggestion & surmission toucheth oure honneur & the pretense therof shuld yeve vs occasion of greet noyse and charge. We certifie vnto you & to eu*er*y of you for trouth þat we knewe neu*er*e such feffement made, ner we consented neu*er*e to such forcible entree. And we dysavoue hit by thees oure le*tt*res signed with oure owne hande. To þentent þat þe parties greeued may haue þaire acc*i*on yif thay bee so aduised, and due processe of law to bee executed, as in such caas hit is required. Right trusty and welbeloued. Oure lord haue you in his keping. Yeven vndr*e* oure signet at London, þe ix day of ffeuer*er*.

(signed) R York

It is quite obvious that the rumour that Daniel was supported in his seizure of Brayston had spread very effectively, and it seems cer-

---

[6] The individuals herein noted were all friends of the Pastons and repeatedly appear in the *Paston Letters*. Most of them were probably also well known to the Duke of York; in Letter 146 it is stated that Calthorp had recently received a letter from the Duke (1450) and William Bokenham, Prior of Yarmouth, was doubtlessly well acquainted with York. Pagrave's Christian name was John.

tain that the Duke of York wished to reassure the Pastons and their allies by this letter that he and the Duke of Norfolk were not the lords who had backed Daniel. The inference is, therefore, that Daniel seized Brayston with the help or connivance of the Duke of Somerset, Lord Scales, Sir Thomas Tuddenham, and John Heydon,[7] a group of men with whom Daniel had more in common than with the Duke of York's party.

The Duke of York's letter adds one more piece of information in that it explicitly states that Daniel entered Brayston "vppon Tuesday last passed." Now, in 1452, February 9 fell on a Wednesday, which would imply that Daniel's raid occurred the day before, but there seems to be satisfactory evidence to show that the raid had actually taken place a week earlier. Item 208 in the *Paston Letters* is a letter from Mundford himself to John Paston informing him that he had heard of Daniel's entry into his manor of Brayston and begging Paston to look after his interests. This letter was, however, written at Calais, of which Mundford was at that time Marshal, and it is also dated February 9. As it is most unlikely that the news of the capture of Brayston could have reached Mundford in Calais within thirty-six hours after the outrage had been committed in Norfolk, it is probable that the previous Tuesday was meant and that Daniel actually entered Brayston on Tuesday, February 1, 1452.

## II

### 173 *bis*

#### INDENTURE MADE BETWEEN SIR JOHN FASTOLF AND HUGH ACTON CONCERNING THE MANOR OF MUNDHAM

#### Dated January 24, 1451

Hec indentura facta Londonie xxiiij die mensis Januarii Anno regni regis henrici sexti post conquestum vicesimo nono inter Johannem/Fastolf militem ex vna parte et Hugonem Acton clericum ex altera parte testatur quod prefatus Johannes Fastolf liberauit predicto Hugoni quandam cartam/feoffamenti manerij de Mundham ac alie terre ibidem cum litera attornata pro seisina inde deliberanda Wallo Episcopo Norwicensi et alijs ad opus eiusdem/Hugo-

---

[7] It is characteristic of those changing and troubled times that after Daniel's first raid on Brayston, Lord Scales wrote to John Paston (Letter 108) that as "Osberd is my tenaunt and homager, it is my part to holde with hym rather than with Danyelle in hise right, which I wylle do to my pouer." Heydon was one of those who helped Mundford to regain Brayston at that time. Two years later both these gentlemen are found in support of Thomas Daniel.

nis ea condic*ione* et intenc*ione* q*u*od idem Hugo lib*er*abit eandem cartam cu*m* lit*er*a attorn*ata* p*re*dict*a* Thome Howis cl*er*ico p*er* quamquidem cartam/ p*er* ip*su*m Thomam *et* alios sigillat*am* et idem Thomas p*ro* CC. marcis sibi soluend*is* deductis inde prius vj S. viij d. p*re*dict*o* Joh*ann*i/Fastolf in manu*m* solut*is* fieri fac*it* p*re*fat*us* Ep*is*copu*s* et al*ii* in p*re*dict*a* carta specificat*i* statum in man*er*io *et* terr*a* p*re*dict*is* sec*undu*m tenorem carte p*re*dict*e*/In cuius rei testi*m*oniu*m* hijs indentur*is* partes p*re*dict*e* alt*er*natim sigilla sua apposu*er*u*n*t. Dat*um* die loco *et* anno supradic*t*o.

Fastolfe.

This indenture is dated January 24, 1451, but even if the date had not been preserved, the approximate day on which the indenture was drawn up could have been easily determined. On November 23, 1450, Sir John Fastolf wrote to the Parson of Castlecombe, Sir Thomas Howys, that he had agreed with the master of St. Giles (St. Giles' Hospital in Norwich) for the sale of "Mundham Maner with appurtenances in Cyselond" for 200 marks (Letter 156). On January 28, 1451, Fastolf again wrote Howys that "Master Hue Acton has been with him for the new evidences ensealed for the manor of Mundham, which F. has sold to the use of the Church of St. Giles that he is master of, etc." (Gairdner's abstract of Letter 174). Even if, then, the date had been lost, the indenture could have been dated "shortly before January 28, 1451." The present document merely fixes the day on which the meeting between Fastolf and Acton took place.

502 bis

THE EARL OF WARWICK TO JOHN PASTON

Dated March 1, [year uncertain]

To my right trusty and welbeloued John Paston, Squyer.

Right trusty and welbeloued I grete yow well, desiryng & praying yow hertily that at the reuerens of God And this my writyng ye wooll shewe your good maist*er*shep And tender frenshep vn-to the right trew s*er*uaunt*es* of God, my oratour*es*, the frer*es* menour*es* of the couent of Norwich in swich maters as my right welbeloued doctour Brakley shall enforme yow mor*e* apleyn, to whoom I praye yow yeue feith & full credens in this bihalf wherin ye shall aswell doo a meritory dede as to me a singuler pleaser and cause me to shewe yow my good lordshep in tyme comyng wherfor in thies ye ne faile as my trust is in yow, and Crist haue yow in his blissed kepyng. Yeuen vnder my signet at London the ferst day of March.

Richard, Erl of

Warrewyk.                                             (signed) R. Warrewyk.

The date of this letter is not definitely ascertainable. It must, however, have been written on some March 1 following the accession
of Richard Neville to the Earldom of Warwick (July 23, 1449) and
before the death of John Paston in May 1466. As the younger John
Paston was knighted in 1463, the letter cannot be presumed to be
one written by Warwick to Sir John after the death of his father,
for it is specifically addressed to "John Paston, Squyer." The letter
is here included with a group to which Gairdner could assign no
definite year, but it may be noted in passing that the only other letter (No. 257) from Warwick to Paston is dated August 24, and to
this the editor assigned the years 1454 or 1455 (*Paston Letters*, II. 331).

### 719 *bis*
#### EDWARD IV TO SIR JOHN PASTON
#### Dated July 23, [1469]

To oure trusti and welbeloued John Paston Knyght.

By the King.
Trusti and welbeloued We grete you wele. And prey and also charge you
that with as many men defensible in array as ye can bring to vs at youre leed-
ing, ye be with vs at oure Towne of Dancastre the iij^de Day of August next
commyng to attende vpon oure personne from thens toward the defence of
oure lande, and repressing of the malice of our ennemyes, traitours and rebelles
entred oure saide lande, not failing hereof as ye wol stonde in the fauour of oure
good grace and vpon peyn of the feith and ligeance that ye owe vnto vs. Yeuen
vndre our signet at oure Towne of Northampton the xxiij^tt Day of Juyl.
(signed at the top with the Royal sign manual)

This letter must surely belong to 1469, the year in which the allies
of Edward IV were defeated at Edgecote on July 26. Gairdner and
Sir James Ramsay[8] have described the King's progress for the month
previous to this battle. On June 21 Edward left Norwich, and, after
having made a pilgrimage to Our Lady of Walsingham, reached
King's Lynn on the 26th. From there he travelled, *via* Wisbech and
Crowland Abbey, to his castle at Fotheringay. Here he collected his
forces and then went on to Nottingham, which he seems to have
reached early in July. On the 9th of that month he addressed from
Nottingham letters to the Duke of Clarence, to the Earl of Warwick,
and to the Archbishop of York (Letter 719 and note). Apparently

---

[8] Gairdner, I. pp. 248–250, and Ramsay, *Lancaster and York*, Oxford, 1892,
II. pp. 340–343.

he stayed in this town for a fortnight awaiting more troops. Upon the arrival of the Earls of Pembroke and Devon, they marched on to Northampton, which was presumed to be the enemies' objective; here Edward made a fresh appeal for more soldiers. From the present letter we can see that Edward planned to attack the "rebelles" in the North after having disposed of Robin of Redesdale, and for this reason sent requests for troops to meet him at Doncaster on August 3. This plan was apparently upset by the defeat of the Earl of Pembroke by Sir William Conyers (Robin of Redesdale) at Edgecote.

The original letter is only a "form" with the name of Sir John Paston filled in by another hand; Edward probably had a great number of these written and sent them to as many of his adherents as he thought might be able to supply him with men.

## 868 *bis*

### Indenture made between the Duke of Gloucester and Edmund Paston concerning Military Service in France

### Dated April 7, 1475

Edmund Paston ar reteyned to serue in the werres vnder the Duke of Glouc. A°.E. iiij^te xv°.

This endenture made the vij daye of Aprile, the xv^th yere of the reigne of Kyng Edward the iiij, betwixt the right high and mighty Prince Rychard, Duc of Gloucestre, Constable and Admirall of Englond, on the on partie, and Edmond Paston, Squyer, on that othyr partie, wyttenessith that the sayd Edmond ys reteyned and withholden with the sayd Duc to do him seruice of werre with the Kyng oure souuerayn lord now in his viage ouir the see for an hol yere at his spere, weell and sufficyently horsed, armed and arrayed as it apperteyneth to a man of armes, and thre archers, well and sufficiently horsed, herneised, habilled and arrayed as it apperteyneth to archers, takyng for hym-self xviij^d a daye and for euery archer vj^d by the daye, of the whiche wages the sayd Edmond hath rescyued for the firot quarter of the sayd hol yere, the daye of the sealing of these presentes, at whiche day the sayd Duc hath yeven knowleche to the sayd Edmond that he shal make moustres of hymself and hys sayd retenue at Portesdown in Hampshire, the xxiiij^ty day of May next commyng or the same daye at any othyr plase vpon resounable warnyng. At that day and tyme, the sayd Edmond byndeth hym by thise presentes to appere in hys propyr personne with his sayd retenue. And if it happen the sayd Edmond, aftyr the reseyte of his sayd fyrst paiement to dicesse or be in suche sykenesse or disease that he may nat be able to come to the sayd moustresse in hys propyr personne, that thanne he shal fynd an able man in his sted with hys sayd retenue to performe his sayd seruise accordyng to

the tenure of this endenture, or ellys to repaye to the sayd Duc that money
by hym reseyued for hym and hys sayd retenue for the sayd quarter. And for
the seconde quarter of the sayd yere, the sayd Edmond shalbe payed by the
sayd Duc of the wage of hym and of yche of his sayd retenue at the makyng
of the mostres of hym, and the same his retenue, afore such comissioners as
shal[9] be deputed ther by the Kyng, oure souuerayn lord, at wiche tyme shal
be-gynne the terme of the sayd hole yere and nat affore. And aftyr the sayd
moustresse and payement, with Goddes grase to go to shyp at suche tyme
as the Kyng and the sayd Duc shal comaunde theim. And for the othyr half
of the sayd yere, the sayd Edmond shal be payed by the sayd Duc for hym-
self and hys said retenue on the yondyr syde on the see, monethly in Englyshe
money or in money there rennyng to the valu of Englysshe money, so all waye
that the same wages be payed with-in x days aftyr the end of eueryche of the
sayd monethes or elles the sayd Edmond to be quited and discharged ayenst
the Kyng and the sayd Duc of eny covenaunt specifeyd in these endentures,
the same endenture natwithstandyng. And the sayd Edmond shal dvely and
truely obeye at the Kynges proclamaciouns and ordinaunces and fulfylle the
comaundment of the sayd Duc to his power and shal make wacche and warde
of hym-self and his sayd retenue frome tyme to tyme, whene and as ofte duryng
the tyme aboue-sayd as he ther-to shal dvly be warned and required by the
sayd Duc or hys comis. And in cas that any moustresse to be mad be-yond the
see by the sayd Edmond of hys sayd retenue lakketh any of his nombre of
the same other wyse than by dethe or sikenesse proued, thane the sayd wages
of theim that so shal fayle shalbe rebated vj on the payement to be made to
the sayd Edmond frome tyme to tyme as the cas shall require. Also the sayd
Duc shal haue the iij[de] parte of wynnynges of werre as well of the sayd Edmond as the iij[de] of iij[de] where-of iche of hys retenue shalbe answeryng vnto
hym of there wynnynges of werre duryng the tyme aboue-said, be yt prysoners,
prayes or othyr goodes or catalles whatsoeuer thei be. And the sayd Edmond
or he or thay that shal so take suche prisoners or prayes shal shewe vnto the
said Duc with-in vj dayes aftir the so tokyng, as well the names of the sayd
prisoners as theire estate, degre or condicioun, and the quantite and valu of the
said gettynges bi estimacion vpon payne of forfacture of the sayd prysoners and
wynnynges aboue-sayd. Also the sayd Edmond shal haue almaner prysoners to
hys propre vse that shal happe to be takyn by him or by ony of his sayd retenue
duryng the tyme aboue-sayd, except the iij[de] of iij[de] aboue-sayd, the Kynge,
oure souuerayn lordes aduersary, and all Kynges and Kynges sonnes, his
aduersariers of Fraunce, and also all lieuetenaunts and chifteyns hauyng the
sayd aduersariers power, whiche shalbe and abyd prisoners to our sayd souuerayn lord, for the whyche he shal make resounable aggrement with the
takers of theym, except also all othyr Kynges, Kynges sonnes, prynces, dukes,
erles and chyef capitaynes nat hauyng the sayd aduersariers power, whiche
shalbe and abyde prisoners to the said Duc, for the whiche he shal make resounable aggrement with the takers of theim. And if it happen the sayd Duc
with-in the sayd yere to dicesse, then the sayd Edmond and hys sayd retenue
shal serue out the yere aboue-sayd vndyr suche a capitaigne as the Kynge shal

---

[9] shal *interlineated*.

assyne and appoynt to haue the rule of hym and hys sayd retenue, and if the sayd Duc be takyn hurt or diseased with-in the sayd tyme so that he shal nat be able to do the Kynge seruise of werre, then the sayd Edmond and his retenue duryng the tyme of hys enprisounment, hurt or disease, shal serue oute the same tyme vndir his lyeuetenaunt or comys. And that all these covenaunts aboue-sayd by the sayd Edmond wele and truly to be obserued and kepte the same Edmond byndeth hymself, his heires and executours, to the sayd Duc in the somme of C^ll. sterlynges by these presentes. In wittenesse where-of the parties aboue-sayd to thise present endentures enterchaungeably haue putte theire seales, the day and yere aboue-sayd.

(signed at top) R. Gloucestre

The present indenture, like the previous letter, is merely a form with the name Edmund Paston and the "thre archers" filled in, but it is here printed *in extenso* as an interesting document relating to military details, showing at least theoretically how, when, and what the average soldier of those days was paid.

That Edmund Paston actually went to France with the King's unfortunate expedition is known from the *Paston Letters*. On May 23, Margaret Paston wrote to her son, Sir John: "For Goddes love, and your brether go over the see, avyse them as ye thynk best for her save garde. For some of them be but yonge sawgeres, and wote full lytyll what yt meneth to be as a sauger, nor for to endure to do as a sawger shuld do" (Letter 871). Some three weeks later Sir John wrote from Calais to his brothers, John and Edmund: "Brother Edmonde, it is soo that I heer telle that ye be in hope to come hyddre, and to be in suche wages as ye schall come lyve lyke a jentylman, wheroff I wolde be gladde" (Letter 873). According to these letters then, both John and Edmund were expected to go to Calais, and it is quite certain that John actually did go and fell ill there (Letter 876). In February 1477 Edmund was clearly in Calais (Letter 900).

1000 *bis*

RICHARD III. TO THE ABBOT OF ST. BENET'S MONASTERY
AND OTHERS

Dated May 31, [1485]

To oure dere & welbeloued in God, thabbot of Saint Benet, the Priours of Norwich, Walsingham, Saint ffaithes, & Ingham, and to euery of thaim.[10]

[10] With one exception, the religious houses here mentioned, all located in Norfolk, are all noted in the *Paston Letters*: St. Benet's Monastery in Holme, the Friars Minors of Walsingham, St. Faith's Priory in Horsham, and, I presume, the "Priours

By the King.

Dere and welbeloued in God. We grete you wele. And for asmuch as we vnderstande by writing from diuerses parties and also by espies such as we haue, howe þat oure enemyes, both of ffraunce & other places, been fulli disposed to entre into this oure lande in diuerses parties to execute thaire malice of long tyme conceiued and ymagined ayenst vs and all this oure lande for the vttre distruccioun therof and we doubte not but ye conceiue wele þat the rediest way and mean for thaire withstanding and rebuke is to haue a mighti armee vpon the see. We therfore, ouere the nombre of shippes & men that oure cousin, therl of Warrewyk,[11] is bounde by endentures to haue vpon the see to resiste the malice of oure said enemyes, haue disposed and ordeigned certain other shippes to bee sette furth in all hast to the same entent with a notable nombre of men, and haue deputed oure vncle, therl of Kent, and other notable lordes, knightes, and squiers of oure hous to haue the guyding and rule of the said shippes and men. And considering the great charges that reste vpon vs both for the keping of the Marches in the North, the bringing into oure handes of such strenghthes as been holden & occupied there by oure rebelles, and also in other diuerses wises, the setting furth of the said shippes & men can not ne may soo sone ner soo redily bee doo, as the necessitee requirith withouten the helpe of oure true subgettes. We therfore hertily desire & pray you þat ye wol put youre good willes & helpe to the vitailling & mannyng of the said shippes in such wise as both we and all that loue the comune wele of this oure lande þat standeth nowe in soo great necessite, may yeve you a perpetuell laude & thankes. And howe & in what wise ye wol shewe vnto vs youre good willes herin, we pray you to certifie vs by the berer herof. Yeuen vnder oure Signet at oure Castell of Leycestre, the last Day of May.

(Signed with the Royal sign manual.)

This letter probably belongs to the year 1485, when Richard III, having heard in January of the proposed invasion planned by the Earl of Richmond (later Henry VII) for the following summer, made his preparations to repel the invaders. In the spring of that year he left London, and seems to have been in Nottingham in June; about the same time he placed Lord Lovel "in command of a fleet at Southampton" (*D.N.B.*, XLVIII. 164). It must, nevertheless, be pointed out that in the spring of the previous year "commissions of muster and array were issued to meet the danger of invasion" which *might* point to the fact that the letter was written in 1484. However, on Twelfth

---

of Norwich" refers to the Priors of the four "houshes of Freres in Norwich" noted in Margaret Paston's Will. Ingham refers to the church in that village, of which we know that "a small College was annexed to this church by Sir Miles Stapleton, for a prior, sacrist, and six canons; their duty was the *redemption of captives*" (*The Beauties of England and Wales*, London, 1810, Norfolk, p. 346).

[11] The Earl of Warwick here referred to must be Edward, the eldest son of George, Duke of Clarence, who was at this time but ten years old.

Night, 1485, Richard received definite information from France that Richmond would cross into England that summer. As this agrees with the statements made in the letter, together with the specific request for aid in providing the fleet (which, as we have seen, was actually at Southampton in 1485), it seems likely that the date is 1485 rather than 1484.

### 1044 *bis*

#### The Earl of Surrey to Sir John Paston

#### Dated September 25, [year uncertain]

To þe worshipfull and my right entierly biloued Cousine, Sir John Paston, knight.

*Lit*era Comit*es* Surrey.

Worshipfull and right entierly biloued Cousine. I com̄maund me vnto you and in my right hartily wise þank you of all kindnes, requiryng you of contynuance. And where-as Edmond Stanhawe, late baillif of Horsford in þe Countee of Norffolk, owghte me at þe tyme of his disceas .xxxvij^lt. x^d, Cousine, I desire and praye you to shewe you of good wille and toward disposicion in þis matier so þat þe rather by your mean I of þexecutours to þe Testament of þe said Edmond may in þis bihalue haue contentatcioun and þat it woll like you to yeue credence touching þe promiss(?) vnto my seruaunt and conseillour Thomas Jenney. And if þinges lye in me for your pleasur, I pray you to be bold ouer me as I am of you, to whom I biseche God to send good fortunes. Written in þe Castelle of Shirefhoton þe xxv Daie of Septembre.

Your louyng Cousin
(signed) Thomas Surrey.

This letter, as well as the two that follow, cannot be accurately dated, but they all belong to the reign of Henry VII. As the three are addressed to Sir John Paston, the younger, they must have been written between 1487 (the year Paston was knighted) and 1503 (the year of his death). They have been intercalated in Gairdner's edition when the form of address, context, or place of writing agreed with that of other letters. In this case the letter was written from the "Castelle of Shirefhoton," from which letters 1043 (see note) and 1044 were also addressed. Edmund Stanhawe is not otherwise found in the *Paston Letters*, though Thomas Jenney appears to have been in Surrey's service as early as 1485/6 (Letter 1004). Horsford Castle, of which Stanhawe had been bailiff, lay within the hundred of Taverham, at no great distance from the city of Norwich.

1052 *bis*

### THE EARL OF OXFORD TO SIR JOHN PASTON

### Dated September 22, [year uncertain]

To the right worshipfull and my right intierly welbelouyd Councello*ur*, S*ir* John Paston, knyght.

Right worshipfull and right intierly welbelouyd Councello*ur*, I comaund me to you and hartely thanke you for your hawk*es* and also for your stork*es* whiche I vndirstond that ye haue sent vnto me to my right great pleasure, acertenyng you that I wolde be right glad to se you in these p*ar*ties. Neuyrtheles I trust in short tyme, doing my pilgrimage to Walsingh*a*m, to se you in tho p*ar*ties and than*ne* to thanke you for yo*ur* right gode and louyng remembraunce, whiche I well vndirstond by these and diuerse otherys nat owt of yo*ur* mynde ne forgotyn, whiche shall nat be in my behalue forgotyn by the grace of God, who haue you in keping. Wretin at my Castell of Heding-h*a*m, the xxij Day of Septembre.

(signed) Oxynford.

As the form of address is similar to that employed in Letters 1049–1051 and the letter is written from "my Castell of Hedingham" as Letter 1052, the present letter has been placed after 1052, near other letters of the Earl of Oxford.[12] It may be recalled that in 1498 Oxford entertained Henry VII at Hedingham, and it may have been for this occasion that Sir John Paston made the present which the Earl here acknowledges.

1063 *bis*

### MARGARET, COUNTESS OF RICHMOND, TO SIR JOHN PASTON

### Dated April 10, [year uncertain]

To oure trusty and right welbeloued S*ir* John Paston, knight.

By the kinges modr*e*.

Trusty and welbeloued, we grete you wele. And pray you in o*ur* name to haue the contynue of a bill herin closed in good and deliberate examinac*i*on. And therupon to set suche cude[13] and ordinate directiou*n* as shalbe consonant to iustice, right, and good conscience, so as for lakke therof the p*ar*tie plaintief haue no cause reasounable to pursue furth*er* vnto vs in that behalue as we trust you. Yeuen vndr*e* o*ur* signet at our Manor of Colyweston, the x^th Day of Aprill.

(signed) Margaret R.

12 The reader should also consult Gairdner's notes to Letters 1049 and 1052.
13 *I.e.* "couth."

Although the above is quite uncertain in point of date, this letter is placed directly below the only other letter written by the Countess of Richmond that appears in the *Paston Letters*. That letter was also written from "Colyweston" and the letter now in The Pierpont Morgan Library *may* refer to the dispute mentioned in the one printed by Gairdner.

Individually the letters and documents here printed may add little to our knowledge of the Pastons and their friends, but they are of interest as a supplement to the most extensive series of letters that have come down to us from the fifteenth century. Though one or two of the present series may have some historical value and though others, such as the last three, are of no importance whatsoever (although they are certainly no less important than some of those printed by Gairdner), yet as a group they are worthy to be printed here, if for no other reason than their connection with the *Paston Letters*.

(From *The Review of English Studies* 14 (1938), pp. 129-142).

# CHAPTER T6

## LYDGATE'S *HORSE, SHEEP AND GOOSE* AND
## HUNTINGTON MS. HM 144

OF Lydgate's shorter poems, the *Horse, Sheep and Goose* seems to have been one of the most popular in its own day. No fewer than a dozen manuscripts of this text as well as five editions printed in the fifteenth century are known to us. Although the poem has been critically edited a number of times,[1] the text preserved in the Huntington MS. HM 144 was not consulted for these editions. A note on this text will not, I think, be found unwelcome.

The text in the Huntington manuscript occupies folios 140$^v$ to 144$^r$; these lines correspond to stanzas 43 through 77 of MacCracken's edition. Following at the end of the poem, there are seven further stanzas in the same hand while a different, though contemporary, hand has added still another.

The merest glance at the variant readings shows that the text in the Huntington manuscript is closely related to that in the printed editions; every variant reading peculiar to the printed editions is also found in the Huntington text. Furthermore the seven stanzas on folio 144 are peculiar to the Huntington manuscript and the printed texts; no other manuscript containing these stanzas is known. If, then, the manuscript actually belongs to the decade (1460-70) assigned to it by F. J. Furnivall and Carleton Brown,[2] it cannot, of course, be a copy of a book printed in 1477. It is equally apparent, though, that this was not the manuscript used by Caxton as it lacks the first 42 stanzas found in the printed text; this omission cannot be the result of a simple lacuna in the manuscript as the poem begins on the verso of a leaf, the recto of which contains the

---

[1] F. J. Furnivall, *Political, Religious and Love Poems* (EETS., O. S. 15, pp. 15-22, and revised edition, pp. 15-42); M. Degenhart, *Münchener Beiträge zur romanischen und englischen Philologie* (Heft xix, Leipzig, 1900); H. N. MacCracken, *The Minor Poems of John Lydgate* (EETS., O. S. 192, pp. 539-66). For the kind gift of a set of photostats and permission to quote from them, I am obliged to the authorities of the Henry E. Huntington Library.

[2] Furnivall, *Notes and Queries, Fifth Series*, ix, 342; Brown, *A Register of Middle English Religious & Didactic Verse*, Oxford, 1916-20, I, 472.

closing lines of Lydgate's *Churl and the Bird*. Under these circumstances the only possible explanation is that the Huntington manuscript was transcribed from the same one used by Caxton or from some "sister-manuscript" of this which also may have lacked the first 42 stanzas. There is, however, no textual evidence to show that the Huntington manuscript derives from any other source than Caxton or his original. In only twelve cases do the Huntington (H) and Caxton (C) texts differ, ten of which are of no importance whatsoever.[3] The only real differences occur in lines 521 and 533. In the first case, the two texts respectively read:

> And though one be more than another stronge (C)
> And though one be weke and another stronge (H)

As no other manuscript has the reading of the Huntington text, it is probable that we are here dealing with nothing more than a scribal emendation. In line 533, the texts read:

> As thus all vertues allone hath not one man (C)
> And thus all vertues allone hathe not one man (H)

Whether these variant readings indicate that the Huntington manuscript derives from a different source than the early printed editions may be seriously doubted. The variations are so slight that they can hardly be more than scribal errors and emendations.

On the other hand, if the dating of the manuscript is wrong and if it be supposed that it was actually written after 1477,[4] a further possibility presents itself; namely that the Huntington manuscript was copied from a printed edition. Of the five fifteenth-century editions, those printed by Wynkyn de Worde may be eliminated at once; that the Huntington manuscript was not copied from these is clear since all three lack stanzas 67 through 77 which are included in the Huntington text.[5] The whole problem therefore resolves itself

---

[3] Line 331, comparison C *and* paiysou II; l. 349, consideren C *and* considere H; l. 380, His C *and* Hi H; l. 399, that pees C *and* pees H; l. 413, thy C *and* the H; l. 434, defenden C *and* defend H; l. 454, spekes C *and* spokes H; l. 468, recoure C *and* recouer H; l. 478, in to C *and* in H; l. 504, hem at C *and* hem H. Although lines 426-7 were originally transposed, this was corrected by the scribe.

[4] I am obliged to the manuscript department of the Huntington Library for pointing out that Prof. Manly dated the MS., though without giving specific reasons, as 1480-1500 (*The Text of The Canterbury Tales*, I, 291). The present paper, therefore, helps to confirm Prof. Manly's dating.

[5] E. Gordon Duff (*The Printers, Stationers and Bookbinders of Westminster and London from 1476 to 1535*, Cambridge, 1906, p. 32) says: "One of these reprints

into the question: was the Huntington manuscript copied from a
Caxton edition and, if so, from which one? Three significant points
seem to indicate that the manuscript was copied from the printed
book. First of all, the text in the Huntington manuscript comprises
the contents of the second quire in the Caxton edition; in short, it
may be argued that the scribe transcribed his text from a copy that
had lost the whole of the first quire. In the second place, the interlinear, rather than marginal, explanations are somewhat more
characteristic of printed books than of manuscripts. Lastly, and
perhaps the most significant of all, is the evidence afforded by a
single line (537). Here the Caxton editions and the Huntington
manuscript agree in the reading:

> Yf charyte gouerne well the rother

I think it is clear that a simple misprint ("rother" for "tother")
in Caxton's first edition was mechanically copied both by the scribe
of the Huntington manuscript and by the compositor who set the
text of Caxton's second edition. As it is difficult to believe that the
scribe could have independently made the same mistake and in view
of the fact that the text wanting in the Huntington manuscript
corresponds exactly to the contents of one quire in Caxton's editions, it seems likely that the Huntington manuscript derives from
the printed edition rather than from Caxton's original.

It is probable, moreover, that the Huntington manuscript was
copied from Caxton's first edition rather than from the second. The
orthography in the manuscript compares more nearly to that in
the first edition than to that in the second. Furthermore in the two
instances where the editions differ textually, the manuscript agrees
with the first edition in each case. In line 411, the manuscript and
the first edition have "circumstaunce" while the second edition has
the plural case; in line 455, the same two texts read "Torned"
while the second edition has "Torneth."

As both Furnivall and Carleton Brown failed to realize that the
additional stanzas were also included in the printed editions of the

---

shows how careless a printer W. de Worde was. He reprints the *Horse, the Shepe,
and the Ghoos*, from a copy of Caxton's wanting a leaf, but never noticing anything wrong prints straight ahead, making of course nonsense of the whole." As
Caxton printed only six stanzas to a leaf and as eleven stanzas are wanting, it is
clear that the Caxton copy used by de Worde lacked not one but *two* leaves; these
leaves were the fifth and sixth of the second quire.

*Horse, Sheep and Goose,*[6] these are here reprinted from the manuscript with the variant readings taken from four of the printed editions:

## I

Hit is ful harde to knowe ony estate
Double visage loketh oute of euery hood
Sewerte is loste Truste is past the date
Thrifte hathe take his leue ouer the flood
5 Lawe can do no thyng withouten good
Thefte hathe leue to goo oute at large
Of the communes mysreule hathe take the charge

## II

And thou desire thy self to auaunce
Poure or riche whether that thou be
10 Be lowly and gentyl in thy gouernaunce
Good reule douteles may best preferre the
Yf thou be gentyl hurte not thy degre
And thou be poure do alle that thou canne
To vse goode maners for maner maket[h] man

## III

15 Atte thy mele be glad in countenaunce
In mete and drynke be thou mesurable
Beware of surfete and mysgouernaunce
They cause men ofte to be vnresonable
Suffre no thyng be sayde at thy table
20 That ony man may hurte or displese
For good mete and drynke axeth Joye and ese

## IV

Yf thy goodes to the not suffyse
Conforme the euer to that thou hast
Gouerne so thy self in suche a wyse
25 In thyn expences make no waste
Grete excesse causeth vnthrift in haste
Beware be tyme bere this in thyn herte
Misrewle maketh ofte many men to smerte

---

[6] The editions are the following: Caxton's first (Duff 261 = 1); Caxton's second (Duff 262 = 2); de Worde's first (Duff 263 = 3); de Worde's second (Duff 264); de Worde's third (Duff 265 = 5). I have been unable to see the only known copy of de Worde's second edition, which is in the possession of the Duke of Devonshire. It may here be pointed out that, though de Worde's first edition follows the Caxton prints very carefully, his third edition contains numerous alternative readings, mostly not very good ones. We may also note that, in line 38 below, the Huntington MS. and de Worde's third edition have the correct reading, while de Worde's first edition follows the misprints of the Caxton editions.

### V

Beware of nouellis that be new brought
30 Though they be plesau*n*t lokke fast thy lyppe
An hasty worde may be to sore bought
Close thy mouthe leste thy tou*n*ge trippe
To thy self loke thou make not a whyppe
Hurte not thy self lest thou sore rewe
35 For thyn owne ese keepe thy tonge in mewe

### VI

The worlde so wyde the ayre so remeuable
The sely man so lytel of stature
The graue and grounde of clothyng so mutable
The fyre so hoote and subtyll of nature
40 The water neuer in oon what creature
That made is of these foure thus flyttyng
Maye endure stable and *per*seuere in abydyng

### VII

The further I goo the more behynde
The more behynde the ner my weyes ende
45 The more I seche the werse can I fynde
The lyghter leue the lother for to wende
The truer I serue the ferther oute of mynde
Though I goo loose I am teyde wi*th* a lyne
Is hit fortune or Infortune thus I fyne

Explicit

[Different hand]

### VIII

50 Wo worthe debate þat neu*er* may haue pease
Wo worthe penau*n*ce þat askith no pyte
Wo worthe vengeau*n*ce whiche m*er*cy may not sease
Wo worthe þat Jugement þat hathe none equite
Wo worthe þat trouthe þat hathe no charite
55 Wo worthe þat Juge þat may no gilt[y] saue
Wo worthe þat right þat may no fauor haue

l. 5 wi*th*outen] without 35; l. 14 maner] maners 5; l. 15 mele] mete 5 coun-
tenau*n*ce] contenance 123; l. 16 dryke (*sic*) 3; l. 19 be] to be 5 thy] the 5; l. 21
good] god *corrected to* good MS axeth] asketh 5; l. 22 goodes] goddes 5; l. 23 Con-
forme] Conferme 5; l. 28 ofte] *omitted* 5 smerte] smarte 3, sterte 5; l. 30 lokke]
loke 2; l. 34 Hurte] Hute *corrected to* Hurte MS; l. 36 remeuable] remuable 1235;
l. 38 grounde of clothyng] gound of clotyng 123; l. 39 suptyll (*sic*) 5; l. 41 fletynge
5; l. 48 louse 35; l. 49 fyne] fynde *corrected to* fyne MS; l. 55 gilt MS.

As the present writer has previously pointed out,[7] the last stanza (which is not included in the printed editions and which is probably written in a different hand) may also be found in the *Court of Sapience* (stanza 67) and in Ashby's *Active Policy of a Prince* (stanza 99). Although the first five stanzas are very Lydgatian in character, a reasonably careful search has failed to identify them. The remaining two stanzas, as Furnivall and Degenhart have already pointed out, are sometimes called "Halsham's Ballad." These lines have a rather amazing "history" behind them. The first of these stanzas occurs in Lydgate's *A Pageant of Knowledge*, of which both a seven and an eight line version are known to us.[8] The second forms part of another of Lydgate's poems, being the first stanza of his *Tyed with a Lyne*.[9] It may also be found as a single stanza in British Museum MS. Addit. 5465, f. 2$^v$, while the first also occurs alone in MS. Addit. 34360, f. 22$^r$. The two are found together as "Halsham's Ballad" (Brown 2252)[10] in MS. Harley 7333, f. 148$^r$, and in MS. Addit. 16165, f. 244$^r$. Combined with Lydgate's *Stanza on Deceit* (Brown 438) and his *Four Things that make a Man a Fool* (Brown 2693), it appears in Bodleian MS. Fairfax 16, f. 195$^r$, while in MS. Harley 7578, f. 20$^r$, these same four stanzas reappear but with Chaucer's *Proverb* (Brown 2510) inserted in the middle. The appearance of the Halsham Ballad in these additional stanzas is merely another example of the extraordinary adaptability of Lydgate's stanzas;[11] they could be combined in any number of ways to form a tolerable poem.[12]

(From *Modern Language Notes* 55 (1940), pp. 563-69).

[7] *The Sources of the Court of Sapience*, Leipzig, 1932, p. 87.

[8] MacCracken, *op. cit.*, p. 730 and p. 734.

[9] MacCracken, *op. cit.*, p. 832.

[10] The references are to Carleton Brown's *Register etc.*, II.

[11] The *Stanza on Deceit* comes from Lydgate's *Fall of Princes*; compare Brown 438. For other extracts from the *Fall of Princes*, see my paper "A New Lydgate-Chaucer Manuscript," *MLN.*, Jan., 1937, p. 2. At least two other versions of *Four Things that make a Man a Fool* are known (Brown 2271 and 2272). *Four Things* and *Deceit* are combined to form a single poem in MS. 775 of The Pierpont Morgan Library (f. 320$^r$), though this was not known to Brown or MacCracken. *Four Things* is furthermore added to some stanzas extracted from another poem (Brown 2081) in MS. Harley 2251, f. 150$^v$, while in MS. R. 3. 19 (f. 205$^v$) of Trinity College, Cambridge, it forms the second stanza of a poem beginning: "O mosy quince hangyng by your stalke" (compare Speght's *Chaucer*, f. 344$^v$). It may finally be noted that *Deceit* occurs attached to a stanza on the uncertainties of this world (Brown 2509) in MS. Douce 45, ff. 115$^v$-116$^r$.

[12] As I have rejected Helen P. South's contention that Halsham was the real

author of the Ballad ("The Question of Halsam," *PMLA.*, L, 362-71), it has been suggested to me that my reasons for this should be made clear. Dr. South based her belief mainly on two factors, namely the testimony of John Shirley and the internal evidence offered by the rhyme in ll. 13-14 of the Ballad. Shirley's attribution is found in MS. Addit. 16165 and is repeated in two manuscripts dependent on Shirley, Harley 7333 and Addit. 34360. It is, however, well-known that Shirley's attributions and texts are not above question. Alternatively, if Shirley is worthy of credence here, it may well be argued that Halsham "made" the Ballad by the simple expedient of borrowing two Lydgate stanzas. Dr. South furthermore believed that MS. Fairfax 16 was the earliest and best MS. of this text. This MS. was, however, recently dated "mid-15th Cent." in the Bodleian *Summary Catalogue* (No. 3896), at which period Shirley was either very old or dead; it may be questioned, then, whether this MS. is older than Addit. 16165. Next it may be noted that in the Fairfax MS. Halsham is not noted as the author and the stanzas are found in conjunction with other Lydgatian lines as noted above. Dr. South believed that the Fairfax text represents the correct version because the rhyme in lines 13-14 is *infortune: Lune* whereas Lydgate's poem is presumed to have *infortune: lyne* (i. e. *line*). It is significant, it seems to me, that in the Shirley MSS., which alone attribute the poem to Halsham, violence is done to the rhyme by the readings *infortune: loyne, loygne, loynne*. On the other hand, is it impossible that Lydgate's poem originally also had *lune* and that *lyne* is no more than a graphic variant or scribal error? In the twelve stanzas of the poem as printed by MacCracken, the last word appears as *luyne* no fewer than six times; while *luyne* is a perfectly good form for *lune* (*OED* records *tuyne* for *tune*, *ruyle* for *rule*, *muyle* for *mule*, etc.), it is difficult to see how it could stand for *line*. As bad as some of Lydgate's verse unquestionably is, it strikes me as entirely unlikely that he would ever have written a poem in which the refrain failed to rhyme. If, then, it is not impossible that Lydgate originally wrote *lune* (> *luyne* > *lyne*), the argument based on the superiority of the Fairfax text collapses. (Of course, the Caxton-Huntington text is very late; here it is made clear that *lyne* stands for *line* by the rhyme *lyne: fyne*). We must also note that the first Halsham stanza corresponds not to the "opening strophe" of *A Pageant of Knowledge* but to stanza 23 of the seven-line version; that these stanzas, listed separately by Brown but printed as one poem by Mac-Cracken, really belong together seems to be indicated by the refrain. Finally it may be pointed out that poems fashioned by combining various stanzas from Lydgate's other works have been fully treated in the previous footnote.

# CHAPTER T7

## ASTROLOGICAL PROGNOSTICATIONS
## IN MS. 775 OF THE
## PIERPONT MORGAN LIBRARY

AMONG the texts illustrating medieval folk-lore, astrological prognostications are perhaps among the most interesting. Numerous texts of this sort, in Old English as well as in various other tongues were printed some years ago by Professor Max Förster[1] and to these may now be added the prognostications which appear in Morgan MS. 775.[2] The text in the Morgan MS. comprises a thunder-book, a prognostication based on the day of the week on which the moon changes and a general discussion of the influence of each planet.

The first of these is clearly the most interesting. Prof. Förster divided the Old English thunder-books or βροντολόγια into five groups, based on the time when thunder was first heard:

 (1) According to the month
 (2) According to the day of the week
 (3) According to the hour of the day or night
 (4) According to the canonical hour
 (5) According to the position in the heavens

A zodiacal thunder-book, to which group the Morgan text belongs, was not printed by Prof. Förster though he referred to a Slavic one in the course of his discussion. It is probable that the source for the present text may be found in the *Summa astrologiae judicialis* by

---

[1] *Archiv für das Studium der neueren Sprachen*, cx, 346-58; cxx, 43-52 and 296-305; cxxviii, 285-91, with important notes. See also R. H. Robbins, "English Almanacks of the Fifteenth Century," *Philological Quarterly*, xviii, 321-31, and Prof. Förster's comment, *ibid.*, xix, 411-2. For further notes on the Morgan MS. see my paper "Sir John Paston's *Grete Booke*, a Fifteenth-century 'Best Seller,'" *Modern Language Notes* LVI (1941), pp. 345-51.

[2] These texts were not noted by Seymour de Ricci in his description of the manuscript in the *Census of Medieval and Renaissance Manuscripts in the United States and Canada* (1935-37), ii, 1501-2.

Joannes Eschuid, or, to give his name in the English form, John of Eschenden.[3] Here the text reads:[4]

Dicit itaque hermes trimegistus libro quarto, capitulo 3. et leopoldus in libro suo tractatu sexto.[5] quod in quocunque signo tonuerit siue in die siue in nocte. unum erit quicquid notauerit anno eodem nisi alter tonitruus in secundo signo ab eo uenerit et tunc prioris non peribunt. Si in ariete tonuerit herbae habundabunt: angustia erit in filiis hominum quadrupedia multiplicabuntur. Sed bestiae agri minorabuntur. Si in tauro tonuerit annonae montium prosperabuntur et in uallibus deficiet uinum et bestiae agri multiplicabuntur.[6] Si in geminis pluuiarum et grandinum copia erit et fulmina legumina habundabunt lanigerae paucae et reptilia multa.[7] Si in cancro erit fames hominum et commotio: locuste quoque fructus terrae uastabunt. Si in leone seditio erit inter regna: annona cara in principio in fine et erit populi seditio et morietur aliquis magnus homo in fine anni. Si in uirgine ferae bestiae hominibus insidiabuntur quadrupedia morientur. Si in libra siccitas erit in ualle in principio anni: deinde descendunt pluuiae et erit annona cara in fine anni.[8] Si in scorpione racemi erunt pauci: oleum uile: pisces et pecudes morientur foemine abortiuos faciunt. uenti magni erunt clima ab oriente obfuscabitur.[9] Si in sagittario pluuiae erunt congruae: fructus arborum cadent: serui regum praeliabuntur. Si in capricorno multae gentes dispergentur magna pestis erit in filiis hominum et mortalitas undique. Si in aquario pluuiae magnae erunt etiam terror in hominibus uentus infrigidet: tussis et scabies et commotio magna erit in saeculo. Et si in piscibus tonuerit erit gelu et siccitas in terra et fructus terrae deficient. uinum tantum habundabit. diuitiae erunt in populo: et homines infirmabuntur nec tamen morientur.[10]

[3] Compare Lynn Thorndike, *A History of Magic and Experimental Science*, vol. III, chap. XXI, New York, 1934.

[4] Quoted from the copy in The Pierpont Morgan Library (PML 20700), Venice, 1489, folio 145 verso.

[5] I have not been able to locate the passage in the works of Hermes Trismegistus, though a similar passage does occur in Leupoldus, *Compilatio de astrorum scientia*, "Tractatus sextus de mutatione aeris." Through the courtesy of the librarian of the College of Physicians in Philadelphia, I have been able to consult a photostatic copy of the edition printed by Erhard Ratdolt in Augsburg, 9 January 1489. As Leupoldus' text occasionally differs, his readings have in several instances been quoted in the footnotes.

[6] In [Tauro] annona bona in montibus: pauca in vallibus: vinum et bestie agri multiplicabuntur. Leupoldus.

[7] In [Geminis] pluuie erunt multe et grandines: frumentum et legumen multum: aues pauce: reptilia multa. Leupoldus.

[8] In [Libra] siccitas in principio: in fine anni pluuie: et annona cara in fine. Leupoldus.

[9] In [Scorpione] racemi pauci pisces et pecudes morientur femine aborcient: venti erunt magni: [Luna] in oriente obscurabitur. Leupoldus.

[10] In [Piscibus] gelu et siccitas in terra: fructus terre deficient: vinum multum abundabit: diuitie erunt: homines infirmabuntur: non tamen multi morientur. Leupoldus.

The remaining astrological predictions are not very unusual and suitable comparisons may be made with any number of medieval treatises on astrology. A number of footnotes have been added, however, to indicate possible sources or parallels and to show where the English text is at fault.

The text printed below is found on folios 280 verso to 282 verso of Morgan MS. 775. The handwriting is of the late fifteenth century and, though carefully written, there are several omissions and slips of the pen, as may be seen by comparing the English and Latin texts.

Whenne it thundreth in Ariete that is to say whenne the Sonne is in Ariete there shall be moche gras moche desese to mon-kynde shall come fowre foted beestes shullen multiplie

Whenne it thundreth in Tauro all thyng that newed in hulles shull been ese And thynges in valeys shullen faylle And wyn feld beestus shull multiplye

Whenne it thundreth in Geminis thenne there shall be moche rayne And hayll whete shall multiplye and mony wormes that crepenne shullen be

Whenne it thundreth in Cancro thenne shall be moche hungre And boturfleus shull distroye fruytus

Whenne it thundreth in Leone there shall be grete desese betwene kyn[g]-dom*es* And dere corne in the begynnyng or in the last ende shall be desese of peple And A grete man shall deye

Whenne it thundreth in Virgine thenne it signifyeth that Weluus [*sic*] shullen doo desese to men And foure fotede beestes shullen deye

Whenne it thundreth in Libra thenne there shall be drowth in the valeyes and in the ende of the yere shall be moche reyne And cornes shall be full dere in the ende &c

Whenne it thundreth [in] Scorpione thenne there shall be lytyll Oyll and ffysshes of the See shullen deye and beestes Wo*m*men shall haue many dede chi[l]dren *with*in here body there shullen be grete wyndes there shall be a m*er*ken*es* in the Mone in the Est p*ar*te of the firmament

Whenne it thundreth in Capricornu thenne shall moche peple be disp*er*ged and grete pestilence in children of men And grete pestylence [in] all the world

Whenne it thundreth in Sagittari thenne reyn*es* shullen be but euene fruytus of treus shullen falle and kynges shullen ʒeuenne batayllus

Whenne it thundreth in Aquario thenne shullen be grete rayn*es* and grete drede of peple the wynd shall engendur the couʒ and the scabbe and grete stryfe shall be in the world

Whenne it thundreth in Pissib*us* thenne shall be grete forstes and dryen*es* in the eyre ffrutus on erth shull fayll wyne shall multiplye moche rychesse shall be amonge the peple many A man shall be seke but they shull not deye

In what signe þat euyr it thundreth whether it by day or be nyght as it is notified it shall be soth but so be that it thundyr in þe next signe aftur thenne the thunder of the furst leseth his strenght And the seconde thunder holdeth his strength and it farith in eche signe

If the mone chaunge on Soneday hit signifieth drye wether fro the furst day tyll the xxxᵗʰ day

If it chaunge on Monday it signifieth neþer drye ne wete

If it chaunge on the Tywysday it signifieth cold weþer And northen wynde

If it chaunge on the Wendysday it signifieth wete wethurs

If it chaunge on the Thurday [sic] it signifyeth bryȝt weþer and clere

If it chaunge on þe ffryday hit signifieth medlyd weþer drye and rayne

If he chaunge on the Seturday hit signifieth rayne weþer

This rewel faylleth not moche if it be well taken in his chaunge tr[e]wlyche[11]

Ye shullen vnderstande there be planettes

Saturnus Jubiter Mars Sol Venus Mercurius Luna

The planet of Saturne is cold and drye and shrewed And whenne he regneth he maketh all maner of Tempast he maketh A man hevy and ȝelowe of complexions And mony other thynges[12]

Jubiter he is hote and moyst and he is good to all thynges And he doth none harme to man he maketh A man good and honest and of wyn colour and he bryngeth all clere wethur and all goodnus

Mars is cold and drye and shrewed he maketh a man croked and wrathfull and malicious And whanne he regneth he signifieth batel and falshed[13]

Sol that is the Sonne he is hoot and drye and temporat he maketh erbes and trews to growe and bere fryȝt he maketh A man to be full of flessh and fayr and manerly of other th[i]nges

---

[11] A similar prognostication may be found in *Batman vppon Bartholome, His Booke, De Proprietatibus Rerum* (London, 1582) in the chapter entitled "De Neomenia," folio 150 recto. Here it reads: "Also of the Prime the common rule is, that Sunday Prime is dry weather, Munday prime wet, Teusday prime, cold and windie, Wednesdaye tempestuous, Thursday faire and cleere, Friday changeable, Saterday rainie, the three dayes from the chaunge, is the prime day." See also the early English version in MS. Cotton Tiberius A III, f. 38ᵛ.

[12] Bartholomaeus Anglicus says that Saturn has "two dedely qualytees, coldnesse & drynesse." He also says that Saturn "makyth a man broun & fowle, mysdoynge, slowe & heuy, eleynge & sory, seldom gladde & mery other laughyng. And therfore Pholomeus [sic] sayth they þat ben subgette to Saturnus haue oft euyl drye chynnes in the hynder party of the fote. And ben yelowe of colour & broun of heere & sharpe in al the body and vnsemely." *De proprietatibus rerum*, Westminster, Wynkyn de Worde, 1495, Lib. VIII, cap. xij.

[13] "Mars est planeta calidus et siccus." Albohazen Haly, *Liber in iudiciis astrorum*, Venice, Ratdolt, 1485, f. 4ᵛ.

Venus that is day-sterre he is hote and moyst and Sangwyn he maketh A man to be whyte colour redy glad and lecherus he loveth all goodnus[14]

Marcurius [*sic*] he is cold and drye his vertue is wi*th* good he is good wi*th* euel he maketh A man wyse and many other dyu*er*se goodnesse he cordeth wi*th* all the planettes[15]

Luna he [is] cold and moyst for why by the Mone we haue encrese and decrese he maketh A man to be mevable neu*er* to dwell in oon place he maketh a man to haue his on hande ay more thenne his other his on fote more thenne his other or any other lymme

Of these planettus there is a table[16] to knowe eu*er*y day whanne any of hem regneth And thus I suppose that this day be called Thursday that is to say Jubit*er* atte the Sonne rysyng that same planet that day is cold aftur reigne [*sic*] And next aft*ur* hym next houre regneth Mars And the next houre aft*ur* hym regneth Sol And aftur hym regneth Venus And aftur hym the next houre regneth Marcurie And aftur hym the next that is the sixte oure regneth Luna And aftur hym the next oure regneth Saturnus And aftur hym regneth Jubit*er* And so eu*er*yche oure tyl þou come to 24 oures eu*er*y planet regneth aftur odur.

(From *Modern Language Notes* 56 (1941), pp. 351-55).

[14] "Venus est frigida et humida," Albohazen Haly, *op. cit.*, f. 5. "Venus est frigida humida et temperata," Vincent of Beauvais, *Speculum naturale*, Strassburg, R-Printer, 1473, Lib. xvi, cap. xlv.

[15] "Mercurius est calidus et siccus," Vincent of Beauvais, *op. cit.*

[16] A manuscript table of this sort in French is written on the title-page of the copy of Leupoldus in the library of the College of Physicians in Philadelphia. It is drawn up for every day of the week. A table drawn up only for Sunday may be found in Albumasar, *Introductorium in astronomiam*, Augsburg, Ratdolft, 1489, signature g4 verso.

# CHAPTER T8

## A MEDICAL MANUSCRIPT PRESENTED TO
## CHARLES VIII OF FRANCE

### CURT F. BÜHLER AND ROBERT H. BOWERS

MANUSCRIPTS specially written for presentation to royal personages are not infrequently found among the treasures of the world's great libraries. Usually these are works of literary or devotional character. Carefully written, beautifully decorated and finely bound, many of these charming manuscripts are as fresh and unsoiled to-day as they were when they left the hands of the scribe, mute testimony to the fact that possibly they were hastily glanced at, certainly little read. On the other hand, manuscripts of utilitarian value, or at least those presumed to have been so in their own day, are much less frequently met with, either because they were not favoured for the purpose of presentation or because their royal owners, putting them to better use than mere preservation, literally "read them to pieces." That manuscript 509 of The Pierpont Morgan Library owes much of its importance to the fact that it represents such a utilitarian gift escaped the notice of Seymour de Ricci.[1] The manuscript may be described as follows:
The Pierpont Morgan Library, MS. 509.

MS. on vellum, written and illuminated in Italy in the last decade of the fifteenth century. The decoration is slight, consisting of a floriated initial S in blue and gold on folio 1$^r$, repeated on 5$^r$; other initials are supplied in gold or blue. On folio 5$^r$ is a coat-of-arms; a green shield surmounted by a gold crown, on which is depicted an ermine, is set on a blue back-ground, covered with gold fleur-de-lis, all of which is encircled by a gold wreath. The lower margin of folio 1, which may have contained another coat-of-arms, has been cut away with some damage to the text.

---

[1] *Census of medieval and renaissance manuscripts in the United States and Canada* (New York, 1935-40), II, 1464. The MS. is described thus:
509. Petrus de Abano, De venenis. Vol. (XVth. c.), 38 ff. (20 x 15 cm.). Written in Italy. Orig. oak boards and dark-red mor., stamped and gilt.
"L. Donini Regimontani D. Medici 1633." Later owned by Courtoys (ca. 1680), Simon Brigault and Agnan Brigault (ca. 1780).—Obtained from Olschki (1912).

The handwriting is very clear; chapter-headings, marginal notes, etc. are written in a brown ink. Catch-words are found at the end of each quire.

38 leaves, the last two of which are blank. Collation: a-d¹⁰, the last two, presumably also blank, having been cut away. The leaves measure 8 x 5¾ inches and there are 25 lines to the full page. The manuscript is bound in a contemporary binding of dark red morocco, stamped and gilt, over oak boards.

Contents: Dedication by Franciscus Pamoleus to King Charles VIII of France (ff. 1ʳ-3ᵛ); Petrus de Abano, *De venenis sive De remediis venenorum* (ff. 3ᵛ-33ʳ); Franciscus Pamoleus, *De lapidibus* (ff. 33ʳ-36ᵛ).

Provenance: the historic device on folio 5ʳ, noted above, belongs to Anne de Bretagne, Queen of Charles VIII. This device appears to be painted over an earlier one, quite possibly the winged stag of Charles VIII. The further history of the MS. is described in the *Census*.

It appears certain that this manuscript was intended for presentation to Charles VIII and his wife, according to the biographical hints which Pamoleus gives us in the dedication. In addition there is a marginal note on folio 33ᵛ which speaks of Francesco Sforza as dead; the manuscript must, therefore, have been written after 1466 (the year of the Duke's death) and Charles VIII was the only king of that name to rule over France between 1461 and 1560. Finally the coat-of-arms, of which we have already had occasion to speak, bears the device of Anne de Bretagne.[2]

It is not easy to determine the exact date on which the manuscript was presented to the King. Charles' marriage to Anne took place in December 1491 and on 8 February, 1492, she was crowned Queen at St. Denis.[3] This fixes the *terminus a quo* roughly as January, 1492. On the other hand, Pamoleus states that he crossed the Alps (superatis alpibus) in order to see the King, which implies that Charles was still in France. Thus the *terminus ad quem* would appear to be September, 1494, since Guicciardini[4] states that Charles arrived in Asti on the ninth of that month. It is difficult to believe that the presentation could have taken place after his return from the disastrous Italian expedition, for by then Milan[5] and the "Moro" (Lu-

[2] Cf. Mrs. Bury Palliser, *Historic devices, badges, and war-cries* (London, 1870), pp. 113-4.

[3] Marie-Anne Pichard, *Anne de Bretagne* (Dinan, n. d.), pp. 14-5.

[4] *Storia d' Italia* (Pisa, 1822), I, 179.

[5] In 1491, Ludovico received the investiture of Genoa, in the name of his nephew, from Charles; thus Pamoleus, as a Genoese citizen, was bound to the fortunes of Milan. Furthermore, there are several references to Milan in the text, showing Pamoleus' vivid interest in Milanese affairs. It seems unlikely, therefore, that Pamoleus would have supported Charles after Milan (and Genoa) had joined the

dovico Sforza) had deserted the cause of Charles and the series of set-backs following hard on the battle of Fornovo could scarcely have earned for Charles the title "Secundus Carolus Magnus." As we have seen, then, the presentation of the manuscript must have taken place between January, 1492, and September, 1494. Since the birth of the Dauphin (10 October, 1492) is not noted, one might be inclined to say that the manuscript could hardly have been written much later, though it must be borne in mind that several months may have elapsed before this news reached Pamoleus in Italy. If a guess is to be hazarded, it is possible that Pamoleus accompanied the great and imposing mission with which Ludovico Sforza hoped to impress the youthful Charles and that the presentation took place some time during the visit of this embassy.[6]

As for the Franciscus Pamoleus of Genoa who presented the manuscript, no further details have come to light, save for the trifling fact that the Pamoleus family is elsewhere spoken of as being native to Liguria.[7]

The text of the dedication is here printed in the usual manner, all abbreviations being expanded with the use of italics; the punctuation and the capitals are those of the original. A number of footnotes have been appended to explain the historical details.

---

Pope, Venice and others to form the League which was to defend the confederates against aggression.

[6] "The Milanese embassy of unusual magnificence that soon afterwards visited France had no compromising instructions. Its object was to win the French courtiers by presents, to make all vague assurances of general devotion, and to secure if possible the protection of the King for the Duke of Bari himself. In all this it succeeded." (*Cambridge Modern History*, New York, 1907, I, 109). In his *Memoires* (Paris, 1552, f. 121), Philip de Commines says: "Et ainsi, comme dict est, l'an mil quatre cens quatre vingts & treize, commença à faire sentir à ce ieune Roy Charles, huictieme, de vingt & deux ans, des fumees & gloires d'Italie: luy remonstrant, comme dict est, le droict qu'il auoit en ce beau royaume de Naples, qu'il luy sçauoit bien blasonner & louer: . . . Leurs paroles en public n'estoyent que visitations, & paroles assez generales: & estoit la premiere Ambassade grande qu'il eust enuoyee deuers ledict Seigneur." Since the Dauphin is not mentioned, it seems unlikely that the presentation took place during the visit of "Messer Galeazzo da San Severino" to Lyons in the spring of 1494, to urge upon Charles the need of haste.

[7] Christian G. Jöcher, *Allgemeines Gelehrten-Lexicon* (Leipzig, 1751), III, 1214, has the following note: "Pamoleus (Joh.), beyder Rechten Doctor, aus Ligurien, florirte im Anfange des 17 Seculi, und gab 1603 zu Genua Praxin judicialem causarum civilium heraus."

Ad Christianissimum Regem Francorum Diuum
Carolum Magnum Secundum[8] Franciscus
Pamoleus l. doc.[9] Januensis.[10]

Semper optaui Christianissime Rex postq*uam* discretionis annos
attigi posse rem gratam facere Ser*enissi*me Familie Regum Francorum; et sub illorum iusto regimine viuere: Delectatusq*ue* sum mira
deuotione audire. legere. Laudare *et* recensere digna facta ip*s*orum
Regum: Adeo q*uod* plurimi admirati s*un*t cur Principes non visos.
non cognitos tanta prosequerer affectione. Ad hoc motus sum: q*ua*
licet scriptum sit bonos Reges et Principes a Deo missos esse: tamen
visum fuit mihi q*uod* ampliorib*us* fauorib*us* et gratijs prosecutus sit
Reges Francoru*m*: *et* se*m*per credidi vnum ex ip*s*is redemptur*um*
sepulcrum D*omi*ni profligatis et domitis hostibus fidei christiane.
Sed postq*uam* venisti in lucem periculu*m*q*ue* de te fecisti motus in-
credibili deuotione om*n*es affectus meos ad te dirrexi: Admiratus
q*uod* amisso p*at*re tercio decimo[11] Anno etatis tue Rex [cre]atus

[8] Charles VIII (1470-1498) dreamt of imitating the Charlemagne of legend and
of becoming the Emperor of Constantinople and King of Jerusalem; his mind had,
according to Guignebert (*Short History of the French People*, I, 425), like Don
Quixote been disordered by the perusal of endless romances of chivalry. He
proposed to claim the rights of the House of Anjou, to which his father Louis
XI had succeeded, to the Kingdom of Naples and to use this as a stepping stone
to the ultimate capture of the East. He sacrificed greatly by signing treaties with
Ferdinand of Aragon, Maximilian of Austria, and Henry VII of England before
embarking on a scheme considered rash by his conservative advisers but he did
succeed in entering Naples in great pomp on February 22, 1495. For general
accounts of the expedition, see *Cambridge Modern History*, I, 104-18, and J. S. C.
Bridges, *A History of France from the death of Louis XI* (Oxford, 1924), vol.
II, as well as the accounts of Commines and Guicciardini, *op. cit.* Further details
may be found in J. Delaborde, *L'expédition de Charles VIII* (Paris, 1888), in
E. Herbst, *Der Zug Karl's VIII nach Italien im Urteil der italienischen Zeitgenossen*
(Berlin, 1911), and in the contemporary tracts (by Pierre Desrey, Jean Burchard,
André de la Vigne, and an anonymous writer) printed in the *Archives curieuses
de l'histoire de France* (Paris, 1834), sér. 1, t. 1, pp. 161-435. Commines (*op. cit.*,
f. 118) says: "Le Roy estoit tresleune, foible personne, plein de son vouloir, peu
accompaigné de sages gens, ne de bons Chefz: & n'auoit nul argent contant."
Compare, also, the unflattering description in Guicciardini, *op. cit.*, I, 180.

[9] The reading of "l. doc." is uncertain. It may mean that Pamoleus was a
"doctor legens" or a "legis doctor," or that he held the "licentia docendi." See
H. Rashdall, *The universities of Europe in the middle ages* (revised ed., Oxford,
1936), I, 112, 205, 221.

[10] The editors are obliged to Dr. George K. Boyce for his kindness in reading the
proof and for several excellent suggestions.

[11] Charles was but thirteen when his father died in 1483 and was therefore
incapable of ruling; his able elder sister, Anne de Beaujeu, ruled in effect until
he became of age.

tanta prudentia ac iustitia Regnum tuum gubernaueris quod Diuum illum Otauianum Augustum superasti: Nam Is regnare cepit Decimo octauo etatis sue anno. Tv Decimo tertio. Ille multa infortunia passus est priusquam summa rerum potiretur. Tu Deo [? bene fauetur][12] (fol. 1ᵛ) superatis omnibus insidijs[13] factus es mirabilis: victorque semper euasisti: Adeo quod merito dici potes non solum vrbium sed Prouintiarum expugnator.[14] Hostium victor et malorum domitor. Speculum vite: et bonorum premiator.[15] Imo et imitatus in hoc Iulium Cesarem: cum sis omnium memor: oblitus iniurie Iis bene fecisti qui contra te arma sumpsere. O magnum et preclarum munus a Deo tibi datum. Perge queso inuictissime Rex vt profitias[16] de uirtute in uirtutem. Increbuit enim per orbem de te fama quod sis maximus cultor iustitie. Prudens et bonus super omnibus. fortis animo. temperatissimusve in omni re tua: et Christianissimus omnium Regum vincis omnes Caritate: Clementia et Liberalitate. Dirrigat Dominus cogitationes tuas in viam suam: tibique semper faueat. Hijs ergo Virtutibus tuis incensus superatis alpibus[17] ad te veni: quo liceret mihi te videre et aloqui: et amoris aliquod inditium deuotionisque testimonium pre me ferrem: vt quotiens donum meum sumeres in manus: totiens clementie et humanitatis in me tue: deuotionisque in te mee renouaretur memoria. Habes animum et Cor meum Preclarissime Rex: Accipere dignetur Maiestas tua et de meis rem delectabilem. Res quidem miranda est: que ex Indis (fol. 2ʳ) ad Italos vecta per multa secula iacens incognita tandem nescio quomodo iam longo tempore ad manus meas peruenit: qui: vt eam

---

[12] As the lower margin of the first folio has been cut away with damage to the text, the reading of these two words is doubtful.

[13] Possibly an allusion to the revolt of the League of the Princes, led by the Dukes of Orleans and Bourbon, against the French Crown (1485-1488). The revolt was quelled when Anne's able general La Trémouille defeated them in a decisive battle near St. Aubin in July, 1488. In May of 1491, Charles foolishly released the Duke of Orleans from confinement in the Tower of Bourges.

[14] This is sheer flattery since by the treaties of Étaples and Senlis, and the ceding of Roussillon and Cerdagne to Aragon, Charles had lost more than he had gained. It may, however, refer to the expectation that Brittany would be formally joined to France following Charles' marriage to Anne.

[15] An allusion to the chivalric (and practical!) obligation of a lord to distribute largess to his followers; Chaucer's Knight loved "fredom." Guicciardini, op. cit., I, 180, in listing Charles' characteristics, states: "liberalità, ma inconsiderata, e senza misura, o distinzione."

[16] profitias, properly deponent: profiteris.

[17] vide supra. This seems to indicate that Charles was still in France and had not yet crossed into Italy.

vidi: Maximo Rege dignam censui. Cum*que* in dies magis atq*ue* magis delectarer super mirabilitate op*er*is: Interim euasisti in Maximu*m* Regem: *et* quem censeo nouu*m* Carolum Magnum: tot rebus feliciter peractis. Hanc rem dicaui Maiestati tue: quo aliquando i*n* ea speculando delecteris *et* illam inter gazas tuas Regias conseruari facias. Est opus hoc mirandum omni ex parte: h*a*b*et*q*ue* hanc precipuam virtutem q*uod* speculantes in eo letificat: tollereq*ue* videtur mesticiam:[18] si qua superuenia*nt*: visumve conseruat propt*er* viriditatem: *et* adeo stupendum mirabileq*ue* est q*uod* ni fallor sub sole res manu facta dignior no*n* rep*er*itur. Et hoc ausim dicere: quia perscrutatus ab hijs qui thesauros Magni Soltani. Regis Turcorum. Grecor*um* Imp*er*atoris: dum regna sua manebant. Su*m*mi Pontificis. Ser*enissi*mi Imperatoris: et aliorum Principum Christianitatis: nusq*uam* sensi rem tam stupendam visam fuisse. Accipias ergo Clementissim*e* Rex a Seruo tuo: qui te preposuit om*n*ibus Principibus Christianitatis: munus Iuditio meo te Rege dignu*m*. Thronus[19] est Presbiteri Joannis Magni Principis Indorum triumphantis in viridario. Sedet ip*s*e (fol. 2ᵛ) Princeps alto tribunali sub columnis quinq*ue* ordinato. Astant Heroes et Famuli: inter quos vnus crucem erectam tenens. Ad eum vadunt Consors *et* filia cum muneribus et Ancillis tanto apparatu: tamq*ue* venusta maiestate q*uod* nemo est qui non miretur i*n* hoc opere speculando. Nam si plures in eo dirrigant oculos. Vni uidetur in multis partib*us* coloris purpurei: ac esset Balasius:[20] et alteri uiridentis tanq*uam* Smaragdus:[21] Alijsq*ue* apparet diuersi coloris: etiam in eadem figura: qua*n*do prospitientes no*n* su*n*t in pari linea. Vestes Regis. Coniugis *et* Filie ad om*n*em aspectum sunt eiusdem coloris. Ast vno aspectu videntur auro intertexto

---

[18] mesticiam, *i. e.* maestitiam.

[19] Prof. Meyer Schapiro suggests that Pamoleus is here speaking of some curio or "piece of virtu" (possibly of a box-shape) with the representation of Prester John's pleasure garden executed in various semi-precious stones. On the back of this, Pamoleus "caused to be painted" a counter-part in which Charles VIII occupies the position held by Prester John in the original. (Cf. Julius von Schlosser, *Die Kunst- und Wunderkammern der Spätrenaissance*, Leipzig 1908). For Prester John, see Friedrich Zarncke, "Der Priester Johannes," *Abh. d. phil.-hist. Cl. d. kgl. sächs. Ges. d. Wiss.*, VII, 827-1030 and VIII, 1-186. Pamoleus' description of the pleasure garden bears a curious resemblance to that of the palace of Susa and its garden given in his account of Prester John by Sir John Mandeville; see the editions of the *Travels* by (Sir) George Warner, Roxburghe Club, 1889, pp. 136-7 and by Paul Hamelius, EETS, 1919, pp. 183-5.

[20] Balase (cf. *NED*), a red-rose ruby; from a district near Samarkand.

[21] An emerald or beryl.

laborate: Alio ex Smaragdo et Balasio. Sed parumper opere reuoluto versicoloris apparent omnes sicut hyris:[22] Cuius splendoris et variationis causam Doctissimi interrogati reddere nesciuerunt. Redeo ad ipsum tribunal: quod est eleuatum per gradus. Ad huius hostium[23] sunt quatuor quasi custodes et duo Adolescentes magna cum reuerentia. Tectum vero theatri totum videtur ex Smaragdo: Columne ex Balasio: repositeque uidentur inter lineas Smaragdi. Parietes omnes videntur diuersis localibus compositi. Quid plura stupenda sunt omnia: et opus uariat in qualibet sui parte ad omnem motum speculantis (fol. 3ʳ) in eo: Adeo quod mirandum est quomodo potuerit manus hominis tam mirabile opus conficere. Si enim opponatur viridens[24] siue purpureus aut cocineus vel auratus color: in oppositum mutatur colorem. A tergo huius operis pingi feci opere non spernendo Leonis Pontificis qui tuum Carolum Magnum decorauit titulo Imperiali et eiusdem Caroli tribunalia etiam in Viridario: et assistit vtri[n]que sua Comitiua In hermis armateque militie: Apparetque ex alio quasi de Celo missus nouus Rex cum radijs solaribus: qui videtur medius fieri inter istos Maximos Principes: et Alcuinus[25] magister Caroli: qui vaticinatus est futurum nouum Carolum Regem Francorum qui redimet Israel acclamat extenso digito. Ecce Carolum quem predixi Sepulcrum Domini recuperaturum.

Cupiens preterea te longeuum esse:[26] quia et mondus te Rege indiget. Data opera Inueni libellum editum per Illustrem Doctorem etate sua Medicorum Principem Petrum de Abano: in quo sigillanti[27] descripsit Species et Remedia Venenorum: et quem summo studio

[22] Hyris, *i. e.* iris, the rainbow or the precious stone of this name, mentioned by Pliny, *Historia naturalis*, xxxvii, 9 (Aldus, 1535, III, 287).

[23] Hostium, *i. e.* ostium.

[24] Viridens, *read* viridans.

[25] The famous English scholar (c. 730-804) who served Charlemagne from 781-790 in the revival of learning in France; cf. J. Bass Mullinger, *Schools of Charles the Great and the restoration of education in the ninth century* (1877) and Max Manitius, *Geschichte der lateinischen Literatur des Mittelalters* (München, 1911-31), I, 273-88.

[26] Charles did not long survive the return of the expedition. On the Saturday, April 7, 1498, while accompanying the Queen to witness a game of ball which was being played in the fosse of the castle of Amboise, Charles struck his head against the low archway of a gallery. Though the blow did not at first appear to trouble him, he was shortly thereafter seized with a stroke of apoplexy and died at the age of twenty-seven. Cf. Commines, *op. cit.*, ff. 167-8.

[27] A neologism (?); a noun formed from the present participle of *sigillare* [transitive], to seal.

compositum dirrexit Nicolao .iii°. Su*m*mo Pontifici:[28] huncq*ue* ad te detuli vt insidias proditorum facilius queas superare. Additis in calce ip*s*ius operis virtutibus nonnullorum lapidum: ex quibus pro tui tueve Clarissime (fol. 3ᵛ) Consortis conseruatione[29] aliquos conduxi. Vale Decus et presidium fidei Christiane.

Though a modern critical edition is badly needed, the second tract in the manuscript, the well-known *De venenis* by Petrus de Abano,[30] is not printed here chiefly because the manuscript is, in point of date, quite late and there are numerous earlier manuscripts[31] and printed editions available.[32]

The Lapidary,[33] however, which Pamoleus adds at the end of the book, is specially noteworthy. Most of the fifteenth-century lapidaries[34] are anonymous, whereas for this text we know not only the author but the purpose for which it was compiled; here the stones were specially selected for a particular individual and for a definite purpose. Although Pamoleus seems to have had little new to add to the then extensive knowledge (if such it may be called) of the medicinal value of stones, the selections show that the compiler had

---

[28] Nicholas III (Giovanni Gaetano Orsini) was Pope from November 25, 1277, to August 22, 1280; he was a politician who contributed little to the dignity of the Church. Cf. A. Demski. "Papst Nikolaus III" in *Kirchengeschichtliche Studien* (Münster, 1903).

[29] After Charles' death, Anne married his successor, Louis XII, on January 8, 1499. With Charles VIII, the direct line of Valois was ended, the crown passing to the Duke of Orleans, of the collateral branch of Valois-Orleans. Anne's life was a tragic one; the Dauphin died in August, 1495, and each of the three children she bore Charles in the succeeding years lived but a short space. By Louis XII, Anne had two sons and two daughters, both sons dying at birth. She died at Blois, January 9, 1514. Cf. Pichard, *op. cit.*

[30] On Petrus de Abano and his works, see Lynn Thorndike, *A history of magic and experimental science* (New York, 1929), II, 874-947 and Karl Sudhoff, *Kurzes Handbuch der Geschichte der Medizin* (Berlin, 1922), p. 197.

[31] Thorndike, *op. cit.*, pp. 922-3.

[32] Arnold C. Klebs, *Incunabula scientifica et medica* (Bruges, 1938), p. 251, no. 774. George Sarton, *The scientific literature transmitted through the incunabula* (Bruges, 1938) notes that Petrus de Abano was one of the twenty-five most popular authors in the fifteenth century (p. 183) and that the *De venenis*, with sixteen separate printings, was his most popular work (p. 190).

[33] For the general history of lapidaries, consult Thorndike, *op. cit.*; Joan Evans, *Magical Jewels* (Oxford, 1922); Mély and Ruelle, *Les lapidaires de l'antiquité et du moyen âge* (Paris, 1898); L. Pannier, *Les lapidaires français* (Paris, 1882); Curt Bühler, *The sources of the Court of Sapience* (Leipzig, 1932), pp. 41-59; and Joan Evans and Mary Serjeantson, *English mediaeval lapidaries* (Early English Text Society, 1933).

[34] See, for example, the texts printed by Evans and Serjeantson, *op. cit.*

at least an intimate acquaintanceship with this field and had, apparently, read widely in it. He quotes from Albertus Magnus, Dioscorides, Matthaeus Silvaticus, Pliny, Marbode, Serapion, Albumasar, Razi, and Petrus Decembrius,[35] though with some of these writers he was, probably, only acquainted at second hand. Oddly enough, Pamoleus even quotes from the *De venenis*, though the work itself immediately precedes the Lapidary and the same passage is thus found twice in the manuscript. He seems also to have known the *De natura rerum* of Thomas of Cantimpré and possibly Vincent of Beauvais' *Speculum naturale*.

The text, then, is illustrative of the firm belief in the curative as well as preventative properties of gems and stones in the late fifteenth century, and as such it may suitably take its place among the numerous lapidaries already published.

Qve sint virtutes eorum lapidum quos detuli. Et Primo. De Allectorio.

Allectorius secundum Albertum Magnum suo libello de Mineralib*us* tractatu secundo libri secundi. Cap*itul*o *pr*imo.[36] est ge*m*ma que uocatur lapis galli: et est albus nitens: cristallo similis sed obscurior. Extrahitur autem de uentriculo gallinatij postq*ua*m excesserit quartu*m* annum: *et* quidam dicunt q*uod* post nouem annos extrahitur et melior qui extrahit*ur* de decrepito. Virt*us* eius est excitare venerem: gratum et constantem victorem et discretum facere: Oratoriam tribuit facultatem: conciliat amicos: tentus sub lingua sitim deprimit: *et* hoc ultimum dicit expertum. Diascorides[37] uero dixit: qui secum

---

[35] Chaucer's "verray parfit praktisour" respected similar authorities (F. N. Robinson, *The complete works of Geoffrey Chaucer*, Boston and New York, 1933, p. 24):

> Wel knew he the olde Esculapius,
> And Deyscorides, and eek Rufus,
> Olde Ypocras, Haly, and Galyen,
> Serapion, Razis, and Avycen,
> Averrois, Damascien, and Constantyn,
> Bernard, and Gatesden, and Gilbertyn.

[36] This passage follows closely the text as printed in Raymond Lull, *De secretis naturae*, Venice, Peter Schoeffer, 1543, where the text of the *De mineralibus* by Albertus Magnus is printed on pages 107-324. The editors are obliged to the courtesy of the New York Academy of Medicine for generously putting their large collection of early medical books at our disposal.

[37] "Hu*n*c q*u*i secu*m* habu*er*it inuict*us* erit ut a m*u*ltis p*r*obatum est. Nam gladiator eu*m* h*a*bens i*n* ore i*n*uict*us* p*er*manet et sine siti. Similit*er* et reges eu*m* h*a*b*en*tes fortit*er* bellaba*n*t et expulsi a regno no*n* solum p*r*opriam domi*n*atione*m* ueru*m* *et* alienam receper*un*t. Mulieribus p*r*od*er*it portat*us* q*ue* uolu*n*t placere

habuerit Allectorium inuictus erit: vt a m*u*ltis est probatum. Nam
gladiator h*a*b*e*ns in ore p*er*manet inuictus. et Reges illum h*a*b*e*ntes
fortiter bellaba*n*t expulsiq*ue* de regno non solum propria*m* domi-
nationem (fol. 33ᵛ) verum etiam alienam recep*er*unt. Mulieribus
que uolunt placere viris suis portatus proderit: na*m* probos et speti-
osos viros reddit portantes s*e*: Ita refert Matheus Siluaticus³⁸ in suo
libro pandetar*um* medicine: quem dirrexit ad Serenissimu*m* Sicilie
Regem Robertum. Cap*itulo* ccccviii°. *Et* Plinius³⁹ in suo de naturali
historia libro .xxxvii°. Cap*itulo* .iiii°. dixit. Milonum crotonensem
vsum hoc Lapide in certaminib*us* victorem euasisse: Et Euax Rex
Arabie⁴⁰ qui scripsit librum de virtutib*us* Lapidum dirrectum Neroni
Imperatori: sequitur hanc opinionem: *Et* scriptum rep*er*itur in
libris antiquissimis:⁴¹ q*uod* si quis vult h*a*b*e*re uictoriam de inimico

---

uiris. Na*m* p*r*obos *et* speciosos redd*it* portantes s*e*." (Dioscorides, *De materia
medica,* Morgan MS. 760, f. 36ʳ.) The text in the Morgan MS. follows that in the
printed edition of Colle, 1478, which is usually attributed to Petrus de Abano
(Thorndike, *op. cit.,* II, 923). On paleographical grounds, it is likely that the
Morgan manuscript was written in Southern France about 1150, almost a century
before Peter's birth. It seems likely, then, that this translation is really by
Constantinus Africanus, to whom it is attributed in a Bamberg MS. (Thorndike,
*op. cit.,* I, 610). For further notes on Dioscorides, see Bühler, *op. cit.,* 47-59.
As the quotation from Dioscorides is also found in the *Pandects* of Matthaeus
Silvaticus to which reference is made immediately below, it is probable that
Pamoleus did not consult the original work but made his extract at second hand.

³⁸ "A great name in this group is Matthaeus Silvaticus, of the early part of the
fourteenth century, surnamed Pandectarius, whose *Liber Pandectarum Medicinae*
appeared at Naples on April 1, 1474, edited by Angelus Cato. This was a com-
pend or dictionary designed to interpret the writings of the Arabs and Greeks,
but Freind remarks that another dictionary would be needed to make it intelligible."
Sir William Osler, *Incunabula medica* (Bibligrapical Society, 1923), p. 24.

³⁹ "Alectorias uocant in uentriculis gallinaceorum inuentas crystallina specie,
magnitudine fabae: quibus Milonem Crotonie*n*sem usum in certaminibus, inuictum
fuisse uideri uolunt." Pliny, *ed. cit.,* III, 288.

⁴⁰ Marbode, *Liber lapidum* in Migne, *Patr. Lat.,* CLXXI, 1742. For a discussion
of "Evax," see Bühler, *op. cit.,* pp. 54-9.

⁴¹ A similar passage may be found in Evans and Serjeantson, *op. cit.,* p. 51.
[Note: as þ and y are indistinguishable in the MS., the editors have printed y
throughout]:
Old me*n* gafe hym a name Electoyr; & he y*t* wyll haue vyctory apon his enmy,
& y*t* he sal noght be ou*er*-comen of no ma*n*, ber yis ston in a rynge of gold on
his ryȝte hand, & on y*t* oy*er* syde of y*e* hond I-graue a knyght armyd, his swerd
in his hand, & ef*t*er y*t* lat syng ix messys apon y*e* rynge, y*t* is to say iij of y*e*
Trinite, iij of y*e* Crosse, & iij of y*e* Martirs; & when a ma*n* has yis ryng a-pon
hym, lok y*t* he make no defayle of synn.
In the notes to the text (p. 155), the editors state: "We do not know of any
source for the instructions." Although no other parallel is known to us, it is
interesting to note that there is a Latin source for the English text, and that this
tradition was quite wide-spread.

suo et ab aliquo non vinci: hunc lapidem portet in anulo aureo
dextra manu: et ex vna parte anuli armatum militem sculpat cum
ense in manu. Postea faciat cantari desuper tres missas de Sancta
Trinitate: et tres de exaltatione sancte crucis: et totidem in honore
omnium Martirum: et quamdiu defert non eat ad turpitudinem.

[*Marginal note*: Fertur quod Franciscus Sfortia[42] Dux Mediolani inuictissimus: et etate nostra omnium fortunatissimus
hunc lapidem continue secum habuit vsque ad ultimum vite.]

De Ethite seu Echite qui uocatur lapis aquileus.

Echites alias Ethites secundum ipsum Albertum[43] eodem tractatu
Capitulo .v°. est optima gemmarum coloris punicei: et uocatur aquileus a quibusdam id est Lapilus aquile: et ab alijs Herodialis: eo
quod (fol. 34ʳ) aquile hunc habent in nido: iuxta oua sua collocantes:
Inuenitur autem iuxta littora maris occeani: et dicitur quod aliquando
in Persia: habens intus alium Lapidem qui sonat in eo quando manu
quassatur. Suspensus autem sinistro lacerto confert pregnantibus et
impedit abortum: periculumve parturitionis mitigat: et dicunt quidam quod caducorum prohibet frequentem casum: *Et* quod mirabilius est: traddunt Caldei[44] quod si de ministratione veneni cibus

---

[42] Francesco Sforza (1401-1466), claiming succession to the Dukedom through
his marriage to Bianca, only daughter of Filippo Maria Visconti, overthrew the
Ambrosian republic and proclaimed himself Duke of Milan in 1450. An able
soldier and statesman, he established the Sforzas firmly in Milan. Pamoleus does
not exaggerate here; compare, for example, the most complimentary note by Pope
Pius II (*Opera geographica et historica*, Helmstadii 1699, p. 357).

[43] This is a somewhat condensed version of Albert's text; cf. *op. cit.*, pp. 181-2.
For a very similar passage, compare Vincent de Beauvais, *Speculum naturale*
[Strassburg: R-Printer, c. 1473], lib. ix, cap. 23:

Arnoldus de saxonia in libro de virtutibus lapidum. Ethites lapis est puniciei
coloris: qui reperitur in aquile nidis. aut in persia aut in litoribus oceani. hic alium
lapidem continet. & in sinistro suspensus lacerto: pregnantibus confert. casum
caducorum prohibet. Contra etiam abortum et laborem pregnantis valet. Si de
veneni fraude aliquis suspectus est. hic lapis sub eius cibo suppositus ipsum deglutire
prohibet: si reus est. Si vero lapidem a cibo ipso subtraxeris: mox eundem cibum
deglutiet.

On Arnoldus de Saxonia, see Valentin Rose, "Aristoteles De Lapidibus und
Arnoldus Saxo" in *Zeitschrift für deutsches Altertum*, XVIII (1875), 321 sqq.;
Thorndike, *op. cit.*, II, 430-2; Bühler, *op. cit.*, 48 sqq.

[44] Dr. Edith von Porada has most kindly pointed out that the belief in the
medical properties of aetites goes back to a much earlier period. The Assyrian
names for the stones are "aban eri" or pregnant stone, with its enclosed "aban
aladi" or birth stone; their virtues in Assyrian days were precisely the same as
those noted by Albertus Magnus. Compare Reginald C. Thompson, *A dictionary
of Assyrian chemistry and geology*, Oxford 1936, pp. 104-9.

sit suspectus positus hic lapis in eo cibo prohibet ne possit deglutiri cibus ille: Sed si lapis subtrahatur: mox deglutitur. Aiunt etiam quidam q*uod* si aliquis suspectus ha*ber*etur de ministratione veneni: si in cibo eius quocu*m*q*ue* lapis inmittitur: statim ad cibum strangulatur: et quando subtrahitur cibum deglutit: si est reus: Sed si est innocens: non glutit cibum in quo lapis missus est. Secundum uero Serapionem[45] uocatur iste lapis a Grecis Aleuians partum: *et* hec proprietas est inuenta in hoc lapide: Et Albumasar[46] in suo lapida*r*io dixit: q*uod* iste lapis est optimus ge*m*marum. Et Serapio procedens ulterius dixit q*uod* Aquila masculus defert hunc lapidem a partibus Indie: et supponit aquile pariture oua: facitq*ue* eam faciliter parere: aleuiatq*ue* dolorem eius: et hoc idem facit Mulieribus: om*n*ibusq*ue* animalibus quando ponitur sub eis in hora p*ar*tus. (fol. 34ᵛ) Et Rasis[47] auctor est q*uod* suspendatur Mulieri in coxia quando debet parere: quia facit accelerare partum cum facilitate: et dicit se hoc expertum: et sic inuenisse: et om*n*es in hoc concorda*n*t: q*uod* aleuiat partum: Evax[48] autem in suo lapidario Cap*itul*o De lapide aquile dicit q*uod* suspensus in brachio sinistro conuenit pregnantibus. Conciliat amorem. Diuitias auget vbi fertur: et pregna*n*tibus impedit aborsum. Ita refert et sequitur Idem Matheus Siluaticus in premisso libro pandetarum Cap*itul*o ccccv°. Et Candidus[49] in suo libello De

---

[45] This passage, as the author notes, is taken from Silvaticus, cap. CCCCV. On Serapion, see Ludwig Choulant, *Handbuch der Bücherkunde für die ältere Medicin*, Leipzig, 1841, p. 345; Sudhoff, *loc. cit.*, p. 144.

[46] Albumasar (Abu Ma'shar Ja'far ben Muhammad al-Balkhi) is best known as an astrologer (Thorndike, *op. cit.*, I, 649-52). The English academic play *Albumazar* (1615) by Thomas Tomkis treats of a quack alchemist in a manner similar to Jonson's delineation of Subtle in *The Alchemist* (1610).

[47] "Next to Avicenna the greatest name in Arabian medicine is Rhazes, who lived in the tenth century and whose description of small-pox is still quoted in our text-books." Osler, *op. cit.*, p. 19. Compare also Choulant, *op. cit.*, p. 340; Sudhoff, *op. cit.*, p. 143.

[48]
> Creditur ergo potens praegnantibus auxiliari,
> Ne vel abortivum faciant, partuve laborent;
> Appensus laevo solito de more lacerto.
> Confert praeterea gestanti sobrietatem.
> Auget divitias, et amari cogit habentem,
> Victoremque facit, populique favoribus ornat.
>                     (Migne, *Patr. Lat.*, CLXXI, 1755)

As these quotations are all found in Silvaticus, it does not necessarily follow that Pamoleus knew these works at first hand.

[49] Petrus Candidus Decembrius (1399-1477), a well-known humanist, translator and author, served Filippo Maria Visconti as a secretary from 1419-47, a position which he also held under the Ambrosian republic. Subsequently he is found

genitura hominis .viii°. Cap*itul*o dicens hu*n*c lapidem esse admiratione dignum: per hec verba laudat. Vidim*us* et ip*s*i ac plerunq*ue* experti sumus: q*uod* lapis Ethites Mulieri impo*s*itus aborsum prohibet. auertit part*us* discrimina: et feminam cum fetu p*r*estat incolume*n*. Et ne quis rem co*m*mentitiam putet: Plurime in Mediolanensi vrbe illius ope liberate sunt Mulieres: cum lapidem ip*s*um a nobis h*ab*uissent.

De Iaspide viridi h*ab*ente venas Rubeas.

Iaspis[50] est lapis multorum colorum: et h*ab*et dece*m* species:[51] melior tamen est viridis transluce*n*s rubeas h*ab*ens venas: et in argento proprie locandus: Expertum tamen est q*uod* stringit fluxum sanguinis et me[n]struum. Aiunt etiam q*uod* tegat (fol. 35ʳ) conceptum et iuuat partum: et gestantem se a luxuria cohibet. In Magicis etiam legitur:[52] q*uod* si consecratus est reddit gestantem se gratu*m* et pote*n*tem ac tutum: fugat febres et ydropesim: *Et* hoc ref*er*t et sequitur idem Matheus dicto libro Pandetar*um* Cap*itul*o .cccclviii°.

De lapide qui reperitur in ventre Bouis.

In ventre Bouis reperitur tophus nigricans ad pille rotunditatem nullo pondere: singulare remedium egre parientibus: si tellurem non attigerit. Ita refert Plinius[53] libro .xi°. de naturali hystoria. capit*ul*o .xxxvii°. in .iiii°. folio. Hic lapis quem detuli apud Corsos

---

in the service of the King of Aragon and later with the Este family in Ferrara (Cf. E. Ditt, *Mem. del R. Ist. Lomb.*, Classe di Lett., XXIV, 2, 21 ff.). Nine editions of his *De genitura hominis* appeared in the fifteenth century according to Klebs, *op. cit.*, no. 327.

[50] "Lapis iaspis secundu*m* Albertu*m* e*st* lapis multoru*m* coloru*m* *et* habet sp*ec*ies dece*m*. melior tame*n* est viridis transpare*n*s hab*en*s i*n* se venas rubeas. debet autem in argento proprie ligari hic in multis p*ar*tibus inuenitur. POSSE. expertu*m* est contra sanguinem et fluxum me*n*struorum. Ayunt autem q*uod* tegat conceptum *et* iuuat partu*m* et q*uod* gestantem se a luxuria p*r*ohibet. Magicis etiam legit*ur* q*uod* si inca*n*tetur portante*m* reddit gratu*m* *et* potentem *et* tutu*m* *et* fugat febrem *et* hydropisim." Matthaeus Silvaticus, *Liber pandectarum medicinae*, Venice, Liechtenstein, c. 1480 (copy in the NYAcMed.). Cf. Albertus Magnus, *op. cit.*, p. 188.

[51] Iaspis has, according to the texts published by Evans and Serjeantson, *op. cit.*, either nine (pp. 23, 43 and 121) or seventeen species (p. 93). Isidore, *Liber etymologiarum* (Migne, *Patr. Lat.*, LXXXII, 572) writes: "Species ejus XVII."; so also Arnoldus de Saxonia, *op. cit.*, p. 437.

[52] Vincent de Beauvais, *Spec. nat.*, lib. IX, cap. 77, quoting from "Philosophus," writes: "Castum hominem se portante*m* tutu*m* facit et gratu*m*: si consecrata sit. noxia quoq*ue* fantasmata pellit."

[53] Pliny, *loc. cit.* (Aldus, 1535, I, 288) says: "Et in iuuencarum secundo uentre pilae rotunditate nigricans tophus, nullo pondere: singulare (ut putant) remedium aegre parientibus, si tellurem non attigerit."

in uentre bouis repertus est. et magna cum diligentia conseruatus immondus.

De Lapide Ematite.

Ematites lapis multas h*abe*t virtutes secundum Albertum[54] libro suo Mineralium tractatu secundo libri secundi. cap*itulo* .v° : *et* maxime quia ualet contra fluxum vesice: ventris *et* Menstruorum: qua*n*do contrictus in aqua mixtus bibitur. Sanat etiam fluxum saliue sanguinee. Limoq*ue* permixtus eius puluis sanat ulcera et vulnera: et etiam carnem superfluam in vlceribus natam corrodit: ac visus hebetes ex (fol. 35ᵛ) humida causa confortat: sanat et temperat asperitatem palpebrarum. *Et* quod mirabilius est: secundum Petrum de Abano[55] in suo libello *p*remisso De remedijs venenorum Cap*itulo* .v°. Scriptv*m* est in libro Regum Persarum. Si sculptus fuerit in hoc lapide Ematit*is* vir genuflexus cinctus serpente: cuius caput teneat dext*r*a manus: et caudam sinistra: posuerisq*ue* lapide*m* hunc in aureo anulo: et sub lapide radicem serpentarie tritam: Portauerisq*ue* hunc anulum ab om*n*i veneno preseruat: Quod quidem se preparari fecisse dixit: *et* ad predictum vsum seruari.

Benedictio et consecratio lapidum seu ge*m*maru*m*.

Omnis[56] creatura in propria natura in qua a Deo est condita: est ab ip*s*o benedicta. S*ed* pro peccato inobedientie corrupto *p*rimo homi*n*e deinde illa que propter hominem i*d est* ad usus homi*n*is creata fuerant: corrupta sunt: *et* sicut homo rep*a*ratur baptismo uel

---

[54] This is a shortened version of the account given by Albertus Magnus, *op. cit.*, p. 183. For "Limoque" Albert has "Vino"; similarly Konrad von Megenberg in his *Buch der Natur* (Augsburg 1475, f. 264ʳ) states: "Wan*n* man sein puluer mit wein mischet, so heylet er die geschwer."

[55] In the text of Petrus de Abano as written in the same MS., f. 15ʳ, the passage reads:

Aliud est etiam quod scriptum e*st* in libro Regum Persaru*m*: q*uod* si sculpire feceris in lapide ematitis viru*m.* genu flexum cinctum serpente: cuius caput teneat dextera manus et cauda*m* sinistra: posuerisq*ue* lapidem hu*n*c in aureo anulo: et sub lapide posueris radicem serpe*n*tarie tita*m*. p*or*taue*r*isq*ue* hu*n*c anulum: ab om*n*i uen*e*no *p*reseruat: quod quide*m* ego q*uan*do*que* prep*a*rari feci et ad predictum usum s*er*uari.

[56] A French version of this text is appended to Jean de Mandeville's *Le lapidaire en francoys*; see I. del Sotto, *Le lapidaire du XIV siècle . . . du Chevalier Jean de Mandeville*, Vienne 1862, p. 127. A German translation is found at the end of the lapidary in the *Buch der Natur, ed. cit.*, f. 280ʳ. Vincent de Beauvais, *Spec. nat.*, lib. IX, cap. 29, says:

Sed sicut in peccato *p*rimi hominis omnis creatura corrupta est. Sic etiam in ip*s*is virtutes que post peccatum in eis remanserant p*er* attactum et vsum im-mund*orum* et impio*rum* homin*um*: precipui *et* lapides corrumpu*n*tur. Sed sanctificat*i*o*n*e consecrat*i*onis ad virtutu*m* efficacias reperantur.

penitentia contrictione et confessione vt dignus efficiat*ur* secu*n*dum statu*m* p*r*imi hom*in*is i*d* *est* vt sit bonus et iustus: sic cetere res quib*us* in natura sua Deus virtutem donauit: co*n*secrari debent: vt per sanctificatione*m* recipia*n*t priorem vim virtutu*m*: que ex parte obfuscate (fol. 36ʳ) fuerant: malis hominib*us* bonis rebus male ute*n*tibus. Debent ergo naturales lapides co[n]secrari. Pone ig*it*ur eos in panno nitido et mu*n*do. Antequ*am* dicatur Pax domini Dicat Sacerdos super illos istam benedictionem.

Oratio.⁵⁷

Deus om*n*ipote[n]s qui etiam per quasdam insensibiles creaturas om*n*ib*us* uirtutem tua*m* ostendis: qui famulo tuo Moysi inter cetera sacerdotalia irrationabiles Duodecim lapides ponere p*re*cepisti: non p*ro*pter illos lapides tantu*m*: sed ut uirtutes quas ip*si* significant hom*in*em h*ab*ere doceres: Quib*us* in Apocalipsi De duodecim Lapidib*us* i*d* *est* de xii virtutib*us* quas ip*si* significant Ciuitatem Celestem Ierusalem beato Ioa*n*ni Eua*n*geliste construe*n*dam significasti. Deprecamur te d*omi*ne s*an*cte p*ate*r et maiestatem et clementia*m* tuam suppliciter exoramus: vt hos lapides sancti✠ficare *et* conse✠crare digneris: vt per sanctificatione*m* tuam: et per tui sancti nom*in*is inuocationem sint sancti✠ficati et conse✠crati: et recipiant effectus illarum uirtutum quas te docente *et* inspirante comp*er*ti sunt: *et* que illos h*ab*ere i*n* libro de virtutib*us* lapidum scribitur: *et* ut q*ui*cunq*ue* illos super se portauerit: tuam per illos v*ir*tutem sibi adesse cognoscat: *et* dona tue gratie tutela*m* (fol. 36ᵛ) q*ue* tue sancte virtutis vbiq*ue* se h*ab*ere congaudeat. Per D*omin*um n*os*tr*um* Yesu*m* Christu*m* filium tuum qui tecum viuit et regnat in vnitate sp*irit*us Sancti Deus.    Per om*n*ia secula seculorum.

De Custodia Lapidum.

Predicta b*e*nedictione facta h*ab*eantur lapides illi et teneant*ur* custodianturve cum magna reuerentia. Quod enim sanctum est nisi cum sanctitate custodiri non pot*est*. Ne ergo sancte rei violator existat

⁵⁷ Except for a few variant readings of a minor sort, this prayer is the same as that found in the *De natura rerum* of Thomas of Cantimpré (Harvard College Library, Riant MS. 19, f. 76). It is also printed in J. B. Pitra, *Spicilegium solesmense*, Paris 1855, III, 337, in the *Histoire littéraire de la France*, XXX, 371, and in *Buch der Natur*, f. 280ʳ. A slightly different prayer is found in Jean de Mandeville's lapidary (del Sotto, *op. cit.*, pp. 127-8). Rose (*op. cit.*, p. 345) notes that in one of the manuscripts (Prague [mixt.] XI C 2) which contains the lapidary by Arnoldus de Saxonia as well as a *De virtute universali* "den Schluss macht (grade wie in dem sogen. Lapidaire français composé par Jehan de Mandeville, und sonst, aus Thomas) ein Steinsegen (consecratio) zur Herstellung der verlorenen Kräfte der Steine."

q*uoniam* aliquod sanctum portat peccare desistat: ne quod sibi prodesse debet noceat. Ne ve bonu*m* in malum: uel dulce in amarum conuertatur. Obsunt e*n*im multotiens bona malis: cum indigni presumu*n*t de bonis. Cum uero bona prosunt malis: misericordia est. Cum mala prosunt bonis: correctio est. Cum autem bona bonis et mala malis dantu[r]: Iustitia est.

De Coralo.

Coralus secu*n*dum Albertu*m*[58] in suo de min*er*alib*us* Cap*itulo* .iij°. exp*er*tu*m* est q*uod* ualet contra que*m*lib*et* fluxu*m* sangui*n*is: *et* collo suspens*us* dicit*ur* valere co*n*tra epilensia*m*: contra *tem*pestates: fulmina *et* grandines: et q*uod* principia expedit et fines negociorum:[59]

If we assume that Charles VIII actually did read the presentation volume, we must either believe that he did not follow the lapidary's advice or we are forced to the reluctant conclusion that the stones did not really possess the virtues which the present treatise claims for them. As thoughtful as Pamoleus unquestionably was in presenting this gift and as useful as Charles may have believed the manuscript to be, it served the king but ill in his short, unhappy career.

(From *Bulletin of the History of Medicine* 11 (1942), pp. 69-86).

[58] Albertus Magnus, *loc. cit.*, p. 177. One of the English lapidaries states (Evans and Serjeantson, *op. cit.*, p. 125):

It waxeth in the sea as a grass, and when it is out of ye sea it is red and lyke a branch. It is no longer nor greater then halfe a foote. And as old m*ai*str*e*s and authors do wryte, it defendeth and kepeth a man from lightning, thunder, and from tempest of wether. It is good in a vinierd or garden, it defendeth it from tempest. It makes ye fruit to encrease. It helpeth a man from faintness. It geueth man a good beginning and a good ending what contry yt he taketh.

[59] Although the manuscript breaks off abruptly, nothing is wanting as the following (original) leaves are blank.

# CHAPTER T9

## AN UNPUBLISHED MIDDLE HIGH GERMAN
## *BANNTAIDING*

CURT F. BÜHLER AND CARL SELMER

NO less a scholar than Jacob Grimm[1] over a century ago called attention to the inherent value of the German *Weistümer*,[2] particularly as outstanding monuments of old local laws. Two decades later, F. I. Mone[3] in a study of these documents emphasized their great age and their connections with the provisions of the Roman law. While these *Weistümer* (also known as *Banntaiding, Ehehafttaiding, Fischtaiding* etc.) are common to most parts of the German-speaking territory, relatively only a few of those once extant have come down to us; of these the greatest number by far were originally written in Austria and the Alpine provinces. For this reason the *Akademie der Wissenschaften in Wien* set itself the task of publishing all the available local laws for the districts of Salzburg, Tyrol, Styria, Carinthia, Upper and Lower Austria.[4] From the point of view of date,[5] the earliest of these belong

[1] J. Grimm, *Dt. Rechtsaltertümer* (Göttingen, 1828).

[2] H. Wiessner, "Sachinhalt und wirtschaftl. Bedeutung der Weistümer im dt. Kulturgebiet," *Veröffentl. des Seminars für Wirtsch. und Kulturgesch. an der Univ. Wien*, 1934, x, 1 defines *Weistümer* as follows: "Unter Weistum verstehen wir das Ergebnis der Weisungen, wobei wir vor allem an die schriftliche Niederlegung des Resultates der Weisung denken. Von Weisung sprechen wir nur dann, wenn alte, erfahrene, rechtskundige Männer auf amtlichen Antrag hin unter Eid eine Aussage über geltende Rechtsgewohnheit abgeben." For the Meaning of *Taiding*, see also Grimm, *op. cit.*, p. 747.

[3] F. I. Mone, "Weisthümer vom 13. bis 15. Jahrhundert," *Zeitschr. für die Gesch. des Oberrheins* (1850), I, 6.

[4] *Oesterreichische Weisthümer*; I, *Die Salzburgischen Taidinge*, ed. H. Siegel und K. Tomaschek, 1870; II–V, *Die Tirol. Weisthümer*, ed. I, v. Zingerle und K. Th. v. Inama-Sternegg, 1875-1888; VI, *Steirische und Kärnthnische Taidinge*, ed. F. Bischoff und A. Schönbach, 1881; VII-IX, *Niederösterreichische Weisthümer*, ed. G. Winter, 1886-1909; X, *Steirische Taidinge (Nachträge)*, ed. A. Mell und E. F. v. Müller, 1913; XI, *Niederösterreich. Weistümer (Nachträge)*, ed. G. Winter, 1913. Abbreviations will be by volume and page of this edition.

[5] Cf. H. Wiessner, *op. cit.*, "Über Kurvenverlauf der datierten Texte der Winterschen Edition für N. O. Weistümer," p. 26. E. Patzelt, *Entstehung und Charakter der Weistümer in Oesterreich* (Budapest, 1924), p. 67 gives the following figures for the Austrian *Weistümer*: fourteenth century, 30; fifteenth century, 287 (Nieder-

to the thirteenth and fourteenth centuries, though no more than a handful of them have survived. The number of extant *Weistümer* increases greatly in the fifteenth century, achieves its greatest total in the following century and then gradually declines, till after 1800 the *Weistümer* disappear entirely.

Though frequently obscure and difficult to interpret, the *Weistümer* are of the greatest interest not alone for the law historian and the student of medieval folk-lore, but for the philologist as well. To the latter their chief claim to notice lies in the fact that they preserve the everyday language of the people for whom they were compiled, thus retaining in every instance the dialectal peculiarities of a particular community. They are consequently relatively independent of normalizing influences, and may be classified as belonging to the *nidern swanc*, to speak in the terms of Engelbert of Cologne. It is chiefly for this reason that the *Weistümer* are of considerable importance for the student of modern and medieval dialects.

*The manuscript.*[6] The *Banntaiding* (MHG *ban* 'district'; *tagedinc* 'meeting') which is the subject of the present discussion is probably the only one found on this side of the Atlantic and is in private hands.[7] It consists of eight unnumbered parchment pages of the size 70x230 mm. The space covered by the script is 50x180 mm. There are some 25 lines to the page and about 15 letters to a line. The manuscript is nicely and evenly written in light-brown ink, with the exception of the last paragraph which, written over a moist spot, appears black. Red ink is used only sparingly, (a) for the initial letters of the words *Item* 22x,[8] *Es* 1, and *Wer* 10, all of which occur at the beginning of a paragraph; (b) for the *er*-hook in *lewgener* 14; (c) for *R* in *Richter* 7. Furthermore, a red line, drawn across the page, separates the single paragraphs. The red ink was obviously applied

---

österreich 191, Tir. 60, Steierm. 22, Salzb. 12, Kärnten 2); sixteenth century, 529 (Niederösterreich 348, Tir. 90, St. 67, Salzb. 8, Kärnten 16); seventeenth century, 298 (Niederösterreich 166, Tir. 70, St. 40, Salzb. 12, Kärnten 10); eighteenth century, 103; nineteenth century, 8.

[6] The editors gladly take this opportunity to express their thanks to Professor Otto Springer for helpful suggestions and valuable advice.

[7] It is now in the possession of Dr. Curt F. Bühler of New York, who obtained it in 1935 from E. P. Goldschmidt & Co., Ltd., of London. Mr. Goldschmidt states in a letter that the MS came from the well-known Figdor collection of Vienna. Nothing else is known about its provenance. It is now Bühler MS 7.

[8] Numbers after words indicate the paragraph of the MHG text in which the word occurs; 'x' after a number stands for 'times.'

after the MS was written, since the scribe did not allow the red ink
to dry, with the result that an off-set repeatedly appears on the opposite side. The MS is bound in modern parchment with the inscription *Taiding Büchel* on the upper cover. On the last page (4v) is
found the inscription *Täding biechel H 65*, written by a hand of the
eighteenth century. Only two minor corrections (13, 23) and one
erasure (17) occur; once a word is crossed out as the result of a
scribal error.

Capital letters are used only for *I* in *Item* at the beginning of each
paragraph, for *E* in *Er* 1, for *R* in *Raynſtayn* 22, *Rayn* 24 (but *rayn*
in 23) and *Richter* 7. No sign of punctuation is used throughout the
MS. nor is word division indicated by any symbol.

As a means of abbreviation the nasal bar appears frequently. It is
used (a) for *m* 7x (only in *aynem* 4, 9, 23, 29 and *ſeynem* 13, 15, 28)
and in the gemmination 2x (*ſrummen* 14, *chommen* 17, each time
with the bar over the preceding vowel); (b) for *n* in *amptman* 23,
*laynen* 23, *vadrung* 17, *von* 11, *pfening* 15, 16, 22, 25; (c) for *e* in
*haben* 1, *meczen* 2, *ſchaden* 5, *geben* 6, *gaſſen* 8, *chnechten* 11, *willen* 12 etc.; (d) for *em* in *Item* 25x; (e) in the word *ſol* (abbr.) 8x.
The *er*-hook is used very frequently, *e.g. wer* 21x, *oder* 15x, *auer*
3x; in the prefix *ver-* (*verpotnew* 14). Except for one isolated case,
where two dots are used above an *a* (*ſnytärn* 23), no diacritical sign
(and no superscription) is visible.

Doubling of consonants is found frequently, (a) of *l: alls* 3x, *willen* 12; (b) of *ſ: dach troſſen* 4, *ſraſſel* 4; finally *auſſ* 5x, *ſunſſ* 3x;
with *-ſt: oſſt* 2x, *lauſſt* 4x, *chauſſt* 11, *auſgerueſſt* 6, *wegreyſſt* 19;
(c) of *t: vertt* 27, *ſpantt* 25, *matt* 24, *ſneytt* 23, *vber ſnitt* 23, *tatt* 23;
(d) of *s: gaſſen* 8; (e) of *p: dewpp, dewppin* 28.

The following symbols have been used to express the *s*-sound: (a)
German long ſ, initially and medially; also in composition, *e.g. auſgerueſſt* 6, *hawſgeſind* 11, *auſtrayt* 12; (b) German round *s* at the
end of words; this symbol sometimes resembles the *sz*-letter of the
so-called Gothic script; (c) *zz e.g.* in *mazz* 1. Only one *r*-symbol is
found, the regular German *r*, which, when used as capital letter, is
merely enlarged.

Some of the striking features of consonantism are as follows: The
*b*-sounds are rendered (a) by *p, e.g. prantew* 1, *pranten* 2, *pot* 3,
*pringt* 10, 28, *peſſrung* 11, 26, *verpotnew* 14, *pey* 14, *pankch* 14,
*panczewn* 20, *pan garten* 20, *prechen* 29; (b) by *w, e.g. wegreyſſt*
19; (c) by *u, e.g. auer* 3x; (d) vocalization is seen in *geyth* 14, *geyt*

17, 27. The *g*-sounds appear (a) as *kch, e.g. dreyſikch* 25; (b) as *k, e.g. leykeb* 1; (c) vocalized, *e.g. auſtrayt* 12. The *k*-sounds are written (a) initially *ch, e.g. chommen* 17, *chumpt* 21, *chayn* 6, *chnechten* 11, *chinder* 11, *chaufft* 11; (b) medially and finally *kch, e.g. czukcht* 5, *ab hakcht* 18, *ſtekchen* 18, *pankch* 14. The labial spirans appears as *v*, or as *f*. Initially *f* is used before consonants, *e.g. fraffel* 4, *fraueler* 14, *frummen* 14, *gefritt* 20; *v* appears before vowels, *e.g. vertt* 27, *vadrung* 17; but *funff* 22, *fenſter* 9, *fuder* 19; at the end of a word always *ff, e.g. auff* 5x, *funff* 3x; doubling also in the nexus *-ft, e.g. offt* 2x, *chaufft* 11, *wegreyfft* 19, *laufft* 4, *auſgeruefft* 6; doubling in the medial position is rare, *e.g. dach troffen* 4, *fraffel* 4. The affricate is indicated by *ph, e.g. phlichtig* 24, *phunt* 5x, but *pfening* 4x. In the writing of the dental sounds no peculiar feature is shown, except once *th* in *geyth* 14. The shifted *s*-sound appears (a) as *ſſ, e.g. peſſrung* 11; (b) as *cz, e.g. czeit* 23, *czway* 25, *czawn* 18; (c) as *zz, e.g. mazz* 1.

Some of the important features of vocalism are as follows: The *i*-sounds are rendered (a) by *y, e.g. dy* 23, *ſnytärn* 23; (b) by *ie, e.g. wiert* 13, 15, 23; (c) by *ye, e.g. dyern* 11; (d) by *j*, chiefly before nasals, *e.g. jn* 6, 13, 14, 26; *jm* 7, 24. The *o*-sound appears as *a, e.g. wart* 14, *vadrung* 17, and *u* is written *ue* (before r) once in *nuer* 29. Occasionally *-ew* appears (a) for acc. pl. masc., *e.g. dew halben* 21; (b) for acc. pl. neuter, *e.g. verpotnew wart* 14; (c) for acc. sg. fem., *e.g. prantew mazz* 1, *allew vadrung* 17, *allew genad* 26. The old diphthongs are expressed (a) by *ai, e.g. aynem* 4, *chain* 6, *gemayn* 25, *czway* 25, *rayn* 23; (b) by *au, e.g. auch* 4x, *chaufft* 11; (c) by *ie, e.g. liecht* 8; (d) by *ew, e.g. dewpp* 28, *dewppin* 28, *ſchweſt* 25; (e) by *ue, e.g. guet* 27, *tuet* 20, etc. The new diphthongs appear (a) as *ei, e.g. czeit* 23; as *ey, e.g. ſeynem* 13; (b) as *au, e.g. auſtrayt* 12; as *aw, e.g. haws* 26; (c) as *ey, e.g. leyten* 14, etc. Umlaut is rarely indicated and appears written (a) as *ä*, only once, in *ſnytärn* 23; (b) as *e, e.g. aws grebt* 22, *vertt* 27; (c) as *ew, e.g. panczewn* 20; (d) as *ue, e.g. tuer* 29.

Apocope and syncope can be observed in the text, *e.g.* (a) with the indefinite article *ain* 12, 14, 18, 28 and with *chayn* 6; (b) in the 3rd p. sg. pr., *e.g. ſneytt* 23, *leyt* 15; (c) in connection with the prefix *ge-* of the past part., *e.g. prantew* 1, *tan* 26 (but *getan* 4 and *genad* 26); (d) with a noun, *e.g. rechtn* 27; (e) with the 3rd p. sg. pr., *e.g. ſiech* 10. Reverse spelling is seen in *halben* 21 for *halm*. Two other dialectal peculiarities are (a) the use of the prefix *der-* (for *er*) *e.g.*

*der get* 5; (b) MHG *gên* is always rendered with the *e*-form, *e.g.* *get* 5, 8, 22; *gen* 13.

*Age of the manuscript:* The date of the manuscript under discussion is not given and is only ascertainable from such paleographical criteria as the handwriting and orthography afford.[9] These would date the manuscript as belonging to the fifteenth century, probably in the first half, but certainly not much after 1450. The first part of the fifteenth century is likewise suggested when one compares the contents and form of the provisions in the present text with those found in the other Austrian *Weistümer*. The regulations are more awkwardly worded and less elaborate in scope than those found in the other printed versions.[10] The manuscript is not, of course, an original composition but is only a copy, possibly extracted from a lost code of local laws.

*Text:*  1 (1r) Es[a] ſchol yeder leykeb ayn prantew mazz haben oder er iſt lxij[b] ϑ zu wandel

2 Item welicher nicht ayn pranten meczen hat der gerecht ſey der iſt lxij ϑ zu wandel

3 Item ain pot wandel lxxij ϑ

4 Item wer aynem laufft vnter ſein dach troffen der iſt ij vnd ſechs ſchillig[c] ϑ czu wandel wen er hat ayn fraffel getan

5 Item wer czukcht der iſt xij ϑ zu wandel iſt das es an ſchaden der get

6 Item es ſchol auch chayn leykeb chayn wein nicht tewrer[d] geben den er jn hat aufgeruefft

7 Item er ſchol jn auch her geben dy weil er wein hat oder der Richter oder der ampt[e] ſchol jm den nemen

---

[a] Abbreviations used in the text were resolved only then when no other resolution was possible. The symbol for penny is here represented by ϑ.

[b] Should read lxxij?          [c] Nasal bar forgotten.

[d] MS reads *tewer* (with *-er* abbr.).          [e] *amptman*; no abbr. visible.

[9] The handwriting resembles most closely that of *Codex Germanicus Monacensis* 576, shown in E. Petzet and O. Glauning, *Deutsche Schriﬀttafeln aus Papierhandschriﬀten des XIV. bis XVI. Jahrhunderts*, v (Leipzig, 1930), Tafel LX. It is a fifteenth-century manuscript of South German origin.

[10] This gradual expansion of the provisions of the single paragraphs should be of great interest not only to the student of law and economics, but also to the Germanist. These *Weistümer* offer many interesting examples for the study of quantitative and qualitative differences between *Konzept*, *Vorlage*, *Niederschrift* and *Überarbeitung*.

8 (1v) Item wer mit liecht get auff der gaſſen der iſt vmb ij vnd vj ſōlᶠ

9 Item wer aynem an ſein haws oder an ſeyn fenſterᵍ der iſt ij vnd vj ſōlᶠ zu wandel

10 Wer das ſiech vnd pringt es nicht an den amptman der iſt vmb lxij ❡

11 Item wer von chnechten oder von dyern oder von ayns chinder oder hawſgeſind chaufft der iſt in meynes herren peſſrung

12 Item wer aym wiert oder wiertin ſein czech auſtrayt vber ſein willen der iſt vmb ij vnd vj ſōlᶠ

13 Item wer ayn wiert oder aynʰ wirtin noten wil jn ſeynem haws vnd wil nicht aws (2r) gen der iſt vmb ij ❡ vnd vj ſōlᶠ ❡

14 Item wer dem andern verpotnew wart geyth oder hayſt jn lewgenerⁱ oder vnendleich oder ſlecht pey frummen leyten jn ayn tiſch oder auff ayn pankch der iſt aynᵏ fraulerˡ ij vnd vj ſōlᶠ ❡

15 Item welicher wiert ſpilen leyt jn ſeynem haws der iſt vmb funff phunt pfening

16 Item wer dan ſpilt der iſt auch vmb funff phunt pfening

17 Item wer nicht allew vadrung geyt alls es von alter her chommen iſt der iſt lxij ❡ zu wandel

18 (2v) Item wer ayn ſtekchen ab hakcht auff aynem czawn der iſt xij ❡ zu wandel als offt er das tuet

19 Item wer czawnholcz fuder trayt es ſein ſpelten oder ſtekchen oder gerten alls offt man jn da mit wegreyfft xij ❡ zu wandel

20 Item Es ſchullen auch all panczewn vnd all pan garten zu ſand Jorigen tag gefritt ſein wer des nicht tuet der iſt lxij ❡ zu wandel

21 Item wer jn dew halben treybt ee das der trayd her awꙅ chumpt der iſt vmb ij ❡ vnd vmb vbj ſōlᶠ ❡ (3r)

22 Item wer Raynſtayn aws grebt oder aws czakcherᵐ get der iſt vmb funff phunt pfening zu wandel

23 Item wer aynem vber ſein rayn ſneytt wer auer das tan dasⁿ der wiert dy ſelbig czeit nicht pey den ſnytärn wer ſo

---

ᶠ Elongated abbr. bar over -*ol*.  ᵍ Verb omitted; suggested: *lost*.
ʰ Abbr. hook for -*er* over *ayn* crossed out.  ⁱ -er hook in red.
ᵏ After *ayn* erasure of three letters.  ˡ MS reads *frauel*; -er hook forgotten.
ᵐ Nasal bar forgotten.  ⁿ Correction: *s* over *n*.

ſchol er den vber ſnitt hin wider dem an ſein trayd laynen tatt er auer des nicht ſo iſt er dem der ſchaden gefallen dem der vber ſnitt geſchehen iſt vnd dem amptman ij vnd vj ſōl° zu wandel

24 Item wer aynē vber ſein Rayn matt[p] vnd lat jms nicht ligen an der mad ſo iſt er jm ſeyner ſchaden phlichtig vnd ij vnd vj ſōl° zu wandel (3v)

25 Item ayner der da ſpantt vnd ſchewſt vnter ayn gemayn der iſt czway vnd dreyſikch phunt pfening zu wandel

26 Wer auer das tan das er aynē[q] jn ſein haws ſchewſt ſo iſt[r] jn meynes herrn peſſrung[s] gefallen[t] an allew genad

27 Item ſo hat meynes herrn guet vnd grunt das rechtn[u] wer aws vertt der geyt ij ϑ der dann jn vertt auch ij ϑ

28 Item wer ayn dewpp oder ayn dewppin jn hat jn ſeynem haws vnd ways das vnd pringt es nicht an dy herſchafft oder an den amptman (4r) der iſt alles des gefallen alls der dewpp vnd dy dewppin

29 Item wer aynē dringt vmb ſein tuer oder vmb ſein tor vnd wil nuer auff dringen oder prechen der iſt funff phunt zu wandel zc

[o] Elongated abbr. bar over -*ol*.     [p] *m* looks like capital *m*.
[q] Probable resolution *aynem*.     [r] Supply *er*.
[s] Word division *pes srung* (two long *s*-symbols), but no division symbol visible.
[t] After *gefallen, auff* crossed out; clerical error?     [u] Nasal bar for *e* missing?

*Contents and comments:* As one may readily perceive from the preceding text, we are here dealing with a *Banntaiding*—that is, a compilation of local customs, rights and privileges, made for the needs of a village or hamlet. The seignoral character of the text is clearly indicated by the use of indicative words, such as *herschafft* (28), *herrn* (26, 27), and *amptman* (7, 10, 23). In view of the fact that this manuscript may be of interest not only to the student of languages but also to the student of medieval law, it has been thought desirable to make the contents of this document available in a free translation rather than a literal one, with the emphasis placed chiefly on the sense. A few explanatory remarks have been appended.

No. 1: "Any one who sells wine must have a gauged (branded) measure or he is fined 62 pennies." Parallel passages with similar wording or in a slightly revised form may be found in other collections of by-laws. A *Taiding* of St. Lambrecht (VI, 237) reads: . . . *soll und mag auch der landrichter die maaß besichten und messen, und ob er die nit recht findet* . . . Another document of Pürg (vi, 23) says: *Item die weinschenk oder leitgeben sollen rechte lantmaß inner und außerhalb dem hauß geben.* Likewise a *Weistum* of Mayenburg (v, 171) stipulates: *Item, wer wein schenkt, der soll die geschworn maß haben, als von alter her recht ist.* Of interest is the word *leykeb* (MHG *lítgebe*; cf. M. Lexer, *Mhd. HWb.* i, 1939) which must have been widespread throughout the South Bavarian territory in the fifteenth century. It occurs in documents from the Wienerwald (*leykgeb* in Kirchschlag vii, 9; *leickab* in Gutenstein vii, 352), through Styria and Carinthia (*leitgeb, leutgeb* in Pürg vi, 23; St. Lambrecht vi, 236; Millstadt vi, 474; Ratten vi, 150), and to Tyrol (*leitgeb* in Vilanders v, 255; Passeier v, 102; Sterzing v, 428). In the last-named territory it is still found as a family name in modern times.[11] It designates a person licensed to sell new wine.[12] The fine (*wandel,* cf. M. Lexer, *op. cit.,* iii, 670) amounting to 62 pennies is quite unusual, since nowhere else in the mass of Austrian *Weistümer* does the odd amount of '62' pennies occur.

No. 2: "Whosoever has not a branded measure of the proper size will be fined 62 pennies." The measure in question is the *Müllermetzen,* a dry measure used chiefly for grain. A miller was allowed the thirtieth part of such a *Metzen* for his work. Many other Austrian documents call attention to a 'right measure,' as *e.g.* a *Banntaiding* of Spital (vi, 57) which reads: *Item, ain jeder so ain mühl hat in der gegent, den leuten mahlt und mahlen will, der soll haben ain gerechts mäßl, der sollen an ainem mezen gehen* xxxij, *damit er seine maut nimbt.*

No. 3: "The fine for a warning or special notification is 72 pennies." The expression *pot wandel* is a legal term and can be identified in this form only in three Austrian *Banntaidinge,* one from Salzburg (Anthering i, 72: *potwandl*), one from Tyrol (Windisch-Matrei i, 306: *pottwandl*), and one from Lower Austria (Pechlarn xi, 421: *Item ain potwandel* 72 *phenning*). In a few parallel cases this expression is resolved, *e.g.* in Ziegersberg (Lower Austria) xi, 3: *Item, welcher verbeut und gett dem verpott nicht nach, der ist.* . . .

---

[11] Concerning *Leikauf, 'Gelöbnistrunk beim Abschluss eines Handels* . . . *auf bayr. österreichischem Gebiet,'* cf. F. Kluge, *Etym. Wb. der dt. Sprache* (Berlin, 1924), p. 301. For other combinations, cf. Lexer, *op. cit.,* i, 1939.

[12] In this respect cf. J. A. Schmeller, *Bayer. Wb.,* i, 1535 (quoting Castelli, *Wbch.* 187): "Wenn die österreichischen Weinbauern ihren Wein geerntet haben, und derselbe trinkbar geworden ist, so wird vom Amte Jedem in der Reihe das Recht ertheilt Wein auszuschenken, und dieses nennt man: *laidgöbn.*"

No. 4: "Whosoever violates another's privacy by entering his house is to be fined '2 and 6 shillings' because (if) he has committed an offence." The word *dach troffen* (eaves) means the passage under the veranda which surrounded the houses on all sides in the Austrian-Alpine districts, this being regarded as the boundary of the house.[12a] The punishment for killing an intruder, who was killed by the owner under the 'eaves,' was rather lenient. In this respect says Franz Arens:[13] "Aber namentlich die feindselige Nachfolge unter eines ehrlichen Mannes 'trupfstal' (Dachtraufe) ist eine schwere Rechtsverletzung, deren Tragweite sich mit dem Eindringen in das Haus noch steigert." The spelling of this word can be various: *dachtropfen, dachtrafn, dachtrauf, tagtrafn,* etc. The examples nearest to the spelling of *dach troffen* of our manuscript are those found in *Taidinge* of Styria and Lower Austria, *e.g.* Pürg (vi, 24): *Es soll niemant dem andern fröflich unter sein tachtropfen nachvolgen, noch schlachen*; Wolkenstein (vi, 31): *So er unter den dachtrophen kumbt*; Neusiedel (Lower Austria), vii, 133: *Als weit der tachtropfen wehrt*; Hettmannsdorf (vii, 181): *unter der dachtropfen*; Krummbach vii, 15: *unter der dachtropfen*. In Tyrol, however, one encounters the spelling *truphstall, e.g.* in Latzfons (v, 360): *unter sein truphstall.*

No. 5: "Whosoever draws (a weapon) is to be fined 12 pennies, if no harm was done." The brandishing of weapons is here called *zucken* (NHG *zücken*) in a general sense, although this word is mostly used in the transitive meaning in other texts. A *Banntaiding* of Edlitz (viii, 47) says: *Item, so ainer zuckt ain stain* ... Another document of Reichenau (vi, 68) reads: *Ob ainer uber den andern ain swert, messer, hackn, stecken, spies, degen, stecher, tiliz oder anderlai weer oder waffen auszuckät* ... Wangen (v, 199), too, forbids the use of weapons, saying: *Item schwert und messer zucken ist die peen funf phunt.* Of interest is the prefix *der-* in *der get,* which replaces the more common prefix *er-*. This specific Bavarian prefix appears *e.g.* in a *Recht* of Gugging, near Klosterneuburg (ix, 3): *ob das ân schaden derget,* and in a *Banntaiding* of Stolzenwert (vii, 264): *als oft ain rain der gedt.*

[12a] Cp. in this respect F. S. Lear, "The Public Law of the Ripuarian, Alamannic and Bavarian Codes," *Medievalia et Humanistica,* Fasc. ii (1944), p. 23, who points to similar old enactments in the *Lex Baiuvariorum,* 10, 1: *Si curtem dissipaverit aut inruperit liber liberi, cum tribus solidis componat, et restituat damnum.*

[13] *Das Tiroler Volk in seinen Weistümern* (Gotha, 1904), p. 161.

No. 6: "No one who sells wine shall charge more than the announced (official) price." This provision, reminding us in some ways of the price regulations of our OPA, binds the seller of wine to the price set at the beginning of the season at a communal meeting. This regulation to 'call out the prices' is reflected in a similar *Weistum*, the *Ordnung* of Hartperg (vi, 126) which reads: *sollen . . . ausgeruefft . . . werden.*

No. 7: "Any one who has wine shall sell it, or the judge or bailiff shall take it away." This is an extension of the preceding regulation and prevents the owner of wine from refusing to sell it.

No. 8: "Whosoever walks with light (burning torches) through the streets is to be fined '2 and 6 sol.'" This regulation, due to the scribe's tendency to condensation which occasionally lends itself to misunderstandings, appears at first glance curious enough. A comparison with other Weistümer, however, affords the necessary explanation, in which it is made clear that only a drunken person, who might become a fire hazard was forbidden to wander around with burning torches. The *Banntaiding* of Edlitz (vii, 48) *e.g.* enjoins every host not to give a drunkard a torch: *So ain leitgebe ainem trunknen ain liecht gibt auß dem hauß* . . . A peculiarity of the manuscript is the use of *sol.*[14] which occurs seven more times in the manuscript, always in the abbreviation and in the nexus *ij vnd vj sol.* The use of *sol.* is open to two interpretations. It may be possible that it represents only a contraction for *solidus (Schilling)*,[14a] reminding us of the present-day use of L.s.d. in English coinage. On the other hand another solution is that *sol.* stands for *soldin* and represents a coin of small value which must have fallen into disuse in Austria toward the end of the fifteenth century, since it cannot be found in any of the hundreds of *Weistümer* of the Austrian territory. The *soldin* does, however, appear in the works of Oswald von Wolkenstein,[15] whose language shows characteristics of the South

[14] Concerning the use of the *solidus pacis* as a fine *(Friedeschilling)* cf. E. Haberkorn and F. F. Wallach, *Hilfswörterbuch für Historiker*, 1935, p. 518. For its name and spread in France and Italy cf. Fr. v. Schrötter, *Wb. der Münzkunde* (Berlin, 1930), pp. 641–642.

[14a] See, for example, the Latin-German gloss "Solidus ein schilling" in the *Vocabularius Arra* of the Sachsenspiegel (Augsburg, 1517), as printed by G. Kisch, *Zeitschr. der Savigny-Stiftung f. Rechtsgeschichte*, German, Abt., vol. 44 (1924), p. 315.

[15] Cf. M. Lexer, *Mhd. HWb.*, ii, 1052. On Oswald's language cf. F. Maurer, "Beiträge zur Sprache Oswalds von Wolkenstein," *Giessener Beiträge zur dt. Philologie*, 1922, iii, 66 ff.

Bavarian, particularly Tyrolian, dialect. This monetary unit, which is known to have been coined in Venice (1329) and Milan[16] (1400), is not the only coin introduced into Austria from the adjacent Italy; one need only recall the *Agler* (coined in Aquileia) and *Berner* (coined in Verona) which are mentioned so frequently in the Austrian *Weistümer.*[17]

No. 9: "Whosoever eavesdrops at someone's house or window makes himself liable to a fine of '2 and 6 sol.'" Due to the scribe's carelessness the verb of this sentence is omitted. Fortunately, a comparison with other *Weistümer* supplies the wanting word. The *Ordnung* of Wolkenstein (VI, 31) reads as follows: *Item wer ainem an seinem hauß und venster lost, den sol man straffen.* A similar verb is suggested in the *Freiheit und Gerechtigkeit* of Krummbach (VII, 15): *Item, welcher an aines erbern man hauß lißnet oder an seinem fenster bei der nacht stet* . . . and in a *Taiding* of Donnersbach (VI, 19): *Das chainer dem andern an den venstern lüsmen sol, noch vensterpret noch tür in stozz.* . . . A synonym is used in a *Taiding* of Spital (VI, 58) which reads as follows: *Item ob ainer aim am fenster zuehört bei nacht oder tag, wierdt er beschrieren, so* . . . The grave aspect of such eavesdropping is elucidated by the sentence immediately following the above (Spital) regulation: *Dan es ist zu schäzen für diept und mörderei.* The slaying of such an eavesdropper was not considered a crime, as a *Weistum* of Stratzing (VIII, 905) reveals: *Item, wer auch aim lusmet an sein haus oder venster und siecht es der wirt und chumpt heraus und slecht den lusmer ze tod, so ist der wirt niemant phlichtig.*

No. 10: "Whosoever observes an eavesdropper and does not call it to the attention of the bailiff shall be fined 62 pennies." This regulation refers obviously to the preceding paragraph.

No. 11: "Whosoever buys from farmhands, servant-girls, children, or domestics is liable to be punished by the lord of the manor."

No. 12: "Whosoever leaves without paying his account to the host or hostess is to be fined '2 and 6 sol.'" The expression *die czech austragen*[18] occurs only once in the Austrian *Weistümer, i.e.* in Altenthan, near Salzburg (I, 19) which reads as follows: *das er die zech*

---

[16] Cf. E. Martinori, *La Moneta* (Roma, 1915), p. 481.

[17] The following *Wandelbeträge* (fines) are used: *Agler, Denare, Schillinge, Dukaten, Gulden, Kreuzer, Thaler, Mark, Pfund, Pfennige, Vierer,* and *Zwanziger.*

[18] Concerning Alemannic parallels cf. H. Fischer, *Schwäb. Wb.*, VI, 1071 and *ibid.,* I, 530: *Wer ainem Wirt Win usstregt in ain Zech oder wa hin das ist.*

*aus hob getragen und nit bezalt.* A similar wording, however, is found in a *Rechtsbuch* of Brixen (v, 390): *Es sol auch niemant chainem leitgeben sein wein auztragen ân seinen willen,* in the *Rechte* of Grinzing (vii, 937): *der einem sein wein austrueg,* and in a *Taiding* of Wienersdorf (vii, 504) which says: *Wer einem seinen wein auß trueg.*

No. 13: "Whosoever abuses a host or hostess in his house and refuses to leave is subject to a fine of '2 and 6 sol.'" In the same sense, the verb *noten* (MHG *noeten,* NHG *nötigen*) is used in other Bavarian documents, *e.g.* in Heinrich von Neustadt's '*Apollonius von Tyrland.*'[19]

No. 14: "Whosoever uses invectives against another or calls him a liar, disorderly or vile in the presence of other (respectable) people in public (at table or on a bench) is an offender (transgressor) and is to be fined '2 and 6 sol.'" The expression *verpotnew wart* is not infrequently found in the Austrian territory, particularly in Styria, Carinthia and Tyrol (*e.g.* in St. Gallen vi, 40; Spital vi, 57; Millstadt vi, 475; Unzmarkt vi, 258; Pürg vi, 23; Donnersbach vi, 18 etc.). The adjective *vnendleich,* however, was used rather sparingly in Austrian *Weistümer* and was replaced by other adjectives at a later date. In the meaning 'useless, disorderly' (cf. M. Lexer, *Mhd. HWb,* ii, 1818) it appears in the *Rechte und Banntaiding* of Matzleindorf, near Vienna (vii, 757): ... *unendleich leut, diep oder wie si genant sein.* ... In the same connection this adjective is used in a *Taiding* of Erdberg (xi, 130). Although it cannot be found in Tyrolian[20] and Styrian *Weistümer,* it may well have been part of the Tyrolese-Styrian vocabulary at the time when our manuscript was written. In the phrase *vnendleich versprochene frauwen* it is used in the fourteenth-century *Würzburger Polizei Gesetzbuch* of Bishop Otto von Wolffskeel.[21] Occasionally it seems to have been displaced by the expression *unehelich,* as shown *e.g.* in the *Rechte des Stiftes Göss* (vi, 299) in Styria (*unehelich leut*).

No. 15: "Any host or hostess who permits gambling in his house is to be fined 5 pounds (pennies)."

No. 16: "Whosoever gambles is subject to a fine of 5 pounds (pennies)." These two regulations dealing with gambling are here

[19] Cf. S. Singer, "Apollonius von Tyrland, nach der Gothaer Handschrift," *Dt. Texte des Mittelalters* (Berlin, 1906), vii, v. 7124.
[20] For its use in the Alemannic territory cf. H. Fischer, *Schwäb. Wb.,* vi, 1, 136 ff.
[21] Ed. A. Ruland (Würzburg, 1851), p. 89.

phrased in very general terms. Other *Weistümer* usually specify the hours or days during which it is forbidden to gamble or play cards. A *Taiding* of St. Lambrecht (vi, 237) *e.g.* reads as follows: *Der wiert und weinschenkn sollen an sambstag nachtens und an andern heiligen abenten, auch hochzeitlichen festen alß unser frawen, zwelfpotten und andern heiligen tagen in irn heüsern nit spillen noch karten lassen bei der pueß des spillgelts und noch darzue lxxij ϑ.* Only Krumbach (vii, 16) has a general regulation: *Item, welcher in den heußern spilt, der ist verfallen 1 tal. ϑ. Item, welcher wiert es gestat ist auch verfallen 1 tal. ϑ.*

No. 17: "Whosoever will not pay his bills according to the custom handed down from olden times is to be fined 62 pennies." The word *vadrung* is found only once in Austrian *Weistümer.* A *Stiftsrecht* of Gasthof, near Rastadt (vi, 2), reads as follows: *vmb meins herren von Admund vadrung*; the form *vodrung*, however, is found more frequently, *e.g. ibid., dinst vnd vodrung*; Donnersbach (vi, 17): *vodrung*, etc.

No. 18: "Whosoever chops off a stick from a fence is to be fined 12 pennies, as often as he does so." This regulation, common to many *Taidinge* of Austria, is found in almost the same wording in Spital (vi, 57): *Item wehr ain steken oder mehr in aim zaun . . . abbricht . . .*

No. 19: "Whosoever removes wood intended for the construction of fences, be it pickets, sticks or twigs, is to be fined 12 pennies, as often as he is caught so doing." This regulation, as well as the preceding one, points out the importance of fences for restraining cattle from doing damage. Wood used for the repair of fences was usually placed along the road wherever it was needed, and the removal of it (*fuder tragen*) was, of course, punishable. The word *fuder* is found occasionally in *Taidinge* of the South Bavarian territory, *e.g.* in St. Gallen (vi, 36), Gstatt (vi, 48), and St. Lambrecht (vi, 225). It is also found in *Apollonius von Tyrland* (*op. cit.*, p. 334) which originated in this section.

No. 20: "All communal fences have to be repaired and all communal gardens have to be fenced in by St. George's Day. Whosoever does not do so will be fined 62 pennies." Here one finds provisions for the care of fences and gardens belonging to the community (situated within the *ban*). The date, when such work was to be finished, was the feast of St. George, April 23rd. This day, a favorite calendar date from which to reckon, is used very frequently not only in Austrian *Weistümer* (*e.g.* Sterzing v, 434, Reichenau vi, 69, Krummbach vii, 16, Spital vi, 57, Erlach vii, 91, etc.) but also in German *Weistümer*.[22] A similar admonition, without stipulating a specific date, is found in a *Banntaiding* of Fischbach, which says as follows: *Wer nitt zu rechter zeit fridt hat* ... A synonym for MHG *friden* is used in a document of Gschaid (vi, 155): *wan einer zeunet ader fridet.* ...

No. 21: "Whosoever uses the fields as pasturage before the crops are removed is to be fined '2 and 6 sol.'" Here extreme care is enjoined lest damage be done to the crops by cattle, which at the end of the harvest were permitted to graze in the stubblefields.[23] In this sense a Tyrolese *Taiding* of Sterzing (v, 431) states: *Item wer dem andern in sein helme treibt, ee er gar geschnitten hat* ... Only after the haulms, left over from the harvest, had been gathered and removed, were the cattle let into the fields. Therefore, *vmb halben rechen* is used in a *Taiding* of Falkenberg (viii, 693). The masculine form for *trayd* (crops), used in the manuscript under discussion, appears only twice in Austrian *Weistümer, i.e.* in Windisch-Matrei (i, 314) in Tyrol: *wen man den getraid verkaufen welle* ... and in Külb (xi, 500) in Lower Austria: *alle jahr und iede zeit als der getraid sein markt hat.*

No. 22: "Whosoever removes or ploughs up a boundary stone is to be fined five pounds (pennies)." This regulation appears in a similar wording in various *Weistümer* in Austria. Thus the *Ordnung* of Wolkenstein (vi, 31) says: *Item welcher die march oder rainstain verkörte oder ausgrueb* ... and a *Banntaiding* of Ziegersberg (xi, 3) reads: *Welche die wärn, die wollten verdilgen march oder rainstain.* ... Another *Taiding,* originating from Spital (vi, 57), stipulates: *Item wehr rainstain mit willen aus grebt, aus reit oder sonst verdilge, der ist umb* v £ ϑ *wandlfellig.* Of some interest is the agglutination of *z* to the verb in *czacker* (NHG *zu ackern*).[24]

No. 23: "Whosoever mows across his boundary line, when the owner is not at that time with the mowers, shall return the over-cut crop onto his neighbor's field (crop); if he fails to do so, he is re-

---

[22] Cf. J. Grimm, *Dt. Weistümer,* i, 1391.

[23] J. A. Schmeller, *op. cit.,* i, 1094 explains '*halm*' as 'die *Stoppeln auf einem abjeärnteten Getreideacker*'; he documents the spelling *Helbemen* in the following passage (*eod. loco*): *Ir Viech in den Helbemen für den hüeter schlagen.*

[24] For its use in Alemannic districts, cf. H. Fischer, *Schwäb. Wb.,* vi, 1, 1272 ff. For Bavarian examples, see O. Mausser, *Mittelhochdeutsche Grammatik* (München, 1932), 515: z'Minga.

sponsible for damages to the one beyond whose ridge the crop has been mowed, and he is to be fined '2 and 6 sol.' by the bailiff."

No. 24: "Whosoever mows across his neighbor's boundary and does not leave the grass or grain at the spot where it has been mown is responsible for the damage done to him and shall be fined '2 and 6 sol.'" This regulation, together with the preceding one, deals with agricultural misdemeanors through reaping beyond boundary lines; such provisions are not infrequently found in the Austrian territory.

No. 25: "Whosoever shoots a cross-bow in a community is to be fined 32 pounds (pennies)."

No. 26: "Whosoever has shot into (in) someone's house, incurs my lord's punishment without mercy." This regulation, as well as the preceding one forbidding the brandishing of arms, clearly refers to the use of a crossbow. Similarly a *Taiding* of Wangen (IV, 200) stipulates: *Item, wer ain armbrust fräventlichen spannt ist funf phunt, er leg ain pfeil auf oder nit, scheust er aber.* . . . Another *Weistum* of Krummbach (VII, 15) says: *Item welcher ain armbst spant und scheust nit.* . . . A document of Reichenau (VI, 69) reads as follows: *Ob ainer ain armst auf einen andern spannet, er schies oder schies nit.* . . .

No. 27: "Whosoever by driving out or driving in crosses my lord's property, whenever he has the right of way, shall pay 2 pennies." Of interest is the form *geyt* (*geyth* in no. 14; *geit* in no. 17) encountered frequently in the Bavarian and Alemannic territories. Examples for Tyrol and Salzburg are given in *Weistümer* of Frauenchiemsee (II, 4), Axams (II, 254), and Partchins (V, 32). But also Styria and Carinthia furnish some examples, *e.g.* Stralleck (VI, 151), Dürnstein (VI, 243), Admont (VI, 269), St. Dionisen (VI, 320), Gmünd (VI, 465), St. Gallen (VI, 36), etc.

No. 28: "Whosoever harbors a thief, male or female, in his house and does not bring it to the attention of the manorial authorities or the bailiff, makes himself as liable as the thief." The legal term *fallen*, as used in this paragraph, is not uncommon in Austrian *Weistümer* and appears in various combinations. The *Landrecht im Zillerthal* (I, 320), *e.g.* offers the following paragraph: *wer des nicht tät, der ist ainem pfleger gevallen mit leib und mit guet* and a *Taiding* of the *Oetzthal und Umhausen* (III, 74) reads as follows: *were das überfür, der ist gevallen umb das wandel.*

No. 29: "Whosoever presses against a door or gate with the (sole) intent of entering the house is to be fined 5 pounds." In this regulation, forbidding illegal entry, one finds the well-known expression *tuer und tor*, so frequently used in *Taidinge*[25] and popular literature.[26]

*Dialect of the manuscript:* Although the manuscript is too short to permit the most outstanding characteristics of a dialect to be represented, it is quite possible on the basis of the preceding discussion to arrive at a definition of the dialect. The following criteria of a grammatical, orthographical and lexicographical nature permit one to draw pertinent conclusions: (a) Shift of initial *ķ*; (b) delabialization of *o*; (c) vocalizations; (d) frequent use of apocope and syncope;[27] (e) use of the prefix *der-*; (f) affricate spelling of the hardened final media.[28] These criteria, together with numerous other examples of specific dialectal words, indicate that the dialect of the manuscript is South Bavarian.[29]

It would certainly not be an easy task would one try to localize the manuscript even more definitely within the periphery of the South Bavarian limits. First of all, the text is not sufficiently long to make a thorough comparison with contemporary texts of the Alpine-Bavarian group possible. In addition, this group itself covers a rather small territory and forms a very homogeneous dialectal unit, making it well-nigh impossible to arrive at further useful subdivisions. Furthermore, the very nature of the text presents considerable difficulties, since we are here dealing with a document not written in the literary language but in the common parlance of its day, which one may call *Sprechbairisch*.[30] Only very few works written in non-literary lan-

[25] Cf. J. Grimm, *Dt. Weistümer*, III, 721.

[26] For an example in an (Alemannic) Priamel, cf. C. Selmer and C. R. Goedsche, "The Priamel Manuscript of the Newberry Library, Chicago," *PMLA*, LIII, 76.

[27] Cf. O. Mausser, *Mhd. Grammatiķ* (München, 1932), p. 53: "Das Bairische ist jenes mhd. Mundartgebiet, in dem am stärksten apokopiert und synkopiert wird." For additional references, see p. 517.

[28] *Ibid.*, p. 63.

[29] Among documents, which are locally and chronologically near the present one, is above all *Seifrits Alexander,* ed. P. Gereke, *Dt. Texte des Mittelalters* (Berlin, 1932), XXXVI, which agrees most nearly in practically all peculiarities with our manuscript. In the following a few agreements are pointed out, the number behind the word indicating each time the verse in Alexander: *chommen: cham* 99; *panķch: danķch* 7; *wegreyfft: offenwar* 365; *phlichtig: phlicht* 68; *wart: wart* 13, 130; *siech: sag* 21; *ain: ain* 685; *der get: derfaullen* 3775, *derwert* 4617, *derschaint* 5320, *derfuer* 233; *dreysiķch: gesanķch* 264; *wiert: wierd* 2105; *dew: dew* 3098; *nuer: nuer* 54, 516; *guet, tuen: guetten* 5; *tuen* 7; *auf-: auf-* 26, 4932, etc. Frequent agreements are also seen in Heinrich von Neustadt's '*Apollonius von Tyrlant*,' *op. cit.*, which points to Tyrol as the place of its origin.

[30] Concerning the language of the Weistümer F. Arens, *op. cit.*, p. 88 says: "Die

guage of this epoch have survived or are available in print. Even if one compares the present manuscript with similar Austrian *Weistümer*, written within the territory where the South Bavarian dialect prevails, one is faced with the additional difficulty that the above text ante-dates almost all of the others by a period of from fifty to one hundred and fifty years, a considerable interval of time with its consequent effect upon language and orthography. Moreover, the Austrian *Weis-tümer* available for comparison were edited many decades ago, at a time when the methods of preparing texts for publication were different from those applied today. It is not improbable that many an editor "emended" his seemingly faulty or misunderstood text, "corrected" the original spelling, and made changes or expanded contractions without bringing such alterations to the notice of his readers. Such a procedure might materially alter the text of the manuscript and make a collation and deduction highly problemati-cal. Finally, as indicated above, due to the homogeneous character of the Alpine-Bavarian dialect, the mere appearance of comparatively unusual words or phraseology is not as helpful as might be expected.

The only word in the present text which offers a definite clue, however small this may be, is the word *sol.* which probably repre-sents the abbreviation for *soldin.* This word is found in the vocabu-lary of Oswald von Wolkenstein, which is South Tyrolese. This fact, combined with the study of the language and the various textual agreements noted in comparing our *Taiding* with other similar Weistümer, supports the supposition that this manuscript originated in South Tyrol.

Thus the manuscript, as short as it is, is of considerable interest both for the philologist and the student of manorial customs. The present discussion, it is hoped, will provide a satisfactory explanation and elucidation not only of the language but also of the legal aspects of the text.

(From *PMLA* 60 (1945), pp. 325-39).

---

Quellen des 14. und 15. Jahrhunderts drücken sich kurz und herb aus, sie scheuen keine Derbheit bewahren in ihrer Schweigsamkeit immer einen Ton schlichten Stolzes. . . . Die Sprache der Weistümer ist von der mündlichen Rede nicht unter-schieden, sie macht die lebhaften Wendungen mit. . . . Das wird im 16. Jahr-hundert anders. Die Höflichkeitsformeln gegen die wohl edlen und gestrengen Amtspersonen beginnen sich zu häufen; die Sprache wird bedächtig und überlegt, sie argumentiert, sie moralisiert."

# CHAPTER T10

## THE *FLEURS DE TOUTES VERTUS* AND
## CHRISTINE DE PISAN'S *L'EPÎTRE D'OTHÉA*

IN preparing my edition of the Middle English *Epistle of Othea* attributed to Stephen Scrope,[1] I have chanced upon some details which apparently have not been previously noticed. The conclusions to be drawn in this paper must necessarily be tentative until exhaustive search in Italian and French libraries can once again be undertaken with the hope of providing the necessary evidence for the satisfactory solution of the present problem. The points which I propose to make, however, are of sufficient importance and interest to present them in their present form to students of comparative literature.

The sources of Christine de Pisan's *L'Epître d'Othéa*, from which the Middle English versions were made, have been outlined by two previous editors of the English translations;[2] in addition, we have the excellent work by Professor P. G. C. Campbell, *L'Epître d'Othéa, étude sur les sources de Christine de Pisan* (Paris, 1924). Campbell settled upon the *Manipulus florum* of Thomas Hibernicus (pp. 155 ff.) as the main source for the quotations from the Church Fathers and upon Guillaume de Tignonville's *Dits moraulx des philosophes* (pp. 172 ff.) as the work from which Christine drew most of her sayings of ancient philosophers. Being quite familiar with the latter text through my edition of two Middle English translations of it (Early English Text Society, Original Series no. 211), I was surprised, while preparing the text of the *Epistle of Othea*, to find that many sayings in that work were either wanting in the *Dits moraulx* or that they had been radically altered in the text or in the name of the philosopher to whom they were attached. Again I was unable to identify many of the quotations from the Fathers in the *Manipulus florum*, at least in the only edition to which I had access.[3] Since it seemed unlikely that much work could

---

[1] See [Sir] George F. Warner, *The Epistle of Othea to Hector* (London: Roxburghe Club, 1904), pp. xxv–xlvii.

[2] Warner, *op. cit.*, pp. xxi–xxv; James D. Gordon, *The Epistle of Othea to Hector . . . edited from the Harleian Manuscript 838* (Philadelphia, 1942), pp. xiv–xvii.

[3] Piacenza: Jacobus de Tyela, 5 September 1483; see Ada Thurston and Curt F.

be done on the notes for these elusive quotations till the European libraries were once again open for consultation, I temporarily put my notes aside. Oddly enough, the routine course of cataloguing some of the manuscripts in The Pierpont Morgan Library brought a text to my notice which, if anything, threatened to bring even further complexity into the problem of Christine's sources for the *Othéa*.

The manuscript in question is Morgan MS. 771 and the particular text with which we are concerned is the first item in that manuscript. Seymour de Ricci[4] described it as *Le Livre de Sapience* and gave the incipit: "Comme par la souveraine sapience." In an endeavor to locate other manuscripts and printed editions of this text, I came across the following items:[5]

Manuscripts[6]
1. Paris. Bibliothèque nationale, fds. franç. 572
2. Paris. Bibliothèque nationale, fds. franç. 1746
3. Paris. Bibliothèque nationale, fds. franç. 1892
4. Paris. Bibliothèque nationale, fds. franç. 1893
5. Lyon. Bibliothèque municipale. MS. 784
6. Brussels. Bibliothèque royale. MS. 10972
7. Chantilly, Musée Condé. MS. 649
8. Chantilly, Musée Condé. MS. 660

Printed editions
9. Caen: Petrus Regnault, no date [XV cent.]
10. Paris: Antoine Caillaut, no date [XV cent.]
11. Paris: unidentified press, no date[7] [XV cent.]
12. Lyon: Guillaume Le Roy, no date[8] [XV cent.]

---

Bühler, *Check List of Fifteenth Century Printing in the Pierpont Morgan Library* (New York, 1939), no. 1327.

[4] *Census of Medieval and Renaissance Manuscripts in the United States and Canada* (New York, 1935–40), II, 1500.

[5] This list represents only such manuscripts as I have come across and does not pretend to be complete. The text is not listed by Gustav Gröber, *Geschichte der mittelfranzösischen Literatur* (ed. by Stefan Hofer, Berlin and Leipzig, 1933–37).

[6] There may be another manuscript in the Bibliothèque d'Albi in Albi (no. 4) but the description in the catalogue (*Catalogue général des manuscrits des bibliothèques publiques de France*) is too vague to warrant its inclusion here.

[7] Marie Pellechet, *Catalogue général des incunables des bibliothèques publiques de France* (Paris, 1897–1909), nos. 3516 (Arsenal), 3517 (Bibl. Nat.), and 3518 (Rouen).

[8] Anatole Claudin, *Histoire de l'imprimerie en France* (Paris, 1900–14), III, 92–94, and *Chantilly, Le cabinet des livres. Imprimés antérieurs au milieu du XVI⁶ siècle* (Paris, 1905), p. 81, no. 413.

13. France: unidentified press, no date[9] [XV cent.]
14. Paris: Philippe Le Noir, c. 1525
15. Paris: Alain Lotrian, c. 1530[10]
16. Paris: Galliot du Pre, 1530
17. Paris: Denys Ianot, 1532[11]
18. Paris: Pierre Vidoue, c. 1532[11a]

These texts are variously labelled: *Chapelet des vertus, Fleurs de toutes vertus, Livre de saigesse, Livre de sapience, Livre du songe, Rommant de prudence* and *Somme le roi.* The incipits are also varied, falling into three groups.[12] While some texts begin as does Morgan 771 with the incipit as cited by de Ricci,[13] others have verse introductions which precede this same prose passage and these are found in two forms:

Ce fut d'avril dix et septiesme jour
En ce temps prim que la rose entre en flour
Gaye saison que tout ce renouvelle
Les prez verdoyent et toute fleur est belle . . . (Chantilly 649)[14]

*and*

En ce printemps que les humains espris
Sont plus agus en science et en espris
Et en vertus qu'en nulle aultre saison
En mon resveil fus de desir surpris
A translater aucun livre de pris . . . (Chantilly 660)[15]

[9] Robert Proctor, *An Index to the Early Printed Books in the British Museum . . . with Notes of those in the Bodleian Library* (London, 1898–1903), p. 650, no. 8809. In the Museum's "General Catalogue" the imprint is given as: [Orleans ? 1480 ?].

[10] Emile Picot, *Catalogue des livres de la bibliothèque de M. le Baron James de Rothschild* (Paris, 1884–1920), III, 351–353, no. 2557, and I, 74–75, no. 136.

[11] Jacques-Charles Brunet, *Manuel du libraire et de l'amateur de livres* (Paris, 1860–80), II, 1286 (two editions).

[11a] See the sale catalogue *Bibliothèque de M. Lucien Gougy,* Paris, 1934, p. 109, no. 168.

[12] Similarly, as Gordon (*op. cit.,* p. xxx) points out, Christine supplied her *Othéa* with four different dedications. Scrope's English text contains three dedications: to Sir John Fastolf (Marquis of Bath, Longleat MS. 253), to Humphrey, Duke of Buckingham (St. John's College, Cambridge, MS. 208) and to an unspecified "hye princesse" (Morgan MS. 775).

[13] So, for example, nos. 3, 4, 6, 11, 12 and 13 above.

[14] This is also the incipit in nos. 1, 2, 9, 10, 14 and 15.

[15] Neither incipit is listed by Arthur Långfors, *Les incipit des poèmes français antérieurs au XVIᵉ siècle* (Paris, 1917).

Emile Picot[16] and W. Nelson Francis[17] state that this text is an abridged version of the *Somme des vices et des vertus* or *Somme le roi* by Lorens d'Orléans;[18] the catalogue of the Cabinet des Manuscrits at Chantilly is less positive.[19]

Apart from the verse incipits, the opening and closing lines, as well as such parts of the texts as the various catalogues reproduce, indicate that these manuscripts and printed books all have the same text as Morgan 771—possibly, in a few cases, slight revisions of such a work. In any event it is certain that the Morgan text is not a revision of the *Somme le roi* but is either a translation of the *Fiore di virtù*[20] with enlargements from other sources by the French translator or a translation of some enlarged version of the Italian *Fiore*.[21] Significantly enough the British Museum lists its fifteenth-century edition (no. 13 above) of this text under the heading: "Fiore. Le liure des vices et des vertus. [A translation of the 'Fiore di virtù']."[22]

[16] *Op. cit.*, I, 75: "Le *Livre de Saigesse* est un extrait, rédigé vers la fin du xive siècle, de la *Somme le Roy*, de frère Laurent."

[17] *The Book of Vices and Virtues*, EETS, OS. 217, pp. xxvii–xxviii. He lists several of the manuscripts noted above and states that they are "abridged versions of the *Somme*." Compare also his note 1, p. xxvii, which needs correction. The *Gesamtkatalog der Wiegendrucke* (Leipzig, 1925–38), VI, 420, intimates that it will also list the incunabula editions under Laurent.

[18] For this work see D. C. Tinbergen, *Des Coninx Summe* (Leyden, 1900–07) and Gröber, *op. cit.*, II, 216 and note, for the early French versions. According to Paulin Paris, *Les manuscrits françois de la bibliothèque du roi* (Paris, 1836–48), v, 9, MS. 572 bears the title: "Aucuns diz des sages, extraiz du livre des Vices et Vertus, nommé la Somme le Roy, et de plusieurs philosophes." However, C. Frati, "Ricerche sul 'Fiore di Virtù,'" *Studj di filologia romanza*, VI, 410–413, points out that the "Somma de' vizi" mentioned in the *Fiore* refers to the *Summa virtutum et vitiorum* by Guillelmus Peraldus; the similarity in the titles perhaps misled the scribe of the Paris manuscript.

[19] "Le présent manuscrit offre un texte disposé de la même façon que l'ouvrage italien *Fiore di virtù*, composé vers 1320, soit d'après frère Laurent, soit d'après une autre Somme, attribué à Tomaso Leoni et plusieurs fois imprimé en Italie au xve siècle." *Chantilly. Le cabinet des livres. Manuscrits* (Paris, 1900–11), I, 236.

[20] For this work, see Adolfo Bartoli, *Storia della letteratura italiana* (Firenze, 1878–89), III, 347–350; Frati, *op. cit.*; N. Cartojan, "Fiore di virtù in literatura românească," *Academia Română, Memoriile sectiunii literare*, seria III, tomul IV (Bucuresti, 1928–29); R. Renier, "Di una ignota traduzione spagnuola del 'Fiore di virtù,'" *Zeitschrift für romanische Philologie*, xviii, 305–318; etc.

[21] Bartoli, *op. cit.*, p. 348 notes that MS. Riccardiano 1084 is an interpolated text; so also is Magliabechiano II. ii. 21 according to T. Casini, "Appunti sul Fiore di virtù," *Rivista critica della letteratura italiana*, III, 154–159. Renier, *op. cit.*, p. 306, speaks of the "incrementi, modificazioni and rimaneggiamenti" found in the Italian manuscripts.

[22] Henry Thomas, *Short-title Catalogue of Books Printed in France . . . now*

Again there is a sixteenth-century work printed by Thomas Colwell in London which is entitled:[23] "The boke of wisdome otherwise called the Flower of Vertue"; on the title-page[24] is the note "Translated fyrst out of Italion into French & out of french into English by John Larke. 1565." This work includes a translation of the usual French verse introduction, beginning:

> It was of Apryll the seuentene day
> In that freshe tyme when the Rose so gay
> Hys Flower begynneth to spred and spryng
> And al other herbes & trees take liking . . .

The prose passage begins: "As by the Soueraine Sapyence, or Wysdome. And hyghe power of god, al thinges reasonable be create, all the same oughte to goo to theyr good and happy ende." This work[25] is clearly a translation of some early French edition of the sort listed above; the English text, furthermore, agrees in all important details with the text of Morgan 771. Thus it seems reasonably certain that all the texts listed above represent a translation into French of the well-known *Fiore di virtù*.

The fact that the Morgan *Livre de sapience*—and consequently the other texts we have noticed—is a translation of the *Fiore* may be even more satisfactorily established by the following excerpts. The French work is not, however, an exact translation from the Italian; the chapters have been rearranged and there is much in the French work which does not appear in the Italian original.[26]

### Amore

Amore beniuolentia dilectatione sono quasi una cosa secondo che proua frate tomaxo d'aquino nella sua som-

Amour beniuolence et deliberation sont comme vne mesme chose selon que dit saint thomas en sa somme

---

*in the British Museum* (London, 1924), p. 166. The book is listed in the *Catalogue of Printed Books* (Filace-Fisgrave. London, 1887, p. 105) under *Fiore di virtù*; the press-mark is C. 27. g. 6.

[23] A. W. Pollard and G. R. Redgrave, *A Short-title Catalogue of Books Printed in England, Scotland, & Ireland . . . 1475-1640* (London, 1926), p. 72, nos. 3357-3358a. The British Museum lists its edition under *Fiore di virtù*, with the press-mark C. 38. b. 1.

[24] Cited from the Harvard copy of STC 3358.

[25] Mary Augusta Scott, *Elizabethan Translations from the Italian* (Boston, 1916), pp. 451-456, no. 373 includes the *Boke of Wisdome* as a translation of the Italian *Fiore di virtù*.

[26] The contrary is also true but this need not concern us here.

ma; gieneralmente lo primaio moui-
mento di ciaschuno amore si e la cog-
noscença.
(*Fiore*, Morgan 770, f. 1)

que le premier mouuement de che-
schune amour est la congnoissance.
(*Fleurs*, Morgan 771, f. 7ᵛ)

### Misericordia

Misericordia secondo santo agostino
sie auere compassione della sua anima e della altruj miseria.
(Morgan 770, f. 6ᵛ)

Misericorde selon que dit saint augustin est auoir compassion de son
ame et de la misere d'aultruy.
(Morgan 771, f. 35ᵛ)

### Castita

Castitade sie una uirtu si chome disse
tulio per la quale ragioneuole si ra-
frena lo stimolo della carne e della
lusuria.
(Morgan 770, f. 23)

Chastete selon que dit tules est vne
vertu par la quelle se refraint raison-
nablement la voulente de la char et de
luxure.
(Morgan 771, f. 18ᵛ)

Of the additional matter found in the French version we shall have
more to say later.

It is rather more difficult to approximate the date of this translation. The Chantilly[27] and Rothschild[28] catalogues both refer to
this as "une compilation du xivᵉ siècle," but such manuscripts as I
have been able to date all belong to the fifteenth century[29] or later.[30]
On the other hand, it is certain that the *Fiore* was available in a
French translation not later than 1437, for such a work is listed in
a catalogue (compiled in that year) of the library belonging to
Nicolò Este (1393–1441).[31]

That the *Fiore di virtù* was translated into French in the late fourteenth century, if one may assume that to be the date of the text, is

[27] *Op. cit.*, I, 236: "Quelle que soit l'origine de cet ouvrage, que l'auteur soit français ou italien, il est certain que nous avons ici une compilation du xivᵉ siècle, dont
on connaît de nombreuses copies."

[28] *Op. cit.*, I, 74–75. Francis, *op. cit.*, p. xxvii, speaks of the *Livre de saigesse* as
"dating from the end of the fourteenth century."

[29] MS. 1893 is dated 1487, while Morgan 771 was probably written about 1440.
MS. 572 is described as late fifteenth century and the two Chantilly MSS. (as also
MS. 1746) are listed as belonging to the same century.

[30] MS. 1892 is said to be a sixteenth century manuscript.

[31] Cf. Pio Rajna, "Ricordi di codici francesi posseduti dagli Estensi nel secolo xv,"
*Romania*, II, 49–58. Under no. 10 (36) is listed: "Libro uno chiamado Fiore de
vertù in francexe—in membrana, cum l'aquila volante et l'arma di Malatesti et
l'aquila volante su la prima carta et su le aleve, coverto de chore roso." No. 12
(55) "Libro uno chiamado el libro de le vertu, in francexe" may represent another
copy of this text. Presumably the translation was made in France and it may have
been many years before the translation reached Italy.

hardly to be wondered at. The *Fiore*, a work dealing with the vices and virtues, enjoyed an almost unparalleled popularity for an Italian work of this period,[32] not only in the fourteenth century but in the subsequent centuries as well. The number of the extant manuscripts of this work is legion[33] and no fewer than 84 editions were published before 1900. Forty of these, it is said,[34] are incunables; in the same period, only fifteen editions of the *Divine Comedy* found their way into print.[35] This is evident proof of the *Fiore's* enormous popularity; it explains the reason why it was translated into Arabic, Armenian, Catalan, English, French, German, Greek, Roumanian, Russian, Serbian and Spanish.[36]

While thus establishing that the Morgan text in MS. 771 was a translation of the *Fiore di virtù* and that it should be properly called the *Fleurs de toutes vertus*, I became increasingly aware that many of the passages in the *Fleurs* seemed remarkably familiar. A hurried comparison of these passages with similar lines in the *Othéa* revealed that they were identical, in many cases word for word. We may, in illustration of this, consider the opening lines of the *Fleurs* in comparison with the parallel passage from the first section of *Othéa*:

| *Fleurs* | *Othéa* |
|---|---|
| Comme par la souuerainne sapience et haulte puissance de dieu toutes choses sont crees raisonnablement et toutes doiuent tendre a la sienne beneuree fin. Et pource que les esperis des creatures raisonnablement sont creez par luy a sa semblance est chose necessaire qu'ilz soyent adornez de vertus par lesquelles puissent paruenir a la fin pour la quelle sont faiz. Et | Comme par la somme sapience et haulte puissance de dieu toutes choses soient crees raisonnablement doiuent toutes tendre a fin de lui. Et pour ce que nostre esperit de dieu cree a son ymage est des choses crees le plus noble apres les anges couuenable chose est et neccessaire que il soit aournez de vertus par quoy il puit estre conuoye a la fin pour quoy il est fait . . . |

[32] Even Leonardo da Vinci made use of the *Fiore di virtù*; cf. Jean Paul Richter, *The Literary Works of Leonardo da Vinci* (London, 1883), II, 313 ff.

[33] Casini, *op. cit.*, lists 38 manuscripts found in the various Florentine libraries.

[34] For the printed editions, see Hermann Varnhagen, "Drei italienische Kleinigkeiten," *Philologische und volkskundliche Arbeiten Karl Vollmöller . . . dargeboten* (Erlangen, 1908), pp. 52–54.

[35] *Gesamtkatalog* 7958–7972. The same total represents the number of fifteenth-century editions of Cavalca's *Specchio di croce* (*Gesamtkatalog* 6414–6428), while only eleven editions of Boccaccio's *Decamerone* (*Gesamtkatalog*, 4440–4450) were produced before 1501.

[36] For the various translations see the works cited above by Frati, Cartojan and Renier; for the Catalan text, see Konrad Haebler, *Bibliografía Ibérica del siglo XV* (La Haya, 1903–17), nos. 274–276 and 274(5).

car prudence est mere & conduiceresse
de toutes autres vertus sans laquelle
nulle des autres n'y pourroit estre bien
gouuernee et est moult chose cou-
uenable et necessaire aux esperis des
creatures estre adornez de prudence.
Salomon en fait mencion en ses prouerbes disant. Si intrauerit sapiencia
cor tuum etc. (Prov. ii. 10, 11).
(Morgan 771, f. 1)[37]

Comme prudence et sagece soit mere
& conduisarresse de toutes vertus sans
la quelle les autres ne pourroient estre
bien gouuernees est il neccessaire a
l'esperit cheualereux que de prudence
soit aournez. . . . Et a ce propos parle
salemon es prouerbes. Si intrauerit
sapientia cor tuum etc.
(British Museum, MS. Harley 4431,
f. 96ᵛ)[38]

Further examination showed that the quotations from the Fathers,
Philosophers and the Bible found in several sections of the *Othéa*
were exactly the same as those found in similar chapters of the
*Fleurs*. One example of this will suffice to prove my point:

*Fleurs* (Ire)

Et dit.[39] garde toy de ire car elle des-
tourbe raison et trouble l'entendement. . . . Saint augustin dit[40] que

*Othéa* (xvii)

Et pour ce dit aristote garde toy d'ire
Car elle trouble l'entendement et
destourne raison . . . & dit saint au-

---

[37] As by the Soueraine Sapyence, or Wysdome. And hyghe power of god, al
thinges reasonable be create, all the same oughte to goo to theyr good and happy
ende. And because that the sprites, or soules of reasonable creatures be create by
god, to his owne semblaunce and lykenes, it is necessarye, that he be adorned
wyth vertues, by the whyche they maye come to the ende, for the whyche they were
made and create. Prudence is mother and leader of al other vertues, without the
whyche none of the other Vertues can be well gouerned. And it is verye nesessarye
and conuenient, to the spyrytes of reasonable creatures to haue Prudence, and be
adorned of the same. For Salamon saythe in makynge mencyon of the same in
hys Prouerbes. Si intrauerit etc. (*Boke of Wisdome*, Harvard copy, sig. B₁).

[38] A[s] be the grete wisedome and hiʒ myghte of God alle thinges that be resonabli
made alle scholde streche to the ende of hym and be-cause that our spirit made
of God to his likenes is made of thinges moost noble aftir the angelis it is behoueli
and necessarie that it be araid withe vertues be the whiche it may be conueid to
the ende wherefore it was made. . . . How prudence and wisedome be moderis and
conditoures of alle vertues withoute the whiche the tothir may not be welle
gouernyd it is necessarie to goostli knyghthood to be araid withe prudence. . . .
And to this purpos Salamon seithe in his Prouerbis Si intrauerit etc. (*Epistle of
Othea*, St. John's MS. 208, f. 4).

[39] The previous philosopher cited by the *Fleurs* and the *Boke* is Varro. This statement may be based on the quotation in the *Fiore* (Morgan 770, f. 5ᵛ): Ira secondo
Aristotile sie turbamento d'animo per discorso di sangue. Compare also Carl Selmer,
"An Unnoticed Version of Pseudo Aristotelian Proverbs," *PMLA*, LIX, p. 586, no.
5. The *Book of Good Manners* (London, de Worde, c. 1520—Morgan 747), sig.
c₁ has: As Seneca sayth, Ire troubleth the vnderstandynge of the creatures.

[40] Epistola ccx (Migne XXXIII, 958): Quia sicut acetum corrumpit vas, si diutius
ibi fuerit; sic ira corrumpit cor, si in alium diem duraverit. This is rendered by
the *Boke of Wisdome* (f. 42ᵛ) as: Saint Augustine saithe, that in lyke case as the

ainsy comme vng mauuais vin corrompt le vaisseau ou l'on le boute.
ainsy Ire corrompt le corps de l'omme
se elle y demeure d'un iour a autre.
Et pour ce dit saint paul. Sol non
occidat super iracundiam vestram.
(Ephes. iv. 26)
(MS. 771, ff. 17ᵛ–18)

gustin en vn epistre que ainsi comme
le vin aigre on boute corrompt le
vaissel ou il est se il y demeure longuement ainsi yre corrompt le cuer
ou elle se boute se elle y demeure de
iour a autre. pour ce dit s[aint] paul
l'apostre / sol non occidat super iracundiam vestram.
(Harley 4431, f. 104ᵛ)

In the final analysis, many of the quotations of the Church Fathers and of the sayings of the ancient philosophers which I had been unable to find in the *Manipulus florum*[41] and in the *Dits moraulx*[42] appeared in practically identical wording in the *Fleurs*.

The question we are now faced with is, of course, whether Christine used the *Fleurs de toutes vertus* as a source or whether the *Epître d'Othéa* was laid under contribution by the French translator of the *Fiore* for those passages not found in the original work. This is, unfortunately, a problem which cannot be solved with complete certainty at the moment; the answer must be sought in Continental libraries. Furthermore, it must be borne in mind that the additions to the text may have been the work of some Italian reviser of the *Fiore di virtù* and that the French text represents no more than a literal translation of an expanded Italian *Fiore*. In that case, of course, it is Christine who is the borrower. However, with the facts we have already established in mind, it is quite possible to arrive at a likely (and reasonable) solution for our problem.

Assuming that the additional matter is the contribution of a

---

euyll wine doth corrupte the vessell wherin it is putte, so Ire dothe corrupte the bodye of the man, if it doe tarye there from one daye to a-nother.

[41] For the quotation from St. Gregory used in section XII (compare Warner, p. 24, and Gordon, p. 31), the *Fleurs* (f. 44ᵛ) has: Saint gregoire dit que nous deuons auoir en grant reuerence ceulx qui preschent la saincte escripture car ce sont les courriers qui vont deuant nostre seigneur et nostre s[eigneur] les suit. La saincte predication vient deuant et apres nostre s[eigneur] vient en visitation de noz coraiges. Les paroles font la cource deuant & la verite est respandue en nostre entendement. The identical quotation may be found in Guillaume Telin, *Bref sommaire des sept vertus etc.* (Paris, 1533), f. cxviii; for Telin's work, see my *Dicts*, pp. xvi–xviii.

[42] Comparable to the Hermes extract in VII (Warner, p. 19, and Gordon, p. 24), we find in the *Fleurs* (f. 20ᵛ—Luxure): Hermes dit que le vice de luxure estaint toutes vertus. For this, the *Boke of Wisdome* (f. 49ᵛ) has: Hermes saithe, that the Vyce of Lechery doth quenshe al vertues.

French writer,[43] it still seems likely that the *Fleurs* supplied material for the *Othéa* and not that the contrary is true. It may be pointed out that the dates which competent scholars have assigned to both works indicate that Christine is the borrower, for the *Fleurs* is assigned to the fourteenth century[44] while the *Othéa* is considered to have been written about 1400[45] and represents her first extensive prose work. The fact that Christine made liberal use of many sources not only for the *Othéa* but for her other works as well[46] lends support to such a theory. Again, if the translator of the *Fiore* was using Christine's work for his supplementary material, it is strange that so many suitable quotations found in the *Othéa* were not incorporated into his translation. Conversely, of course, there are many sayings in the *Fleurs* which, though perfectly apt, Christine did not include in her book. However, by the nature of her work, Christine was limited to a hundred quotations from the Fathers and a similar number for the sayings of the philosophers,[47] so that when she had reached that total she needed no more. This readily accounts for the fact, assuming that Christine used the *Fleurs*, that many quotations found in that work do not appear in *Othéa*. The French translator of the *Fiore*, on the other hand, was bound by no such limitation and if he did use the *Othéa* as a source, it is indeed strange that he did not utilize it more fully.

Another aspect which may support the theory that Christine was acquainted with the *Fiore*, either in its French or its Italian form, is that this work is very similar in form to the *Othéa*.[48] Each chapter of

[43] It has occurred to me that this French translation of the *Fiore di virtù* might be an early exercise by Christine; however the awkwardness of the style seems to be an argument against this assumption.

[44] I am obliged to M. Henri Malo, the Conservateur-adjoint of the Musée Condé, for informing me that the catalogue is the result of the combined efforts of the Duc d'Aumale, Leopold Delisle and Paul Meyer.

[45] So Campbell and Gordon. Ph. Aug. Becker, "Christine de Pizan," *Zeitschrift für französische Sprache und Literatur*, LIV, 129–163, places the date of composition as 1402, while E. M. Robineau, *Christine de Pisan* (St.-Omer, 1882), p. 89, assigns the work to 1406.

[46] See Gröber, *op. cit.*, II, 14–40; Mathilde Laigle, *Le Livre des trois vertus de Christine de Pisan* (Paris, 1912), pp. 74–103; Maurice Roy, "Le debat de deux amans," *Œuvres poétiques de Christine de Pisan* (Société des anciens textes français), II, p. 49 ff. and notes.

[47] In four instances (III, XXVI, LXVII, and LXXI) there are two quotations from the philosophers in one section.

[48] Gordon, *op. cit.*, pp. xvii–xxix, mentions a number of other works which may have served as a model.

the *Fiore* is divided into three parts which may be described as: the exposition (definition of the virtue or vice), the simile (identification of the virtue or vice with some animal or bird, followed by quotations from the Fathers and philosophers), and the exemplum (a story illustrative of the matter discussed). Each of Christine's hundred sections, it will be recalled, is similarly divided into a "texte," "glose" and "allegorie." Thus the *Fiore di virtù*, either in the original or in the translation, may have helped to suggest to Christine the form for the *Epître d'Othéa*.

Finally, it may be noted that in at least two instances[49] the French *Fleurs de toutes vertus* is found bound together with Tignonville's *Dits moraulx des philosophes*, a work which unquestionably supplied Christine with many of her "sentences." It is not impossible, then, that even in Christine's day these works were sometimes bound together, being of a similar nature, and some such manuscript may well have been accessible to Christine while she was writing the *Othéa*.

We have, thus, a number of good reasons for believing that Christine used the *Fleurs* to obtain desirable quotations rather than that the contrary is true. A final word may, I think, be said about some of the passages in the *Fleurs* which have no counterpart in the original Italian text. It is apparent that many of the sayings from the ancient philosophers in such additions were taken from the *Dits moraulx des philosophes* or (rather more probably) from the *Dicta philosophorum*,[50] the work from which Tignonville made his translation.[51] The *Fiore* itself is largely indebted to the *Dicta philoso-*

---

[49] Bibl. Nat., MS. 572 and Morgan 771.

[50] Ezio Franceschini, "Il 'Liber philosophorum moralium antiquorum.' Testo critico," *Atti del Reale Istituto Veneto di scienze, lettere ed arti* (Anno accademico 1931–1932, tomo XCI, parte seconda), pp. 393–597 (also numbered 1–205).

[51] The fact that *Othéa* occasionally has quotations which agree with the *Fleurs* and differ materially from Tignonville's translation of the *Dicta* may be illustrated by the following example. In LXXXVII we find: A ce propos dit omer le poete par grant diligence vient on a hon*neur* & perfeccion (Harley 4431, f. 135). Scrope has: To this purpoos Omer seyeth, Be greet diligence a man cometh to perfeccio*un* (Morgan 775, f. 266). Similarly the *Fleurs* (Morgan 771, f. 16) states: Omere dit. par grant diligence vient l'*omme* a parfection: the *Boke of Wisdome* (f. 38ᵛ) has: Homer saythe that by greate dylygence, a man commeth to perfeccyon.

The *Dicta philosophorum* and its translations present quite a different version. The Latin (p. 27) says: Et dixit: per [cautionem] magnam consequitur homo quod vult. This is rather literally translated by Tignonville as: Et dit par gra*nt* diligence vient on a so*n* i*n*tentio*n* (Morgan 771, f. 59). In Scrope's *Dicts* (p. 38, ll. 11–12) it reads: And he saithe: bi grete diligence men may come to their entent;

*phorum* although the author often materially altered the text and attributed the sayings to whomsoever it pleased him, as, for example, in the following instances:[52]

| *Fiore* | *Dicta philosophorum* |
|---|---|
| Giulico disse questo e quello che signoreggiaua la terra dal leuante al ponente e ora in due passi si contiene. Barbariccio disse / Alesandro come pvo essere cio niuno s'ardiua di fauellare contro al luj / Ora ciascuno s'ardiscie affauellare perche ogi non puo udire. Dalfino disse quegli che non uidono maj Alessandro ebono paura di luj e ora queglj che il uegono nol temono di niente. (Morgan MS. 770, f. 5)[53] | Et dixit alius: hic est qui totam perambulavit terram, nunc vero duobus continetur passibus. Et dixit: heri Alexander audire poterat et nullus coram eo loqui presumebat, hodie unusquisque loquitur coram eo, et ipse non audit. [Et dixit alius alius: quanto altitudo Alexandri excellencior fuit, tanto gravior est casus]. Et dixit alius; non videntes Alexandrum consueverant eo terreri, nunc qui eum aspiciunt non terrentur. (p. 132) |
| Anchora [Plato][54] disse d'un altra che inparaua a scriuere non multiplicare lo male collo male. (f. 3$^v$) | Et [Socrates] vidit quandam puellam discentem scribere, cui dixit: non multiplices malum cum malo. (p. 63) |

The expanded French text[55] is dependent on the *Dicta* in exactly the same fashion:

---

the Helmingham Hall text states: And seith: by grete diligence a man cometh to haue his entente (*Dicts*, p. 39, ll. 14-15). Earl Rivers' translation (Westminster, Caxton, 1477, f. 15) also has: And sayde by grete diligence som men atteyne to their purpose.

Thus all the versions of the *Dicta* have "entent" for "quod vult," while *Othéa* and the *Fleurs* have "perfeccioun" for the Latin phrase. The English translation of *Othéa* printed by Gordon (p. 130) similarly has: Wherfore seyth þe noble poete Omere: By grett diligence comet a man to þe grett hye estat of perfeccioun. See also note 56 below.

[52] See also the notes to my *Dicts* for 38/2, 146/17 and 242/16.

[53] Cf. the *Dicts*, p. 210, ll. 6-24, and the notes to this passage. In addition to the works cited there, this story may also be found in the following: *Speculum laicorum* (by John of Hoveden?), MS. Addit. 11284, f. 55; Petrus Alphonsus, *Disciplina clericalis*, MS. Addit. 24641, f. 226$^v$; Robert Holkot, *Convertimini*, MS. Royal 7 C I, f. 117$^v$; the German *Gesta*, MS. Addit. 10291, f. 69; and Ranulf Higden, *Polycronicon* (Westminster, 1495), f. cxxiii$^v$. The Spanish *Fiore* (Renier, *op. cit.*, p. 318) names the philosophers thus: Gullicio, Bartolico, Delphian, Preciano, Archito, Drusiano, and Bernardo. In the *Fleurs*, which borrows the story from the *Fiore*, it is found under "Tristesse" (Morgan 771, f. 16).

[54] In some editions of the *Fiore*, this quotation is attributed to Avicenna; so Rome, Bulle, 1478 (Morgan Check List 665) and Venice, Nel Beretin Convento, 1474 (Morgan 838).

[55] For other French works which borrowed from the *Dicta*, see my *Dicts*, pp. xvi-xviii.

*Fleurs*               *Dicta philosophorum*

Aristote dit que iustice est vne mesure que Dieu a establie en terre pour limiter les choses. (MS. 771, f. 30)[56]

Et dixit [Aristotiles]: iusticia est mensura quedam quam Deus statuit super terram, cuius suffragio debilis a forti, et verax eripitur a mendaci. (p. 102)[57]

Et ainsi comme nous veons communement les femmes sont plus toust corrocees que les hommes et les malades que les sains et les jeunes que les vieulx. et pource peut on bien penser que ire vient de mauuais couraige. (MS. 771, f. 18)[58]

Et dixit: invenimus mulieres citius quam viros irasci, et infirmos quam sanos, senesque quam iuvenes; propter que perpendere valemus iram ex debilitate anime pervenire. (p. 176)[59]

Our investigations, then, lead us to the following conclusions. As we have seen, the *Fleurs de toutes vertus*[60] is a translation of the *Fiore di virtù* with certain additional passages, part of which are taken from the *Dicta philosophorum*.[61] The *Fleurs* and the *Epître*

[56] Telin (*op. cit.*, f. 61ᵛ) has the identical quotation under "La vertu de justice" as it here appears in the *Fleurs*. The *Boke of Wisdome* (f. 71) renders this as: Arystotyl sayth, that Iustice is a measure, that god hath stablished in earthe, for to lymyte all thynges. *Othéa* (IV) has the text of the *Fleurs*, not that of the *Dicta* or its French translation.

[57] Apparently based on Diogenes Laertius (v, 21): Τὴν δικαιοσύνην ἔφη ἀρετὴν ψυχῆς διανεμητικὴν τοῦ κατ' ἀξίαν. William Baldwin, *A treatise of morall phylosophie* (London, Whitchurch, c. 1550—copy at Harvard), sig. N₃, translates the *Dicta* thus: Iustice is a measure whiche god hath ordayned on the yearth, to defende the feble from the myghtye, and the true from the vntrue, and to roote out the wicked from among the good. Baldwin attributes this saying to Plato; cf. *Dicts*, 158/15 and 159/15. Tignonville's translation is a close rendering of the Latin text.

[58] Compare this with Tignonville's translation: Et dist Nous veons communement les femmes estre plus tost courouciees que les hommes, les malades que les sains, les vieulx que les jeunes pourquoy on peut pensser que Ire vient de foiblesce de couraige. (Royal 19 B IV, f. 70ᵛ.)

[59] Baldwin, *op. cit.*, sig. O₁, agrees with the Latin text: Women are sooner angrye than men, the sycke sooner than the healthy, and olde folke be soner moued than the younge—Plato. The *Dicts* (274/12) does not specify the philosopher to whom this saying is attached.

[60] The *Othéa* itself was enlarged from other sources by Jean Mielot; see Gröber, *op. cit.*, II, 219. Picot (*op. cit.*, III, 351–353) points out that some of the editions of the *Fleurs* were augmented by portions of the chapter on Sedechias, also borrowed from the *Dits moraulx*. The *Dits* in turn, was also expanded; see my *Dicts*, p. xix and note. William Worcester supplied additions to Scrope's English translation of this work.

[61] The *Fleurs* (under "Seurte") is also indebted to Seneca's *Liber de remediis fortuitorum*, though probably only indirectly. In Seneca this work has the sub-title "Dialogus sensus et rationis," while the personifications in the *Fleurs* are Paour and Seurte. The French work may have borrowed this passage from the *Moralium dogma philosophorum* (Migne CLXXI, 1028–1031), where it appears under the title

*d'Othéa,* moreover, have extensive sections in common. Although definite proof cannot be produced, it seems rather more than likely that the French *Fleurs* is the earlier and that it may well have supplied not only many of the quotations which Christine used but also provided her with a model for the form in which the *Epître d'Othéa* came to be written.

(From *PMLA* 62 (1947), pp. 32-44).

## THE *FLEURS DE TOUTES VERTUS*

With the intention of confirming certain tentative assumptions which I had set forth in my paper "The *Fleurs de toutes vertus* and Christine de Pisan's *L'Epître d'Othéa*" (*PMLA*, LXII, 32-44), I devoted a large part of this past summer to intensive research in the most important European libraries. The results of these studies have been, in the main, to confirm my beliefs though these had, during the war years when the material for this paper was gathered together, been necessarily based upon an examination of library catalogues and a study of reference works and of various learned papers. An investigation of the manuscripts themselves, which had to be deferred until now, necessitates a modification of my paper in two respects. Though minor from my point of view and not directly connected with my problem, they may seem serious inasmuch as they affect the actual title of my article.

The theory that I set forth was that Christine de Pisan had borrowed extensive portions from a certain text (represented in Morgan MS 771) for her *Epître d'Othéa* and that this original text was based on the Italian *Fiore di virtù* either through an altered and rearranged Italian version or through alterations and modifications made by a French translator. Actually it develops that the *Fiore di virtù* was literally translated into French, that this French translation was recast into the text found (for example) in Morgan MS

---

"Dialogus inter securitatem et timorem." For the authorship of the Latin text, see my *Dicts*, p. xvii, and Theodore Silverstein, "The *Tertia philosophia* of Guillaume de Conches and the authorship of the *Moralium dogma philosophorum*," *Quantulacumque*, 1937, pp. 23-33. An Italian translation of this Dialogus appears at the end of a work entitled *Libro della vita de philosophi* printed at Florence in 1488 (*Gesamtkatalog* 8387). This work has been incorrectly assumed to be a translation of Diogenes Laertius, whereas it is, in the main, no more than a translation of Walter Burley's *Liber de vita et moribus philosophorum*; on this, see my paper "Greek philosophers in the literature of the later Middle Ages," *Speculum*, XII, pp. 451-452.

771, and that this text was then extensively cited by Christine in her *Epître d'Othéa*.

Thus far, then, my tentative assumptions were found vindicated—but by relying (unfortunately) upon the Chantilly catalogue I was sadly misled in other respects. The catalogue assures us that MS 649 contains "le même ouvrage" (1, 126) as MS 660; again, it is explicitly stated elsewhere that the texts in the two manuscripts are the same, though that in MS 660 has "un autre prologue et une autre disposition des chapitres" (1, 236). Unfortunately this is not at all true, the text of MS 660, which is called the *Fleurs de toutes vertus* and which has the verse incipit "En ce printemps que les humains espris," is an exact translation of the *Fiore di virtù* and is quite distinct from the work found in MS 649. Other manuscripts of this text are to be found in Paris (Bibl. Nat. franç. 1021 and 24785) and at Maihingen (MS I. 4. [n. a. Spr:] fol: 6). The Chantilly MS 660 must therefore be deleted from the list of manuscripts containing the text as found in Morgan MS 771, while Arsenal MS 2676 and Bibl. Nat. nouv. acq. fr. 1157 can be added to that list.

Most unfortunate of all, of course, was my choice of the title *Fleurs de toutes vertus* for the text of the Morgan manuscript; this was selected because it was closest to the Italian, although it was justified only by Chantilly MS 660. The *Fleurs* title must henceforth be reserved for the text represented by MS 660, while that found in Morgan MS 771 may be called *Livre de sapience* or *Chapelet des vertus*. I should vote for the latter as it is found in some manuscripts and in most early printed editions, while the *Livre de sapience* might lead to confusion with the book by the same name in the Bible and the work with the very similar title by Frère Laurent.

The confusion that has existed as to these two related texts is very ancient indeed. Nearly four hundred years ago the text found in Chantilly MS 660 was identified as being the same as that in Morgan MS 771; for example, the first English edition (1565) has the title: "The boke of wisdome otherwise called the Flower of Vertue." Even then, obviously, the *Livre de sapience* and the *Fleur(s)* were believed to be one and the same work.

While I am not solely responsible, therefore, for creating this confusion, I have certainly been guilty of perpetuating it—and for this I wish to apologize to my readers and hasten to offer these corrections. My slip is the horrid result of trusting the descriptions found in a catalogue and of not going to the original works themselves;

my excuse (if there be one) is that this was absolutely impossible at the time when the paper was written. It is well for the research worker to engrave upon his mind the observation that Alfred W. Pollard made of his great friend and colleague, Robert Proctor, "that in matters of bibliography he would not have taken the results of an archangel upon trust." I have quoted these words of wisdom for many years and now, alas, I too am found "in flagrante delicto," though I would very much prefer to view this paper as just another casualty of the war.

(From *PMLA* 64 (1949), pp. 600-01).

# CHAPTER T11

## A SURVIVAL FROM THE MIDDLE AGES:
## WILLIAM BALDWIN'S USE OF THE
## *DICTES AND SAYINGS*

WILLIAM BALDWIN'S[1] *A Treatise of Morall Phylosophie*, judging from the number of editions which were called forth, seems to have been extremely popular among Tudor and Stuart readers, no fewer than twenty-three editions[2] having been issued between 1547 and 1651. The *Treatise* is divided into four parts, the first containing 'The Lives and Witty Answers of the Philosophers' and the remainder devoted to 'Precepts and Counsells,' 'Proverbs and Adages' and 'Parables and Semblables,' in that order. It purports to be, in the main, a collection of suitable quotations from the writers of classical antiquity. The authors thus represented include, among others, Aristippus, Aristotle, Bias, Chilon, Hermes, Isocrates, Pythagoras, Plato, Plutarch and Socrates.[3]

---

[1] For an account of Baldwin's life, see Eveline I. Feasey, 'William Baldwin,' *Modern Language Review*, xx (1925), 407–418. His literary works were discussed by Wilbraham F. Trench, 'William Baldwin,' *Modern Quarterly of Language and Literature*, I (1898), 259–267. Trench found that 'the plan of Books I and III [of the *Treatise*] seems to be derived from the *Apophthegms* of Erasmus, of which Nicholas Udall's English translation was in print since 1542; while Book II is modelled upon Erasmus's *Adagia*' (p. 260).

[2] Compare the *Short-Title Catalogue of Books Printed in England, Scotland & Ireland . . . 1475–1640* (STC), (London, 1926), nos. 1253–1269. William W. Bishop, *A Checklist of American Copies of "Short-Title Catalogue" Books* (Ann Arbor, 1944), cites four additional editions not in STC, viz., 1257.1, 1259.1, 1265.1 and 1267.1. The edition of 1651 is listed by Donald Wing, *Short-Title Catalogue . . . 1641–1700* (New York, 1945), no. B 547.

[3] A study of Baldwin's sources was undertaken by D. T. Starnes, 'Sir Thomas Elyot and the "Sayings of the Philosophers,"' *Texas University Studies in English*, XIII (1933), 5–35 (especially 13–17). Starnes concluded (p. 24) that Baldwin had drawn 'from Laertius, Burley and, to a less extent, from Caxton and Erasmus.' Elsewhere (p. 14) it is stated that 'the indebtedness to Laertius is the heaviest' and that 'certain of the precepts and sayings seem also to derive from Burley.' Only in the case of Hermes does Starnes mention specific borrowing from the *Dictes*. Actually the debt to the Caxton edition is very great, as will be brought out below. Of the 144 lines in the chapter on 'Wisdom' in STC 1255, sixty-two lines are certainly derived from the *Dictes* and thirteen additional ones possibly so.

On signature M8 recto of the edition printed by Edward Whitchurch about the years 1550–1555[4] there will be found the following proverb, accompanied by a commentary and without attribution to any philosopher:

Wrathe leadeth shame in a lease.[5]
What might there be saide to cause a man more to refraine his wrathe? For euery man naturally hateth shame, which sithe it is the folower & ende of anger, and thereto ioyned inseperably, euen as the shadowe is to the bodye, what man consyderyng the ende, wyll vse hymselfe thereto?

This somewhat curious adage can, with certainty, be traced back not to a classical source but to the popular *Liber philosophorum moralium antiquorum*, a thirteenth-century treatise from which the first dated book printed in England, the *Dictes and Sayings of the Philosophers*,[6] was derived. In the Latin text, the proverb is attributed to Plato and reads thus: 'Et dixit: ira est honor adducens post se dedecus.'[7] When, late in the following century, Guillaume de Tignonville made his French translation, he rendered this Latin line fairly literally, and in some manuscripts (thus Morgan 771, f. 90[v]) we find: 'Et dit ire est honneur qui mainte honte.' A subsequent scribe—possibly the translator himself—apparently decided that it was necessary to clarify or amplify this saying in order to explain its meaning in a more satisfactory manner. Exactly what happened is not quite clear, but it is certain that the proverb was altered either by the addition of the words 'en leesse'[8] ('into joy'— which came to be read as 'en lesse,' i.e. 'in a leash') or by 'en lesse'[9] which was subsequently misread by some scribes as 'en leesse.'

The *British Museum MS Royal 19 B IV*, f. 31[v], for example, preserves the reading: 'Et dist ire [est] honneur qui meine honte en

[4] STC 1255, copies seen: Harvard and Folger. Also consulted were the copies of STC 1258 (Union Theological Seminary) and Wing B 547 (Columbia).

[5] This saying is also found in the chapter 'Of anger, wrath, etc.,' sign. O1.

[6] For this work, consult the Introduction to my edition of the *Dicts and Sayings of the Philosophers*. Early English Text Society, Original Series 211. Starnes's statements that (p. 8) 'What de Tignonville's source was, we do not know' and that the *Dictes* was a work 'related to that of Burley' (p. 22) need correction. In this paper *Dictes* is used only for the Rivers translation, the other versions being cited as *Dicts* as in my edition.

[7] Ed. Ezio Franceschini, 'Il "Liber philosophorum moralium antiquorum." Testo critico,' *Atti del Reale Istituto Veneto di Scienze, Lettere ed Arti*, xci (1932), parte seconda, 393–597; see p. 466.

[8] See Frédéric Godefroy, *Dictionnaire de l'ancienne langue française* (Paris, 1880–1895), under 'leece.'

[9] Cf. *NED* 'leash.'

leesce' and this was translated in the anonymous version of the Helmingham Hall MS[10] as: 'And seith: such angre is worshipful þat bryngeþ oftetymes shame to gladnesse.' Stephen Scrope, although he mistranslated the first half of this saying, similarly has: '. . . þat ledithe shame in-to gladnes.'[11]

Some French manuscripts, on the other hand, preserve the other reading and so *Morgan MS 10*, f. 29, quotes this as: 'Et dist ire est honneur qui mainte honte en laisse.' In the later printed editions of Tignonville's French rendering, we find the proverb still further corrupted to read: 'Et dist ire est le veneur qui mene honte en liesse.'[12]

When Anthony Woodville, Earl Rivers,[13] made his translation of the *Dits Moraulx*, he apparently had a fairly corrupt French manuscript[14] before him and one that preserved a different tradition than that familiar to Scrope and the anonymous translator. In this instance he translated the French proverb[15] in the identical words found in Baldwin's *Treatise*: 'And sayd wrath ledeth shame in a lese.' Thus it is certain that the quotation in the *Treatise of Morall Phylosophie* was borrowed from the *Dictes and Sayings of the Philosophers* in the translation made by Earl Rivers.

Another example will suffice to show, I think, that Baldwin did not make use of the Latin or French texts or of either of the other two English versions for his *Treatise* but that he unquestionably borrowed heavily from the Rivers translation.[16] Among the quotations attributed to Tac in the *Liber philosophorum* there is to be found: 'Et dixit: homines regis sunt cum eo velut ventus cum igne, nam ignis, quando accenditur absque vento, eius opus debilitatur et tardatur eius crematio' (p. 416). Tignonville rendered this as: 'Et dist les subges du roy sont auecques lui comme le vent auecques le feu et quant le feu est alume ou il n'a point de vent il tarde de tant plus ardoir.'[17] Scrope's translation, for example, has: 'And he saithe: þe subiettis of a king is with him as þe winde is with the fire; whan a fire is kindeled wher þere is no wynde, it tariethe lenger of bren-

[10] *Ed. cit.*, 119. 11–12. [This is now Glazier MS 66. CFB]

[11] *Ibid.*, 118. 14–15 and notes p. 349.  [12] Paris: Pierre Leber, 1533, folio 58.

[13] See Rudolf Hittmair, 'Earl Rivers' Einleitung zu seiner Übertragung der *Weisheitssprüche der Philosophen,'* *Anglia*, XLVII (1935), 328–344.

[14] Compare my *Dicts*, pp. xlvii–lix.

[15] Pierpont Morgan Library, no. 673, sign. [e5].

[16] My statement in the *Dicts* (p. lxviii, n. 2) to the effect that Baldwin had made fresh translations from the French or Latin texts is quite incorrect.

[17] MS *Royal 19 B* IV, f. 10[v].

nyng.'[18] Rivers, on the other hand, supplied the following reading: 'And saide. the people ar to the kyng as the wynde to a grete fyere. for the more the wynde is. the strenger is the fyere.'[19] This passage seems to have been modified by Baldwin, who attributes it to Pythagoras (sig. L4), to read: 'The subiectes are to theyr kyng, as a wynd is to a fyre: for the stronger that the wynde is, the greater is the fyer.'

It is quite true that Baldwin occasionally quoted the Rivers text *verbatim* together with the correct attribution; thus, for example, he assigns to Socrates (sig. L3) the saying: 'The profite of sylence, is lesse than the profite of speche: and the harme of speche is more than the harme of silence.'[20] The identical words, apart from minor orthographical differences, will be found on signature [d6] of the Caxton edition. However, in common with many writers of mediaeval days who found it desirable or expedient to use the *Liber philosophorum* (or its various descendants) as a source book,[21] the Tudor compiler often took liberties with his original. As we have seen, he did not hesitate to alter the name of the philosopher to whom a proverb was attributed.[22] And the instance cited above is, by no means, a solitary example! Thus we find 'There is no goodnes in a lyer' attributed to Seneca (sig. N7), though in the Caxton edition these are the concluding words in the chapter on 'Omer.' Again 'It is better to be in company with a serpente, than with a wicked woman' is given to Socrates (sig. O2[v]), probably on the strength of the many similar, unkind remarks attached to him in the *Dictes*; the philosopher is not specified in the original text.[23] In many cases,[24] also, the wording has been slightly altered; in the first edition,[25] the above example reads: 'And another saide It were better

---

[18] *Ed. cit.*, 32, 26–28.        [19] Morgan 673, sign. [b5[v]].

[20] Scrope, following his French manuscript, has badly mistranslated this; cf. 96. 14–16 and notes, p. 344.

[21] Compare my paper 'The *Fleurs de toutes vertus* and Christine de Pisan's *L'Epitre d'Othéa*,' supra, and my *Dicts*, pp. xvii–xviii.

[22] Starnes, *op. cit.*, p. 15, n. 25, correctly states that 'Baldwin is quite unreliable in his ascriptions of the sayings.'

[23] *Ed. cit.*, 280. 15–17.

[24] Another misattribution by Baldwin is found on sign. N8[v]: 'Syckenes is the prieson of the bodye, but sorowe the prieson of the soule. Hermes.' In the *Dicts* (71. 12–13) this saying is found under Diogenes.

[25] STC 6826, sign. [i6]. On two occasions (*The Library*, xv [1934] 316–329, and xxi [1941], 284–290) I have maintained that this was the second edition and that the actual first edition was STC 6828. Some years ago a piece of evidence came to

to be in companye & conuersaunt with a serpent. than with an euil woman.'

Another innovation which Baldwin introduced[26]—and one which certainly improved in no way on his original—was to transform the prose proverbs into what he must have fondly believed was verse. In Rivers' text Sedechias is credited with the line (sig. [a5$^v$]): 'And saide/bettir is a woman to be bareyn than to bere an euill disposid or a wikked childe'; for this Baldwin offers (sig. P2$^v$):

> Better it is for a wyfe to be barraine
> Then to bring foorth a vyle wycked carrain. Hermes.

Another bit of doggerel[27] is attributed by Baldwin to Socrates (sig. O8):

> He that to wrathe and anger is thrall,
> Ouer his wit hath no power at all.

whereas in the *Dictes* the line reads (sig. [b5]): 'Tac sayd he that can not refrayne his Ire hath no power ouir his witte.'

Whatever interest the *Treatise of Morall Phylosophie*[28] may have

---

my attention which may indicate that my belief was quite wrong. The final solution of the problem awaits an opportunity for a thorough examination of *Lambeth MS 265* and a collation of all the known copies of both editions.

[26] In his own words (STC 1255, sign. M8): 'And suche thynges as I thought moste proper, I haue drawen into Metre, & ioyned with them diuers other, by other men doen already: to the intent that such as delite in Englishe Metre, and can retayne it in memorye better than prose, mighte fynde herein somewhat accordyng to their desyres: whiche booke & Meters I submit to the correccion of all fine witted and well learned menne: desyring them herein to pardon myne ignoraunce, and to beare wyth my boldenesse, which thought it better, though rudely, to doe somewhat, than to be idle, and to do nothing.'

[27] As another example, we may cite from sign. o8:

> Be mery and glad, honest and vertuous,
> For that suffyseth to anger the enuious. Hermes.

The attribution is quite correct; cf. my *Dicts*, 22. 25–26.

[28] The *Treatise of Morall Phylosophie*, in turn, was extensively used as a source book for *Politeuphuia; Wits Commonwealth* (variously attributed to Nicholas Ling and John Bodenham), as Starnes has adequately demonstrated. This work was also very popular. Of the twelve editions apparently printed before 1640, seven have survived (STC 15685–15690 and Bishop 15687.1). The catalogue of the Carl H. Pforzheimer Library (*English Literature, 1475–1700*, New York, 1940, III. 826) states that there were issued 'some eighteen editions before the end of the seventeenth century' and the last edition in the Library of Congress is dated 1699.

Starnes has also made the claim (p. 8, n. 12) that *Wits Commonwealth* borrowed directly from Rivers' *Dictes*, but I have found no conclusive proof for this. The two quotations cited by Starnes as evidences of direct borrowing are also to be

for us, this does not rest upon the dreary list of moral common-places which forms the subject matter of the volume. But as an example of the survival of mediaeval literary traditions[29] into the days of the Commonwealth, it is highly significant. By 1640, as Miss Palmer's list[30] adequately shows, a very considerable body of classical literature, both in Latin and in translation, had been printed in England. Yet the first edition of Baldwin's *Treatise* appeared in the same year (1547) as did Robert Whittington's translation of Seneca's *De remediis fortuitorum* (STC 22216) and 1640 saw the appearance of both Horace's *Ars poetica* in the translation by Ben Jonson (STC 13798) and the twenty-second edition of the *Treatise of Morall Phylosophie* 'now the sixt time inlarged.'

For more than four hundred years, the literary descendants of the Arabic *Mokhtâr el-Ḥikam* had influenced the thoughts and writings of many people in Western Europe, though it is scarcely probable that this compilation, in the form of Baldwin's *Treatise*, enjoyed the esteem of George Chapman, Philemon Holland, or Ben Jonson. The simplicity of its style, however, appealed to Thomas Nashe.[31]

---

found in the *Treatise*, the former on sign. N1 of STC 1255 and the latter on p. 148 of Wing B 547 (though, at least in the 1651 edition, the saying is attributed to Seneca).

[29] Starnes is of the opinion that the influence of the *Dictes* can even be traced, through *Wits Commonwealth*, to Bodenham's *Bel-vedére, or the Garden of the Muses* (STC 3189-3190). With this opinion the writer does not concur. True enough, many of the sayings in the *Garden* seem quite similar to those in the *Dictes* but this is not, in view of the commonplace nature of these adages, sufficient to prove even indirect kinship. Indeed, identity of wording is itself not proof of inter-relationship, as the several English translations of the *Dictes* amply demonstrate. If an example from the *Garden* may be cited, we find in the chapter 'Of Friend-ship' (STC 3189, sign. G7ᵛ):

> The summe of friendship is, that of two soules
> One should be made, in will and firme affect.

This might, of course, have been based upon the *Dicts* (compare anonymous version, 65. 18-20) but it is also found in Diogenes Laertius (v, 20), of whose work many editions in Greek and Latin were in print before 1600. The adage also occurs in the *Rudimentum Novitiorum* (Lübeck, 1475, f. 257ᵛ) and in various other works of the 'Vincent tradition' (cf. my 'Greek Philosophers in the Literature of the Later Middle Ages,' *Speculum* (1937), XII, 440-455). Thus, for example, it is found in the German translation of Burley (Augsburg, Sorg, 1490, f. 91ᵛ): 'Ward gefraget. was ist ein freünd. Er sprache ein sele in zweÿen leÿben wonent.' Similarity of thought and wording, thus, is not proof of kinship and I have noticed no quotation in the *Garden* which could be solely traced to the *Dictes and Sayings*.

[30] Henrietta R. Palmer, *List of English Editions and Translations of Greek and Latin Classics Printed before 1641* (London, 1911).

[31] In his preface to *Haue with you to Saffron-Walden*, Nashe states that he wanted

In the seventeenth century, the *Treatise* had become one of those 'Handbooks to Improvement' for the middle classes about which Mr Louis B. Wright[32] has written so learnedly and entertainingly. A hundred years after the appearance of the twenty-third edition of Baldwin's book, the *Dictes and Sayings* was once again claiming the attention of readers but by this time solely as an object of antiquarian interest, for Joseph Ames included an account of this work in his *Typographical Antiquities* (London, 1749).

(From *Speculum* 23 (1948), pp. 76-80).

---

to keep 'a smooth plain forme in my eloquence, as . . . Baldwin in his morrall sentences (which now are all snatcht vp for Printers posies),' (Ronald B. McKerrow, *The Works of Thomas Nashe*, London, 1904-1910, III, 20).

[32] *Middle-Class Culture in Elizabethan England* (Chapel Hill, 1935), pp. 121-169.

# CHAPTER T12

## FOUR ELIZABETHAN POEMS

IN the series of historical documents known as the "Rulers of England" which form part of the manuscript collections of the Pierpont Morgan Library, items of literary interest are occasionally encountered. Such a literary document is the subject of the present study.[1] It is preserved in volume I of the documents pertaining to the reign of Queen Elizabeth[2] and consists of a single folio sheet of paper, written on both sides. It was apparently extracted many years ago from some commonplace book but the earlier history of the leaf, before it entered the Morgan Library in 1905, is unknown. The watermark of the paper is quite similar to Briquet 12801 (*Pot à une anse*);[3] this mark occurs frequently on paper used in the neighborhood of Rouen, Amiens, and Paris from the middle of the sixteenth century onwards. The handwriting is certainly that of the first quarter of the seventeenth century, and probably belongs to the first decade of that century, as we shall see later. At the top of one side of the sheet is found a draft for a power of attorney, of no literary interest whatsoever; unfortunately it supplies no further clue for the dating of the document.

### I

Underneath the draft referred to above is found a version of a poem which has been rightly called "one of the most popular Elizabethan lyrics"—Christopher Marlowe's *The Passionate Shepherd to his Love*.[4] This is followed, as usual, by the "Reply" generally attributed to Sir Walter Raleigh.[5]

[1] For their kind assistance in the preparation of this paper, I am much obliged to William H. Bond, James G. McManaway, and Edwin Wolf, 2nd.

[2] Seymour de Ricci, *Census of Medieval and Renaissance Manuscripts in the United States and Canada* (1935–40), ii, 1622, enters this under the title: "Ralegh (Sir Walter). Contemporary copy of verses by him, 2 pp."

[3] Charles M. Briquet, *Les Filigranes* (Paris, 1907), iv, 624, adds the note: "Cette marque est essentiellement française; elle abonde à Paris dans les manuscrits et dans les imprimés."

[4] Compare J. W. Hebel and H. H. Hudson, *Poetry of the English Renaissance 1509–1660* (1936), pp. 137–8 (notes pp. 938–41) and p. 168 (notes pp. 945–6). For the enormous bibliography, see Samuel A. Tannenbaum, *Christopher Marlowe: A Concise Bibliography* (1937), with Supplement, especially pp. 22–4 and 26–7. A

Poemes written in the Reigne of Queen Elizabeth
A sonnet Madrigal by Sᵣ Philipp Sydney[6]

Come live with me and be my love,
and we will all the pastimes prove,
That valleis, mountaines, woods or feld*es*,
or groves, or pleasant pastures yeild*es*.

5 Wher we will sitt vpon the rock*es*
and see the Shepherds feede their flock*es*.
By shallowe rivers to whose falles
Melodious bird*es* singe Madrigalls.

Wher we will make the bed*es* of roses
10 and a thowsand fragrant poses.
a cappe of fflower & a kirtle:
Imbroydred all with Leaves of mertle.

Her belt*es* of strawe with Ivy bud*es*[7]
Corrall clasp*es* & amber Stud*es*.
15 All this Ile giue thie mynde to move
to liue with me and be my Love;

### Response

But if the world & love were sound
and truth in eu*er*y Shepherd found.
Then thes delight*es* might me much move.
to Live with the & be thie love.

5 Thie belt*es* of Strawe, thie bed*es* of roses
thie caps, thie kirtles & thie poses.
Sone break*es*, sone withers, sone forgotten
with follie ripe, with reason rotten.

Could youth long[8] last, & love but feede
10 Had tyme no death, nor age no neede

---

useful study of the sources and influence of this poem is by R. S. Forsythe, "*The Passionate Shepherd* and English Poetry," *P.M.L.A.*, xl (1925), 692–742. [For the present discussion, see the new note 15a. CFB].

[5] See Thomas Birch, *The Works of Sir Walter Ralegh* (1751), ii, 394; Sir Egerton Brydges, *The Poems of Sir Walter Raleigh* (Lee Priory, 1813), pp. 24–7; Agnes Latham, *The Poems of Sir Walter Ralegh* (1929), pp. 39–40. Hyder Rollins, *England's Helicon* (1935), ii, 186–9, is hesitant about assigning it to Raleigh.

[6] The titles are written by another (and probably later) hand. Capitals and punctuation are those of the MS.; contractions have been expanded and are printed in italics.

[7] This stanza is written crosswise in the margin at the right by the same hand.

[8] By correction *currente calamo* from "but."

Then thes delight*es* might my mind move
to live w*i*th thee & be thie love:>

The Morgan versions of these poems differ from all the other known texts in the number of stanzas, in the rhyme-words, and in an extensive list of variant readings. The [fourteen] early texts that have come down to us differ so widely from each other that the list of variant readings obtained from a preliminary survey produced nothing more than a bewildering and fruitless result;[9] this list has consequently been discarded. The dubious reader may be convinced of the wisdom of this by casting a glance at the *variae lectiones* listed by Samuel A. Tannenbaum[10] from just a few of the early texts; these clearly reveal the futility of attempting to arrive at any valuable conclusion from the multitudinous variety of the textual variants of all the early versions. On the other hand, it seems likely that an understanding of the relationship between the various texts can be more readily achieved by listing the order in which the stanzas occur in the several versions.

Hitherto only five manuscripts[11] of the two poems have been known to scholars and there are at least [eight] important printed versions which appeared before the year 1800. In their fullest form, as they were printed in Izaak Walton's second edition of *The Compleat Angler* (London: T. M[axey] for Rich. Marriot, 1655),[12] the poems by Marlowe and Raleigh consisted of seven stanzas each. Below there are listed the first lines of each stanza (with the rhyme-words in brackets) as they are found in Walton's full text; this is followed by a tabular arrangement which indicates the presence and order of the stanzas in their various other appearances.

[9] Even Walton's text shows variant readings. For example, the last line of stanza 2 of Raleigh's *Reply* reads in the first edition: "The rest complains of cares to come." In the 1676 edition of *The Compleat Angler* this line reads: "And age complains of care to come."

[10] "Unfamiliar Versions of Some Elizabethan Poems," *P.M.L.A.*, xlv (1930), 815-7.

[11] Ashmole 1486, ii, fol. 6ᵛ; Rawlinson Poet. 148, fol. 96ᵛ; Folger 621.1, fol. 2; Folger 297.3, fol. 100; and Dr. Rosenbach's MS. (Cf. John Bakeless, *The Tragicall History of Christopher Marlowe* (1942), ii, 150, and Rollins, *op. cit.*, ii, 188.) L. C. Martin, *Marlowe's Poems* (1931), pp. 299-300, refers to only "five different early versions."

[12] For a bibliographical description, see the Carl H. Pforzheimer catalogue (*English Literature, 1475-1700* (1940), iii, 1084-5). The first edition (1653) is described, *ibid.*, no. 1048, and the fifth edition (1676) under no. 1052.

## The Milk maids Song

1. Come live with me and be my Love       [: prove / field : yield]
2. Where we will sit upon the Rocks       [: flocks / falls : madrigals]
3. And I will make thee beds of Roses      [: posies / kirtle : mirtle]
4. A Gown made of the finest wool         [: pull / cold : gold]
5. A belt of straw, and ivie buds          [: studs / move : love]
6. Thy silver dishes for thy meat          [: eat / be : me]
7. The Shepherds Swains shal dance & sing  [: morning / move : love]

## The Milk maids Mothers Answer

1. If all the world and Love were young     [: toung / move : love]
2. But time drives flocks from field to fold [: cold / dumb : come]
3. The flowers do fade, and wanton fields    [: yields / gall : fall]
4. Thy gowns, thy shooes, thy beds of roses  [: posies / forgotten : rotten]
5. Thy belt of straw and ivie buds           [: studs / move : love]
6. What should we talk of dainties then      [: men / good : food]
7. But could youth last, and love stil breed [: need / move : love]

| | As above Walton, pp. 108–11 | Passionate Pilgrim[13] | Morgan MS. | Rosenbach MS. | Ashmole MS.[14] | Rawlinson MS. | Raleigh[15] London, 1751 | Folger 621.1[15a] | England's Helicon[16] | Angler, 1653[17] | Percy's[18] Reliques, 1765 | Roxburghe Ballads[19] | Folger 297.3[20] |
|---|---|---|---|---|---|---|---|---|---|---|---|---|---|
| 1 | 1 | 1 | 1 | 1 | 1 | 1 | 1 | 1 | 1 | 1 | 1 | 1 | 1 |
| 2 | 2 | 2 | 2 | 2 | 2 | 2 | 2 | 2 | 2 | 2 | 2 | 2 | 2 |
| 3 | 3 | 3 | 3 | 3 | 3 | 3 | 3 | 3 | 3 | 3 | 3 | 3 | 3 |
| 4 | – | – | – | – | – | 4 | 4 | 4 | 4 | 4 | 4 | 4 | 5 |
| 5 | 4 | 4 | 4 | 4 | 4 | 5 | 5 | 5 | 5 | 5 | – | 4 | |
| 6 | – | – | – | – | – | – | – | – | – | – | 5 | 6 | |
| 7 | – | – | – | – | – | – | 6 | 6 | 6 | 6 | 6 | 7 | |

**REPLY**

| | As above Walton, pp. 108–11 | Passionate Pilgrim[13] | Morgan MS. | Rosenbach MS. | Ashmole MS.[14] | Rawlinson MS. | Raleigh[15] London, 1751 | Folger 621.1[15a] | England's Helicon[16] | Angler, 1653[17] | Percy's[18] Reliques, 1765 | Roxburghe Ballads[19] | Folger 297.3[20] |
|---|---|---|---|---|---|---|---|---|---|---|---|---|---|
| 1 | 1 | 1 | 1 | 1 | 1 | 1 | 1 | 1 | 1 | 1 | 1 | 1 | |
| 2 | – | – | 3 | 3 | 3 | – | 2 | 2 | 2 | 2 | 3 | 3 | |
| 3 | – | – | 2 | 2 | 2 | 2 | 3 | 3 | 3 | 3 | 2 | 2 | |
| 4 | – | 2 | 4 | 4 | 4 | 3 | 4 | 4 | 4 | 4 | 4 | 4 | |
| 5 | – | – | – | – | – | 4 | 5 | 5 | 5 | 5 | – | – | |
| 6 | – | – | – | – | – | – | – | – | – | – | 5 | 5 | |
| 7 | – | 3 | 5 | 5 | 5 | 5 | 6 | 6 | 6 | 6 | 6 | 6 | |

It will be noted that the new Morgan text is, next to the version in *The Passionate Pilgrim*, the shortest of all; those in Dr. Rosenbach's volume and in the two Oxford manuscripts supply two additional stanzas for Raleigh's *Reply*.[21] But the fact that these versions are quite

[13] See Charles Edmonds's reprint, "The Isham Reprints" (1870), Sig. D5, and Joseph Q. Adams, *The Passionate Pilgrim by William Shakespeare, Reproduced in Facsimile from the Unique Copy in the Folger Shakespeare Library* (1939), Sig. D5.

[14] Through the courtesy of Mr. R. W. Hunt, I learn that the Ashmole MS. can be dated *ca.* 1600, which is also the date of the Rawlinson MS. (cf. *A Summary Catalogue of Western Manuscripts in the Bodleian Library at Oxford* (1895–1937), iii, 421). Although Dr. Rosenbach's MS. and the two at Oxford have the same stanzas, they do not agree *verbatim*.

[15] Birch, *loc. cit.*; the same text occurs in the edition by Brydges.

[15a] It is almost inconceivable—but, alas, true—that the most familiar of all the printed versions of these poems was accidentally omitted; see Shakespeare's *Poems* (London, 1640), sigs. K4ᵛ-K5. This text is similar to Folger 621.1. CFB].

[16] Rollins, *op. cit.*, i, 184–6.

[17] Though the versions in *England's Helicon*, Walton, and Percy agree in the number and order of the stanzas, the texts differ widely from each other.

[18] Thomas Percy, *Reliques of Ancient English Poetry* (1765), i, 199–202.

[19] A facsimile of this appears in Charles Norman, *The Muses' Darling* (1946), opposite p. 106. The sheet bears the note: "Printed by the Assignes of Thomas symcock" and may be dated *ca.* 1620. For Thomas Symcock, who flourished between 1619 and 1629, see McKerrow, *A Dictionary of Printers and Booksellers in England . . . 1557–1640* (1910), pp. 261–2.

[20] Cf. de Ricci, *op. cit.*, i, 294. This, the Thornborough MS. version, was printed by John H. Ingram, *Christopher Marlowe and His Associates* (1904), pp. 222–6, and was called by the editor the "oldest and contemporaneous" copy. It is, however, considerably later.

[21] The gradual growth in the number of stanzas may, perhaps, be best noted in the case of line 5 of Raleigh's "Reply" as printed above; practically the identical line occurs in the Rosenbach and Oxford MSS. The stanza, of which this is the first line, is clearly enough an answer to lines 9–14 of Marlowe's poem in the Morgan MS.

When an additional stanza appeared in Marlowe (as represented in the state found in Raleigh's *Works*, 1751), Raleigh's second stanza of the Morgan MS. became two stanzas. "Thy belt(es) of strawe" was deleted in favor of a reference to the gowns and slippers corresponding to the new stanza 4 of Marlowe, but the other words and original rhymes were retained. Around "Thy belt of straw," a new stanza was supplied for the "Reply" with the same rhyme-words of what had then become the fifth stanza in Marlowe (ll. 13–6 above).

It may, of course, be argued that the two stanzas of the "Reply" (the fourth and fifth of the final version) were originally present and were only combined as the result of an eye-slip by an early scribe. But the numerous differences between the Rosenbach and Oxford MSS. argue against a common prototype for these three; furthermore, the Morgan MS., both in the number of the stanzas and in the text, represents a different origin and tradition. It seems highly improbable that two or three scribes could have made the identical slip, and it is thus easier to believe that one stanza became two rather than that the reverse procedure took place.

distinct and present different traditions is amply demonstrated by the third and fourth lines of Marlowe's poem. For these lines, Dr. Tannenbaum has given us five different versions in all and yet the Morgan manuscript offers still other readings.[22] The new manuscript, then, is interesting as apparently representing one of the earliest versions, as may be judged both from the dating of the manuscript and from the number of stanzas there present, and is a valuable addition to the body of Marlovian literature.

## II

At the top of the reverse side of the leaf is a poem entitled (by a hand other—and probably later—than that of the original scribe) "On the State of France under y$^e$ Administration of y$^e$ Guises by S$^r$ Walter Rawleigh." Two other manuscripts of this poem have come to the writer's attention, British Museum (Harley MS. 3787, fol. 212)[23] and Folger (MS. 1.112, fol. 16$^v$);[24] the variant readings in these manuscripts are given below under the sigla H and F.

> The state of ffraunce as nowe it stand*es*
> is like primero at ffower hand*es*.
> wher some doe vie and some doe holde
> and best assurid maye prove to bolde.
>
> 5　The kinge was rashe without regarde
> and being flush would not discarde.
> but first he passed it to the guise,
> and he of nought straight waie it vies
>
> Navarre was next and would not oute,
> 10　for of his Card*es* he had no doubt.
> The Cardynall faintlier held the vie
> and watched advantage for to spie;

[22] Still another reading may be found in Joseph Ritson, *A Select Collection of English Songs* (1813), i, 263–6, where he prints:

> That vallies, groves, or hills and fields,
> And all the steepy mountain yields.

[23] The text of the poem is printed in *A Catalogue of the Harleian Manuscripts in the British Museum* (1808–12), iii, 78, following an item with the curious title: "A coppy of a Lettre sent by the great Lord to the King of Navarre, translated out of Greek into Frenche & soe into Englishe."

[24] See de Ricci, *op. cit.*, i, 272, where the MS. is dated *ca.* 1590, and Adams, *op. cit.*, pp. liv–lvi. [Through the kindness of Professor William Ringler, I have now learned of the following manuscript versions: Harley MS. 7392 (ff. 60$^v$ and 62$^v$); University Library, Cambridge, MS. DD. 5. 75 (f. 29); Marsh's Library, Dublin MS. Z. 3. 5. 21 (f. 22); and Bodleian Library, MS. Rawlinson Poet. 85 (f. 104). CFB].

ffor to goe out his frend*es* him bid*es*
but Cardynall*es* hatt*es* makes busie head*es*
15 all rest were vp and all were in
and Phillip wrought that guise might wynne.

Quene mother stode behind his backe,
and taught him howe to make his packe,
The king that all their word*es* did knowe
20 said what, goe lesse before we showe,

He profers dalyaunce for to make,
to saue himself & Guises stake
and we that sawe him at this staie
Did leave him there & rune our waie:>

4 and] the F    prove] be FH    6 flush] shyhe H    not] nedes FH    7 but]
yet F Guyse F, Gwyes H    8 of . . . waie] straightwayes of naughte F    9 Navar
F next] in F    11 faintlier] fayntlye FH    held] holdes F    12 and watched]
waitinge F    13 out] on F    bid*es*] leades F    14 but] for F    makes] make
H    15 When rest*es* F, All rests H    all] vyes F    16 and] then F, Till H
sought H    17 *By correction from* Quene mother taught him how to packe
standethe at his backe F    18 his] a F    19-22 *omitted* H    19 their wordes]
the cardes F    20 we] yow F    21 profered F    22 himself] his owne F    23
sawe . . . staie] did see all this playe F, sawe them and ther playe H    24 him]
them FH    rune] wente F, dance H    our waie] awaye F

The poem describes a game of cards, popular in its own day under
the name of Primero[25] and apparently a progenitor of Poker as it
is played today. The four players are, of course, the King of France,
the Duke of Guise, the King of Navarre and a Cardinal; the by-
standers are Catherine de' Medici and King Philip II of Spain. While
the rules under which Primero was played are today not clearly
understood and appear to have varied widely from place to place
and from time to time, the meaning of the allegory in this poem is
tolerably certain. The stake in this case apparently represents the
control of France, since the King holds a "flush" which, as today,
means a whole hand in suit and was the highest hand in Primero—
naturally the King would not discard. The opportunity to discard and
draw then passes to Guise, who "stands pat" and immediately bids
his hand. Navarre, confident of his cards, "stays in" as also does
the Cardinal, with less certainty but with more devious plans. Lines

[25] For details concerning this game, see Samuel W. Singer, *Researches into the
History of Playing Cards* (1816), pp. 244-58; Joseph Strutt, *The Sports and Pastimes
of the People of England* (1876), pp. 433-4; the articles on "Card-playing" by
Daines Barrington, John Bowle, and Richard Gough in *Archaeologia*, VIII, 133-58;
*Shakespeare's England* (1916), ii, 472-4; and especially J. S. McTear's notes on
Primero in *Notes and Queries*, 11th ser., vii, 1-3, 23-4, and 41-3.

15-8, it may be interpreted, mean that a break has occurred in the dealing, that all are in the pool and that Queen-Mother Catherine and King Philip are attempting to "influence" the game to their own advantage. The final outcome is left to the reader's imagination.

The approximate date of the poem can be determined fairly closely from the content.[26] The *terminus a quo* must be 10 July 1559, when, upon the death of Henry II from wounds received in a joust, Catherine de' Medici became the Queen-Mother; at the other extreme, the *terminus ad quem* may be fixed as 2 August 1589,[27] for on that day Henry III died from a fatal stabbing, and with the accession of Henry IV the Kingdom of Navarre was merged with that of France. Between these two terminal dates only two periods can supply satisfactory historical backgrounds for the plot of our poem; the earlier is from 10 July 1559 to 17 November 1562 and the later from 9 June 1572 to 23 December 1588. On 17 November 1562, Anthony of Bourbon, King of Navarre, died at the battle of Rouen and was succeeded by his wife (Jeanne d'Albret) who was Queen in her own right. The future Henry IV only became King of Navarre upon the death of his mother (9 June 1572);[28] thus, in this interval of nearly ten years there was no King but only a Queen of Navarre. Again, with the murder of Henry, Duke of Guise (also known, as his father was before him, as "Le Balafré"), on 23 December 1588, the second period may be considered closed. His successor, the young Prince of Joinville, was immature and in any event promptly imprisoned; the new Duke of Guise thus represented no immediate threat in the political struggles of the day.

It seems rather unlikely that the earlier of these two periods could supply the proper setting for the poem. The two French Kings who reigned during this period were both young boys. Francis II (who

[26] The historical notes are based, in the main, on *The Cambridge Modern History* (1907-10), vol. ii, chap. 9, and vol. iii, chap. 1; Martha W. Freer, *Henry III, King of France and Poland* (1858); Bernard de Montfaucon, *Les monumens de la monarchie Françoise* (Paris, 1729-33), v, 65-434; Pierre de Lanux, *La vie de Henri IV* (Paris, 1928); and Walther Tritsch, *Heinrich IV, König von Frankreich und Navarra* (Frauenfeld, 1938). Interesting and more popular accounts may be found in Milton Waldman, *Biography of a Family; Catherine de Medici and Her Children* (1936), and Quentin Hurst, *Henry of Navarre* (1938). See also Paul F. Willert, *Henry of Navarre and the Huguenots in France* (London, 1929).

[27] This date might have been set at 5 January 1589, the date of the Queen-Mother's death, but since it is not necessary to suppose that she was there in the flesh, it seems better to adopt the date of Henry III's death.

[28] Concerning her death, possibly by poison, see Freer, *op. cit.*, i, 92-3.

died at the age of sixteen in 1560) was entirely in the power of the Guises, and Charles IX (who was only ten years old at his succession) was under the complete control of the Queen-Mother. They, in short, held no cards at all. Again Anthony, King of Navarre, was not the great political leader that his son was to be at a later date. Indeed the struggle for power in 1559–62 did not rest so much between Navarre and Francis, 2nd Duke of Guise,[29] as between the latter on one side and Condé (Louis I of Bourbon and brother of Navarre) and Admiral Gaspard de Coligny on the other. It is significant to note that neither of these historically prominent opponents of "Le grand Guise" is even mentioned.

Thus it seems probable that the poem refers to the second period and can, perhaps, be still further limited as to date. When Henry ascended the throne of Navarre, he was not yet nineteen years old and was of little political significance; his bitter rival, Henry, 3rd Duke of Guise, was only three years older. At that time, also, Coligny and Henry, 2nd Prince of Condé, were still the leaders of the Huguenot party; the former, of course, perished not long after in the massacre of St. Bartholomew (24 August 1572), while Condé continued his active life until 1588.[30] If our poem belongs to the earlier years of this period, one might expect some reference at least to Condé. Finally, in February 1576, the young Navarre escaped from court and abjured Catholicism; thereafter he absented himself from the French court for many years. These historical facts seem to preclude the earlier years of this epoch, as they do not provide a suitable setting.

Not until 1584, after the death of Francis, Duke of Anjou[31] and (as brother of Henry III) the heir apparent, did the King of Navarre become the logical successor to the crown of France. This, of course, caused the Catholic party considerable anxiety and on 2 January 1585, at the Treaty of Joinville, King Philip of Spain undertook to support the party of the Guises (now headed by Henry) with contributions of money; at the same time Charles, Cardinal of Bour-

[29] "Le grand Guise" was shot 19 February 1563 by the Huguenot Jean Poltrot de Méré and died five days later.

[30] He died, probably by poison, on March 5th. The unsavory scandal centering around Condé's wife, Charlotte de la Tremouille, is told by Freer, op. cit., iii, 74–7. Pierre Matthieu, Histoire des Derniers Troubles de France (Lyon, 1597), fol. 81ᵛ (i.e., 71ᵛ), says that Condé died on May 5th.

[31] If the poem was written before his death, one might expect that it would have included some mention of him either as Anjou or as Alençon.

bon, was chosen successor to Henry III by this alliance.[32] Lines 11–16 of our poem seem to refer to the provisions of this treaty. It is, thus, likely that the poem was composed during the "War of the Three Henrys" and one may see in lines 21–2 a reference to the summer of 1588, when Guise was in Paris and Henry III was trying to placate him while attempting to improve his own position.

We can, then, with some confidence date the poem as having been written about 1588. As political poems of this sort rapidly lose their interest, once the events which they depict are no longer familiar to the eventual reader, such poems are rarely found carefully written out in manuscripts of much later date. The problem posed in the poem was solved by the murder of Henry "Le Balafré" on 23 December 1588 and by the similar death of Henry III, at the hands of Jacques Clément, eight months later. By 13 September 1598[33] all the characters noted in these lines were dead except Navarre himself, who survived only to be assassinated by François Ravaillac on 14 May 1610. It seems logical,[34] therefore, to assume that the poem as here written was set down not later than 1610.

### III

The lower half of the same page contains a copy of Thomas Campion's well-known poem "What if a day," here with the title by the later hand "On the Brevity of Humane Happyness." Two other manuscripts of this poem are in America, Folger (MS. 452.5, fol. 137)[35] and Rosenbach Company (*olim* Phillipps MS. 9549, p. 198);[36] the variant readings (with the abbreviations F and R) are noted below.[37]

---

[32] According to Martha W. Freer, *History of the Reign of Henry IV* (1860), he was proclaimed King Charles X on 7 August 1589 (i, 38) and died nine months later, 31 May 1590 (i, 171).

[33] This is the date of the death of Philip II.

[34] Raleigh, of course, ascended the scaffold on 29 October 1618 (*D.N.B.*, xlvii, 200). The attribution of the poem to Raleigh is by the later hand and is of no critical importance.

[35] De Ricci, *op. cit.*, i, 319, dates the MS. as *ca.* 1630.

[36] My thanks are due to Dr. A. S. W. Rosenbach for his generosity in permitting me to quote the variant readings and to Edwin Wolf, 2nd for supplying me with a transcript of this version. The MS. is described in the Rosenbach Company's catalogue, *English Poetry to 1700* (1941), p. 47, no. 187, and is dated 1630.

[37] In the manuscript itself, lines 5–12 and 17–24 are doubled up, these sections amounting to only 4 lines each in the original. They have been rearranged to conform to the manner in which they are usually printed.

What if a daie, or an night, or an hower,
Crowne thie delight with a thousand wisht Contentinge*s*
Cannot the Chau*n*ce of a night, or a*n* hower
Crosse thie delight*es* w*i*th a thowsand sad tormentinge*s*
5      ffortune, hono*ur*, beawtie, youth,
     are but blossomes dying
     Wanton pleasures, doting love,
     are but shadwes flying.
     All o*ur* ioyes are but toyes,
10     idle thought*es* Deceaving.
     None hath power of an hower,
     in their lives bereaving.

Earth is but a point to the world, & a man
is but a point to the world*es* compared center
15 shall then a point of a point be so vaine:
as to triumphe in a sillie point*es* adventure.
     All is hazard that we haue,
     ther is nothing byding
     Daies of pleasure are like streames
20     through faier medwes glyding
     weale or woe, tyme doth goe
     in tyme no returning.
     Secret fates, guide o*ur* states
     both in mirth & mourning.

1 or . . . hower] or a month or a yeare FR     2 delight] delights R, desires F
wisht] sweet FR    3 Cannot] May not FR    4 thie] those F    delight*es*] desires
R    a thowsand] as many FR    7 pleasure FR    12 his lifes breathing F
13 The earth F, Earth's R    to] of R    16 in] on R    18 ther] heer F
abiding F    21 weale or woe] wel we or F    or] & R    22 in tyme] time is
R    no returning] theres no turning F, neuer turninge R

In A. E. H. Swaen's thorough study of the poem,[38] twenty-nine
versions were listed (to which these three may now be added) and
twelve of these were printed by him in full. As the result of mis-
dating a manuscript, however, Swaen denied the authorship of
Thomas Campion.[39] The poem is now generally regarded as the

[38] "The Authorship of 'What if a day' and Its Various Versions," *M.P.*, iv (1907),
397–422 and v (1908), 383–5.
[39] Percival Vivian, *Campion's Works* (1909), p. 378, points out that Swaen
believed MS. Addit. 33933 could not be later than 1578, and adds "but he is mis-
informed as to this. Whatever the date of the MS. Scottish Metrical Psalter, the
jottings in the subsequent leaves" are later. The *Catalogue of Additions to the Manuscripts in the British Museum* (1894), p. 132, dates Addit. 33933 as "in an early 17th-
century hand." The Lute MS. (Dd. iv. 23) is dated about 1610 in the *Catalogue
of the Manuscripts Preserved in the Library of the University of Cambridge* (1856–
67), i, 228, and is thus also not as early as Swaen thought. The copy in MS. Lans-

work of this poet, and it is attributed to him in anthologies[40] and is printed amongst his poems in the standard critical editions.[41] The Morgan manuscript is perhaps the earliest text of this poem now known save for that found in Lansdowne MS. 241 of the British Museum. According to Swaen's findings,[42] the Morgan text is also that of the earliest state of the poem, for it contains but two stanzas and preserves the "oldest form of the first line."

The leaf under discussion, then, can be confidently dated as belonging to the first decade of the seventeenth century[43] and contains new copies of several poems already well known to students of Elizabethan verse. Unfortunately nothing more is known of the earlier history of this leaf; it would indeed be interesting to know what else was written in the commonplace book to which it once quite obviously belonged.

(From *Joseph Quincy Adams: Memorial Studies* (Folger Shakespeare Library, 1948), pp. 695-706).

---

downe 241 (the diary of John Sanderson, 1560–1610) appears on f. 49 and can thus be dated *ca.* 1592; see *A Catalogue of the Lansdowne Manuscripts in the British Museum* (1819), p. 86.

[40] Hebel and Hudson, *op. cit.*, pp. 446 and 984–5.

[41] So in A. H. Bullen, *The Works of Dr. Thomas Campion* (1889), p. 398 ff., and in Vivian (*vide supra*).

[42] "We may safely say that the poem originally counted two stanzas only," *loc. cit.*

[43] This date is assumed on palaeographical grounds. The literary content, however, gives good reasons for believing either that these texts were written down before 1600 or that the present MS. was copied *ca.* 1610 from another commonplace book of 1588–1600.

# CHAPTER T13

## ROBERT WALDEGRAVE AND THE
## PIRATES OF DUNKIRK

ROBERT WALDEGRAVE[1] was apprenticed as a printer to the stationer William Griffith in London on June 24, 1568, and ten years later his first entry appears in the Register of the Stationer's Company. Subsequently he was attracted to the Puritan movement, and agitated against the privileged printers. On at least two occasions he was thrown into prison for printing unlicensed books or Puritan tracts; and in 1588 his press and types were seized and defaced. Following this seizure, Waldegrave began his peripatetic career, printing several of the Martin Marprelate tracts in various places of refuge, and always keeping just one step ahead of the pursuivants of the church and of the Company of Stationers.

Eventually Waldegrave fled to Scotland, apparently by way of Rochelle, where he may have printed other Puritan tracts. In Edinburgh, he became an almost immediate success, for he was appointed printer to the King (James VI) on October 9, 1590, and from that date to James's succession to the throne of England (March 24, 1603) he printed over a hundred books. He apparently followed James to London, for on June 11, 1603, a book was entered to him in the Stationer's Register. Waldegrave died before January 5, 1604,[2] probably during December of the previous year.

In the historical collections in the Pierpont Morgan Library (Rulers of England, James I, vol. i), is a document concerning Robert Waldegrave which is of considerable interest in the history of print-

---

[1] For further particulars of Waldegrave's career, see *A Dictionary of Printers and Booksellers in England, Scotland, and Ireland . . . 1557-1640*, London, 1910, pp. 277-279; Ronald B. McKerrow, *Printers' & Publishers' Devices in England & Scotland*, London, 1913, p. 183; Robert Dickson and John P. Edmond, *Annals of Scottish Printing*, Cambridge, 1890, pp. 394-474; Edward Arber, *An Introductory Sketch to the Martin Marprelate Controversy*, London, 1879; J. Dover Wilson's chapter on "Martin Marprelate" in *CHEL*, III, chapter xvii, and two other articles by the same writer: "A Date in the Marprelate Controversy," *The Library*, 2nd ser., VIII, 337-359, and "A New Tract from the Marprelate Press," *ibid.*, X, 225-240.

[2] This date is given by Robert Steele, *A Bibliography of Royal Proclamations of the Tudor and Stuart Sovereigns*, Oxford, 1910, I, xxxviii.

ing in Tudor and Stuart England. It is a communication addressed, on the verso, to "Serenissimo Principi Domino Alberto Dei gratia Archiduci Austriæ: Duci Brabantiæ Burgundiæque fratri et consanguineo nostro charissimo"; at the end is written in King James's own hand: "*Servus Vester* frater amantissimus Jacobus R." The body of the letter[3] reads in translation:

James, by the grace of God, King of the Scots, to the most Serene Albert,[4] by the same grace Archduke of Austria, Duke of Brabant and Burgundy, our most beloved relative and brother, greeting and continual increase of all happiness.

O most serene Prince, relative and brother most dear, when in the past year, our subject John Smaillie, a citizen of Edinburgh, was captured by a Dunkirk[5] ship, he obtained our recommendations by which means he procured easier access to your Serenity and he more easily effected that the property stolen by the Dunkirkers both from him and from those others our subjects in the same ship was restored. Nevertheless, when he was not able to identify the individual seizures from the rest, he abstained in the petition of them, though he obtained with great ease an appraisal of those wares which he stated belonged to him, so that for damage received he obtained compensation wholly through your clemency. When Smaillie returned to his homeland, Robert Waldegrave our printer and his son-in-law Robert Barnett, whose property (valued at a thousand[6] guldens) had been plundered in the same ship with Smaillie, made entreaties to us that we might deign to recommend their cases to your Serenity, which on behalf of the probity of these men we have not been able to decline, we, therefore, first give thanks—to the greatest extent of our power—to your Serenity both on behalf of this Smaillie and also we beg for a singular inclination of good-will towards all our [subjects], so that by the same clemency in whatever manner the procedure has hitherto been towards our remaining subjects may be extended to Waldegrave and his son-in-law and their agent William Murray, an Edinburgh merchant. And because we deem ourselves not lightly devoted to your Serenity, we will give an undertaking that (in turn) we may confirm to your [subjects] our thanks

[3] The letter came to the Morgan Library from the collection of Augustus Frederick, Duke of Sussex. See reproduction in Plate 16.

[4] Albert (1559-1621) was one of the younger sons of the Emperor Maximilian II. He served as governor of the Spanish Netherlands from February 1596 until his death.

[5] The pirates operating out of Dunkirk were a source of constant irritation to the seafaring nations. About this time the States General undertook an invasion of Flanders with the object of capturing the town and destroying this "nest of audacious pirates." Compare *Cambridge Modern History*, New York, 1907, III, 634 ff. There is a record in the Public Record Office (*Calendar of State Papers Relating to Scotland*, London, 1858, II, 796) which notes that the Dunkirkers had taken a prize ship on April 22, 1601, which may be the one referred to in this letter.

[6] According to the *Glossarium mediae et infimae latinitatis* of Du Cange, Niort, 1883-1887, I, 485, "aureus" is the normal Latin equivalent of "gulden."

and favor when the suitable time comes about. May the Lord most powerful preserve your Serenity unharmed. Given at our Palace Holyrood, the seventh day of the month of January in the year of human salvation 1603.[7]

This letter provides us with several new details regarding the Martinist printer. The fact that Waldegrave had six children as early as 1588 and that his son Robert[8] was baptized in Edinburgh on September 26, 1596, has been common knowledge for some time. Robert Barnett is, however, new to the printer's biography. We must conclude, of course, either that Barnett had married a Waldegrave daughter or that he was Mrs. Waldegrave's brother, since *gener* usually means son-in-law, though it has also been recorded with the sense of brother-in-law. Neither John Smaillie[9] nor William Murray is to be found in the local records of their day so far as these have been published or calendared.

But much more significant than these family details are the goods valued at a thousand guldens which were stolen by the Dunkirkers. What were these goods, and how much does this figure represent in our currency? One can only surmise that the merchandise must have had something to do with Waldegrave's professional activities. It is known that he employed Dutch types[10] and, in common with other printers of the time, he probably used paper from the Netherlands; thus it may have been either paper or types, or even books printed on the continent for sale in Britain, which the Dunkirkers had confiscated.

As to the value of these goods, it is possible to be more exact. Fynes Moryson's *Itinerary* (London, John Beale, 1617, sign. ¶8) informs us that "20 stiuers [make] a gulden or three shillings foure pence, being two shillings English"; consequently the thousand guldens which constituted Waldegrave's loss were equal to two thousand English shillings, one hundred pounds, or two hundred golden angels. In order to arrive at the present-day value of this sum, it is

---

[7] The date here given must be New Style, since by January, 1604, James was King of England as well as of Scotland, and Waldegrave was dead.

[8] See the *Scottish Antiquary*, IV, 174. The witnesses were the "Lord Ambassidour" and Nicoll Uddart, merchant. Robert Waldegrave, Sr., was witness to the baptism of Robert, son of Dr. James Skarchinner, "Chirurgeon," on October 22, 1595, and of Violet, daughter of John Jackson, an "Inglishman," in July, 1600.

[9] This name (Smelius) can be rendered in various ways in English or Scots; compare George F. Black, *The Surnames of Scotland, their Origin, Meaning, and History*, New York, 1946, particularly under Smalley and Smellie.

[10] Frank Isaac, *English Printers' Types of the Sixteenth Century*, Oxford, 1936, pp. 48-50.

generally customary to multiply the total by some arbitrary figure. This has always seemed to me a most unsatisfactory procedure, especially so for this particular period, since more practical standards for comparison are available. These will make it more apparent than any arbitrary figure can ever do that in 1603 a thousand guldens or a hundred English pounds was a very handsome sum indeed. In 1618 the house rent of a London baker's family was estimated at thirty pounds annually.[11] The chatty Moryson has preserved for us a wealth of detail in regard to the cost of living and travelling expenses in the closing years of the sixteenth century. For more or less permanent expatriates, Moryson estimated (sign. 3E6) that "fifty or sixty pounds sterling yeerely, were sufficient at the time when I was beyond sea, to beare the charge of a Trauellers diet, necessary apparrell, and two iournies yeerely, in the Spring and Autumne." Again, at Leyden in 1592, Moryson says (sign. D5ᵛ) that he paid for his "diet and chamber in this French-mans house three guldens, and fifteene stiuers weekely, but in the common Innes they pay ten or fifteene stiuers a meale, according to the quantity of beere they drinke, and ordinarily twenty stiuers or more, if they drinke wine." Finally he states in his general summary (sign. 3I4): "In the publike Innes a passenger paies some ten or fourteene stiuers each meale: but if he drinke wine, that will cost as much more, by reason of the great impositions vpon the Wines. Besides that, the Flemmings his consorts drinking beare stiffely, especially if they light vpon English beare, and drinke being put into the common reckoning of the company, a stranger shall pay for their intemperancy."

The sum of a thousand guldens, then, was the equivalent of a three-years' rent for a London baker; for this amount a traveller could live abroad for nearly two years, or five Englishmen could live "American plan" at Leyden for a period of twelve months; and, finally, with this much money one would have been able to give a banquet complete with wines for a thousand guests in the fair city of Amsterdam. A thousand guldens was, in short, a very considerable sum of money in 1603, and one might conjecture that it had the purchasing power of approximately six to eight thousand dollars of our money.

When one considers that Waldegrave's means two decades earlier were not sufficient to prevent his being thrown into jail at least twice,

[11] *Shakespeare's England, An Account of the Life & Manners of his Age,* Oxford, 1916, I, 318.

that he had appeared in Edinburgh as a fugitive just a dozen years before, and that the goods which the Dunkirkers had appropriated could hardly have represented the entire capital of the firm, one can only conclude that Waldegrave had done very well for himself in the Scottish capital. His return to London shortly after the date of this letter must have been a great personal triumph for the former vagrant-printer, and it is safe to assume that he was no longer quite so opposed to the rights of the privileged printers or to the principles of the established church as he once had been.

(From *The New Colophon* I (1948), pp. 377-82).

# CHAPTER T14

## NOVELLO CATTANIO: *UN VIAGGIO FATTO ALLI PAESI DEL CONTINENTE NUOVO*

IN the collection of mediaeval and renaissance manuscripts in the Pierpont Morgan Library, there is one codex (M 555) which, by some strange circumstance, has aroused no curiosity among the students of the earliest period in the discovery and exploration of America.[1] One might have expected that the published description of it[2] would have sent staid scholars scurrying to investigate the text —but if anyone has made a study of this manuscript, it is not known to the Library. Seymour de Ricci records it in the following terms:

Novello Cattanio. Viaggio alli paesi del continente nuovo, 1531–1533. Pap. (late XVI[th] c.), 33 ff. (22 x 16 cm.). Written in Venice. Orig. dark-red mor. From the Soranzo family library, Venice.

This description requires only two modifications; I would judge that the handwriting suggests a date not earlier than the second quarter of the seventeenth century, and there is no evidence to the effect that the manuscript actually belonged to the Soranzo family, though this may very well have been the case. On the inside of the upper cover we find inserted a note apparently in the hand of Count Camillo Soranzo (1826–1902), sometime "sottobibliotecario" of the Biblioteca Marciana in Venice;[3] this reads:[4]

Novello Cattanio descrive un suo viaggio fatto nel 1533 su una nave veneta (cocca da mercantia) nei paesi che ora si chiamano Florida, Virginia, Carolina, Nuova Yersey, e pare anche le prime terre del Canada, descrive peripetie di viaggio, ritrovi e scambi coi selvaggi, scene di pesca, caccia, costumi ecc. C. Soranzo.

[1] For their kind help and useful suggestions, I am most obliged to Miss Sarah Dickson, Miss Helen Gunz and Mr. Arnold Bank. It is, also, a pleasure to recall the welcome reception and the helpful assistance given this enquirer by the authorities of the Biblioteca Marciana and the Archivio di Stato in Venice.

[2] Seymour de Ricci, *Census of Medieval and Renaissance Manuscripts in the United States and Canada*, New York, 1935–1940, II, 1471.

[3] Compare Carlo Frati, *Dizionario bio-bibliografico dei bibliotecari e bibliofili italiani dal sec. XIV al XIX*, Florence, 1933, page 520.

[4] The heading in the manuscript reads: Del viagio fatto da me Novello Cattanio in ocidente alli paesi del continente novo dal zugno 1531 al zener 1533.

While this may indicate that the manuscript once formed part of the rich collections of that distinguished Venetian family, it does not appear in the catalogue of the Soranzo manuscripts preserved in the Marciana (Codice Marciano Latino, XIII.77). It is equally possible, of course, that the note is merely a statement by Soranzo in his professional capacity.

In the Morgan manuscript, Novello Cattanio[5] begins his account by informing us of the reasons which persuaded him to set down this narrative. In his own words (p. 3) he explains:

ho voluto lasciare ai posteri con questa mia faticha una testimonianza della mia diligentia non imitando io da libri ma piutosto dal fruto delle mie ricerche considerate nel mondo chose nuove, non altrimenti imaginate e questo che dicho è vero.

Repeatedly he refers to the truthfulness of his account, specifying that he has put down only what he himself has seen and that he has excluded everything fabulous or fictitious.[6] Following this short preface, Cattanio's story commences with his departure from Venice one hour before sunrise on June 24, 1531, aboard a Mediterranean-style bark named the *Santa Catharina*.[7] The ship stopped at Malaga for supplies and, passing unchallenged through the straits of Gibraltar,[8] arrived safely in the Canaries.[9] After further provisioning

[5] No further particulars regarding Novello Cattanio have come to light in the Archivio di Stato nor is he cited by that chatty diarist Marino Sanuto (*I diarii di Marino Sanuto*, Venice, 1879-1903, 58 vols.). This name does not appear in the standard books of reference, though in the form Cattaneo the name is common enough not only in Venice but also in Liguria (e.g., Oberto Cattaneo was Doge of Genoa in 1529) and in Lombardy (Camillo Cattaneo, for example, was secretary to the Duke of Milan in 1532). This author and text are unknown to G. Fumagalli and P. Amat di S. Filippo, *Bibliografia degli scritti italiani o stampati in Italia sopra Cristoforo Colombo, la scoperta del nuovo mondo e i viaggi degli italiani in America*, Rome, 1893 (in: R. Commissione Colombiana. Raccolta di documenti e studi. Parte VI, vol. I).

[6] In his own words (p. 1), Cattanio states that he has recorded only: ciò che io ho veduto & escluso tutto ciò che è favoloso.

[7] A dì 24 zugno 1531 un' hora avanti il levar del sole si mise in ordine ogni chosa e dopo levate le anchore la cocca da mercantia chiamata sancta catharina prese la sua via per il viagio col nome di Dio & in bona ventura si parti da Venetia (pages 5-6). This ship is not otherwise reported by Sanuto or recorded in the Archivio di Stato.

[8] After the edict of April 10, 1495, all ships bound for America were to sail from Cadiz. It is unlikely that the Spaniards would have permitted an Italian ship to sail for America, and this would only have been possible if they did not know of the probable destination of the Santa Catharina. Compare John Fiske, *The Discovery of America*, Cambridge (Mass.), 1892, I, 486-487.

[9] Dette isole Canarie sono habitate da christiani quali sono di differenti linguaggi

in the "Isole Fortunate," the travellers set sail on July 30 for the New World, which they reached shortly after September 23. Here they made their first contact with the natives, whom they found to be completely terrified at the sight of the Christians and who were (if possible) even more unclothed ("quasi ignuda") than frightened. In need of a safer harbor, the ship set sail once more and on October 8 again reached land (p. 11): "Eravamo dunque alla terra che scoperse il Ponze & chiamò Florida[10] & vicino alla fortezza dell'isola di san Giovanni." The description of the Indians found there, and given at this place, warrants our attention:[11]

gli habitatori sono di color giallo olivastro molto forti & ben proporzionati. Il vestire di questa gente è solo una pelle di cerva che li copre a metà del corpo anco nella stagione fredda. i capelli li hanno neri & molto lunghi che cascano sulle loro spalle, l'arma è l'arco & la freccia. hanno per loro Signore Iddio il sole & la luna come altri popoli selvatici. ogni floridiano ha la sua donna ma il capo ne ha benanco tre o quattro, esse curano la chasa & i propri

---

(page 7). Compare the *Paesi novamente retrovati & novo mondo da Alberico Vesputio Florentino intitulato*, Milan, 1508, sig. a4ᵛ: questi habitanti de queste .iiii. isole de christiani sonno pur canarii: & sonno differente de lenguazo.

[10] No mention of this landing is made by Woodbury Lowery, *The Spanish Settlements within the Present Limits of the United States, 1513–1561*, New York, 1901, nor does Cattanio's name appear in the second part of Lowery's work (*Florida 1562–1574*, New York, 1905). Both are also unknown to the distinguished bibliographer who is honored by the present volume (cf. Lawrence C. Wroth, "Source Materials of Florida History in the John Carter Brown Library of Brown University," *Florida Historical Quarterly*, XX [1941], 3–46). This Italian explorer is also not recorded by Bruno Roselli, *The Italians in Colonial Florida [1513–1821]*, Jacksonville, 1941; according to Roselli, the first Italian to land in Florida was the (unnamed) servant of Don Martin Francisco Lopez de Mendoza Grajales, the chaplain and historian of Menendez' expedition of 1565.

[11] Compare René de Laudonnière, *L'histoire notable de la Floride*, Paris, 1586, sigs. A4-A5: Les hommes sont de couleur oliuastre, de grande corporance, beaux sans aucune difformité & bien proportionnez. Ils couurent leur nature d'une peau de Cerf bien couroyée. . . . Ils portent les cheueux fort noirs & longs iusques sur la hanche . . . ils n'ont autres armes que l'arc & la flesche. . . . Ils n'ont cognoissance de Dieu ny d'aucune religion, sinon, que ce qui leur apparoist comme le Soleil & la Lune. . . . Ils se marient chacun à sa femme, & est permis aux Roys d'en auoir deux ou trois. . . . Les femmes font tout le mesnage. . . . Quand ils vont à la guerre, leur Roy marche le premier, auec vn baston en vne main, & son arc en l'autre, auec son carquois garny de flesches. Verrazzano also reports (according to Giovanni Battista Ramusio, *Delle navigationi et viaggi*, Venice, 1565, III, 421ᵛ): vanno nude fuor che le parte vergognose, lequali cuoprono con vna pelle di ceruo ricamata. As for their weapons, Girolamo Benzoni (*La historia del mondo nuovo*, Venice, 1565, f. 8) observes: Le arme principali che portano, sono archi, con saette auuelenate.

figlioli . . . quando vanno alla guerra il capo marcia alla testa dei guerrieri con la freccia in una mano & l'arco nell' altra & un' altra freccia o giavellotto nelle treccie dei capelli.

The fauna and the flora of the country also attracted the notice of Cattanio;[12] he writes of the alligators (pp. 15–16) in these words:

I fiumi sono richi di pesci & vi abondano i cocodrilli, alla notte bisogna tenersi in guardia perchè questi scendono a terra per cerchar il loro cibo e se si inchontrano in qualche huomo verso la riva lo assalgono & lo tragono nell' aqua lo uccidono & interamente lo mangiano.

After having rested and refreshed themselves sufficiently in these parts, Cattanio and his colleagues sailed ever north, touching land at various intervals, and conversing and trading with the natives. Thus they stopped at the land of the Choriba[13] (apparently the Caribs), where the author met his first tobacco-smoking Indian;[14] the latter was further adorned by a necklace of vari-colored shells not unlike the description of the "quipu" which we find in Fiske's *Discovery of America*.[15] Continuing their course northerly, they encountered on St. Stephen's day (December 26) still another tribe of natives, residents of the land called Baria;[16] of these we shall have more to say

[12] The parrots found in Florida to which Cattanio refers may be the now extinct Carolina Parrakeets (Conuropsis carolinensis carolinensis). The author also agrees with Giovanni Boemo (*l costumi, le leggi et l'usanze di tutte le genti*, Venice, 1585, f. 204) that: i Papagalli . . . son buonissimi da mangiare. Cattanio also relates how the Indians caught the parrots (pages 16–17): Per prenderli con facilità senza che algun possi sfuggire gl' indiani mettono un ragazzo di dieci o dodici anni sopra un albero con un papagallo vivo, pongono sulla testa del ragazzo un po' d'herba e della paglia e toccando della mano sulla testa del papagallo, egli grida subito come che piangesse, & gli altri che stanno in quantità attendendo quello dell' albero si arrabiano e percuotono sull' albero; il ragazzo tiene in mano una specie di lenza quale è attacato un lungo filo al capo del quale è fatto uno laccio, getta il laccio al collo di ciaschun papagallo e tirando doppo il filo prende quanti papagalli vuole. A very similar account is given by Peter Martyr (*Historie of the West-Indies*, London, Hebb, c. 1625, folio 153).

[13] Actually the word appears to be Choniba (page 18), which is likely to be due only to the carelessness of the scribe and may thus indicate that the author of the text and the scribe of the present manuscript were not one and the same.

[14] Con la pippa in bocca quale vien rimpita di foglie seche & bruciate & il fumo di quelle vien respirato (page 19).

[15] Compare Fiske, *op. cit.*, II, 298 ff.

[16] Several interpretations may be given for the name of this place. It may be a scribal error for Paria, which is frequently mentioned by the early explorers. Alternatively, it may be the author's emendation of the notorious slips in Vespucci's account, "badia di tucti e sancti" or "Lariab"; for Vespucci, see below.

later on. February 27 found our voyagers at an Indian village built (like Venice) on piles over the water;[17] here Cattanio (p. 33) noted the following landmark:[18]

a tre leghe discosta da noi vi era una altissima rocha dalla quale veniva fuora molta aqua la quale cadeva con tanto romore & asprezza che si sentiva assai distante.

Cattanio next speaks of arriving at a place called Faiale,[19] which he quitted on April 13. The sixteenth of May a further tribe of Indians was met with, whose curious marriage habits will be discussed later. Still sailing north, the ship reached cold and stormy waters—and the sailors deemed that they had reached the land "che fu scoperta da Sebastian Gavoto venetian" (p. 44).[20] The land discovered by Cabot seems to be the most northern point mentioned in Cattanio's account; from thence, after a few more landings (including one at Porto Gomiz[21] on November 26, where Cattanio joined an Indian hunting expedition), the hardy adventurers finally decided to return home.[22] They set sail from the New World on the night of November 23–24 ("due hore circa prima di mezanote"),

[17] Cattanio (page 32) states as follows: molte chase ad uso capanne erano fondate sopra pali assai grossi sopra l'aqua come venetia & da una chasa si poteva correre su tutte per causa di certi ponti levatoi che gittavano di chasa in chasa.

[18] Nostre descente en terre fut ioignant vn fort haut rocher duquel procedoit vne petite riuiere d'eau douce & bonne au possible: le long de laquelle nous demeurasmes quelques iours, pour recognoistre les choses dignes d'estre veuës, en trafiquant tousiours auec les Indiens (Laudonnière, *op. cit.*, sig. E3). Compare also the report by Verrazzano (*ed. cit.*, f. 422ᵛ): Tornando dipoi verso mezzo dì, all'entrata del porto dall'uno & l'altro lato, sono amenissimi colli con molti Riui, che dalla eminentia di quelli conducono chiarissime acque al mare. nel mezzo di detta bocca si troua vno scoglio di viua pietra, dalla natura prodotto, atto a fabricarui qual si voglia fortezza per custodia di quello.

[19] Cattanio (page 34) says they arrived: ad una terra dove alguni christiani havevano fabrichato chase & piazze molto larghe chiamata faiale. The name of this place would seem to be related to Portuguese *faial*, a forest of beech-trees (Spanish *hayal*). Both an island and a town (on the island of São Miguel) in the Azores bear this name.

[20] Ramusio (*loc. cit.*, III, 417) notes the discoveries of: Signor Sebastian Gabotto nostro Venetiano, ilquale a spese del Re Henrico 7 d'Inghilterra scorse tutta la detta costa fino a gradi 67, ma per il freddo fu forzato a tornare a dietro.

[21] Perhaps a reference to the Arcipielago or Tiera of Estevam Gomez, which appear on the Ribero maps.

[22] Eravamo già da 17 mesi in viaggio & già la nave & li ordegni erano molto consumati & gli huomeni stanchi così che il domani si prese determinatione di fare il viagio di ritorno (page 60).

reached the Azores on Christmas Eve, and lay off Madeira on the
last day of the old year. From there they sailed to Cadiz and, passing
once more safely through the straits of Gibraltar on January 21, returned to Venice in good time. Truly, this is a most fascinating and
informative account, with a wealth of specific details as to the Indians of the North American continent. There is, however, but one
thing entirely certain about this "relazione"; in spite of the author's repeated assertions as to the truthfulness of his account (some
of which have already been quoted), the whole thing is fictitious.
When, where, by whom and why the work was fabricated has not
yet been determined.

With the very first perusal of the text, suspicions are aroused in
the mind of the reader;[23] making all due allowances for the possibility that Cattanio might not have been a well-informed geographer
or naturalist, one still finds several statements contrary to common,
familiar knowledge. Florida, for example, is qualified in these terms:
"Il paese è montuoso . . . vi sono molti uccelli ma manca affatto la
gru" (p. 16). How and where Cattanio managed to acquire the
notion that mountains were near the coastline of Florida (when
the highest "peak" in the entire state attains an altitude of only 324
feet) is a mystery; certainly Laudonnière and de Soto knew better.[24]
Cranes, furthermore, are certainly to be found in the Peninsula
State, for the Florida Crane (Grus canadensis pratensis) is indigenous and is confined to that state, or to the immediately adjacent
areas. Again Cattanio speaks of cinnamon trees (p. 35) and wild
pigs (p. 37),[25] neither of which are native to that region, I am in-
informed. As still another instance of gross misinformation, we may
cite what appears to be a botanical impossibility, for in connection
with certain trees the author says (p. 15) that "li loro rami [sono]
di diversi aspetti quantunque vengano tutti di uno stesso troncho &

[23] The similarity of wording between Cattanio's account and, for example, that
by Laudonnière is in itself suspicious.

[24] Le païs est plat, decoupé de plusieurs riuieres, pour ceste cause, humide, &
sablonneux vers le riuage de la mer (Laudonnière, sig. A3). In Richard Hakluyt's
English version of the de Soto narrative (*Virginia Richly Valued*, London, 1609,
page 177), Florida is described in these terms: [It] is a verie plaine Countrie, and
hath many lakes and thicke woods, and in some places they are of wild pinetrees;
and is a weake soile: There is in it neither Mountaine nor hill.

[25] Pigs were not found in Florida before the time of Columbus, though the related peccaries may have been there.

sono così strani che quella diversità delle loro forme è la maggior meraviglia del mondo & in un solo albero sono di cinque o sei forme diverse."[26] Lastly, there is the obvious confusion as to the date of departure from America, for at one point we are told that Cattanio sailed for home on November 23, when, twelve pages earlier, we had been informed that on the twenty-sixth of the same month Cattanio had gone off on a hunting expedition with forty Indian friends.[27]

Two facts revealed by the text, however, make it perfectly self-evident that Novello Cattanio never came to Florida in October, 1531. If Cattanio had made the trip he recounts, one wonders why it was necessary for him to copy, practically verbatim,[28] the descriptions of the New World and its inhabitants which we find in the "Soderini Letter"[29] of Amerigo Vespucci,[30] especially as told in the first two voyages. For example, the Indians claimed to have been found in the land reached on St. Stephen's day are the very same ones described in Vespucci's account of the Isola de' Giganti. One need only cite the first meeting, as told by Cattanio (p. 28), to see how close the text is to Vespucci's:[31]

[26] There is a possibility that this statement may be due to a misunderstanding in regard to the dimorphic character of the sassafras tree. It may also be some mistranslation of such a comment as Jacopo Foresti's (Et in arboribus reperiuntur fructus diuersi generis) which will be found in his *Supplementum chronicarum*, Venice, 1503, f. 442.

[27] This may again be taken to be evidence for the misreading of copy, and hence that M 555 is not written out by the author of the text; see above, note 13.

[28] It is evident that the author of the Cattanio narrative was quite a scholar. As George T. Northup has pointed out in the preface to his translation of the Soderini Letter (*Amerigo Vespucci. Letter to Piero Soderini*, Princeton, 1916 [Vespucci Reprints, Texts and Studies, vol. IV], page 30): "Many passages in the Soderini Letter cannot be understood by an Italian unversed in Spanish." As we shall see below, some of the Hispanicisms of the original were replaced by the author with correct Italian forms. Although absolute proof is wanting, I am reasonably certain that "Cattanio" was also familiar with Laudonnière's account, which does not appear to be available in an early Italian version.

[29] The first and only early edition in Italian was produced in Florence about the year 1505; the book is attributed by Proctor-Isaac (no. 13324) to the press of Tubini and Ghirlandi, and in Sabin to the publisher Pietro Pacini da Pescia.

[30] The book is described in Sabin, no. 99353, XXVI, 461–463. Four copies are cited there: British Museum, Biblioteca Nazionale (Florence), Princeton and Rothschild. The Princeton copy was used for the facsimile (Vespucci Reprints, Texts and Studies, vol. II, Princeton, 1916). To his great sorrow, the present writer must here confess that in searching for sources for the Cattanio narrative, he read likely authors in an alphabetical sequence; a chronological one would have saved him much unnecessary labor!

[31] Uedemmo in una ualle cinque delle lor capanne | che ci pareuon dispopolate:

vedemmo in una valle cinque capanne che ci parevano disabitate & trovammo cinque donne che per meraviglia ci guardavano con paura & ebber animo di fuggire ma poi vedendo la nostra amicitia & alguni doni cominciarono con parole a convitarci portandoci molte chose da mangiare & adunandosi in una capanna.

Here, too, we have (apparently) conclusive evidence that the author was using the original edition of the Soderini Letter and not the reprint supplied by Bandini,[32] for the reprint omits the words "che ci pareuon dispopolate" of the original. It seems incredible that the author of this narrative could, by sheer coincidence, have supplied practically the identical words carelessly omitted by Bandini.

In other passages,[33] the text of the Soderini Letter reappears in practically identical wording in the Cattanio narrative; of the language spoken by the Indians, Morgan MS 555 (p. 30) reports:[34]

Essi parlarono poco & con bassa voce, usano i medesimi accenti come noi, perchè formano le parole o nel palato o nei denti o nelle labbra salvo che usano altri nomi alle chose.[35]

Here the differences between the Soderini and the Cattanio accounts are so slight that they concern only Romance philologists. There can be no doubt but that this is the chief source from which the author of the Morgan text took most of the details as to the habits[36] and appearances of the American Indians.

---

& fumo ad epse | & trouammo solo cinque donne | & due uecchie & tre fanciulle di tanto alta statura | che per marauiglia le guardauamo: & come ci uiddono | entro lor tanta paura | che non hebbono animo a fuggire: & le due uecchie ci cominciorono con parole a conuitare | traendoci molte cose da mangiare | & messonci in una capanna (Soderini Letter, sig. b5).

[32] Angelo Maria Bandini, *Vita e lettere di Amerigo Vespucci*, Florence, 1745, pages 1–63.

[33] The description of the Venetian-style village is borrowed from sig. a5ᵛ (including the word *levatoi*) of the Soderini Letter; compare note 17 above. The decision to return home (note 22) is almost identical with the Soderini account (sig. b1ᵛ). Sometimes the text is altered as, for example: Sono liberali nel dare | che per marauiglia ui nieghano chosa alchuna: et per contrario liberali nel domandare (Soderini, sig. a4ᵛ) *versus* sono liberi nel domandare ma nel dare è difficile che vi neghino chosa alguna (M 555, page 37).

[34] Parlano poco | & con bassa uoce; usono e medesimi accenti come noi | perche formano le parole o nel palato | o ne denti | o nelle labbra: saluo che usano altri nomi alle cose (Soderini, sig. a3ᵛ).

[35] The text continues: & quando vuotano il ventre fanno ogni chosa per non esser visti cosichè sono netti & schifi. This is similar to the Soderini narrative (sig. a3ᵛ) except that the author has replaced Spanish *vaciar* with Italian *vuotare*.

[36] Quivi non usano matrimoni ciascuno piglia la moglie che vuole & quando la vuole ripudiare la ripudia senza che gli sia tenuto ingiuria o alla donna vergogna,

The final certainty as to the spurious nature of this "voyage" will be found on pages 58 and 59 of M 555, where we read:

il capo di detto villagio si sedette circondato dai suoi havendo dinanzi a se il gran chalumit quale è una gran pipa fatta di una certa pietra o di marmo rosso o nero o bianco di figura simile a quella di una massa d' armi. li selvaggi se ne servono per gli affari di negoziato e sopratuto ne viagi potendo andar dovunque co' gran sicurezza portando in mano detto cholumit. egli è hornato di penne gialle bianche & verdi & i selvaggi terrebero di haver commesso un gran delitto capace di attirare le più grandi calamità sulla loro natione se havessero violati i diritti di questa venerabile pippa.

Here, of course, we have without question a detailed description of the calumet[37]—but this celebrated pipe was not known, nor had it received this Gallic name,[38] before the North American explorations of the seventeenth century. Indeed, the earliest appearance of the word *calumet* in the *Oxford English Dictionary* is in the French

---

che in questo tanta libertà tiene l'huomo che la donna, non sono molto gelosi & le donne mostravansi anco desiderose di congiungersi con noi christiani (page 36). The corresponding text may be found on sig. a4 of the Soderini Letter.

[37] See, for example, the description of the calumet given by Alfred Dunhill, *The Pipe Book*, London, 1924, Chapter V (esp. pages 56–65). Cattanio's account is close to Father Louis Hennepin's as given in his *Nouvelle decouverte d'un tres grand pays situé dans l'Amerique*, Utrecht, 1697, pages 149–151: Ce Calumet est une espece de grande Pipe à fumer, qui est faite de marbre rouge, noir, ou blanc, & il ressemble assez à un marteau d'armes. La teste en est bien polie, & le tuyau long de deux pieds & demi, est une Canne assez forte, ornée de plûmes de toutes sortes de couleurs. . . . Jamais on ne fait d'Ambassade parmi les Sauvages qu'on ne porte cette marque exterieure. C'est le Symbole de la paix. Tous ces Barbares sont generalement persuadez, qu'il leur arriveroit de grands malheurs, s'ils avoient violé la foy du Calumet. Toutes leurs entreprises de paix & de guerre, & leurs Ceremonies les plus considerables sont seellées, & comme cachetées du Calumet. The Italian *Descrizione della Luigiana*, Bologna, 1686, is a literal translation of Hennepin's earlier version, and differs from both Cattanio and the French text given above in mentioning only the red catlinite for the bowl of the pipe and omitting to add its similarity to the mace. The text (pages 81–82) reads: Questo Calumetto è una specie di pipa à fumare, la testa della quale è d'una pietra rossa ben polita, e'l tubo longo due piedi, e mezzo è d'una canna assai dura, abellita di piume d'ogni sorte di colore disposte leggiadramente. . . . Un Calumetto di questa sorte è un passaporto sicuro appresso tutti i confederati di quegli, che l'hanno dato, e li Selvaggi sono persuasi, che accaderebbero loro disgrazie rilevanti, se violassero la fede, come dicono del Calumetto, col quale sono solennizzate, e sigillate tutte le loro imprese in guerra, e in pace piu considerabili, facendo fumare in esso quelli, con i quali concludono qualche affare di conseguenza. Certainly the French text is nearer than the Italian to the description given in the manuscript.

[38] This word (the Norman-French form of the literary French *chalumet*) is a parallel of *chalumeau* (for *chalemeau*) or Old French *chalemel*, from the low Latin *calamellus*, a diminutive of Latin *calamus*: reed. It was applied by the French in Canada to those plants of which the stems served as pipe-tubes and to the pipe

"Jesuit Relations" of 1638, though the scholarly catalogue of the Arents' collection notes a somewhat earlier instance.[39]

It is truly unfortunate that Cattanio's account is fictitious, since there are many details which one would have been delighted with, had they been true. Cattanio's description, for example, of the dinner which the Florida Indians tendered him, though not (perhaps) of the "haute cuisine" which might have appealed to Brillat-Savarin, is sufficiently amazing to be recounted here. Four dishes, it is said, were prepared and placed before Cattanio: the first contained some white fishes simply boiled in water, the second a cutlet and a tongue (similarly boiled) of a roebuck, the third roast meat—composed of two "royal hens," the foot of a bear[40] and the tail of a beaver,[41] and the fourth dish an abundant meat broth, the whole washed down with a maple-syrup cup. If this had been their steady diet, the Carlos would certainly have deserved their reputation of being hardy, self-reliant Indians!

Again, one may quote from Cattanio's account (pp. 25–26) of the sugar-cane, probably true enough in its statement as to the introduction of the cane into the West Indies and significant in the Italian's (perhaps just) appraisal of the colonizing methods of his Mediterranean neighbors:

Si dice che li spagnoli ne portassero le prime piante nelle isole di Madera & Canarie donde essi le specie trapiantarono nella nuova Spagna dopo la scoperta & conquista del nuovo mondo, ma questo sia credo un parere senza fondamento giacchè qualche volta i selvaggi portarono ai naviganti parechie sorte di fruti & fra altro delle canne di zucaro & è certo che gli Spagnuoli mai hanno coltivato un pollice di terra nelle loro nuove conquiste.

---

itself (*Tobacco. Its History Illustrated by the Books, Manuscripts, and Engravings in the Library of George Arents, Jr.*, New York, 1937–1943, I, 24, *n.* 10).

[39] In Sagard Theodat, *Le grand voyage du pays des Hurons*, Paris, 1632. Miss Dickson kindly informs me of an even earlier citation. This is found in Urbain Chauveton's translation of Benzoni (*Histoire nouvelle du nouveau monde*, [Geneva], 1579, f. 309ᵛ): Les autres Indiens ont des chalumeaux faits de cannes pour le mesme effect.

[40] Apres qu'il eust acheué sa harangue, nous sortismes de sa Cabanne, & eux commencerent à faire leur Tabagie, ou festin, qu'ils font auec des chairs d'Orignac, qui est comme boeuf, d'Ours, de Loumarins & Castors, qui sont les viandes les plus ordinaires qu'ils ont, & du gibier en quantité (Samuel Champlain, *Des sauuages*, Paris, 1604, f. 4ᵛ). Père Marquette describes a somewhat similar four-course dinner in his account (printed in Melchisedec Thévenot, *Recueil de voyages*, Paris, 1682, page 19).

[41] It is doubtful, I am told, whether or not beavers were indigenous to Florida.

The narrative of Cattanio's voyage contained in Morgan MS 555 may be of little factual value to the student of early American history, but as an indication of the interest taken in the discovery of a new continent by a Venetian scholar,[42] the manuscript certainly possesses some historical significance. When we come to the possible date of composition of this "voyage imaginaire," it is not possible— anyway, it is not possible for me—to make a final statement.[43] According to the script, the (unwatermarked) paper, and the obviously original, seventeenth-century binding, a date past the middle of the seventeenth century would seem not improbable. The text also supports such a date for, when the author refers to the Christian colonists of Cabot's land who were subject to the King of England and who were troubled by native opposition, he must have had in mind a period certainly after August, 1585 (the settlement of Roanoke island) and probably before 1652 (the first Dutch War).[44] One may indeed accept the author's own words as an explanation of his interest in American exploration and of his reasons for writing this account (p. 4):

Nella mia vita la lettura delle diverse relationi di viagi & fattioni fu per me un diletto & le scoperte di terre sconosciute hanno sempre mossa la mia curiosità. . . . Non pretendo di non esser caduto in qualche errore ma spero che si vorrà scusarlo se si considera che è impossibile di non arenarsi qualche volta su un mare così pieno di scogli difficile & poco conosciuto.

The works he refers to were probably the very ones cited above and in the various notes; by the eighteenth century, other handbooks had superseded these accounts of the earliest days on the American continent.

Since the manuscript is not what it represents itself to be, it may,

[42] Both the style of the handwriting and the dialect of the text, as well as the several references to Venice in the narrative, make it certain that the writer was a Venetian.

[43] As we have had several occasions to note, the date of composition is not necessarily that of the date of the writing of this manuscript, though it is unlikely that much time had elapsed between the two events.

[44] The fact that there is no mention of the Dutch settlements (but only of the English) may be significant for the dating of the text. The chronological inaccuracies in the narrative (that is, the note on the English colonies and the reference to the calumet) suggest a late seventeenth-century date for the writing of this narrative dated 1531–1533; a later fabricator would have been better informed in regard to such details.

of course, be argued that it is a forgery—and that, as such, it could well have been made at any time. This argument may be plausible enough, but I do not believe it is applicable in this instance. A *terminus ad quem*, as well as some guarantee that its apparent antiquity is genuine enough, is afforded by the professional opinion of a former librarian of the Marciana, a specialist in local history[45] and consequently (one may well suppose) an expert in Venetian palaeography. Indeed, the narrative is too full of gross inaccuracies to warrant considering it as a nineteenth-century production; more detailed and accurate information on what the early adventurers found in America than that contained in the Soderini Letter was by that time available to a prospective forger. By then, too, the Vespucci text in its original edition was probably as rare as it is today, and no copy seems ever to have been available in a public library in Venice. It is certain, as we have seen, that the author did not use the first modern reprint (Bandini's edition of 1745), so that the second half of the eighteenth century also seems an unsuitable date. On the whole, the last quarter of the seventeenth century is perhaps the only period comfortably to fit the facts that we have passed in review. The physical state of M 555 is consonant with such a dating, the factual knowledge concerning Florida and the Atlantic Seaboard would then still have been (in part, at least) sufficiently fantastic and dubious to account for the serious flaws in Cattanio's text, and the supply of sixteenth-century printings would certainly have been far greater then than at any subsequent time. The author may well have owned one of the surviving copies[46] of the Soderini Letter—or some example which has not been preserved to us. It is, therefore, the reasoned belief of the present writer that the text of M 555 was composed and written out some time before 1700.[47] Whether this be the correct view or not must abide a final verdict;

[45] Soranzo was a "socio effettivo della Deputazione di Storia Patria di Venezia."

[46] Six copies are noted in Sabin but five by Northup (*op. cit.*, page 5), viz. London, Florence, Princeton and two copies formerly in private hands (Marchese Gino Capponi and Francisco Adolfo de Varnhagen, Baron de Porto Seguro).

[47] There is a conflict of evidence here. On the one hand, the handwriting seems to point to a date not much later than 1650; on the other, if the author really used a Hennepin account of the calumet as his source, this argues for a date after 1697. It is easily possible, of course, that both Hennepin and the narrator of the Cattanio voyage used a description of the Indian pipe with which the present writer is not acquainted.

on that score, as Peter Martyr reminds us (Dec. I, Lib. VI): "But tyme shall speake, which in tyme appoynted, reuealeth both truth and falsehod."

(From *Essays honoring Lawrence C. Wroth* (1951), pp. 85-99).

[Note: Mr. Colton Storm points out (*PBSA*, xlvi [1952], 274-275) that still further details were borrowed by Cattanio either from the *Nouveaux voyages* of the Baron de Lahontan (La Haye, 1703) or perhaps from a common source, since Lahontan too "was probably a plagiarist." CFB].

# CHAPTER T15

## THE *FASCICULUS TEMPORUM* AND
## MORGAN MANUSCRIPT 801

AMONG the manuscripts once forming part of the valuable
collection belonging to Henry Hucks Gibbs (later the first
Baron Aldenham) there was one which was described in
these words in the catalogue issued by its former owner:[1]

Universal History (in Latin) on the plan of Martinus Polonus. 51 folios MS.
on paper, with 32 drawings. Also a Diary of Events at Naples from its foundation to 1498 (99 pages), written in curious Italian. Without [*sic*] about 130
very remarkable drawings of Processions, Battles, Armies, Shipping, Towns,
&c., with much detail of Costume. Given me by Mr. Heeren, and bound for
me at the British Museum in *green morocco.*

This description was based upon notes supplied to Gibbs by the
celebrated palaeographer E. Maunde Thompson, then Keeper of
Manuscripts and subsequently Director and Principal Librarian of
the British Museum; his letter to Gibbs, dated 5 June 1880, is still
kept with the manuscript.[2] This entry was repeated practically
verbatim in the catalogue of the Aldenham Collection compiled
by Helen Rudd[3] and again in the sale catalogue when the collection
was broken up at auction.[4] The volume was purchased at the Aldenham sale for the Pierpont Morgan Library, which valued the manuscript primarily for the extremely interesting and important drawings illustrating the second tract; the manuscript is now numbered
M 801 in the Library's collection.[5]

---

[1] *A Catalogue of Some Printed Books and Manuscripts at St. Dunstan's, Regent's
Park, and Aldenham House, Herts, Collected by Henry Hucks Gibbs* (London,
1888), p. 185.

[2] Thompson stated in his letter that he had arranged the leaves in their correct
order but had been unable to discover either the identity of the authors of the
two tracts or that these chronicles had ever been printed. He also suggested that the
*Universal History* was modeled upon that by Martinus Polonus.

[3] *Catalogue of the Aldenham Library mainly Collected by Henry Hucks Gibbs,
First Lord Aldenham* (Letchworth, 1914), p. 461.

[4] *The Aldenham Library, Catalogue of the Famous Library, the Property of the
Rt. Honourable Lord Aldenham. The First Portion* (London, Sotheby & Co., 24
March 1937, lot 250).

[5] Compare *The Pierpont Morgan Library. Review of the Activities and Acquisitions of the Library from 1936 through 1940* (New York, 1941), pp. 39-40.

In connection with another matter under investigation in M 801,[6] the present writer happened to discover the identity of the first tract, the 'Universal History in Latin.' It is a manuscript of the familiar *Fasciculus temporum*, a summary of world history compiled by the scholarly priest Werner Rolewinck who,[7] at the time of the writing of this manuscript,[8] was still very much alive and continuing his studies at the Carthusian monastery in Cologne. Despite the assurance given Gibbs by Thompson, the leaves are even now not in the correct order; there are, also, *lacunae* in the history caused by the loss of several sheets of paper. Compared with the text found in the first Louvain edition of the *Fasciculus temporum*,[9] the following portions of Rolewinck's work appear in M 801:

> ff. 5–20 of M 801 = text of ff. 11–26$^v$ of the printed edition
> f. 1 of MS should be inserted between ff. 12–13
> f. 2 should be inserted between ff. 18–19
> f. 3 should be inserted between ff. 19–20
> f. 4 does not belong to the *Fasciculus temporum*
> ff. 21–43 of M 801 = text on ff. 32–46$^v$ of the printed edition; one leaf wanting between ff. 28–29 and its apparent conjugate between ff. 34–35 is also wanting
> ff. 44–51 of M 801 = text on ff. 50$^v$–55$^v$ of the printed edition

Once the text had been identified, it naturally became a matter of some concern to discover how the version in the Morgan manuscript

[6] The second portion contains a 'Trattato de li bangni de pezolo et de treppergola,' upon which the present writer has done considerable research; I hope to publish my findings in the near future. This text is a manuscript version of the *Cronaca di Partenope*; compare Gennaro Maria Monti, 'La "Cronaca di Partenope" (Premessa all'edizione critica),' *Annali del Seminario Giuridico Economico della R. Università di Bari*, Anno V (1932), fasc. II (reprint of 51 pages). It seems highly probable that this text was copied from the edition printed at Naples by Francesco del Tuppo *circa* 1488, but the edition is not illustrated and the illustrations in the manuscript appear to be original. *Vide infra*, Chapter T16.

[7] For notes on Rolewinck and a discussion of the earliest editions of his work, see Margaret B. Stillwell, 'The Fasciculus Temporum, a Genealogical Survey of Editions before 1480,' *Bibliographical Essays, A Tribute to Wilberforce Eames* (Cambridge, Mass., 1924), pp. 409–440.

[8] The *Fasciculus temporum* appears on the list of books recommended to the contemporary reader by Marco dal Monte Santa Maria; compare my paper, 'A Fifteenth-Century List of Recommended Books,' *The New Colophon*, 1950, pp. 48–53.

[9] The Louvain edition was printed by Jan Veldener who took as his model the edition printed at Cologne by Arnold Ther Hoernen in 1474 (cf. Stillwell, *loc. cit.*). In the colophon of his edition, Ther Hoernen states that he set up his copy 'secundum primum exemplar quod ipse renerabilis [*sic*] autor proprijs conscripsit manibus ad finem' (PML 20812, f. 74). The Louvain edition is dated, 'secundum stilum romane curie,' the 4 Kal. Jan. 1476, or 29 Dec. 1475 according to our reckoning.

stood in relation to the very many printed editions produced before
the close of the fifteenth century. No fewer than 33 such printings
are on record,[10] of which at least 25 are in Latin.[11] The Italian origin
of the manuscript, apparent from palaeographical and artistic evidence[12] and confirmed by the vernacular text found with the *Fasciculus temporum* in the manuscript, suggested that the enquiry might
best be begun with a study of the editions produced in the Peninsula
itself. Five or six[13] such editions are familiar items to bibliographers
conversant with the period; still another edition is *believed* to have
been produced but no copy of this printing has ever come to light.
The list of recorded editions is the following:[14]

1. Venice: Georgius Walch, 1479, [H 6924; Sander 6525; BMC V:274]
2. Venice: Erhard Ratdolt, 1480 [H 6926; Sander 6526; BMC V:283]
3. Venice: Erhard Ratdolt, 1481 [H 6928; Sander 6527; BMC V:285]
4. Venice: Erhard Ratdolt, 1483 [H 6933; Sander 6528; no copy known][15]
5. Venice: Erhard Ratdolt, 1484 [H 6934; Sander 6529; BMC V:288]
6. Venice: Erhard Ratdolt, 1485 [H 6935; Sander 6530; BMC V:290]
7. [? Aquila]: Adam de Rottweil, 1486 [Sander 6531; BMC VIII:413]

[10] Stillwell, *op. cit.*, p. 409.

[11] This, in any case, is the total of editions represented in America (Margaret B.
Stillwell, *Incunabula in American Libraries*, New York, 1940, pp. 435–436; nos.
R245–R269).

[12] The Italian editions supply cuts of local interest which do not appear in the
North European printings, such as the realistic views of Venice, the Pantheon at
Rome, etc.

[13] The edition formerly assigned to Aquila degli Abruzzi (no. 7 below) may
have been produced in Piedmont or even in Southern France; on this, see the interesting article by Victor Scholderer, 'Adam Alamanus,' *The Library*, 5th ser., 1
(1946–1947), 237–242.

[14] The bibliographical references are to: Ludwig Hain, *Repertorium bibliographicum* (Stuttgart, 1826–1836); Max Sander, *Le livre à figures italien depuis 1467
jusqu'à 1530* (New York, 1941); and the *Catalogue of Books Printed in the XV*th
*Century now in the British Museum* (London, 1908–1949). The discussions of the
cuts which appear in the several editions as given by Sander, the British Museum
Catalogue and Wilhelm Schreiber (*Catalogue des incunables à figures imprimés en
Allemagne, en Suisse, en Autriche-Hongrie et en Scandinavie*, Leipzig, 1910, pp.
220–225) are incorrect and misleading; a new account and tabulation would prove
useful and instructive.

[15] Gilbert Redgrave, *Erhard Ratdolt and his Work at Venice* (London, 1894), p.
38, lists this work with hesitation under his no. 39. He remarks: 'According to
Panzer, in this [edition] no printer's name is given. The whole is perhaps due to
an error in reading the date of No. 43 [the 1484 edition—no. 5 above].' Since all
the other Ratdolt editions are fairly common books, it is singular (to say the least)
that no copy of this edition should have survived to our day! Redgrave's table on
p. 47 (Note A) gives the location of cuts in the four extant Ratdolt editions—but
it is not always clear from this chart how very much the arrangement of the cuts

A comparison of the six extant editions reveals that, for the sections of text present in the Morgan manuscript, all the Italian editions[16] have the same page-for-page contents; this is equally true of the Louvain edition cited above. Obviously Walch set up the first Venetian printing from the one produced by Jan Veldener;[17] Ratdolt, in turn, copied Walch's volume and at least three times reset his type from an earlier edition of his own; and, finally, Rottweil took the last Ratdolt edition as the prototype for his own production, wherever that may have been printed. Though all these editions are inter-related, they nevertheless all differ in detail, the one from the other. The chief differences lie in the arrangement of the cuts used to illustrate the work and the amount of 'current information' supplied at the end of the chronicle.[18] Furthermore, one can also detect a gradual increase in the amount of text per page from edition to edition. Thus, though the text on each page of one edition corresponds to that on the same page in another, the later printing will —as often as not—include additional or supplementary information for the period represented on that page.

When the Morgan manuscript was compared with the Italian editions, it could be seen at a glance that the manuscript differed notably from the 1479 and 1486 printings. The Walch edition has fewer illustrations than are found in M 801, while the cuts in the Rottweil production differed in character and arrangement from the figures in the manuscript.[19] Furthermore—and equally as strange —both these editions have the scene of Venice in reverse;[20] that is,

---

differs (from edition to edition), and what they were meant to represent in the first instance and in the subsequent repetitions. [See also Chapter B23.]

[16] All four Ratdolt editions were compared in the Biblioteca Nacional, Madrid (*Catalogo de incunables*, 1945, nos. 1615–1618) and the first one can be seen in the library of the Santa Iglesia Catedral at Segovia (Inc. no. 384). Nos. 1, 3, 5, and 7 above are also found in the Pierpont Morgan Library (*Check List*, nos. 883, 853, 838, and 1343); at Salamanca, I saw nos. 3, 5, and 6.

[17] Compare Stillwell, *op. cit.*, p. 419, and the BMC citations.

[18] Each edition adds notes on current happenings which took place since the appearance of the preceding edition. The last entry in the 1481 edition records the death of Mohammed II, the Conqueror (of Constantinople), with the confident note 'descendit ad inferos tertia die mai.'

[19] BMC VIII: 413 states that 'the cuts are suggested by those of Ratdolt but are more carefully executed,' while Sander (no. 6531) remarks that the cuts are 'grossièrement copiés sur l'édit. précédente.'

[20] The 1479 edition was, of course, printed in Venice and it is thus very strange that this slip was not discovered and rectified. The original sketch may have been made directly on the block which, when cut and printed, would have produced a

the facing view places the two pillars with the statues of St Theodore and the Winged Lion of St Mark to the right of the Palazzo Ducale, while the bridge leading to the Riva degli Schiavoni appears on the left side of the Doge's palace. As our Plates 17a & b show, the Morgan manuscript does not err in this respect—and neither do the Ratdolt editions.

It is obvious from the very first inspection that M 801 has a close affinity to the editions printed by Erhard Ratdolt. The next step was to identify, if possible, the particular edition most closely parallel to the manuscript version.[21] Since all the editions differ from one another in specific details, it was a relatively simple matter to determine that the text of the *Fasciculus temporum* in M 801 was a direct copy of Ratdolt's 1481 edition of this work.[22] The accompanying Plate 18 shows that even the woodcuts were copied with scrupulous fidelity by the scribe, though in some cases the manuscript supplies supporting figures or 'putti' further to embellish the illustrations.[23]

Not only do the woodcuts connect the 1481 edition with Morgan MS 801, but the text itself offers corroborative proof.[24] On folio 5

---

picture in reverse. It is equally curious that the cut is also reversed in the 1486 edition no matter where printed, since Adam de Rottweil spent at least five years in the Republic. The cut is reproduced in Scholderer's article cited in note 13.

[21] As we have seen (note 9 above), all the Italian editions are descended from the author's holograph manuscript. It is impossible to believe that any edition was set up from Morgan M 801, since the printings all agree page-for-page while the page contents of the manuscript are entirely independent of the editions.

[22] It will suffice to cite three examples where M 801 shares misprints with the 1481 edition, and *all* the other editions (including the Veldener one) have the correct facts. On folio 6 (f. 12$^v$ of the edition), the two B.C. dates are cited as 118 & 785 (the other editions correctly have 811 & 785); on f. 10 (f. 16 of the edition), the two B.C. dates are 5416 & 540 (the other editions correctly have 540 & 516); and on f. 35 (f. 41 of the edition), the A.D. date is 494, where all the others correctly have 594.

[23] On f. 31$^v$ there is a figure of a dolphin, which does not appear in the printed edition, and on f. 43 there are handsome border designs in the manuscript which are not present in the edition. It is, of course, possible that these were manuscript additions which the scribe of M 801 found in *his* copy of the printed volume.

[24] One of the peculiarities of the printed editions is cited by Miss Stillwell (p. 415) in these words: 'The historic paragraphs seem to occupy whatever space may have been available in their proper period. When space proves insufficient the last word is followed by a symbol, at the reappearance of which, on the following page, the text of the incomplete paragraph continues.' The scribe of M 801 did not seem to understand his text very well, so he simply copied what he saw, or thought he saw, without paying much attention to the sense. Thus, instead of completing paragraphs for which he had plenty of room (he did not, it will be recalled, follow his original page-for-page and could thus dispose of his space as he wished), the scribe

of the manuscript we find the note: 'Anno M° C 10 post natiuitatem abraham ante xp̄i natiuitatem annis dommine CCCC 23 helias propheta auriga israel et origo religionis carmelite eliseo uidente rapitur.' This is a direct quotation from the 1481 printed version (folio 11),[25] save for the fact that the scribe senselessly expanded the 'd' of the roman date 923 to read 'dommine' [*sic*]. No other Italian edition includes this bit of information in its text.

Again on folio 38 verso one reads: 'Et santus [*sic*] clodolphus eius filius episcopus metens [*sic*] dicunt quidam quod fuit auus karoli magni sed hoc maro non ad mittit [*sic*] necron [*sic*] temporis *con*sonat set karolus marcellus fuit pater pipini illius qui erat karoli magni pater.' This too is found only in the 1481 edition (folio 43) and not in any of the other Italian printings. The scribe not only copied the misprint 'necron' (for 'necnon')[26] appearing in the printed text, but also preserved the authority 'Maro,'[27] though Virgil could scarcely be the source for this denial. Since the information here supplied was admittedly doubtful, it is self-evident why the note was not reprinted in the subsequent Ratdolt editions. Curiously enough, however, if 'avus' is not taken in the specific meaning of 'grandfather' but rather in the equally correct sense of 'ancestor,' this bit of genealogy is not quite so wrong as one might expect. St Clodulphus was the son of St Arnulphus of Metz and his wife Doda;[28] their younger son Ansigisus (brother to St Clodulphus) married Begga, the daughter of Pepin I (of Landen). From this

---

made the divisions exactly as he found them in his *Vorlage*. For example, on f. 45 of the printed edition, the text ends: '. . . nec etiam dispu-✠' and, at the foot of the verso, it continues '✠tatione*m* promisit iniqua*m* facie*n*dam: . . .' In the manuscript, f. 42 recto, line 9 reads: 'nec eciam dispu✠' and the rest of the line (5¾ inches of it) remains blank; to the utter confusion of the sense, a new paragraph begins on the verso of the same folio, half way down the page, with the words: 'Stacionem promisit iniquam faciendam.'

[25] Ratdolt, f. 11: '¶ Anno M°. c. 10. post natiuitatem abrahā añ xp̄i natiuitatē annis .d. cccc. 23. helias propheta auriga isrl': & origo religionis carmelite heliseo vidente rapitur.' Compare IV Reg. 2 and the *Catholic Encyclopedia*, v, 382: 'The Carmelite monks long cherished the belief that their order could be traced back in unbroken succession to Elias, whom they hailed as their founder.'

[26] The scribe had, apparently, a very uncertain knowledge of Latin; compare note 24 above.

[27] I have been unable to discover to whom this reference (Maro) may refer. There was a thirteenth-century Marco whose *Chronicon Venetum* is cited by Max Manitius (*Geschichte der lateinischen Literatur des Mittelalters*, München, 1911–1931, II, 251).

[28] Compare the *Acta Sanctorum* for 8 June and 18 July.

union came Pepin II (of Heristal), the father of Charles Martel; the latter's son, Pepin III (the Short), was, of course, the father of Charlemagne. Thus it develops that St Clodulphus was the grand-uncle of the grandfather of Charles the Great, strictly speaking not an 'avus' but sometimes so regarded by those who use the term loosely.

Morgan MS 801, as an illuminated manuscript faithfully copied from a printed text, may thus be identified as a characteristic example of a strange but not-uncommon phenomenon.[29] Why such manuscripts—and there are rather more of them preserved to us than was formerly believed to be the case—were transcribed with scrupulous care from printed matter is not completely apparent to the present writer.[30] The only plausible explanation for the existence of such a manuscript as M 801 that I can suggest is that the volume was prepared for presentation to a person of such eminence that a printed text was considered improper and unworthy for this purpose. If there be a better explanation for the origin of such calligraphic curiosities as M 801, I should be very glad to hear of it.

[*Postscript.* Since the present paper was written and too late for insertion in the typescript, the writer has set forth his reasons for believing that no edition was printed by Ratdolt in 1483. It seems extremely likely that the supposititious edition was 'created' as the result of the misunderstanding of a statement made by Ratdolt in his issue of 1484. There Ratdolt spoke of the three earlier editions printed by him. It seems probable, however, that Ratdolt was simply

---

[29] See my notes, 'An Unusual Fifteenth-Century Manuscript,' *La Bibliofilia*, XLII (1940), 65–71, 'Lydgate's *Horse, Sheep and Goose* and Huntington MS HM 144,' *supra*, and 'New Manuscripts of *The Dicts and Sayings of the Philosophers*,' *MLN*, LXIII (1948), 26–30. A manuscript transcript of Henricus de Herpf, *Speculum aureum decem praeceptorum*, Mainz, Schoeffer, 10 September, 1474, was listed in a recent bookseller's catalogue (Dawson, Cat. 243, June 1950, no. 13). The following manuscripts appear to be, wholly or in part, copies of Caxton printings: *British Museum*—Harley 149; Harley 6149; Royal 18 B 26; Sloane 779; Addit. 10,099; Addit. 22,718; and Addit. 29,729. *Lambeth*—MS 264 and MS 306. *Glasgow*—Hunterian 410. *Cambridge*—ULC Kk.1.7 and Nn.3.10.1. *Dublin*—TCD D.4.12. *Edinburgh*—Advocates MS 31.52 and 31.3.20. *Oxford*—Balliol 354; Oriel 79; Queen's 161; Bodleian Library, Fairfax 16 and Hatton 51. *etc.*

[30] The Lambeth manuscript of the *Dictes and Sayings of the Philosophers* (MS 265) has often been cited in the past (especially by the present writer) as a copy of a Caxton edition. For reasons which I have set forth in my paper 'Some Observations on the *Dictes and Sayings of the Philosophers*,' *vide supra*, it seems more probable that this manuscript is *not* a copy of a printed text but rather a manuscript version with editorial emendations made from the author's holograph text.

referring to the 1480 and 1481 editions signed by himself, together with the 1479 edition which, though signed by Walch alone, was probably produced at Walch's expense but with Ratdolt acting as the actual printer. See my note 'The Laying of a Ghost? Observations on the 1483 Ratdolt Edition of the *Fasciculus Temporum*,' reprinted *supra*.]

(From *Speculum* 27 (1952), pp. 178-83).

# CHAPTER T16

## THE THIRTEENTH RECORDED MANUSCRIPT
## OF THE *CRONACA DI PARTENOPE*

TO the dozen MSS. of the *Cronaca di Partenope* previously known to students of medieval Neapolitan literature,[1] one may now add a thirteenth codex of this "prima opera scritta nel dialetto napoletano."[2] This text is found in M 801 of the Pierpont Morgan Library,[3] a MS. as well known to the art historian as it is (apparently) unfamiliar to literary historians. For the past half-century the *Cronaca di Partenope* in M 801 has been described as a "diary of events at Naples," a title which was fathered upon the present tract by no less an authority than Sir Edward Maunde Thompson.[4]

The fact that this text remained unidentified for so long a time may well be attributed to the circumstance that it is incomplete at the beginning and badly misbound at the end. The *Cronaca* occupies folios 52–87 of the MS., but the following defects should be noted:

---

[1] Besides the five MSS. discussed in the text below, there are recorded these: Palermo MS. 1.D.14; Modena (Estense) MS. viii.B.4; Paris, Bibl. Nat. MS. Italien 303 and MS. Italien 304; Vatican MS. Vat. Lat. 4061; Naples, Società napoletana di storia patria, MS. xxxii.D.14 bis; and collection of the late Professor Giuliano Vanzolini of Pesaro. Compare Gennaro Maria Monti, "La 'Cronaca di Partenope' (Premessa all 'edizione critica)," *Annali del Seminario Giuridico Economico della R. Università di Bari*, Anno v (1932), fasc. ii (reprint of 52 pp.), and Tammaro de Marinis, *La biblioteca napoletana dei Re d'Aragona* (Milano, 1947), ii, 56–57.

[2] Bartolomeo Capasso, *Le fonti della storia delle provincie napoletane dal 568 al 1500*, ed. Mastrojanni (Napoli, 1902), p. 137.

[3] For a further discussion of this MS., see my paper "The *Fasciculus temporum* and Morgan Manuscript 801," *supra* [and Riccardo Filangieri, *Una cronaca napoletana figurata del quattrocento* (Naples, 1956). CFB]

[4] It was thus described in a letter from Thompson, then Keeper of MSS. in the British Museum, to Henry Hucks Gibbs (later Lord Aldenham), dated 5 June 1880, and this title was subsequently adopted in the several catalogues of the Aldenham Library. See *A Catalogue of Some Printed Books and Manuscripts at St. Dunstan's, Regent's Park, and Aldenham House, Herts. Collected by Henry Hucks Gibbs* (London, 1888), p. 185; *Catalogue of the Aldenham Library mainly collected by Henry Hucks Gibbs, First Lord Aldenham* (Letchworth, 1914), p. 461; and *The Aldenham Library. Catalogue of the Famous Library, the Property of the Rt. Honourable Lord Aldenham. The First Portion* (Sale catalogue—London, Sotheby & Co., 24 March 1937, lot 250).

(1) before folio 52, one leaf is wanting; (2) between folios 57–58, two leaves are wanting; (3) between folios 71–72, two leaves are wanting; (4) folios 79–81 are improperly inserted and do not form part of the *Cronaca di Partenope*—they seemingly belong to the third tract in the MS., which is a continuation of the chronicle to 1498; (5) folios 82–87 are misbound and should appear in the following order: 83, 82, 87, 85, 86 and 84.

In common with five other MSS. of the *Cronaca*, the Morgan MS. concludes with an account of the Baths of Pozzuoli. This treatise was edited by Erasmo Pèrcopo[5] from three not too dissimilar Neapolitan MSS. (Biblioteca Nazionale MS.i.63 and MS.xiv.D.7; Società napoletana di storia patria MS.xx.C.5). A fourth MS. at Naples (Bibl. Naz. MS.xiii.AA.39) turns out to be a copy of the 1526 printed edition,[6] as Professor Monti had suspected.[7] The version in MS. Italien 301 of the Bibliothèque Nationale, Paris, is dated 1479 and belongs to the same redaction as the text printed by Pèrcopo, with no more than the normal quota of variant readings which we are bound to allow.[8]

Since the Paris MS. is the only one of these texts which is not available in print, it is necessary to reproduce a portion of the text so that this version may conveniently be compared with the others. For this purpose, the chapter on the bath of Arco has been chosen:

Lo bagnio d'arco haue l'acqua multo dolce la quale acqua ha multe virtù & è assai vtile: Questo bagnio [è] restauratiuo & retorna multo le virtù perdute: & dà gran forza alo stomaco: & refresca li membri desiccati: & fa gran prode & vtile ad chi hauesse defecto ale extremità: Aduisandote che fa prode ad chi hauesse lo ventre grosso per infermità: & ad chi agrauasse & dolesse la melza o uero hauesse intorzato lo fecato: ma io parlo cosa experta la quale oculatim [? agio] veduta ad testimonio de multo populo lo quale lo vede con meco, primo scriptore: Jo vidi vn'omo alquale scarsamente restata li era la pelle con l'ossa: et venuto ad questo bagnio: niuno lo jodicho che veuesse longo tempo

---

[5] "I bagni di Pozzuoli, poemetto napolitano del secolo xiv," *Archivio storico per le province napoletane*, xi (1886), 597–750.

[6] The work was printed, according to the colophon, "in la Inclita Cita de Neapole per M. Euangelista di Presenzani de Pauia adi xxvii. de Aprile. xiiii. indictione dala Natiuita del nostro Signore M. D. xxvi." Quoted from the copy belonging to the writer, sig. X5ᵛ.

[7] Monti (op. cit., p. 15) remarks that the MS. was a "copia—a noi pare—dell'edizione del 1526." My own study of the MS. confirms Monti's observation.

[8] The text in this MS. ends with the account of "La Spelonga"; this is also the case in the two early MSS. of the Biblioteca Nazionale, while Pèrcopo supplies seven more chapters found in the Società MS., as well as still another (no. iv) on "La fommarola d'Agnano."

et bagna*n*dose i*n* questo bagno i*n* breue te*m*po lo vidi restaurato & sano como mai fo.[9]

The variant readings show that the Paris MS. is much closer to Naples MS.xiv.D.7 (and MS.1.63) than to the one belonging to the Società napoletana di storia patria, the basis of Pèrcopo's edition.

From all these MSS. of the *Cronaca di Partenope* which provide the account of the Baths of Pozzuoli, the Morgan text differs—and differs materially.[10] Happily, however, there is still another such version of the *Cronaca* which we have not paused to examine; this is the first printed edition, produced at Naples by Francesco del Tuppo circa 1486–90.[11] With this version the Morgan text agrees throughout, making due allowance for minor slips and omissions.[12]

Having thus established the kinship of M 801 with the first printed edition of the *Cronaca di Partenope*, the question that next arises is, of course, what the exact relationship of the MS. to the edition may be. Can this be the MS. used by the printer, is it related (to a greater or lesser degree) to the printer's original copy, or is it simply a MS. copy made directly from the printed text? These questions may

---

[9] This text is found on folio 158ᵛ of the MS. Two corrections have been made: the [è] is wanting in the MS. and [?agio] has been supplied where two wormholes have consumed enough of the text to make the original word illegible. The scribe of the MS., one Bernardinus de Turricella de Capitulo, adds the words "primo scriptore" (not found in the other MSS.) apparently so that the reader will understand that it was not he himself who saw this miraculous cure, but that he found the story in his source.

[10] In Appendice ii (pp. 726–729), Pèrcopo prints a chapter from the *Cronaca* on Virgil and the Baths of Pozzuoli. This chapter occurs as no. 26 in the Naples MS. xiv.D.7 and Società MS. XX.C.5, while it is numbered 29 in M 801 and Del Tuppo (sig. b2). The Morgan-Del Tuppo text differs notably from the Neapolitan codices but shows a close affinity with the Palermo MS. 1.D.14 of 1380.

[11] This edition is described by Mariano Fava and Giovanni Bresciano, *La stampa a Napoli nel XV secolo* (Leipzig, 1911–12), ii, 59, no. 68. Two copies are preserved in the Biblioteca Nazionale, Naples (ix.B.34 and xiv.B.46).

[12] The account of Arco in M 801 (f. 85) agrees completely with the Del Tuppo print (sig. i2), apart from minor orthographical variations; it reads: "Ala sinistra parte delo lato de tre pergole e un bangnio chiamato arco doue se restaurano li hommini debili. restaura le menbre. conforta lo stomaco et aiuta tutti le interiore." (Del Tuppo prints "hōi" and "mēbre"!) The 1526 edition offers the following: "Nella sinistra parte dello laco di auerno nello quale: e alta profundita & gra*n*de copia de diuersi pesci: sono de ce [i.e., diece] bagni de lequale lo primo dala forma e chiamato archo del quale e mirabile uirtu in restaurare li defecti: etiam dio in gli corpi guasti Restaura le membra: conforta lo stomacho: aiuta a tutti li interiori: non ioua alo uentre infiato ne melza: ne allo fecato infiato" (sig. V2).

best be answered by citing three significant, parallel excerpts from the MS. and the two printed editions:[13]

Et secondo la singioria de quel ulgare [sic] & usato peruerbio (MS., f. 53) [e]T secondo la snĩa de quel vulgare & vsato p'uerbio (Tuppo, sig. a5ᵛ) Et secõdo la sententia de quel vulgare & usato prouerbio (1526, sig. B2)

Pone iusto ancora de lassare insilencio quello miracolo (MS., f. 58) [ ]One iusto anchora de lassare insilencio quello miraculo (Tuppo, sig. c2ᵛ) Non e iusto anchora de lassare in silentio quello miraculo (1526, sig. F1)

A chiãndo[14] lo ditto Re Carllo in ungaria lo ditto Re de ungaria et la Regina Johanna procurano de auere una despensasione da lo papa (MS., f. 78ᵛ)

[ ]Tãdo lo dicto Re Carolo in vngaria lo dicto Re d'vngaria & la Regina Johanna procurano de hauere vna dispensatione da lo papa (Tuppo, sig. h3ᵛ)

STando lo dicto Re Carlo in Vngaria lo dicto Re de vngaria & la Regina Ioanna procurarono de hauere una dispensatione da lo Papa (1526, sig. S2).

In each case, the reader will rightly surmise that the readings in the MS. can be explained only by assuming that the scribe did not fully understand his "copy" (*Vorlage*). In the first instance, he misread a perfectly simple and quite common contraction,[15] while in the other two cases he supplied the wrong initial letter where the printed edition had failed to provide a "guide-letter."[16] As so many chapters begin with the word "Po" (Poi), it is no surprise that the scribe supplied a capital P (in the second example) for the blank space of the original, although the resulting text destroys the sense of the passage. I can offer no easy explanation for the third citation other than that the writer quite carelessly copied out what he thought he saw without reference to any possible sense. The MS., then, is a copy of the printed book.

[13] Since it is clear from the confusing slips and occasional omissions in the MS. that the text of the printed book cannot have been set from M 801, it again follows that the MS. must be a copy of the edition. Furthermore the MS. often repeats misprints found in the printed text, as for example: folio 54 "constolatione" and "costellatione" (so in Tuppo, sig. a7ᵛ, ll. 20 and 28; 1526 edition, sig. C1, has "constellatione" twice); folio 64ᵛ "Guiscandi" (so Tuppo, sig. d6, l. 16; 1526 ed., sig. I3ᵛ, has "Guiscardo") and "tranchedo guascardo" (so Tuppo, sig. d6, l. 21; 1526 ed., sig. I3ᵛ, has "Tanchredo Guiscardo"); etc.

[14] Probably the scribe intended this to be read "A chia*ma*ndo . . ." which would give an entirely different (and incorrect) meaning to the passage.

[15] See Adriano Cappelli, *Dizionario di abbreviature latine ed italiane* (Milano, 1912), p. 355.

[16] For the appearance and use of these "guide-letters," compare Konrad Haebler, *Handbuch der Inkunabelkunde* (Leipzig, 1925), pp. 91–92.

As Pèrcopo had pointed out, the version of the *Trattato dei Bagni di Pozzuoli* in the editio princeps is a translation in brief of the *Libellus de mirabilibus civitatis Putheolorum et locorum vicinorum*, while a fuller Italian rendering, in part practically a literal translation, of the same Latin text is included in the second edition, that of 1526. The text of the Baths of Pozzuoli found in four of the five previously recorded MSS., however, was derived from an entirely different source; it is a prose version in Italian of the *De balneis puteolanis* of Peter of Eboli,[17] a work upon which the *Libellus de mirabilibus* itself was based.

The first edition of the *Libellus* had appeared in 1475 from the press of Arnaldus de Bruxella,[18] a printer and scribe who was a contemporary (and a fellow-resident of Naples)[19] of the Francesco del Tuppo who first printed the *Cronaca di Partenope*. Apparently when Del Tuppo obtained his MS. of the *Cronaca* and set up his type from this, he was displeased with the antiquated account[20] of the Baths of Pozzuoli of his original and commissioned a new version to be made from the *Libellus,* which must have been thoroughly familiar to him. When the second edition of the *Cronaca* (based on the Del Tuppo print) appeared in 1526, the editor[21] or printer improved on the text of the editio princeps to the point of including a new and (sometimes) literal translation of the relevant parts of the *Libellus de mirabilibus*. A MS. copy of this version is, of course, found in the Naples MS.XIII.AA.39.

[17] For further details and bibliography, consult George Sarton, *Introduction to the History of Science* (Baltimore, 1927–48), II, 438–439. The work is sometimes known under the title *De balneis terrae laboris,* a title which is also justified by the Paris MS. Italien 301 (f. 156ᵛ, col. 2, l. 22): "la prouincia de terra de lauore haue bagni che curano li malati."

[18] See Fava and Bresciano, op. cit., p. 81, no. 92. I am deeply obliged to Dr. Dorothy M. Schullian of the Army Medical Library for her truly remarkable kindness and generosity in lending me her typescript copy of this edition. Such scholarly cooperation is as rare as it is appreciated!

[19] Arnold of Brussels was working in Naples in his capacity as scribe as early as 10 July 1455 and as late as 26 May 1492. For further details, see Konrad Haebler, *Die deutschen Buchdrucker des XV. Jahrhunderts im Auslande* (München, 1924), p. 137 ff.

[20] It seems likely, from Pèrcopo's discussion, that the Italian prose version of the *Cronaca* MSS. belongs to the closing years of the 14th century, nearly a century before the appearance of the first printed edition.

[21] According to Monti, op. cit., p. 16, the editor was Leonardo Astrino of S. Giovanni Rotondo (Gargano) and the work was undertaken at the instance of Antonio de Falco and Giacomo Bondino. See Astrino's letter on verso of title page of 1526 edition.

The account of the Baths of Pozzuoli in Morgan MS. 801, in turn, agrees throughout (save for the *variae lectiones* due to haplography, dittography, homoeoteleuton, and other human frailties) with the editio princeps of the *Cronaca di Partenope*. This agreement offers at once further proof of the kinship between M 801 and the printed edition as well as affording additional evidence (which need not detain us here) that the MS. was copied from Del Tuppo's edition.[22]

The "continuation" to the *Cronaca di Partenope*, which fills the remaining sixty-odd leaves of the volume, contains no fewer than 120 colored drawings, many of these remarkable and realistic full-page illustrations of events described in the accompanying text. These are of the greatest historical and artistic importance and interest. This continuation should also be of value for the historian, as it contains such significant items as an eye-witness account (fully illustrated) of the entry of King Charles VIII of France into Naples (22 February 1495). A thorough study of this text and its drawings would seem to be a suitable subject of investigation by a competent historian. Such research might reasonably be expected to yield some new items of significant importance for the complicated history of the Neapolitan kingdom of the fifteenth century.

(From *PMLA* 67 (1952), pp. 572-84).

[22] The present writer has in hand a lengthier study of the Baths of Pozzuoli and Ischia, where further reasons will be listed in support of this contention. For a possible explanation as to why this copy of a printed book was made, consult my paper cited in note 3 above.

# CHAPTER T17

## REPAIRS TO CALSHOT CASTLE IN 1612

FOR the better defence of his realm King Henry VIII erected along the southern coast of England a series of forts, not the least important of these being Calshot Castle, which still stands guard at the mouth of Southampton Water. It is, too, the first Tudor Castle which has greeted many an American tourist about to land at Southampton, though to-day it is somewhat disfigured by the encroachments of the Royal Air Force.

Although Calshot Castle was built with stone quarried from the ruins of the nearby Beaulieu Abbey no earlier than the reign of Henry VIII, it seems to have fallen into disrepair so quickly that Henry's daughter, the great Queen Elizabeth, was compelled to undertake certain restorations. Evidence of this work may be seen in the letters "E. R." which are still found on a water-spout of the castle.[1] In the reign of the first Stuart king, too, repairs were needed at Calshot Castle, and it is to these restorations that a document in the Pierpont Morgan Library refers.[2] It is the official "An estimate of the charge of the repayringe of Cawlshott Castle withe the Breache there 23 Januarij 1611 (*i.e.*, 1612)"[3] made by His Majesty's surveyor, John Norden.[4]

The document consists of a single sheet of paper, measuring 395 x 285 mm., folded in half. On what one may term "page 1" are the specifications set forth below, and the middle opening contains the sketch herewith reproduced (Plate 19); the last page is blank save for the endorsement: "A certificat of the supposed charge of the repayringe of Cawlshott Castle. Sowtht[5] 1611." The estimate reads as follows:

---

[1] Compare *A History of Hampshire and the Isle of Wight* (Victoria History of Hampshire), Westminster, 1900–14, III, 292.

[2] The document is included in the series: Rulers of England, James I, Treasury.

[3] Until 1752 the English Civil and Legal year began on March 25th, so that the date of this document is 1612 according to our reckoning.

[4] For an account of Norden's career see the *Dictionary of National Biography*, XLI, 105–108, and further details in *The Library*, 4th series, VII (1927), 233–252.

[5] This contraction apparently stands for "Southampton."

Com. Sowtht. An estimate of the charge of the repayringe of Cawlshott
Castle withe the Breache there 23 Januarij 1611.

ffirste the plotforme, beinge leaded couered with
beames, Justes[6] and planckes all decayde, con-
tayninge in the whole 1332 foote, wherof aboute
300 foote may be supplyed with the beste olde
planckes and Justes that shall arise, where the new
are to be layde: So there wilbe required 20 tuns[7]
of timber to repayre the residue, beinge 1032 foote,
The workmanship wherof will coste     –     –   xvj £

The bridge, for the moste parte to be made new,
and will require in plancke 90 foote with Justes,
beames and rayles, about 3 tuns of timber, the
workmanship wherof will cost –     –     –     lxvj *s* viij *d*

The warde howse, to be new wetherborded will
require about 1/2 tunne timber, the workmanship     xiij *s* iiij *d*

The gate of the wardhowse, to be new made, will
require 1/2 tun timber, the Iron and workmanship     xx *s*

The poyntinge[8] and tylinge of the wardhowse, and
workmanship, and stuffe     –     –     –     xxvj *s* viij *d*

The mendinge of the defectes of the leade, beinge
now hidden may amount vnto     –     –     –   iiij £

The poyntinge of some parte of the parapits, and
walls of the castle, for lyme and workmanship –     xiij *s* iiij *d*

The mendinge of the defectes of the particion walls
within the Castle; in lath, lime, nayles and workmanship about –     –     –     –     –     xx *s*

The Ironworke about the castle, beinge mouldred
with rust by reason of the salt water –     –     lx *s*

ffor the Caryage of 24 tuns of timber out of the
new forest where it is fitteste to be taken –     –   vij £

ffor mendinge of the scluces, and the wall of the
moate, lyme, supplie of stones, and workmanship   xxx £

ffor a peere to be new made before the moate, to
haue woode and pyles out of the new foreste, and
for workmanship     –     –     –     –   xiij £   vj *s* viij *d*

[total][9]     –     iiij$^{xx}$j £   vj *s* viij *d*

The "breach" made by the sea is illustrated in the sketch, to which the following descriptive note is attached:

> This Breache being a thinge muche to be respected for that if it be not repayred, there wilbe shortlie noe passage without boate, to or from the Castle—as yet there is passedge for horse and man at a lowe water, and it will coste the repayringe, eyther with stones or claye (but I take clay the surest & fitteste) with some ayde of the Countrye whome also it doth much concerne about   CCl   £

> There muste be wood allowed out of the foreste, to make a defensiue hedge agaynste the violence of the sea while the worke is in hande, according as occasion shall require.
>
> J. NORDEN.

Finally the document bears the "memorandum" from Sir Julius Caesar[10] (Chancellor of the Exchequer) to Mr. John Bingley (Remembrancer of the Exchequer) to the effect:

> 3 febr. 1611.

> Mr. Bingley, Let there bee a privy seale drawen vp for the payment of the said two summes, amounting to three hundred thirtie one *lib'*. vj *s*. 8 *d*. to Mr.        Smith captan of the Castle vppon imprest.
>
> JUL. CAESAR.

From documents preserved in the Public Record Office of Great Britain it is evident that the repairs to Calshot Castle were part of a large-scale rehabilitation of the forts and castles on the south coast of England undertaken in the first two decades of the 17th century. In 1609[11] repairs were made to Sandown and Yarmouth Castles by order of the Earl of Southampton in his capacity as Governor of the Isle of Wight. A warrant was issued on December 6th, 1611, to pay John Norden himself £125 for reparations done to "Sand-

---

[6] This is certainly Norden's way of spelling "joist" although this variant is not recorded by the *New English Dictionary*.

[7] According to *NED* a "ton of timber" is defined as "usually equivalent to 40 cubic feet (or for hewn timber, 50)."

[8] A good graphic variant for "painting."

[9] In Arabic numbers the total amounts to £81. 6*s*. 8*d*.

[10] For Sir Julius Caesar's career see *D.N.B.*, VIII, 204–207.

[11] *Calendar of State Papers, Domestic Series, of the Reign of James I,* 1603–1610, *Preserved in the State Paper Department of Her Majesty's Public Record Office,* London, 1857, pp. 528, 551. (The *Calendar* for the years 1611–1618 appeared the following year.)

ham" Castle,[12] although just a year and a half earlier (June 2nd, 1610)[13] Norden had received £412 for repairs to the same castle as well as for reconstruction in the parks at Farnham.[14] A further document in the Public Record Office—bearing the same date (January 23rd, 1611/12)[15] as the estimate printed above—consists of a note by Norden estimating the amount of munitions necessary for Calshot Castle, apparently a corollary to the document now preserved in the Pierpont Morgan Library.

It seems absolutely certain that the repairs to Calshot Castle were duly undertaken and completed. From Sir Julius Caesar's memorandum, as printed above, one would conclude that the sum of £331. 6s. 8d. was to have been paid to the keeper of the castle. The captain at that time, according to the estimate, was a "Mr. Smith," whose Christian name is supplied by documents in the Public Record Office. On January 31st, 1608,[16] Richard Smith received the reversion, after Sir Edgar Conway, of the captaincy of Calshot Castle. On February 22nd, 1610, Conway (now cited as Thomas Conway)[17] was still the "present captain,"[18] while on April 13th, 1614, the cap-

---

[12] *Cal. S. P. Dom.*, 1611–18, p. 97.　　　[13] *Cal. S. P. Dom.*, 1603–10, p. 616.

[14] *Cal. S. P. Dom.*, 1611–18, p. 108, records a document of uncertain date (? 1611) which contains an estimate "by John Norden of expenses of repairs done or to be done about Castles in Hampshire and Dorsetshire."

[15] *Ibid.*, p. 113.　　　　　　　　　[16] *Cal. S. P. Dom.*, 1603–10, p. 400.

[17] *Ibid.*, p. 588.

[18] The printed *Calendar*—or the records themselves—are somewhat confused here. Before turning to the entries, it is well to recall that Calshot is located in Hampshire, while Bagshot with its mansion and park (a favourite resort of King James I) is found in Surrey. Now for 21st July, 1603 (*Cal. S. P. Dom.*, 1603–10, p. 23), one finds in the Public Record Office a "grant to Thos. Conway, and Edward his son, of the office of Constable and Keeper of Bagshot Castle, co. Hants (*sic*), for life." This is apparently a misreading for Calshot Castle for, on 11th January, 1604, Sir Henry Guildford was granted "the office of Keeper of Bagshot Park co. Berks (*sic*), for life" (*ibid.*, p. 65). Again, on 25th November, 1609 (*ibid.*, p. 562), there is recorded a "warrant to pay to Sir Wm. Harmon, Keeper of Bagshot Park, co. Surrey, the necessary sums for finishing the repairs of the lodge." This apparent contradiction is explained by a later record (*Cal. S. P. Dom.*, 1611–18, p. 159) whereby, on 30th November, 1612, there is noted a "grant to Sir Noel de Caron of the office of Keeper of Bagshot Park, Surrey, on surrender of Sir Wm. Harmon, to whom it was assigned by Sir Hen. Guildford." It thus becomes evident that between 1604 and 1612 the Keepers of Bagshot were successively Sir Henry Guildford and Sir William Harmon. Since Thomas Conway was appointed Keeper of Calshot Castle in 1603 and was still the Captain in 1610, it would seem certain that the "Sir Edgar" Conway of the document cited in the text above is either a misreading in the calendar or a mis-citation in the official record.

taincy was conferred upon a certain James Mills.[19] It is evident that Richard Smith enjoyed the keeping of Calshot Castle for only a brief period between these terminal dates.

Although the Morgan document suggests that payment was to be made to Richard Smith as captain of Calshot Castle, one finds in the Public Record Office[20] a warrant made out on February 17th, 1612, to John Norden for the payment of £81. 6s. 8d. for repairs about to be made to the castle and of £250[21] for the repairing of the "breach" made by the sea. Still another record,[22] with date March 5th, 1611/12 (*Pells Order Book*, Vol. 11 [E 403/2731], fo. 122), seems to offer conclusive proof that the payment was finally made to John Norden, despite the request as noted above that payment be made to Richard Smith.

(From *Proceedings of the Hampshire Field Club and Archaeological Society* 17 (1952), pp. 247-251).

[19] *Cal. S. P. Dom.*, 1611–18, p. 231.

[20] *Ibid.*, p. 121. Mr. J. E. Fagg of the Public Record Office confirms my suspicion that the £251 as printed in the *Calendar* is a slip for £250.

[21] The figure in the Morgan document is difficult to read but is certainly "CCl" pounds. That this is the correct sum is made plain by the memorandum of Sir Julius Caesar, which calls for a total payment of £331. 6s. 8d. Since the itemized repairs to the castle itself correctly total £81. 6s. 8d., it is quite certain that the estimated repairs for the "breach made by the sea" amounted to £250.

[22] Mr. Fagg has also most kindly supplied me with information concerning this entry.

# CHAPTER T18

## THE APOSTLES AND THE CREED

TO each of the twelve Apostles is assigned a specific section of the Creed in the text of the fifteenth-century *Epistle of Othea* by Stephen Scrope; a new edition of this work is in preparation by the present writer. As these attributions seemingly required annotation, a search for possible sources or parallels for these citations naturally suggested itself. This quest led to such interesting results that they were judged of sufficient value for separate publication, since the findings were in no way directly connected with the text of Scrope's translation.

As always when faced with such problems, one searches first in the works of Montague Rhodes James for a possible explanation of any symbolism of this sort—and, as usual, one is not disappointed. In his *Suffolk and Norfolk* (London: Dent, 1930), pp. 218-219, James wrote:

In the relics of painted windows we find a somewhat different treatment, namely, when each Apostle bears a sentence from the Creed. A legend grew up (how early I do not know, but it was being used in the twelfth century) that after Pentecost the Apostles composed the Creed which goes by their name, each contributing a clause. Peter begins: *Credo in deum Patrem*, and Matthias ends: *Et vitam aeternam Amen*. Paul is, of course, excluded from this series: he was not yet a Christian . . . the division of the Creed among the Apostles is fairly well fixed.

With this opinion and the arrangement of the Apostles and the Creed as given by James, several eminent authorities have concurred; one may, for example, point specifically to Wilhelm Molsdorf (*Christliche Symbolik der mittelalterlichen Kunst* [Leipzig: Hiersemann, 1926], p. 187 and pp. 189-191), who refers to this 'Verteilung' as being 'traditionell.' Yet, upon comparing the arrangement in the *Epistle of Othea* with the traditional one noted by James-Molsdorf, it becomes readily apparent that Christine de Pisan, the authoress of the French original, was quite unaware of this fixed tradition. Indeed, she assigned only to Peter and James the Greater precisely the same sections of the Creed as did James the Englishman. It thus seemed necessary and desirable to examine this bit of symbolism in greater detail.

The tradition that each Apostle contributed one section of the Creed is found as early as the fourth century. This belief is certainly implied by Rufinus in his *Expositio in symbolum apostolorum* (Oxford, Rood, '1468' [i.e. 1478], sig. a2), and his observations were repeated by St Augustine, *Sermo de symbolo* (Migne, *PL*, XL, 1189–90). In two sermons printed among the supposititious works of St Augustine (Migne, *PL*, XXXIX, 2188–91) are found what appear to be the earliest definite attributions, at least so far as I am aware. Such identification of parts of the Creed with specific Apostles is also to be found in the *Sacramentarium gallicanum* (Mabillon, *Museum italicum* [Paris, 1687–89], I², 396) and thus is clearly placed in the seventh or eighth century, to which period this service book is assigned (*Lexikon für Theologie und Kirche*, IX, 96). But the most significant feature of all is that each of these three early accounts is completely at variance with, and independent of, the others; not even Pseudo-Augustinus can agree with Pseudo-Augustinus!

The natural corollary to this discovery was to institute a search for as many different combinations as possible; the results of this investigation are set forth on the table printed here above. These fifteen varying 'traditions' were found in the following places:

1. Pseudo-Augustinus, *Sermo de symbolo*, Migne, *PL*, XXXIX, 2190.
2. Bodley MS. Lat. th. c. 57, fol. 16ᵛ (*Ignorancia sacerdotum*); Pseudo-Augustinus, *Sermo de symbolo*, Migne, *PL*, XXXIX, 2189; *Symbolum apostolicum*, third blockbook edition (compare Schreiber, *Manuel de l'amateur de la gravure sur bois*, IV, 239–244); single woodblock no. 1759 (Schreiber, II, 196–197); Montague Rhodes James (see above).
3. *Cura clericalis*, London: Wynkyn de Worde, 1532, sig. B3ᵛ.
4. *Le livret des consolations*, Paris: Gui Marchand, 1497/8, sigs. f8ᵛ–g1; *Boke of Comforte agaynste all Trybulacyons*, London: de Worde, [1505], sig. f4.
5. Babyngton's *Epistle of Othea* (ed. James D. Gordon, Philadelphia, 1942, pp. 46–59).
6. MS. Wisbech 6, fol. 52ᵛ (*Qui bene presunt* by Richard Wetherset); *Symbolum apostolicum*, first blockbook edition (Schreiber, IV, 239–244).
7. *Erklärung der zwölf Artikeln des christlichen Glaubens*, Ulm: Dinckmut, 1485; Wotton, *Speculum christiani*, London: Machlinia, [1486], sig. a6; *Compost et calendrier des bergers*, Paris: Marchand, 1493, sigs. f5ᵛ–f6; *Kalender of Shepherdes*, Paris: Vérard, 1503, sig. f2ᵛ (facsimile ed.).
8. *The Royal Book*, [Westminster: Caxton, 1486], sigs. c2ᵛ–c3ᵛ.
9. Rolewinck, *Fasciculus temporum*, Morgan MS. 801, fol. 3ᵛ; *Rudimentum novitiorum*, Lübeck: Brandis, 1475, fols. 313ᵛ–315ᵛ; *La mer des histoires*, Paris: Le Rouge, 1488, II, 96–98; *Chronicles of England*, Saint

| Migne, xxxix, 2190 | Credo in Deum Patrem omnipotentem | Creatorem coeli et terrae. | Credo et in Jesum Christum Filium eius unicum Dominum nostrum. | Qui conceptus est de Spiritu sancto, natus ex Maria virgine. | Passus sub Pontio Pilato, crucifixus, mortuus et sepultus. | Descendit ad inferna, tertia die resurrexit a mortuis. |
|---|---|---|---|---|---|---|
| | I | II | III | IV | V | VI |
| 1 | Peter | John | James | Andrew | Philip | Thomas |
| 2 | " | Peter | Andrew | James | John | " |
| 3 | " | " | " | " | " | Philip/Thom |
| 4 | " | " | " | " | " | " |
| 5 | " | " | " | " | " | " |
| 6 | " | " | " | " | " | Philip |
| 7 | " | " | " | " | " | Thomas |
| 8 | " | " | " | " | " | John/Thoma |
| 9 | " | " | " | John | James | Thomas |
| 10 | " | " | " | " | " | " |
| 11 | " | " | " | " | " | " |
| 12 | " | " | " | " | " | " |
| 13 | " | " | John | James | Andrew | Philip/Thom: |
| 14 | " | Andrew | Andrew | " | John | Thomas |
| 15 | | | | | " | |

Albans: [Schoolmaster Printer, 1485], sigs. g1ᵛ-g2; Schedel, *Liber chronicarum*, Nürnberg: Koberger, 1493, woodcut on 'Folium CI'; *L'art et science de bien vivre et de bien mourir*, Paris: Caillaut, [1505], sigs. c1-c4.

10. *Die cronijcken van ouden tijden* [*Fasciculus temporum*. Dutch], U-trecht: Veldener, 1480, fols. 72-73; *La fleur des commandemens de Dieu*, Paris: Vérard, 1500, fol. 7; single woodblock no. 1852 (Schreiber, ii, 241-242).

| Ascendit ad coelos, sedet ad dexteram Dei Patris omnipotentis. | Inde venturus judicare vivos et mortuos. | Credo et in Spiritum sanctum, / sanctam Ecclesiam catholicam. | Sanctorum communionem, / Remissionem peccatorum. | Carnis resurrectionem. | Vitam aeternam. Amen. |
|---|---|---|---|---|---|
| VII | VIII | IX | X | XI | XII |
| Bartholomew | Matthew | James² (the Less) | Simon | Jude | Matthias |
| ames the Less | Philip | Barth./Matthew | Matthew/Simon | " | " |
| Bartholomew | Matthew | James the Less | James²/Simon | " | " |
| " | " | " | Simon | " | " |
| " | " | James²/Simon | Simon/Jude | Matthias | " |
| " | Thomas | Matthew/James² | James²/Simon | Jude | " |
| ames the Less | Philip | Barth./Matthew | Simon | " | " |
| " | " | " | " | " | " |
| " | " | " | " | " | " |
| " | " | " | Matthew/Simon | " | " |
| " | " | Barth./Jude | Jude/Simon | Matthew | " |
| James | " | Barth./Matthew | Simon/Jude | Matthias | " |
| Bartholomew | Matthew | James²/Simon | " | " | " |
| ames the Less | Philip | Barth./Matthew | Thomas/Simon | Jude | " |
| | | | | | Thomas |

11. *Catechismus ex decreto Concilii Tridentini*, Venice: Aldus Manutius II, 1575, pp. 1–40.
12. Schedel, *Liber chronicarum* (in German), Nürnberg: Koberger, 1493, 'Blat CII.'
13. *Sacramentarium gallicanum* (see above); Balbus, *Catholicon*, Mainz: [? Gutenberg], 1460, under 'Fides'; Christine de Pisan, *L'épitre d'Othéa*, Harley MS. 4431, fols. 107ᵛ–111ᵛ (thus in Scrope's translation, Morgan MS. 775, fols. 219–225ᵛ); Roye, *Doctrinal of Sapience*, Westminster:

Caxton, [1489], sigs. A3–A4; Laurent, *Summe le roy of des conincs summe,* Delft: [van der Meer and Yemantszoen], 1478, fol. 6; Michel, *The Ayenbite of Inwyt,* London: Roxburghe Club, 1855, pp. 6–9; *The Book of Vices and Virtues,* EETS, OS 217, pp. 6–9.

14. *The Flower of the Commandments of God,* London: de Worde, 1521, fols. 16ᵛ–17.
15. Single woodblocks nos. 2748a and 2751 (Schreiber, III, 192–193). Although only the impressions of John and Thomas have survived to our day, it seems entirely reasonable to assume that a full series was originally printed.

Amazing as the variety of the traditions may be, it is even more startling to note that different editions or renderings of the *same* work present differing arrangements. Quite obviously, local tradition would influence a translator or editor to alter the version given him in accordance with what was familiar to him. We have already seen that Pseudo-Augustinus fails to agree with his namesake, but even more noteworthy divergencies must claim our attention. The English translation of the *Fleur des commandemens de Dieu* varies markedly from its original; again, the Dutch rendering of the *Fasciculus temporum* differs from the text found in the Morgan manuscript of the Latin source and in the dozen printed editions, both in Latin and in French, found in the same library. Two blockbooks of the *Symbolum apostolicum* cannot agree as to the arrangement, though the editions may well be artistically related. The Latin edition of Schedel's famous 'Nürnberg Chronicle' entirely omits the clause 'Remissionem peccatorum' and thus differs from its German counterpart. Finally, both the German and the Latin printed texts of Schedel offer a version quite different from that found on the woodcut which appears on the page facing these texts.

The arrangement of the clauses of the Creed here followed is that found in one of the two Pseudo-Augustine sermons (Migne, *PL,* XXXIX, 2190); thus Peter is the only Apostle who is invariably identified with the same article (no. I). If the other traditional grouping be observed, which combines articles I and II (dividing one of the other sections into two parts), one notes that *no* Apostle would be definitely linked with any specific phrase, since classes 1 and 14 would split the new clause I between Peter/John and Peter/Andrew. Truly the variety seems infinite!

For the two examples cited above from the Bodley and Wisbech manuscripts, I am indebted to Mr R. W. Hunt, Keeper of Western Manuscripts in the Bodleian Library; the other citations were all collected from books found in the library with which I have been connected for almost a score of years. The number of examples which could be gathered together by persistent search in any large European library would, no doubt, be legion—but the importance of such search would not lie in the heaping up of examples but rather in the variety which could be produced. I should be most happy indeed to learn of still other combinations in the apportioning of the articles of the Creed amongst the several Apostles.

(From *Speculum* 28 (1953), pp. 335-39).

[For still further examples, see my *Epistle of Othea*, EETS, OS 264 (1970), p. 146. CFB]

# CHAPTER T19

## A PROJECTED BUT UNPUBLISHED EDITION OF THE "LIFE AND WORKS" OF ROBERT BOYLE

THE bibliography of the works of that distinguished chemist and scientist at large, Robert Boyle, was given final form not many years ago through the researches, both meticulous and extensive, of Dr. John F. Fulton.[1] Under these circumstances, one may consider it most unlikely that any future study will provide really significant additions to the list of Boyle's published works; items of ancillary interest to the canon may, however, be expected to come to light at any time.[**]

An autograph letter in the Pierpont Morgan Library[2] does provide such an additional footnote to Dr. Fulton's great bibliography. The letter, written by John Williams (the future Bishop of Chichester)[3] to John Evelyn (the diarist),[4] is transcribed below and takes note of preliminary discussions for a proposed folio edition of Boyle's "Life and Works." The text of the letter is provided with such explanatory notes as seemed necessary, but a few further comments may also prove welcome.

No record of the edition to which Williams referred in his letter of 1696 has come down to us; since it is not listed in Dr. Fulton's definitive bibliography, one may rest assured that this edition never was issued from the press. The study of Boyle upon which, as Williams recounts, Bishop Burnet[5] was engaged did indeed appear—

---

[1] "A Bibliography of The Honourable Robert Boyle," *Oxford Bibliographical Society, Proceedings and Papers*, 3, 1–172 (1931), 339–365 (1933); *Oxford Bibliographical Society Publications*, New Series, 1, 33–38 (1947).

[**] *Ed. note:* E.g., Margaret E. Rowbottom, "The Earliest Published Writing of Robert Boyle," *Ann. Sci.*, 6, 376–389 (1950).

[2] R-V, Clarendon's Rebellion, Vol. I (part 3), p. 456.

[3] For his biography, see "Dictionary of National Biography" (abbreviated below as "D.N.B."), Vol. 61, p. 420. Williams was responsible for the posthumous publication of Boyle's "A Free Discourse against Swearing," London, 1695 (Fulton no. 197).

[4] See "D.N.B.," Vol. 18, pp. 79–83. Evelyn was a close acquaintance of Boyle's for some forty years.

[5] Compare "D.N.B.," Vol. 7, pp. 394–405, for the biography of Gilbert Burnet, Bishop of Salisbury. According to Anthony À. Wood, "Fasti Oxonienses, or Annals

but apparently not as part of an edition of the "Opera." It seems to have first been printed in Eustace Budgell's "Memoirs of the Lives and Characters of the Illustrious Family of the Boyles . . . With an Appendix, Containing the Character of the Honourable Robert Boyle . . . By Bishop Burnet, and Others" (London, 1737). The only folio edition of the "Opera omnia" of Boyle known to Dr. Fulton was not published until 1744,[6] long after the deaths of Evelyn (1706), Williams (1709) and Burnet (1715). Furthermore, the life of Boyle included in that edition was prepared by Thomas Birch,[7] who at the time of the writing of the present letter had not yet been born. Thus we may conclude that the discussions and plans to which Williams referred in his letter to Evelyn were abandoned and that this projected edition of the "Vita et opera" of Boyle failed to materialize.

The address of John Williams' letter reads as follows: "For M$^r$ Evelyn at William Draper's[8] Esq. in Surrey street near Norfolk Buildings in the Strand London." This leaf is further stamped with an encircled "IV.20," representing (apparently) the date April 20th; it also bears a partially undecipherable note of later date which refers to the contents of the letter.

John Evelyn, as we know from his own diary, held a high opinion of the sixty-year-old cleric and voluminous controversialist. In his capacity as Trustee of the Boyle foundation, which sponsored an annual series of lectures "to prove the truth of the Christian religion against infidels," Evelyn had had a hand in having Williams appointed lecturer in 1695 and again in 1696.[9] The present letter is

---

of the University of Oxford" (second part, 1641–1691; 3rd ed., by Philip Bliss, London, 1820, p. 287), Boyle bequeathed him a "Hebrew bible with silver clasps"; Wood also speaks of "the life of him the said Mr. Boyle, about to be published by the said doctor [Burnet]." Louis T. More ("The Life and Works of the Honourable Robert Boyle," New York, 1944, p. x) observes that "shortly before his death, Boyle appointed his friend Evelyn as one of his literary trustees, and gave to Bishop Burnet material for his biography."

[6] Fulton no. 240.

[7] Dr. Thomas Birch ("D.N.B.," Vol. 5, pp. 68–70) was a voluminous writer, historian, and biographer, but his account of Robert Boyle is not particularly successful.

[8] William Draper was Evelyn's son-in-law, having married his daughter Susanna on 27 April 1693. They were wedded by Dr. Thomas Tenison, then Bishop of Lincoln. (For further notes on him, see below.)

[9] On 23 November 1695, Evelyn entered in his diary the note: "I went to Lambeth to get Mr. Williams continued in Boyle's lectures another year." ("Diary of John Evelyn," edited by Henry B. Wheatley, London, 1906, Vol. 3, p. 126.)

obviously the reply to an earlier one from Evelyn to Williams, the contents of which are not known to us. The text of Williams' letter reads as follows:

Canterb.[10] 19. 1696[11]

Hon[rd] S[r]:

I esteem it as a particular mark of your Friendship, that you are pleased to acquaint me with the report, w[ch] I perceive by your's, is abroad, concerning my writing the Life of the Hon[ble] M[r] Boyl: A report that there is no ground, but what there is some reason for, through the mistake of what I said concerning the publishing a new these[12] of his works which had heretofore been printed. The short story of which is this. About a month since I received a Letter from D[r] Charlet[13] Master of University College Oxoñ; in which he told me that some of the works of M[r] Boyl having grown scarce, it had been advised that it would be of good use & be very acceptable to the Learned; if there were a Collection of all his works set forth together in Folio; & that[14] it was desired[14] I would consider of it, & consult with the Trustees[15] or others, how it might be best accomplished. Toward the promoting of this I waited on my Lord of Cant. & in the next place had so on you; but that I thought you were out of Town. In the mean time I lighted on S[r] H. Ashurst[16] in the street, & afterward waiting on him at his house, I told him of it; & withall that it would be convenient that some enquiry might be made of what might be found among his papers, fit for the press; & he promised me to advise with the E. of Burlington[17] about it. While I was there, came in M[r] Warr;[18] & he very readily offerd his service [about][19] the papers; this was the week before

[10] In addition to his other dignities, Williams was made a prebendary of Canterbury and chaplain to William and Mary about this time.

[11] Apparently Williams forgot to include the month, but it seems certain that the letter was written in April. This is indicated not only by the stamp already referred to but also by the correspondence between Evelyn and William Wotton which will be discussed later.

[12] According to the "New English Dictionary," this is a good 17th-century variant for "thesis."

[13] Arthur Charlett (cf. "D.N.B.," Vol. 10, pp. 119-120).

[14] These words are interlineated.

[15] See Evelyn's diary for 2 May 1696 (Vol. 3, pp. 129-130): "I din'd at Lambeth, being summon'd to meete my co-trustees, the Abp. [Thomas Tenison, now Archbishop of Canterbury], S[r] Hen. Ashurst and Mr. Serjeant [Sir John] Rotheram, to consult about settling Mr. Boyle's lecture for a perpetuity."

[16] According to Dr. Fulton (p. 125), Sir Henry Ashurst was one of Boyle's executors, in addition to being a trustee of the Boyle foundation.

[17] Robert Boyle's elder brother Richard, first Earl of Burlington (1612-1697).

[18] Robert Boyle's last will and testament (as cited by Anthony Wood, *loc. cit.*) named "John Warr, jun." as one of the three executors, the others being the Earl of Burlington and Lady Ranelagh (Robert's sister Katherine). She, however, predeceased her famous brother by exactly a week, dying on 23 December 1691.

[19] A tear has made this reading not absolutely certain, though it seems to be the only word that would fit the existing pen-strokes.

I came out of Town; & farther we went not. So that all y$^t$ could be said of a preface was presumption; & no more of y$^t$ thought of, I believe, than what in cause might be done by the Oxford Gentlemen. As for my own part, I was so far from thinking of writing a Life (which I knew to be in the Bps[20] hands) that I thought not of so much as a preface. The design is worthy of a better pen, & what I have alwaies thought a way of writing not without great difficulties. For he y$^t$ will write a Life, if possible, should have had an intimate acquaintance with the person, & should know that of his air, his Genius & way; that can no more be wrote than he himself can be drawn by description only; & must be if not intimate enough, yet led into all the particulars which you speak of by one y$^t$ was inward with him. Now I had not the honour of any thing like this, never having been in the Company of that great man but once that I know of, many years since; & which I afterward blamed myself for, having been encouraged by him to make an acquaintance there. I am well pleased that at last it's likely to be done, & to be undertaken by one so well qualified for it as M$^r$ Wotton;[21] to whom it being necessary to peruse his papers, he may at the same time promote the Oxford design by a farther Collection. When I return to Town, which will be, God willing, about 14 daies hence, I shall wait on you, with my acknowledgments for your obliging letter, to

S$^r$

y$^r$ faithful & humble servant

John Williams

The projected biography of Robert Boyle by William Wotton which is mentioned in Williams' letter also failed to be issued, though we know from Evelyn's correspondence that Wotton was at work on it, off and on, for many years. On 30 March 1696,[22] Evelyn wrote out a sketch of Boyle's life and character for Wotton's use, the receipt of which the latter acknowledged on April 7th.[23] A year later Wotton complained to Evelyn that the Earl of Burlington had failed to make the Boyle papers readily available to him,

[20] See note 5 above. The "D.N.B." (Vol. 6, p. 123) states that Birch's biography of Boyle was "founded on materials collected with abortive biographical designs by Burnet and Wotton."

[21] For William Wotton, see "D.N.B.," Vol. 63, pp. 61–62. More (op. cit., p. x) remarks that "we know that Evelyn advised the other trustees, Bishop Burnet and the Archbishop of Canterbury, to choose William Wotton, F.R.S., as their authorized biographer [of Boyle]."

[22] "Diary," Vol. 3, pp. 479–487. More (pp. 134–135) cites portions of this account, but his Index (p. 313) wrongly indicates that the letter was sent to Sir Henry (not William) Wotton. A second use of the letter (p. 148) is correctly entered in the Index.

[23] Wotton adds (Evelyn's "Diary," Vol. 4, p. 1): "If my L$^d$ Archbishop of Canterbury encourages me, & I can get those materials out of Mr. Warre's hands, w$^{ch}$ I was speaking of. I will set about it [the biography]." His letter of 24 May 1696 indicates that Dr. Tenison did approve of the choice of Wotton.

though he still had hopes of completing his work.[24] As late as 13 August 1703, Wotton referred to his biography of Boyle[25] in a letter to Evelyn; however, the project was never completed, and Wotton's materials were dispersed. Thus the high hopes and ambitious plans which form the substance of John Williams' letter to John Evelyn were left unfulfilled—and like so many other projects of this nature, the final completion of this undertaking was left for another age and to different hands.

(From *Chymia* 4 (1953), pp. 79-83).

[24] "Diary," Vol. 4, pp. 18–19, letter dated 2 January 1698.

[25] "The discouragements I met with since I undertook it were so many, that I have often wished that I had let it alone or never thought of it" (Vol. 4, p. 30). He also asked for further details, which Evelyn provided in his reply of 12 September 1703 (Vol. 4, pp. 32-42).

# CHAPTER T20

## THE MIDDLE ENGLISH TEXTS
## OF MORGAN MANUSCRIPT 861

BY a most happy coincidence, the Pierpont Morgan Library was so fortunate as to secure recently a Middle English manuscript comparable in character and importance to the newly-found first edition of the *Abbey of the Holy Ghost* which, a few months earlier, had become part of the Library.[1] Since the new Morgan manuscript will surely prove to be of considerable interest to students of the period,[2] a brief but sufficiently detailed description of it is given below:[3]

M 861. Manuscript on vellum (6½ × 4½ inches); 33 leaves; 32 lines to the full page; written in a neat English book hand of the middle of the fifteenth century. Bound in calf, with sides panelled in blind.

CONTENTS:

ff. 1–3ᵛ. Treatise on the Ten Commandments.
[Printed below].
ff. 3ᵛ–4ʳ. Ten Vengeaunces of God.
[Printed below].
f. 4. Seven Deadly Sins.

---

[1] Wynkyn de Worde's *Abbey of the Holy Ghost* corresponds to the work by that title printed by Horstman, I, 321–337, but it is, in the incunable, inserted into the *Charter of the Abbey of the Holy Ghost* (Horstman, I, 337–362). Most of the text of Horstman's *Abbey* appears in the de Worde print after the "Explicit carta" (Horstman, I, 340). Thus, de Worde prints Horstman's *Charter* to this point; then (sig. a3) inserts almost all of the *Abbey*; and (on sig. b1ᵛ) continues with the rest of the *Charter*. A full description of the new Wynkyn de Worde edition may be found in the writer's "The First Edition of *The Abbey of the Holy Ghost*," reprinted *supra*.

[2] The first mention of the MS. to appear in print seems to be the notice in a bookseller's catalogue of Feb. 1925 (P. J. and A. E. Dobell, Catalogue 42, item 18). Thereafter the manuscript apparently disappeared from sight till acquired by the Morgan Library.

[3] The following works are cited in shortened form in this paper: Hope Emily Allen, *Writings Ascribed to Richard Rolle* (New York, 1927); Thomas Arnold, *Select English Works of John Wyclif* (Oxford, 1869–71); Carl Horstman, *Yorkshire Writers; Richard Rolle of Hampole and his Followers* (London, 1895–96); and John Edwin Wells, *A Manual of the Writings in Middle English, 1050–1400* (New Haven, 1926) and nine supplements.

*Heading:* Heere bene þe seuene dedly synnes þat euery man most flee. if he wolde be saued. for þei ben þe large weie to helle.

*Incipit:* Pride wraþe and enuye ben synnes of þe feend . . .

*Comment:* Corresponds in large part to the text (from the Vernon MS.) printed by Horstman, ii, 344.

f. 4ᵛ. Seven Works of Bodily Mercy.

*Heading:* Heere bygynneþ þe werkys of mercy bodily. whiche god wole reherse at þe day of doom to alle hem þat schullen be saued.

*Incipit:* There ben seuen werkys of bodily mercy. and oþer seuene of goostly mercy. And þese loueþ criste more . . .

*Comment:* compare the tract printed by Arnold (iii, 168–169).

f. 5. Seven Works of Ghostly Mercy.

*Heading:* Teche. Counceile. Comforte. Castise, fforȝeue. Suffre and Preye.

*Incipit:* A man techith an oþir by þe lawe of charite whanne he tellyþ hym for loue þe byddynge of god . . .

*Comment:* compare Arnold (iii, 177–182).

ff. 5–5ᵛ. Five Outer Senses.

*Heading:* Herynge. Seynge. Smellynge. Tastynge & Touchynge.

*Incipit:* Herynge þat is here þou gladly þe lawe of god and alle maner goodnes and truþe . . .

*Comment:* compare Arnold (iii, 117).

f. 5ᵛ. Five Inner Senses.

*Heading:* Mynde. Resoun. Understondynge. Ymagynacion and Wille.

*Incipit:* And who þat wole be saued he muste chastise his wittes . . .

*Comment:* compare Arnold (iii, 117–118).

f. 5ᵛ. Four Cardinal Virtues.

*Heading:* Riȝtwisnes. Temperaunce. Prudence. and Strengþe.

*Incipit:* Wherynne stondith Riȝtwisnes. in iuste deemynge . . .

f. 6. Seven Sacraments.

*Heading and Incipit* (combined): Baptym. Confermacioun. þe sacrament of the auter þat is cristes fleisch and his blood . . .

ff. 6–6ᵛ. The Eight Tokens of Good Character.

*Incipit:* The fyrste tokene is. þat he hath no dedayn or is yuel apaied. þouȝ he be vndirnome of oon þat is of lasse degre . . .

ff. 6ᵛ–7ʳ. A Prayer.

*Incipit:* God þat by power of þi vertue hast maad alle þinges of nouȝt. And whanne þou haddiste maade bygynnynge of alle þinges . . .

*Comment:* At the end is found an inscription which reads "Amende thi liffe in time ‖ amend that eacke [sic] man ‖ E M."

ff. 7ᵛ–33ʳ. Contemplations of the Dread and Love of God.

*Heading:* Ardeat in nobis diuini feruor amoris.

*Incipit:* This schorte pistelle þat foloweþ is deuyded in sundry maters eche matere by him selfe in titlis as þis kalendere schewiþ . . .

*Comment:* printed by Horstman, ii, 72 ff. Compare Wells (xi, 48) and Allen (p. 357).

f. 33ᵛ. Blank.

As will be noted, The *Contemplations of the Dread and Love of God* is by far the longest tract in the manuscript; furthermore, we can be quite certain that this text will be the one of greatest value and interest to literary historians. Indeed, it seems clear that a new edition of this work stands high in the list of Middle English *desiderata*, since the only edition of which the present writer is aware is that printed by Carl Horstman more than half a century ago from the comparatively late Wynkyn de Worde print of 1506 (STC 21259). The text in the Morgan manuscript is somewhat shorter[4] and probably contains an earlier form of the treatise. The other recorded manuscripts of the *Contemplations* are: *British Museum*, Royal 17 A xxv; Arundel 197; Harley 1706; Harley 2409; *Cambridge University Library*, Ee. ii. 12; Ii. vi. 40; *Huntington Library*, HM 127; and (present location unknown to the writer) Stonor MS.

In order to give some idea of the nature and character of M 861, the text of the commentary on the Decalogue is printed below.[5] Numerous comparable treatises, both in verse and in prose, are recorded in Wells' *Manual of the Writings in Middle English*, most of which have already appeared in print. As we shall see, the Morgan text shares certain lines with the similar treatise held to be by John Wyclif[6] and has others in common with the discussion of the Ten Commandments given in the *Lay-Folks' Catechism*;[7] further, some of the citations from the Bible were also used in this connection by still other tracts treating of the same subject.[8] Nevertheless, the large bulk of the present text does not seem to be paralleled by any version

[4] Morgan MS. 861 omits, for example, the following passages printed by Horstman: 96.17–98.21 (at bottom of f. 29r); 98. up 2–99.28 (at line 2 of f. 30r); and 102.30–104.5 (at line 21 of f. 31v). The text in the MS. ends at the "Amen" printed at 105.14.

[5] Capitals are supplied in accordance with modern practice, while the sometimes erratic punctuation has been standardized to conform with the scribe's apparent intention. Paragraphs (¶) are reproduced as they appear in the MS.

[6] Printed by Arnold (III, 82–92). The present tract may possibly be the "pre-existing commentary" which Arnold believed Wyclif may have used. For a different view, see Samuel A. Ives, "The Genuine and Unpublished Version of Wyclif's Treatise on the Ten Commandments," *Rare Books*, III (New York: H. P. Kraus, 1942), 3–9.

[7] Ed. Thomas F. Simmons and Henry E. Nolloth, EETS, OS 118 (1901), pp. 33–57.

[8] Compare for example the *Speculum Christiani* (ed. Gustaf Holmstedt, EETS, OS 182 (1933), pp. 16–39) and *The Book of Vices and Virtues* (ed. W. Nelson Francis, EETS, OS 217 (1942), pp. 1–6).

as yet printed. Some twenty-five years ago and in regard to another manuscript, William P. Cumming[9] made an observation which may suitably be quoted here: "The interest of the Ste. Geneviève MS lies in the number of 'Wycliffite tracts' in a non-Wycliffite form which it contains, and in a hitherto unnoted text of Richard Rolle's *Form of Perfect Living*." If for the latter work we substitute the [Pseudo-Rolle] *Contemplations of the Dread and Love of God*, this statement would fit the new Morgan manuscript quite perfectly.

* * *

Here begynneth the ten commaundementis of God þe whiche euery man mote kepe if he wulle com to blysse. and so the Gospelle M. 19 & Luc.[10] is þat a man askyd Crist. Quid faciendo vitam eternam possidebo. þat is what he schulde do to haue euer-lastyng lyffe. And Crist answerid to þat man and seid þus. Si vis ad uitam ingredi serua mandata. þat is if þou wolte entre in-to lijffe kepe þe commaundementis.

¶ þe ffirst commaundement of God is þis.[11] the Lorde spake of þes wordes. I am þi Lord God. þat ladde þe oute of þe londe of Egypte fro þe house of seruage. þou schalt not haue oþir goddys bifore me. þou schalt make to þe no grauen ymage neþir eny liknes of þingys whiche ben in heuen aboue and whiche ben in erþe beneth. neþer of þingis þat ben in watris vndir erthe. þou schalt not herye neyþir worschip þoo as god. for I am thi Lord God a stronge gelouse louere. And I visite the wicke[d]nesse of ffaders in-to her sonnes in-to the

---

[9] "A Middle-English MS in the Bibliothèque Ste. Geneviève, Paris," *PMLA*, XLII (1927), 862–864.

[10] Matthew 19.16–17 and Luke 10.25.

[11] The Biblical citations are not exactly the same as they occur in either version of the so-called Wyclif Bible, though they are closer to that rendering attributed to John Purvey. The quotation from Exodus 20.1–6 was also used by Wyclif in the treatise on the Ten Commandments (Arnold, III, 82–92), though this passage differs both from those in M 861 and in the ME Bible. In the Purvey version (Forshall and Madden, *The Holy Bible . . . in the Earliest English Versions made . . . by John Wycliffe and his Followers* [1850], I, 238), the text reads: "And the Lord spak alle these wordis, Y am thi Lord God, that ladde thee out of the lond of Egipt, fro the hous of seruage. Thou schalt not haue alien goddis bifore me. Thou schalt not make to thee a grauun ymage, nethir ony licnesse *of thing* which is in heuene aboue, and which is in erthe bynethe, nether of tho thingis, that ben in watris vndur erthe; thou schalt not herie tho, nether thou schalt worschipe; for Y am thi Lord God, a stronge gelouse louyere; and Y visite the wickidnesse of fadris in to the thridde and the fourthe generacioun of hem that haten me, and Y do mercy in to a thousynde, to hem that louen me, and kepen myn heestis."

thridde and fourthe generacioune of hem that haten me. And I do mercy in-to a þowsand of hem that louen me and kepen myne heestis. ¶ Who brekith þis commaundement. proude men. worldly men. and fleischly men.[12] ¶ Why proude men. for þei maken þe feend her god as Iob seiþ in þe .xlj. c°. the deuel is prince ouer alle þe children of pride.[13] Why worldly men. for þei maken worldly goodys [? her god?].[14] as Poul seiþ to Effesices þe .v. c°. an auerouse man is a seruaunt of mawmentis. ¶ Why fleischly men. for þei maken her belyes her god as Poul seid to Philipenses .iij. c°. þer ben many þat walken þat ben enemyes of Cristis Cros whoos end is deeþ. and her bely is her god. ||

[f. 1ᵛ] Thou schalt not take Goddis name in veyne. for God wole not haue him vnpunyschyd. þat takith His name in ydel. ¶ Who brekyth this heest. veyn spekers. idil swereris. and wickyd worchers. ¶ Why veyn spekers. for her wordes ben not meedful for Crist seiþ Matheu .xij. c°. of eny idil word þat men speken. þei schullen yelde resoun þerof at þe day of doome. ¶ Why idyl swereris. for her oþis ben not needful for þe Wise Man seiþ Ecc¹ .xxiij. c°. a man myche swerynge schal be fulfilled wiþ wickydnes. and veniaunce schal not go fro his hous.[15] ¶ Why wyckyd worcheris. for her werkys ben vnlefulle. for Poul seiþ to þe Romayns .xvj. c°. awaite ye hem þat letten the lawe of God. and dele ye not with hem for by her softe speche þey disseyuen þe hertys of innocent men and wymmen.

---

[12] As an editorial note to the *Lay-Folks' Catechism* (p. 115) points out, the query "Who breaks this Commandment" is raised for each section and conforms to a tradition which survived through Archbishop John Hamilton's Catechism of 1552. The several sets of "breakers" in the present text are identical with those in the *L-F Catechism* except as indicated in n. 23. The *Catechism*, however, merely lists the "breakers" without giving the Biblical texts that support or enlarge upon these selections.

[13] The reference is, of course, to the Leviathan (Job 41.25) and occurs in both Wyclif versions (II, 733) in these words: "he is king vpon (ouer) alle the sones of pride." In the *Catechism* we find the same extract in this connection: "þe fynd ys prince of alle þe childryn of pride" (p. 33).

[14] These two words are omitted in the MS. but are included in the *Catechism* (p. 35). The following quotation is also found in Wyclif's treatise (Arnold, III, 83– "as Poul seiþ þat averyce is service of mawmetis") and in the tract on the Decalogue printed by W. N. Francis (EETS, OS 217, pp. 318–319—"An Auerous mon. or a couetous: is þraldam of maumetes").

[15] This extract agrees almost verbatim with Wyclif's in his treatise (Arnold, III, 84), and both differ from the two Bible versions. The *Speculum Christiani* (p. 20) has: "A man mych swerynge schal be filled wyth wykydnes, and veniaunce schal not departe frome his hows."

Haue mynde to halowe þin haly day.[16] sixe daies þou schalt worche
and do þin owne werkys. the seuenþe day is þe rest of þi Lord God /
in þat dai þou schalt do no seruyse werke. þou ne þi sone ne þi
douȝtir ne thy seruaunt ne þi mayden. ne þi werke beest ne þi gyst
that dwellith wiþinne þin yatis. for in six daies God made heuen and
erþe and þe see. and alle þat is wiþinne hem and restide on þe seuen þe
day and blessyde þat day and halowide it. ¶ Who brekyþ þis heeste.
men þat þenken not on God hertely. ne p[r]eyde Him not deuoutly.
and don not þe werkys of mercy iustly. ¶Why men þat þenken not
on God hertely. for þei ocupien her þouȝtes in vaniteis for [Micah][17]
þe profete seiþ in his booke .iij. c. wo to you þat þenken vnprofitable
þouȝtes worchynge yuelle in youre couchis in þe morowe liȝt. ¶Why
men þat preien wiþ her lippes and noȝt with her hertys. as Criste seiþ
in þe Gospelle of Mathew || [f. 2ʳ] .xv. c. þis puple worschipiþ me
wiþ lippes but her hertys ben fer fro me. ¶Why men þat don not þe
werkys of mercy iustly. for þei leuen uertues and yeuen hem to vicis
as Seint Ion seiþ in þe Gospel .iij. c°. liȝt cam in-to þe world and men
loueden more derkenesse þanne liȝt. for her werkys weren yuelle.

Worschippe þi fadir and þy modyr. þat þou be of longe lyffe upon
þe lond þat þe Lord þi God wole yeue to þee. ¶Who brekyth this
heest. vnkynde men. frowarde men. and rebel men. ¶Why vnkynde
men. for þey helpen not her eldres as þey schullen / for þe Wise
Man seiþ Ecc¹ .iij. c°. he is cursed of God that terriþ þe fadir or moder
to wrathe. ¶Why frowarde men. for þei wollen take no goostly
techinge as Ysaie seiþ in þe .xxx. c°. sones of frowardnes not willynge
to here þe lawe of God seien. speke ye to us plesaunt þingys þouȝ
þei ben errouris. ¶Why rebel men. for þey ben vnbuxum to Crist
and to His Chirche for Goddis lawe tellith[18] that Daton and Abiron
for vnbuxumnesse to Moises and Aaron sonkun doun to helle al
quike wijff and child and alle þat longen to hem.

Thou schalt not sle. ¶Who brekyth þis heeste. enuyouse men.
wrathful men. and auerouse men. ¶ Why enuyouse men. for þei

---

[16] Wyclif (Arnold, III, 85) quotes: "In sixe daies þou miȝte worche, and in þe
sevenþe day is reste of þe Lord God. In þat day þou schalt do no servile werk, ne no
werk of synne, þou, ne þi sone, ne þi douȝter, ne þi servaunt, ne þin hand-mayden,
ne þi werk-beest, ne þe straunger in þin hous. For in sixe daies God made hevene
and erþe, and al þat is þerinne, and restide in þe sevenþe day." (Exodus 20.9–11).

[17] MS. has "miache"? The extract comes from Micah 2.1 (not c°. iij) and reads
in the earlier Wycliffite version thus (III, 716): "Woo to ȝou, that thenken vnprofitable thing, and wirchen yuel in ȝoure couchis; in the morew liȝt thei don it, for the
hond of hem is aȝeinus God."

[18] Numbers 16.27–33.

haten or bacbiten her breþeren. as Ion seith in his Pistle .iij. c°. he
þat is wroth to his broþir. is a mansleer. and he þat seiþ he loueþ
God and hatith his brother is a lier. ¶Whi wraþful men. for þei
smyten or dispisen her brethern as Seint Austyn seith.[19] a wrathe- ||
[f. 2ᵛ] fulle man is hateful to God. and he is made felowe of feendis.
¶Why auerouse men. for þei releuen not in neede her euen-Cristen.
as þe Wise Man seiþ Ecc[1] .xviij. c°. haue mynde of pouerte in tyme
of plente. and of þe neede of pouerte in þe daye of richesse. for fro
eerly vnto euen the tyme schalle chaunge.

Thou schalt do no lecherye. ¶ Who brekyth þis heeste. fornycatouris.
auoutreris. and halowris. ¶ Why fornycatouris. for þei defoulen her
bodies in lecherie as Tobie seiþ .iij. c°. how þe deuel Asmodeus slou3
seuen men for o woman. for þey token hir not in forme of clene wed-
lok. ¶ Why auoutreris. for þei breken þe sacrament of trew wedloke as
the Wise Man seith in þe Booke of Sapience .iij. c°. þe children of
avoutry schullen be outlawid. and if þey be of longe lyffe. att nou3t
þei schullen be acountid and þe laste eelde of hem schal be wiþoute
honoure and bileeue. ¶Why holouris. for þei wasten her bodyes vn-
kyndely as Poul seith to Effesies þe .v. c°. þis þinge wite ye þat holouris haue noon eritage in þe kyndom of heuenes.

Thou schalt do no þefte. ¶ Who brekyth this heeste. mycheris, rob-
beris. and extorcioners. ¶Why mycheris. for þei stelen priuely as þe
prophete Osee seiþ .iiij. c°. truþe is not in erþe. but cursidnes and
þefte. mercy is awey and science of þe Lord. for þis þinge schulen
morne alle þat þerynne dwellen. ¶Whi robbers. for þey robben
openly as the prophete Isaye seiþ .xxxiij. [c°.][20] wo to þe þat robbest.
whether || [f. 3ʳ] thou schalt not be robbyd whanne þou hast fulle
rubbyd. þanne schalt þou be robbed. ¶Why extorcioners. for þei
spoilen men of her goodis falsly as þe Wise Man seiþ Sapience .ij. c°.
þe vnpitouse man seiþ. vigile we þe ri3twis man. for vnprofitable
he is to us. and contrarie to oure werkys. by moost foule deeþ con-
dempne we hym. and priue we so þe pacience of hym.

Thou schalt not seie fals witnes ayens thy nei3bore. ¶Who brekyth
þis heeste. liers. glosers. and fals questmongers. ¶Why liers. for þey

---

[19] Compare the comment on 1 John 3.15 by St. Augustine cited by Thomas
Hibernicus in his *Manipulus florum*, example "d" of Ira (Piacenza: Jacobus de
Tyela, 5 Sept. 1483, sig. 13ᵛ).

[20] The extract suffers from excessive cutting. In the earlier version of the Bible
(III, 281), the passage from Isaiah 33.1 reads: "Wo! thou that robbest; whether
and thi self shalt not be robbid? and thou that dispisist, whethir and thiself shalt
not be dispised? Whan thou shalt han ful endid robbing, thou shalt be robbid."

haten þe treuþe as Poul[21] seiþ in þe Deedis of Apostalis .xxj. c°. I woot þat after me rauischynge wolues schullen come techinge lesynges desseyuable to make oþer to folowe hem. ¶Why glosers. for þey hiden þe treuþe. as Poul seith to Tymothe .iiij. c°. tyme schal come. whanne men schullen not susteyne holsum techynge. and þei schullen turne awey þe heringe fro treuþe. ¶ Why false questmongers. for þei sillen þe truþe as þe prophete Ysaye seiþ .lix. c°. turned is bacward doom. for truþe is fallen in þe strete. and equite may not go ynne / & he þat ceessiþ fro synne. is deemed worthy to be dispised.

Thou schalt not coueite þi neiȝboris hous[22] ne his lond / And þis heeste breketh þo men þat coueiten in herte. þouȝ thei done it not in deede for þe Wise Man seiþ Ecc[1] .v. c°. wille þou not wrongfully coueite possessiouns. ne folowe þou not in þi strengþe þe coueityng of þin herte.[23]

Thou schalt not desire þi neiȝboris wijf. And þis heest breken þoo men that desiren || [f. 3ᵛ] in herte. and to her power don it in deede for Crist seiþ in þe Gospelle of Matheu .v. c°. euery man þat seeþ a woman to coueite hir. hath now don lecherie bi hir in his herte.[24] Ne þou schalt not coueite þe seruaunt of þi neiȝbore. his oxe ne his asse ne no þinge þat is his þou schalt not coueite it wrongfully.

Here enden the ten comaundementis. And here bygynnen þe ten veniauncis þat God toke vppon men of Egipt for brekynge of hem as þe Booke of Exodi techiþ. þe .vij. c°.[25]

[21] The citation is incorrect, as the text comes from Acts 20.29–30. The Purvey version (IV, 568–569) offers: "Y woot, that aftir my departyng, rauyschinge wolues schulen entre in to ȝou, and spare not the flok; and men spekinge schrewid thingis schullen rise of ȝou silf, that thei leden awei disciplis aftir hem."

[22] MS. reads "hous hous."

[23] The ninth and tenth Commandments of Catholic belief are combined by one version (L) of the *Lay-Folks' Catechism* (p. 55) into a single group (as in the Protestant Catechism of today). The *L-F Catechism* here cites three "breakers": those that covet in their hearts, those that covet both in heart and do so in deed, and those that take pleasure in wrongful coveting. The text of the Morgan MS. follows the order of Exodus at the close, in which regard it agrees with Archbishop Thoresby's Catechism (T of the *L-F Catechism*). The Wycliffite adaptation (L of the *L-F Catechism*) takes the sequence of Deuteronomy (5.21), though it alone lists the "breakers." Thus M 861 follows Thoresby as to order but agrees with the Wycliffite adaptation in listing the violators of the Commandments. For the ninth and tenth Commandments of the Morgan MS., one "breaker" is cited in each case; thus this text omits only a single one of all those listed in the *Lay-Folks' Catechism*.

[24] The same Biblical citation is used in this connection (though as the ninth Commandment) by the *Speculum Christiani* (p. 34) and by the *Book of Vices and Virtues* (p. 5).

[25] Compare Exodus 7.19 to 12.30.

For brekynge of þe fyrste heeste. God turned alle þe waters of Egipt into blood. boþe freische water and salt. alle was blood. ¶The secounde veniaunce for brekynge of þe secounde maundement. God multiplied froggys uppon alle þe lond of Egypt in housis and oute of housis. uppon mennes beddes and uppon her metys and drynkes. saue where þe children of Israel weren. ffor brekynge of the þridde heeste. God turned pouder of þe erþe to gnattis. greuous uppon alle þe lond of Egipt. ¶ffor brekynge of the fourthe commoundement [sic]. God sente of alle kynde of flyes. dogge flies and other. ¶ffor brekynge of þe fyue[t] heest. God sent pestilence uppon her beestis. for brekynge of þe sixte heeste. God sent bocchis bilys and bleynes. ¶ffor brekynge of þe seuenþe heeste. God sent þundris hailynge and liȝtnynge þat distroiden muche of the grene fruyt of alle Egypt / for brekyng of þe viij heeste. God sente so grete multitude of brucis þat neuer man sawe bifore ne schalle after att onis so grete þat distroiden alle þe grene frutys that þe || [f. 4ʳ] liȝtnyngys hadden left in Egipt. ¶ffor brekyng of þe nynþe heeste. God sente palpable þicke derke-nesse þat no man myȝte see is broþir. ne moue hym-selffe fro the place þat he was ynne in þre daies. ¶ffor breken [sic] of þe tenþe heeste. God slouȝ alle þe firste goten / bothe of men and of beestis. /

(From *PMLA* 69 (1954), pp. 686-92).

# CHAPTER T21

## A LETTER FROM EDWARD IV TO
## GALEAZZO MARIA SFORZA

AMONG those pilgrims who visited Rome during the winter
of 1475/6 was Anthony Woodville, second Earl Rivers and
brother-in-law to King Edward IV of England.[1] Apparently
the earl was a man of devout faith, for this pilgrimage was but one
of several upon which he embarked. In July 1473 the earl journeyed
to Saint James of Compostella; it was on this trip, it will be recalled,
that Rivers first read the *Dits moraulx des philosophes* by Guillaume
de Tignonville.[2] A few years later Anthony Woodville was to translate this work into English, a translation famous in the annals of
literary and bibliographical history as the first dated book to be
printed in England.[3] In the epilogue to another of the earl's translations (the *Cordyale*), William Caxton listed the pilgrimages
which Rivers had made; the Roman one of 1475/6 is, of course, noted
there.[4]

In his account in the *Cordyale*, however, Caxton failed to mention
what must surely have been one of the most noteworthy events of
the earl's Roman pilgrimage. Such important news did this make
at the time that it was widely reported back home, and Sir John

[1] The fullest biographical sketch of Anthony Woodville is that given by Rudolf
Hittmair, "Earl Rivers' Einleitung zu seiner Übertragung der *Weisheitssprüche
der Philosophen*," *Anglia*, XLVII (1935), 328–344.

[2] Compare the introduction to my edition of *The Dicts and Sayings of the Philosophers*, Early English Text Society, Original Series 211 (London, 1941), for an
account of this text.

[3] See William Blades, *The Life and Typography of William Caxton* (London,
1861–63), II, 36–41. The latest discussion as to the order in which the Caxton editions appeared will be found in my note "Some Observations on *The Dictes and
Sayings of the Philosophers*" (reprinted in Chapter B3 above). In a note, I have expressed the belief that Lambeth Ms No. 265 is very probably an independent authority and is not copied (as was hitherto believed) from some Caxton edition.

[4] "And it is to be noted that sythen the tyme of the grete tribulacion and ad-
uersite of my saide lord / he hath been ful vertuously occupied / as in goyng of
pilgremagis to Seint James in Galice. to Rome. to Seint Bartylmew. to Seint Andrew.
to Seint Mathew. in the Royalme of Naples. and to Seint Nicholas de Bar in Puyle.
and other diuerse holy places." (Westminster: William Caxton, 1479–PML 677,
f. 76ᵛ).

Paston wrote of it to his mother on 21 March 1476, in these words:[5] "ffyrst, the Lorde Ryverse was at Roome right weell and honorably,[6] and other Lords off Ynglonde, as the Lord Hurmonde, and the Lord Scrope, and at ther departyng xij. myle on thysehalff Roome, the Lorde Ryverse was robbyd off alle hys jowelles and plate, whyche was worthe m[le.] marke or better, and is retornyd to Rome ffor a remedy." The hold-up took place at Torre di Baccano, just north of Rome, and some of the booty subsequently turned up in Venice. Upon representation being made to the Signoria, the Venetian authorities undertook to restore to the earl whatever property could be identified, and to do so gratuitously.[7] By these and other means, the Italians sought to restore the confidence of English pilgrims in respect to their personal safety on future trips to the Peninsula.

A number of documents have been recorded relative to the pilgrimage of Earl Rivers to Rome in 1475. One of these, the nature of which has been known for many years through a summary printed in 1864, became the property of the Pierpont Morgan Library (MA 1346–93)[8] some years ago by the acquisition of the Fairfax Murray collection of autograph documents.[9] The contents of this document have been summarized thus:[10]

"Edward IV. to Galeazzo Maria Sforza, Duke of Milan.

Announces the departure thitherwards of Anthony Earl of Rivers, one of his chief confidents and the brother of his dear consort. On his way to or from Rome, he purposes visiting the city of Milan and other places belonging to the Duke, whom he would see and converse with, if not inconvenient. The King therefore recommends him strongly, promising to reciprocate towards any Milanese coming to England with letters from the Duke."

[5] James Gairdner, *The Paston Letters* (London, 1904), v, 258.

[6] Something seems to be omitted here—perhaps "received"?

[7] *Calendar of State Papers and Manuscripts, relating to English Affairs, existing in the Archives and Collections of Venice* (London, 1864), I, 136, nos. 454 and 455.

[8] See the account by Frederick B. Adams, Jr., *Second Annual Report to the Fellows of the Pierpont Morgan Library* (New York, 1951), pp. 49–52.

[9] A number of other documents from this collection were described by George K. Boyce in *Italian Manuscripts in the Pierpont Morgan Library* (New York, 1953), nos. 104–106, 111–114, and 118–119.

[10] *Calendar of State Papers . . . Venice*, I, 133, no. 448. The editor, Rawdon Brown, had apparently not seen the original and relied upon a transcript made for him by Luigi Osio, then director of the Milan archives. This caused Brown to state that the document contained 37 lines (apparently the total of Osio's copy); actually there are eleven lines and a signature. When the *Calendar of State Papers and Manuscripts, existing in the Archives and Collections of Milan* was printed (London, 1912), Allen B. Hinds reported that he had been unable to locate the original.

Since royal documents of this period are not overly common, at least in the U. S. A., and the full contents of this letter from the king of England to the duke of Milan have not been available in the original Latin,[11] the document appears worth printing. On the verso, the letter bears the address: "Illustrissimo ac potentissimo principi Domino Duci Mediolanen*si* amico n*ost*ro carissimo." The text is transcribed below in the usual diplomatic fashion.

Edwardus dei gr*atia* Rex Anglie & ffrancie et Dominus Hibernie Illustrissimo ac potentissimo || principi Domino Duci Mediolanen*si* amico carissimo salu*tem* plurima*m* & feliciter prosp*er*ari / Proficiscitur || istuc Illustris vir domin*us* Antonius Comes de Riparijs. quem non modo diligim*us* s*ed* amam*us* in pri- mis || tum ob suam in nos fidem & egregia m*er*ita tum q*u*od carissime consort*is* n*ost*re frater est; Iter p*er*egri- || nacionis facturus. is noster dominus Antonius Romanam vrbem versus. vel eundo. vel redeundo. ad || p*re*claram mediolani Ciuitatem atq*ue* alia v*est*re dom*in*acionis loca se diuertet vos quatenus id comode || pot*er*it visurus alloquuturusq*ue* Rogamus iccirco serenitatem v*est*ram maiorem in modu*m* quatenus || cum ad eas access*er*it regiones non modo no- bilitat*is* virtutu*m*q*ue* suar*um* ver*um* eciam n*ost*ra contemplacione || commen- datissimu*m* eum suscipia*tis*; p*er*inde atq*ue* istiusmodi viros si ad nos forent accessuri comm*en*- || datos haberi cup*er*etis. qua in re vices grato quidem animo rependemus si quando dabitur || oportunitas Valete feliciter Ex vrbe n*ost*ra Londoniar*um* kalendis Octobris. 1475$^{to}$. || [Signed] Edwardus R. ||

(From *Speculum* 30 (1955), pp. 239-40).

[11] At the head of the sheet, a different hand has written: "1475. Kal. 8bris."

# CHAPTER T22

## THREE LETTERS FROM HENRY VII
## TO THE DUKES OF MILAN

THE collection of historical documents in the Pierpont Morgan Library[1] contains three letters from King Henry VII of England to the dukes of Milan, one being addressed to Gian Galeazzo Maria Sforza, the other two to Lodovico Maria Sforza, known to us more familiarly as "Il Moro." Extremely summary accounts (two being quite inaccurate) of these letters have previously appeared in print, but no detailed discussion of these letters now in the Morgan Library has so far been published.

### I

The first of the three letters was acquired by the library very recently, having been sold at a Sotheby auction on 12 October 1954.[2] The document is slightly damaged on the right hand margin, with the result that the date is defective so far as the year is concerned. Fortunately this can be determined from outside sources, and the document may thus be dated 21 December 1490. Save for one other instance, where the supplied details can hardly be questioned (C[elsitudine]), the editor has made no attempt to provide the missing letters; it was deemed preferable to indicate *lacunae* by dots rather than to supply conjectural readings of dubious value. The texts are printed in the normal fashion, all contractions having been expanded with the use of italics; punctuation and capitalization of the original have been retained in the transcripts.

[Address, on verso]: Ill*ustrissi*mo ac Pote*n*tissimo pri*n*cipi D*omi*no Joha*n*ni galeaz Maria Sfortia Vicecomiti: || Duci Mediolani &c / Papię anglerięq*ue* Comiti: ac genuę & Cremonę || domino: Consanguineo et confęderato nostro Carissimo. / ||

[Text, on recto]: Ill*ustrissi*mo ac Pote*n*tissimo pri*n*cipi D*omi*no Joha*n*ni galeaz maria sfortia uicecomiti Duci mediolani &c / Papię anglerięq*ue* comiti: ac genuę et cre-||monę domino, co*n*sanguineo et co*n*fęderato nostro car*iss*imo

---

[1] For a similar discussion, compare the writer's "A Letter from Edward IV to Galeazzo Maria Sforza," *supra*.

[2] W. Westley Manning sale, p. 40, lot 211, with reproduction of the letter.

Henricus dei gratia rex anglię et francię: ac dominus hybernię Salutem: et prospera uotorum || incrementa. Intelleximus tam ex litteris uestris quam etiam ex relatione nobilis uiri benedicti spinulę, uestro nomine nobis facta, quam beni||gne quamque humaniter et amice dominus dauid gulielmus orator noster ad sedem apostolicam missus istuc diuertens a uestra Celsitudine fuerit || susceptus: nec minus etiam cognouimus / quam grato animo et quam iucunda mente mutuam nostram redintegratam necessitudinem uestra Sublimitas || acceptarit: quę sane omnia licet antea ab eodem oratore nostro litteris fuissent nobis demonstrata summa tamen cum nostra uoluptate atque animi || dulcedine ex litteris uestrę Celsitudinis et eius nuncio benedicto spinola, uiro nobis admodum grato audiuimus Equidem Illustrissime princeps non || possumus imprimis non ingentes gratias uestrę Sublimitati habere quod oratorem nostrum istac transeuntem nostro intuitu et precipuo nostro amore tam || libenter uiderit: tanque honorifice susceperit. Vestra nanque Celsitudo tot nobis et tam manifesta integerrimi sui erga nos amoris indicia || sępe antea et nuper quoque nobis ostendit: ut maiori declarationi uix pateat locus. Quod autem ueteris nostrę coniunctionis redint . . . || uestrę Celsitudini tantopere grata accesserit: et eadem proinde litteris suis sit nobis gratulata ex animo: gaudemus profecto supra quam litteris . . . || ri possit, hoc nostrę societatis et amicicie fędus initum tantopere gratum et iucundum aduenisse. Nos autem quantum ad nos . . . || plane intelligimus eam ipsam contractam inter nos amiciciam, non posse gratiore unquam animo aut placabiliori mente a uestra C[elsitudine]* || accipi, quam a nobis ipsis: Tantus est noster amor erga uestram Celsitudinem et tam feruens gratificandi uoluntas: Faxit deus . . . || hęc nostra fędera sicuti ab optimo animo profecta sunt ita indies magis et magis coalescant: fecundentur et exube . . . || fiant immortalia. Id uero nos pro uirili nostra contendemus semper: atque ita in officio perstabimus: ut uel facile omnes . . . || possint Illustrissimum dominum ducem mediolani consanguineum nostrum carissimum, usque adeo intimum esse nobis et propinquum: ut . . . || non mediocri iniuria nemo in eum aliquod aduersum moliri possit. Reliquum est ut fęlicissime ualeat ad uota uestra Celsitudo . . . || sui beniuolentissimos esse: ac perpetuo fore sibi firmiter persuadeat. Ex Regia nostra Windesorę die .xxj. decembris M[CCCCLXXXX]* || [signed] Henricus R ||

In the *Calendar* of the English state papers preserved in Milan,[3] the letter now in the Pierpont Morgan Library (MA 1578) is noted under date 21 December 1490 together with this brief summary: "Returns thanks for the honourable reception given to Sir David Williams, English ambassador to Rome, on his passage through

* Letters supplied where text is certain.

3 *Calendar of State Papers and Manuscripts, existing in the Archives and Collections of Milan* (London, 1912), p. 272, no. 428. The letter had previously been cited in the *Calendar of State Papers and Manuscripts, relating to English Affairs, existing in the Archives and Collections of Venice* (London, 1864), 1, 202, no. 602. When Allen B. Hinds prepared the Milanese calendar, he reported that he was unable to locate the document and quoted the contents from the Venetian calendar.

Milan." Even if this entry had not been available, it would have been relatively easy to supply the correct year for the letter from other records.

On 26 July 1490[4] Henry VII wrote to Gian Galeazzo Maria Sforza that he was sending "Dominus David Gulielmus" to Rome with instructions to stop in Milan on the way. David Williams was identified as the Master of the Rolls ("rotulorum nostrorum custos"). In the king's letter, it was further set forth that Williams would be accompanied on his trip by Johannes de Giglis (Giovanni Gigli),[5] the collector in England for the pope; some years later, Gigli was identified as the "Orator regis Angliae in Rom. Curia"[6] and subsequently became bishop of Worcester.[7]

On 4 October of the same year[8] Giacomo Gherardi, the papal nuncio in Milan, wrote to the Apostolic Secretary Giovanni Pietro Arrivabene that the (unnamed) "legatus ab Anglia, clericus, ut mihi refertur" had indeed arrived in Milan that day, though his colleague Giovanni Gigli, having been seized by an attack of podagra, had remained at Lyons. He also reported that the ambassador had previously conferred with the duke, who had been attending a hunt near Somma Lombarda, province of Varese.[9] Three weeks later (25 October)[10] Gian Galeazzo himself wrote to Henry, explaining that Williams had been there and had received from the duke letters setting forth the nature of the business which had been transacted; furthermore, the duke stated that he had asked Benedetto Spinola to report directly to the king on these matters. [Spinola, as the Morgan letter shows, duly performed this service.] Finally,[11] we learn from a letter written by Giacomo Botta, bishop of Tortona, to the duke on 31 October that the English ambassador had at last arrived in Rome

---

[4] *Calendar of State Papers . . . Milan*, p. 262, no. 411.

[5] For a short account of his career, compare the *Dictionary of National Biography*, XXI, 311.

[6] Conrad Eubel, *Hierarchia catholica medii aevi* (Münster, 1913–23), II, 268, Wigornien., n. 4.

[7] Pope Alexander VI appointed him bishop of Worcester on 30 August 1497, and he was consecrated in Rome. Giovanni Gigli died in Rome on 25 August 1498 without ever having visited his see. He was succeeded by his nephew, Silvestro Gigli. Cf. Eubel, *loc. cit.*, and Bonifacius Gams, *Series episcoporum ecclesiae catholicae* (Leipzig, 1931), p. 200.

[8] Enrico Carusi, *Dispacci e lettere di Giacomo Gherardi*, Studi e Testi, XXI (Rome, 1909), pp. 550–551.

[9] "Audio honorifice et amanter receptum" as Gherardi observes (Carusi, p. 551).

[10] *Calendar of State Papers . . . Milan*, p. 265, no. 417.

[11] *Ibid.*, pp. 265–266, no. 418.

but that his companion had fallen ill en route. Clearly, the ambassador here referred to was David Williams. All these details, then, make it evident that the king's letter to Gian Galeazzo printed above was written on 21 December 1490.

## II

The second letter (Plate 20; Morgan Library, R. of E., Vol. I, No. 40), written slightly more than six years later (10 February 1496/97),[12] deals with an event of greater historic significance.[13] It concerns the English entry as participants in the League founded in the summer of 1496 to combat the threat of French aggression.[14]

[Address, on verso]: Ill*ustrissi*mo ac Potentissimo pr*i*ncipi D*omi*no Ludouico Maria Sforcia anglo || Dei gr*ati*a Duci mediolani &c / Papi*ę* angleri*ęque* comiti: ac genu*ę* et || Cremon*ę* D*omi*no: amico n*os*tro carissimo. /. ||

[Text, on recto]: Ill*ustrissi*mo ac Potentissimo pr*i*ncipi D*omi*no Ludouico ma-ria Sforcia anglo Dei gr*ati*a Duci mediolani &c / Papi*ę* angleri*ęque* comiti. ac genu*ę* et cremon*ę* || D*omi*no amico n*os*tro car*issi*mo Henricus eadem gr*ati*a Rex angli*ę* et franci*ę* ac d*omin*us hybern*i*ę Salutem et prospera uotor*um* in-crem*en*ta. Vidimus perlibenter || litter*a*s u*e*str*ę* Cel*situdi*nis quintodecimo de-cembr*is* mediolani datas / quib*us* intelleximus litter*a*s n*os*tras fuisse uob*is* red-ditas / quib*us* continebat*ur* Instrum*en*tum confirmatio-||nis et ratificationis f*ę*deris rom*ę* initi: Item et nom*i*na colligator*um* adher*en*tium ac comm*en*dato-r*um* pro parte u*e*str*ę* Cel*situdi*nis fuisse nobis reddita. Insuper || f*ę*dus ips*um* solem*n*iter processionaliter*que* nos *e*ss*e* i*n* festo om*n*ium sanctor*um* celebraturos (qu*o*d et re ipsa effecimus pr*o*ut S*an*ctissimo D*omi*no N*os*tro tam*quam* capiti totius lig*ę* || multo a*n*tea litter*i*s n*os*tris latissime declarauimus) L*ę*tamur au-tem q*uo*d hui*u*smodi n*os*tra f*ę*deris publicatio u*e*str*ę* Cel*situdi*ni iucu*n*da ex-titerit. Q*uo*d u*er*o eadem u*e*stra || Cel*situd*o Oratorem ad nos su*um* propediem sit missura: Expectabimus illi*u*s adue*n*tum / quem sane / ubi applicuerit ni*hil*omin*us* hilari uultu q*uam* grato et iu-||cu*n*do a*n*imo uisuri sumus et audi-turi. Ex Palatio n*os*tro Iuxta Westmon*ast*erium die x febr*uarii*. M°ccccl*xxxx*vj°. /. || [signed] Henricus R ||

---

[12] The English legal and official year began on Lady Day (Feast of the Annun-ciation, 25 March) until the reform of the calendar in 1752.

[13] The document bears the suggestive, modern note: "Enrico VII dal 1485 al 1509." This notation in Italian points strongly to the conclusion that the document was once in some Italian collection. The letter came to the Morgan Library as part of a collection entitled "Royal House of Tudor," which seems to have been ac-quired by the Library in the early years of the present century. The letter is listed by Seymour de Ricci, *Census of Medieval and Renaissance Manuscripts in the United States and Canada* (New York, 1935–40), II, 1578, with the date "10 Feb. 1496."

[14] For a concise account, see the *Cambridge Modern History*, I, 118 ff.

This letter is, as the text implies, a reply to one written by Il Moro on 15 December 1496;[15] a draft of this communication is preserved in the Milan archives. Furthermore, the letter from Henry VII to Lodovico Sforza printed above, forms part of the correspondence dealing with the English entry into the coalition formed to protect Italy from French invasion. On 12 August,[16] the duke of Milan wrote to the king of England expressing his satisfaction at the English decision to join the League. This was followed two weeks later (27 August)[17] by another letter from the duke, informing King Henry that Milan had ratified the English participation and that he was sending herewith all the pertinent information concerning the articles and agreements together with a detailed list of allies and adherents to the League. On 29 October[18] Henry acknowledged receipt of this material, adding the note: "We ourselves intend to celebrate this league publicly within three days, on the feast of All Saints, in the church of St. Paul's, the metropolitan of the realm, with a state procession, making public declaration of our joy; and there we shall receive the Sword and Cap of Maintenance, sent to us by his Holiness with all due respect." Il Moro, in turn, acknowledged receipt (on 15 December)[19] of the king's letter of 29 October, expressing the usual cordial greetings of friendship and warm affection.

The entry in the *Calendar* of the English state papers in Venice, which first described the Morgan letter, reads:[20] "[Henry VII] has received the names of the Duke's colleagues and adherents and of those recommended by him." Here is no mention, however, of the king's report concerning the promulgation of England's entry into the League, and the nature of and reason for the events which took place. Henry's letter is, of course, largely a recapitulation of his note of 29 October.

It is not at all clear why Henry waited so long before informing Lodovico Sforza of the events of 1 November. As early as 5 December, the forthcoming publication of England's participation in the League was known to the Venetian statesman Marino Sanuto,[21]

---

[15] *Calendar of State Papers . . . Milan*, p. 310, no. 519.
[16] *Ibid.*, p. 302, no. 500.      [17] *Ibid.*, p. 303, no. 501.
[18] *Ibid.*, p. 309, no. 515.      [19] *Ibid.*, p. 310, no. 519.
[20] *Calendar of State Papers . . . Venice*, 1, 252, no. 734. Again the editor of the Milanese calendar, Allen B. Hinds, was unable to discover the original in the Milan Archives (Potenze Estere. Inghilterra) and simply repeated the description in the Venetian inventory. The letter is listed on p. 310, no. 520.
[21] *I diarii* (Venice, 1879–1903), 1, 420: "Vene lettere de Ingeltera de 17 novembrio,

and the report was duly entered in his diary. By 19 January 1497,[22] an account of the English promulgation had reached Venice through the republic's ambassador in Spain, Jacopo Contarini. Certainly the duke of Milan must have been just as fully informed of what had taken place by his own representatives in England. In view of these facts, it is strange indeed that the king of England delayed until 10 February before forwarding the official statement to Milan. Possibly Henry thought that his letter of 29 October setting forth what he planned to do was sufficient notice—until the arrival of the letter from Il Moro of 15 December required an acknowledgement and a more complete and formal account.

## III

The third letter (Pierpont Morgan Library, MA 1346–125) is dated 16 June 1498 and is not listed either in the Venetian or in the Milanese inventories of state papers relating to England. Nevertheless it seems highly probable that this document too must once have formed part of the Sforza archives.

[Address, on verso]: Ill*ustrissi*mo ac Potentissimo Principi do*mi*no Ludouico Maria Sfortia || Anglo Duci mediolani papię Anglerię*que* comiti ac genuę || et Cremonę Domino amico nostro car*issi*mo. ||

[Text, on recto]: Henricus Dei gr*ati*a Rex Anglię et francię ac d*ominu*s hybernię &c. Ill*u*strissi*mo ac Potentissimo principi Domino Ludouico Maria || Sfortia anglo Duci Mediolani: papię Anglerię*que* Comiti ac genuę et Cremonę Domino. amico *n*ostro car*issi*mo. Sal*ute*m et prospera || votor*um* Increme*n*ta. Legimus perlibenter *litte*ras vestrę Cel*situdi*nis xvj Maij mediolani datas / quas pr*esentium* lator vester Nuncius|| nobis reddidit / quibus q*ui*dem primu*m* cognouimus domi*n*u*m* Raymu*n*du*m* oratorem ve*st*rum istuc applicuisse et nostram quam || gerimus erga v*estram* Cel*situdi*nem affectionem Demo*n*strasse / quod sane no*n* mediocriter nobis gratum extitit / eo*que* magis accep-||tum q*uod* huiusmodi Relatio vestrę Subl*imi*tati fuerit no*n* Iniucunda: Q*uod* vero eadem v*est*ra Cel*situd*o ip*s*um domi*n*u*m* Raymu*n*du*m* oratorem || suu*m* sit propediem ad Nos remissura / gratus nempe erit Nobis eius adue*n*tus quotienscum*que* applicuerit / Cui quicq*ui*d || paulo antea Impe*n*dimus / id profecto v*estr*ę Cel*situdi*nis Intuitu libenter fecimus / habemus aute*m* gr*ati*as

---

dil piacer havea abuto il re di la demostration fata per i confederati di la publication di la liga. E dovea publicarsi de lì a Londra al primo dil mexe presente di dezembrio, et il re scrisse a la Signoria in responsion di una lettera congratulatoria *de eadem materia*, la qual è avanti scripta." Sanuto seems to have misunderstood the dates, for the letter could hardly have reached Venice thus quickly. The letter was probably sent from England on 17 October and refers to the events of 1 November.

22 *Ibid.*, I, 470.

non mediocres vestrę || Sublimitati quod sua omnia tam libere nobis offerat / nostramque amicitiam adaugere cupiat. Ceterum audiuimus quę Augustinus || Spinola pro parte vestra nobis exposuit / a quo mentem superinde nostram intelligere poterit vestra Celsitudo quę fęlix semper vale[at]* || ad vota. Ex Palatio Nostro Iuxta Westmonasterium xvj Die Junij M°cccclxxxxviij°. / || [signed] Henricus R ||

The summary given in the catalogue of a former owner of this document is very misleading,[23] viz.: "He [Henry VII] has read with pleasure his correspondent's letters of May 16th brought by Signor Ramondi, with whom he was before acquainted, and who has assured him of the Duke's affectionate sentiments towards him." For example, it is clear from the Morgan letter as well as from documents still preserved in Milan that, far from Raimondo de' Raimondi's having brought anything to England from Milan, he had actually returned to Milan, having been summoned thither by Lodovico. The events that actually occurred are these:

According to a draft in the Milanese archives, dated 11 May 1498,[24] Lodovico Sforza wrote to his agent in England, Agostino Spinola, that he had received the report of Raimondo de' Raimondi and that the duke wished Spinola to congratulate King Henry on his "well-being and prosperity." Spinola was also to inform the king that the duke had written to his brother (Cardinal Ascanio Maria Sforza) on behalf of Giovanni Gigli, bishop of Worcester, whose promotion to the cardinalate the king was anxious to secure. Another draft of a letter, dated 16 May,[25] indicates that Lodovico wrote to Henry informing him that Raimondo had arrived in Milan with good news and kind greetings from the king of England. The duke wished Henry to know that Raimondo had been recalled for the sole purpose of discussing matters of mutual interest to England and Milan.

The Morgan document is clearly a reply to this letter from Il Moro, though it is no less certain that, even prior to this, Henry had urged that Raimondo be sent back to England. On 11 June,[26] Lodovico Sforza wrote to Ambassador Raimondo de' Raimondi that he had wanted him to attend to some diplomatic functions in Italy, but that the king of England had so strongly urged the return of Raimondo to England that the duke had decided to accede to

---

* Lacuna as result of a tear in the paper; letters supplied.

[23] *Catalogue of the Collection of Autograph Letters and Historical Documents formed . . . by Alfred Morrison* (London, 1883–1897), ii, 256.

[24] *Calendar of State Papers . . . Milan*, pp. 343–344, no. 559.

[25] *Ibid.*, pp. 344–345, no. 563.      [26] *Ibid.*, pp. 345–346, no. 565.

Henry's wishes. Raimondo was to inform the king that Il Moro would be happy to accept the Order of the Garter. However, a letter of 15 June from Raimondo to Lodovico makes it clear that the ambassador was then still in Milan.[27]

As a sequel to Lodovico Sforza's letter to Agostino Spinola, we find a report from the latter to the former, dated 20 June,[28] informing the duke that Spinola had proceeded to Westminster immediately upon the receipt of instructions from Milan and had been granted an audience by the king. Henry was most pleased at Lodovico's efforts, especially with the help of Cardinal Sforza, on behalf of Giovanni Gigli. Henry was indeed very anxious for the bishop of Worcester to be made a cardinal, and the king hoped that the duke would continue to work for the successful conclusion of this worthy cause. This meeting between King Henry VII and Agostino Spinola is clearly the one referred to in the Morgan letter of 16 June 1498. It is also certain that Henry was successful in his insistence upon the speedy return of Raimondo de' Raimondi to England, as noted in the text under discussion. On 12 September 1498,[29] Raimondo wrote to the duke of Milan that he was now in England, having safely arrived there despite the considerable dangers and difficulties encountered in the course of the journey.

The three Morgan documents, here printed *in extenso* for the first time, thus correct previous statements as to the contents of the letters and provide additional facts of historic interest. The first two letters were written by Pietro Carmeliano, Latin secretary to King Henry VII.[30] These will be of particular interest to students of calligraphy, for they are fine examples of writing from the pen of the man who brought the Italian hand into England.

(From *Speculum* 31 (1956), pp. 485-90).

[27] *Ibid.*, p. 346, no. 567.      [28] *Ibid.*, pp. 347–348, no. 571.
[29] *Ibid.*, p. 352, no. 583.
[30] In the summary of a letter from Il Moro to Pietro Carmeliano (*Calendar of State Papers . . . Milan*, p. 344, no. 561), the latter is described as "Latin Secretary of the Duke of Milan." This is an accidental slip by the editor, for Carmeliano was certainly secretary to King Henry at this time. Compare *DNB*, IX, 127-128.

# CHAPTER T23

## BELLE DA COSTA GREENE

BELLE DA COSTA GREENE was born in Alexandria, Virginia. After a brief apprenticeship at Princeton University, she became Mr Pierpont Morgan's librarian in 1905. For forty-three years, Miss Greene was connected with this collection, serving as head of the incorporated institution for a quarter-century. She was elected a Fellow of the Mediaeval Academy in 1939, an honor which she greatly esteemed. In place of the usual memoir, it has been suggested that I might offer (with minor changes) the "appreciation" which, as representing the staff, I presented at the celebration given by the Library in her honor on 4 April 1949.

"Whether or not"—Andrew Lang once observed·—"Whether or not a lady can love books is a question that may not be so readily settled." Clearly Andrew Lang wrote down this *mot* before his first meeting with Belle da Costa Greene. Once he had met this particular lady, Lang could not possibly have made this statement—save with his tongue in his cheek. Indeed, had he ventured to do so, he would certainly never have survived his second encounter with her.

If Belle da Costa Greene has been elsewhere described—and with much justification—as being of imperious temperament, one may observe with equal candor that she, in common with the Emperor Hadrian, "fuit memoriae ingentis, facultatis immensae." If her nature was ebullient and dominant—and though blessed with eminent and ample gifts—nevertheless she was never, to my knowledge, unbecomingly haughty. Our great American shibboleth that a thousand-dollar man ought not to waste his time on a hundred-dollar job, had no appeal for Miss Greene. No matter how trifling the matter in hand, she always undertook it with the obvious feeling that it demanded the very best there was in her—and once the task was accomplished, it was scrutinized with an unsparingly critical eye. It was nice working for a boss who never asked one to do anything that she was not prepared to do herself—and no task was too menial for Miss Greene to attend to personally if HER library could better be served thereby. One hot July, I recall, we found it necessary to move our largest and heaviest tomes (the oversize incunabula) from one gallery in the East Room to another. This transfer involved a veritable "bucket brigade," one in which "B G" insisted upon taking her place. At the end of a typically sultry, New York summer day, she was still fresh and full of energy. I cannot say as much for several of her bulkier, and presumably more vigorous, juniors.

One never knew quite what to expect from Miss Greene—and one was rarely disappointed. From the moment a newcomer set foot in the Library, he came face to face with the unexpected. Well do I remember my own first day, when she had reluctantly intrusted me with a key to the Library treasures and I had spent several happy hours making my first acquaintanceship with just a few of them. As I turned to leave the building that evening, Miss Greene with characteristic enthusiasm *roared* at me: "Where are you going with that key?? Not even Mr Morgan is permitted to leave the Library with one in his pocket." Conspicuous above all else was Miss Greene's enthusiasm—that, in the broad Platonic sense of the Phaedrus, "eine gottgesandte Begeisterung," was the secret of her success.

In fifteen years at the Library, one came to observe many changes taking place and one noted how easily Miss Greene was able to make these difficult adjustments. In the early nineteen-thirties, the motto of The Pierpont Morgan Library might well have been that Greek inscription which decorated the old gateway to the Library in Berne: μή τις βέβηλος εἰσίτω. "Let not the profane enter!!!" Ten years later the wealth of the Library was lavishly spread out for the visitors of all sorts and classes—from nearby and from the far reaches of the land—who came to attend the New York World's Fair! Education, according to Plato's great fundamental principle, is a life-long process—and Belle Greene was forever learning.

Her success in the bookmarts and in the auction places of two Continents is familiar to all; for us of her staff, it was ever a fascinating experience to see Miss Greene in action. Watching her deal with the preliminary mechanics of an auction sale—appeasing the auctioneer, quieting (or, with skillful hand, misleading) the opposition, and selecting the proper agent for each special transaction—some of us came to wonder, indeed, how Miss Greene escaped being made a partner in J. P. Morgan & Co. Beyond all else, however, her emphasis on quality made a profound impression on friend and friendly foe alike. Not for Belle Greene was the elegant trash—the "scruta scita" as Petronius was pleased to call it—which fills the catalogues of many an antiquarian bookseller. Deeply engraved upon her heart was the dictum of Seneca's that "it matters not how many books you have—but how good those are which you do possess."

Miss Greene's disposition, as everyone knows, was chivalrous—that is, it was at once generous and combative. We had our differences, and Miss Greene was ever ready, in her forceful way, to call me "that mule in sheep's clothing." But I do not recall a controversy tainted with rancor. No matter how serious the difference, debate was tempered with wisdom. That there was much disputation, the hearty expression of strongly-felt opinions, is natural. Indeed, it could hardly have been otherwise with Miss Greene—for, as Milton reminds us: "Where there is much desire to learn, there of necessity will be much arguing, much writing, many opinions; for opinion in good men is but knowledge in the making."

No man, we are told, is a hero to his valet—but let me assure you of the equal truth that any Director of the calibre of Belle da Costa Greene can easily win the total, respectful admiration of every member of her staff. Alas, there have been but few such in the World! It was a wonderful privilege to be for fifteen years on the staff of one who could enjoy the devotion and respect of friends and colleagues without pride, who could greet success with due humility, and who could face heartbreak and pain—alas, all too frequently in later years—with the unflinching courage befitting a man. In the words of the Classicist, the inscription on Belle da Costa Greene's memorial should read:

VIS VIRIDIS VIRIS VIVIS VIRESCAT

May the Greene power em*bell*ish humanity!

(From *Speculum* 32 (1957), pp. 624-44).

# CHAPTER T24

## 'AT THY GOLG FIRST EUT OF THE HOUS VLYSSE THE SAYNGE THUS'

IN examining a number of books of hours for the use of Sarum printed on the continent for sale in England,[1] the writer noted with some amazement the peculiar English often to be found in these volumes.[2] It therefore seemed worth while to record, in this journal and thus for the benefit of a wider audience, some of the choicer specimens found in these printings,[3] together with other poems which came into English religious books as translations from foreign sources. The title of this study, a typical example of the cruder continental spelling (for 'At thy going first out of the house bless thee saying thus'), is to be found on folio 8 (signature A8) of the *Horae ad usum Sarum* printed in Rouen about the year 1506 by Richard Goupil for William Candos.[4] In glancing over the foreign *horae*, one is continually astounded that such truly fantastic orthography[5] could find a market in the British Isles in competition with

[1] Though this study is based chiefly on materials in the Pierpont Morgan Library (PML), I have drawn heavily on the resources of the British Museum (BM), the Bibliothèque Nationale (BN), the Bodleian Library (Bodl.), and the University (CUL) and college libraries at Cambridge. For his ready willingness to assist, both in person and by letter, I am deeply obliged to Dr. Dennis E. Rhodes of the British Museum.

[2] The poetry is mentioned in passing, without further explanation or quotation, by Helen C. White, *The Tudor Books of Private Devotion* (Madison, Wis., 1951). The French stanzas printed in sections III and IV are briefly noticed by Rosemond Tuve, *Seasons and Months: Studies in a Tradition of Middle English Poetry* (Paris, 1933), p. 210.

[3] Sarum *Horae*, Paris: for Francis Byrckman, 14 April 1519 (STC 15923; Bodl. Douce BB. 141. [1]), sig. H4ᵛ: 'Thys epystell of our sauyour sendeth our holy father pope leo vnto te emperour Carolo magno of the wyche we fynste wyrten who that bereth thys blessyng vpon hym and says yt ones a day schall opteyne .xl. yere of pardon and .lxxx. lenttyg. And he schal not peryshe wyrth soden deeth.'

[4] This edition is not listed by the STC (*A Short-Title Catalogue of Books Printed in England, Scotland, & Ireland and of English Books Printed Abroad 1475–1640*, London, 1926), but it is included by William W. Bishop, *A Checklist of American Copies of 'Short-Title Catalogue' Books* (Ann Arbor, 1950), p. 195. Copy at PML (no. 30004).

[5] 'O Blyssed trinite the fadre the sonne et the holy good thre persones and one god. I by leue vvith my hert et confesse vvith my moulth al tat holy church byleueth and holdeth of the and as a gode catholike and cristen man ougth tho fele

the editions put out there by the native presses; yet no fewer than 120 editions[6] of the surviving *horae* (almost exactly half of those recorded by the *Short-Title Catalogue*, nos. 15866–16109) were printed abroad. Not all of these, of course, were so ignorantly composed by the pressman as the example cited here,[7] but it is evident that even the poorer specimens of English were so well received that reprintings were found commercially desirable.

I

Under no. 940, the Brown-Robbins *Index*[8] records only a single manuscript for the familiar prayer 'God be in my head and in my understanding' (Magdalene College, Cambridge, MS. F. 4. 13, ff. 27ᵛ–28). In that manuscript, the prayer reads:

> God be in my hedde and in my vnderstandyng
> God be in myn eyen & in my beholding
> God be in my mouthe & in my spekyng
> God be in my herte & in my thinkyng
> God be with me in all my lyuyng & at and after my departyng

The catalogue of the Magdalene College manuscripts,[9] however, maintains that this book of hours belongs to the sixteenth century (1518); to the present writer it seemed unlikely that this was the

---

and byleue of the' (PML 30004, sig. D12; the 'et' corresponds to an ampersand in the prototype).

[6] At least 19 came from the Low Countries, 71 from Paris, 29 from Rouen, and a single one from Venice.

[7] On occasion it is perfectly evident that the pressman did not understand the text he was setting. For example, in the Sarum *Horae*, [Paris]: Johann Philippi, 1497 (BM IA. 40487), we find the following lines on sig. i4 (the double-stroke marking the end of a line): '. . . I crie the mercy || vvyth hert contrit of mygret vnkinde- || nesse that. || ¶ I haue had to the. || The most svvetest spouse of mi || so vvle crist iesu destring hertly || euermore for to be vvyth the in mynde || et vvylle et to le te non erthely thyng be || soo nygh myn hert as thou crist iesu.' This same treatment of '¶ I haue had to the' is found in Vostre's Sarum hours of 20 October 1501 (BM C. 29. h. 12) and those of [? 1510] (BM C. 41. a. 20). In the Pigouchet edition of 1495 (STC 15880; Bodl. Douce 24, sig. h2), this is treated as a full rubric.

[8] Carleton Brown and Rossell Hope Robbins, *The Index of Middle English Verse* (New York, 1943), p. 151: 'A Prayer of St. Richard of Chichester—six lines.' In the quotations I have silently expanded the contractions throughout, since they are in all instances perfectly normal and usual abbreviations.

[9] Montague Rhodes James, *A Descriptive Catalogue of the Manuscripts in the College Library of Magdalene College, Cambridge* (Cambridge, 1909), p. 24: 'Cent. xvi (1518), beautifully written by or for Jasper Fyloll, a London Dominican.' On f. 1ᵛ, a reward of 3s. 4d. for the return of the MS. is promised to the finder.

very first appearance of this prayer in English. Some years ago, Mr. Frederick J. H. Sutton of Amenia, New York, persuaded me to undertake the search for the earliest extant text of this stanza, and I deeply regret that the results of my investigations could not have been presented to him before his death on 10 March 1958.

The oldest surviving appearance of the poem, so far as I have been able to determine, is that on the title page of the Rouen *Horae ad usum Sarum* noted above:[10]

> God † be in mihede And in min vnder ston dyng[11]
> God † be in myn hyyesse And in min lokeyng
> God † be in mi movthe And in myspekeyng
> God † be in my hartt And in my thovgvt
> God † be at myneyende And ad myde partyng

Although undated, this edition almost certainly was issued no later than the year 1506, since the calendar prefixed to the volume covers the years 1506–1517. It is most improbable that the edition could have been produced much later than the first year for which the calendar supplied the pertinent information. Both Goupil and Candos were active in Rouen in the early years of the sixteenth century.[12] According to Georges Lepreux,[13] Richard Goupil only began to print in the year 1510; the evidence of this book seems to prove that Lepreux gave too late a date for the beginnings of this press. Edouard Frère[14] supplies an address 'la 5ᵉ *échoppe* du portail des Libraires' for the shop of Guillaume Candos in the years 1504–1505, while the Morgan *Horae* (see note 11) provides a different location.

[10] With minor errors, the text of this edition was printed in the *Third Report of the Royal Commission on Historical Manuscripts* (London, 1872), p. 256; cf. Brown-Robbins, p. 151. The errors in this edition suggest that the text was set up from an earlier printing, perhaps that of [Rouen: Guerin, *c.* 1505], the only known copy of which (BM c. 35. a. 2) lacks the title page. The later Rouen edition (Jacques Cousin, 28 July 1525; CUL Syn. 8.52.36, sig. a1) provides an almost perfect version.

[11] The prayer is printed in ten lines. The colophon reads: '¶ Impressum Rothomagi in officina Richardi goupil pro Guillermo candos | hac in vrbe in vico sancti nicolai commorante. G c.' (sig. I12ᵛ).

[12] Compare the *Catalogue of a Collection of early French Books in the Library of C. Fairfax Murray* (London, 1910), nos. 321 [*c.* 1500], 509 [*c.* 1502], and 447 [*c.* 1520], and the *Catalogue des livres composant la bibliothèque de feu M. le baron James de Rothschild* (Paris, 1884–1920), nos. 3223 (17 January 1511/12) and 3225 ('Ad ix. Idus Augusti'—more correctly, the nones, 5 August—1511).

[13] *Gallia typographica* (Paris, 1909–1914), III, 64, n. 3, and 186–187.

[14] *Des livres de liturgie des églises d'Angleterre (Salisbury, York, Hereford), imprimés à Rouen dans les XV et XVIᵉ siècles* (Rouen, 1867), p. 26. He cites a Sarum missal of 2 August 1509.

Though this seems to be the first appearance of this text in English, the prayer had long formed a part of the French *horae*.[15] Its first printed appearance is in a *livre d'heures* which was printed at Paris by Antoine Vérard on 3 April 1488/9,[16] the only extant copy of this edition being now preserved in the Bibliothèque Municipale at Toulouse (Inc. 654).[17] With minor variations, Vérard continued to print this prayer in his various *horae* for the next decade;[18] it also appeared in the editions published by Thielmann Kerver (e.g., Rome use, 9 May 1501—PML 582)[19] and by Gillet Hardouyn (Rome use, 24 November 1503—PML 19286).[20] On folio 1ᵛ of Vérard's edition, the stanza reads:

Jesus soit en ma teste & en mon entendement
Jesus soit en mes yeulx & en mon regardement
Jesus soit en ma bouche & en mon parlement
Jesus soit en mon cueur et en mon pensement
Jesus soit en ma vie & en mon trespassement

The prayer was first printed in England itself by Richard Pynson (12 May 1514—STC 15917, on the title page of the work),[21] the sole surviving copy of this edition being in the library of Clare College, Cambridge (Kk. 8. 3):

God be in my heed And in myn vnderstandynge
God be in myn eyen And in my lokynge
God be in my mouthe And in my spekynge
God be in my herte And in my thynkynge
God be at myn ende And my departynge

[15] It is included in a book of hours for the use of St.-Brieuc (BN ms. fr. 14396, f. 33); cf. Victor Leroquais, *Les livres d'heures, manuscrits de la Bibliothèque Nationale* (Paris, 1927), II, 298. This is a fifteenth-century manuscript.

[16] John Macfarlane, *Antoine Vérard* (London, 1899), p. 98, no. 198.

[17] I should here like to express my thanks to the *conservateur*, M. Caillet, for his kindness in permitting me to examine the volume in May 1958.

[18] In the editions of 20 August 1490 (Macf 202; PML 566) and [1498] (Macf 222; BN Vélins 918), the first line reads: 'Jesus soit en ma teste et mon entendement.' In that of [?1497] (Macf 215; BN Vél. 1631), the first line also has this text, while the last line now provides: 'Jesus soit en ma vie et mon trespassement.'

[19] Has the first line like PML 566, and the second line now reads: 'Jesus soit en mes yeulx: et mon regardement.'

[20] With the first two lines like the Kerver edition, and the last line as in BN Vélins 1631. See also Félix Soleil, *Les heures gothiques et la litterature pieuse aux XVᵉ et XVIᵉ siècles* (Rouen, 1882), p. 239.

[21] This edition is described by Edgar Hoskins, *Horae Beatae Mariae Virginis, or Sarum and York Primers* (London, 1901), no. 44. The text of this version was also printed by Charles C. Butterworth, *The English Primers (1529-1545)* (Philadelphia, 1953), p. 6.

In England, this prayer was often reprinted in the old Sarum primers (at least until 1558). The words from this edition were set to music, which was not copyrighted until 1910, by H. Walford Davies, who was the organist at St. George's, Windsor, and the master of the king's music.[22] A copy of a printed edition of this song, with the date 'July, 1923', is in the possession of Professor Allan G. Chester of the University of Pennsylvania, who most kindly placed it at my disposal. This text, almost identical with that of Pynson's volume except for its present-day orthography, reads:

> God be in my head, And in my understanding;
> God be in mine eyes, And in my looking;
> God be in my mouth, And in my speaking;
> God be in my heart, And in my thinking;
> God be at mine end, And at my departing.

## II

Another poem often included in the French *livres d'heures*,[23] as well as in books of a religious nature printed in France, is a decalogue in French verse.[24] The poem appears, for example, on sig. l7ᵛ of a book of hours for Le Mans use,[25] apparently printed in Paris about the year 1492:[26]

> Vng seul dieu tu adoreras et aymeras parfaictement
> Dieu en vain ne iureras n'autre chose pareillement
> Les dimenches tu garderas en seruant dieu deuotement
> Pere et mere honnoureras affim que viue longuement
> Homicide point ne feras[27] de fait ne voluntairement
> Luxurieux point ne seras de corps ne de consentement

[22] I owe these details to the kindness of Professor Chester.

[23] See for example, BN ms. lat. 1373, f. 131 (Paris use, middle or second half of fifteenth century, Leroquais, *op. cit.*, I, 193) and BN ms. lat. 18031, f. 113ᵛ (a similar manuscript, Leroquais, II, 222).

[24] An entirely different verse rendering is given by Soleil, *op. cit.*, pp. 230–231.

[25] See the *Catalogue of Manuscripts and Early Printed Books from the Libraries of William Morris, Richard Bennett, Bertram, fourth Earl of Ashburnham, and other Sources now forming Portion of the Library of J. Pierpont Morgan* (London, 1907), III, 4–6, no. 567. It has now been determined that the book is for Le Mans use.

[26] In very similar form, this stanza occurs in the *Compost et calendrier des bergers*, Paris: Gui Marchand, 18 July 1493, sig. f6ᵛ (PML 508). It is also included in the edition of Geneva: [Jean Bellot, after 1497]; compare the facsimile edition (*Le Grand Calendrier des Bergiers von Jean Belot, Genf 1497*, Bern, 1920, p. 50).

[27] The *Compost* agrees in having 'feras', while the *Fleur* text offers 'seras'.

L'auoir d'aultruy tu n'embleras ne retiendras a escient
Faulx tesmoignage ne diras ne mentiras aucunement
L'oeuure de chair ne desireras qu'em mariage seulement
Biens d'autruy ne couuoiteras pour les auoir iniustement

The same poem, with almost identical wording, was included in various early editions of the *Fleur des commandemens de Dieu*.[28]

This French stanza on the ten commandments was soon translated into English[29] and can be found in many of the Sarum *horae* which were produced abroad for importation into England. In this English rendering, the lines read:[30]

One god onely thou shalte loue: & worshype perfytely.
God in vayn thou shalt not swere nor by that he made truly.
The sondayes thou shalt kepe in sernynge [*sic*] god deuoutly.
Fader and moder thou shalte honour and shalt lyue longely.
Mansleer thou shalte nat be in dede / ne willyngly.
Lecherous thou shalte not be of thy bodi / ne consentyngly.
No mannes goodes / thou shalte nat stele / nor with holde falsly.
False wytnesse thou shalte nat bere / in any wyse lyengly.
The werkes of the flesshe desyre nat but in maryage only.
The goodes of other coueyte nat / to haue them vniustly.

When the *Fleur des commandemens de Dieu* came to be translated into English (by Andrew Chertsey),[31] a different translation was made for use on the title page of this work. It appears in identical form in both Wynkyn de Worde printings of this text. This rendi-

---

[28] Paris: Nicole de la Barre, 31 January 1498 (BM C. 22. b. 4, f. 26ᵛ) and Paris: Antoine Vérard, 7 March 1500/1, sig. AI (Macf 64; PML 42037). Presumably it also occurs in the first edition (Rouen: Le Bourgeois, 1496), but I have been unable to examine the only recorded copy, that in the Bibliothèque Municipale at Rouen (Inc. mm. 54).

[29] This is not listed by Brown-Robbins, *op. cit.*, and the first mention of it by Hoskins (*op. cit.*, p. 133) is in the Kaetz edition of *c.* 1523 (STC 15935).

[30] Antwerp: Christopher Endovienses for Pieter Kaetz (London), 27 November 1523, sig. ✠8. Hoskins 66 and STC 15938 give the date 22 November, but the Morgan copy (PML 17690) is certainly dated the 27th. A hand of the early sixteenth century has written this stanza in the margin of sig. b2ᵛ of the Morgan copy (PML 698) of *The Royal Book*, [Westminster: William Caxton, 1486]. It will also be found on sig. N3ᵛ of the 1532 Salisbury *Prymer* (Paris: Yolande Bonhomme vidue T. Kerver, August 1532) (PML 1046). Different texts on the same theme will be found in Emmanuel College, Cambridge, MS 27 (I. 2. 6, f. 111ᵛ—Brown-Robbins 2694); in BM Royal MS. 8 F VII, f. 47 ('On God I byde the worchyp ay'); and, in two differing recensions, in the English *Kalender of Shepherdes* (cf. facsimile by H. Oskar Sommer, London, 1892—sig. f3 of the Paris 1503 edition and p. 78 of the reprint of Pynson's 1506 printing). Compare also Butterworth, *op. cit.*, p. 6 and p. 89, n. 4.

[31] See *DNB*, x, 191-192, and H. G. Pfander, 'Dives et Pauper', *The Library*, 4th ser., XIV (1933), 299, note.

tion is somewhat more elaborate than that used in the editions of the *horae*:[32]

¶ Thou shalt worshyp one god onely
　And loue hym with thy herte perfytely
¶ God in vayne swere not wylfully
　Ne by nothynge that he made veryly
¶ The sonday kepe and halow holyly
　Herynge gods seruyce on them deuoutly
¶ Fader and moder honour thou lowly
　And in theyr nede helpe them gladly
¶ Slee thou no man malycyously
　Nor to his dethe consent wytyngly
¶ Thou ne shalte commyt lechery
　But with thy wyfe in wedlocke onely
¶ Thy neyghbours goodes stele not falsly
　Nor nothynge withholde vntruely
¶ Fals wytnesse bere thou not slyly
　Nor fals recorde for none enuy
¶ Other mennes wyues take not flesshely
　Ne other women to knowe carnally
¶ Other mennes godes coueyt not lightly
　Nor holde from them vnryghtfully

Both the French text and its English renderings seem ultimately to have been inspired by a much earlier Latin stanza which also appears occasionally in the English *horae* and in certain devout tracts.[33] As a manuscript entry, this stanza was written into the lower margin of sig. ✠8 in the Morgan copy (PML 17690) of STC 15938:

Vnum crede deum Ne Jures vana per ipsum
Sabbata sanctifices, Habebis in honore parentes
Ne sis occisor fur Mecus Testis inJ[us]tus[34]
Alterius Nuptam, Rem nec Cupias alienum

While the English versified decalogues in the continental publications are obviously not corrupt as to orthography or rhyme, it is

[32] London: Wynkyn de Worde, 14 September 1510 (STC 23876; CUL Sel. 3. 18, title page). This is identically the same as that found on the title of De Worde's second edition, 8 October 1521 (PML 748).

[33] This also occurs in Robert Grosseteste's *Templum Domini* (BM Royal MS. 8 D IV, f. 77—fourteenth century) and in slightly different form in Royal MS. 16 E IX, f. 1v (XIV cent.). It is also written out in the Morgan copy of *The Royal Book* (see note 30) and is printed in the Salisbury *Primer*, Rouen: Richard Valentinus, 1555 (STC 16072; PML 1047, sig. D8v).

[34] This is written 'inJcus' (?). The texts of the *Royal Book* and of the 1555 *Primer* have 'iniquus'.

nevertheless interesting to observe how the publishers of the continental printings influenced the literary content of books designed for the English market.

## III

Frequently there were attached to the calendar some mnemonic verses which were intended to recall the saints venerated in the several months. Félix Soleil[35] supplies this succinct explanation for the French text found in the Parisian printed *horae*:[36]

C'est une suite de mauvaises rimes françaises, fort bizarres, n'offrant généralement aucun sens raisonnable, mais ayant pour but, sous leur enveloppe ridicule, d'aider, en les récitant de mémoire à défaut de calendrier, à se rappeler l'époque exacte des Fêtes fixes de chaque mois. Il suffit pour cela de scander, en comptant sur ses doigts, ces quatrains puérils qui contiennent autant de syllabes, qu'il y a de jours dans le mois auquel se rapporte chacun d'eux. La première syllabe du nom de chaque saint chômé répond à la date du jour consacré à sa fête.

For the Salisbury hours, these verses were transformed (*not* translated, since the text differs) into English;[37] in these printed editions,[38] the names of those saints most venerated in England were, of course, specially singled out for mention.[39]

### January[40]

| | |
|---|---|
| En ian uier que les Roys ve nus sont | Cir. cum. staunt. ly. thre. Kings. |
| Glau me dit fre min mor font | came. by. nynght |
| An thoin boit le iour vin cent fois | By. an. hye. hell. or. day. light |
| Pol us en sont tous ses dois | An. tho. vvoull. graffe. ony. good. |
| | vyne |
| | Paule. call. for. Tho. mas. Al. quyne |

[35] *Op. cit.*, p. 155.

[36] It is included in a book of hours for Rome use written in France early in the sixteenth century (BN ms. lat. 13268, f. 1ᵛ; Leroquais, *op. cit.*, II, 60).

[37] A different version is given in the *Calendrier des bergers* (PML 508, sig. a6, and the Bern facsimile, p. 9). A Latin version, perhaps the prototype, appears in the English *Kalender of Shepherdes* (1503 ed., sig. a6, and 1506 ed., sig. A6ᵛ).

[38] The French text is taken from the Rome *Horae*, Paris: Pigouchet, 19 April 1494 (PML 18558), corrected from the Rome *Horae* (Paris: Pigouchet, [1495]; PML 570) and Soleil, *op. cit.*, 155–157. The English stanzas have been copied from the edition printed at Rouen by Florentinus Valentinus, [1557/8] (Bishop, *op. cit.*, p. 195; PML 1036). Hoskins first mentions the verses on p. 209 of his book (no. 130; cf. note 52).

[39] A single stroke (|) is printed where a period is wanting or omitted in the text. In the Vérard edition of Macfarlane 198 (Toulouse Inc. 654), 'Guillau. me' appears in line 2 of January.

[40] There are only 30 'syllables' here, although the French (correctly, of course)

## February[41]

| | |
|---|---|
| Au chan de lier A ga the beut | Bryde. ma. ry. gil\| bert. har. de. ly |
| Mais le vin si fort les meut | All. thy. frendes. stan. dyng. the. by |
| Qu'il tu a pres dau si | And. pray. vvith. the. tho. dyne |
| Pier res Ma thi as aus si | Pe. ter. ma. thy. and. au. gu. styne |

## March[42]

| | |
|---|---|
| Au bin dit que mars est pril leux | Da. uid. of. wales. lo. neth. vvel. lekes |
| C'est mon fait gre goir il est feux | That. wil. make. [gre.] go. ry. lene. chekes |
| Et tout prest de don ner des eaux | If. ed. warde. do. eate. some. with. them |
| Ma ri e dit il est caux | Ma. ry. sende. hym. to. bed. lem |

## April

| | |
|---|---|
| En a uril am broi se s'en vint | In. A. pryll. am. broise. is. fayne |
| Droit a Le on la se tint | To. se. vs. vvas. shed. vvith. rayne |
| En son temps estoit en bal le | Os. vvalde. forth. vvith. sent. vic. tore |
| Geor ge Marc hant de go dal le | Uvith. George. and. Marke. to. do. so. no. more |

## May

| | |
|---|---|
| Ja ques Croix dit que iehan est moy[43] | James. Toke. Crosse. vvas. ters. iohn. to\| kyll[44] |
| Ni co las dit il est vray | Ni. co. las. sayd. do. hym. none. yll |
| Hon no rez sont sai ges et sotz | But. vvith. that. came. fayre. he\| layne |
| Car mes au gu stins et bi gotz | And. fran. ceys. to. de. parte. them. tvvayne |

---

has 31. St. Anthony is properly set down for the 17th, but the Conversion of St. Paul falls on the 25th (not the 24th, as here noted). The Sarum *Prymer* of 1529 (Paris: [François Regnault]—not in stc; pml 28432) and that of 1532 (see note 30) agree with this text, though they have 'nyght', 'hyll', and 'wull' in the appropriate lines.

[41] Here Gilbert is spelled as one word, though it should be divided as in the 1529 and 1532 editions in order to have the days come out right, so far as the saints are concerned. This now provides 29 days for February in our text. The other editions have 'Austyne' for 'Augustin', thus making a total of 28 'syllables' for this month.

[42] All editions have 'loneth' for 'loueth'. Only the edition here used omits 'gre' at syllable 12, though this is necessary to mark the feast of St. Gregory on that day.

[43] Soleil, *op. cit.*, p. 156, prints 'en. May.'

[44] The text omits the period after 'to' in line 1 and prints 'helayne' as one word. As it now stands, May has 31 days, and correctly noted for the 9th is the Translation of St. Nicholas. However, St. Helen is now assigned to the 22nd (instead of the 21st) and the 25th is given to St. Francis (in place of the 24th, on which his translation is venerated).

## June

En iuing a l'on bien sou uent
Grant soif ou bar na be ment
En son temps fut prins com ler res
Damp iehan e loy et damp pier res

In. June. e. ras. mus. dyde. tynke
For. to. gyue. Bar. na. be. drinke
Buth. than. bo. tulph. thougth. it.
  me| ter
That. Joh. sholde. drinke. be. fore.
  Pe| ter

## July

En iuil let Mar tin se com bat
Et du be noi tier sainct vaast bat
La sur vint Mar guet mag de lain
Iac mar dor An ne et Germain

Uvhan. ma. ry. vi| si. ted. Tho. mas
The. fre. ers. lete. their. dogs. out. pas
Than. came. forth. mar. get. mag. da.
  lain
James. An. marth. &. o. ther. tvvayne

## August

Pier res et os on get toit
A pres lau rens qui bru loit
Ma ri e lors se print a brai re
Bar the le mi fait Jehan tai re

Pe. ter. cal. led. for. Je. su
And. bade. Lau. rence. for. to. say. tru.
Ma. ry. se. yng. all. their. de| bate
Made. Bar. thyll. mevv. to. breke.
  Johns. pate

## September

Gi les a ce que ie vois
Ma rie toy se tu me Croix
Et pri e des nop ces Ma thieu
Son filz fre min cos me mi chieu

Gy. les. vvas. cut. to. his. losse
Ma. ry. sayd. nay. by. this. crosse
For. e. dith. savve. how. that. ma.
  thew
Did. beat. fre. myn. cos. me. mygh.
  evv

## October[45]

Re mis sont fran cois en vi gueur
De nis n'en est point bien as seur
Car luc est pri son nier a han
Cre spin et sy mon a quen

Full| lygh| vvas| fran| coys| fayth| at|
  come
De| nis| conde| not| ed| vvard| our|
  come
Tyll| luke| vvith| a| leuen| thou|
  sande
Made| crys| pin| and| Sy| mon| to|
  stande

[45] The 1529 and 1532 primers both have 'lyght', 'at Rome', and 'oure. come' (overcome). The Rouen compositor entirely forgot to mark the syllables with periods in this month.

November[46]

| | |
|---|---|
| Sains mors sont les gens bien eu rez | Saints. soules. in. heuen. ben. fic. ker |
| Com dit Mar tin du biez | As. fay. eth. Mar. tyn. bryc. er. |
| Aus si fait por rus de mil lan | Re. corde. hue. and. besse. that. tell. |
| Cle ment Ka the rin et sat An | can |
| | Cle. ment. Ka. the. ryn. and. sat. An |

December

| | |
|---|---|
| E loy fait bar ba co lart[47] | Loy. vvas. bar. ber. to. Ny. coll |
| Ma ri e cri e Lu ce art | Ma. ry. pray\| thou. for\| lu. cas.[48] soll |
| Dont en grant i re Tho mas meut | And. for. grace. pray. good. Tho. mas. |
| De No E Jehan In no cens fut | ynde |
| | To. Crist. Steuen. iohan. Chylde. to. be. kynde |

In the course of transforming the French quatrains into English (or what passed for such), some errors crept into the text. Thus, the month of August is, of course, divided into thirty-one 'syllables';[49] those with a correct correspondence are St. Peter ad Vincula (1st), the Transfiguration of our Lord (6th), and St. Lawrence (10th). However, the Assumption of the Virgin is here noted in the sixteenth syllable (for August 15th), St. Bartholomew in the twenty-fifth (for the 24th), and the Decollation of St. John the Baptist in the thirtieth (for the 29th).

The English text has been printed exactly as it appears in the original without the correction of misprints, for this alone gives the reader an idea of what the sixteenth-century purchaser got for his money. By puzzling a bit over the readings, most (if not all) of the text becomes reasonably intelligent. Nevertheless, one cannot help feeling sorry for the contemporary reader—presumably a child—who was obliged to commit these lines to memory.

## IV

Another set of verses was just as frequently attached to the calendar. In these quatrains, the course of human life was compared to the months of the year, six years of a man's life being allotted to each

---

[46] Both other editions have 'syc. ker' and 'say. eth.' The Rouen *horae* misprints 'corde' as 'cor. de.'

[47] In the Vérard edition at Toulouse, the first line reads: 'Dic. E. loy. fait. barb. a. colart.' However, it seems likely that the French editions specifically called attention to the Feast of St. Éloi de Chatelac, which is celebrated on 1 December.

[48] Since St. Lucy is venerated on the 13th, the other editions more obviously have the reading 'lu. ces.'

[49] In error the Rouen *horae* prints 'debate' as a monosyllable.

month.[50] So far as the present writer is aware, these lines first appeared in the *horae*, both manuscript[51] and printed.[52] The same theme, though expressed in a different verse form, will be found in the several editions of the *Calendrier des bergers*, also printed in the closing years of the fifteenth century.[53]

Below is given an original French text from an edition of the *horae* together with its English equivalent, the misprints of which have again been left uncorrected:[54]

### January

| | |
|---|---|
| Les six premiers ans que vit l'homme au monde | The fyrst .vj. yeres of mannes byrth and aege |
| Nous comparons a Januier droictement | May well be compared to Janyuere For in this moneth is no strength noȝ courage |
| Car en ce moys vertu ne force habonde | More than in a chylde of the aege of .vj. yere |
| Nemplus que quant six ans a vng enfant | |

### February

| | |
|---|---|
| Les six d'apres ressemblent a Feurier | The other .vi. yeres is like February |
| En fin duquel commence le printemps | In the ende therof beguyneth the sprynge |
| Car l'esperit se ouure prest est a enseigner | That tyme chyldren is moost apt and redy |
| Et doulx deuient l'enfant quant a douze ans | To receyue chatysement nurture and lernynge |

[50] Compare Joseph Morawski, 'Les douze mois figurez', *Archivum romanicum* x (1926), 351–363; the Rothschild Catalogue, I, 344, no. 531; and Émile Mâle, *L'art religieux de la fin du moyen âge en France* (Paris, 1922), pp. 303–306.

[51] The French text occurs in the *Horae* for Rome use (BN lat. 13268—Leroquais, *op. cit.*, II, 60; and in Morgan MS. 813) and those for Chartres use (BN MS. Smith-Lesouëf 39—Leroquais, suppl., p. 37). All three manuscripts belong to the early sixteenth century.

[52] The first mention of the English lines by Hoskins (*op. cit.*, p. 209, no. 130) is from the edition printed in London by John Byddell about the year 1537 (STC 15999). Through the kindness of Dr. Rhodes, I learn that they also appear in the edition of Paris: François Regnault, 27 June 1527 (Hoskins no. 77; BM C. 42. e. 7). The lines appear *in French* in the edition of the Sarum *Horae* printed at Paris by Philippe Pigouchet for Simon Vostre, 20 October 1501 (STC 15896; BM C. 29. h. 12).

[53] See p. 90 of the facsimile edition of the 1497 *Calendrier des bergers*. Two different English versions were printed in the English *Kalender of Shepherdes* (facsimile edition, sig. l4ᵛ–l5, and pp. 153–155).

[54] The French text is taken from the *Horae ad usum Noviomensem* (Noyon), Paris: Pigouchet for Vostre, 8 August 1498 (PML 46606), and the English stanzas from the Sarum *Horae*, Paris: François Regnault, 10 October 1527 (STC 15954; PML 17603).

## March

Mars signifie les six ans ensuiuans
Que le temps change en produisant
   verdure
En celluy aage s'adonnent les enfans
A maint esbat sans soucy ne sans cure

Marche betokeneth the .vj. yeres
   folowynge
Arayeng the erthe with pleasaunt
   verdure
That seasou youth thought for
   nothynge
And wothout thought dooth his
   sporte & pleasure

## April

Six ans prochains vingt et quatre en
   somme
Sont figurez par Auril gracieux
Et soubz cest aage est gay & ioly
   l'homme
Plaisant aux dames courtois &
   amoureux

The nept .vj. yeres maketh foure and
   tvventy
And fygured is to ioly Apryll
That tyme of pleasures man hath
   moost plenty
Fresshe and louyng his lustes to fulfyll

## May

Au moys de May ou tout est en
   vigueur
Autres six ans comparons par
   droicture
Qui trente sont: lors est l'homme en
   valeur
En sa fleur / force / et beaulte de
   nature

As in the mouth of Maye all thyng
   in myght
So at .xxx. yeres man is in chyef
   lykyng
Pleasaunt and lusty to euery mannes
   syght
In beaute and strength to vvomen
   pleasyng

## June

En Juing les biens commencent a
   meurir
Aussi fait l'homme quant a trente-six
   ans
Pour ce en tel temps doit-il femme
   querir
Se luy viuant veult pourueoir ses
   enfans

In June all thyng falleth to rypenesse
And so dooth man at .xxxvj. yere olde
And studyeth for to acquyre rychesse
And taketh a wyfe to kepe his
   houscholde

## July

Saige doit estre ou ne sera iamais
L'homme quant il a quarante-deux
   ans
Lors la beaulte decline desormais
Comme en Juillet toutes fleurs sont
   passans

At .xl. yere of aege or elles neuer
Is ony man ende vved vvith vvysdom
Forthan forthon his myghat fayleth
   euer
As in July dooth euery blossome

### August

| | |
|---|---|
| Les biens de terre commence l'en cueillir | The goodes of the erthe is gadred euer more |
| En Aoust: aussi quant l'an quarante-huit | In August. so at .xlviij. yere |
| L'homme approche: il doit biens acquerir | Man ought to gather some goodes in store |
| Pour soustenir vieillesse qui le suit | To susteyne aege that than dravveth nere |

### September

| | |
|---|---|
| Auoir grans biens ne fault plus que l'homme cuide | Lete no man tynke for to gather plenty |
| S'il ne les a a cinquante-quatre ans | Yf at .liiij. yere he haue none |
| Nemplus que s'il a sa granche vuide | Nomore than yf his barne vvere empty |
| En Septembre: plus de l'an n'aura riens | In septembre / vvhan all the corne is gone |

### October

| | |
|---|---|
| Au moys d'octobre figurant soixante ans | By Octobre betokenet .lx. yere |
| Se l'homme est riche ce la est a bonne heure | That aege hastely dooth man assayle |
| Des biens qu'il a nourrit femme et enfans | If he haue ougth / than it dooth appere |
| Plus n'a besoing qu'il traueille ou labeure | To lyue quyetly aster his trauayle |

### November

| | |
|---|---|
| Quant a soixante-six ans vient | Vvan man is at .lxvj. yere olde |
| Representez par le moys de Nouembre | whiche lykened is to bareyne Nouembre |
| Vieux et caduc et maladif deuient | He wexeth vnweldy sekely and colde |
| Lors de bien faire est temps qu'il se remembre | Than his soule helth is tyme to remembre |

### December

| | |
|---|---|
| L'an par Decembre prent fin & se termine | The yere by Decembre taketh his ende |
| Aussi fait l'homme aux ans soixante-douze | And so dooth man at thre score and twelue |
| Le plus souuent: car vieillesse le myne | Nature vvith aege vvyll hym on message sende |
| L'heure est venue que pour partir se house | The tyme is come that he must go hym-selue |

Occasionally the calendar also contained Latin stanzas, based on the *Regimen sanitatis Salernitanum*,[55] but I have found no translations of these lines in the considerable number of English books of hours which I have consulted.

These, then, are the principal English 'poems' often included in the preliminary matter of the *horae ad usum Sarum*.[56] Thousands of Englishmen must have read these lines—but what they thought of them when they read them, we shall probably never know.[57] Fortunately it seems clear that these verses had little effect on the poetry of their own day—and no influence at all upon the great writers of the later decades of the sixteenth century.

(From *Studies in the Renaissance* 6 (1959), pp. 223-35).

[Note: See also the article by Jos. Maria Wagner, "Französischer Cisiojanus des XVI. Jahrhunderts," *Serapeum*, xxiii (1862), 297-299. CFB]

[55] Compare Soleil, *op. cit.*, pp. 31–41. They also appear in the BN MS. Smith-Lesouëf 39 and in the 1532 primer (see note 30 above). These verses were likewise included in books printed for the French market (e.g. *Horae ad usum Romanum*, Paris: Kerver for Gillet Remacle, 14 May 1501; PML 582, and in the *Calendrier des bergers*, PML 508, sig. b1–b6). In agreement with the French text, the stanzas also appear in the English *Kalender of Shepherdes* (facs. ed., sig. b1–b6 and pp. 21–32).

[56] Since these poems were not listed by William Ringler ('A Bibliography and First-Line Index of English Verse Printed through 1500', *PBSA* xlix, 1955, 153–180), it is clear that they were not printed in the English incunabula. Elsewhere in the *horae*, English verse may also be found (in the hours of the cross, as descriptive lines for the woodcuts, etc.). It is planned to print these in a separate publication. The hymn of Richard de Caistre (Brown-Robbins, 1727) is included in the 1532 primer (PML 1046, sig. ††6–7) and was printed by Sir Egerton Brydges, *The British Bibliographer* (London, 1810–1814), iv, 139–140, though this printing was not listed by Brown-Robbins in their *Index*.

[57] Quite good English is found in the prayers of the *horae* for Sarum use printed in Paris by Wolfgang Hopyl (at the expense of William Bretton of London), 24 March 1506 (Bodl. Arch. B e 37; STC 15903, with date 9 April for ix Kal. Aprilis).

# CHAPTER T25

## THE NEW MORGAN MANUSCRIPT OF
### *TITUS AND VESPASIAN*

UNDER their number 1881, Carleton Brown and Rossell Hope Robbins[1] listed ten manuscripts which contain the romance of *Titus and Vespasian* written in couplet form. Since the publication of the *Index*, however, at least two more manuscripts of this work have come to light, the Earl of Derby (Knowsley Hall) codex[2] and another recently acquired by the Pierpont Morgan Library. The present investigation concerns the latter manuscript, for which the following description may be supplied:

M 898, collection: The Pierpont Morgan Library, New York. Manuscript on vellum (5⅝ × 3⅞ inches). *Collation:* a–m⁸ n⁵, wanting a1 = 100 leaves. 20 lines. Written (black ink with chapter headings or résumés in red, and rubrication[3] in blue) in England in the fifteenth century. Bound in nineteenth-century brown morocco by F. Bedford. With the book-plate of Sir Henry Hope Edwardes (his library was sold at Christie's, 20 May 1901).[4]

NOTES. *Misbinding:* the vellum sheets are misbound in the following manner. The eleventh quire has two sheets signed "l₁₁₁ⱼ" and the twelfth quire (m) has the fourth sheet signed "l₁₁ⱼ." The last-mentioned sheet is correctly signed and has the text proper to the third sheet in quire "l." The second of the two sheets signed "l₁₁₁ⱼ" (the first being the correct l4) should have been signed "m₁₁₁ⱼ" and includes the text which belongs to the fourth sheet of the twelfth quire. This misbinding has existed since the late fifteenth century, as manuscript notes of that period call attention to this fact.

*Handwriting:* the manuscript is written in the close-knit gothic book-hand current in the first half, or towards the middle, of the fifteenth century. The writing has many points in common with the script illustrated on C. E. Wright's Plate 20.[5] The following details may be singled out:

---

[1] *The Index of Middle English Verse* (New York, 1943), p. 296.

[2] Sold at Christie's (Christie, Manson & Woods, Ltd., London) on 19 October 1953, lot 301. The incipit and the description indicate that this is a manuscript of the "long-version." This manuscript is now in the library of Mr. James M. Osborn of New Haven, Conn.

[3] The original "guide-letters" for the convenience of the rubricator are often visible underneath the painted-in initials.

[4] Cf. Seymour de Ricci, *English Collectors of Books & Manuscripts (1530–1930)* (Cambridge, 1930), p. 177.

[5] *English Vernacular Hands from the Twelfth to the Fifteenth Centuries* (Oxford,

*th* is often written in the "wyn" form; ȝ is used both for *y* (ȝe) and *gh* (noȝt).
*y* has a hook over it (same hook serves as the *er* contraction, e.g., after the "wyn" for *ther*); *i* is stroked.
*g* has the "8" form.
*h* is very like a perpendicular Ij (with latter undotted, of course).
*l* is straight (not looped); *ll*, not crossed.
*r*, second form after letters rounded to the right.
*s*, long but with Greek form finally; capital *S* like a dollar sign.
*Fusion:* in *de, do* (but not in *be, bo*).
*Contractions: Jerl'm* for *Jerusalem;* for *per, p* with a heavy dot on either side of the descender.

Since the first leaf is missing, it is clear that forty lines of writing are wanting. The first line of a2 corresponds to line 846 of J. A. Herbert's text.[6] Allowing for a proper heading (perhaps 9 lines), this suggests that the Morgan MS originally began with line 815 of the Roxburghe Club edition. Thus, this MS never contained the account of the closing events in the life of Jesus, with the Passion and the Resurrection. Similarly, these lines never formed part of the romance as preserved in Pepys MS. 2014,[7] and it can also be shown that they were originally never included in BM Additional MS. 10036.[8] In this MS, the first line of the existing leaf signed d1 is line 1977 of Herbert's edition. Assuming the original quires a–c were quaternions (as the subsequent quires are) and that each leaf had twenty-four lines to a page, then only 1152 lines could have been accommodated in the twenty-four folios. As a result, it is evident that, after making allowance for a possible heading and the occasional omissions of lines peculiar to the Herbert text, the first line on a1 must have been line 815 (the first line of the Pepys MS and the probable incipit of the Morgan volume). In the Morgan MS, the poem ends at line 4 on folio n5 recto.

---

1960), p. 20. The script also has points of similarity with the hand displayed on his Plate 22.

[6] *Titus & Vespasian, or The Destruction of Jerusalem, in Rhymed Couplets* (London, 1905).

[7] Edited by Rudolf Fischer, "Vindicta Salvatoris," *Archiv für das Studium der neueren Sprachen und Literaturen,* cxi (1903), 285–298 and cxii (1904), 25–45. The manuscript is described in detail by Montague Rhodes James in *Bibliotheca Pepysiana, a Descriptive Catalogue of the Library of Samuel Pepys* (London, 1914–23), iii, 65–67, citing the editor as Rudolph Fricker.

[8] For a full description of Additional 10036, see H. L. D. Ward and J. A. Herbert, *Catalogue of Romances in the Department of Manuscripts in the British Museum* (London, 1883–1910), i, 187–189, and pp. xxvii–xxx of Herbert's edition of the romance.

The Morgan text is unique in that it divides the romance into eighteen chapters, each of which is provided with a suitable heading; occasionally, short prose summaries are introduced within the body of the text. Taken as a whole, these rubrics are invaluable, since they permit us to view the story in a form considered acceptable to the fifteenth-century reader, very possibly, indeed, in the very form preferred by him. The summary, as presented here, can also be conveniently compared with the marginal commentary as supplied in Herbert's edition, this representing a twentieth-century account of the plot.

The first chapter-heading (wanting, of course, in M 898) would have related the threefold punishment of impenitent Israel (pilgrimage, servitude, and dispersion), together with the prophecy of Josephus. The remaining résumés read as follows:

Of diuers tokynnes & veniaunces þat was shewyd or þe sege byganne. and of þe lyffe & martirdome of seynt Jame oure lordes cosyne. Capitulum .2ᵐ. [M 898, a3ᵛ; before line 915].

Of waspasyanes name & his sykenes. and of þe iewes complaynt of Pylate to þe emperoure syr Tyberius. Capitulum .3ᵐ. [b2; line 1163].

Of waspasianes sonne Tytus. how he mette Nathaan at Burdax. whiche brouȝt fro Jerusalem trewage & letter fro pilate to þe emperoure. & of velosyan þe styward þat stoode and herde al her talkynge. Capitulum .4ᵐ. [b4ᵛ; l. 1271].

Howe pilate bygoten was & of his cursed maners boþe in ȝoungþe & in age & of þe blody fluxe onn þe iewys & al her kynde. Capitulum .5. [c2; l. 1489. On c2ᵛ, a later hand has written: howe pylate was begotten off a milners dawghter by one Tirus a kinge off spayne].

Now turneþ Nathaan to Jerusalem home a-ȝen. & of Tytus & Velosyan. how þei tolde to syr waspasyane al þat Nathaan to hem seid of Jhesu crist þe gret prophete of Jude þat leched al mortual sykenes of soule & of body. Capitulum .6ᵐ. [c6; l. 1631].

Now goþ Velosian to Jerusalem to þat Cytee to speke wiþ pilate þat tyraunte. And howe Jacob & dame Veronye þat were preuy cristen folke welcomed and chered syr Velosyan þat come to seche some holy sanatyf⁹ for his lord þat lay sore syke. Capitulum .7ᵐ. [c8ᵛ; l. 1737].

    Now Jacob ledeþ velosian vn-to pilate. [d3ᵛ; l. 1851]. Of the iewes howe thei bosted, and in what manere thei dude Jhesus to his bitter passioun. [d8ᵛ; l. 2047].

⁹ Earliest recorded use of *sanative* (a remedy) by *OED* is c. 1440.

Nowe ledeþ velosian Seynt clement & dame veronye to syr waspasian to teche him of Jhesu. & so þoruȝ vertu & byleue to hele him of his sykenys. Capitulum .8ᵐ. [e7; l. 2311].

Nowe waspasian grauntteþ commyssyon to alle cristen in pees to dwelle in Gaskoyne. and shippe he takeþ. he and alle his hoste ouer the see to passe to þat stronge cytee of Jerusalem. Capitulum .9. [f7ᵛ; l. 2685].

Nowe is waspasian J-londed & þe towne of Japhet he haþ taken. wherfor pilate fortefieþ stronge þe cyte of Jerusalem with men of armes & vitaille. ffor nowe begynneþ waspasian to ley Sege to that noble cytee of Jude. Capitulum .10. [g3; l. 2829].

Nowe waspasian leuyþ Tytus his sone to kepe þat Sege. and to rome nowe he turneþ to be crowned emperoure. And howe god of his myȝt delyuered Jacob out of prisoun & out of þat cyte fro pilate þat cruel traytoure. Capitulum .11. [h4; l. 3165].

Of two women of holy fame dame claryce & marye. & of þe iewes euerychone howe þei ete her tresoure. & how þei eche oþer ete in defaute of mete. Capitulum .12. [i1ᵛ; l. 3391].

Howe Pilate þinkeþ a tretys to make. and howe Josephus þat noble clerke of þat cyte ouer þe walle telleþ Jacob of alle her sorowe wiþ-in. and nowe Jacob telleþ to þe emperoure waspasian euerydel. Capitulum .13. [i5ᵛ; l. 3547].

Nowe Josephus counselleþ Pilate to ȝelde vp þat cytee. and how þe comynte eche sleeþ oþer wiþ his knyffe for þe gret myschieff þat þei beþ in. in þat cytee. [k1ᵛ; l. 3703].

Nowe þe emperoure makeþ gret ioye & gladnys þat þe cyte vp hem ȝelde & how Archilaus him-self he sleeþ. [k4; l. 3807].

Howe al þat ben in þat Cytee þei ryden out wiþ Pilate and Tytus and his hoste wiþ hem mette. & how Josephus is J-take and brouȝt to-fore waspasian. and how he heleþ tytus of a Cardiakel. Capitulum .14. [k5; l. 3843].

Nowe pilate begynneþ a profer to make for him & þat cyte. & how tytus nowe takeþ þer þat traytoure Pilate. & how he fyndeþ Joseph of Armathie. and how Jacob þe god man gaddreþ to-geder alle the cristen of þat cytee & ledeþ hem alle to-fore þe emperoure waspasian. Capitulum .15. [l1ᵛ; l. 4027].

Howe þe emperoure welcomed al þe cristen & cloþed hem also. & how he comaunded eche man to bye his ware. þe iewes to turment with wicked peynes tyl þei dye euerychone. [l6; l. 4155].

Howe Pilate is nowe brouȝte to-fore þe emperoure. & put in stronge prisoun. & how þe deuels him fecheþ after he haþ him-self J-sleyn. Capitulum .16. [l8ᵛ; l. 4292].

Nowe is þe sege ended. & þe emperoure makeþ capteyns good al Jude for to kepe & þer he doeþ al þe iewes swere fewte to him for to bere. & also þer he

maketh lawes good. now after al þis he turneþ to rome a-geyn. Ca*pitulu*m
.17. ["l" = m5ᵛ; l. 4885].

Nowe þe emp*er*oure & al his men taken of Seynt clement cristendome.
[m8; l. 4981].

After þe Sege was ended & þe emp*er*oure home passed. nowe laste of al what
veniau*n*ce god toke on*n* þe iewes whiche wolde haue edefied vp a-ʒen þe
Cytee of Jer*usa*lem. whiche þe emp*er*oure had down felled. Ca*pitulu*m .18.
[n2; l. 5075].

Though not pertinent to the text of *Titus and Vespasian*, it seems
worth recording that, so far as M 898 is concerned, three different
hands of the sixteenth century have contributed the following lines
(all carefully written) as marginalia:

> Bewty is subiect vnto age
>   Sicknes the same will stayne
> And whoso wythered is with yeares
>   cannot be younge agayne   [folio i3][10]

> The ape the lyon the foxe the ase
> Descrybes manes nature as in a glase
> Lyke apes wee be toyinge till xx & one
> As furious as lyons till xl be gon
> As wylie as foxes till lx & three
> And after as asses accounted we be   [k6ᵛ][11]

> He that in youthe no care will take
>   some goodes to get and keepe
> in age perhappes he may goe begge
>   and mourne full ofte and weepe   [l7ᵛ][12]

The text of *Titus and Vespasian* in the new Morgan manuscript
presents us with a number of interesting facts and surmises. Even
the most cursory examination quickly reveals that the Additional
MS. 10036, Pepys MS. 2014, and the Morgan MS are closely related
and clearly all derive from a common ancestor. All three agree in
the omissions and transpositions of lines (and in the unique readings) as indicated by Herbert in the *variae lectiones* as peculiar to
the British Museum manuscript. Both the Pepys and the Morgan
MSS accidentally omit lines 2553/2590, it being probable that the

[10] Written as two lines in the MS.
[11] The same hand has written the first three lines only on the folio signed i4.
[12] Written as three prose lines in the MS. Compare, also, Brown-Robbins 1151.

scribe of the archetype common to them happened to skip over a leaf (or two pages) in the exemplar he was copying.[13] If my estimate be correct, these lines were once also wanting in the British Museum manuscript, though they were subsequently supplied by means of an inserted leaf written by another hand.[14]

Although these codices can thus be identified as "sister-manuscripts," it is equally probable that the relationship between them is no closer than this. Specifically, it seems reasonably certain that none of these MSS was copied from another. That neither the British Museum (B) nor the Morgan (M) texts derive from the Pepys MS (P) can be argued from the fact that the Cambridge MS omits six lines (3771/76)[15] as the result of an "omissio ex homoeoteleuto," a fault which occurs in neither of the other two. Similarly, it is unlikely that the London and Cambridge MSS were copied from the

[13] Pepys lines 1724/25 read (and almost identically in M, f5):

> To þi seruice I schal [wol M] me ȝeue
> I prey þe lord ȝif hit be þi wylle

These correspond to lines 2552 and 2591 of Herbert's text.

[14] Dr. C. E. Wright, Deputy Keeper of Manuscripts in the British Museum, kindly informs me that the inserted leaf (folio 16) contains the lines corresponding to 2557-94 inclusive of the Roxburghe Club edition. This raises an interesting and unusual problem, which only a thorough study and detailed comparison of the original manuscripts may be able to explain. Both B and PM at this point omitted thirty-eight lines—but they are *not* the same lines. All three MSS agree in omitting thirty-four lines (2557-90), but PM have four lines not originally in B (2591-94), and that MS originally included four lines (2553-56) not present in PM. See Addendum.

[15] Both M (k3) and B (Herbert, p. 171, n. 1) omit lines 3773/74, but they do have the other four. One may also cite two examples (apparently of dittography), where the slips in P are not carried over into the other two MSS:

> My leve freend for hem sende þan
> I prey þe sire þat I had herd
> With Jesu Crist how þei ferd   (Herbert, 2080/82)

> I prey þe send for hem þan
> þat I myȝt her dedes here
> Wiþ Jhesu crist howe þei fere   (M, e1)

> I pray þe þat þou sende for hem þan
> I praye þe þat I had yherde
> With Jesu crist howe þat þei ferde   (P, ll. 1254/56)

Herbert cites no variants for B here. The other example concerns lines 2377/78 of Herbert's text:

> þat if man shulde to helpe be broght
> With mannes deth he most be boght

Here Pepys (line 1550) has "brouȝt" for "bouȝt" in the second line above, an error not found in M (e8ᵛ) and apparently not in B.

one now in New York; had they descended from that text, the other two would certainly have preserved the chapter-headings.[16] Further, the manuscript here under discussion contains two lines apparently not found in B:[17]

> Of good mete & good drynke
> And a man hit him for to brynge to þe brynke = (Herbert ll. 4375/76)
> Of þat ylke depe prysoun
> Þere he lay ful hard J-boun    (M 898, sig. m2ʳ)

Since P breaks off at line 4010, we do not know what its reading at this place might have been.

It is rather more difficult to show that the other two texts do not stem from B, since direct proof for this has not come to my notice. However, the following facts are significant. In many lines, M and P share readings[18] not present in the third manuscript as, for example, in:

> Þan þei ete her tresoure al
> Boþe hey & corne wiþ-al
> 3it [And 3it P] for al þat dyde [dyed P] many one
> In euery strette wel gret wone
> ffor hit was no kyndely fode
> In no stedde it hem stode
> But þei [hem P] al to be kylde
> Whan þe towne schulde be [was P] 3elde    (M, sig. i4ʳ)[19]

[16] It is most unlikely that a professional scribe (such as the one who wrote the Morgan manuscript) would have supplied the rubrics under his own initiative. It must be presumed, I think, that they were present in the "Vorlage" which he was copying.

[17] At least no variants are cited by Herbert to indicate that B contains any extra lines after his line 4376.

[18] For lines 617/18 of Fischer's edition, P and M (c1) have:

> Wherfor Syr wiþout reson
> Haueþ [Haue M] no3t me in suspeccyon

Here, Herbert prints no variants for his lines 1433/34:

> Wherfore sire by noo resoun
> Haveth me in noon suspectioun

For Herbert's line 3204, P (l. 2338) and M (h5) agree in the reading: "Wiþ ioye and myrþe gret plente," while B (Herbert, p. 145, n. 1) has: "With murþe gret plente." At Fischer's lines 2781/82, M (i8) provides the identical reading:

> But it be any pryue cristen-man
> Late J-turned to god þan

The corresponding lines in Herbert (3661/62) are quite different, and the recorded variants do not show that B has the same rhyme words.

[19] These lines correspond to 3501/10 of Herbert's text, though BMP all omit lines 3503/4 of the Roxburghe Club edition. Fischer lines 2629/36.

For the second line, B alone has: "Bothe hewe and corn smalle"; also, B has as the rhyme words in the last two lines "bifelde: ȝelde."

Again, line 2256 reads in M (and P agrees verbatim):[20] "In his worshippe for soule game" (e5ᵛ). The Herbert edition has: "And in his worshep for soules frame," with the variant "saule fame" given as peculiar to B. Finally, M (sig. f3) and P have at Herbert's line 2467: "Kyngges beþ J-flocked to a-wreke his dede,"[21] while Herbert prints: "Kynges þei kest to wreke his deed," with the variant for B given as "Kynges ben ylokid."

Since neither M nor P was a copy of the other, it is evident that the readings they share descended to them from a common ancestor, and since B provides different texts at these places, it is equally evident that B could not be the direct source for either of the other manuscripts.

It may also be noted that, in some spots, all three MSS present a different text. Thus, Herbert prints as lines 2247/48, with only the reading "Therfore" as a variant from B:

> Forþi from Rome hider I flay
> And soo I holde me here alwey

Here M and P offer the couplets:

> þerfore fro rome hyder I fledde soþe to say
> And here I holde me alwey    (M, e5ᵛ)

> Therfor fro Rome hyder I fleiȝ on a day
> And here I holde me alway    (P, ll. 1419/20)

All three differ in their readings for Herbert line 3624:

> And þat was he seide first þurgh me    (B)
> And hit was first þoruȝ me    (M, i7ᵛ)
> And he seid hit was firste þoruȝ me    (P, l. 2746)

Finally, it may be noted that M sometimes is as close to Herbert's text as it is to B:

> Me liketh þou art lives man    (Herbert, l. 4972)
> Me ioyeþ þat þou art a lyues man    (M, m7ᵛ)
> Mynde þat þou art a lyves man    (B in Herbert, p. 223, n. 3)

All these examples speak for the independence of BMP from one another.[22]

---

[20] Fischer's line 1428.    [21] Line 1639 of Fischer's text.

[22] Frequently also, B holds with P in opposition to M. Thus, in line 2148, B reads: "Than wol I þee of frenschip hede" (Herbert, p. 98, n. 4) with which P (line 1320)

So much for the probable relationship between the three manuscripts. In concluding this analysis, a word should be said, however,
concerning the importance of the text as represented by BMP in
comparison with the longer version made familiar through Herbert's
edition. The editor of the Roxburghe Club volume, who knew only
of the B manuscript of the three we have been discussing, asserted
firmly that the Additional MS. 10036 represented (p. xlii) "an
abridged version of the original text." His arguments are not completely convincing.

As we have seen, the shorter version (beginning at line 815 of the
Herbert text) omits the life of Christ which seems extraneous to the
narrative of the destruction of Jerusalem. Similarly, the MSS of this
version omit the life of Judas which,[23] as Herbert himself suggests
(p. xlii), is "not strictly relevant" to the story. Many of the lines
found only in the full text seem to be no more than expansions, often
using the common stock of aureate phrases (e.g., ll. 2115/16, 3389/90,
3875/78, 5071/72, etc.).[24] Elsewhere, one meets with examples more
easily explained as augmentations rather than as the result of condensation. For example, in lines 4925/30, Herbert prints:

> The riche he gaf landes and rentes
> To meene men grete avauncements
> His pouer servandes þat litell wonen
> Þat kepte withinne and noght oute ronen
> Hem he feffede fair and well
> With þe citezines los cattell

Here, the Morgan text (m6ᵛ) offers the following lines (with similar
omission in B):[25]

---

agrees exactly; here M (e3) has: "Þan wol I shewe þe frenshiphede." Again,
Fischer's lines 1179/80 offer:

> For I wyst I had him forgo
> Therfor in hert me was wo

B (Herbert, p. 92, n. 1) agrees *verbatim* with this, but M (d7ᵛ) provides the text:

> ffor wel I wyste I schulde him forgo
> þerfor in hert me was wo.

[23] Elsewhere (p. xli), Herbert remarks: "First, the omission of the Life of Judas
(ll. 4487–4884) by B alone, out of the six MSS. (for Add. 36983 is included here),
raises the question whether this formed part of the original poem, or was inserted
in a later and expanded version." With the discovery of two more "short-text"
manuscripts, the proportion given above is materially altered.

[24] Some lines, of course, may have been accidentally omitted in the shorter version.

[25] Herbert, p. 221, n. 3, shows that B also omits the third and fourth lines of
this quotation. It will be recalled that P breaks off at line 4010.

þe ryche men he ʒafe londes & rentes
þe meen men oþer a-vauncementes
He a-vaunced hem feyre & wel
Wiþ þe cyteʒeynes goodes & here catel

It seems more logical to assume that the middle couplet was added to the original (as referring to a group which the original text had slighted) than to argue that some scribe needlessly deleted these lines.

To the present writer, it seems more likely that the longer text is due to accretion than that the shorter text resulted from abridgement. Technically, the longer text is rather a sorry poem.[26] Indeed, Herbert has remarked (p. xliv), that "for the sake of brevity I have frequently alluded to the present metrical composition as a poem, but the justice of Dr. Brandl's description of it as 'void of artistic aspiration' cannot be gainsaid."[27] It is conceivable, therefore, that a new edition based on the three short-text manuscripts may provide a poetically happier version of *Titus and Vespasian*[28] than the longer one familiar to us through the Roxburghe Club edition, a text (unfortunately) often difficult to find in the rare-book market.

## ADDENDUM

An examination of the two manuscripts in October 1960 enables me to supply the necessary information called for in note 14. The facts relative to Additional MS. 10036 are both unusual and interesting. Originally, this manuscript also lacked lines 2553–90, but these

[26] Occasionally, Herbert's text preserves the gross errors of his original; thus, for example, Saint Clement appears as "Sire Clement" in ll. 4961, 4983, 4999, and 5023, though most manuscripts correctly have "Seynt."

[27] To this writer anyway, the shorter text often provides a more satisfactory and smoother rendering than that printed by Herbert. Compare, for example, his lines 5055/62 with the text printed below (M, n1ᵛ–n2):

> As we in storye mowe rede & fynde
> þere were J-heled boþe lame & blynde
> And after him reigned tytus his sonne
> Emperoure of rome gret of renown
> þat euer ʒitte was so I holde
> As men in gestys haue J-tolde
> Hit witnesseþ þat he was alweyes
> Of ʒiftes boþ good & curteys.

[28] Of Additional MS. 10036, Herbert writes (p. xxix): "It is much to be regretted that this MS. is so imperfect, for it is one of the two earliest extant copies of the poem, and the text, though abridged (see below), seems fairly good. The scribe is exceptionally uniform in his orthography and inflections." The latter sentence is also applicable to the Morgan manuscript.

were supplied, by an early corrector, in a skillful and quite exceptional manner.

In the manuscript, the fifth signed quire (e) was originally a quaternion ($e^8$). In line 20 of $e4^v$ we find: "To þi seruyse I schal me ȝyue," which corresponds to line 2552 of Herbert's text. The first line of signature e5 parallels Herbert's line 2595. Clearly what happened was this: lines 21–24 of $e4^v$ (as first written) contained Herbert's lines 2591–94, with omission after the twentieth line of lines 2553–90 as in the Pepys and Morgan MSS. When the corrector noted this, he expunged the last four lines on $e4^v$; over this erasure, he then wrote lines 2553–56 of the full text, as an examination of the manuscript makes evident. He then inserted a leaf, on the recto of which he wrote 20 lines (2557–76). On the verso of this leaf, he wrote but 18 lines, of which the first 14 contained Herbert 2577–90 (the remainder of the omitted text). In the last 4 lines, he copied out once again lines 2591–94, which he had previously erased from $e4^v$; these therefore needed to be written out once more. The corrector thus supplied the wanting section of text in a rather clever manner, least calculated to disturb the reader. Thus Dr. Wright is quite right in stating that the inserted leaf contained lines 2557–94—though it is equally certain that the original lacuna in the manuscript comprised lines 2553–90 (after line 20 of $e4^v$). It seems likely that only a direct examination of the manuscript could have determined this sequence of events in the history of the volume.

The omission in the Pepys MS. 2014 occurs at folio 30, column 1, between lines 46 and 47; in the Morgan MS, at signature f5, between lines 14 and 15. Since the Additional MS has 24 lines to the page, and the Pepys MS is written in 2 columns of 60 lines each, it is evident that none of the MSS is a direct (page-for-page) copy of the original exemplar. As Herbert suggested (p. xxviii), this manuscript was apparently written with 19 lines to the page.

(From *PMLA* 76 (1961), pp. 20-24).

# CHAPTER T26

## A MIDDLE ENGLISH MEDICAL MANUSCRIPT
## FROM NORWICH

THE manuscript which is the subject of the present investigation is not entirely unknown to the world of scholarship. The first apparent mention of the volume is the brief notice given in the catalogue of the Phillipps manuscripts:[1] "Kalendarium. ¶ An English Poem on Medicine. *Incip.* 'These Lechys for seke mannys sake. Divers medicynys sumtyme gun make.' 18*mo. V. S.* xv. *in a blue paper case.*" Subsequently it appeared in two Sotheby sales (July 17, 1950, lot 27, and February 28, 1955, lot 169), being acquired, on the latter occasion, by the present writer. Since the manuscript was not recorded by Brown-Robbins,[2] and since it contains Middle English verse of medical interest, differing in minor details from related texts previously published, a full description of the volume seems to be warranted.

MS. 21, collection: Curt F. Bühler. Manuscript on vellum (6 1/8 x 4 1/2 inches). *Collation:* 1⁶ (wants 1), 2⁶ (wants 2–3); 3⁸, 4⁸ (wants 7–8); 5⁸ (wants 3), 6–8⁸, 9⁸ (wants 8) = 61 leaves (folios i–ix; 1–52). *Note:* though leaves are wanting (possibly blank and cut away), there are no lacunae in the texts. Written by various hands in East Anglia, fifteenth century. Bound in the original binding of leather over oak boards, in a brown morocco case. *Contents:* ff. iʳ–iiʳ, blank.

iiᵛ, colored emblematical drawing (crown with spiral branches beneath, containing grotesques and mottoes). Three names in the same hand: Thomas Cotfold, Johannes Rothe, Robertus Halle;[3] also signature of Johannes Landes.

iii–vi, verses, proverbs, and medical recipes, English and Latin. Signature of Johannes Wylton on iiiʳ.

vii–ix, blank.

---

[1] Sir Thomas Phillipps, *Catalogus librorum manuscriptorum in bibliotheca D. Thomae Phillipps* (Middlehill, 1837), p. 106, no. 7008.

[2] Carleton Brown and Rossell Hope Robbins, *The Index of Middle English Verse* (New York, 1943).

[3] None of these Norfolk individuals can be identified. A Robert Hall is named in a letter written by Margaret Paston on February 7, 1465, but there is no reason to believe that this is the same person. Cf. James Gairdner, *The Paston Letters* (London, 1904), IV:127.

1–14, Calendar, Use of Norwich Cathedral; table for finding Easter; tables for finding Lunar (1429–1479) and Solar (1429–1462) eclipses.

15$^r$, recipe "ffor the tothe ache"; remainder of leaf, blank.

16, treatise on urines, English prose.[4]

17–25, Computus manualis:[5] "Incipit compot*us* manualis. In primis scien-*dum* est quod pro litt*ere* dom*in*icalis invenc*i*one sec*un*dum ordine*m com*poti ... ffilius esto dei celu*m* bon*us* accipe grates ..."

26$^r$, blank.

26$^v$–45$^v$, English Metrical Herbal [for details, see below].

45$^v$–49$^v$, English Metrical Medical Treatise [for details, see below].[6]

50–52, English Prose Treatise on the Rosemary.[7] Begins: "Of þe v*er*tu of rose mary. þe god erbe Rose mary is boþe tre & erbe boþe hot & drye ... [ends]: Schrede hy*m* not ne make hym not to bare of heys branchys but as it is seyd and if þou noryche hy*m* þus thow schalt haue Rose mary in plente & gret help & comfort þerby."

The first entries in the manuscript to draw our attention are the short texts on folio iii, recto. The first of these reads:

> I loue and y dare nouȝt
> y þenke and y sey nouȝt
> y spende and I paye nouȝt
> y wolde and I maye nouȝt
> do wel and dred nouȝt
> pley sekyr and sey nouȝt
> and be meke & stylle
> and þou shalt haue alle þy wylle[8]

This stanza is not included in the *Index of Middle English Verse*, at least as a separate poem under the present incipit.

Below these lines (written as four in the MS.), we find the following:

---

[4] An unprinted treatise on urinoscopy, which may be related to this tract, occurs in the Stockholm MS. (for which see note 25), ff. 123–26.

[5] Listed in col. 266 of Lynn Thorndike and Pearl Kibre, *A Catalogue of Incipits of Mediaeval Scientific Writings in Latin* (Cambridge, Mass., 1937).

[6] For a poem of similar nature but more specific in character, see R. H. Bowers, "A Middle English Mnemonic Plague Tract," *Southern Folklore*, XX (1956):118–25, with important references.

[7] A treatise on the Rosemary, unpublished except for an extract, is also to be found in the Stockholm MS. X. 90, ff. 80–86 (Brodin, p. 60; cf. note 25). The extract was printed by Ferdinand Holthausen, "Rezepte, Segen und Zaubersprüche aus zwei Stockholmer Handschriften," *Anglia*, XIX (1897):75–88.

[8] For similar proverbial rhymes with "nought," see Brown-Robbins no. 1163 and George L. Apperson, *English Proverbs and Proverbial Phrases* (London, 1929), p. 595.

Sey þe best or be stylle[9]
Wyth thy tonge noma*n* thou qwelle
Suffyr and haue thy wylle[10]

Optima*m* dic ve tace
nullu*m* p*er*imat tua ling*ua*
suffer pacifice
sic vota carpe tua

The English lines, obviously a translation of the Latin text, may be considered as verse, though the rhyme "still/quell/will" is very poor. In the fourth Latin line, another hand has interlineated the imperative "carpe" after "vota."

The calendar, which occupies folios 1–14, is a typical one of the early fifteenth century.[11] Since it specifically notes the feasts of St. Cuthbert (March 20), St. Dunstan (May 19), St. Ethelbert, king and martyr (May 20), St. Etheldreda (June 23), etc.,[12] the *Calendarium* was clearly of English origin. Pointing directly to Norwich is the entry for September 24 "Dedicac*i*o ecclesie Norwic*ensis.*" Providing further evidence for the Norfolk origin of the calendar is the notation for the feast of Little St. William of Norwich. This entry ("Passio *sa*nc*t*i will*ia*mi norwic*ensis*") also confirms the fact that, in the fifteenth century anyway, the feast of St. William was celebrated on March 24; the *Acta Sanctorum* and other authorities now cite the following day.[13]

On folio 15ʳ, one finds the remedy for a toothache which may

[9] Compare Alexander Dyce, *The Poetical Works of John Skelton* (London, 1843), I:17: "A prouerbe of old, say well or be styll" ("Agaynste a Comely Coystrowne," l. 64). For an earlier citation (c. 1480), see Apperson, p. 551.

[10] Apperson, p. 608, cites "Suffer and expect" (Herbert, 1640).

[11] Calendars from various dioceses are printed by Francis Wormald, *English Kalendars before A. D. 1100* and *English Benedictine Kalendars after A. D. 1100* (Henry Bradshaw Society nos. LXXII, LXXVII, and LXXXI; London, 1934–1946).

[12] The Dog Days (*dies caniculares*) are here given as July 14–September 6.

[13] Official sources are not in complete agreement on the date. The *Acta Sanctorum* (Paris, 1863–1931), IX:586–88, lists St. William for March 25, while Paul Guérin, *Les petits Bollandistes* (Paris, 1880), III:619, prefers March 24. March 25 is chosen by Sabine Baring-Gould, *The Lives of the Saints* (London, 1897–98), III:461–66, and Sir Nicholas H. Nicolas, *The Chronology of History* (London, 1833), p. 102—though on p. 165 he adds the note: "According to Butler, March 24." Franz von Sales Doyé, *Heilige und Selige der römisch-katholischen Kirche* (Leipzig, 1929), II:546, cites both March 24 and March 25, while Frederick G. Holweck, *A Biographical Dictionary of the Saints* (St. Louis, 1924), p. 1035, suggests that the feast was transferred from March 25 to March 26.

appeal to the reader's interest, though it is unlikely that this will prove to be very beneficial in the hour of need:[14]

#### ffor the tothe ache

Take smythis synder & make yt rede hote in the ffyre Than put them in a vesselle with a lytylle water but leve iij partes of the synder drye than cast henbane sede upon the brennyng synder than hold thi mouthe opyn there-ovyr & lett the ffume go yn-to thy mouthe as myche as ye can but ye must couer your hed clene yn with a schete & vse this for it is as gode as ony ys probatum est.

The two chief items in the manuscript are the Metrical Herbal and the Metrical Medical Treatise, both in the vernacular. Under different incipits, these poems are both listed by Brown-Robbins, under the respective numbers 2627 and 1408. The incipits of the poems as given in the present manuscript are not, however, cited in the Index of Middle English Verse; they will be found below at the appropriate places.

The herbal describes the following herbs: Betany (f. 26ᵛ), Centory (f. 28ᵛ), Goolde (f. 29),[15] Celydonye (f. 30), Pympernol (f. 31), Modyrwort (f. 31ᵛ), Verveyn (f. 33), Mortulaga[16]/Mortagon (f. 34), Perwenke (f. 34ᵛ), Rose (f. 35),[17] Lyly (f. 36ᵛ), Henbane (f. 37ᵛ),

[14] This recipe does not appear in Gottfried Müller, Aus mittelenglischen Medizintexten. Die Prosarezepte des Stockholmer Miszellankodex X. 90 (Kölner Anglistische Arbeiten no. X; Leipzig, 1929); Herbert Schöffler, Beiträge zur mittelenglischen Medizinliteratur (Halle, 1919); Ferdinand Holthausen, "Rezepte, Segen und Zaubersprüche aus zwei Stockholmer Handschriften," Anglia, XIX (1897):75-88; Gösta Frisk, A Middle English Translation of Macer Floridus de Viribus Herbarum (Upsala, 1949; Upsala Universitet, Essays and Studies on English Language and Literature, III); The 'Liber de Diversis Medicinis' in the Thornton Manuscript (ed. Margaret S. Ogden, EETS, OS 207 [1938], pp. 16-19, esp. 17, 11-18); etc.

[15] Marigold. Modern English equivalents for the herbs are mostly not given here, since these can easily be ascertained through the OED.

> Goolde is goode in sauour
> Fayer & yelew is his floure
> The golde flowyr is goode to sene
> It makyth syght bryght & clene          (ULC MS. Dd. 10. 44)

[16] Not in OED, though Mortulaca is cited under Mortagon.

[17] Except for the last two lines, which appear in the Stockholm MS., the lines here printed are unique in this manuscript:

> To make þis playster ho-so wyl cunne
> He hangyt in a glas in þe hete of þe sunne
> And thour þe eyr & sunnys hete
> þe gressys xul moystyn & waxin wete
> And castyn [h]ere water alle be-dene
> Into þe glas ful fayr & clene

Affodylle (f. 38ᵛ), Dragaunce/Serpentin/Nedderystong[18] (f. 39), As-
trologia (f. 40), Baldemonye (f. 40ᵛ),[19] Egrimonye (f. 41),[20] Mynte
(f. 41ᵛ),[21] Sauge (f. 41ᵛ),[22] Rue (f. 42), Fenkel (f. 43ᵛ), Violet (f.

---

þis water is good for eyne smertyng
And for þe syth claryfying                    (ll. 453–60)

Besides rose leaves, the glass was to contain Celidony, Rue, Fennel, and Vervain.

[18] Or Adder's-tongue; see OED under Serpentine.

[19] Baldmoney; more commonly known as the Gentian.

[20] In the short version (c. 300 lines) in Sloane MS. 2457, the poem ends on f. 7ᵛ
with the lines:

Of egrymonye y schal telle al-so
ffor it nedeth and is to do
Egrymonye to dringes and plastres is goode
Als telles the maister of mylde mode
Hit remewes postemes dronke wit wite wyne
And washeþ the splene and the venyme
Lay it vndere a mannes hed
He schal slepe als he were ded
He schal neuer of slepe a-wake
Til hit fro vnder is hed he take

Similarly, Trinity College Cambridge MS. 1117 (112 verses) concludes with these
lines:

It remeuyth postymes dronkyn with wyne
And wascyth the splene & oþer venyme
Lay it vnder a monnis hede
He shalle slepe as he were dede
There shalle no drede hym wake
Tylle fro vnder þe hede it be take.

[21] The Additional MS. (ll. 607–12) includes some verses on Mint which do not
appear in the Stockholm text. The present manuscript also includes this text on
Mint, together with six lines on Rue which are not in the other two MSS. (lines
732–43):

Menta iuuat stomacum cor salgia ruta cerebrum
Ambiger extirpat tussym pectus stomacum
Mynte is for þe stomak good
As seyth þe mayster with mylde mood
Sauge makyth þe herte clene
þus seyn þis vers both be-dene
Rue also is good for syth
And for þe kernele & makyn eyne bryt
It is no nede þese gres to discrye
þis vers wytnessyth here maystrye
Saue þat sauge wyl don more ȝet
þer-fore of hym xal I speke bet

For the "cerebrum" of the new MS, read "celebrum"? The first six English lines
are also to be found in TCC, MS. R.14.51, f. 44.

[22] Cur moritur homo dum salgea crescit in orto
þis vers is ful of gret pryce

44), Scharpe Burre (f. 44ᵛ), Isope (f. 44ᵛ), Fymeter (f. 45), and Columbyne (f. 45).[23]

Of the thirteen manuscripts listed by Brown-Robbins under number 2627,[24] only the Stockholm manuscript is of comparable length (965 lines).[25] The next longest are BM Addit. 17866 (753 lines)[26] and Cambridge University Library MS. Dd. 10. 44 (some 600 lines). The remaining manuscripts, all but one of which (Society of Antiquaries MS.) I have examined, are much shorter, some extending to only a few lines.

---

And is þus to seyn on englische
ffor defaute whi deyyth man
þat sauge myth to his helpe han                                        (ll. 758-62)

The Latin line occurs in both other MSS., though neither of the next two lines are found there. For the English translation they offer:

For defaute whi dies þe mane
þat sauge & mynte to helpe hane                          (Addit. 624-25)

Why of seknesse deyith man
Whil sawge in gardeyn he may han          (Stock. 832-33)

[23] Columbine is present in the Addit. MS., though not in the Stockholm one. In TCC, MS. R.14.51, f. 46, the text reads:

Of columbyne I wil you telle
Hys floure blewe ys like a belle
Thys columbyne berith a blak seede
That ys gode dronken for squynnasy at nede.

[24] Thirteen is the number given by Brown-Robbins, but eleven would seem to be the more correct total. The herbal in Pepys MS. 878 is in prose, not in verse. Thus the description of Betony reads (p. 176): "Beteyne is a[n] herbe of many uertuys qwat manere of man þat beres beten up-on hym þer schal no manere venomys best doo hym an harme whil he beryt it and qhow drynkes þe water I-styllid it schal make hym a gode colowr & of all þing it is gode for þe stomake & he use to drynke it fastyng it is gode for þe dropsye." The text in BM Additional MS. 12056 is also a prose herbal, if I read my notes correctly. Sloane MS. 147 of the British Museum has a long text (some 600 verses), but it is both late and poor.

On the other hand, not noted in Brown-Robbins is Trinity College Cambridge, MS. 921 (R.14.51). This contains the metrical herbal in just under 600 lines, having 22 pages with (normally) 27 lines to the page, beginning with folio 35 verso. The MS. is cited by Brown-Robbins under acephalous poem *40 as "A Book of Receipts in English verse and prose."

[25] The text of Stockholm MS. X. 90 was printed by Ferdinand Holthausen, "Medicinische Gedichte aus einer Stockholmer Handschrift," *Anglia*, XVIII (1896):293-331. For further particulars as to this MS., see Gösta Brodin, *Agnus Castus: A Middle English Herbal* (Upsala, 1950; Upsala Universitet, Essays and Studies on English Language and Literature, VI).

[26] Printed by Robert M. Garrett, "Middle English Rimed Medical Treatise," *Anglia*, XXXIV (1911):163-93.

The manuscript here under discussion contains 918 lines,[27] most of which are identical with (or closely comparable to) lines either in the Stockholm manuscript or in the London one, or to be found in both these texts. Nevertheless, 132 lines in the present manuscript find no counterpart, at the same places, in the other codices. At least a third of these provide no new information, consisting mostly of conventional couplets of hackneyed phrases which serve chiefly as padding.[28] If three examples may be cited, these are typical lines of this nature:

> Of his flour wyl I not seye
> But grene it waxith be wode & weye
> > (Egrimonye, 716-17)

> Thow ne haue y not prouyd i-wys
> þe book tellyth þat soth it is
> > (Scharpe Burre, 889-90)

> þis gres wel for to discrye
> To me it is a gret maystrye
> ffor I knowe no-thyng of his flour
> Ne of his smellyng ne of his sauour
> And þou wold I þat hey & lowe
> Myt þis gres kendely knowe
> þer-fore haue I gretly in mende
> To tellyn of him & of his kende
> > (Dragaunce, 622-29)

Despite this fact, there are a good many lines in this herbal which are of more than passing interest and which do not occur either in the Stockholm or in the London texts; of these, we may print the following as typical examples:

> These lechys for seke mannys sake
> Diuers medicynys sum-tyme gun make
> Of alle þe gressys þat growyn on rote
> þat mown man & woman helpyn to bote

---

[27] A line is omitted at line 477, and the proper numbering is restored by the introduction of the single Latin line at l. 758.

[28] Such lines are not, of course, peculiar to this text but are present in the other manuscripts. Thus, the Stockholm MS. has at lines 409-10 of the Medical Tract:

> þis medycyne full well prowyd is
> As tellyth maystyr Galyeen i-wys

All three MSS. have the lines found at 825-26 of the new text under Fenkel:

> As tellyth mayster Macrobius
> He is a gres ful precyous

> If þey kondyn þese gressys knowe
> And had hem prouyt on hey & lowe
> þey dedyn hem wryte wysly in boke
> þat leryt & leuyt þeron myth loke
> þerfore a leuyt man thour grace at nede
> May help a sek man to wysse & rede
> So þat he knowe his gressys alle
> And thynggis þat þerto wyln be-falle
> Now at betany I wyl begwynne[29]
> þat many vertuys beryth hym with-inne      (ll. 1–14)

> A gracious grees is betany
> ffor oþer vertuys hath he many
> Weche þat I haue not in mende
> þerfore of hym here I make an ende
> At anothyr gres I wel be-gynne
> þat on hunderyt vertuys hath hym with-inne
> Centory it is nemelyd be name
> It may don helpe to blynd & lame
> To seke & fayre it may don helpe
> I may not þer-of to fele ȝelpe
> But þer-on a lytyl wyln I dwelle
> And sumdel of his vertuys wel to telle
> If it be sothyn in good wyn clerleche[30]
> And drunkyn XV dayys contuneleche
> So þat it be mad cler & thynne
> Wath maner of venym be man with-inne
> It schal dystroye it & breke þe flesche
> And dryuyn out þe venym nesche
> Ley no thyng elles be þat wonde
> Tyl þat he be heyl & sownde      (ll. 99–118)

---

[29] Line 13 corresponds to line 7 of the Stockholm text.

[30] At this point, the text in the University Library Cambridge MS. Dd. 10. 44 (and almost identically in Pepys MS. 1661, pp. 290–291) reads:

> At betony ende I
> And begynne at Centory
> In gode wyne sodyn centory
> And be dronke 15 dayes by and by
> So þat it be made clere & thynne
> What maner venym be man wyth-Inne
> It shalle verili brest the fleshe
> And drevyn owt the venym neshe

In Trinity College Cambridge Ms. 1117 (O.2.13), the next two lines read:

> Lay no thynges be þat wounde
> Tyll it be made hole & sounde

The other manuscripts have comparable lines for the last eight as printed here.

The English version here under consideration also has some general remarks to make on the subject of herbalists which seem to find no counterpart in the Stockholm or London texts:

Ho-so xal warkyn with gressys to sen[31]
fful wyse & ware he must been
But if he knowe hym in gressis wel
He xal for-lesyn his warkys eche deel
But if he wete what he xal done
He may for-lesyn his craft ryt sone
But he kendys of gressys knowe
And here vertuys of hey & lowe
Ho-so kendys of gressys knowe can
He may be told a mayster þan
ffor fewe leue noow vndyr sunne
þat alle gressys mown knowe kunne
þerfore be hym þat hath me bowth
In here craft ne spede he nowth
ffor he cun neyþer hende ne fare
Knowe thynggis þat longyn to þe mayster
Sweche mown be lekenyt to a blynd man
þat may not seen but felyn he can
þow he be felyng alone may goon
Sone he may stumbelyn on a ston
So faryth a leche man or woman
þat wenyth to cun good & noon he can[32]
Of feythful fenkel & of his kende
I wele telle as y wrete fynde      (ll. 801–24)

For the Hyssop, the present manuscript adds these lines which do not appear in the printed versions of the other two texts:[33]

[31] In Addit. MS. 17866, lines 660–63, the first four verses read:

Who so shal wyrke with gres to sene
War & wyse he moste bene
But he hym knawe in gres welle
He schal for lese his werk ilke dele

This passage is preceded by two French lines (plus six of English translation) which do not seem to appear elsewhere. Following it are the lines:

Fenkill says maister Macrobius
Is a gres ful precious

These compare to lines 825–26 of the new manuscript and 874–75 of the Stockholm text.

[32] After "he," another hand has interlineated "or thee."

[33] In place of these, Sloane MS. 2457, f. 4, supplies the lines:

And fro the fende hit schal the schelde
In hous in toun in wod and felde

It may be etyn & drwnk also
But if his betyrnes it for-do
þan men may sethyn it in swet lycour
þat xal it make of betyr sauour    (ll. 897–900)

The medical treatise in the manuscript from Norwich consists of 202 lines, as compared with the 496 in the Stockholm manuscript and 370 in the London volume. The only other recorded manuscript to preserve this text is Trinity College Cambridge MS. 911, "a dis-arranged and defective text" (Brown-Robbins 1408), containing some hundred verses.

Twenty-six lines in the manuscript under consideration are not duplicated in either printed version.[34] Here again some couplets are introduced for the evident purpose of padding the text, such as:

Anoþer medecyn y fynde redende
þat mannys heryng may mekyl mende    (ll. 133–34)

Also y fynde for þis peyne
þat prouyd is a fayre medecyne    (ll. 157–58)

Nevertheless, other lines provide material not previously recorded in print, of which the following appear to be the most interesting:

Now haue y told ȝou þow y it ȝelpe
Of gressys þat most mown men do helpe
How þei waxyn hey & lowe
And wherby a man may hem knowe
Of here vertuys & of here kende
In diuers bokys as wretyn I fynde
But for þe loue of a lewyt man
More xal I telle ȝet as I can
And as I fynde wretyn in book
þat leryd & lewyd moun on loke
In iiij parteys of eche a man
Be-gynnyth þe sekenes þat þei han

Pepys MS. 878, p. 177, here reads: "Isop is a gode herbe for þe stomake & for þe lyuere & for þe longis & for þe dropsye. stampid and temperyd it wiþ water & ȝif it a womman to drynke þat is trauelyng wyþ child she schal haue gode deleueraunce be þe grace of god."

[34] A great many lines are duplicated in either the Stockholm or the Additional texts but not by both. Forty-four lines of the new text are not in the Stockholm one (but in Addit.), while twenty-two are not found in the Additional MS. (but do occur in Stockholm). The last twenty-two lines of the new text compare with the others as follows: four lines (181–82 and 189–190) are found in neither of the other texts; lines 183–88 and 191–96 = Addit. 884–95 (not in Stock.) and lines 197–202 = Stock. 133–38 (not in Addit.).

In heed in wombe or in þe splene
Or in þe bledder þese iiij I mene[35]         (ll. 1–14)

Through some inexplicable circumstance, the present writer's manuscript preserves the lines on the Euphrasy in the very middle of the medical treatise (f. 47ᵛ). In the Additional MS., they appear, in almost identical wording, at the end of the herbal, the appropriate place for these couplets; they are not, however, included in either poem in the Stockholm MS. This would seem to be the earliest description of the Euphrasy in English, since the *O.E.D.* cites only a mention of this herb in a vocabulary of "circa 1475." In the new manuscript, the lines read:

[E]ufras is of bytter sauour
A lytyl smal gres whit is his flour
In metys & drynkys if he be doon
He is medecynabyl boþe morwe & noon
He castyth wel to eye his syth
þis medecyn is prouyd wel I plyth
For helpe of syth mekyl haue I sowt
And more to telle let wyl I nowt[36]         (ll. 95–102)

The first six lines also occur in Trinity College Cambridge, MS. R.14.51, f. 46, as the closing lines of the herbal.

The particulars here given set forth the chief characteristics of the newly discovered texts and emphasize the importance of this manuscript vis-à-vis those whose contents have already been printed. A line-by-line comparison reveals that the new manuscript stands in close relationship to the Additional MS. 17866, though it is slightly longer and (here and there) seems to offer more satisfactory readings. When the exhaustive treatment and critical edition of these poems is eventually undertaken, the present manuscript will serve, together with the Stockholm manuscript and Additional 17866, as the basis for the definitive edition of these poems of great medical interest.

(From *Studies in Medieval Literature in Honor of Professor Albert Croll Baugh* (1961), pp. 285-98).

[35] Lines 11–14 correspond to lines 1–4 of the Stockholm "Gereimte Heilkunde."
[36] Lines 101–102 do not occur in Addit. but are paralleled by Stock. lines 85–86:

For helpe of syth mekyl I hawe sowth
And more to telle let wil I no[w]t[h].

# CHAPTER T27

## TWO MIDDLE ENGLISH TEXTS
## OF THE *SOMNIA DANIELIS*

CONSIDERING the somewhat slight nature of the text, the influence of (and the literature on) the *Somnia Danielis* has been exceptionally great.[1] Dream-books of this variety were familiar to the Akkadians[2] and to other peoples of the ancient Near East.[3] They were current in Byzantium and in Alexandria (as, for example, the writings of Artemidorus bear witness).[4] The scholar who wishes to search out the dark antiquity of the dream-book so popular throughout Western Europe in the fifteenth century, the *Dreams of Daniel*, is referred to the studies of Krumbacher,[5] Hélin,[6] and particularly Max Förster.[7] The purpose of the

[1] Compare Lynn Thorndike, *A History of Magic and Experimental Science* (New York, 1923–58), I, 679–680; II, 162–163; etc. See also F. Drexel, "Das Traumbuch des Propheten Daniel nach dem cod. Vatic. Palat. gr. 319", *Byzantinische Zeitschrift*, XXVI (1926), 314ff., and the same writer's "Achmet und das Syrische Traumbuch des Cod. Syr. or. 4434 des Brit. Mus.", *ibid.*, XXX (1929–1930), 113 ff.

[2] A. Leo Oppenheim, "The Interpretation of Dreams in the Ancient Near East, with a Translation of an Assyrian Dream-Book," *Transactions of the American Philosophical Society*, New Series, vol. XLVI, Part 3 (1956), 179–371. See also the French translation (by Jeanne-Marie Aynard): *Le rêve, son interprétation dans le Proche-Orient ancien* (Paris, 1959).

[3] See, for example, E. L. Ehrlich, *Der Traum im Alten Testament* (Berlin, 1953).

[4] Cf. George Sarton, *Introduction to the History of Science* (Baltimore, 1927–1948), I, 295; also his review in *Isis*, XXV, 476–478.

[5] Karl Krumbacher, *Geschichte der byzantinischen Literatur* (München, 1897), 629–630.

[6] Maurice Hélin, *La clef des songes: fac-similés, notes et liste des éditions incunables* [Documents scientifiques du XVe siècle, Tome II] (Paris, 1925). Hélin lists 36 editions, while the *Gesamtkatalog der Wiegendrucke* (Leipzig, 1925–1940), VII, 240–249, records 38. According to the GW, Hélin no. 33 (French trans., [Paris: Jean Trepperel]) belongs to the XVI century. In turn, Hélin did not know the three Latin editions recorded by GW:

> GW 7906. [Venice: Christoph Arnold, c. 1476]
> GW 7907. [Padua: D. S., c. 1480]
> GW 7937. [Vienna: Johann Winterburg, c. 1500]

There is a copy of Hélin 22 in the University Library, Cambridge, which is not recorded by GW; see J. C. T. Oates, *A Catalogue of the Fifteenth-Century Printed Books in the University Library Cambridge* (Cambridge, 1954), p. 591, no. 3532.

[7] Especially in his "Beiträge zur mittelalterlichen Volkskunde", *Archiv für das*

present article is primarily to print for the first time, so far as the writer is aware, a short Middle English oneirocritical text from a Lansdowne manuscript in the British Museum and, secondly, to correct a major and extensive slip in Förster's otherwise minutely accurate study of the English prose version which he had printed half a century ago.

## I

The previously inedited text is found in MS. Lansdowne 388, folio 372$^v$, and this differs in many respects from the version printed by Max Förster. This is, in itself, not the least surprising, since Maurice Hélin (p. 78) has correctly remarked that "les versions latines, manuscrites ou imprimées, diffèrent assez sensiblement les unes des autres." As a result, the various recensions in the several national tongues often display remarkable discrepancies from one another.

The Middle English text printed below, however, provides a number of almost exact parallels for prognostications included in the Latin text provided by Hélin and in two vernacular incunables preserved in the Pierpont Morgan Library.[8] Readings from these sources are cited in the notes under the following sigla:

G—German text. [Augsburg: Johann Schönsperger, 1497]. Morgan Check List 371.

H—Latin text, as per Hélin's facsimile of: [Vienne: Eberhard Fromolt, c. 1481]. GW 7922.

I—Italian text. Bologna: Bazalerius de Bazaleriis and Angelus de Rugeriis, 31 May 1487. Morgan Check List 1208.

[also a number of manuscripts noted below in Section II.]

The English text, though much shorter than any of those here cited (it may only be an extract made by the scribe from a fuller text for his own purposes), is nevertheless interesting in its own right.

---

*Studium der Neueren Sprachen und Literaturen*, CXXV (1910), 39–70; CXXVII (1911), 31–84; etc. Consult Herbert Schöffler, *Bibliographie der wissenschaftlichen Veröffentlichungen Max Försters* [Kölner Anglistische Arbeiten, vol. XXXV] (Bochum, 1939), for other articles on this subject.

[8] Ada Thurston and Curt F. Bühler, *Check List of Fifteenth Century Printing in the Pierpont Morgan Library* (New York, 1939).

Lansdowne MS 388, f. 372ᵛ.

### Danyelles dremys.

1. Yef þou dremyst of Armery it be-tokenyth chaunge of sum þinge.
2. Yef þou dremyst þou bere armour it by-tokenyth worship.
3. To clime on a tre by-tokens worshipe.
4. to se a grete tre by-tokens worshipe.
5. to se birdes fyght by-tokens wrethe.
6. to se byrdes fyght with hem-self by-tokens chydynge.
7. to se birdes sit on a tre betokens good tydynges.
8. to se byrdis bytokens harme.
9. to se⁹ siluer & haue it not bytokens chidinge.
10. to se a gardyn by-tokenyth good tydynges.
11. to se þe ayre clere by-tokenys¹⁰ wynynge.
12. to se þe ayre dark betokens shame.
13. to geve a rynge betokens harme.
14. to hold a rynge by-tokens securnes.
15. to eyre land by-tokens besenes in þe world.
16. to ete roste fleshe by-tokens harme.
17. to se lambes or kydis by-tokens good counsell.
18. to se þe fyrmament bytokens joy.
19. to se an egill on þi hed tokens worship.
20. to se ganders & take hem tokens joy.
21. to haue good wynnynge tokens worshipe.
22. to se gold tokens gret worshipe.
23. to se gold or syluer tokens envy.
24. to haue a longe berd tokens strengthe.
25. to se thy berd newe shaue tokens harme.
26. to do a messe tokens joye.
27. to syt on a staf tokens seknes.
28. to syt on a whit ox tokens worship.
29. to se a blak ox tokens pereles.
30. to se a gret ox tokens wynynge.
31. to speke with a woman tokens wynynge.
32. to set on an hors tokens wynynge.
33. to rede on a boke bytokens joy.
34. to se a white hed tokens wynynge.
35. to se the hed shore tokens longynge.

⁹ "syul" cancelled in MS.        ¹⁰ "wynng" cancelled in MS.

## Notes to the Text

### (with all contractions expanded)

2. Arma in sompnis portare, honorem [tutamentum = Cotton-Tiberius] significat — ULC Gg. 1. 1; arme portar in li insonio, significa honore — I.

3. Arbores videre vel ascendere significat honorem — H; arbori veder ouer montar su essi significa honor — I; ein baum steigen, bedeüt eer — G; arbores ascendere, aliquam dignitatem optinebit — Cotton.

10. According to Förster, the Vienna MS. reads: Hortos facere uel edificare, iocunditatem uite significat. Also: Hortum videre leticiam significat — Harley 3902; ortum videre gaudium significat — Egerton 847; see note to Horrea in section II.

11. To se cler eyre, by-tokeneþ honoure — TCC, o. 9. 37, f. 29$^v$; aerem clarum videre significat lucrum — H; aere chiaro veder significa guadagno — I; schön wetter sehen, bedeüt gewin — G.

13/14. Annulum tollere significat securitatem. Annulum dare significat damnum — H; anel receuere significa securita. Ma darlo significa danno — I; Fingerlin geben oder verlieren, bedeüt schmertzen. Fingerlin annemen, bedeüt sicherheyt — G.

15. Arare qui se uiderit, labores maximas ei obueniunt — Cotton; arare se videre significat labores — H (Similarly Vienna MS); arar se veder significa fatiche — I.

16. Carnes. To eete or se ete fleshe betokneth þat þi enymys shall speke euyll of the — Royal 12. E. XVI, f. 2; carnes commedere qui se viderit quod inimici sui male de illo loquuntur — Royal 13. D. 1; carne aroste manzar significa peccato ouer danno — I; gebraten fleisch essen oder sehen, bedeüt schaden — G. See Förster's note in section II below, and: Carbones qui se uiderit edere inimici tui de te mala loquuntur — Cotton MS., Tiberius A. III, f. 27$^v$.

24. Barbam prolixam habere, fortitudinem significat — Vienna MS; barbam longam habere significat fortitudinem vel lucrum — H; barba longa hauer significa forteza — I; ein langen bart haben, bedeüt störckin [also: ein langen bart heben, bedeüt gewalt] — G.

26. Missam celebrare tribulationem significat — Hélin, p. 88; qui songe de mort messe chanter ou ouyr, s'il est prestre, ioye lui vient — Hélin, p. 87.

34. Caput album habere, lucrum significat — Cotton; caput valde album videre significat lucrum — II; capo biancho hauere significa alegreza — I; ein weyss haubt sehen, bedeüt gewin — G.

## II

In 1911,[11] Max Förster printed an English prose *Dreams of Daniel* based upon MS. Sloane 1609, ff. 29$^v$-32, as corrected (and supplied with variant readings) from manuscripts Trinity College, Cambridge, o. 9. 37, ff. 26–30 and Royal 12. E. XVI, ff. 1–2$^v$. By a curious

[11] "Ein me. Prosatraumbuch des 14. Jahrh.", *Archiv*, CXXVII (1911), 48–84.

slip, unusual in the work of so meticulous a scholar (to whose wise counsel, generous help, and learned instruction, the present writer is heavily indebted), the text as found in the Royal MS. is very imperfectly set forth.

Förster observed (p. 48): "Die letztere [Royal] Handschrift stellt überdies ein Fragment dar: nicht nur, weil sie mehrfach einzelne Traumgesichte ausläßt und nach Nr. LI sogar 24 Nummern, also eine ganze Seite oder (bei Annahme weitläufigerer Schrift) ein ganzes Blatt der Vorlage, überspringt, sondern auch weil sie mit Nr. CXV überhaupt abbricht." This statement is incorrect in both respects, since the two blocks of text which Förster presumed to be wanting are actually found on folio 2 verso of the manuscript.[12] This text is supplied below, in the hope of completing Förster's edition. According to his account, the Royal manuscript failed to provide 42 "omina" of dreams; actually only 14 are missing,[13] and the Royal MS. includes one prognostication not present in Förster's text.[14]

The apparent reason for Förster's oversight is the jumbled state of the text in the Royal MS. The alphabetical order is here greatly upset. In accordance with Förster's numbering, the order of the prognostications in the Royal MS. is:[15] I–XXXIV (Aves–Citharam), LXXVI–CXV (Nauem–Volare), XXXVIII–LXXIV (Calciamenta–Metuentem), and CXVII–CXXIV (Uxorem–Zonam). The very probable explanation for this anomaly is that the archetype had been misbound before the scribe of the Royal MS. had made his copy. One may assume that the exemplar consisted of two sheets, containing the following portions: Folio 1 = I–XXXIV; folio 2 = XXXVIII–LXXIV; folio 3 = LXXVI–CXV; and folio 4 = CXVII–CXXIV.[16] Now if the innermost sheet had, by mischance, become reversed, the order of the folios then being 1, 3, 2, and 4, and this text had been mechanically copied by the scribe, then this would fully account for the jumbled order in the Royal MS. Förster may,

---

[12] No. CXVIII precedes CXVII and XCI and XCII are combined into one number in the Royal MS.

[13] The following numbers are wanting in the Royal MS.: IX, XXXV–XXXVII, XXXIX, XLVII, LV, LXVIII, LXXV, LXXXIV, C, CXIII, CXVI, and CXXIV.

[14] Printed here as number LI-bis.

[15] The "Vorlage" may—or may not—have contained the prognostications wanting in the Royal MS.

[16] Thus there must have been approximately 17–19 entries per page in the Vorlage.

quite understandably, have lost his way in the upset state of the text and have overlooked the prognostications still preserved on the verso of the second leaf.[17]

In one other respect, it seems permissible to disagree with Förster's edition of this text. For the parallel Latin version, the editor made use of six manuscripts (Vienna, Nationalbibliothek MS. 271; Cambridge, University Library, MS. Gg. 1. 1, and Pembroke College, MS. 103; Oxford, Digby 81; Munich, Clm. 5125; Paris, BN Lat. 7349) and prepared his text "nach der ältesten Wiener Handschrift." But what we have come to realize nowadays as important for any vernacular text is not the most ancient—nor even the most correct —Latin version, but that one which can explain some of the peculiarities of the "vulgar" rendering. The English prose would have been more satisfactorily elucidated if use had been made of the Cambridge and Paris manuscripts, the closest to the English text[18] and the furthest removed from the *textus receptus*. The Latin version in MS. Royal 13 D. 1, ff. 247ᵛ-248 (not cited by Förster) is especially close to this translation and extracts from it will be cited in the notes for the sake of comparison.

In a way, Förster was aware of this problem ("Immerhin muß die Lateinvorlage unseres mittelenglischen Prosatextes eine Reihe von Sonderlesarten gehabt haben, die mir bisher noch in keiner Handschrift begegnet sind"), but he did not pursue this matter any further. For example, he cites as a note to item XLI (p. 62, n. 1): "*Carnes* ist verderbt aus *Cardones*; doch lehrt die Übersetzung mit *flesh*, daß schon die Vorlage des Engländers diese Korruptel aufwies. Die Lateinhandschrift P führt übrigens ein Traumgesicht mit *Carnes* [48ᵃ] neben einem solchen mit *Cardones* auf." In this case, the British Museum manuscripts Sloane 1009 (f. 58) and Addit. 15236 (f. 161ᵛ) supply "Cardones vel Carbones," while the latter variant is alone cited by Harley 3902 (f. 31), Egerton 847 (f. 21ᵛ), and Cotton Tiberius A. III (f. 28ᵛ). Royal MS. 13. D. 1 (f. 247ᵛ) clearly has *Carnes* (see Section I, no. 16 and note).

Again,[19] as a comment to item XCII (p. 72, n. 3), Förster remarks:

[17] Förster, correctly noting the confusion in the MS., states (p. 60) that nos. "XXXVIII–LI stehen in R hinter CXV".

[18] "Wir dürfen also sagen, daß die Lateinvorlage des Engländers der jüngeren Textform, wie sie etwa durch die Cambridger [Pembroke 103, ff. 75–77ᵛ] und Pariser [Bibl. Nat. Lat. 7349] Handschrift repräsentiert wird, näher gestanden zu haben scheint." (Förster, p. 50).

[19] See also the textual notes to Horrea, Metuentem, etc.

"*Pontem* ist beidemal verderbt aus *Portum*. Doch lehrt die Übersetzung mit *a brygge*, daß schon die Vorlage des Engländers jene
Lesart von G aufwies." Here G identifies Cambridge University
Library, MS. Gg. 1. 1. In addition, the Cotton, Egerton,[20] Harley,
and Royal MSS. (among others) also have *Pontem*.

The text of the section overlooked by Förster is printed below. A
few notes have been appended to this, in order to explain some of
the peculiarities of the English rendering.

### Royal MS 12 E XVI, f. 2ᵛ.

| | | |
|---|---|---|
| [LI-bis] | Flumen. | To passe a stondyng whater bytokenyth sykyrnes. |
| LII | [Flumen].[21] | To passe a whatyr full of tempest & rowe[22] bytoknyth drede & streytnes. |
| LIII | Fontes. | To se a whell or therof drynk betoknythe whynnyng. |
| LIV | Fossas. | To se a dyche & þer-yn fall betokneþe gret sclaundyr. |
| LVI | Gaudere. | To yoy in slepe betokneþe heuynesse. |
| LVII | Grandinem. | To se hayle & tempest betokneþe harme. |
| LVIII | Gladiatores. | To se men pley at þe bukler And with them play betokenyth gret anguysche. |
| LIX | Horrea. | To se a berne or to make [one] betoknyth jocundenesse. |
| LX | Hominem. | A man to be turnyde yn-to a beste betokneþe offence of God. |
| LXI | Bellum. | To goo [to] or to se batell betokneþe gret anguisshe. |
| LXII | In aqua. | To be whasche yn whatyr clene betokneþe gret gladnes. |
| LXIII | [In aqua.] | & to be whasche yn fowle whater betokneþe accusyng & harm. |
| LXIV | Lunam. | To se a feyr moone betokneth thy power shall encresse. |

[20] The Egerton manuscript was one of the manuscripts taken by J. O. Halliwell
from the library of Trinity College, Cambridge, having once formed part of that
library's MS. O. 8. 16. For a most interesting account of this theft, see D. A. Win-
stanley, "Halliwell Phillipps and Trinity College Library," *The Library*, 5th series,
II (1948), 250–282.

[21] Words enclosed in brackets are wanting in the MS.

[22] A worm has consumed what must originally have been a final "e".

| LXV | [Lunam.] | To se a blody moone betok*neth* p*er*yll. |
| LXVI | [Lunam]. | To se þe moone fall fro*m* heuy*n* betok*neth* gret tr*a*uayle. |
| LXVII | Ligar*e*.[23] | To se þe bounde betokneþe letty*n*g. |
| LXIX | Mar*e*. | To se a blake see betok*neth* gret speede. |
| LXX | [Mare]. | To se a row3e see betok*neth* gret hardnes. |
| LXXI | Man*us*. | To se ha*n*d*es* defowlyd betok*neth* sy*n*ne & harme. |
| LXXII | Migrar*e* | To passe owt of þe worlde i*n* þi slepe betok*neth* to cha*n*ge þi dwelly*n*g. |
| LXXIII | Mortuu*m*. | To se a dede body & þ*er*-wi*th* to speke betok*neth* joy & gladenes. |
| LXXIV | Metue*n*te*m*. | To dreme þ*at* þou hart i*n* grete fer*e* hit betok*neth* gret letty*n*g. |
| CXVIII[24] | Uxore*m*. | A ma*n* to whedde a wyffe bytok*neth* harme. |
| CXVII | Veste*m*. | To mete þ*at* þou hast a feyr cloth hyt betok*neth* gr*a*ce & whurshuppe. |
| CXIX | Expoliatu*m*. | A ma*n* þ*at* dremyth þ*at* he ys robbyd of fry*n*d*es* he shalbe made bare. |
| CXX | Yrcos. | A ma*n* to se gete or wedyrys h*i*t betok*neth* ple*n*te. |
| CXXI | Ydreas. | To se pott*es* full of wat*er* betok*neth* co*n*solaci*on* & ple*n*te. |
| CXXII | Zona*m*. | To be gyrde wi*th* a sylu*er* gyrdyll bytok*neth* wy*n*ny*n*g. |
| CXXIII | [Zonam]. | A gyrdyll p*a*rtyde betok*neth* langor & e*n*vye. |

## Notes to the Text
(with all contractions expanded)

LI-bis; LII.  Flumen pacificum transire securitatem significat. Flumen turbulentum vel tempestuosum transire timorem et anxietatem significat. (Royal MS. 13. D. I, f. 247ᵛ). LI-bis is not in Förster's English text.

LIV.  Förster's text adds: "of peeple", but his Latin parallel reads: Fossas uidere et in eas cadere, calumniam grauem significat.

LIX.  Förster provides the note: "*Horreum* und die Übersetzung mit *a beerne* lehrt, daß des Engländers Vorlage mit GP *horrea(m)*

---

[23] Perhaps read "ligar*i*" as Förster suggests.
[24] The incorrect order is that of the manuscript.

las, was aus ursprünglichen *Hortos* 'Gärten' verderbt ist." The Royal MS., agreeing with ULC Gg. 1. 1 and BN Lat. 7349, reads: Horrea videre vel edificare iocunditatem significat. See Section I, note to no. 10.

LXVI.    The Royal MS. has: Lunam de celo cadere laborem maximam significat, while MS. Digby 81 offers: "cadere videre".

LXXIV.   Förster (p. 68, n. 1) remarks: "*Metuentem* und die Übersetzung *to seeme, that thou haue dreed* lehrt, daß die Vorlage des Engländers ein Traumgesicht *Metuentem se videre, impedimentum grave significat* enthielt. Ein solches ist mir nirgendwo begegnet; doch bietet die Handschrift G [ULC, Gg. 1. 1] ein Traumgesicht [94ᵇ] *Mutum se videre factum, impedimentum s.*, aus dem die Fassung des Engländers sich leicht erklärt durch eine Verlesung metuentem für *mutum*." The assumption of a misreading is not necessary, since the Royal MS. (f. 248) has: Metuentem se videre factum impedimentum grave significat.

CXIX.    Förster's English and Latin texts read: Expoliatum. A man, that metith, that he is robbed, by-toknith, of his freendis he shal be mad bare. Exspoliatum qui se uiderit, a propriis denudatur. To this he adds the note (p. 78, n. 1): "*of his freendis* gegenüber dem lat. *a propriis* 'Eigentum'. Entweder hat der Engländer seine Vorlage wieder mißverstanden, oder diese las *a propinquis*." The Royal MS. (f. 248) has: Videre sese expoliatum a propinquis parentibus vel amicis denudari significat.

CXXII.   According to Förster, the parallel Latin text is: Zona aurea accingere, lucrum significat. Here the editor adds the note (p. 78, n. 3): "*silveren*, also muß die Vorlage *argentea* statt *aurea* gelesen haben, oder der Übersetzer hat das Latein mißverstanden." Though the Royal MS. has: Zonam auream cingere lucrum significat, it is not necessary to assume that the English writer made such a crude mistranslation. In Harley MS. 3902, f. 33ᵛ, we find: Zonam argenteam habere lucrum significat.

CXXIII.  For the Latin text (Zona Partica accingere, languorem et iniuriam significat), Förster (p. 80, n. 1) remarks: "Me. *partid* 'verschiedenfarbig' lehrt, daß die Vorlage des Engländers *partita* 'verschiedenfarbig' statt des vielleicht früh unverständlich gewordenen *Partica* 'Parthisch' las. Im Altertum wurde das von den Parthern bearbeitete scharlachrote Leder gern zu Gürteln und Wehrgehängen benutzt." The Royal MS. has: Zonam partitam cingere languorem & iniuriam significat.

(From *Anglia* 80 (1962), pp. 264-73).

# CHAPTER T28

## PRAYERS AND CHARMS IN CERTAIN
## MIDDLE ENGLISH SCROLLS

SCROLLS containing Middle English texts are among the most interesting and unusual of the late mediaeval manuscripts[1] which have come down to our day. Certain texts, it would seem, were particularly suited to be written in this form, this being especially true of the "Arma Christi" poems,[2] chronicles and genealogical texts[3] (especially those portraying the descent of the English crown),[4] cookery books,[5] estate rolls,[6] and a wide variety of religious

---

[1] Other manuscripts in roll form, which seem to be unrelated to those here discussed, include the "exultet rolls" of the eleventh and twelfth centuries (cf. Myrtilla Avery, *The Exultet Rolls of South Italy* [Princeton, 1936]) and the "obituary rolls" (Léopold V. Delisle, *Rouleaux des morts du IXe au XVe siècle* [Paris, 1866] and E. P. Goldschmidt, "An Obituary Rotulus from York, 1405," *Studies in Art and Literature for Belle da Costa Greene* [Princeton, 1954], pp. 379–383). For a discussion of the rolls in classical times, see Theodor Birt, *Die Buchrolle in der Kunst* (Leipzig, 1907). The invention of printing did not put an end to the production of rolls and some were even issued by the press; thus the so-called "Astronomischer Kalender" printed at Mainz either in 1448 or 1458 (cf. Carl Wehmer, *Mainzer Probedrucke* [Munich, 1948] and Aloys Ruppel, *Johannes Gutenberg, sein Leben und sein Werk* [Berlin, 1947], pp. 121–123) and the English Calendar of about 1521, printed on both sides of the roll in xylography, in the Morgan Library (PML 22918).

[2] Compare Carleton Brown and Rossell Hope Robbins, *The Index of Middle English Verse* (New York, 1943), p. 405, no. 2577. Two such roll manuscripts, not recorded by Brown-Robbins, are now owned by Dr James M. Osborn (Box 22, no. 17); cf. C. U. Faye and W. H. Bond, *Supplement to the Census of Medieval and Renaissance Manuscripts in the United States and Canada* (New York, 1962), p. 99. See also Rossell Hope Robbins, "The 'Arma Christi' Rolls," *Modern Language Review*, xxxiv (1939), 415–421 and his "Private Prayers in Middle English Verse," *Studies in Philology*, xxxvi (1939), 466–475.

[3] For example, Petrus Pictaviensis, *Compendium historiae in genealogia Christi*, MSS: Morgan M 367, M 628, M 689; Harvard fMS Typ 216H; Free Library, Philadelphia, MS. E 202 and John F. Lewis MS. 181 (Edwin Wolf II, *A Descriptive Catalogue of the John Frederick Lewis Collection of European Manuscripts in the Free Library of Philadelphia* [Philadelphia, 1937], p. 78, no. 72). See also Walther Merz, *Die Wappenrolle von Zürich* (Zürich and Leipzig, 1930). Statutes, too, appeared in this form; cf. the MS of the *Statutes of England* (Sotheby sale, 10 June 1963, lot 160).

[4] Compare Sotheby sale, 10 June 1963, lot 153; Marston MS. 242; Huntington MS. HM 264; and Bühler MS. 30 (the latter two mounted in book-form). Also Harvard bMS Typ 40 and (in French) bMS Typ 41. Consult also Frank J. Mather,

prayers and supplications,[7] in verse as well as in prose.[8] The present discussion centers on a number of scrolls which contain texts of interest to the literary historian, to the folklorist, and to the student of medical history.

The religious texts (chiefly supplications) here set forth obviously possess a very ancient[9] and widespread heritage,[10] though by the ephemeral nature of these physical objects, relatively few examples of such amulets have been preserved to our times. The prayers appear to be the literary descendants of such curiosities as the Letter of Christ to Abgar[11] and that "Himmelsbrief" which, it is said, Pope

---

"Two Manuscript Rolls," *Record of the Museum of Historic Art, Princeton University*, v (1946), 6–9.

[5] Such manuscripts as British Museum Addit. 5016 and Bühler MS. 36.

[6] Cf. Sotheby sale, 10 June 1963, lot 161 (Survey and Rent Roll of the Manors and Lands belonging to the See of Canterbury).

[7] See, for example, Morgan MS. 486 (Curt F. Bühler, "A Middle English Prayer Roll," *Modern Language Notes*, LII [1937], 555–562) and that curious and unidentified manuscript listed in the Bodleian *Summary Catalogue* under no. 8460: "A Parchment Scrolle, of the Adoration of the five Principal Wounds of our Saviour, &c. B.38." The Morgan Library also possesses a French Legend of St Margaret (MS. 779), which probably served as a talisman for pregnant women: cf. *The Pierpont Morgan Library, Review of the Activities and Acquisitions of the Library from 1930 through 1935* (New York, 1937), pp. 93–94. There are such rolls of Italian origin (Adolf Deissmann and Hans Wegener, *Die Armenbibel des Serai, Rotulus Seragliensis Nr. 52* [Berlin and Leipzig, 1934]). For a characteristic example of a later roll (BM Addit. 25,311), see W. Sparrow Simpson, "On a Magical Roll of the Seventeenth Century," *Journal of the British Archaeological Association*, XL (1884), 297–332.

[8] Robbins (*Arma Christi Rolls*, p. 415) remarks: "No other religious poem or prayer [other than the Arma Christi ones] occurs in more than a single text." He probably meant versified supplications, since (as we shall see) prose ones often occur in more than one manuscript.

[9] See especially Walter J. Dilling, "Girdles: their Origin and Development, particularly with Regard to their Use as Charms in Medicine, Marriage, and Midwifery," *The Caledonian Medical Journal*, IX (1912–14), 337–357 and 403–425.

[10] Among sixteenth-century manuscripts, one may cite the Brig "Himmelsbrief" (D. Imesch, "Zwei alte Besegnungen," *Schweizerisches Archiv für Volkskunde*, IV [1900], 340–341) and that in a Tegernsee MS of 1507 (Adolf Jacoby, "Heilige Längenmasse: Eine Untersuchung zur Geschichte der Amulette," *SAVk*, XXIX [1929], 1–17 and 181–216 [esp. p. 8]).

[11] Cf. K. C. A. Matthes, *Die Edessenische Abgarsage auf ihre Fortbildung untersucht* (Leipzig, 1882). According to the catalogue, BM Royal MS. 2 A XX, f. 12, contains the text "with added remarks on the value of the letter as a charm." Similarly the Greek text in Morgan MS. 499; according to Sirarpie Der Nersessian ("La légende d'Abgar d'après un rouleau illustré de la bibliothèque Pierpont Morgan à New York," *Bulletin de l'institut archéologique bulgare*, x [1936], 98–

Leo III sent to Charlemagne as a "porte-bonheur dans les batailles."[12] But both the popes and their worldly counterparts vary from text to text, even from version to version of the same text, according to the date of writing and the nationality of the scribe or the patron who commissioned the amulet. Thus we may note the indulgence which "Jhon the .iij. pope of rome at the requeste of the quene of englo*n*de hath grau*n*ted to all them that deuoutly say thys prayer before the ymage of our lorde crucified."[13] We know, of course, that the papacy of the third pope of that name extended from 560 to 574, but a more recondite scholar than the present writer will be required to discover who the contemporary queen of England may have been. One of the charms noted below names Innocent VIII (1484–1492) and King Charles VIII of France (1484–1498),[14] while Innocent II (1130–1143)[15] and Clement VIII (1592–1605)[16] appear elsewhere.

Though the texts here discussed are not completely unfamiliar to all mediaevalists, the various studies dealing with them have appeared in a great number of different journals and reference works, many of which are not normally consulted by literary historians.

---

106): "Le rouleau de New York renferme une énumération de tous les périls qui seront écartés grâce à la lettre et, surtout, des maladies variées contre lesquelles elle sera un remède."

[12] Louis Gougaud, "La prière dite de Charlemagne et les pièces apocryphes apparentées," *Revue d'histoire ecclésiastique*, xx (1924), 211–238. An eighteenth-century charm of safety in Latin, Irish, and English is found in BM Sloane MS. 3323, ff. 288–289, where it is set forth that Leo Papa wrote this prayer for "Caralus mhoir Ri Franc" (Charles the Great, King of France). The *Horae ad usum Sarum* (Paris: for F. Regnault, 10 Oct. 1527—PML 17603), f. lxxj, prints: "Thys epystell of our sauyour sendeth our holy father pope Leo to the emperour Carolo magno of the whiche we fyndest wryte*n* who that bereth thys blessynge vpo*n* hym et sayth it ones a daye shall obteyne xl yere of pardo*n* et lxxx lenttyge & he shall not perysshe wyth soden deth." For the curious English found in books printed abroad, consult my "At thy golg first eut of the hous vlysse the saynge thus," *supra* (Chapter T24).

[13] 1527 Sarum *Horae*, f. lxxvj. Perhaps the antipope John XXIII (1410–15) was meant, in which case the queen would have been Joanna of Navarre.

[14] See below, note 48.

[15] The 1527 Sarum *Horae* (f. lxxxvj) includes a prayer of Innocent II in the worship of the wound in Christ's side. According to Jacoby (*op. cit.*, p. 211), this pope authenticated the relic of the "holy nails" belonging to the Viennese court.

[16] Jacoby (*op. cit.*, p. 1) has a German text, printed at Augsburg in 1655, based on the measurement of Christ's length as ordered to be determined by Pope Clement VIII.

Thus, in 1918, Professor C. T. Onions[17] could write of the Latin "prayer in collect form, [which] I have been unable to trace elsewhere; it was probably composed specially for the occasion." Actually, this same prayer (with but minor textual differences) had been printed a number of times in the preceding half-century.[18] That other investigations of the charms and the prayer remained unfamiliar to scholars concerned with them is underlined by the fact that a recent discussion of these pieces (1962)[19] mentions but two of the very considerable number of studies noted in the present article. Then again, the English texts were heretofore printed (with minor slips) in the style favored by nineteenth-century editors, so that one finds (on the one hand) such disturbing forms as "yyne," "yis" and "yem" for þyne, þis and þem, while (on the other hand) scribal mistakes were silently emended, giving a very imperfect picture of the original. Finally, this investigation calls attention to a few incipits not recorded by Brown-Robbins and to an extensive number of manuscripts and early printed pieces not previously examined in connection with the subject matter of this essay.

The scrolls (together with the sigla here used)[20] which are particularly studied are the following:

(1) Harley Rot. 43 A 14—A[21]
(2) Harley Rot. T 11—T[22]

[17] "A Devotion to the Cross written in the South-west of England," *Modern Language Review*, XIII (1918), 228-230.

[18] For example, by Philip Bliss (*Reliquiae Hearnianae, The Remains of Thomas Hearne, M. A.* [2nd ed.; London, 1869], I, 193-198); W. de G. Birch ("On two Anglo-Saxon Manuscripts in the British Museum," *Transactions of the Royal Society of Literature*, 2nd ser., XI [1878], 463-512) and also in the *Journal of the British Archaeological Association*, XXXI (1875), 105-106; and W. Sparrow Simpson ("On a Magical Roll Preserved in the British Museum," *ibid.*, XLVIII [1892] 38-54), where he refers to Birch's printing of the full text.

[19] S. A. J. Moorat, *Catalogue of Western Manuscripts on Medicine and Science in the Wellcome Historical Medical Library* (London, 1962), I, 491-493. A familiarity with the other texts would have prevented such misreadings as "grew" for "greve" and "sengter" for "length."

[20] H stands for the text of the Pullen MS. as transcribed by Hearne, and B for the text from Bodley MS. 177 printed by Onions.

[21] The texts were printed by Birch and Simpson in the articles cited in note 18 above.

[22] Printed by Simpson in his 1892 article.

(3) Wellcome MS. 632—W[23]
(4) Glazier MS. 39—G[24]

The texts of the scrolls are printed below in the usual fashion, all abbreviations having been expanded with the use of italics. Where necessary, scribal slips have been corrected, the readings of the original being supplied as *variae lectiones*. Capitalization and punctuation are mainly editorial.

## I

The amulet[25] based on the measurement of the length of the body of our Lord is a most curious piece,[26] traces of which may be found from Iceland to the Balkans. A Celtic version of the text is extant,[27] and the charm makes its appearance on both sides of the Alps (in

[23] See the catalogue (note 19) and my review of this in the *Journal of the History of Medicine and Allied Sciences*, XVIII (1963), 182-183. I there suggested that a plate from this manuscript would have been desirable, but having now seen the roll, I realize that the text was so badly rubbed out that reproduction would have been impossible.

[24] Described by John Plummer, *Manuscripts from the William S. Glazier Collection* (New York, 1959), pp. 24-25. Most (but not all) of the English text was printed by W. Heneage Legge, "A Decorated Mediaeval Roll of Prayers," *The Reliquary and Illustrated Archaeologist*, x (1904), 99-112. A short extract from it was printed by the present writer in SPECULUM, XXXIV (1959), 637-638. I should here like to express my grateful thanks to the late Mr Glazier for his kindness in placing his manuscript at my disposal. The Glazier Collection is now on deposit at the Pierpont Morgan Library, New York.

[25] The charm based on the measure of the length of Christ was once also contained in the Wellcome MS but most of it is now quite illegible. So much of it as can be read has been printed in the catalogue.

[26] The literature on the subject is very extensive. See, for example, the following studies (where the reader is referred to still further monographs): Gustavo Uzielli, *Le misure lineari medioevali e l'effigie di Cristo* (Florence, 1899) and his "Sulle misure e sul Corpo di Cristo come campione di misura nel medio evo in Italia," *Atti del Congresso Internazionale di scienze storiche*, XII (1903), 191-201; Jacoby, *op. cit.;* Jean Baptiste Thiers, *Traité des superstitions* (Paris, 1704), I, 272, and IV, 88; Louis Réau, *Iconographie de l'art chrétien* (Paris, 1955-59), II², 22-23; Hanns Bächtold-Stäubli, *Handwörterbuch des deutschen Aberglaubens* (Berlin and Leipzig, 1927-41), II, 63-64 and V, 899-902; *Lexikon für Theologie und Kirche* (Freiburg, 1957-62), VI, 785; and the other articles cited below. The *Lexikon* recalls the interesting fact that so late as "1908 wurde dieses Amulett in Bayrisch-Schwaben in grossen Mengen verlegt."

[27] Cf. Kuno Meyer, "Die Leibeslänge Christi," *Zeitschrift für celtische Philologie*, x (1915), 401-402. The text, in MS. Rawl. B 512, f. 52ᵛ, affirms that, the day you see the measure, you will suffer no sudden death, Jesus will be kind to you, and the Devil will do you no harm.

Germany as well as in Italy).[28] In its earliest form (in such manu-scripts as Cotton Titus D. XXVI, f. 3,[29] and Pluteo XXV, 3 of the Laurenziana),[30] we find no promises given in return for the (im-plied) veneration of the measure.

It seems highly probable that such texts as those here printed were used as medical charms, and the Wellcome roll, from the severe usage which it has obviously undergone (as its present, largely il-legible, state makes evident), may well have seen service as a "birth-girdle."[31] Religious texts of all sorts have often been put to such profane purposes, as even so famous a manuscript as the "Book of Durrow"[32] will recall to our minds.

## Rotulus Harley 43 A 14

This cros XV tymys metyn ys þe lenght of oure Lord Ihesu Criste. And þe day þat þou beryst it vpon þe or lokist þer-vpon, þou shalt haue þise gret giftis þat folowyth: The furst is þou schalt die no soden deth; The seconde is þou

---

[28] A number of Italian versions were printed. Compare Curt F. Bühler, "An Orazione della misura di Cristo," *La Bibliofilia*, xxxix (1937), 430–433; Gustavo Uzielli, "L'Orazione della misura di Cristo," *Archivio storico italiano*, ser. 5, xxvii (1901), 334–345; and Alphonse Aymar, "Le sachet accoucheur et ses mystères," *Annales du Midi*, xxxviii (1926), 273–347. Aymar (p. 276) writes of "un ruban en soie . . . sur lequel sont imprimés, en capitales romaines noires, les mots italiens: *Longhezza di Nostro Signore Giesu Christo.*" This yields a measurement of about 180 centimeters. Aymar maintained: "nous ignorons l'emploi de ce ruban."

[29] Though no measurement is given and no rewards are promised, the text reads: "Haec figura sedecies multiplicata perficit mensuram Domini Nostri Ihesu Christi corporis."

[30] "Hec linea bis sexties [*sic*] ducta mensuram dominici corporis monstrat. Sumpta est autem de constantinopoli ex aurea cruce facta ad formam corporis Christi." Cf. Angelo Maria Bandini, *Catalogus codicum latinorum bibliothecae Mediceae Lau-rentianae* (Florence, 1774–78), i, 748–754. The measure is multiplied sixteen times in such manuscripts as Riccardiano 1294 (1760), f. 103, and Ricc. 1763, f. 56ᵛ.

[31] On these, see the description of MS. 632 given in the Wellcome catalogue, Dil-ling (*op. cit.*, 403–425), and particularly the work by Alphonse Aymar (see note 28). Such a girdle is probably the item referred to "in the 'Privy Purse Expenses of Elizabeth of York' in December, 1502, [where] is the entry:—'To a monke that broughte our Lady gyrdelle to the Quene in reward, vjs. viijd.'" (Dilling, p. 421).

[32] MS. A.4.5 of the Library of Trinity College, Dublin. In the seventeenth cen-tury, Conall MacEochagáin reported that he "saw the Ignorant man that had the [Book of Durrow] in his Custody, when sickness came upon cattle, for their Remedy putt water on the booke & suffered it to rest there a while & saw alsoe cattle returne thereby to their former or pristin state & the book to receave no loss" (*Evangeliorum quattuor codex Durmachensis* [Olten, 1960], ii, 66). Unhappily, the last statement is not quite true, since water-stains may be seen in various parts of the volume; some leaves have suffered quite severely.

schalt not be hurte nor slayne with no maner of wepyn; The iij$^d$ is þou shalt haue resonabull godis & helth vn-to þy lyuys ende; The iiij$^{th}$ is þyne enmys shall neuer ouyr-com þe; The v$^{th}$ is no maner of preson nor fals wytnes shall neuyr greve þe;[33] The vj$^{th}$ is þou shalt not die with-oute the Sacramenttes of the Chirche; The vij$^{th}$ is þou schalt be defendid from all maner of wykkid spirites, tribulacions, & dissesis, & from all infirmitees & sekenes of þe pestilence; The viiij$^{th}$ is yf a woman be in trauell of childe lay þis vpon her wombe & þe childe schall haue Cristendom & þe moder schall haue purificacion, ffor Seynt Cerice & Seynt Julitt, his moder, desirid þise graciouse gyftis of God, which He grauntid vn-to þem, and þis is regestird in Rome.[34]

Salue decus paruulorum, miles regis angelorum.[35] O Cerice, cum beata Julitta. Christe & Maria nos saluet in hora mortis nostre. Amen.

Preciosa est in conspectu Dei mors sanctorum eius.

Deus qui gloriosis martiribus tuis Cerico & Julitte tribuisti dira nephandi iudicis tormenta superare tribue michi Willelmo famulo tuo humilitatem in virtute gloriose longitudinis tue et venerabilis crucis tue preciosique corporis & sanguinis tui & omnipotenciarum & virtutum per intercessionem sanctorum tuorum concede[36] michi triumphum omnium inimicorum meorum vt possum semper retinere constanciam per Christum Dominum nostrum Amen A.M.E.N.

For the sake of comparison, the text found in Glazier MS. 39 is given below, since it was only partially (and not entirely correctly) transcribed by Legge,[37] who also omitted to reproduce the Latin prayer. Furthermore, it differs sufficiently from the Harley roll to warrant its being printed here for the sake of comparison. The Glazier text is closer to that found in MS. Bodley 177[38] than to that of the British Museum supplication, but the Oxford version, in turn, is longer and more detailed than in the account here given.[39]

## Glazier MS. 39

This crose .XV. tymes metyn is þe trew lenth of our Lorde Ihesu Criste. And þat day that þou lokes on it er beris it a-pone the, that day sall no wekid

---

[33] In the prayer to the nails in G, the following is promised to the supplicant: "þat no posom [sic] ne fals wittnes shall not grefe þaim." The prayer of St Augustine in the 1527 Sarum *Horae* (f. lxxvj$^v$) sets forth that "who that . . . bereth [it] aboute them shall not perysshe in fyer or water nother in batyll or iugement et he shall not dye of sodyne dethe et no venym shall poysinne hym that daye. . . ."

[34] This passage is quoted (with slips) by Gougaud, *op. cit.*, p. 221. He discusses these saints on pp. 221–222. A fifteenth-century French account of their lives and martyrdom may be found in Morgan MS. 674, ff. 278–279.

[35] Anglorum [!] (Birch, *JBAA*, 1875, 105).

[36] concedas BGHTW.     [37] *Op. cit.*, p. 103.

[38] As printed by Onions; see note 17.

[39] As Uzielli (*Archivio*, p. 341) states: "Veramente può oggi sembrare strano che si avesse fede in una scrittura secondo la quale Cristo sarebbe stato quasi un nano."

sprete haue pou*er* to hurte þe. Thono*ur* ne leuenyng, slepyng ne wakyng, shal not harme the. In batell þou shalt not be slayn, ne dy of no man*er* of wepyn, with-outen the Sacramentes of the Kirke ne þou salt not dy no sodan ne evill dede. Fire ne water salt not hurte the. And if a woman tra*w*ell of childe, take þis crose and lay[40] it one hyr wome and she shalbe hastely be delyu*e*rede with joy with-outen p*e*rell, the childe to haue Cristendom and þe moder purificac*io*n of Haly Kirk. For Seynt Cerice and Seynt Julite, his moder, desired thes of almyghty Gode, the wich He gr*a*untede þame. This is registrede at Rome in Seynt John Laternence.[41]

Ant*iphona*. Salue decus p*a*ruulor*um* miles reges [*sic*] angelorum. O Cerice cum beata genitrice tua Iulitta. Chr*iste* et Maria nos saluet in hora mortis. Amen. V*ersus*. Preciosa *est* in con[spectu Domini mors sanctorum eius]. Deus qui gloriosis m*arti*ribus tuis Cerice & Julitte dira nephandi iudicis tormenta sup*er*are fecisti, tribue michi famulo tuo N humilitat*em* et virtutem gloriose longitudinis tue, & ven*er*abilis crucis tue, pr*e*ciosiq*ue* corp*or*is & sang*u*inis tui, & *om*nipotencias & v*ir*tutes tuas, et p*er* intercession*em* s*an*ct*orum* tuo*rum* concedas michi triumphu*m* *om*nium inimicorum, vt et possim s*em*p*er* retinere constanciam. Amen.

The dialect of the text in Bodley 177, Professor Onions pointed out, is that of the southwest of England in the late fourteenth century.[42] The scribe of the Glazier manuscript, as we shall see, was a native of—and continued to reside in—the North Riding of Yorkshire; he "flourished" in the closing years of the fifteenth century. Several words in his text, therefore, call for comment. For the Bodley "dunder ne lyȝtnyng" which Onions discussed, we here have "thonour ne leuenyng." These two forms, together with the spelling "wome," do not seem to be recorded by the *OED*—but whether we here have true dialectal variants or merely words ignorantly written seems debatable. "Haly Kirk" and "dede" are certainly Northern, and "salt" seems to be a characteristic variant for the East Midlands.

Some slips may be certainly identified as the fault of the several scribes, such as the "Dei" for "Domini" in the Harley roll, and the "reges" for "regis" in the Glazier MS. The *Reliquiae Hearnianae* prints "Speciosa est in conspectu domini mors seculorum ejus" for the versicle from the Psalms (CXV, 15), which may be due either to the ignorance of the mediaeval scribe or to the carelessness of Thomas Hearne.

[40] "lay" is repeated (and cancelled) in the MS.

[41] Laterens H; Latoranensez T; Lateranence W. Similar "pardons" were said to be registered in the "Ara Celi" at Rome (Robbins, *Arma Christi*, p. 418).

[42] Due to a misprint, Dom Louis Gougaud places the manuscript in the nineteenth century.

## II

The second Harley roll, after still another version of the Middle English veneration based on the length of Christ (now no longer very legible),[43] contains two further supplications. The first is connected with the length of the nails[44] with which our Lord was fastened to the Cross,[45] and the second with that of the wound[46] which the spear of Longinus made in the side of His body.[47] Both of these belong to a very long-lived and widespread tradition.

[43] Printed (so far as it could be deciphered) by Simpson, *JBAA*, 1892, 50–51. The text appears to be very close to that in the Glazier MS.

[44] The number of nails varies in the mediaeval period. Aymar (p. 284, n. 2) suggests that the number "three" arose in the thirteenth century in Italy. Émile Mâle, *L'art religieux du XIIe siècle en France* (Paris, 1922), p. 84, also states that four nails appear in the twelfth century, but that it was in France that the number was reduced to three within the next hundred years. Gabriel Millet (*Recherches sur l'iconographie de l'Évangile aux XIVe, XVe et XVIe siècles* [Paris, 1916], p. 413) believes that the tradition of the three nails came "du Nord." See also Réau, *op. cit.*, II², 480; Géza de Francovich, "L'origine e la diffusione del crocifesso gotico doloroso," *Kunstgeschichtliches Jahrbuch der Biblioteca Hertziana*, II (1938), 143–261; Joseph W. Hewitt, "The Use of Nails in the Crucifixion," *Harvard Theological Review*, XXV (1932), 29–45; etc. Three nails also appear on the British fifteenth-century indulgences known as the "Image of Pity"; cf. Henry Bradshaw's essay in his *Collected Papers* (Cambridge, 1889), pp. 84–100.

[45] A printed version (in German) of the measure is given by Paul Heitz, *Pestblätter des XV. Jahrhunderts (Einblattdrucke des fünfzehnten Jahrhunderts*, Band II; Strassburg, 1918), fig. 1, and a Dutch one by Wilhelm L. Schreiber, *Handbuch der Holz- und Metallschnitte des XV. Jahrhunderts* (Leipzig, 1926–30), IV, 2, 1785.

[46] Compare W. Sparrow Simpson, "On the Measure of the Wound in the Side of the Redeemer, worn anciently as a Charm," *Journal of the British Archaeological Association*, XXX (1874), 357–374, and Réau, *op. cit.*, II², 23. A characteristic indulgence on the *five* wounds was in the former Pullen MS. (see *Rel. Hearn.*, I, 193–198, item 12). An English poem on the five wounds of Christ (eleven couplets; not listed by Brown-Robbins) was printed by Henry H. Gibbs from a fifteenth-century French manuscript belonging to the Earl of Verulam (Gorhambury) in *Notes and Queries*, 6th ser., VIII (1883), 443. Recently Douglas Gray has printed a detailed discussion of the cult of the Five Wounds ("The Five Wounds of our Lord," *Notes and Queries*, CCVIII [1963], 50 51; 82 89; 127 134; and 163 168). According to Simpson (*JBAA*, 1892, 45–46), Lansdowne MS. 96, art. 44, f. 104, contains two six-line stanzas also not in Brown-Robbins; the first begins "God that made boythe daye & neight," while the second has the incipit "In nomine patris at my Crowne." Although the manuscript is chiefly of the sixteenth century, these stanzas appear to belong to the previous one. The *Catalogue of the Lansdowne Manuscripts in the British Museum* (London, 1819), p. 188, describes these as "some ridiculous Popish charms or spells, in miserable rhyme, the recital of which is to procure pardon for sins, protection from spirits, &c."

[47] Lambeth MS. 545, f. 79ᵛ, has a representation of the wound, around which is written: "The mesure of þe wonde of oure Lorde Ihesu Crist he suffride on þe crose for oure redempcioun." Similarly in French, Morgan MS. 90, f. 130, one finds: "Ci

## Rotulus Harley T 11

Pope Innocent[48] the viij hath grauntyd that who-so-euer, man or woman that beth, beryth the lenght of the naylis upon hym & worshipith deuoutly the iij naylis of oure Lord Ihesu Crist with .v. Pater Noster & .v. Auez & a Crede, he shall haue grauntyd hym vij yeftiz: the first yefte, he shall[a] not dey of no soden deth nor evyll deth; the second yeft, he shall not be slayn with no swerd nor with no wepyn; the iij, that his enemys shall haue no power to ouer-comme hym; the iiij, that no poyson nor fals wyttenesse shall not greue hym; the v[th] yefte, he shall haue suffycient gooddes & honest lyuyng in this world; the vj, he shall not dey without receyuyng the Holy Sacramentes of the Church;[49] the vijþe yefte, he shall be deleueryd from all wykyd spyritz, feuers, pestelens & other malicyeus. And thys ys the very lengh[t][b] of Cristiz naylis which most be holdyn as[c] relekys & worshipid deuoutly with saying of v Pater Noster & v Auez & a Crede.

This is the mesur of[d] the blessyd wounde[e] that oure Lord Ihesu Crist had in his right syde, the whiche an angell brought to Charlamayn, the nobyll emperour of Constrantyne,[f] wyth-in a cofer of gold, saing this in hys tityll, that who-so-euer, man or woman, hauyng this mesur on hym shall not be slayn wyth no swerd[g] nor spere, nor no shot shall not hurt the[h], nor no man shall not ouercomme hym in batell, nor fire nor water shall not noy hym, & yf a woma[n][i] be trauelyng of child that day, that she shuld haue sayn the sayd mesur, that day she[j] shall not perysh, but the child to haue Crestendom & the modur puryfycacion, for this ys provyd for euery man that goth to a sault[k] of ar[mes], hauyng thys mesur on hym, shall haue the victory[l] & honour upon hys enemys.

---

est la mesure de la plaie du coste nostre seigneur qui pour nous souffrist mort en la crois." On the facing page a later hand has written: "haec est mensura plagae sacratissimi lateris Christj, quae a Constantinopoli B. Carolo Imperatorj allata fuit in capsa aurea, ad ejus ab inimicis in bello protectionem." A very similar passage is printed in the *Enchiridion Leonis papae* (Mainz, 1633), p. 129. Morgan MS. 488, f. 61, provides the figure and text: "Icy dessus est la mesure de la digne et precieuse plaie du couste de noustre seigneur Ihesucrist, laquelle fut a-portee de Constantin-noble, a noble homme empereur Charlemaigne dedans vne casse dor affin que nulx ennemis ne luy puissant nuyre en bataille." Here it is further asserted that he who carries this figure or says the prayer will die no evil death; will be safe from lightning, fire, water, spear, knife, and so forth; that women in childbirth will be protected; etc. For printed representations, see Schreiber, *loc. cit.*, nos. 1788, 1789, 1795, etc.

[48] The Glazier MS. begins with the words: "Theis er the veray trew lenth of the thre nailis of our Lorde Ihesu Criste to whame Pape Innocent sent this same lenth vn-to Kyng Charls." This would seem to refer to Innocent VIII (1484–1492) and Charles VIII (1484–1498), rather than to Innocent VII (1404–1406) and Charles VI (the Mad; 1380–1422), the only others of that name to be contemporaries. See A. Cappelli, *Cronologia, cronografia e calendario perpetuo* (Milan, 1930), pp. 295 and 457–459. T specifies Innocent VIII and thus supports the above conjecture.

[49] "The vj is he shal se our Lady in bute & comforth to hys saluacion" (G).

*Textual Notes* (a) MS reads "sh shall" (b) MS has "leñgh" (c) MS reads "as a relekys & worshipith deuot deuoutly" (d) "of of" MS (e) MS apparently reads "wound*es*" (f) thus in MS (g) "sw swerd" MS (h) note change of person in MS (i) MS reads "woma be traueuely*ng* of ch child" (j) "sh she shall s not be perysh" MS (k) the reading "sault of ar" is not absolutely certain but highly likely (l) MS has "vic victory."

The reader will not have failed to notice that the "gifts," which these several charms promise to provide for the devout supplicant, are all very similar in nature.

## III

The Glazier MS concludes with a poem (consisting of twenty rhymed lines of indifferent verse) which, though first printed by Legge,[50] was not listed by Brown-Robbins. Though both the rhyme and the meter falter, the autobiographical details will, no doubt, be of considerable interest to the student of dialects.

### Glazier MS. 39

Noghte to lyke þow me to lake
For this schrowyll by-hynd my bake
Bot whare ȝe fynde that I offende
I pray þow mekely it amende
For ilk a sere man hath a wyte
And thare-by he shall wyrke it
For vnto powre erudicione
I make thys symple formac*ione*
Chanon in Coue*rha*m wi*th*owten le
In þe ordere of Premonstre
þat tyme þis schrowyll I dyd wryte
Whare-fore I p*ray* þou me not wyte
In haste done so trewle
Thare-fore it apperyth full symple
In Rudby towne of my moder fre
I was borne wyth-owtyn le
Schawyn I was to þe ord*er* clene
The vigill of All Halo*es* evyn
My name it was Percevall
Ih*es*u to þe blys be bryng vs all[51]

[50] His text, together with comments on Canon Percival and Coverham Abbey, appears on pp. 111-112.

[51] An unfortunate erasure of three lines occurs at the very end of the scroll.

These lines establish the fact that the scroll[52] was written by a certain Percival, born in Rudby in Cleveland (not far from Stokesley in Yorkshire), who had entered the Premonstratensian Order on Halloween (year unspecified) and had become a canon of Coverham Abbey[53] (two miles from Middleham, also in Yorkshire) by the time the scroll was written. Percival must have undertaken to write this manuscript some time after 1484, since Pope Innocent VIII and King Charles VIII of France (each of whom ascended his throne in that year) are both mentioned therein. From these facts it becomes clear that the dialect of the Glazier scroll must be that which was current in the northeastern Midlands about the year 1500.

(From *Speculum* 39 (1964), pp. 270-78).

[52] According to *OED*, this must be one of the earliest appearances of "scroll" in English. The form "schrowyll" is not recorded by *OED*. This may well be a Northern form, as "schawyn" (shaven) certainly is (*OED*, VIII², 642).

[53] Cf. L. H. Cottineau, *Répertoire topo-bibliographique des abbayes et prieurés* (Mâcon, 1939), I, 906–907.

# CHAPTER T29

## THE VERSE PROLOGUE TO THE MIDDLE
## HIGH GERMAN MACER

A PECULIARITY of some Middle High German scientific
and didactic treatises, as Karl F. Bartsch has pointed out,[1]
is that these are provided with metrical prologues. This
feature is exemplified, we are informed, by the versified prefaces to
the *Lucidarius* and the *Sachsenspiegel* (both of the thirteenth century), as well as to the fourteenth-century *Buch der Natur*. Another
instance of this tradition may be observed in the case of the German
translation of that popular herbal entitled *De viribus herbarum* and
attributed to Macer Floridus.[2] A definitive edition of the versified
prologue to this "Macer" was printed by Bartsch, basing his eclectic
text (cited here as H) on the readings of the following five manuscripts:

A. Heidelberg, Universitätsbibliothek. Cod. pal. germ 213
B. Heidelberg, Universitätsbibliothek. Cod. pal. germ 226
C. Frankfurt, Stadtbibliothek. MS. germ. IV. 82
D. Berlin, Preussische Staatsbibliothek. MS. germ. fol. 817
E. Breslau, Universitätsbibliothek. MS. III. Fol. 22.

The purpose of the present note is to call attention to three more
manuscripts of this prologue and to print the version found in the
Morgan manuscript (M 900),[3] together with a few comments on
the two manuscripts preserved in the British Museum[4] (Addit. 16892,
f. 37 = F and Addit. 17527,[5] f. 73ᵛ = G). All three appear to belong

[1] *Beiträge zur Quellenkunde der altdeutschen Literatur* (Strassburg, 1886), pp.
171-75.
[2] For a discussion of this text, see Cyrill Resak, *Odo Magdunensis, der Verfasser
des "Macer Floridus" und der deutsche Leipziger Macer Text* (Leipzig, 1917) and
the literature cited there.
[3] Bought at the Sotheby sale, July 11, 1960, lot 129, with income from the Trust
Fund of Lathrop Colgate Harper, Litt. D. For a further account of the manuscript,
see Frederick B. Adams, Jr., *Eleventh Report to the Fellows of the Pierpont Morgan
Library* (New York, 1961), pp. 16-17.
[4] The manuscripts are described by Robert Priebsch, *Deutsche Handschriften in
England* (Erlangen, 1896-1901), pp. 160 and 167.
[5] This text has the heading: "Incipit hic macer qui docet virtutes herb*arum*. Hy

to the fifteenth century.[6] Interestingly enough, the two texts in the British Museum are written out as prose. In the Morgan manuscript, fifteen verse lines, appearing on folio 60 recto (lines 19–30), are similarly written, but beginning with line 16 of the prologue on the verso, the scribe apparently became aware of the rhyme and metre, and wrote the remainder of the text as verse. The dialect in M 900 appears to be Middle Rhenish[7] and supports Bartsch's conjecture that the lines were the work of "eines mitteldeutschen Verfassers." Taken all in all, the version in BM Addit. 17527 agrees reasonably closely with the Morgan text (as printed below); however, that found in Addit. 16892 extends to only 38 lines. The first 26 lines correspond to the standard text, as do also the last 10 lines. The couplet[8] found between these two groups seems to be a combination of lines 36–38 and 43–44 of the definitive edition.

The text of M 900 is unreliable in a number of places.[9] The present editor has nevertheless decided to print the text with a minimum of emendations, though he has appended a few suggested readings or explanations as notes:

---

lert der meiſter macer alle togunt der crew*ter*. vnde alle ir crafft. et cetera. In nomine *pa*tris & filij & ſpir*itu*s ſancti. Amen solame*n*."

[6] M 900 has the watermarks: "Lettre P gothique à fleuron à quatre feuille" (Briquet group 8588–8653, much used in Rhine valley in mid-fifteenth century; closest perhaps no. 8599) and "Lettre p gothique simple" (Briquet 8566–8581, same place and time; closest perhaps 8571). G has watermark "Lettre M" (Briquet 8341–8354, Italian paper also used in the north; closest perhaps 8346, recorded in Holland, 1386).

[7] Bartsch (*loc. cit.*) observes that the rhyme *nente: irkente* is typically Mitteldeutsch (same rhyme in G and see lines 31–32), as well as the reading *unpfliht* which is foreign to Oberdeutsch. Compare line 21 (*vnplichte*) where *p* has not shifted to *pf*; on this, see Hermann Paul, *Mittelhochdeutsche Grammatik* (Halle, 1929), § 92/3. Note also the readings *worcze* (Paul § 98.3 and Matthias Lexer, *Mittelhochdeutsches Taschenwörterbuch* [Leipzig, 1930], p. 329) and *eme* (Paul § 102); the addition of *i* to indicate a long vowel (*hait*, line 20; Paul § 101); the survival of Old Teutonic *d* (*godis, mudis;* Paul § 91.4); and the presence of *a* for *o* (*ab, ane;* Paul § 99). Lexer (p. 137) lists *meinster* as an Alemanic variant. These details suggest that the manuscript was written in the region between Koblenz and Bonn, probably towards the middle of the fifteenth century.

[8]     Dûrch got ſo wil ich ſcriben
Der worze tûgint vnde ir craft ob ich mochte vortriben

[9] An abbreviated form of the German prose Macer follows the prologue (folios 61–69). The same text, in a longer form and under the heading "Virtutes herbarum. Der kruder crafft," appears also on folios 100ᵛ–118ᵛ, with the colophon:

Hye hait diß medicinal eyn ende
Got vnß ſyne wyßheyt ſende

An eyner ſtat geſchrieben ſtat
Das got ſelbir geſprochin [hait]
Das mercke wyp vnd man
Iſt yman der icht gudes kan
5   Ob der das nyemant leret
Syn vnglucke er meret
Recht als eyn man er thut
Der da begrebit ſyn ſelbis gut
Das nach eme nyeman en wirt
10   Godis fluch er nit enbiert
Das mercke wer gelert ſÿ
Secht dem iſt godis fluch by
Wer ſyne kunſt nyeman enleret
So wirt auch lychte ſyn heyle gemerit
15   Wer da lerit was er kan
[f. 60ᵛ]   Da wil ich gedencken an
Durch got vnd durch myn heÿll
Ab ich noch mochte eyn deyll
Gebuſſen myner myſſetait
20   Der myn munt geſprochen hait
An worten mit vnplichte
Der muß vor dem gerichte
Mit angiſt czu antworten han
Da mag vorſprechin keyne man
25   Abe ich ſie nit hie hab gebußit
Da manchis vnſanfftes wirt gegrußit
Auch bath eyn frauwe mich
Daz durch ÿren willen ich
Der ich dynſtes byn bereyt
30   Beſtunde dyſße arbeyt
Das ich yr die worcze nent
Was ich der erkent
Vnd ir crafft wolt ſchriben
Das ſolde nit beliben
35   Vnverſchuldit widder mich
Durch got vnd durch ſie wyll ich
Schriben der worcze macht
Ir dogent vnd auch ir crafft
Was ich der han erkant
40   Als ich iz geſchrieben fant
Von eynes wyſen meynſters hant
Ich nente yn woll was ſall er genant
Dis will ich durch das ſchriben
Ab ich mochte alßo vertriben
[f. 61]45   Myner ſchweren ſunde eyn deyll
Geſchee ymant da von eyn heyll
Daz mir der bede auch godis

Nu bidden ich das des ſelbin mudis
Der gene mir woll weſen
50    Daz er iz gerne hore leſen
Ich ſchriben iz ane vnd durch das
Daz man es vorneme deſte baß
Vnd daz yme czwifel ſy czu ſtorit
Der es leſit odir horit

*Textual notes.* Line 2: MS. reads "hoit"; cf. footnote 7. Line 8: Der do begibt ſeines ſelben mut (G); F = MS. Line 11; MS. inverts, reading "ſÿ gelert." Line 12: H (similarly G) has "Seht, dem ist gotes fluoch bî." Line 14: Sin heil wirt ouch lichte gemerit (F); G (omitting "auch") = MS. Line 19: Geleschen (H; also GF). Line 21: vnpflichte (G; so by correction in F). Line 22: Der ich muoz vor gerihte (H); Der mus ich vor dem gerichte (G); Der ich mûz vor deme richte (F). Line 24: Da nieman mac vürsprechen hân (HG; similarly F). Line 26: Da maniger vnſanfte wirt gegrûzit (F); Do man vnſanft wirt gegruſſet (G). Line 38: G (with "togunt" and omitting "auch") as MS.; Ir tugent und ir kraft geslaht (H). Line 49: gein (HF = gên/gegen). Line 51: for "iz ane vnd" read "iz ane rîm" (as HGF).

The verse, to say the least, is not very inspiring. The passage is prolix despite its brevity and contains a good many stock phrases and trite rhyme-tags, highly characteristic of the period. But the poet (if such he may be called) does assert that, knowing the evils of concealing knowledge and the danger of incurring God's wrath by not spreading learning, he undertook this work as penance for the wickednesses he has uttered. For such he will be judged, unless he should atone. A lady, too, has asked him to set down for her what he knows about herbs and their virtues, even as he found this information compiled by a wise master. Thus the rhymester had hopes of absolving himself from the burden of a part of his heavy sins. If the suggested reading for line 51 be accepted, then the poet also states that he wrote the herbal in prose,[10] so that it might be better understood, without uncertainty, by whoever reads or hears the text.

(From *Philological Quarterly* 44 (1965), pp. 113-16).

[10] For the verse translation, see J. G. Thierfelder, "Zwei Handschriften des Macer Floridus mit Uebersetzung in deutsche Reime," *Serapeum*, 1862, 23: 7-12, quoting from two manuscripts in the possession of the author. Resak, pp. 19-20, refers to two other manuscripts of this text in Gotha and Vicenza.

# CHAPTER LI

## LIBRI IMPRESSI CUM NOTIS MANUSCRIPTIS

### Part I

IN the field of early printed books, there are few bibliographical problems left to be solved. These books have been so thoroughly examined from a textual and typographical point of view that few great discoveries can be expected to be made in the future. To this general rule, there is, however, one outstanding exception and that concerns the manuscript entries frequently met with in the earlier books. It is true, of course, that these are mostly only of bibliographical interest, but every now and again small jottings that have some literary value come to light in the margins or on the blank pages of these books. These are usually dismissed with a few words or entirely omitted in the various descriptive catalogues of the books, but they have as much claim as any other piece of literature to some form of permanent record. It is proposed, therefore, to publish from time to time, under the present title, such manuscript entries as may be presumed to have any literary interest. The books in which these entries are found are preserved, unless specially noted to the contrary, in The Pierpont Morgan Library, and for the convenience of those wishing to examine or confirm these for themselves the accession numbers of the books are given together with the symbol *PML*.

### I

The first book to be so noticed is the English translation of the *De consolatione philosophiae* printed by William Caxton about the year 1478 (*PML.*, 775). On the last printed page there are two short entries, written by the same hand and probably in the first half of the sixteenth century. The first reads:

> Love þat is powre it is with pyne
> Love that is riche it is ethe for to tyne
> Love that is hot it can no skyll
> Love that is cold it waxys sone ill
> Love that is changeable þat is ryght nawght
> Love dangerowse þat is dere bowght
> Love that is false it will a-way
> Love that is trwe it lastythe aye.

This stanza is not included in Carleton Brown's *A Register of Middle English Religious & Didactic Verse* (Bibliographical Society, 1916–20), and I do not recall off hand that it forms part of any longer work. The lines are obviously of no great poetic merit. (Cf. Carleton Brown, *Eng. Lyrics of 13th Cy.*, No. 53.)

The second piece, which is incomplete at the end but is of some interest because of the reference to Lydgate, reads as follows:

### Out of a sermon prechid at Powls Crosse

Ther was a vertuous monke of Bury called Lydgate, whiche wrot many notable historis & made many vertuous ballettes to þe encrease of vertwe & oppressyon of vyce. And amonge other he made a treatyse called Galand & all þe kyndred of Galand he discryved ther-in. I suppose yf galantes vnderstonde þe progeny, they wolte refuse to be of that felowshyp & kyndrede. The occasion of makynge this boke was whan Englysshe men were set out & loste Fraunce, Gascoyne, Gyone, & Normandy & came home dysgwysed[1] in theyr garmentes in every parte of theyr bodyes, whiche Engleshe men sawe never before, and many folowed the lewde & abhomynable garments in so moche þat all good men [? were wroth with] them, and this good monke in detestacion of theyr synne & wretchidnes made þe sayd boke in balad wyse. And þe repete of every balet was this: Englond may wayle that ever galand came here.[2] And in short[3] season after were grete surrections & murdre of lords & other, as I doubte not many that lyvethe can remember it. I praye God they maye amend them, that we be not punysshed for them & wayle theyr wretchidnesse, for bycause we suffre the sub- . . .

The ballad here referred to is apparently the one printed in Sir Egerton Brydges' *Censura Literaria* (second edition, London, 1815, Vol. I, pp. 62–66). The poem is also found in a manuscript of the third quarter of the fifteenth century and was subsequently printed by Wynkyn de Worde. This ballad is now no longer believed to have been written by Lydgate. Professor MacCracken says of it:

Bishop John Alcock (*d.* 1500), in a sermon preached in his old age, attributed this poem to Lydgate, saying that he remembered it in his youth. Alcock was about 19 years old when Lydgate died. It is of course not absolutely certain that the Ballade we possess is in the original form, or precisely the one Alcock had in mind, though the refrain he quotes is that of our poem.[4]

[1] *After* dysgwysed *MS. reads:* in theyr garmandye & came home disgwysed. *This obvious copyist's error was subsequently cancelled.*

[2] *The MS. originally read:* Englond may wayle that every balet was this galand came here. *Another scribal error, later corrected.*

[3] *After* short, *the scribe wrote* space *which he then cancelled.*

[4] *The Minor Poems of John Lydgate*, E.E.T.S., E.S., cvii, p. xxxii.

The sermon here printed is probably the same one noted by Mac-Cracken, although it is not, in this entry, directly ascribed to Bishop Alcock, and is consequently not an independent authority for ascribing such a poem to Lydgate. We may note, however, that the refrain differs slightly from that printed by Brydges, where it reads:

Englonde may wayle that ever it came here.

This is clearly insufficient evidence for assuming that a different (and earlier) version of the poem existed in addition to the one that has come down to us, but it does not preclude the fact that there may have been some such version.

## II

On the blank fly-leaves of Henry Bull's *Christian Prayers and Holy Meditations* (London, H. Middleton, 1570–PML., 7768), there are several interesting entries written in an artificial "writing master" style. At the end of the last entry is written, apparently with the same ink and at the same time, the name: T. Heneage. The signature is that of Sir Thomas Heneage,[5] a favorite of Queen Elizabeth's and vice-chamberlain of her court, and this gives fair reason for believing that the verses printed below were actually composed by Queen Elizabeth. On the first fly-leaf is written:

GENUS INFOELIX VITAE

Multum vigilaui, laboraui, presto multis fui,
Stultitiam multorum perpessa sum,
Arrogantiam pertuli, Difficultates exorbui,
Vixi ad aliorum arbitrium, non ad meum.

A haples kynde of lyfe is this I weare;
Moch watche I dure, and weary toilinge daies;
I serue the route, and all their follies beare;
I suffer pryde, and suppe full harde assaies;
To others wyll, my life is all addrest;
And no ware so, as might content me best.

This aboue was written in a booke by the Queenes Ma^tie.

On the second fly-leaf are the following lines by Sir Thomas to an unidentified "noble Lady":

[5] I am obliged to Dr. Robin Flower of the British Museum for confirming my belief that the signature was that of Sir Thomas Heneage.

Madam, but marke the labours of our lyfe,
And therewithall, what errours we be in;
We sue and seeke, with praiers, sturre and stryfe,
Vppon this earthe a happie state to win.

And whilst with cares, we trauell to content vs
In vaine desires, and sette no certaine scope,
We reape but things whereof we oft repent vs,
And feede our wylles with moch beguilinge hope.

We praie for honours, lapt in daungers handes;
We striue for riches, which we streight forgoe;
We seeke delyte, that all in poison standes;
And sette with paines, but seedes of synne and woe.

Then noble lady, need we not to praie
The lord of all, for better state and staie.
                 Your La: moch bound
                    T. Heneage.

Although perhaps not comparable to the finest Elizabethan verse, the lines are not without a certain charm. Sir Thomas was on intimate terms with many of the literary lights of the period (including Sir Philip Sidney, Sir William Fleetwood, John Foxe, and others) and it is pleasant to note that he was also able to turn out quite tolerable verse.

             (From *Modern Language Notes* 53 (1938), pp. 245-49).

# CHAPTER L2

## SIXTEENTH-CENTURY PROGNOSTICATIONS[1]

IN SEYMOUR DE RICCI's *A Census of Caxtons* (Bibliographical Society, 1909, p. 93), there is a short notation to the effect that a copy of CAXTON's *Myrrour of the World* [Westminster, ca. 1481] in The Pierpont Morgan Library (PML 776) has "16 ff. of old MS. added at the end." Written in the mid-sixteenth century,[2] this manuscript contains the following items:

1. Treatise on geography,[3] etc., ff. 1ᵃ–3ᵇ
2. Table of the regnant planets,[4] f. 4ᵃ
3. Lists of unlucky days and a thunder-book, f. 6ᵃ
4. Astrological tables and figures, mostly in Latin, ff. 6ᵇ–11ᵇ
    4ᵃ. Order of the planets, in English, f. 8ᵇ
    4ᵇ. Weather prognostications, in English, f. 10ᵇ
5. Order of the planets, f. 12ᵃ
6. Effect of the planets, ff. 13ᵃ–15ᵃ
7. Astrological notes and diagrams, in Latin, ff. 15ᵇ–16ᵇ

As the English items are unusually interesting, it seems eminently desirable to make these texts available in print.

### I

Turning first of all to the astrological tracts, we note that the first item discusses the unlucky days which occur annually. Reaching as far back as the earliest days of Mesopotamian culture,[5] the "dies fasti

---

[1] The second publication in the series *Libri impressi.*

[2] The manuscript is written in the usual sixteenth-century "secretary" hand except that important words, place names, etc. are picked out in what was then the new "italic" script.

[3] Included in the text is a reference to "this yeare 1549." Of course the present manuscript may only be a copy, preserving the date of the original, but on palaeographical grounds this date suits the style of the handwriting.

[4] A MS. note states that the table was "calculated by JOHN SOMUR, Ann° 1364." According to *DNB* (LIII, 218), JOHN SOMER compiled the table in 1380; so in MS. Royal 2 B VIII (cf. WARNER and GILSON, *Cat. of Western MSS.* etc., London, 1921, I, 47). According to MS. Cotton Vespasian E VII, the table appears to have been compiled for 140 years from 1367; see the note in CHAUCER's *Treatise on the Astrolabe* (EETS, 1905, p. 73).

[5] For the best general discussions, see LYNN THORNDIKE, *A History of Magic and Experimental Science*, New York, 1929; HUTTON WEBSTER, *Rest Days*, New York, 1916; MAX FÖRSTER, "Die altenglischen Glücks- und Unglückstage" in *Studies in*

et nefasti" have formed part of European folklore certainly since the time of Hesiod's Ἡμέραι. In Roman times and in the earlier Middle Ages, the twenty-four "Dies Aegyptiaci" were believed to occur annually,[6] each month having two unlucky days; in the following centuries an incredible number[7] of varying lists of evil days made their appearance. The present manuscript reads as follows:

fy[n]ding this in an olde wrytten Booke / and as vntrue as olde, I it tooke Marking in eche Monethe Malignant dayes and in forme following thus it sayes /
The dayes in January daungerus and Mortall is the 1, the 2, the 4, the 5, the 7, the 15 and the 19, continualy as it acompteth /
In February is the 3, the 8, the 17, and the 18 /
In Marche the 6, the 15, and the 18 /
In Aprill the laste day /
In May the 8, the 15, the 16, and the 20 /
In June only the 8 day /
In July the 15 and the 19 /
In August the 19 and the 20 /
In September the 16 and the 18 /
In October the 6 day allwayes /
In Nouember the 15 and the 19 /
In December the 6, the 8, and the 15 /

Among the numerous lists of unlucky days which the present writer has come across, the closest to the present text appears to be that found in THOMAS MOULTON's *Myrrour or Glasse of Helthe*,[8] which lists the following: January 1, 2, 4, 5, 10, 15, 17, 19; February 8, 10, 17; March 15, 16, 19; April 16, 21; May 7, 15, 20; June 4, 7; July 15,

---

*English Philology, a Miscellany in Honor of Professor Frederick Klaeber*, Minneapolis, 1929, pp. 258–77.

[6] Compare BEDE, MIGNE XC, 960, and the eleventh-century English version from MS. Vitellius E XVIII printed by FÖRSTER, *op. cit.* BARTHOLOMAEUS ANGLICUS (Westminster, 1495, IX, 21) states: "And for there ben .xxiiij. Egypcyans dayes . . . The dayes Egyptiaci ben sett in the Kalender of holy chyrche & ben callyd Dies mali, euyll dayes."

[7] To quote two fifteenth-century examples, the Vienna MS. (Cod. 5327, f. 161[b]) states: "Nota quod in quolibet anno sunt dies 30 pericolosi." SYDRACH, *La fontaine de toutes sciences*, Paris, 1486, cap. 907, lists 35 unlucky days, viz.: Jan. 1, 2, 4, 6, 11, 15, 16, 19; Feb. 15, 16, 19; Mar. 4, 15, 16, 17, 18; Apr. 11, 17; May 15, 16, 18; June 16; July 15, 19; Aug. 14, 20; Sept. 16, 19; Oct. 16; Nov. 15, 17; Dec. 6, 7, 8, 17.

[8] London, WYER, ca. 1540, sig. d₈ (*STC* 18217; copy PML 6455). Another edition, perhaps a year later, was printed by WYER (*STC* 18218; copy NYAcMed). I have seen two other editions, one printed by ELYSABETH REDMAN (*STC* 18219; copy Huntington) and the other by W. MYDDELTON (*STC* 18220; copy PML 6456). These two have March 17 instead of 16 and add December 3 to the list.

20; August 19, 20; September 6, 7; October 6; November 15, 19; December 6, 7, 9, with the added note "Et alii dicunt xv, xvi." A substantially similar list is found in *Batman vppon Bartholome*,[9] who omits December 15 and 16 as evil days but adds the warning "take heede of the 15, 17, 22" of the same month. LEONARD DIGGES, in his *Prognostication*,[10] also omits December 15 and 16 but here January 29 appears instead of the nineteenth, possibly the result of a misprint. Curiously enough, lists of unlucky days similar to the above continued to appear in print for well over two hundred years, some of them being published in America. I have seen two editions of the *Erra Pater*[11] printed respectively at Worcester, Mass. (ca. 1796)[12] and at Suffield, Conn. (1799),[13] where the following list appears: Jan. 1, 2, 4, 5, 10, 15, 17, 19; Feb. 8, 10, 19; Mar. 15, 16, 21; Apr. 15, 21; May 15, 17, 20; June 4, 17; July 15, 20; Aug. 20, 25; Sept. 6, 7; Oct. 6; Nov. 5, 19; Dec. 6, 7, 11, or 15, 19.

The writer of the Morgan manuscript expressed, at the head of his list, a certain doubt as to its value. In the sixteenth century,[14] it will be recalled, opposition to astrology and prognostications in general became more and more pronounced. A typical instance is the opinion expressed by WILLIAM FULKE (apparently a contemporary of the writer of the Morgan manuscript) in his *Antiprognosticon*:[15]

Good dayes to bye and selle, bee market dayes, and all other whensoever a manne canne gette a good bargayne with honestie. I thynke but fewe marchantes wyll leese their mart in waightyng for heavenly healpe frome the starres.

On the other hand, almanacks and prognostications continued to be printed throughout the sixteenth and seventeenth centuries;[16] judg-

[9] London, T. EAST, 1582, f. 147[b] (*STC* 1538).

[10] *A Prognostication of right good effect*, London, THOMAS GEMINI, 1555 (Old Ashmolean Reprints, No. III, London, n.d., pp. 42–4).

[11] See G. L. KITTREDGE, *The Old Farmer and his Almanack*, Boston, 1904.

[12] CHARLES EVANS, *American Bibliography*, Chicago, 1903–34, no. 30393; copy NYAcMed.

[13] EVANS, no. 35451; copy NYPL.

[14] WEBSTER (*op. cit.*, p. 301) states: "After the Reformation the old unlucky days appear to have abated much of their malevolence, and to have left behind them only a general superstition against fishermen starting out to fish, or seamen to take a voyage, or landsmen a journey, or domestic servants to enter a new place—on a Friday." The *Erra Pater* seems to contradict this.

[15] Quoted by S. V. LARKEY, "Astrology and politics in the first years of Elizabeth's reign," *Bulletin of the History of Medicine*, III, 184.

[16] See E. F. BOSANQUET, *English Printed Almanacks and Prognostications*, Bib-

ing from the number of editions produced, these must have found a ready market. The mere fact that our author found it worth while to write out the list of unlucky days despite his expressed doubts seems to indicate that he was not quite as certain of the untruthfulness of his original as he would have us believe.

## II

Directly below the list of unlucky days, the scribe has added the following note on the three most perilous days of all:

> And of theis said daungerus dayes the worste ben the last Munday of Aprill, the first Munday of August and the last Munday of September. And the Reuolucion of howses in theis dayes sheweth a suddayne Ruyne of them in theis dayes begune.[17]

A very similar passage is found on the title-page of MOULTON's *Myrrour*:[18]

> These ben the .iii. peryllous Mondayes in the yere to let blod or to take any medycyn or purgacion on, that is for to sayne, The fyrste Mondaye of August and y^e seconde is y^e last Monday of Apryll. And the thyrde is the last Mondaye of Decembre.

While it is quite possible that the scribe accidentally wrote September instead of December, it may also be true that he, by mistake, confused the last evil Monday with one found in another list. MAX FÖRSTER[19] printed such a list of three perilous days from a fifteenth-century manuscript (Ashmole MS. 342, f. 136^b), reading:

> These ben .III. perlous monedayes in þe ȝere: on ys þe fyrst monday of Feuerere; and oþer is þe last monday of May; *and* þe þryde ys þe last monday of Septembre.

---

liographical Society, 1917, and his papers in the Society's *Transactions* (*Library*), 1928, 456–77 and 1930, 361–97; CARROLL CAMDEN, "Elizabethan Almanacs and Prognostications," *Library*, 1931, 83–108 and 194–207; F. P. WILSON, "Some English Mock-Prognostications," *Library*, 1938, 6–43. Compare also LOUIS B. WRIGHT, *Middle-Class Culture in Elizabethan England*, Chapel Hill, 1935.

[17] The sense seems obscure here; see note 63. I believe the writer is trying to say: "things undertaken in these days will end badly."

[18] Compare the early English and Latin texts printed by FÖRSTER, *op. cit.* The version printed by COCKAYNE, *Anglo-Saxon Leechdoms*, etc., Rolls Series 1866, III, 76, lists the last Monday in April, the first in August and the first in January.

[19] *Op. cit.*, p. 276. MOULTON (d₃ verso) also names these three Mondays with the warning "that yf any man or woman ete of any gose flesshe on any of these .iii. dayes, they shall haue the fallynge euyll, & no bodely werke shall come to good ende that is begon in any of these .iii. dayes."

It is not inconceivable that both lists were found in the manuscript from which the scribe made his copy and that his eye slipped by accident from one to the other while he was copying out the list.[20]

## III

At the foot of the same page containing the lists of unlucky days, the writer has added a thunder-book[21] based on the month in which thunder is heard. This was a very popular form of prognostication in the Middle Ages and the exact source is not easy to ascertain. Perhaps the greatest similarity to this version is displayed by the Latin text found in the *Compilatio de astrorum scientia* by LEU-POLDUS:[22]

Januarij tonitrua ventos validos & abundantiam frugum significant. Februarij mortem multorum hominum et maxime diuitum pronunciat. Marcij ventos validos: & abundantiam frugum: et lites in populo. Aprilis bonum & iocundum annum. Maius famem signat. Junius frugum copiam & maxime annone: & malas infirmitates. Julius anno illo annonam bonam: sed fructus pomorum peribit. Augustus rei publice prosperitatem: sed multum homines egrotabunt. September abund[a]ntiam frugum: & occisiones potentum. October ventum validum affert & annone & fructus arborum inopiam. Nouember abundantiam frumenti et iocunditatem anno illo. December annone abundantiam: pacem in populo & concordiam.

LEUPOLDUS' text is closely like the early English thunder-book included in MS. Vespasian D XIV, f. 103[b], of the early twelfth century,[23] which is in turn paralleled by the Middle English version (ca. 1440) in the Thornton manuscript[24] and that published in GOD-FRIDUS' *The Boke of Knowledge*, ca. 1530.[25] The Morgan text reads:[26]

---

[20] MOULTON, *ibid.*, notes two further series of unlucky days. One lists August 1, December 31 and the VIII Kal. of April (March 25); the other notes the "Canyculers dayes" (see BEDE, *De minutione sanguinis*, Migne XC, 959–62).

[21] For notes on "thunder-books," see my paper "Astrological Prognostications in MS. 775 of the Pierpont Morgan Library," *supra*, and the works referred to there.

[22] Augsburg, RATDOLT, 1489, sig. f8 verso. I am deeply obliged to the authorities of the Walters Art Gallery in Baltimore for permitting the Walters' copy to be brought to New York for my use. A similar prognostication may be found in ESCHUID, *Summa astrologiae judicialis*, Venice, 1489, f. 146. Though based on LEUPOLDUS, this text varies in detail.

[23] Printed in EETS, OS 152, p. 91.

[24] Printed in EETS, OS 26 (revised ed. 1913), p. 114.

[25] London, R. WYER, ca. 1530, sig. D3 (*STC* 11931; copy Huntington).

[26] A marginal note reads: Theis thunders ar to be deamed more extreme then usuall and mor [? common] then ben accustomed and so to be expounded.

If in January it thundereth it forshoweth plenty of Grayne and war that yeare

If it Thunder in february mutche it forshoweth deathe

If it thunder in Marche plenty of frute & grayne & stryfe amonge the peple

If it Thunder in Aprill it betokeneth a frutefull and Joyus yeare[27]

Yf it thunder in May it betokeneth the wante of Corne and all-so warre

If it thunder in June plentie of Corne and sycknesse of people

If it thunder in July want of corne & death of Cattell[28]

If in August maladies many & stryfe

If in September plentie of Corne & death of noble men

If in October Corne plentie & littell frute

If in Nouember plentie of corne & frute

If in December plenty and peace

Oddly enough, in several cases, the different thunder-books foretell completely divergent events, one prophesying want of food and hunger where the other predicts plenty. The present writer believes the explanation for this to be both simple and curious. As c's were frequently written with two strokes of the pen,[29] it would sometimes be difficult to tell whether the original word in a manuscript was "īopia" (contraction for "inopia") or "copia."[30] A choice of reading was thus offered the copyist or compositor, as the case may be, and differing prognostications may thus have come into being.

## IV

On folio 10[b] of the added leaves, following on the Latin astrological notes, tables, etc., we find a weather prognostication which reads:

> Sunday pryme fayre wether and drye
> Munday pryme moyste and no lye

[27] GODFRIDUS says: Thondre in Apryll, sygnyfyeth that same yeare to be fruytefull, and mery, and also deth of wycked men.

[28] The early English version reads: On Jvlius monðe, hit bodeð wæstme wel gewænde, & oref forfærð. In the Thornton MS., it reads: Thonour In Iuly, sygnyfyes, þat same ȝere, a gode ȝer; and grete synner schalle spytt. Godfridus has a curious note: Thondre in July, sygnyfyeth that same yeare shalbe good corne, & fruytes of Beastes, that is to saye, theyr strength shall perysshe. The only likely explanation that occurs to me is that GODFRIDUS, or his source, misread the "fructus pomorum," appearing in both LEUPOLDUS and ESCHUID, as "fructus pecorum."

[29] See S. A. TANNENBAUM, *The Handwriting of the Renaissance*, New York, 1930, p. 34, especially type 4 of *c*.

[30] GODFRIDUS, differing from the Morgan text, has: "Thondre in Octobre sygnyfyeth the same yeare, great wynde and scantnes of Cornes, and fruytes of trees." The opposite prophecy is in ESCHUID: "Octobris uentum ualidum & annonae & fructus copiam," while LEUPOLDUS reads "inopiam."

Tewesday pryme wynde and colde
Wednesday pryme moste strange said of Olde
Thursday pryme fayre and Cleare
Fryday pryme fowle & fayre that yeare
Saturday prime geven to Rayne
W*h*ich may be true as all-so vayne

The only unusual feature about this prognostication is that it is rhymed; a similar one, without the note of incredulity expressed in the last line and written in prose, occurs in MS. 775 of the Pierpont Morgan Library.[31] Since the author[32] noted on the same page that he had made his extracts on magical numbers from the "Book of Knowledge," it is not unlikely that this work also served as the direct source for this prophecy. GODFRIDUS writes:[33]

Sondaye Pryme drye wether
Mondaye Pryme moyst wether
Tuesdaye Pryme colde and wynde
Wednesdaye Pryme meruaylous
Thursdaye Pryme fayre and clere
Frydaye Pryme fayre and fowle
Saturdaye Pryme Rayne

Nevertheless it must be noted in passing that almost identical prophecies are also found in BATMAN (*op. cit.*, f. 150) and in DIGGES (*op. cit.*, p. 7).

# V

The two remaining English items in the manuscript added to the Morgan copy of CAXTON's *Myrrour* are closely related. The first explains the order of the planets and the hour in which each one reigns;[34] the second tells of the influence each planet exerts on the children born in the hours of his rule.

[31] See my paper, *supra*, Chapter T7.
[32] On folio 10[b] is the note: "I finde the *Lettres* thus Numbered in a Printed Booke called the Book of Knowledge." These tables of magical numbers are not printed here; they may be consulted in GODFRIDUS, quires I and K.
[33] *Op. cit.*, sig. I₃.
[34] For further particulars, see W. GUNDEL, "Stundengötter," *Hessische Blätter für Volkskunde*, XII, 100–31; G. K. BAUER, *Sternkunde und Sterndeutung der Deutschen im 9.–14. Jahrhundert*, Berlin, 1937; PAULY-WISSOWA, VII, 2547 et seq., under Hebdomas; WEBSTER, *op. cit.*, pp. 217–8. This is the third time the table of "hour-gods" is explained in the Morgan MS., as the table of regnant planets is found on f. 4 and another (shorter) description occurs on f. 8 verso.

It is impossible to be quite certain what the immediate source for this passage is. As early as the second century, VETTIUS VALENS[35] had set forth his theory of the ἑπτάζωνος and a similar system of chronocratories may be found in DIO CASSIUS.[36] Every mediaeval astrological treatise, with hardly an exception, contains either a table or some such description as we find here. From among the works already cited, we find tables of regnant planets in LEUPOLDUS, ESCHUID, MOULTON, GODFRIDUS, *Erra Pater*, and CHAUCER's *Astrolabe*. The direct source may be such a manuscript as is described in *Almanac for the year 1386*,[37] since the writer of the Morgan MS. states elsewhere that he had obtained his information from "an olde wrytten Booke." This belief is further strengthened by the fact that the MS. *Almanac* also contains notes on the influence of the planets in words and phrases strongly reminiscent of the Morgan text. A number of such similar passages will be found in the footnotes, together with further parallels taken from other works. The text reads:[38]

It is to be thowght, if eny man be borne in eny howre[39] of the day in the whiche regneyth eny of the vij Planetes, he shalbe disposed to goode, or to evill, after thinfluence of that planet vnder the which he was borne; Neverthelesse there is none of them that bringeth eny Necessitie. But as how they shalbe bent & Inclyned this extracte maketh Demonstracion as folloeth.—

[35] *Astrologus*, ed. W. KROLL, Berlin, 1908, 144.14.
[36] *Historiae Romanae*, XXXVII. 18–19.
[37] *Almanac for the Year 1386, transcribed, verbatim, from the original antique illuminated Manuscript, in the Black Letter*, London, 1812. On the title-page appears the note: "The Manuscript to be disposed of.—Apply to the Printer." Whoever made the transcription had only a slight acquaintance with Middle English MSS. None of the abbreviations are expanded; there are numerous obvious misreadings; and occasionally blank spaces are left, apparently to indicate the presence of words which the transcriber failed to decipher. It is, however, quite possible to reconstruct the probable readings of the original. I have enclosed my own emendations in square brackets except that I have, without further indication, substituted the thorn for the "y" wherever necessary.
[38] Compare, also, the seventeenth-century rhymed version in Canterbury Cathedral MS. Y. 8. 3 [EETS, OS 48, pp. 114–6].
[39] "*Dominus* hore est planeta qui *est dominus* hore *cum* incipit res vel nat*us* est puer," LEUPOLDUS, sig. d₈. "It es to understande, þat if a man be born in any owre of þe day in whilk on of þe 7 planetys has d[omi]nacyon he sal be more styred and redyar by hys complexion eyther to gode or to ill after þe influens of þat planet in þe whilk he es borne. An[d] nev[er]-þe-lesse ther es none of þem 7 þat causys any necessyte or disposicyon bot þat a man by hys fre wylle and grace of Almyghty God goyng before and wirky[n]g in hym may do wele and leve ille, or be hys frewyll and concupyscence of his hert havyng lust and lykyng in syn may do ill," *Almanac*, p. 36.

## De ordine Planetarum.

In the order of planetes Luna is loweste, nexte is Mercurius, then Venus, then so foll[o]ing Sol, after Mars, then insueth Iupiter, and lastly Saturnus, so ever going their curse in the howres of Dayes & Nightes, But in a day Naturall is contayned xxiiij^ti howres so hathe every of the vij planetes iij howres of the 24 howres in government as in Computacion to explycate their curse first as in exemple if this Day were saterday then Saturnus to haue the first howre, Jupiter the 2 howre, Mars the 3 howre, & Sol the 4^th howre, Venus the 5^th howre, Mercurius the 6 howre & Luna the 7 howre, then to recompt Saturnus agayne to the 8 howre, Jupiter the 9^th, Mars the 10^th, Sol the 11^th, Venus the 12, Mercurius the 13^th, Luna the 14, and so to Reuerte to saturnus agayne, to haue the 15^th, Jupiter the 16^th, Mars the 17^th, Sol the 18^th, Venus the 19^th, Mercurius the 20^th, and Luna the 21^th. And then Reiterat Saturnus to the 22^th, and Jupiter to the 23^th, and Mars to the 24^th. so is thartificiall day fynesed And Sol that folloeth shall haue the firste in the nexte day folloynge and is called Dies solis.[40] And what so of the said 7 Planetes Ryseth so orderly in curse that daye shall beare the name of the same planet possessing the said firste howre, as playnely to yow now hereby apereth.

## De Planetis qui Boni qui mali et qui mediocres[41]

The best in birthe by thinfluence of the planetes be those borne vnder Jupiter and Venus, the nexte vnder Sol, Mercurius and Luna, the worst vnder Mars and Saturnus.

## De Planeta Solis.

This planet Sol is the Eye of the worlde,[42] and fayrnese of the firmament, lighte gever to all other planetes and all thinges earthly on him take virtue as man also In the generacion of his semblante. And he that is Borne[43] vnder

[40] "Et cossi la prima hora del di sequente, cioe de la dominica, apertiene al Sole," REGIOMONTANUS, *Calendario*, Venice, 1476, f. 30^b.

[41] The Greeks divided the planets into benign (ἀγαθοποιοί)—Sun, Jupiter and Venus; malignant (κακοποιοί)—Saturn and Mars; and indifferent (κοινοί)—Moon and Mercury. Similarly SERVIUS on VERGIL, *Georgica* I, 335: "Sciendum autem (ut diximus) de planetis quinque, duos esse noxios. Martem et Saturnum; duos bonos, Jovem et Venerem; Mercurius vero talis est, qualis ille cui jungitur." "Jupiter unde Venus sint geluckehaft, Saturnus unde Mars ubil, aber die sunne unde der mane unde mercurius sint etwenne guot, etwenne ubil," *Meinauer Naturlehre* (ed. W. WACKERNAGEL), Stuttgart, 1851 (BLV 22), p. 3. So also MOULTON (b₂ verso) and *Almanac*, p. 37.

[42] "Oculus est enim mundi, jucunditas diei, coeli pulchritudo, naturae gratia, praestantia creaturae," AMBROSIUS, *Hexaemeron*, MIGNE XIV, 188; "þe Son es þe eye of all þe firmament; þe fairness of þe mone and all þe planetys; of whom þe day has hys beyng," *Almanac*, p. 38.

[43] "Under whos constellacyon, by dysposicyon, schal a man be benyng and buxo[m], meke, and anone receyve conyng and kepe it, of an excellent wyt, most duryng, in hys speky[n]g moderately and sad, by getyng micul gode and w[i]t[h] a mery chere þat he h[a]s getyn expend it w[i]t[h]owte any bost, mycul loved and wyse; bot nev[er]-þe-lesse he schal be luffi[n]g women ouer mycul, al oþer

Sol is Boxome, a man meke, fayre, of goode literature, of a noble wytte, and well spoken, of good gettyng, plentuus, and bountefull in spendinge with ffrancke harte, welbeloved and of a goode discrecion, and hath reason to his guyde, And is Venerius something. the signes of him in a man be theis. A cleare fface, well cowllered, large lyppes and red, with comlynesse in corpes.

### De Planeta Lunae.

Luna is a Planet that hath virtues deryved from the sonne, a sollas gever to way goers, a shower of Eville, and her Constellacion[44] geveth them borne vnder her to be travaylers and wanderers dyversly Journeying, and well can wache & muche Imagenyng in mynde, a rashe speker onlesse staied with muche experyence, In subiection to skicknesse (sic), lightly Bent to brabling, and his wrathe sonne past over, And no wastefull spender, But Rather disposede to be a getter of Riches, or at the leste a keper, and lothe to departe with that he once possesseth,[45] And vnstedfaste in manners & condicions,[46] not covetyng to contynewe longe in one place, the Tokens[47] in bodyes of her governement be theis, a Pale visage & whyte, a lyttell mowthe, an high nose, And sone to haue hoore heres And in his latter yeares covetous.

### De planeta Mercurii.

The Mercuristes[48] by Constellacion ar geven to learning & sciences,[49] wise, politike, Eloquent, Ambicius, singuler in all thinges, Delyver and Quyke of

---

thy[n]gys w[i]t[h] discrecyon doyng," *Almanac*, p. 38. GREGORIO DATI, *La Sfera*, Morgan MS. 721, p. 4b, writes:

> Coloro in cui lo sole ha sua potença
> Sicondo lor concepti o nascimenti
> Homini sono di grande intelligença
> Che danno lume a tucte laltre genti
> Di gran doctrina & di gran sapiença
> Et al bene operar non son mai lenti
> Feruenti sono & pieni di karitade
> Et ne quai regna somma ueritade

[44] "Und[e]r whos constellacyon and a man be born naturally sal be mycul waking, and in hymselfe passyn[g] mycul thynkyng, unwysely spekyng, for cold son be seke, a lytel cause take for a grete cause and lyghtly wrong forgyfing, not gladly w[i]t[h] his go[d]e departyng, gederyng togyder mycul siluer, not expending, not syttyng or restyng, w[i]t[h] hys wyll in his hart unstabul," *Almanac*, pp. 38-9.

[45] But compare Prince Hal's speech in *I Hen. IV*, I. ii. 35.

[46] PONTANUS (*De rebus coelestibus*, ALDUS, 1519, III, f. 156) points out the moon's inconstancies, adding the note: "uarietates hae in hominum actionibus euentisque contingunt."

[47] "þe token[s] of þe Mone in a man be þise: his face pale and su[m]-what whyte, a litel mouth and nose, sone waxis gray heyrd, and to worldly thyngys hav[i]ng grete mynd," *Almanac*.

[48] The first example of this form cited by *NED* is 1602.

[49] "Und[e]r whos constellacyon be born philosofyrs of all þe 7 scyences and men þat be p[er]fyte of warks of hand. M[er]curi ma[k]ys men born und[e]r hys constellacyon to be proude and fayer spekars, of gode wytte and reme[m]bera[n]c[e],

bodie, in agilitie passing others. Desierus of the knolege of straunge thing*es*
and to se straunge Regions, Apsicorus,[50] allwayes presuming muche of his
owen wytte, leaning to his owen devise and contemnyng others, muche getting
and ffrancly departing therw*i*th. The signes in bodys vnder this planet*es*
governement be theis. A cleare fface and a fayre, well coulored, greate lippes,
w*i*th tethe vn-even or vncumly, Blacke Eyen, a straighte Nose, and geven to
venerie.

### De Planeta Veneris.

Venus is a plesant planet and they vnder her Borne[51] shall muche delighte
in Musike and hermony and muche delighte in merthe, delicate p*e*rsones, and
esteminge muche try*m*me apparaile, Ornamente*s* and Jvelles, as also vayne
Glorius, their Anger lightly kindeled, and when in them it is begowne [*sic*]
it is sonne fforgotten, their wrathe wereth sonne Away, And trusting muche
other mens Jud[g]mente*s* more then to credite his owen in eny cawse, And
if he be of habilitie he shall distribute muche a-monge the Powre, And their
compassyon shalbe muche wheare substance exstendeth not to it, they shall
Rather pitie povertie to their helpe in that they can Rather then to supporte

---

movyng and lyghtly passyng into diverse contryes, þ*a*t he may every new thyng
lerne and specially thing þ*a*t ben neuer hard of byfore," *Almanac.* "Der sechst planet
ist zu lateyn geheyssen Mercurius das ist zu teutsch der kauffherr oder der kaufflewt
herre darumb das sey*n* kind die er macht in der muter leib wol gespräch sind wann
wol gesprächikeit gehört die kauffleut an," *Buch der Natur,* Augsburg, 1475, II,
6. G. M. Tolosani, *Compendio di Sphera,* Florence, ca. 1515, f. 4, writes:

> La sua uirtu sopra dell' huomo spande
> Et fa quel nel parlar tutto elegante
> Buon giudice & rectore & mercata*n*te.

[50] Written in italic, this word may come from some Latin source, though it is
not noted by Forcellini or Du Cange. Apparently of Greek origin, it is not in
*NED* though it may be related to "apsychical." The meaning is quite uncertain,
perhaps something like "unspiritual"?

[51] "The native will be of a quiet, even, and friendly disposition, naturally inclined to neatness, loving mirth and cheerfulness, and delighting in music; amorous,
and prone to venery, though truly virtuous if a woman; yet she will be given to
jealousy, even without cause," Ebenezer Sibly, *A new and complete Illustration
of the Celestial Science of Astrology,* London, 1784, p. 119. "Much addicted to sing-
ing and gaming, and spends his money in courting the female sex," *Erra Pater,*
p. 32. Dati, *op. cit.,* says:

> Poi seguita di venere el pianeta
> Lucente stella & parche sempre rida
> E suoi son tucti di natura lieta
> Leali & chiari adchi di loro si fida
> Vaghi se adornar doro & di seta
> Cortesi & larghi & nimici dimida
> Inclinati al luxuria & uan dilecto
> Se lascian la ragion dell' intellecto.

the substanciall persones, And they be very Oblivius, And perhumayne[52] in maners and very curtice in condicions, As also excedinge Luxurius et Fluxurus.

### De Planeta Martis.

The Marcialistes[53] ar Inclyned to be covetus and of Cruell disposition. And moste generalye kinges ar borne vnder this planet Mars And all warryours,[54] And ar Politike and quicke in Judgement and not lightly sedused, or begyled, And ar Ambycius muche contemnyng the Actes of other men & in exaltinge their owen, And this note generally is founde moste trwe, and certayne. Who that is Borne vnder Mars, he shalbe ether a Royall persone, in pryncely dignitie, or elles as Basse as the lowest in lyving, he holdeth those extremities. And allwayes Cruell and indevoreth hym to battell.[55] The tokens of A Marciall man in Boddie be theis. a Blake fface and a leane, a greate mowthe, a longe Nose somtyme Botteled,[56] And take this Rule for Righte certayne that who so hathe a hawke nose[57] naturally shalbe gylefull, full of fraude and discepte, therfore be hedefull & yow shall so fynde in them.

### De Planeta Jouis.

Jupiter is a worthy planet, for the Jovistes[58] be goode, plesunt and merry men[59] and godly and Relygeus & devoute, well lovinge and Belowed [sic],

---

[52] This word is not in NED; apparently it means something like "very benevolent."

[53] First example of "Martialist" in NED is 1569.

[54] "L'enfant qui est ne en ceste planet . . . sera grant homme et de gros entendement; il aymera moult les armes et les gens d'armes; il escheuera fort les gens de mestier large sera et donnant et fel et meslif et de chaulde nature," SYDRACH, cap. 929. "This planette, und[e]r whos constellacyon be born kynges þat be v[er]tyus men in batell . . . praysing and bostyng [v]aine dedys, and oþ[e]r mennys dedys despysyng," Almanac.

[55] REGIOMONTANUS, Kalender, Venice, 1476, sig. f₂, notes:

> Zu streit vnd vnseuberkeyt bin ich bereit
> Als auch allhie erzeygt mein kleydt
> Meine kind machen manigen hass
> Sy wissen nit wie warumb oder was.

[56] Protuberant or swollen (cf. NED "bottled," first ex. 1594). The description here given of the Martialist closely parallels that in the Almanac.

[57] "A hawks nose signifieth magnanimity and courage, cruelty, rapacity, and boldnesse, which thing commeth of heate. And therefore they that have this Hawks Nose, are commonly angry, full of revenge, and give themselves to unlawfull things," Book of . . . Arcandam (tr. W. WARDE), London, 1649, sig. L₂.

[58] Not in NED, which only notes "Jovialist."

[59] "Iouis uero sydus quando solum gubernationem animi nanciscitur in felici situ, efficit magnanimos, gratiosos, pios reuerentes, hilares, humanos, magnificos, liberos, iustos, misericordes, affabiles, etc.," Ptolemy, Quadripartitus, Louvain, 1548, sig. M₂. "Et significat animam vitam leticiam & religionem & veritatem patientiam & omne preceptum bonum pulcrum & preciosum & quicquid ad honestatem pertinet. Et significat abundantiam veneris," BONATUS, Decem tractatus astronomiae, Augsburg, 1491, sig. f₇ verso.

gentell and prudent, Naturally delyting in wemens Intisment*es* But their sage wisdome Refrayneth fancie to chastitie by that virtue in wisdome, and shalbe in estimac*i*on therby. And their tokens in bodie be theis. a cleare face, well cowlered, tethe vn-even, a longe nose boteled and Redde, and well ly*m*med.

## De Planeta Saturni.

They that be Saturnyne,[60] be covetus, sedicius, svbtile, slye & vaferus, tymerus and dissymelynge in sayinge one thinge and thinckynge an other, thowghtfull and hevie, Irus & wrathefull, drawen vehemently to[61] Reuenge, full of Impetuositie, Dulle in sence, and not of a per*fi*te Rememberance to Retayne, his tokens be theise. pale in hve, and leane.[62]

Hereby yow may preve the constellac*i*ons and the Influences of theise planet*es* in bodies, As in their coniunctions in thoppocitions so placed in the howses in figure sett showen[63] at the Natiuitie, mans Inclynac*i*on, & by theise Celestiall sygnes his dispocition, by their stac*i*ons and mocions in their Aspectes, man-asynge Evyll or enlargeing goodnesse, w*h*iche the Auctors as Guydo Bonatus[64] geven Judgement of, whiche moste generally and Naturally man so fframeth and fashyoneth him-selfe as in curse a Bias[65] is to the Bowle, so onlesse God his grace dothe contrepaies being therto excited dothe Refrayne suche af-feccions,[66] But Tholomeus sayth the wyse may governe and haue lordship over the sterres And w*i*thstand that they dyspose. Vt dicit*ur*. sapiens domina-bit*ur* astris.[67]

## Exodium.

## De stella Cometa.

When the Comete rv*n*nethe,[68] it is a starre in showe castinge owte flambes of lengthe somtyme, otherwise lyke to brighte Beames, And his apparance

---

[60] "Facit homi*n*es inflatos spiritu: sublatos honorib*us*: raro ridentes: ira*m*que diu seruantes: boni co*n*silij: & quorum fides recto semper iuditio comprobet*ur*: etc.," ANGELI, *Astrolabium*, Augsburg, 1488, sig. t$_1$. "L'enfant qui sera ne en ceste planette sera . . . couuoiteux et fel et courouceux mais son courroux passera trop legiere-me*n*t et sera couuert et aura fors reins et foible teste et sera paourreux de nuyt, etc.," SYDRACH, cap. 908.

[61] "be" is incorrectly interlineated in the MS.

[62] "Meine chind sein durr plaich vnd kalt," Vienna MS. 3085, f. 20.

[63] This seems to indicate that the writer had an imperfect knowledge of astrology, as the passage makes little sense.

[64] On GUIDO BONATUS (1230–1296), see Thorndike, *op. cit.*, II, 825–35, and my note in *Gutenberg-Jahrbuch*, 1937, p. 92.

[65] See *NED* Bias², first example 1570. This appears to support the belief that *bias* originally referred to the "oblique one-sided structure or shape of the bowl."

[66] See note 39 above.

[67] JACOB BURCKHARDT (*The Civilization of the Renaissance in Italy*, Vienna, Phai-don Press, n.d., p. 269 and note 1013) states that LODOVICO IL MORO had a cross made bearing this inscription. See also KITTREDGE, *op. cit.*, p. 50.

[68] "An steorra ys genemned *cometa*. þonne he ætywð, þonne getacnað he hungor oððe cwealm oððe gefeoht oððe tostencednyss þæs eardes oððe egeslice windas," *Byrhtferth's Manual*, EETS, OS 177, p. 132. Compare ISIDORE (MIGNE LXXXII, 180)

sheweth somme wofull calamities, as greate Penurie, warre, Pestilence, Distruccion of the Cuntrie, Alteracion[69] & sedicion of it or of their prynce and Ruler, Godes forshow of his Displeasure bent, onlesse of his benignitie by the Repentance taken dowth stay suche cawse and asswage suche grevus punyshementes from the peple by his greate mercie, to whome be all glorie in all his workes as it hath byn from the begynynge and shalbe evermore Amen.

### Finis.

The moone is the vj[th] parte of the Earthe,[70] And theighte parte of the sonne,—

This is as far as the writer got and the manuscript ends thus abruptly. It seems evident that the leaves were inserted by the scribe in order to make entries supplementing the text of CAXTON's *Myrrour of the World* and thus to prepare for his own use a handy encyclopaedia of such "scientific" knowledge as he possessed. The geographical tract, it is expected, will be printed in a future issue of this series.

(From *Isis* 33 (1942), pp. 609-20).

---

and BEDE (MIGNE XC, 243-4). A similar belief was expressed by LEONARD DIGGES, *op. cit.*, p. 5: "Cometes signifie corruption of the ayre. They ar signes of earthquakes, of warres, chaunging of kyngdomes, great derth of corne, yea a comon death of man, and beast." In his "Bericht von dem Cometen des Jahres 1607" (*Die Astrologie des Johannes Kepler*, München, 1926, pp. 84-9), the great astronomer states (p. 86): "Dies halt ich also die Ursach zu sein, warum Cometen Kriege, Pestilenz, Teuerung, Erdbeben, Trockenheit, oder dagegen grosses Gewässer gemeiniglich miteinander kommen, und eins das ander zu bedeuten habe." In MS. Royal 12 B XV, there is a contemporary *De cometis commentaria* by one JOHN ROBYNS. For Elizabethan beliefs, compare CAMDEN, *op. cit.*, pp. 201-7: and for the earliest American ones, see INCREASE MATHER, *Kometographia or a Discourse Concerning Comets*, Boston, 1683.

[69] Read "altercacion"?
[70] A marginal note reads "Dubito."

# CHAPTER L3

## A SOUTH GERMAN "SAMMELBAND"
## OF THE FIFTEENTH CENTURY

NEARLY a decade ago, the present writer began to collect manuscript items of interest found in early printed books and proposed printing these from time to time under the heading which forms the sub-title of this paper.[1] It seemed likely that such search among early printed books for manuscript notes and texts would prove to be a fruitful field of investigation—and such, indeed, it has proved to be. Although two papers in this series have already appeared, it has been found difficult to place the results of several of these studies in learned journals, largely (I expect) because these discoveries rarely presented a homogeneous unit corresponding to the interests of the various editors. The bibliographical quarterlies (rightly or wrongly) consider these manuscript studies to be solely of literary consequence. The literary journals, on the other hand, find that these investigations have little unified interest; the manuscript items in such books are often written in more than one language (Latin and the language of the country where the "Sammelband" was gathered together), the texts in one volume may cover a wide range of topics (science, classics, geography, sermons, popular verse, theological studies, etc.), and the items can belong to the literatures of many ages. The study of the book *per se*—be it all manuscript, all printed work or part of each—has not, it seems, been considered a proper subject for special research by American scholars, although on the Continent (notably through the patient and meritorious efforts of Hauréau, Lehmann, Collijn and others) it has achieved its rightful and respected place. In the libraries themselves, these books present problems, for such volumes (in which the chief item is apt to be an incunabulum) are generally not placed with the manuscripts and, if the book is shelved among the early printed books, the manuscript insertions are often lost sight of. These texts do not appear in the catalogues of manuscripts, and the incunabula lists have no room for descriptions of the often valuable, scribal additions. The obvious result is that such manuscript texts remain undescribed

[1] As no. 3 of *Libri impressi*.

and inaccessible to scholars who might otherwise find them of considerable interest and importance. It is to be hoped that this journal may supply a means for bringing to the attention of a wider circle the possibilities inherent in this form of research as well as the presence of texts that might otherwise be hidden away in some unsuspected quarter.

The volume we are about to consider (Pierpont Morgan Library, accession number 35456) includes four printed works and seven manuscript texts. The incunabula are all bound together in the first part of the volume and represent the following editions:

1. Petrarca, Francesco. *De remediis utriusque fortunae.*
   Printed at Esslingen by Conrad Fyner about 1475.
   References: Hain[2] 12790; Morgan Check List[3] 468 +.

2. Albertanus Causidicus Brixiensis. *De arte loquendi et tacendi.*
   Printed at Strassburg by an anonymous press (called The Printer of Henricus Ariminensis) about 1476.
   Ref.: Gesamtkatalog[4] 532; Morgan Check List 98 +.

3. Turrecremata, Joannes de. *Meditationes.*
   Printed in Cologne, probably by Johannes Solidi, about 1474.
   Ref.: Hain 15721; Morgan Check List 228 +.

4. Henricus de Hassia. *Expositiones super Ave Maria, etc.*
   Printed in Basel by Michael Wenssler, not after 1474.
   Ref.: Hain 8395 & 2107; Morgan Check List 1362 +.

Thereafter follow the manuscript additions, written in several hands:

5. Cicero, Marcus Tullius. *De amicitia*, with notes.
   Begins: Quintus Mucius Augur Sceuola multa narrare de gaio lelio socero suo memoriter . . .
   ff. 1–19[v]. Dated: 1467.
   *Census*[5] lists 17 MSS of this text in America.

6. Seneca, Lucius Annaeus. *De beneficiis* [extracts].
   Begins: Inter multos et varios errores temere et inconsulte viuencium . . .
   ff. 20–24[v]. XV cent., third quarter.
   *Census* lists only Garrett 114 and Michigan 163.
   [Note: these two tracts are written, by different hands, on two quires of paper: a–b[12]].

[2] Ludwig Hain, *Repertorium bibliographicum* (Stuttgart, 1826–38).
[3] Ada Thurston and Curt F. Bühler, *Check List of Fifteenth Century Printing in the Pierpont Morgan Library* (New York, 1939).
[4] *Gesamtkatalog der Wiegendrucke* (Leipzig, 1925–38).
[5] Seymour de Ricci, *Census of Medieval and Renaissance Manuscripts in the United States and Canada* (New York, 1935–40).

7. Cicero, Marcus Tullius [Pseudo]. *Rhetorica ad C. Herennium.*
   Begins: Etsi negocijs familiaribus impediti, vix satis ocium studio
   suppeditare possimus . . .
   ff. 25–67ᵛ. XV cent., third quarter.
   *Census* lists 9 manuscripts.

8. *Carmen de littera Y.*
   Title: Publij uirgilij maronis carmen de y litera pitagore.
   Begins: Litera bitagore (*sic*) discrimine secta bicorni, Humane vite
   speciem preferre videtur . . .
   Printed: Alexander Riese, *Anthologia Latina*, Leipzig, 1869–70, II,
   no. 632.
   f. 68. XV cent., third quarter.
   *Census* lists only Garrett 110 and Wagstaff 21.

9. *Hexasticha (12) de Cicerone post mortem illius.*
   Title: Versus duodecim sapientum positi in epidafio (*sic*) tulij.
   Begins: Hic jacet arpinas manibus tumulatus amici, Qui fuit orator
   summus et eximius . . .
   Printed: Riese, *Anth. Lat.*, nos. 603–614.
   ff. 68ʳ⁻ᵛ. XV cent., third quarter.
   [Note: the writers are named as follows—Baxilius, Vinennius, Hyo-
   manus, Euforbius, Julianus, Hylasius, Palladius, Asclemas, Eusenius,
   Pompelianus, Maximinus, and Vitalis.]
   *Census* lists only Library of Congress 35.

10. *De officijs et dignitatibus urbis Romae.*
    Begins: Reges primo fuerunt in urbe . . .
    Contents: notes on the Roman kings, senators, consuls, etc.
    f. 69 (verso is blank).
    *Census*: compare Chicago University 471.
    [Note: items 7–10 are written by several hands on four paper quires:
    c–e¹² f¹⁰⁻¹].

11. Aristoteles. *Physica* (anonymous Latin trans., with notes).
    Begins: Quoniam quidem scire et intelligere continuegit (*sic*) circa
    omnes sciencias . . .
    ff. 71–144. Incomplete; ends in Lib. VIII, cap. 58.
    *Census* lists 6 MSS of text and 9 of commentaries.
    [Note: written on six quires, viz. g¹² h¹⁴⁻¹ i¹⁰⁻⁵ (paper) and k¹⁶ l¹⁴
    m¹⁸⁻¹ (paper, with outside sheet of each quire of vellum). ff. 144ᵛ–
    146 are blank; f. 70 is blank save for some scribblings.]

The binding[6] is an interesting example of contemporary South
German work, consisting of stamped brown leather over boards.

---

[6] On the front cover is the fifteenth-century label: Franciscus petrarcha de Re-
medio vtriusque fortune Et alia quamplura valde vtilia. During the restoration of
the binding in 1940, another label of about the same date was found under the
cover, reading: Tractatus Alb. mag de doctrina dicendi et docendi. This title re-

Included among the stamps is a scroll bearing the word "Pancracius," probably the name of the binder; other stamps include a ram's head on a shield (perhaps the arms of some unidentified abbey), a stork and a bird upon a twig. The palmette stamp at the point where the bands at the back come into the sides is characteristic of work done around Augsburg; this is partially confirmed by the manuscript inscription "S. Magni in Fuessen" indicating that the volume was at one time in the Benedictine abbey of St. Magnus in Füssen, diocese of Augsburg.[7]

The volume as a whole is of value as illustrating what works were of interest to a South German monastery in the last years of the Middle Ages. The pages and the binding both attest the fact that the volume, though much read, was carefully handled as a treasured possession. Usually it is the rather uninspired theological texts, which the monasteries bought to fill their shelves or which may have been considered proper for their libraries to have, that have come down to us in immaculate (and apparently unread) condition. In this instance, it is clearly respect for the written and printed word that accounts for the unusual state of preservation of this volume.

The printed section of the present volume includes, among somewhat dull theological and didactic works, the first edition of Petrarch's *Phisicke against fortune*, as it is entitled in the first English edition of 1579.[8] It seems singularly curious that the *editio princeps* of this work should have been produced in a comparatively small and obscure Württemberg town some seventeen years before the Italians themselves took an edition in hand.[9] The manuscripts, on the other hand, are without exception of classical nature—and some, indeed, are of rather uncommon occurrence. The inference to be drawn from the texts in this "Sammelband" is that in at least some

---

appears in the partial and contemporary manuscript list of contents on the first fly-leaf and appears to refer to the second tract of the volume.

[7] See L. H. Cottineau, *Répertoire topo-bibliographique des abbayes et prieurés* (Mâcon, 1935–8), p. 1235.

[8] Printed in London from the translation of T. Twyne by R. Watkyns (Pollard and Redgrave, *A Short-Title Catalogue of Books Printed in England, Scotland & Ireland* etc., [London, 1926] no. 19809).

[9] Edited by Nicolaus Lucarus and printed at Cremona by Bernardinus de Misintis and Caesar Parmensis, 17 November 1492. Cf. Mary Fowler, *Catalogue of the Petrarch Collection Bequeathed by Willard Fiske* [to Cornell University], (Oxford, 1916), p. 13.

monasteries of South Germany towards the close of the fifteenth century, an affection and respect for the works of classical antiquity were part of the monastic tradition, though the frequent slips and grammatical errors do not speak highly for the Latinity of the scribes.

(From *Medievalia et humanistica* 4 (1946), pp. 107-10).

# CHAPTER L4

## A RHENISH 'SAMMELBAND' OF THE FIFTEENTH CENTURY

UNDER the title 'A South German "Sammelband" of the Fifteenth Century'[1] the present writer recently published an analysis of a composite volume of early printed books and manuscript texts in the Pierpont Morgan Library. Another volume of the same sort also found in the Morgan Library (PML 22222) presents a similar problem for investigation; the results of such study seem sufficiently important to justify the publication of the pertinent details. Only one other manuscript of but one of the eleven manuscript texts found in the volume is listed as being in America, thus indicating that these works are not of common occurrence. Neither the incipits nor the titles are noted in the standard works of reference,[2] though the literary contents of the volume are varied in scope and interest.

The two printed works, bound before the manuscript section, represent copies of the following editions:

1. *Defensorium fidei dialogos septem contra Iudaeos, haereticos et Sarracenos continens.* [Utrecht: Nicolaus Ketelaer and Gerardus Leempt, 1473].
   Also contains: Johannes de Turrecremata, *De salute animae*, and Cassiodorus, *Historia ecclesiastica tripartita* (Lib. V, cap. XVII–XVIII).
   References: Gesamtkatalog 8246;[3] Morgan Check List 1627.[4]

[1] *Supra*, Number 3 in the series *Libri impressi*.

[2] Marco Vattasso, *Initia Patrum* (Rome 1906–8); A. G. Little, *Initia Operum Latinorum quae Saeculis xiii. xiv. xv. attribuuntur* (Manchester 1904); Warner and Gilson, *Catalogue of Western Manuscripts in the Old Royal and King's Collections* (London 1921) III, 286–366; Seymour de Ricci, *Census of Medieval and Renaissance Manuscripts in the United States and Canada* (New York 1935–40) III, 155–160; Lynn Thorndike, *A Catalogue of Incipits of Mediaeval Scientific Writings in Latin* (Cambridge, Mass. 1937) with supplements in *Speculum* (vols. XIV and XVII). The texts reproduced in full below are not printed by Barthélemy Hauréau, *Notices et extraits de quelques manuscrits latins de la Bibliothèque Nationale* (Paris 1890–3) vols. I–VI, nor are they to be found in the 41 volumes of the *Notices et extraits des manuscrits de la Bibliothèque Nationale et autres bibliothèques* (Paris 1787–1923).

[3] *Gesamtkatalog der Wiegendrucke* (Leipzig 1925–38) vols. I–VII.

[4] Ada Thurston and Curt F. Bühler, *Check List of Fifteenth Century Printing in the Pierpont Morgan Library* (New York 1939).

2. *De communione et conversatione Iudaeorum et Christianorum.* [Strassburg: Printer of Henricus Ariminensis, not after 1476].
References: Gesamtkatalog 7259; Morgan Check List 100.

The manuscript texts appended to the printed works are contained in 48 leaves of paper and were written by four different hands on four different sorts of paper. Written in the second half of the fifteenth century, they are:

3. Carolus IV. *Bulla aurea.*
Heading: 'Incipit Aurea bulla de electione Romanorum.'
Begins: 'In nomine sancte et indiuidue Trinitatis feliciter Amen Karolus quartus diuina fauente clemencia Romanorum Imperator semper Augustus et Romanorum Rex . . .'
Signatures: a–b$^{12}$ c$^2$ (folios 1–26).
Paper: similar to Briquet[5] 15101 'Tête de boeuf à yeux et à narines surmontée d'un trait étoilé.' Probably manufactured in Lorraine.

The only other manuscript of the 'Golden Bull'[6] in this country is at Harvard (MS *Lat.* 121).[7] Although several editions of this work were printed before the year 1501,[8] the present manuscript seems to be earlier in date than any of the printed ones now known and is thus probably not a copy of such a book.

4. *Herbarius cum rationibus conficiendi medicamenta.*
Begins: 'Herba sigillum sancte marie Quecumque persona creuata usum habuit comedendi radicem huius herbe cum ouis per dies 30 liberabitur . . .'
Signatures: d$^{10-4}$ (folios 27–32).
Paper: very like Briquet 14446 'Tête de boeuf à yeux'. Probably made at or near Venice.

This *Herbarius* is one of extraordinary interest and the present manuscript appears to be the only one of this text in America. Though

---

[5] Charles M. Briquet, *Les filigranes* (Paris 1907) vols. I–IV.
[6] This work sets forth the regulations for the election of the Emperor, promulgated at the Diet of Nuremberg in January, 1356. The standard work on the subject is by K. Zeumer, *Die goldene Bulle Kaiser Karls IV* (Wien 1908); for other works, see Louis J. Paetow, *A Guide to the Study of Medieval History* (New York 1931) 319, and Dahlmann-Waitz, *Quellenkunde der deutschen Geschichte* (Leipzig 1931–2) I, 524.
[7] De Ricci, *op. cit.* I, 984. A manuscript of the German translation is found in the Philadelphia Free Library, Lewis MS 191 (de Ricci II, 2060).
[8] Apparently three editions were printed in the fifteenth century (Ludwig Hain, *Repertorium Bibliographicum*, Stuttgart 1826–38, nos. 4074–6). In chronological order the editions appeared thus: Nuremberg, Creussner, 1474; Nuremberg, Koberger, 24 May 1477; and Cologne, Cornelis de Zierikzee, about 1500.

written by a North European (? Rhenish)[9] scribe, the herbal is certainly of Italian origin. As the text is both unusual and important, a more detailed description seems warranted.

The text contains 72 herbs, of which at least 50 (and possibly all of them) bear either the same or very similar names[10] to those found in a manuscript in Pavia, Bibl. Un. 130 E. 31 (211), according to the list given by Giacosa.[11] The only printed extract available from the Pavia MS corresponds closely to the Morgan text:

> Herba lucea et de novem una et habet folia media virida et media alba
> (Giacosa, p. 448)
> Herba lucea Et est de ix vna & facit folia media virida & media alba[12]
> (Morgan, f. 31ᵛ)

Giacosa (p. 473) also points out that an Italian version of this text is preserved in a manuscript at Padua, Bibl. Un. MS N. 604. It thus seems rather more than likely that these three are manuscripts of the same text.

In his valuable *Mittelalterliche Pflanzenkunde* (München 1929), Hermann Fischer has singled out three manuscripts for special mention in the section devoted to Italy (pp. 60–61); these are: Vicenza, Biblioteca Bertoliana (Codex 224-2, 9, 9) and Venice, Biblioteca Nazionale Marciana (*It.* 2. 12 and *It.* 3. 11).[13] The first of these is in Latin and the two Venetian manuscripts are in Italian. The few extracts cited by Fischer establish the connection between these manuscripts and the Morgan herbal:

> Herba tiles—reperitur in saltorona et in aliis alpibus (Vicenza)
> Herba tilles—in terrenos alpestros id est in falthorana[14] & in alijs locis satis
> (Morgan 27ᵛ)

[9] The Vicenza manuscript according to Fischer (*vide infra*) was also written by a German.

[10] Unusual herbs common to both manuscripts (minor orthographical variants being disregarded) include: lunaria grecha, liminellas, illocharias, illoloris, metries, arthethica montana, etc. For the mandrake (here 'Herba lucea dicta madragola'), the author adds the usual note of warning: 'sta ad longum quod tu non audias stridorem suum quando exijt de terra. si tu audisses stridorem suum tu morieris.'

[11] Piero Giacosa, *Magistri Salernitani nondum editi* (Torino 1901) 447–452.

[12] The Morgan text continues: 'Et quecumque persona habet malos oculos Accipe folia de ista herba et facias aquam ad lambicum & pone in oculos statim liberat Et est probatum.'

[13] Fischer also notes a fragment in Munich, Staatsbibliothek, *Cod. it.* 149.

[14] This seems to be a mention of Monte Falterona, the highest point (5425 ft.) in the Casentino and at no great distance from Florence.

Herba fologas—nasce questa erbe in montagne maxime nella macchia nelle montagne di fabriano[15] (*It.* 2. 12)

Herba folegas—in marcham de anthonam in monte fabriani (Morgan 27ᵛ)

Herba canallaria—nasce nelle montagne di cicilia (*It.* 2. 12)

Herba chanalarthas—in montibus de zecilia in locis asperissimis (Morgan 29ʳ)

For 'herba antolla minor' Fischer notes 'dass es auf mageren Boden wachse, in der Nähe von Kastanienbäumen;' the Morgan manuscript states that the herb 'Ad tolam minore' is found 'in terrenis nigris ubi sunt castagari (*sic*).'

The Mediterranean origin[16] of the original text is made evident by the geographical references. Italy, Sicily and Greece are each cited as the home of two of the herbs, while one herb is assigned to Spain. That the herbal in its final form was compiled in Italy is not only indicated by the specific Italian localities already mentioned[17] but also by the vocabulary of the Morgan herbal. For example, we are informed that the herbs are found 'in montibus scuris (scurissimis) or salvadicis' and 'in locis erboxis (sabientis, discopertis)'; as far as I can judge, these words seem to be Latin neologisms[18] from Italian *scuro, salvatico, erboso* (Venetian *erboxo*), *sabbia* (Latin *sabula* > *sabla*) and *discoperta*. The inference seems to be, as Fischer has already pointed out, that such Latin texts as the Morgan manuscript presents, are a translation of a fourteenth-century herbal originally written in Italian. An edition of this herbal, preferably from one of the illustrated manuscripts, would be most desirable not only from the botanical point of view but also for the lexicographer, since many of the herbs obviously retain their local or familiar names.*

[15] Apparently a reference to Fabriano, a town noted for its paper mills and for the manufacture of playing cards. It is located in the Marches, province of Ancona, and is surrounded by the foothills of the Central Apennines.

[16] Twenty-nine of the herbs are to be found in mountainous country, according to this herbal.

[17] The only authority cited (under *Herba conflexurias*) is 'Magister Thadeus de florentia doctor in arte medicina.' This is clearly Taddeo Alderotti (c. 1223–1303), one of the most successful doctors of his day. See George Sarton, *Introduction to the History of Science*, (Carnegie Institution of Washington Publication no. 376, Baltimore 1927–31) II, 1086–7; Arturo Castiglioni, *A History of Medicine* (New York 1941) 333–5; Karl Sudhoff, *Kurzes Handbuch der Geschichte der Medizin* (Berlin 1922) 195; etc.

[18] Already cited are *alpestros* (Italian *alpestre*) and *lambicum* (Italian *lambico* from Arabic *ambiq*). We may also note the use of *o* (for *aut*), *brodio* ('broth'), etc.

* See following article.

5. Rodericus Zamorensis. *Epistola de expugnatione Euboeae.*

Heading: 'Incipit epistola lugubris et mesta: simul et consolatoria de infelice expugnacione ac misera irruptione et invasione Insule Euboye dicte Nigropontis a perfido crucis Christi hoste Turcorum impijssimo principe & tyranno nuper inflicta: Ad Reuerendissimum patrem ac sapientissimum dominum Dominum Bessarionem sacrosancte Romane ecclesie Cardinalem Sabinum & patriarcham Constantinopolitanum. edita a roderico Santij Episcopo Palentino Hyspano. pro sanctitate domini nostri Pauli secundi pontificis maximi in castro suo sancti Angeli de urbe Castellano.'

Begins [greeting from Sancius to Bessarion, followed by a quotation from Habacuc 3.16]: 'Audiui & conturbatus est venter meus . . .'

Signatures: $e^{12}$ (folios 33–44, last two blank).

Paper: belongs to the group Briquet 8588–8653 'Lettre P gothique à fleuron à quatre feuille'. These papers were all apparently made in Alsace-Lorraine.

As the letter concerns the capture of Euboea (Negroponte)[19] by Mahomet II in 1470, this manuscript must be dated subsequent to this event. It is quite possible that the present text was copied from the edition printed by Ulrich Zell at Cologne, about 1475 (Voulliéme 1024).[20] No other manuscript of this work is recorded as being in the United States.

Items 6–14 are short texts contained in quire 'f⁴' (folios 45–48) and are written on paper with a watermark similar to (though smaller than) that of the previous number. The handwriting is of the late fifteenth century. Several of the texts are short and, as their incipits are not recorded, apparently quite unusual; they are accordingly printed in full.

6. *Moralia dogmata philosophorum.*

Begins: 'Autor. Juuenis in timore et parentum in amore[21] . . .'

Folios 45–46ᵛ.

Following a leonine quatrain by the Autor, the names of thirty-six philosophers, to each of whom a leonine couplet is ascribed, are listed. In addition to the sages usually found in such compilations

[19] A full account of the history and fall of Euboea may be found in J. B. Bury, 'The Lombards and Venetians in Euboia (1205–1470),' *Journal of Hellenic Studies* 7, 309–352; 8, 194–213; 9, 91–117.

[20] Ernst Voulliéme, *Der Buchdruck Kölns bis zum Ende des fünfzehnten Jahrhunderts* (Bonn 1903).

[21] Another manuscript of this text is contained in Paris, Bibl. Nat. *Nouv. acq. lat.* 431; cf. Léopold Delisle, *Manuscrits latins et français ajoutés aux fonds des nouvelles acquisitions pendant les années 1875–1891* (Paris 1891) II, 508. Two further manuscripts are at Sankt Gallen, Stiftsbibliothek, nos. 630 and 936.

(such as Plato, Aristotle, Seneca, Tullius, Socrates, etc.), the list includes these more unusual names: Sebastianus, Pausilius, Citaro, Minorius, Plantorius, Agellius and Aubtanus. The following couplet is characteristic of the text:[22]

### Virgilius
Mundo peior inimicus non est quam princeps iniquus
Sepe perdit sua bona gens stans sub parua persona

At the end is the note 'Expliciunt moralia dogmata philosophorum' and this title has been retained, though the present work has no connection with the better known *Moralium dogma philosophorum*.[23]

7. *Florilegium.*
Begins: 'Ambrosius. A circulo lune vsque ad centrum terre non est perfecta securitas . . .'
Folios 46ᵛ–47ᵛ.

The work consists of a number of commonplace extracts from Ambrosius, Boethius, Isidorus, the Bible, etc.

8. *Heptastichon on the varieties of fools.*
Title: 'Septem sunt genera stultorum.'

[22] The Paris manuscript differs in some detail from the Morgan text, according to the extracts printed by Hauréau, *op. cit.* VI, 265–266. For example, he prints:

### Horatius
Amicum tuum ne tentes
De re de qua non indiges;
Non diligit legaliter
Amans pecunialiter.

In the Morgan manuscript the text reads:

### Plato
Amicum corde diligas non ut res eius exigas
Non diligit legaliter amans pecunialiter.

With similar major differences, the Paris quotation for Plato is found in the Morgan text under 'Aristotiles'—and that for Aristoteles is in the Morgan manuscript under 'Tulius'.

[23] Cf. Hauréau, *op. cit.* I, 99–109; Curt F. Bühler, *The Dicts and Sayings of the Philosophers* (Early English Text Society, Original Series 211) xvii; Anders Gagnér, *Florilegium Gallicum* (Skrifter utgivna av Vetenskaps-Societeten i Lund, no. 18, Lund 1936) 53–60; Theodore Silverstein, 'The *Tertia Philosophia* of Guillaume de Conches and the Authorship of the *Moralium Dogma Philosophorum*,' *Quantulacumque* (1937) 23–33. The standard text is printed by John Holmberg, *Das Moralium Dogma Philosophorum des Guillaume de Conches* (Uppsala 1929).

Qui tantum minatur quod ipse non timetur
Qui tantum Jurat quod sibi non creditur
Qui tantum dat quod ipse depauperatur
Qui de rebus amissis vltra commodum affligitur
Qui Impossibile facere nititur
Qui se exaltat dum ab alijs deprimitur
Qui credit illud quod verisimilem non videtur

Folio 47ᵛ.

9. *Heptastichon on the courtesies of the world.*
Title: 'Septem sunt curialitates mundi'
>In priuato sobrietas
>In publico hylaritas
>In externeis affabilitas
>Inter socios omnis benignitas
>Inter prospera et aduersa stabilitas
>In fortunis iocunda liberalitas
>Inter adulantes discreta dapsilitas

Folio 47ᵛ.

10. *Heptastichon on the discourtesies of the world.*
Title: 'Septem sunt incurialitates mundi'
>Nimia loquacitas in conuiuio
>In paupertate alterius derisio
>Beneficij accepti obliuio
>Inter ignotos presumpcio
>Inter amicos et socios elacio
>Pro utilitate commune²⁴ consilij occultacio
>Et in necessitate cordis obduracio

Folios 47ᵛ–48.

11. *De natura musculorum.*
Begins: 'Musculi dicuntur capita neruorum ex sanguine et neruis com-
pilata . . .'
Folio 48.

This is an extract from the *Catholicon* of Johannes Balbus (Januensis) and agrees exactly with the definition (under *Musculus*) as
given in the edition presumably printed by Johann Gutenberg at
Mainz, 1460 (PML Check List 39).

12. *De natura equorum.*
Begins: 'Item de natura equorum loquens ysydorus 12 ethymologiarum sic
dicitur Viuacitas equorum multa . . .
Folio 48.

²⁴ The reading is uncertain; perhaps read 'communis'?

Though the ultimate source for this description is Isidore's *Etymologiarum libri XX* (PL 82, 430) as noted above, the explicit indicates that the scribe took his quotation from the *Catholicon* (under *Equus*) where the identical passage is also attributed to Isidore.

13. *Versus de bonitate equorum.*[25]

    Nobilitas in equis signis cognoscitur istis
    Auris acuta breuis caput exiguum caro dura
    Et grandes oculi calx durus spissaque cauda
    Recta breuis parui testiculi flexibilia ruma
    Et nares ample densa coma ac solidata
    Et grossum latus bonis hijs cognoscitur equus
Folios 48–48ᵛ.

14. *Versus de vicijs mali equi.*

    Sese interferiens[26] corda[27] super ossa laborans
    Morbidus vmbrosus consurgens durus in ore[28]
    Aque cubans vix serrandus calcaribus obstans

[25] As befits a country fond of horses and fox-hunting, there are many Middle English passages (in prose and verse) on the properties and natures of a good horse. Characteristic of these is the one contained in Huntington MS HU 1051, f. 62ᵛ, of *circa* 1485, a transcript of which I owe to the kindness of Mr. H. C. Schulz of that library; it reads:

    A horse hath .xviij. proprietees. iij of an Ox. iij of an asse. iij of a fox. iij of an hare & vj of a woman.

| thre of an | Ox. brod yed. brod fronted. & syde garnesyde |
| | Asse strong chynede. towgh hovyde & well etynge |
| | fox smale moseled. pryke eryd & fayr sterede |
| | hare. wyght. well brethed. & nemely of turnyng |

    Sex of A woman. well chered. fayr herede. well Brestede. Cloven croped. Esy att sterop. & soft beryng &c

The number of good properties of a horse varies considerably in the several texts. There are seven in *Cotton* MS Galba E IX, f. 113ᵛ (printed by William Hulme, EETS, ES 100, p. xxv). Fifteen is the total in *The Book of St. Albans*, St. Albans, 1486, sig. f₅ (Morgan Check List 1845) and, in what appears to be a transcript of it, in MS *Lansdowne* 762, f. 16 (printed by Wright and Halliwell, *Reliquiae Antiquae*, London 1841–3, I, 232–3). Also with fifteen properties but differing in detail is the passage in *The Proprytees and medycynes for hors*, London, Wynkyn de Worde, c. 1502 (E. Gordon Duff, *Fifteenth Century English Books* [Bibliographical Society, 1917] no. 353—copy now at Huntington); in turn the text in Trinity College, Cambridge, MS 0.9.38, f. 49 (printed by Carleton Brown, *Modern Language Notes* 27, 125) also differs from de Worde. MS Galba E IX also contains a version listing twenty-five good properties (printed by Hulme, *loc. cit.*). The total reaches fifty-four in John Fitzherbert, *The boke of husbandry* (English Dialect Society, no. 37, London 1882, pp. 63–5). There is an apparently unpublished treatise on horses listed by Brown and Robbins, *The Index of Middle English Verse* (New York 1943) no. 3318; see also Balliol (Oxford) MS 354, f. 7.

[26] Under 'Calx', Thomas Cooper (*Thesaurus Linguae Romanae et Britannicae*, London 1578) notes: 'Terere calcem calce. Virg. In an horse to enterfyer.' The *New*

Nota corda est vicium quo equus quis dicitur incordatus
est quid rigor neruorum in parte anteriori et huiusmodi
rigor Impedit flecti tibeas & est frequens occasio ad
precipitacionem sui ad lapsum

Folio 48$^v$.

The manuscript is bound in a late fifteenth—or early sixteenth—
century stamped leather binding, now rebacked and repaired. The
stamps are those frequently found on books bound on either side
of the Rhine; one of a pelican feeding her young is especially characteristic of German work of the period. The contemporary manuscript quiring in the printed parts probably indicates that these had
been bound twice before they were enclosed in the present binding.
The first four quires of the *Defensorium fidei contra Judaeos* have
the cancelled signatures M-P,[29] the remainder having been cut off
by the binder. Another set of quire marks (D-P), also cancelled,
runs through the two printed works; however, a note on the first
leaf reads 'A B & C non stabunt,' apparently a memorandum to the
binder that some work which was at one time bound before this
tract was not to be included in the new binding.

The handwriting, paper and binding thus show that the volume
under discussion attained its present form in the closing years of
the fifteenth century, somewhere in the neighborhood of the Rhine.
The nature of the texts perhaps indicates a Germanic[30] rather than
a French locality as the place of origin. In any event, the subject-
matter of this 'Sammelband' is one of uncommon variety, including
items of historical, political, social and scientific interest. It is thus

---

*English Dictionary*, under *interfere*, defines this as 'to strike the inside of the fetlock
with the shoe or hoof of the opposite foot'; this is now generally called 'overreach-
ing'. According to *The Proprytees*, this results in 'a taynt in the hele'; the earliest
previously recorded usage of *taint* in this sense given by NED is 1565 (*attaint*, 1523).

[27] Fitzherbert, *op. cit.* 67: 'The cordes is a thynge that wyll make a horse to stum-
ble, and ofte to fall, and appereth before the forther legges of the body of the horse,
and may well be cured in .ii. places, and there be but fewe horses but they haue
parte thereof.'

[28] This may be what the 1502 *Proprytees* calls 'gygges' or 'lampas'; the earliest
occurrence of *giggs* in NED is 1580 and of *lampas* is 1523.

[29] This of course indicates that at one time quires A–L preceded the *Defensorium
fidei.*

[30] Hauréau (*op. cit.* VI, 266), perhaps influenced by national pride, says of the
*Moralia dogmata philosophorum*: 'Comme on le voit, ces philosophes, ces grands
sages parlaient les uns et les autres une très mauvaise langue. . . . Nous la croyons
plutôt d'un clere germain que d'un français.'

a manuscript volume of considerable literary value in its own right —though, according to the usual library practice, it is classed and shelved as a volume of printed books.

(From *Traditio* 4 (1946), pp. 429-35).

# AN ANONYMOUS LATIN HERBAL IN THE PIERPONT MORGAN LIBRARY

SOME years ago and in another journal,[1] the writer called attention to a botanical text in the Morgan Library which appeared suitable for further investigation. The hope was expressed that the publication of the whole herbal from an early illustrated manuscript (such as the one preserved in the University Library at Pavia) might ensue. This has now materialized in a most satisfactory form under the editorship of TULLIA GASPARRINI LEPORACE, GINO POLLACCI and SIRO LUIGI MAFFEI.[2]

As I had surmised, the Morgan text (bound with PML 22222) is indeed closely related to the Pavian herbal; furthermore it apparently supplies those passages which had been erased "ferociter, a quodam religioso homine" as the former owner of the Pavia manuscript, PIER VITTORIO ALDINI,[3] rightly asserted. The purpose of the present article is, then, to accomplish the following ends: 1) to print a few sections of the Morgan text in juxtaposition to the corresponding herbs in the edition in order to indicate the degree of relationship between them; 2) to list the herbs of the Morgan manuscript alphabetically, indicating the equivalent names of the Pavia version; 3) to print three characteristic passages from the Morgan text which probably correspond to the erased lines of the Pavia manuscript; and finally 4) to reproduce in full the account of the nine herbs of the Morgan manuscript which are not found in the printed text.

Before turning to the extracts themselves, a word must be said about the nature of the Latin text. As Dr. TULLIA GASPARRINI LE-

[1] See previous article.

[2] "Un inedito erbario farmaceutico medioevale," *Biblioteca della "Rivista di storia delle scienze mediche e naturali,"* vol. V (1952).

[3] *Op. cit.,* p. 9.

PORACE has justly remarked,[4] the grammar of the fourteenth-century text in the Pavia manuscript is quite unpredictable. A century of transcription (and re-transcription) has not aided the cause of pure Latinity, and the fifteenth-century version in the Morgan manuscript records instances of "Küchenlatein" which even its prototype could not tolerate. Relative pronouns are often completely unrelated to their "relatives." One finds such truly remarkable phrases as "ex virtutem ista herba," where one had reason to expect "ex virtute istius herbae." "Nascor" is not only properly used as a deponent verb, but exhibits an active voice as well (perhaps *per analogiam* to "cresco"). Words like "predoxi" used in modifying "locis" defy both grammar and meaning, though the shrewd reader may perceive a corruption of the "petrosis" often encountered in the Pavia text. Indeed, there is hardly a sin peculiar to syntax which is not only licensed but also perpetrated in the Morgan version, and every form of accident seems to have befallen the accidence. Lastly, the text includes several unmistakably Italian words in place of the proper Latin ones; thus, for example, "soup" appears not as the Latin "jus" but as "brodo" (a word derived from Old High German "brod"); again, "o" displaces "aut" as the equivalent of "or." Despite the grammatical absurdities, the meaning of the text is seldom in doubt.

For these reasons, it seems impossible to emend without, to all intents and purposes, completely re-writing the text. In conformity with the wise decision of the Italian editors, the text is printed verbatim from the manuscript. I have followed Dr. GASPARRINI LEPORACE's method (pp. 24–5):

Nel fare la trascrizione ho creduto opportuno riportare fedelmente il testo che ci offre il manoscritto, sia perchè non era semplice poter distinguere gli errori dello scriba da quelli del testo originale, sia perchè proprio l'insieme di questi errori possono fornire al filologo elementi per determinare la località, ove l'erbario fu compilato, e per individuare l'autore di esso.

A few lines further on, the opinion is expressed that in its day this herbal probably enjoyed a wide diffusion throughout Northern

[4] "Continuamente si notano consonanti doppie al posto delle semplici e viceversa, lettere aggiunte o omesse, diversa grafia per una stessa parola, la traslitterazione dei nomi greci e arabi delle piante fatta quasi sempre con numerosi errori. Gli errori di sintassi sono poi ancora più frequenti: il genere e il numero dei sostantivi e l'uso dei casi sono trascurati; nella stessa proposizione il verbo è ora al singolare ora al plurale e le preposizioni reggono ora un caso ora un altro" (p. 24).

Italy. The Morgan manuscript gives every indication of having been written north of the Alps, and thus confirms the popularity of the text and widens the boundaries of its influence.

The following two examples, characteristic of the texts found in the two manuscripts, make it patently clear that the two versions descend from a common ancestor:[5]

| Morgan MS., $4^v.2$ | Edition, p. 60, no. 75 |
|---|---|
| Herba Chabalaricos. Ad faciendum bonam aquam ad omnem infirmitatem de oculis. Accipe folia huius herbe & facias aquam ad campanam, & de ista aqua pone in oculos per dies XX, resclarauit lucem & accipit omnem dolorem. Et accipe istam herbam ad xij dies madio si tu vis adoperare per medicinam. | Herba Capallarices. Ad faciendum aquam bonam ad omnem infirmitatem occulorum. Accipe florem istius herbe et fac aquam ad campanam, et de ista aqua pone in occulis per spatium XX dierum, clarificabuntur occuli et removebitur omnis infirmitas. Et hoc est probatum. . . |

| Morgan MS., $5^r.2$ | Edition, p. 50, no. 43 |
|---|---|
| Herba Patrisechas uel Galicinas. Ad wlneraturam de serpente, pista istam herbam & pone super wlneraturam, acepit dolorem & venenum de carne. Et est probatum. Et habet istam virtutem, si tu portas tecum, nullus serpens tibi approximabit; quando sentit odorem de ista herba, fugit extra. Accipe istam herbam ad punctum de luna que vocatur thaurus, qui habet cursum suum de madio. Et crescit in montibus frigidis. | Herba Paroischas. Ad sanandum morsuram serpentis. Accipe de ista herba et implastra super morsuram, removet dollorem et venenum. Et hoc est probatum. Item ista herba habet istam virtutem, quia si quis portaverit eam supra se serpens non potest sibi apropinquare sed fugit cum sentit odorem istius herbe. Et coligi debet de mense maij in ponto lune, quod vocatur taurus. Nascitur in montibus frigidis. |

The Morgan text contains 72 herbs, of which all but nine are found (or were probably once contained) in the Pavia manuscript. Due to the erasures already referred to, some herbs in this codex are not represented by text but survive only as sketches. Further, the lost text may well have corresponded to some of the nine Morgan herbs for which clear parallels have not been found. Of the herbs numbered 1–78 in the Pavia manuscript whose *text* is printed in the edition, only four are not present in the Morgan version;[6] the

---

[5] The citations for the Morgan manuscript refer to the leaf (recto or verso), followed by the numerical position of the herb on that page.

[6] The herbs omitted in the Morgan text are: Herba Mulla Campana (no. 52), Herba Occulus Domini (no. 54), Herba Rigano (no. 70) and Herba Ruschasia (no. 77).

numerical discrepancy is due to the fact that the numbering in the "pictorial" index of the Pavia manuscript is erratic and for some herbs, of course, no text is found.

| Morgan MS. | Printed Edition |
|---|---|
| Ad tolam minore (2ᵛ.5) | —Antolla minor (p. 35, no. 1) |
| Angalos (1ʳ.7) | —Angales (p. 48, no. 39) |
| Angalos (2ʳ.5) | —Angalles (p. 41, no. 13) |
| Arthethica montana (4ʳ.6) | —Areticha montaria (p. 54, no. 51) |
| Atharo (5ʳ.4) | [Not present] |
| Atolas (4ᵛ.6) | —Antollas (p. 44, no. 24) |
| Atolas luparias (4ᵛ.7) | —Antolla lupanas (p. 44, no. 25) |
| Beletolis (2ʳ.3) | —Belletolis (p. 57, no. 59) |
| Bertonatha (3ʳ.3) | —Betoniga (p. 38, no. 7) |
| Bonifacia & ligna pagana (2ᵛ.7) | —Bonifatia (p. 38, no. 6) |
| Bortines (1ᵛ.3) | —Bortines (p. 36, no. 2) |
| Bossiles (2ʳ.8) | —Boxoxilles (p. 41, no. 12) |
| Brancha degenam (6ʳ.2) | [Not present] |
| Brancha lupina (5ᵛ.5) | —Brancha lupina (p. 46, no. 29) |
| Bustania (4ᵛ.1) | —Bustania (p. 59, no. 73) |
| Capalias (4ᵛ.4) | —Capalias (p. 56, no. 57) |
| Carteralis (2ʳ.2) | —Tortorolis (p. 42, no. 16) |
| Chabalaricos (4ᵛ.2) | —Capallarices (p. 60, no. 75) |
| Chanalarthas romana (3ʳ.5) | —Canalaritas romana (p. 39, no. 9) |
| Chanarolis (5ᵛ.3) | —Cancealis (p. 45, no. 27) |
| Conflexurias (5ʳ.1) | —Cofflexanas (p. 45, no. 26) |
| Costoias (5ᵛ.4) | —Toffanas (p. 45, no. 28) |
| Cros amorosos (2ʳ.6) | [Not present] |
| Dictoonem album (1ʳ.2) | —Ditimo biancho (p. 46, no. 35) |
| Ferus (6ʳ.1) | —Forus (p. 60, no. 74) |
| Folegas (1ᵛ.5) | —Folleas (p. 48, no. 38) |
| Folia (2ᵛ.4) | —Follio (p. 52, no. 48) |
| Granchias (1ʳ.4) | —Gratia (p. 41, no. 15) |
| Illilocris (2ᵛ.1) | —Illiboris (p. 49, no. 41) |
| Illotharias (1ᵛ.4) | —Illocharias (p. 48, no. 37) |
| Istanucia (3ʳ.6) | —Instanutia (p. 39, no. 8) |
| Istaturis (1ᵛ.6) | —Ystatoris (p. 57, no. 61) |
| Lingua coruina (3ᵛ.1) | —Lingua corvena (p. 42, no. 17) |
| Lucea (5ᵛ.1) | —Lucea (p. 33, no. 34) |
| Lucea madragola (1ᵛ.2) | —Luza mandragora (p. 48, no. 40) |
| Lucea minor (2ᵛ.6) | —Bazea minor (p. 52, no. 47) |
| Luinaria grecha (5ʳ.6) | —Lunaria grega (p. 56, no. 56) |
| Luminelas (3ʳ.4) | —Luminelas (p. 60, no. 76) |
| Metries (2ʳ.4) | —Metries (p. 57, no. 60) |
| Nastrucio (4ᵛ.5) | —Narscurso (p. 56, no. 58) |
| Nigras (3ʳ.2) | —Nigra (p. 37, no. 4) |

| Morgan MS. (*cont.*) | Printed Edition (*cont.*) |
|---|---|
| Oriola (3$^v$.3) | —Ariolla (p. 43, no. 19) |
| Palma Christi (1$^r$.5) | —Palma Christi (p. 51, no. 46) |
| Panis porano (4$^r$.5) | —Pane porcino (p. 53, no. 50) |
| Paris (4$^r$.1) | —Paris (p. 44, no. 22) |
| Patrisechas (5$^r$.2) | —Paroischas (p. 50, no. 43) |
| Pionia (3$^v$.6) | [Not present] |
| Polorinas (1$^v$.7) | [Not present] |
| Rapalis (5$^r$.5) | —Rapilis (p. 58, no. 72) |
| Rena (2$^v$.3) | —Rena (p. 40, no. 10) |
| Requilicia (1$^r$.6) | —Riquilizie (p. 47, no. 36) |
| Rigola (4$^r$.4) | —Rigogola (p. 52, no. 49) |
| Rudicam saluadicam (5$^v$.2) | [Not present] |
| Sanam inuersa (3$^v$.5) | —Faba inversa (p. 43, no. 21) |
| Sancta Maria (6$^r$.3) | —Santa Maria (p. 55, no. 55) |
| [name omitted] (4$^v$.3) | —Scudaria (p. 60, no. 78) |
| Sebastrela (5$^v$.7) | —Sabastrella (p. 46, no. 31) |
| Serpentilla (4$^r$.3) | [Not present] |
| Sigillum Sancte Marie (1$^r$.1) | —Sigillo de Santa Maria (p. 58, no. 71) |
| Sisicham (5$^v$.6) | —Salsifica (p. 46, no. 30) |
| Stellana (2$^r$.1) | —Stellaria (p. 38, no. 5) |
| Superna (3$^v$.4) | —Superva (p. 43, no. 20) |
| Teloga (4$^r$.2) | —Ciloga (p. 44, no. 23) |
| Terogas (3$^r$.1) | —Torogas (p. 36, no. 3) |
| Thoherbabelis (2$^v$.2) | —Carborelis (p. 50, no. 44) |
| Tilles (1$^v$.1) | —Tilles (p. 49, no. 42) |
| Trefolios (3$^v$.2) | —Trifolio (p. 42, no. 18) |
| Tregodera maior (1$^r$.3) | [Not present] |
| Triachos (2$^r$.7) | —Triacho (p. 40, no. 11) |
| Trodorissos (5$^r$.7) | [Not present] |
| Zenciana (4$^r$.7) | —Zinzana (p. 54, no. 53) |
| Zipolam marinam (5$^r$.3) | —Cipola marina (p. 51, no. 45) |

The list itself, it is hoped, will be of interest to the philologist; it may well be of value in identifying related herbals or serve in the clarification of hitherto obscure literary allusions or uncertain scientific citations.

The nature of the deletions in the Pavia manuscript may be clearly judged by examining those passages in the Morgan manuscript which seem to correspond to erased sections in the other codex. Some early owner methodically went about deleting all passages concerned with magic and most of those dealing with sex. For example, under Herba Forus, only "Nascitur in montibus frigidis et petrosis" is preserved in the Pavia text, while the Morgan text has for Herba Ferus:

Qui portaret secum semper istam herbam erit uenturatus & omnis homo & femina portabit sibi magnum amorem. Accipe istam herbam ad punctum de luna que vocatur geminis o thaurus. Quando tu accipis, dic ista verba: Herba ferus, veni ad me pro parte de spiritu sancto per deum viuum & verum. Et nascitur in montibus frigidis & predoxi.

Similarly, for Herba Lunaria Grega, all that survives in the Pavia manuscript is "Si quis . . . ," while in the Morgan version one finds:

Herba luinaria grecha. Quecumque persona secum portaret istam herbam, semper gauderet. Et numquam erit homo neque femina qui videret se. Et nascit ista herba in locis occultis in montibus frigidis.

Finally, one finds the following passage in the Pavia manuscript under Herba Belletolis:

Ad sanandum mallum dentium. Accipe de ista herba et tene in ore, statim facit venire foras dentem. Item... Nascitur in montibus frigidis.

Here the Morgan text reads (Herba Beletolis):

Ad malum de dentibus, tene in ore de ista herba, statim sanat dentes. Ad faci-endum quod omnis persona que tibi placet tibi portabit magnum amorem, accipe ad iij dies de luna ad nomen illud quod tu uis quod portat tibi amorem & quando habebis illam herbam, pone sibi in aliquo loco quod nullus te videt. & nascit in montibus frigidis.

Lastly, there is printed below in alphabetical order the full text of the nine herbs which the Morgan manuscript alone preserves. Again the text is reproduced exactly as it appears in the original, no corrections having been attempted for reasons already set forth.

Herba atharo. Ad malum de scabiam. Accipe istam herbam cum radice & cum sonzia porci senis; facias vnguentum; vnge scabiam per xv dies, sanat. Et quecumque persona que habet gossam ad gulam, accipe radicem & tene in ore & sputa satis illa res que uenit tibi ad os & in isto modo erit sanus per spacium xx dierum. & probatum est.

Herba brancha degenam. Quecumque persona portaret istam herbam super capite, numquam habebit infirmitatem de illo pro calore solis; unquam de foco non potest nocere ad oculos. Quando aquila vadit in altum, portat istam herbam propter solem, quod non offendat ad oculos. Et nascitur in montibus asperissimis.

Herba cros amorosos. Ad wlneraturam de serpente, accipe folia & pone super malum, acepit extra dolorem & inflaturam sanat; et est probatum. Et quando tu accipis hanc herbam, dic hec verba: gloria forma floriano, & statim accipe herbam per ✠ deum viuum & verum; venias ad me cum tua virtute. Item ad omnem maculam de oculis, accipe succum de ista herba cum vino miste per spacium xv dierum, liberatus est. et est probatum. Et nascit in montibus altissimis in locis frigidis. Ad malum de dentibus, comede de ista herba quod est bona; et firmat dentes & sanat zencinias. Et accipe in die veneri de mense madio ad ieiunium.

Herba pionia. Quecumque persona que habet malum de madrono o de matre, accipe radicem et fac puluerem & da sibi ad bibendum cum bono vino ad ieiunium per spacium xv dierum, liberabitur. Ad sciendum si nulla femina esset indemoniata, pone istam herbam. quod portet secum, non poterit sufferre & nunquam non facit nisi exclamare. Ad sanandum vnam plagam, accipe istam herbam cum lardo & pista inseme & pone super plagam & sanabit cito. Accipe radicem & fac bulire cum vino pauco & postea bibe & liberabit per spacium de xl dierum. Et nascit in montibus ubi dant solem in locis perdoxi.

Herba polorinas. Ad malum caput & frigus, accipe istam erbam & comede cum ouo de sero & mane sanat, et est probata. Ad malum nastencium qui non possit sanare, facias de herba puluerem, pone de isto puluere super plagas, cito sanat omnem malum per spacium x dierum.

Herba rudicam saluadicam. Ad guttas frigidas, accipe istam herbam cum herba stela, coque insimul cum vino vermilio, & postea ponas super malum, liberabitur per spacium de xv dies et est probatum. Ad dolorem de renibus et de flanchos, accipe istam herbam & venedolam & folia de asencio marino & istas res pone in olio senex de v annis & pone super malum per spacium xiij dierum, sanat. Ad figadum infirmus, accipe istam herbam & comede ad ieiunium crudam de xiij dies, sanat. & nascit in terrenis domesticis.

Herba serpentilla. Quecumque persona habet malum de ganbis, id est ruptis, et implagate, accipe radicem huius herbe & pista & pone de zera natura & cum olio & cum lardo de porcho & facias vnguentum & pone super ganbas, cito liberabitur & sanat bene.

Herba tregodera maior. Ad malum de matrona, accipe radicem huius herbe & facias puluerem; da sibi bibere cum vino calido per spacium v dierum & sanabitur. Ad malum de morbo chaducho, accipe herbam & coque in aqua, da sibi ad bibendum de ista aqua omni die ad ieiunium per spacium xij dierum, liberabitur. Ista medicina probata est. Ad malum de tosicho, comede folia huius herbe quando fuisset insalatam per spacium xv dierum, liberabitur; et omnes malos ad malum de flanchis. Et crescit in montibus frigidis.

Herba trodorissos. Quecumque persona esset malesana, da sibi ad comedendum de ista herba cum ouo o cum olio quod possit comedere. & accipe ad tres dies de luna de mense Junio & porta semper tecum & omnes malas facturas te fugerent ante te. Et nascit in montibus de Cecilia & de nocte facit magnum lumen & splendorem, et si tu non scires quod esset ista herba, videret te esse fantasma & haberes magnum timorem.

As Dr. GASPARRINI LEPORACE has pointed out,[7] the body of the Pavian manuscript seems to have been gathered together by two

---

[7] *Op. cit.*, p. 10.

different compilers. The first part is contained in the first 58 folios of the manuscript; it includes drawings of 88 herbs (misnumbered to 96), most of which are subsequently provided with full descriptions. Only this part of the Pavian text is represented in the Morgan manuscript. However, as we have seen, about ninety per cent of the material preserved in the Pavia manuscript, and large parts no longer surviving therein, may be consulted in the Morgan manuscript. For these reasons, it is not at all unlikely that this manuscript may turn out to be of great value for the history of botanical literature.

*Postscript:*

Since the above essay was written, the writer had the opportunity to consult two manuscripts in the Biblioteca Nazionale Marciana at Venice, which contain Italian renderings of this same text. They are: MS. It. II. 12 and MS. It. III. 11. A sample extract from each is cited below to indicate the degree of kinship:

Herba brancha dagina. Qualuncha persona la portassi adosso in suso la testa, non auerià infermitade de queli per calore del solle; ne per focho zamai non li ofender chi alli ochi; quando l'aquilla vola in alto, porta questa erba in bocha per paura ch'el solle non li ofenda alli ochi; e nase in montagne asprissime. (MS. It. II. 12, f. 75; compare "brancha degenam" above).

Erba capaloricco. Affare acqua a ogni infermita et malattia degli occhii. Toglie il fiore de questa erba et stillala nella campana; pone poj sulla malattia et negli ochi, bagnando bene, et in venti dì sia guarito, et l'occhio rimarà chiaro. (MS. It. III. 11, f. 149ᵛ; compare "herba capallarices" above).

It is, of course, quite possible that the Morgan text is simply a retranslation from an Italian version into Latin. This may explain the similarity of thought but difference in expression between the two accounts, as well as the presence of a number of unusual words and grammatical forms in the Morgan text.

(From *Osiris* 11 (1954), pp. 259-66).

# CHAPTER L5

## A *RELATIO BREVIS*
## OF THE LIFE AND MARTYRDOM
## OF ST. THOMAS À BECKET[1]

THE copy of the first printed edition of the *Polycraticus*[2] by John of Salisbury (Joannes Sarisburiensis, d. 1180) found in the Pierpont Morgan Library[3] contains at the end of the volume a fairly long manuscript text, the nature of which has not hitherto been made public. The tract found there is written out below the "Et sic est finis" of the last printed page (f. 249ʳ); it continues on the original last (blank) leaf of the volume and is concluded upon a vellum sheet inserted thereafter as a fly-leaf. The manuscript has the heading:

> Relatio breuis de vita et passione thome cantuariensis per Dominum Johannem salisberiensem de qua fit mentio in prima huius operis pagina.

These words refer, of course, to the prefatory note printed on f. 1ʳ, which speaks of John of Salisbury in these terms: "Hic socius fuit sancti thome martiris Cantuariensis archiepiscopi, cuius vitam et passionem descripsit." A colophon was, in turn, supplied to the manuscript tract and reads:

> Scriptum ex codice fratrum de septem fontibus vbi non habebatur titulus Anno Domini M vᶜ xxxiiij iij decembris.

Unfortunately there is no clue as to the nature or antiquity of the manuscript then owned (3 December 1534) by the Austin friars of the priory of Sept-Fontaines, situated in the forest of Soignes.[4]

---

[1] The fifth number in the series *Libri impressi*.

[2] For bibliographical descriptions, see HAIN-COPINGER 9430; POLAIN 2314; and CAMPBELL 1045. The work is attributed to the Brussels press owned by the Fratres Vitae Communis and was printed about the year 1482.

[3] The present copy is described, but with no statement as to the presence of the manuscript tract, in the *Catalogue of Manuscripts and Early Printed Books . . . now Forming Portion of the Library of J. Pierpont Morgan*, London, 1907, III, 114–115, no. 639. It is listed as no. 1696 in Ada THURSTON and Curt F. BÜHLER, *Check List of Fifteenth Century Printing in the Pierpont Morgan Library*, New York, 1939, p. 157.

[4] According to L. H. COTTINEAU, *Répertoire topo-bibliographique des abbayes et prieurés*, Mâcon, 1935–38, II, 3011, there are several monasteries by this name, but

It is not, of course, pure chance that moved the scribe to write out, in his copy of the *Polycraticus*, an account of the life and martyrdom of St. Thomas à Becket. One can simply assume, plausibly enough, that the note in the printed preface was the chief (possibly even the sole) reason for the copyist's efforts. But if this be true, the scribe was sadly misled for, as we shall see, the account of St. Thomas à Becket here carefully written out is certainly *not* that one which was composed by the Archbishop's close friend, the great English church-man and the "central figure of English learning," John of Salisbury, Bishop of Chartres. Perhaps even more suggestive was the nature of the story and the peculiar timeliness of its particulars; this latter fact may well have suggested to the scribe that the *Relatio brevis* might suitably be included here. At this particular moment of his-tory, the citizens of the Low Countries would certainly have been well aware that the earlier quarrel between the English King Hen-ry II and the Church closely paralleled the contemporary struggle between Henry VIII and the Papacy, while the downfall of Cardinal Wolsey (in 1529–1530) would inevitably recall the tragic end of his great predecessor in the Chancellery, a fate which Wolsey fortu-nately (considering the temper and disposition of the incumbent of the royal throne) managed to escape.

The text of the *Relatio brevis* begins thus:

Cum primo Henric*us* anglor*um* monarchie et interiace*n*tibus transmarinis etia*m* parti*bus* presideret, b*e*atus iste martir thomas ex londonie ciuib*us* no*n* infimis oriu*n*d*us*, canthuarie archidiaconatu*m* sub theobaldo archipresule regebat, qui q*uonia*m eloquentia*m*, qua*m* a natura habebat, su*m*me prude*n*tie maritauerat, vultu pulcher et amabilis, mitis asp*ec*tu, op*er*e iustus, cultu venustus, corpore procerus, et rebus regendis o*m*nino aptus videbatur, in breui a prefato rege in ta*n*tam familiaritate*m* est admissus, ut p*er* diuersas regiones et se b*e*atos reputare*n*t, qui ei ut co*n*siliario et cancellario dom*ini* sui obsecun-dare potuissent.

This is quite manifestly an entirely different text than the *Vita S. Thomae* attributed to John of Salisbury, at least as it is printed by John Allen Giles[5] and in the *Patrologia latina* (vol. CXC, cols. 195–208). A comparison with the other extant lives of St. Thomas à

---

it seems probable that the one here referred to is the priory in the province of Hainaut, not far from Brussels.

[5] *Vita S. Thomae Cantuariensis Archiepiscopi et Martyris*, Oxford, 1845, I, 318–339. GILES prints "agendis" for the above "regendis." For further particulars, see Louis HALPHEN, "Les biographes de Thomas Becket," *Revue historique*, CII, 35–45.

Becket shows that, in the main, the version here cited is a much condensed account of the text printed under the heading *Passio quinta*, also edited by Giles[6] and reprinted by Migne (CXC, 335–344). It is, however, not only a condensed summary of this account but it also includes sentences and phrases which are not printed in the standard (Giles-Migne) text. Migne's two-column edition (not counting the prologue) contains 540 short lines; apart from material in the Morgan manuscript which is omitted from the standard text, only 220 of these lines appear in the Morgan copy of the *Polycraticus*. The text concludes with these words:

> O pastorem dignum, qui ne oues laniarentur, seipsum luporum morsibus tam confidenter exposuit! Et quia mundum abiecerat, mundus volens eum opprimere nescius sublimauit. Deinde alio ictu in capite recepto, martir genua flexit, et cubitos, seipsum hostiam viuentem deo offerendo, dixit: "Pro nomine Ihesu et ecclesie tuicione libentj animo mortem amplectj paratus sum." Ac tercius ita procumbentj graue vulnus in ceruicem impressit. Quartus coronam, que ample erat latitudinis, ita a capite separauit, vt sanguis albens ex cerebro et cerebrum rubens ex sanguine lilij et rose coloribus virginis et martiris[7] ecclesie faciem in confessoris et martiris vitali morte purpuraret. Quintus autem de capite cerebrum quod remanserat effodit; ne ei quinta plaga deesset, qui in alijs christum imitatus est. Itaque dej sacerdos a seculo migrans, celis nascitur iiij° calendas Januarij, Anno ab incarnatione Domini Millesimo centesimo lxxj, die proxima post solemnitatem innocentum; vt qui diu innocenter vixerat, post innocentes tempus celebre sortiretur.

While this is mostly identical with certain sentences in the *Passio quinta*, some parts are not found in the standard version of this account. The second sentence here quoted does not, for example, form part of the anonymous *Passio*, though it does occur in the eyewitness account of the murder as related by Edward Grim.[8] Similarly, the words "Ac tercius ita procumbenti" occur in this form in Grim[9] but not in the *Passio*, while the adjective "vitali" is found in neither version, though (apparently) it seems to be no more than a corruption or a misreading of the "vita et morte" of the standard form of Grim's text. Naturally enough, the *Passio quinta* itself is depend-

---

[6] *Op. cit.*, II, 164–180.　　　　　　[7] Giles prints "matris."

[8] This account is also printed by Giles, *op. cit.*, I, 1–90.

[9] Compare the edition by Giles, p. 77. These words are also to be found (p. 436) in the "Passio Sancti Thomae Cantuariensis e codice Sublacensi descripta" printed by James Craigie Robertson, *Materials for the History of Thomas Becket, Archbishop of Canterbury*, London, 1875–79, (Master of the Rolls, *Chronicles and Memorials*, no. 67), IV, 431–441.

ent on Grim's narrative,[10] and it is possible that some manuscripts of the *Passio* contain portions of the account as given by Grim which are not found in other copies. This may explain the presence in the Morgan text of lines not forming part of the accepted version of the *Passio quinta*.

Though the Morgan text offers no new details as to the life and martyrdom of St. Thomas à Becket, it is interesting and valuable to us for quite other reasons. First of all, it serves as evidence for the nature and extent of scholarly research as it was practised in the first half of the sixteenth century.[11] To some extent anyway, it was the obvious intention of the scribe to amplify his copy of the works of John of Salisbury by adding to the texts included in the Brussels edition a manuscript version of still another work by the famous Bishop of Chartres. One may further suppose that the earlier owner of the Morgan copy of this *Polycraticus* was interested not only in the events of his own day but also in the history of the past. One may therefore conjecture, with some justification, that it was the state of affairs then current in England which prompted the scribe not only to search out the Sept-Fontaines manuscript of the life and martyrdom of St. Thomas à Becket, but also that he might properly write out this text for inclusion in his own copy of the *Polycraticus*.

(From *Scriptorium* 6 (1952), pp. 274-76).

[10] GILES (*op. cit.*, II, x) refers to the *Passio quinta* in these terms: "This was first printed in MARTENE's *Thesaurus Anecdotorum*, t. iii, p. 1737, and by the rubric at the end it might be thought to be the work of Edward Grim . . . But if the reader will take the trouble of examining it, he will certainly come to the conclusion that it is a compilation, written at a later period, as a lectionary for the use of the Church, and like all such compilations, contains numerous passages borrowed without scruple from the original writers."

[11] For further notes on such research, compare E. Ph. GOLDSCHMIDT, *Medieval Texts and their First Appearance in Print*, London, 1943. On pages 59 and 68-69, Mr. Goldschmidt gives some interesting details in regard to the Brussels edition of the *Polycraticus*.

# CHAPTER L6

## A SATIRICAL POEM OF THE
## TUDOR PERIOD

THE satirical poem which forms the subject of the present
study is to be found on the verso of the first (blank) folio
in the copy of Caxton's *The Life of St. Winifred* belonging
to the Pierpont Morgan Library.[1] Apparently the first mention of
this poem is in the early catalogue of the library of Edward Harley,
second Earl of Oxford, which had been bought by the bookseller,
Thomas Osborne, some years earlier (1743).[2] The citation is:

> At the Beginning of the Book there is written, in an old Hand,
> about the Time of the Reformation, a satirical Poem, describing
> what a graceless Age it was wrote in.[3]

The approximate period here assigned to the handwriting seems
reasonable enough, and the writer would judge that a dating of
"second quarter of the sixteenth century" were a conservative estimate.[4]

Although the dating of the script seems to be easily ascertainable,
that of the composition is not so simple to determine. It is plain,
from the evidence of the scribal errors and the carelessness in transcription (cf. lines 15, 41 and 45), that the present text is a copy
and not an original composition; it is not necessary, therefore, to
presume that the composition was coeval with the transcription. The
body of the verse gives no indication of the characteristically Protestant attitude towards religion and morals; the spirit of the poem is
rather that of the typical fifteenth-century complaint on the state of

---

[1] Robert of Shrewsbury, *The Life of St. Winifred*, [Westminster: William Caxton, 1485]. Compare Ada Thurston and Curt F. Bühler, *Check List of Fifteenth
Century Printing in the Pierpont Morgan Library*, New York, 1939, p. 169, no. 1787.

[2] Compare Seymour de Ricci, *English Collectors of Books & Manuscripts*, Cambridge, 1930, p. 35. Harley himself had died in 1741, and the books were sold by
his widow, the daughter of the Duke of Newcastle.

[3] *Catalogus Bibliothecae Harleianae*, London, Thomas Osborne, 1743–1745, III,
29, no. 411.

[4] The script has certain resemblances to that of the manuscript of *Wit and Science*
(c. 1550) as shown on Plate IX of Samuel A. Tannenbaum, *The Handwriting of
the Renaissance*, New York, 1930.

morality amongst the laity and the clergy.[5] The hesitation shown by
the scribe in line 6 seems to result from his uncertainty as to whether
the character represented was the late fifteenth-century form of the
"thorn" or the normal sixteenth-century shape of the "y". In lines
27 and 28, both a singular and a plural third person pronoun appear where either one or the other is required. This suggests that,
in the original, the Scandinavian forms had not been used consistently; this may again point to a fifteenth-century origin. Though
the poem is not listed by Brown-Robbins,[6] it is almost certainly very
much earlier than the date of writing; for these reasons, then, it is not
impossible that the poem belongs to the fifteenth century. We are
here, however, admittedly verging on speculation.

The text is printed below in the usual fashion. All contractions
have been expanded with the use of italics; the punctuation and the
use of capitals is editorial. Though the poem is manifestly of no
great poetic merit, it is an interesting example of the literary composition of the Tudor period. It must, however, be admitted that the
metre is weak and the rhyme is poor; in lines 33/35, a nearly identical, feminine rhyme may also be noted.

O pereles Prynce of Peace
    And Lorde of Lordes all,
Beholde *our* great desese
    O Kynge celestyall.
5    Theese people be so unruly
    To whom You sent *Your* sawes,
So few of them do truly
    Obs*erve* and kepe Thy lawes.
For by misgou*er*nau*n*ce,
10    That is in eu*er*y place,
We see full great dysturbaunce
    And all for lake of grace.
Pryde is malaperte
    By help of ambycyou*n*,
15    And prelates vnexpert
    For money sell remyssyou*n*.
Couetusnes is the hede,
    And wrath wilbe wroken;
They thinke that God is dede,
20    For trouth may not be spoken.

[5] Some pointed references to the conflict with the Papacy might be expected in
a poem written between 1530 and 1553.

[6] Carleton Brown and Rossell Hope Robbins, *The Index of Middle English Verse*,
New York, 1943.

Thus avarice to haue all
    By collo*ur* of blynde deuocioun,
Clymyng to cache a fall
    And all to gett promocyou*n*.
25    Glotonye ys gull,
    As hungrye as an hogg,
To ffed here belly full,
    W*h*ich is ther very god.
Slouthe is very slyee
30    And sleapeth in here houde;
She reacheth not a flye
    Thoughe she doo neuer good.
Lecherye full lothe is
    That men shulde here aspye
35    And spareth for no othes
    Here ded*es* for to denye.
Relygion is a rouer
    Ronnynge euery where,
Castynge eu*er*y border
40    For chaunging of chere.
Fayth doth gretly faynte,
    & charyte is full colde;
& trouthe is nere attaynt,
    For beinge boughte and soulde.
45    Peace is but awaye,
    And plenty oute of plase,
And pou*er*tie may goo playe,
    & all for lake of grace.
    Finis.

## Notes to the lines

6 MS. has "you" crossed out and then written in above; after "y$^R$" MS. supplies "y$^i$". Apparently the scribe was uncertain whether "you" or "thou" (or "your/thy") was the reading of his *Vorlage*, since the late fifteenth-century thorn had degenerated into the appearance of a "y".

15 MS. has "vneppert", a word not recorded by NED and certainly a scribal error.

18 "wrath", the probable reading though a hole in the paper has destroyed the second letter.

23 "cache", cf. NED, catch, sense 19$^b$.

25 "gull", the mouth (see NED, sb$^4$, 1$^b$).

27/28 see discussion above.

30 "houde", i.e. hood.

31 "to reach not a fly", to be worth nothing (not worth a fly).

37 "rouer", a pirate (NED, since 1390); a marauder, robber (since 1550).

40 "chaunge chere", to change countenance (NED, 2ᵇ).

41 MS. has "faute" or "fante", but rhyme requires "faynte".

45 MS. has "peayce", a variant not found in NED and probably not a good form.

(From *Anglia* 72 (1954), pp. 419-22).

# CHAPTER L7

## SAVONAROLA'S ARREST AND THE
## THEFT OF A BOOK

ON the eve of Palm Sunday, April 8, 1498, Florence wit-
nessed a wholly disgraceful exhibition of primitive savagery
and brutal instincts. The ordeal by fire, which Savonarola
and his opponents had been scheduled to undergo, had failed to
take place on the previous day; consequently the populace was in a
particularly ugly frame of mind on being deprived of this ghastly
spectacle. That Sunday night, the Florentines, and those citizens
of the neighborhood who had flocked to the Tuscan capital in the
hope of sharing in the promised looting, broke all bonds of restraint
and the city endured a veritable 'Walpurgisnacht' of horror. Murder,
brutal assault, arson, robbery and most other forms of violence
were the order of the night; the events are recounted not only by
contemporary chroniclers but by modern historians as well.[1]

A reminder of this 'grauenvolle Nacht' is preserved in the Pierpont
Morgan Library (PML 21682).[2] This is an edition of the *Orthographia*
by Joannes Tortellius printed at Venice by Nicolaus Jenson, 1471;
a manuscript note inserted in the lower cover of this volume offers
the following information:

Tempore quo frater Hieronymus captus fuit, nocturno tempore, quidam
asportabat res quasdam, qui aggressus a quodam alio, coactus est deponere
rerum sarcinam. Tunc aggressor ille sibi appropriauit librum hunc Joannem,
scilicet Tortelium. Qui postea ad confessionem accedens, mihi domino Benin-
case priori in Camaldulo Florentino, eundem librum presentauit, et ipsum
auctoritate Vicarij Archiepiscopi Florentini meum feci. Quem postea Reveren-
dissimo Domino Petro Delphino Generali Camaldulensi dedi, et ipse loco
eiusdem libri, quandam bibliam in maternum sermonem transcriptam concessit.

> Ego Dominus Benincasa
> manu propria suprascripsi.

Whence the book was stolen on the night of April 8, 1498, is not
clear; it was probably not taken from the Convent of San Marco itself,

[1] Joseph Schnitzer, *Savonarola, ein Kulturbild aus der Zeit der Renaissance*,
München, 1924, 1, 526–531, gives a full account and lists the early sources.
[2] Ada Thurston and Curt F. Bühler, *Check List of Fifteenth Century Printing in
the Pierpont Morgan Library*, New York, 1939, p. 66, no. 751.

since the Signoria (while the rioters were outside the walls) had placed its own guard in the monastery to protect the library and its valuable contents.[3] In the border at the foot of the first printed page is a coat-of-arms which a description found with the volume identifies as that of Corvino of Venice.[4] This is not, however, identical with the Corvino arms as given by Johannes Baptist Rietstap.[5] The Pietro Benincasa who received the Tortellius from that individual who had 'recovered' the book from an earlier plunderer was, as he himself notes, a prior of a Camaldolese monastery (probably San Salvatore) in Florence; he is listed by Ulysse Chevalier.[6] The Pietro Delphino to whom Benincasa presented the Tortellius in exchange for a copy of the Malermi Bible was the general of that Order (1480–1515), a writer of some merit and a notable opponent of Savonarola's.[7]

The history of the volume in more recent times is clearer. Below an unidentified Italian bookplate is written the note: 'Edizion rara e ricercata. Ne fù venduto un' esemplare lire settantacinque Tornesi nell' anno 1767.' This worldly note would seem to indicate that the book was no longer at Camaldoli in the late eighteenth century.[8] In the year 1902, the eminent biblical scholar, Herman Charles Hoskier, bought the volume in Munich, according to an entry in his hand; another note shows that it was sold to the London firm of Bernard Quaritch, apparently in 1908. This incunabulum was subsequently in the collection, and contains the bookplate, of Walter Thomas Wallace. It then appeared in the sale of Mr. Wallace's library (March 22, 1920), the Pierpont Morgan Library obtaining the volume through Dr. Joseph Martini. One may now hope that its wanderings have come to an end.

(From *Renaissance News* 7 (1954), pp. 95-97).

[3] Schnitzer, I, 531.

[4] The arms are described as: 'Azure on a chief or, a raven sable membered gueules.'

[5] *Armoiries des familles contenues dans l'Armorial général*, Paris, 1903-1926, II, planche CXXXII. The raven is here distinguished by bearing a branch in its beak; this is not present in the border of PML 21682.

[6] *Répertoire des sources historiques du moyen âge . . . Bio-bibliographie*, Paris, 1905–1907, I, 511.

[7] Compare Chevalier, I, 1163, under 'Delfino'.

[8] A manuscript note of ownership reads: 'Camaldoli No. 13058' and also the number 'CLXXV'. Presumably Delphino gave the book to the parent monastery of his Order.

# CHAPTER L8

## A VOLUME FROM THE LIBRARY OF
## SEBALD PIRCKHEIMER

THE Pierpont Morgan Library recently[1] acquired a copy of Ovid's *Metamorphoses* printed at Parma by Andreas Portilia in 1480 (Hain 12160). Below the colophon on the last printed page of the volume (PML 46607) there is a note which now reads: "Rubrica per me sebaldum Pirkeymer anno m cccc lxxx & Octaua epiphanie."[2] It is with the identity of the Sebald Pirckheimer who rubricated the volume that we are now concerned.

This copy of the *Metamorphoses* also bears the stamp of the Royal Society in London, which plainly tells the history of the volume.[3] It will be recalled that Wilibald Pirckheimer's[4] library remained in the family till 1636, when Hans Hieronymus Imhoff sold the books to Thomas Howard, second Earl of Arundel. Thirty-one years later, his grandson, Henry Howard (sixth Duke of Norfolk), presented his library (including the Pirckheimer books) to the Royal Society. The greatest part of these books was sold by the Society in 1873 to the antiquarian bookseller Bernard Quaritch, and the present volume appears in his *General Catalogue of Books* (London, 1874, p. 1444, no. 18109) with this description: "Ovidii Metamorphoseos libri, folio, with MS. notes by Pirckheimer, who writes his Christian name Sebald, a few rude drawings on the margins, bd. Rare £12. Parma, Andreas Portilia, 1480."

However, to return to the inscription as quoted above, history records only three contemporary Sebald Pirckheimers, all descended from Hans Pirckheimer the second (d. 1400). His grandson Sebald,[5] through the family of his first marriage (to Katharina Graser), died

---

[1] In January, 1955.

[2] Below this is written the distich:
   Bis sex millenos versus in codice scriptos
   Sed terquinque minus continet ouidius.

[3] For further details, see Seymour de Ricci, *English Collectors of Books & Manuscripts* (Cambridge, 1930), p. 25, and Emile Offenbacher, "La bibliothèque de Wilibald Pirckheimer," *La Bibliofilia*, XL (1938), 241–263.

[4] On Wilibald, compare the *Allgemeine Deutsche Biographie*, XXVI (1888), 810–817, and Arnold Reimann, *Die älteren Pirckheimer* (Leipzig, 1944), *passim*.

[5] Reimann, p. 40 ff.

at an early age shortly after the turn of the century and can thus be excluded from our consideration. Sebald's nephew and namesake, in turn, was married to Katharina Praun, became a member of the "grosser Rat" of Nürnberg in 1477, suffered a catastrophic bankruptcy in 1492 and thereupon retired to the Carthusian monastery in Nürnberg.[6] He also appears in the records as "Sebald the Carthusian," but such books as he had (mostly on moral philosophy) he left to his Charterhouse. The third Sebald[7] was Wilibald's younger brother, concerning whom precious little is known; he and Wilibald were, of course, the great-great-grandsons of Hans Pirckheimer II by his second wife (Katharina Teufel). Dr. Hans (d. 1501), the father of the boys, records Sebald's birth (Arundel MS. 449, f. 278ᵛ) as "Anno *domini* 1475 qu*into* k*alendas* februarii, q*uae* fuit dies sabathi."[8] In 1475, January 28th did fall on a Saturday, thus establishing the fact that Dr. Hans was using the "style of the Circumcision" (January 1st) as the beginning of the year;[9] this was then the customary style at Nürnberg. This Sebald was certainly still alive on 26 April 1485, when he was mentioned in the will of his step-grandmother, Walpurg Dönninger (Doniger).[10] It is generally assumed, on what authority I have been unable to discover, that he died before his mother; the death of Barbara Löffelholz Pirckheimer took place on 21 March 1488.

Since the Ovid we are discussing subsequently turned up with other books from Wilibald's library, it seems reasonable to suppose that his brother was not only the former owner of the volume but also the author of the note. But on 13 January 1480, Sebald Pirckheimer was not yet five years old; even in the fifteenth century children were not so precocious that they could rubricate volumes at this early age!

Fortunately, modern technology can here come to our aid and offers a solution for our problem. In studying the inscription, one notes that the "-aua" is written in a different colored ink, with the last

---

[6] Reimann, p. 43, and (as the Carthusian), p. 187.

[7] Mentioned repeatedly by Reimann, this Sebald is the only one noted by Emil Reicke, *Willibald Pirckheimers Briefwechsel* (München, 1940).

[8] Reimann, p. 241, cites the entry in full. I am most obliged to Mr. T. J. Brown, of the Department of Manuscripts in the British Museum, for a new and full transcript of this entry in the Arundel manuscript.

[9] On this point, compare Frederick R. Goff, "The Dates in Certain German Incunabula," *PBSA*, XXXIV (1940), 17–67 (esp. p. 18).

[10] Reicke, p. 38; Reimann, p. 112. The date of the death of Sebald's mother is given by Reimann, p. 132, note 4.

two letters written beyond the edge of the type-page and extending well into the inner margin. Examination by microscope suggests that another letter lies below the first "a". Further, only the characters "aua" have offset on the opposite (blank) page. The fourth letter of "epiphanie" seems to have been an "f" over which another hand has written a "p". The "-hanie" may also have been written at the same time and with the same ink as the "-aua". In the infra-red photograph of the inscription taken by the Library's expert photographer, Mr. Mark D. Brewer, almost the entire passage disappeared, the only characters clearly surviving being the "-aua" and "-phanie." Incidentally, the rubrication in the colophon (capital strokes and underlinings) made by the same ink also disappeared in this process.

It is plain by now that the original inscription has been tampered with. Furthermore, close examination reveals that it is equally probable that the original letter under the beginning of "-aua" was an "o". This now suggests that the inscription be read as: "Rubrica per me sebaldum Pirkeymer anno m cccc lxxx & Octo. epif." It would, of course, have been quite possible for Sebald Pirckheimer to have rubricated the volume, and drawn some of the crude but interesting sketches in it, by 6 January 1488 when he was almost thirteen years old. In any event, that is how the present writer reads the inscription. But why, then, was the date altered? The only explanation that is at all plausible is that some later reader "corrected" the date to agree with the year of the colophon (M.CCCCLXXX) without noting that the inscription now proclaims the astonishing fact that the book was rubricated before it ever was printed (Idibus Maiis = May 15th)!!

Since we are now assured that Sebald Pirckheimer was alive in January 1488 and did not die shortly after 1485,[11] a further deduction becomes possible. Among the "carmina mea quae Paduae composui anno domini 1491," there is a poem by Wilibald addressed to his "most gracious" grandfather ("Ad avum obsequentissimum") in which reference is made to the "iuvenes nepotes."[12] Now Wilibald arrived in Padua to commence his studies there in the autumn either

---

[11] No date for Sebald's death is given by Reimann ("Er ist wohl jung gestorben", p. 142, n. 1) or by Reicke ("er starb jung, wenn auch schon über zehn Jahre alt," p. 289).

[12] Compare Reicke, pp. 36–38. The poem was written down by Wilibald on the flyleaves of an Italian incunable. These leaves, removed from the book, were in 1940 in the possession of Dr. Erik Waller of Lidköping, Sweden (Reicke, p. 32).

of 1488 or 1489 (the authorities disagree).[13] Dr. Emil Reicke, in editing this poem, assumed that the word "nepotes" had to refer generally to descendants rather than specifically to grandsons, since he maintained (without offering evidence to that effect) that by this time Wilibald was the sole surviving grandson. May one not assume, just as readily, that Sebald was still alive at the time of the writing of this poem or, at least, that Wilibald in far-off Padua still thought that his brother was alive in Nürnberg? Such an interpretation would certainly underscore the words "avus" and "nepotes", and give them a natural and proper relationship. In that case, it is clear that Sebald was either still alive or Wilibald believed he was so when Wilibald was a student at Padua.

(From *Studies in Bibliography* 8 (1956), pp. 212-15).

[13] Offenbacher, *loc. cit.*, states that Wilibald was in Padua in 1488 (p. 241), while Reicke (p. 8) maintains that he did not reach Italy till 1489.

# CHAPTER L9

## A TUDOR "CROSSE ROWE"

A "Sammelband," composed of thirteen quartos printed in Cologne in the fifteenth century and located in the British Museum,[1] preserves a number of early English entries. At the end of the last tract in the volume (Pius II, *Dialogus contra Bohemos* [Cologne: Ulrich Zell, not after 1472], fols. 270$^v$–271$^v$ of the volume), there is written the Cross Row[2] which is the subject of the present discussion. The precise date of the handwriting is uncertain, though the fact that the thorn still retains its original and separate form, and has not degenerated into a "y", makes it possible that the text was written into the incunabulum before 1501. On the other hand, Brown-Robbins[3] fail to record this—or, apparently, any other—alphabetical poem of this nature. Furthermore, the poem contains some words for which the earliest recorded instance in the *OED* supplies a date well after 1500.

It is as difficult to assign a date for the composition of this piece as it is to fix the date of transcription. The strong evidence of an originally well-worked-out alliteration in the poem perhaps implies an origin of no later than the fifteenth century. There is, too, the additional fact that the textual and metrical corruptions also suggest that the present text may be a late copy of a considerably earlier composition.

Because of the nature of the poem and its ribald character, some of the allusions are obscure. The humor is certainly broad—possibly not always very funny to our way of thinking. Indeed, such poems as the present Cross Row were usually considered too insignificant, or too coarse, for inclusion in the traditional literary manuscripts; hence they are very infrequently met with. As an example of the sort

[1] Compare the *Catalogue of Books Printed in the XVth Century now in the British Museum* (London, 1908–49), I, 215, IA. 3420. The provenance is there given as: "From the old Royal Library (with the 1542 catalogue-number)." Since the volume was out of general circulation as early as 1542, it seems likely that the manuscript notes were written into the book prior to that date by some earlier owner.

[2] See the Explicit. The earliest instance of Cross Row recorded by *OED* is "a. 1529 Skelton."

[3] Carleton Brown and Rossell Hope Robbins, *The Index of Middle English Verse*, (New York, 1943).

of humor which appealed to the average reader of that day, however, this poem has an importance quite out of proportion to its literary value.

Explanatory notes, by line number, have been added at the end of the text where such seemed necessary or useful. I am not so sanguine as to believe that all instances of attempted humor or all possible examples of wordplay have been discovered and annotated—nor that there is in all cases a need to do so.

Crystys crosse be my spede and saynt Nicholas / Crystys cursse be with yow all for I haue faryn the worsse bothe for saynt Gregorye & saynt Nicholas for betyng of myne Arsse.

> A for Alyn Mallson þat was armyde in a matt
> and rode to rychmar for to fyght with a gnatt
> B for bartem the baker þat brostyn mutt he be
> he claymed hys haeritage vpon the Pyllere
> 5 C for charles the chaltar þat neuer lye made
> he chode with a chorles son for brekyng of a spade
> D for danyell þe dastard was dubled in hys hornes
> and a grett drynkar he was of newe ale in cornes
> ff for phelypp þe flaterer þat first be-gan to stynk
> 10 he prayde to God & to the deuyll þat hys dame shuld synk
> G for gyklard & lawer [sic] with her one Eye
> the hyssyng of gander made hym ron a-way
> H for harry hangman þat gelldyd wele an hogg
> for etyng of a puddyng he hong vp hys dogg
> 15 J for jenkyn japer jaggyd with hys hodd
> he justyd downe a joggler with a bene kodd
> K for cok-lossell þat vsed knaves to chesse
> he lepyd fro howsse to howsse & sumwhat he kechesse
> L fo[r] lewys lyght-fote that lepte at a carte
> 20 and broke bothe hys Shynnes for fere of a fart
> M for Margret þe mowmbler þat was a bold stott
> she brake her husbondes hede with a fowlle pyse-pott
> N for Nicholas blere-eye þat was bell[y]ed lyke a gorrell
> he had an hed lyke a brasspan & shapyd lyke a barrell
> 25 O for oliuer þe otemell-makyr þat had oylle for to sell
> he bore lyght in a lampe be-fore the hand-bell
> P for petyr the pere-monger with hys crokyd thombe
> ffor crackyng of wall-notes there he brake hys gom
> Q for all quareleres & questmongeres þat walkythe be þe sond
> 30 ffor with there euyll-gotyn goodes þei purchasse boþe howsse & lond
> R for rawllyn the reuelar þat ran with a spere
> he clothed hym in a cowhes-pawnche & ran to the were
> S for Symkyn the sowtter þat no good can
> he fyll vpon [an] shoo last & brake hys hede pan

35  T for Thomkyn tynker þat dranke owt hys cloke
with the lynnyng of a bottell he made hole hys throte
W for wylkyn þe waster þat wantyd muche of hys wytt
he wrote vp hys wynnynges on the bottom of a posnett
X for Christofor kowys-snowtt þat was chodeyn of hys dame
40  for crachyng of her rompe þat afterward was lame
Y for yaferye jackson þat hadd an hard halpp
and what-so-euer þat he can kache he puttythe hyt in-to hys lapp
& for the hethe-cok þat bredyth in the marysshe
and watkyn þe wyer-drawer þat all-ways ys but haryshe
45  Ɔ for all maydys that wyll haue no blame
God geue ye all ill marage for ye ar past shame.
Explicit þe crosse rowe.

ANNOTATIONS TO THE TEXT

Heading: *OED* Christ-cross 3. "*Christ's cross me speed:* a formula said before repeating the alphabet." Used by Lydgate; compare Brown-Robbins, No. 604.

1. Mallson] cf. *OED* malison.
2. rychmar] Richmond? Only "Riche hill" is cited by Käte Heidrich, *Das geographische Weltbild des späteren englischen Mittelalters*, Freiburg im Br., 1915.
3. brostyn] pa. pple. of burst.
4. Pyllere] pillery (pillage) vs. pillory (punishment).
5. chaltar] connected (?) with "iolte head" or chowter/jouter; cf. *OED* chalter (vb.).
6. chode] strong past tense of chide.
7. dastard] a sot. Horns of a cuckold vs. drinking vessels.
9-10. stynk . . . synk] stink (be abhorrent)/ sink (go to hell); a favorite combination or rhyme.
11. This line is very corrupt. If we read "an lawyer" and the feminine pronoun "her," then the "hym" in the next line is inexplicable. This is equally true if we assume that two persons are meant and "her" is a 3rd pers. pl.
16. kodd] bean-pod or bean-bag vs. cod (*OED* sb. 1, sense 4).
17. losel] a scoundrel; cock-lorel (cf. lorel, *OED* 1515). chesse] chase?;

cf. *OED* jess, but not recorded as verb before 1860.
18. kechesse] catches?
19. fo[r]] MS has "fo."
21. mowmbler] mambler (*OED* 1400-50) or mumbler (*OED* 1543). stott] "term of contempt for a woman" (*OED*, last use ca. 1500).
23. gorrell] a fat-paunched person.
29. þat . . . sond] that walk by (past) the shond (disgrace, scandal; *OED* last used 1450) *or* that walk by (according to) the sound (of quarrelings)? Sand does not make sense.
34. [an]] MS has ampersand.
35. cloke] cloche (bell) vs. cloak vs. claw (cf. *OED* clutch).
36. lynnyng . . . bottell] lining of a bottle (i.e., liquor) vs. "linen made from a bottle (bundle of hay)."
38. posnett] a small metal pot for boiling.
41. halpp] hap?
43. hethe-cok] heath-cock (*OED* first use 1590). marysshe] marish = marsh.
44. haryshe] foolish (*OED* first use 1552), or harsh?
45. ɔ] contraction for *con*, often forming part of the medieval alphabet, together with the ampersand (as above), the *rum* abbreviation, and other such compound forms.

(From *Journal of English and Germanic Philology* 58 (1959), pp. 248-50).

# CHAPTER L10

## MIDDLE ENGLISH APOPHTHEGMS
## IN A CAXTON VOLUME

AVOLUME in the British Museum, composed of two of
Caxton's[1] French publications (issued while he was still at
work in Bruges),[2] contains English manuscript notes which
have not previously been investigated. Included in this potpourri of
literary scraps are no fewer than five metrical pieces listed in the
*Index of Middle English Verse;*[3] these items, however, escaped entry
in that most useful work, since the compilers confined their search
to the manuscript field. But obviously, these too are manuscript
texts, even if found written into printed books. The script may be
judged to belong to the reign of Henry VII rather than to that of
Henry VIII.[4] The manuscript entries may even have been written
into the incunables a year or two before the turn of the century.

From the fact that the same texts are found printed in the identical
order in another English incunable, one might conclude that the
apophthegms in the British Museum's volume were simply copied
into it from the so-called "Boke of St. Albans" (*The Book of Hawk-
ing, Hunting, and Blasing of Arms*).[5] This may, indeed, be so—
but if this be the origin of our maxims, then the "variae lectiones"
here appended give some indication of the liberties which a copyist
felt free to take with his "Vorlage." But the possibility must not be
overlooked that the *Boke of St. Albans* and the manuscript texts
here quoted could both go back to a common original. The texts in

---

[1] For his publications, see William Blades, *The Life and Typography of William
Caxton* (London, 1861–63).

[2] Compare the *Catalogue of Books Printed in the XVth Century now in the
British Museum* (London, 1908–62), IX, 131. The two undated works are: Petrus
de Alliaco (Pierre d'Ailly), *Meditationes circa septem psalmos poenitentiales*, in
French (IB. 49408) and the *Cordiale quattuor novissimorum*, in French (IB. 49437).

[3] Compiled by Carleton Brown and Rossell Hope Robbins (New York, 1943)
and here cited as B-R.

[4] For the dating of the handwriting, I am much obliged to Dr. C. E. Wright
of the British Museum's Department of Manuscripts.

[5] For the various early editions, see STC 3308–18. The variant readings here
cited are taken from the copies in the Pierpont Morgan Library of the editions:
Saint Albans, [Schoolmaster Printer], 1486 (PML 721) and Westminster, Wynkyn
de Worde, 1496 (PML 732).

MS. Lansdowne 762,[6] for example, have comparable differences from the work sometimes ascribed to Dame Juliana Berners,[7] and it may not be unreasonable to postulate that a manuscript tradition of these apophthegms[8] existed prior to their insertion into the printed text, apparently to take up space which would otherwise have remained blank in the incunabulum.[9]

*Alliaco, folio 34 verso.*

Aryse erly[10]
Serue God deuotly
& the worlde besyly
Do þi woork wysely
Yeue thyn almesse secretly
Go by the way sadly
Answer the peple demuerly
Go to thi meat appetently[11]
Sit ther-at dyscretly
Of thi tounge be not liberally[12]
Aryse therfro temperatly[13]
Go to thi super soberly
Go to thi bed merely[14]
& be ther iocondly[15]
Please thi love duly
& slep suerly.

[6] Printed by Thomas Wright and J. O. Halliwell [-Phillipps] in *Reliquiae antiquae* (London, 1841–43), I, 233.

[7] For this attribution, see (for example) the note on authorship in the facsimile of the first edition by William Blades, *The Boke of Saint Albans by Dame Juliana Berners* (London, 1899), pp. 7–15, and the article cited in note 9 below.

[8] The following sigla are used: S for the Saint Albans edition; W for that by De Worde; L for Lansdowne MS. 762 (as printed in *Rel. ant.*). The reprint of the De Worde texts in Joseph Ames and Thomas F. Dibdin, *Typographical Antiquities* (London, 1810–19), II, 59, contains both some errors and modernizations.

[9] E. F. Jacob, "The Book of St. Albans," *Bulletin of the John Rylands Library*, XXVIII (1944), 99–118, similarly accounts for the presence of these maxims amongst the (otherwise unrelated) texts of this volume.

[10] Listed under B-R 324 and as no. 7 in William Ringler, "A Bibliography and First-Line Index of English Verse Printed through 1500," *PBSA*, XLIX (1955), 153–180. Variae lectiones are confined to substantive ones, and purely orthographical variants are not recorded. An eleven-line version was printed by William Caxton in his edition of Lydgate's *Stans puer ad mensam* [Westminster, c. 1477], and this is reproduced by William Blades, *The Life and Typography of William Caxton* (London, 1861–63), II, 50.

[11] Go to thy mete appetently (Caxton); appetideli (S; similarly WL).

[12] to liberalli (SWL).          [13] temperally (L).

[14] And to thy bed merily (Caxton; SWL).

[15] And be there iocondly (Caxton; MS reads "ioconly" [*sic*]); Be in thyn Inne Iocundely (SWL).

Ther[16] be fower thynges to be marked of euery wyseman: the furst ys the curse of the pope; the seconde the indygnacion[17] of a prince, quia indignacio regis mors est; the thyrd ys the fauour of a judge; the forthe ys the slander of the mutacion of a cominaltie.

Who[18] þat makyth in Crystynmas a dogge to his lardere
& in Marche a sow[19] to his gardyner
& in May a foole to be a wyse manes consell[20]
He shall neuer haue good larder
Fayre gardyn nor well kept councell.

ffer[21] fro thi kynsmen caste the
Wrath not thi neabors next the
In a good corne contry thress[22] the
& syt doune[23] & rest the.

### Cordiale, folio 1 recto.

Who[24] that buldyth his howse of sallowes[25]
And prykyth a blynde horse ouer the ffalowes
And sufferyth his wyff to seke many halowes
God sent hym to the blysse of euer lastyng gallowes.[26]

Ther[27] ben iiij° thynges full harde for to knowe whiche way that they wyll drawe: the furst ys the wayes of a younge man; the seconde þe course of a

---

[16] Merke wele theys .iiii. thynges. Ther be .iiij. thynges principall to be drad of euery wise man. The first is the curse of owre holy fader the pope. The secunde is thindignacion of a prince Quia indignacio regis vel principis mors est. The thridde is the fauor or the will of a Juge. The .iiij. is Sclaunder & the mutacion of a comynalte (SW; pryncypally W; this maxim apparently not in L).

[17] indyngnacion (MS).     [18] B-R 4106; Ringler 89.     [19] show (MS).

[20] And in May a fole of a whise mannys counsell (SWL; similarly MS. TCC o. 9. 38, f. 46).

[21] B-R 761; Ringler 13. (L has "kyn" and "neighbor").

[22] threste (SW); rest (L). Sense seems to require "thresh."

[23] Something illegible is written after "doune," perhaps "you"; downe Robyn (SWL).

[24] B-R 4101; Ringler 88. These lines appear to be very ancient and are cited by Chaucer in the Wife of Bath's Prologue, ll. 655-658 (Skeat's edition, London, 1933, p. 573).

[25] byldys (S); buyldeth (WL). all of (SWL).

[26] God sende hym the blysse of euerlastyng galowis (SWL)).

[27] SW (apparently not in L) have the heading: If theis be not directid then go thei at aventyr. The first sentence is considered to be a couplet (Ringler 71; not in B-R), but the rhyme may be accidental. The text differs very considerably in L:
There been thre thinges full harde to be knowen which waye they woll drawe. The first is of birde sitting upon a bough. The second is of a vessell in the see. And the thirde is the waye of a yonge man.

Two wymen in one howse
Two cattes and one mowce

vessell in the see; the thyrde of an adder or of serpent sprent;[28] the fforth of a ffowle sittyng of any thynge.

> Too wyffes in one howse
> ij cattes & one mouse
> ij dogges & one bone
> These shall neuer accorde in one.

> Who that manyth hym with his kyn[29]
> & closyth his croft with cherytres
> Shall haue many hedges broken
> & also full litell good seruys.

It seems difficult, if not impossible, to determine with certainty whether these maxims found in the British Museum's volume were copied from the *Boke of St. Albans* or go back to an earlier manuscript tradition. Whichever may be the correct answer, it seems important to make these lines available to Middle English scholars either as texts predating the familiar early-printed versions or as an illustration of the free and easy manner in which the scribes were wont to treat their sources.[30] The fact that, in at least two instances, the readings here set forth are identical with those printed by Caxton a half-dozen or more years before the first appearance of the *Boke of St. Albans* should not be overlooked, as these must be regarded as evidence of independent and special value.

The presence of these English notes in two French incunabula is also an oddity which will not escape the notice of the investigators of mediaeval books.[31] May we conclude from this that, when Caxton moved his press to Westminster in 1476, he brought with him from Bruges the still unsold stock of his publications?

(From *English Language Notes*, I (1963), pp. 81-84.)

---

> Two dogges and one bone
> Maye never accorde in one

This quatrain is listed by B-R 3818 and Ringler 79.

[28] or a (S); or of a (W). serpent sparent (MS)?

[29] Not in B-R and (apparently) not in L; Ringler 90.

[30] Compare my *The Fifteenth-Century Book* (Philadelphia, 1960), pp. 37-38.

[31] On folio 1ʳ of the *Cordiale*, there is written: "To my master Doctor Shorton," which presumably refers to the Robert Shorton (d. 1535) noted in *DNB*, LII, 158-159.

# CHAPTER L11

## OWNERS' JINGLES IN EARLY PRINTED BOOKS

AMONG the most amusing of literary strays are the occasional jottings one finds in the margins and blank portions of leaves in mediaeval and renaissance manuscripts. A small body of literature has grown up which concerns itself with such material.[1] The subtitle of the present article[2] will suggest that similar literary bits can be found in early printed books and may further suggest that the search for such items could well bring profitable results. The present examples are all taken from volumes in the Pierpont Morgan Library.

### I

On the verso of the last leaf (PML 22102, f. 8ᵛ) of the *De disciplina Christiana* by St. Augustine [Cologne: Ulrich Zell, c. 1470], there is written:

> Pastor tabene wilhelmus mentis amene
> Hunc librum plene legat poscitque serene
> Vt *Christi* cene bona gustet non mala pene

The second word of this stanza is taken to be a feminine genitive[3] and thus identifies the Reverend William as a member of the monastery of Taben,[4] founded by Abbot Wigger of St. Maximin in 960,

---

[1] See, for example, the section "Corollaria Metrica" in Joachim Feller, *Catalogus codicum manuscriptorum bibliothecae Paulinae in Academia Lipsiensi* (Leipzig, 1686), pp. 438–450; Wilhelm Wattenbach, *Das Schriftwesen im Mittelalter* (Leipzig, 1896), p. 327 ff. and p. 491 ff.; Leo Jordan, "Das Verleihen von Büchern im Mittelalter," *Zeitschrift für Bücherfreunde*, IX (1905/6), 455–458; H. S. Bennett, *England from Chaucer to Caxton* (London, 1928), pp. 160–162; Lynn Thorndike, "Copyists' Final Jingles in Mediaeval Manuscripts," *Speculum*, XII (1937), 268 and his "More Copyists' Final Jingles," *ibid.*, XXXI (1956), 321–328; and the articles cited in note 14. A nineteenth-century poem along these lines has recently been published by Albert Ehrman ("An Admonition to Borrowers," *The Book Collector*, XIII [1964], 211).

[2] Published as no. XI of the series *Libri impressi*.

[3] A dative is, of course, possible, suggesting that the book had been left to Taben. However, in view of the leonine rhyme with the certainly genitive *amoenae*, it seems more probable that *Tabenae* is also a genitive.

[4] Consult L. H. Cottineau, *Répertoire topo-bibliographique des abbayes et prieurés* (Mâcon, 1939), col. 3111, and H. Höfer, "Die Benedictinerstiftungen in den

half-way between Trier and Saarlouis. The beneficiary of this dona-
tion is not specified,[5] though it may well have been William's own
monastery, and we can only hope that the donor's prayer was
granted. This is not, however, the only book which was owned by
Father William, for the inscription "Domino wilhelmo de tabena
pertinet" is recorded in a copy of the *Speculum sacerdotum* by Her-
mannus de Schildis (Trier, 1481) now in the University Library at
Cambridge.[6]

## II

A variety of entries[7] (in English and Latin, with even a bit of
Greek) will be found in the Morgan copy (PML 695) of William
Caxton's edition of the *Royal Book* [Westminster, 1486].[8] Thus,
on signature k1 recto, one finds the following (somewhat ill-spelt)
lines:

> When Jesus Christ was tewle yeare olde[9]
> As holie skripters plainelie tolde
> He then disputted braue & bolde
> Amongste the larned docters
> Who wondered greatly at his wit
> As in the temple he did sit
> For no man mite compare whit it
> Is wisdome whare so heuenly
> Then praise the lord both hie and loe
> That all the wondrous woe . . .

---

Rheinlanden," *Studien und Mittheilungen aus dem Benedictiner- und dem Cis-
tercienser-Orden*, IX (1888), 462.

[5] This book remained for many centuries in the neighborhood of Taben. The
volume bears the stamp of the Stadtbibliothek, Trier, on folio 1 recto and has a
shelf-mark "2304. VI." It was acquired by the Morgan Library in October, 1923,
from the firm of Joseph Baer and Company of Frankfurt.

[6] Cf. J. C. T. Oates, *A Catalogue of the Fifteenth-Century Printed Books in the
University Library Cambridge* (Cambridge, 1954), p. 237, no. 1267.

[7] These items are not described by Seymour de Ricci, *A Census of Caxtons* ([Lon-
don], 1909), pp. 89–90, no. 89.1, nor in the *Catalogue of . . . Early Printed Books
from the Libraries of William Morris, Richard Bennett, Bertram, Fourth Earl of
Ashburnham, and other Sources, now forming Portion of the Library of J. Pierpont
Morgan* (London, 1907), III, 177–178, no. 698.

[8] A stanza on the Ten Commandments is also written on signature b2 verso.
This has been printed, from other sources, by the present writer ("At thy golg
first eut of the hous vlysse the saynge thus," see above [T24]; cf. note 30). On
i8 verso, there is written the word: "honorificabilitudinitatibus" (on which see
*OED*, V, 367). On t4 verso, one finds the proverb: "When henes goe to caklinge
louke to ther neast."

[9] The first line is repeated on signature o2: "When Jesus Christ wase tewlue yeare

This unfinished poem may well have been written by the same person who, on signature l2 verso, wrote the somewhat commonplace:

> Thomas Albone is my name
> With hande and pene I write the same
> And yf my pene had bine beter
> Then I woulde haue mended my letter

According to Wilhelm Wattenbach[10] (citing the Wright-Halliwell *Reliquiae Antiquae* [London, 1841–43], II, 164), MS. Harley 3118 contains a very similar stanza, reading:

> Thomas Beech is my name
> And with my pen I write the same
> Yf my pen had been better
> I would have mended it everey lettere

On signature q2, the same hand has written "Thomas A gentilm" and the following lines:

> In hand and [? hart][11] true loue keepe
> If hart do falle true loue will wepe
> Then[12] hart in hand doth not a-mise
> Then think of her that gaue you this[13]

## III

A French curse[14] against a possible book-thief is found written on the inner, upper cover of PML 18206 (*Hours for the Use of Lyons*, Paris: Simon Vostre, [c. 1502]):

> Descire soit de truyes et porceaulx
> Et puys son corps trayne en leaue du Rin
> Le cueur fendu decoupe par morceaulx
> Qui ces heures prendra par larcin

---

olde." Albone was given to adding an improper final *e*, as in *bine, a-mise*, etc. None of the "poetry" here cited is listed by Carleton Brown and Rossell Hope Robbins, *The Index of Middle English Verse* (New York, 1943).

[10] *Op. cit.*, p. 521.          [11] Omitted from the original.

[12] Query: read "When"?

[13] The writer adds: "or sent you this, chouse you which. Amen so be it."

[14] On such curses, see Heinrich Meisner, "Der Bücherfluch," *Zeitschrift für Bücherfreunde*, I (1897/8), 101–103; Graf zu Leiningen-Westerburg, "Zum Kapitel vom 'Bücherfluch,'" *ibid.*, 431–433; G. A. Crüwell, "Die Verfluchung der Bücherdiebe," *Archiv für Kulturgeschichte*, IV (1906), 197–223; and Lawrence S. Thompson, "Notes on Bibliokleptomania," *Bulletin of the New York Public Library*, XLVIII (1944), 723–760.

In modern orthography, these lines would read:

> Déchiré soit de truies et pourceaux
> Et puis son corps traîné en l'eau du Rhin
> Le coeur fendu découpé par morceaux
> Qui ces Heures prendra par larcin

As the objurgation stresses the river Rhine, this may possibly indicate that the curse was written in Northeastern France. However, it is just as likely, to say the very least, that this name was specially chosen for its convenient rhyme. It is somewhat doubtful that such a *de luxe* item as is this vellum *Book of Hours* would have found its way into a predominantly German-speaking diocese at some remove both from the place of its printing or the locality which its text was meant to serve.[15]

## IV

The copy of the *Greate Herball* (London: Jhon Kynge, 1561; STC 13179) formerly in the collection of Mrs. J. P. Morgan[16] and presented to the library by Mr. Henry S. Morgan in 1962 (now PML 53095) preserves two jingles which seem to be worth noting. In the inside of the upper cover, there is twice written:

> Helpe hande
> I haue [no] lande
> For grace I do desyar
> Yf mi hand
> Were no better then my lande
> I myght loke to lye in the myar
> In the fere of God is my desyar

Only the earlier version of the two (much worn and partly illegible) has the "no" which appears to be required by the sense.

Similarly the lower cover of this volume provides the stanza:

> Yff auye man aske a questone [*sic*] of the
> In thine answer makinge be nott to hastye
> Eles may he joudge [*sic*] in the little wytte
> To aunswer to a thynge and nott here ytt

[15] The volume also contains the note of ownership (written later in the sixteenth century or early in the next) of "Joseph Perrier l'aine prestre et societaire du bourg," indicating continued possession of the volume by French owners.

[16] On this, see Frederick B. Adams, Jr., *Fourth Annual Report to the Fellows of the Pierpont Morgan Library* (New York, 1953), pp. 27-29.

The first two lines only are repeated here, though in this case the word is correctly spelled "questyon." The first line[17] is also written out on the verso of the last printed leaf (signature Bb2 verso) with the heading "Not to hasty."

## V

The edition of the *Liber precum publicarum* (London: John Jackson, 1594; STC 16428) is represented in the Morgan Library by a copy (PML 16053) in its original calf binding. In the center of both covers (decorated by gold and blind line-borders on the sides), one finds the crowned Tudor Rose badge of Queen Elizabeth I. On the first fly-leaf, there is written out, in a fine and careful calligraphic script, the lines:

> Discipulus teneris est instituend*us* ab annis,
>      Hæc q*uoque* sunt illi mente tenenda tria.
> Sæpe sacrum genib*us* flexis ut nume*n* adoret,
>      Sit bene moratus, deditus atq*ue* libris.
> In templo, ludo, mensa, stet, sessitet, oret,
>      Mente pius, cultus moribus, artis amans.
>
> A scholer muste in youth bee taughte,
>      And three thing*es* keep in minde full sure,
> Gods worship that it first bee saught,
>      And manners then w*ith* knowledg [*sic*] pure.
> In church, in schole, at table must hee
>      Devout, attent, and handsome bee.

Commonplace advice of this sort was, of course, immensely popular in the fifteenth and sixteenth centuries, as we may see from Lydgate's *Stans puer ad mensam*, Hoccleve's *The Regiment of Princes*, Ashby's *Active Policy of a Prince*, Caxton's *Book of Curtesye*,[18] and the numerous texts (both earlier and later in date) pub-

---

[17] So far as it can be made out (though the first word is lost in a worm-hole and the reading of the last is doubtful), a second line here reads: "[In] makyng answer abie."

[18] Though William Blades has pointed out (*The Life and Typography of William Caxton* [London, 1861–63], II, 64) that "on the final blank [of the copy in the Cambridge University Library] are two verses in manuscript by 'J. F.'" and these are reproduced in the rare facsimile of the unique copy of the first edition (Cambridge: University Press, 1907), they do not seem to have been printed in modern form. Indeed, they do not even appear in the Early English Text Society's edition of this poem (Extra Series III, 1868), though the text of the Caxton printing is included therein. The lines read:

lished by Frederick J. Furnivall.[19] However, no other copy of the present English stanza has been located through the first-line indices in the Bodleian Library and in the British Museum,[20] neither is this verse to be found in the list of English incipits of the Tudor period compiled by William A. Ringler, Jr., nor in the similar one assembled by Edwin Wolf, 2nd.

(From *Studies in Philology* 62 (1965), pp. 647-53).

---

To the reader

Here maist thou learne thyselfe howe to be-haue
Within this curteous booke of curtesie
Then this is all the sum that he doth craue
For this his painfull industrye
Whoe did compile this booke for use of the
That nowe he's dead thou courteously him vse
Which for thy gaine did not his paine refuse

Whose booke though it be old defac'd and torne
By space of tyme which ruinates all thinges
This little treatise therfore in no wise scorne
For to the reader it great prouffitt bringes
If thou but marke of what he treats and singes
For oftentymes an old and a god tree
Bringes better fruit then those that younger be

Finis                                    J. F.

For "he's" the poet may have intended to write "lies," while "a god" can be read as "aged" though this would provide an entirely unwanted redundancy. One should also recall the Biblical "Sic omnis arbor bona fructus bonos facit" (Matthew, vii.17) and the many proverbial expressions dependent on this. The initials J. F. may refer to the John Fawler who owned the copy of the Caxton *Stans puer ad mensam* formerly bound with the *Book of Curtesye* (cf. Blades, II, 49–52), but this person has not been further identified. The writer of the Cambridge lines does not seem to be the same individual as the John Fawler listed by Alfred B. Emden, *A Biographical Register of the University of Oxford to A. D. 1500* (Oxford, 1957–59), II, 672. This Fawler became a deacon as early as 1480, and the handwriting of the verses appears to belong well into the next century.

[19] Compare, for example, those printed in Early English Text Society, Original Series No. 32 and Extra Series VIII.

[20] For a report on the Bodleian index, I am obliged to Miss Margaret C. Crum, while Mr. M. A. F. Borrie has examined the Museum's list on my behalf. I am under similar obligation to Professor Ringler and to Mr. William H. McCarthy, Jr., who has inspected Mr. Wolf's list of initia now on deposit at the Rosenbach Foundation in Philadelphia.

# A REVIEW

Ludwig Bieler, *Ireland: Harbinger of the Middle Ages*. London (New York): Oxford University Press, 1963. Pp. viii, 148; 18 color plates, 12 full-page photographs, 3 maps, numerous cuts and figures.

THIS volume is a most attractive addition to the reference literature on mediaeval Ireland. It is a re-working, rather than an exact translation, of the author's *Irland: Wegbereiter des Mittelalters* (1961), with practically the same (and very excellent) color plates and other illustrations. The decision not to include the rather crude sketch of the Fulda MS. Bonifatianus 3 (p. 24 of the German edition) will be regretted by no one.

The volume sets out to explore the nature of the mediaeval Irish civilization and its impact on that of the Continent. So far as Christianity and the church, missionaries and scholars, script and illumination, and related topics are concerned, this is an excellent account and supplies, in condensed form, precisely the information which the reader will be most likely to seek. The volume, in short, is just what one might expect from the expert scholarship of its distinguished author, the professor of palaeography at University College, Dublin, and a Corresponding Fellow of the Mediaeval Academy of America. The book was not planned, however, for the professional historian, and details which a scholar might require are, therefore, not included. Thus, Ludwig Traube's identification of the marginal glosses in Reims MS. 875 as in the handwriting of Eriugena is noted, but we are not told where this information may be found in Traube's published writings. The "Sources" (p. 145) include only his *Peronna* (or rather, *Perrona*) *Scottorum*, which does not treat of this matter.

It may surprise some readers to find no mention, in a work devoted to mediaeval Ireland, of Cúchulainn, Deirdre, Fland mac Lonáin, Finn mac Cumaill, and other celebrated names—at least, so far as this reviewer could discover, and the volume unhappily lacks an index. It is true, of course, that the direct influence on continental civilization of the secular Irish literature in the vernacular may not be readily discernible. Only the famous *Pangur Bán* is here briefly mentioned, yet this utterly charming and whimsical little piece (written at Reichenau on the shores of Lake Constance) by itself demonstrates that some Irish literature can even *be* continental. If it be true, however, that one "cannot understand the Middle Ages unless you know something about Ireland" (p. vii), then it may well be argued that one cannot understand the Irish without some knowledge of their vernacular literature. May not the fantastic legends of the Irish heroes find an echo in some of the "fantastic miracles" (p. 109) of the Irish saints? Professor Bieler (p. vii) also takes his stand with those who deny the Irish origin and dissemination of the Grail romances, though it is certain that, for the "matter of Britain," the ancient Irish epic tales provide many analogues, perhaps (in some cases) even the ultimate sources. It is a pity that some discussion of the vernacular elements in mediaeval Irish literature and history is not included in the book under review.

The interest of the volume has been greatly heightened by the inclusion of a number of magnificent photographs, including one of the incredibly fantastic Great Skellig (the farthest outpost of mediaeval Europe). Except in the calmest and finest of weather, to land on this craggy and rugged island is virtually impossible, though two more or less modern light-houses now rise amongst the ruined habitations of ancient hermits. The eremites have long ago gone away, possibly driven off by the Norsemen who attacked the *sceilig* (rock) early in the ninth century. Now only shearwaters and gannets claim it as their home. But the beehive-cell of the early Irish monks survived even into our day as the *púicín* (hut for storing tools), still to be found, not many years ago, on Dingle peninsula and the Blaskets. The chief island of this group (*An Blascaod Mór*), too, may have seen early settlements of hermits, if the surviving ruins, known to the natives as *na clocháin gheala* (the bright stone houses), should prove to be remnants of such early monasticism.

(From *Speculum* 39 (1964), pp. 489-90).

# SELECTIVE INDEX

## COMPILED BY GABRIEL AUSTIN

The following abbreviations are used:
B refers to the forty Bibliographical studies, T to the Textual papers,
and L to the *Libri impressi* series

# INDEX TO MANUSCRIPTS